CONSTITUTIONAL CRISIS IN THE EUROPEAN CONSTITUTIONAL AREA

The concept of a European Constitutional Area has been used in legal scholarship to describe a common space of constitutionalism where national and international constitutional guarantees interact to maintain the common constitutional values of Europe. This concept has not yet been tested in a case where the constitutional order of a Member State of the European Union seems to develop systemic deficiencies. The present volume aims to assess recent constitutional developments in Hungary and Romania, as well as the interplay of national, international and European constitutionalism which react to the loopholes in national constitutions. Accordingly, a core part of the volume is an in-depth analysis of the situation in Hungary and Romania. Based on that, the volume offers an account of the different reaction mechanisms of the European Union and of the Council of Europe. Beyond a detailed stock-taking of these mechanisms, their legal and political frameworks are explored, as well as different ways to extend their reach. In this way, the volume contributes to a little studied aspect of European constitutionalism.

Constitutional Crisis in the European Constitutional Area

Theory, Law and Politics in Hungary and Romania

Edited by
Armin von Bogdandy
and
Pál Sonnevend

·HART·
PUBLISHING

OXFORD AND PORTLAND, OREGON
2015

Published in the United Kingdom by Hart Publishing Ltd
16C Worcester Place, Oxford, OX1 2JW
Telephone: +44 (0)1865 517530
Fax: +44 (0)1865 510710
E-mail: mail@hartpub.co.uk
Website: http://www.hartpub.co.uk

Published in North America (US and Canada) by
Hart Publishing
c/o International Specialized Book Services
920 NE 58th Avenue, Suite 300
Portland, OR 97213-3786
USA
Tel: +1 503 287 3093 or toll-free: (1) 800 944 6190
Fax: +1 503 280 8832
E-mail: orders@isbs.com
Website: http://www.isbs.com

Hart Publishing is an imprint of Bloomsbury Publishing plc.

British Library Cataloguing in Publication Data
Data Available

ISBN: 978-1-84946-464-2 (Hart Publishing)
978-3-8487-1996-9 (Verlag CH Beck)

Typeset by Compuscript Ltd, Shannon
Printed and bound in Great Britain by
CPI Group (UK) Ltd, Croydon CR0 4YY

Preface

The dominant understanding of the relationship between European Union Law and national constitutionalism has been to conceive European integration as a threat to national constitutional values, first to fundamental rights, and later to democracy.[1] Whatever steps the framers of the Treaties or the European institutions have taken, this understanding has remained alluring, particularly for high courts all over Europe. This is well demonstrated by the series of constitutional challenges to the European Arrest Warrant in several jurisdictions,[2] and some reactions to the Lisbon Treaty.[3]

Like every successful and long-living frame of understanding certain phenomena, this narrative has had solid grounds in reality. How to safeguard democracy in the framework of European integration is indeed a thorny issue. It also remains beyond doubt that the Court of Justice of the European Union has been reluctant to embrace the role of a supreme court with a full constitutional function. The traditional understanding of the European Union as a functional legal order still underlies much of its jurisprudence. The European Union certainly does not provide a sophisticated system of fundamental rights protection, similar to that of several national constitutions.

The present book, while not denying that there is truth in the understanding of the European integration being the threat to, and EU Member States the protectors of, fundamental values, will lay out a very different one. It focuses on national systemic deficiencies in respecting the founding values of Article 2 of the Treaty on European Union (TEU). The concrete examples of Hungary and in Romania demonstrate that this converse narrative is more than justified: Member States being the threat to, and European institutions the possible protectors of, fundamental rights, rule of law, and democracy.

[1] For an overview see the contributions in G Martinico and O Pollicino, *The National Judicial Treatment of the ECHR and EU Laws* (Groningen, Europa Law Publishing, 2010).

[2] See Scott Siegel, *Courts and Compliance in the European Union: The European Arrest Warrant in National Constitutional Courts*, *Jean Monnet Working Paper* No 5 (2008), available at http://www.jeanmonnetprogram.org/papers/08/080501.pdf; C Grasso, The European Arrest Warrant Under the Scrutiny of the Italian Constitutional Court (2013) 4 *New Journal of European Criminal Law*, 120ff; A Torres Perez, 'Constitutional Dialogue on the European Arrest Warrant' (2012) 8 *EuConst* 105ff. See also Decision 32/2008. (III. 12.) AB határozat (Constitutional Court of Hungary) which found the international agreement extending the substantive rules of the European Arrest Warrant to Iceland and Norway to be in violation of the *nullum crimen* principle of the Hungarian Constitution and thus indirectly challenging the European Arrest Warrant, see http://www.mkab.hu/letoltesek/en_0032_2008.pdf.

[3] Most outspoken is the Federal German Constitutional Court, decision of 30 June 2009, BverGE 123, 267.

Indeed, these two understandings are not mutually exclusive, but can be combined because Europe is not homogeneous. This heterogeneity requires to leave behind the traditional, far too simplistic frame of understanding of the relationship between national constitutionalism and European law. Constitutional crises in some EU Member States highlight the need to understand EU law also, and, given the depth of the crises, perhaps even mainly, as a chance of preserving the core values of every constitution in Europe: democracy, the rule of law and respect for fundamental rights.

Systemic deficiencies in the rule of law in Member States not only threaten the foundations of the EU legal order but also rattle the trust in the core values underlying all national constitutions in Europe. Accordingly, effective reactions by European institutions equally serve the preservation of the foundations of the European Union and the maintenance of the principle of the rule of law in times of crisis in Member States. This is no threat to national constitutionalism. The Union's structure of competences and institutional set-up ensures that the primary responsibility for maintaining constitutional values rests with the Member States. Equally important is, however, the understanding that constitutional crisis may warrant common action and the effective reactions by European institutions.

The examples of Hungary and Romania indicate that, at present, European institutions do not yet possess a sufficiently effective set of instruments to address constitutional crisis. In Hungary, the constitutional developments of the last few years have been marked by at least three crisis symptoms: a permanent constitution-making by the governing majority in Parliament, a gradual deterioration of the guarantees of fundamental rights, and a lack of effective checks and balances (see Chapter 2, Pál Sonnevend, András Jakab and Lóránt Csink, 'The Constitution as an Instrument of Everyday Party Politics: The Basic Law of Hungary' and Chapter 3, Kim Lane Scheppele, 'Understanding Hungary's Constitutional Revolution'). The result is a constitutional system in which constitutional values become freely disposable, the constitution serves everyday political interest, and constitutional culture is in the decline (see Chapter 1, László Sólyom, 'The Rise and Decline of Constitutional Culture in Hungary'). The problem is exacerbated by concerns relating to the freedom of the media (see Chapter 4, Gábor Polyák, 'Context, Rules and Praxis of the New Hungarian Media Laws: How Does the Media Law Affect the Structure and Functioning of Publicity?').

Romania might, in a certain sense, face less severe difficulties in that the constitution itself is not jeopardised. Yet, the separation of powers, rule of law, and constitutionality have acquired surprisingly pliable and unstable meanings in the current Romanian climate. Political crises easily turn into constitutional ones, and the Romanian Constitutional Court has thus far not proven able to develop a consistent case law to create a clear point of reference for the constitutional system (see Chapter 5, Bogdan Iancu, 'Separation of Powers and the Rule of Law in Romania: The Crisis in Concepts and Contexts'). It is also argued that the 2012 events were a crisis only in relation to the intensity and the scope of the measures undertaken in a relatively short period of time and that the generalised practice of quasi-illegal political manoeuvres systemically validates further breaches of law (see Chapter 6, Cosmina Tanasoiu, 'Romania in the European Union: Political Developments and the Rule of Law after Accession').

By contrast, reactions by European institutions so far have remained rather isolated and mostly lacked teeth. European institutions have commonly felt trapped by a lack of appropriate competences and instruments, though this is changing.[4] With a few exceptions, only narrow issues linked to the internal market have been targeted (see Chapter 7, Frank Hoffmeister, 'Enforcing the EU Charter of Fundamental Rights in Member States: How Far are Rome, Budapest and Bucharest from Brussels?'). Institutions of the Council of Europe have addressed a wide range of issues, yet here the enforcement mechanisms are far less effective. This is especially true for the Venice Commission which has thoroughly dealt with a variety of questions relating to Hungary, but many of its concerns and requests remain unanswered (see Chapter 11, Joakim Nergelius, 'The Role of the Venice Commission in Maintaining the Rule of Law in Hungary and in Romania'). Although the European Court of Human Rights may develop and apply the European Convention on Human Rights as a constitutional document (see Chapter 9, Christoph Grabenwarter, 'The European Convention on Human Rights: Inherent Constitutional Tendencies and the Role of the European Court of Human Rights'), the length of its proceedings and its focus on individual cases prevent it from providing a sufficient answer to systemic deficiencies in the rule of law (see Chapter 10, Mahulena Hofmann, 'Central and Eastern European Member States of the EU and the European Convention on Human Rights').

This volume does not only diagnose the problems, but also makes proposals on how to deal with the crises. For example, Article 2 TEU may serve as a basis for judicial enforcement of the foundational values of the EU within the framework of a reverse-*Solange* doctrine (see Chapter 8, Armin von Bogdandy, Carlino Antpöhler, Johanna Dickschen, Simon Hentrei, Matthias Kottmann and Maja Smrkolj, 'A European Response to Domestic Constitutional Crisis: Advancing the Reverse-*Solange* doctrine'). The European Convention on Human Rights can be strengthened to provide a common constitutional minimum in Europe (see Chapter 13, Tilmann Altwicker, 'Convention Rights as Minimum Constitutional Guarantees? The Conflict between Domestic Constitutional Law and the European Convention on Human Rights'). Furthermore, legitimate national constitution-making needs to respect comparative, European and international standards (see Chapter 12, Matthias Hartwig, 'What Legitimises a National Constitution?'). The existence of such standards allow the concept of unconstitutional constitution

[4] See European Commission presents a framework to safeguard the rule of law in the European Union European Commission—IP/14/237, 11 March 2014, http://europa.eu/rapid/press-release_IP-14-237_en.htm; in detail A von Bogdandy and I Ioannidis, 'Systemic deficiency in the rule of law' (2014) 51 *Common Market Law Review* 59.

on the basis of core European values (see Chapter 14, Catherine Dupré, 'The Unconstitutional Constitution: A Timely Concept').

Ultimately, the chapters in this volume will join in the discourse on systemic deficiencies in Europe by demonstrating the examples that warrant this discourse, and by indicating possible ways of addressing such deficiencies.

Heidelberg/Budapest, March 2014
Armin von Bogdandy and Pál Sonnevend

Contents

List of Contributors

Tilmann Altwicker is a lecturer at the University of Basel.

Carlino Antpöhler is a research fellow at the Max Planck Institute for Comparative Public Law and International Law, Heidelberg.

Armin von Bogdandy is Director at the Max Planck Institute for Comparative Public Law and International Law, Heidelberg

Lóránt Csink is an associate professor of Law at Pázmány Péter Catholic University, Budapest, and a Head of Department at the Office of the Commissioner of Fundamental Rights, Hungary.

Johanna Dickschen is a research fellow at the Max Planck Institute for Comparative Public Law and International Law, Heidelberg.

Catherine Dupré is a senior lecturer at the University of Exeter.

Christoph Grabenwarter is a Professor of Public Law, Business Law and Public International Law, Vienna University of Economics and Business Administration and judge at the Austrian Constitutional Court.

Matthias Hartwig is a research fellow at the Max Planck Institute for Comparative Public Law and International Law, Heidelberg.

Simon Hentrei is a research fellow at the Max Planck Institute for Comparative Public Law and International Law, Heidelberg.

Frank Hoffmeister is the Deputy Head of Cabinet in Commissioner De Gucht's Cabinet.

Mahulena Hofmann is a professor at the Faculty of Law, Economics and Finance, University of Luxembourg and the SES Chair in Satellite Communications and Media Law.

Bogdan Iancu is an associate professor (Comparative Constitutional Law and Constitutional Theory), University of Bucharest, Faculty of Political Science

András Jakab is Schumpeter Fellow at the Max Planck Institute for Comparative Public Law and International Law in Heidelberg, and the Director of the Institute for Legal Studies at the Centre for Social Sciences of the Hungarian Academy of Sciences in Budapest.

Matthias Kottmann is an attorney and was a research fellow at the Max Planck Institute for Comparative Public Law and International Law.

Joakim Nergelius is a professor at Örebro University School of Law, Psychology and Social Work.

Gábor Polyák is an associate professor at the University of Pécs.

Kim Lane Scheppele is the Rockefeller Professor of Sociology and International Affairs, as well as the Director of the Program in Law and Public Affairs, at Princeton University, and also a Faculty Fellow at the University of Pennsylvania Law School.

Maja Smrkolj is a research fellow at the Max Planck Institute for Comparative Public Law and International Law, Heidelberg.

László Sólyom was President of Hungary from 2005 until 2010. Previously he was president of the Constitutional Court of Hungary from 1990 to 1998.

Pál Sonnevend is a Professor of European and International Law at ELTE University Faculty of Law.

Cosmina Tanasoiu is an Associate Professor of Comparative European Politics at American University in Bulgaria, Department of Politics and European Studies.

Part I

Setting the Scene

The New Basic Law of Hungary

1

The Rise and Decline of Constitutional Culture in Hungary

LÁSZLÓ SÓLYOM

I. THE RISE

A. Why Recall the Short History of Constitutional Culture in Hungary?

WE ARE AT a turning point in the history of Hungarian constitutionalism, when its achievements have been endangered. To use T.S. Eliot's words, in this time of distress of nations and perplexity it may be useful to recall the formative period of Hungarian constitutional culture, when the scene was set in the 1990s. I do that not in order to show what could be lost. Rather I search into the source from which the vitality of constitutional culture draws. Obviously, it must have inner resources of its own. Yet there was an original intertwining, too, the embedding of Hungarian constitutionalism into international constitutional culture, professional and cultural impacts that had standardising effects, and also mutuality that nourished this culture. After 20 years the context is different. But under the present demolition of what has been built so ambitiously and carefully since the democratic change, identification of determinative traits of that constitutional development is crucial. It helps to form a clear picture of the present situation. Furthermore, one can see which factors may be vital for the survival of constitutionality. Even the differences of the two époques will be instructive.

Thus, this chapter will enlarge upon two subjects. First I describe the formation of constitutionalism in Hungary, especially the influence of examples from abroad. The taking over and adaptive reshaping of foreign legal materials, doctrine and norms and the active integration into the European constitutional culture I will call this 'reception', hoping that this shorthand expression will not hide the complexity of the process. The remote reference to once receiving Roman law may even recall that complexity. Then I touch upon the topical question of the life expectancies of constitutional cultures founded on this basis.

B. 'Reception' of European Constitutionalism

As to my first subject, the so-called reception, we have scholarly works written on it, among others, by contributors to this volume. Catherine Dupré presented a book on the Hungarian Constitutional Court and the German Bundesverfassungsgericht. Kim Scheppele wrote on the 'supranational constitutionalism' of the Hungarian Court. Pál Sonnevend compared the constitutional status of the right to property and social rights in Germany and Hungary.[1] First, I would like to reinforce the usefulness of dealing with this already historical subject, reception. It does have relevance to today's discussions. We may see it as an example of the meeting of constitutional cultures, and the manner in which this worked. It embraced both taking over foreign legal materials and undertaking international obligations. We can also see the power of domestic legal traditions and, at the same time, the political importance of international embeddings. One can discover how steps of constitutional development repeat themselves, in many cases without knowing their predecessors, but in other cases explicitly as if following a model. And if we consider that in the history of the great ideals for the new constitutional courts there also have been periods of political pressure and temporary decay, there may be lessons to be drawn as to realistic expectations about the present situation in Hungary.

Reception is a subject strongly capable of feeding myths around constitutional justice. It is similar to the saga of the 'three generations of European constitutional courts'. These two are interlinked: the time of reception has shortened exponentially from generation to generation. It is then supposed that the legal material has been taken over from the previous generation. The proliferating new generations join the older ones more and more rapidly and a common constitutional culture spreads in this way. This supposition is, on the one hand, realistic, even natural. On the other hand, it needs correction. We shall look at the latter.

C. Correcting the 'Three Generations of Constitutional Courts' Schema

Looking at the development of constitutional review in Europe as the emergence of three generations of constitutional courts—the German, Iberian and post-communist countries' constitutional courts—has by now become general wisdom. A *bon mot* of Roman Herzog made the three generation concept popular. The former President of the Bundesverfassungsgericht claimed that the Spanish

[1] C Dupré, *Importing the Law in Post-Communist Transitions: The Hungarian Constitutional Court and the Right to Human Dignity* (Oxford, Hart, 2003); KL Scheppele, 'Constitutional Negotiations: Political Contexts of Judicial Activism in Post-Soviet Europe' (2003) 18 *International Sociology* 219; P Sonnevend, *Eigentumsschutz und Sozialversicherung: Eine rechtsvergleichende Analyse anhand der Rechtsprechung des Bundesverfassungsgerichts und des ungarischen Verfassungsgerichts* (Berlin, Springer, 2008).

and Portuguese courts were the daughters of Karlsruhe, and the Polish and Hungarian courts, the granddaughters.

It is similarly accepted that all three generations are inseparable from democratic changes. Moreover, the constitutional courts were seen, and they regarded themselves, as symbols and guarantors of the new, democratic system. This connection was well known and consciously used by the German, Italian and Austrian constitutional courts even in the beginning as, before the birth of the 'classic' second generation courts in Spain and Portugal, in 1972 they established the originally four-member Conference of the European Constitutional Courts in order to promote democratic development in Yugoslavia. The link between democratic change and constitutional justice today has become institutionalised. The Council of Europe considers the existence of a constitutional court as proof of the rule of law and has made it a membership criterion as regards the post-Soviet republics.

However, the democratic changes were of a different nature in the case of each generation. In Germany and Italy, the Nazi and Fascist regimes were destroyed in a war and democracy was set up from a level of zero under the tutelage of the victors. Yet the change from the Fascist regimes of Franco and Salazar in Spain and Portugal into democracy in the 1970s was a 'peaceful transition', as was two decades later the 'velvet revolutions' in the communist dominated Central and East-European states and indeed, in parts of the former Soviet Union. The institutions of the ancient regime were not abolished nor were its political players banned.

What is more, the system change in Poland and Hungary was based on negotiations between the Communist Party and the democratic opposition. Especially in Hungary, the system change was based on the principle of legality: each step of the negotiated revolution had to have a clear legal ground, and in 1989 the new democratic constitutional changes were issued by the still communist-dominated Parliament, before the free elections. So the new regime started with contradictions between many mechanisms of formal and institutional continuity and, at the same time, with the presence of decisive, radical and indeed revolutionary change as regards the substance of the law, the state and the economy. The Hungarian Constitutional Court expressed this situation by the phrase 'revolution under the rule of law'.[2]

This historical peculiarity had paradoxical consequences for the Constitutional Court, as well. For instance, not all constitutional judges were chosen from dissidents to the old regime, as was the case in Germany, where

[2] 11/1992 (III.5) AB határozat (Constitutional Court of Hungary) (Decision 11/1992). Translations of the most important decisions of the first Constitutional Court (1990–98) can be found in L Sólyom and G Brunner, *Constitutional Judiciary in a New Democracy: The Hungarian Constitutional Court* (Ann Arbor, MI, University of Michigan Press, 2000), accompanied by two introductory studies and headnotes. As for Decision 11/1992 see ibid 214, 221. For a more extended selection of judgments from 1990–93 in German see G Bunner and L Sólyom, *Verfassungsgerichtsbarkeit in Ungarn: Analysen und Entscheidungssammlung 1990–1993* (Baden-Baden, Nomos Verlagsgesellschaft, 1995).

the election of many former emigrants gave additional symbolic force to the first Bundesverfassungsgericht. On the other hand, even the compromises in the transition helped the Constitutional Court to appear as a symbol of the new regime. The majoritarian institutions of the democratic state had predecessors in the old system where they were corrupted and misused. The Constitutional Court was, in contrast, totally new, created for the new regime, free from inherited distrust. The Court also benefited from the in itself negative trait of the pioneering countries of democratisation in that they started with amendments of the Constitution and reached a formal new constitution later.[3] In such a situation, the Constitutional Court represented the new constitutional order even in the absence of a formally new constitution, and in fact it performed that role through its creative and extensive interpretation of the constitutional rules. The text of the Constitution was negotiated at the National Round Table in a hurry, and thus it was partly based on not always correct translations of international agreements and contained gaps and inconsistencies. This created occasions for developing and enforcing unwritten principles and filling gaps with new rules by the Constitutional Court.

Furthermore, the second and third generation courts immediately obtained the high status of a constitutional court as 'constitutional organ', that is, an equal rank to the parliament and government that in the 1950s the German Constitutional Court had with some trouble fought out for itself.[4]

As a final remark regarding the three generations, one can see that the family members turned out to be very different. This is especially true for the populous cohort of the post-communist courts. The mere existence of a constitutional court says little about the role and performance of the court, or of the quality of democracy, in a given state.[5]

D. Revival of the Kelsenial Model and its Consequences

While accepting the three generations schema one must not forget that even the 'grandfather', the German Federal Constitutional Court, must have had a father. For Europe, the great ancestor is surely the Austrian Constitutional Court, which was set up in 1921. This was the first constitutional court in

[3] In 1989, the Round Table Negotiations in Hungary drafted the text of a brand new Constitution that was, however, passed on political grounds as an amendment of the communist Constitution. In Poland, the 'Small Constitution', which contained the inevitable amendments to the system change, was replaced only in 1997 by a new Constitution. In Hungary a formally new Constitution was passed as late as 2011.

[4] *Cf* the texts of the famous 'Statusbericht' and the 'Statusdenkschrift' with further documents on the struggle between the Constitutional Court and the Federal Government in G Leibholz, 'Der Status des Bundesverfassungsgerichts' (1957) 6 *Jahrbuch des öffentlichen Rechts* 109.

[5] This has become a formal proof for the democratic character of a state, see n 2 above. The Conference of the European Constitutional Courts does not evaluate the members, either. The membership criterion is the power to review and annul Acts of Parliament.

Europe, and its legal foundation greatly relied on the rich contribution of Hans Kelsen. The so-called new constitutional courts in Central and Eastern Europe are no doubt the offspring of Kelsen. Their main activity is *a posteriori* abstract norm control. In contrast, the German Constitutional Court of 1951 united the Kelsenian form of a self-standing constitutional court with the power to annul Acts of Parliament, with an individual remedy for infringement of constitutional rights and the power to review judgments of ordinary courts. As a result, the European development of constitutional justice branched off.

The revival of the Kelsenian model in the post-communist constitutional courts, especially the Hungarian Constitutional Court, had far-reaching consequences. First, the inherent counter-majoritarian difficulty has been enormously aggravated; the conflict between the Constitutional Court, as the Kelsenian 'negative legislator', and the democratic legislator, that is, the Parliament, has become obvious and provocative. Through the declaration of laws as null and void on a large scale[6] the power of the constitutional judges did not remain 'hidden'[7] and for lack of individual complaints this power demonstrated itself solely vis-à-vis the Parliament. However, the legislators were also well aware of their freshly obtained and impeccable democratic legitimacy and inherited the doctrine of unlimited parliamentary supremacy from socialist legal theory as well. In the first 20 years, the Court succeeded, but after the 2010 elections the two-thirds government majority in fact has enforced its supremacy over the Constitutional Court even as it has over the Constitution itself.

Secondly, Hungary not only followed the abstract model; it introduced an *actio popularis* for abstract constitutional review. This meant unlimited standing for everybody. To challenge the constitutionality of a law the applicant was not required to show any violation of his/her rights or interests. He/she acted in the pure interest of constitutionality. Due to this, there was a continuous flow of abstract reviews with an unprecedentedly high rate of declaring laws null and void. As new legislation could immediately be brought before the Constitutional Court, the Court gained a disproportionate role in current politics. On the other hand, through this open door citizens could directly participate in the constitutional transformation of the entire legal order. No wonder that politicians continually criticised the *actio popularis*. Still it was eliminated only in 2011 as a part of the overall constitutional changes.

[6] In the first four years, nearly one-third of the reviewed laws and ministerial decrees (122 out of 420) were annulled; among them 21 Acts of the new Parliament.

[7] The famous remark of Tocqueville in A de Tocqueville, *Democracy in America* (Cambridge, Sever and Francis, 1835) vol 1, ch 6 that the power of the American judges over Congress lays hidden behind the decisions taken in individual cases was frequently mentioned by the first constitutional judges in Hungary.

E. Interplay of the Abstract Review and *actio popularis* and the Self-understanding of the Constitutional Court

The abstract review and the unlimited standing to trigger it had a direct impact on the reception of a common European constitutional culture. As the interplay of these two peculiarities aggravated the conflict with the legislature, the Constitutional Court badly needed the feedback of international parallels and examples. It had to show that such a 'difficulty' is inherent in any democratic order.

Considering cases without any concrete controversy or infringement of individual rights resulted in abstract reasoning by the Court. Because the case was not about the rights of the petitioner the Constitutional Court felt itself not limited to the dimensions of the petition but used it as a starting point and extended the investigation to a complex problem and even to other respective norms. One may say the Court posed questions to itself and answered them. One may even say the Court used the petitions to produce a commentary on the Constitution for use by state authorities and for the citizens of the new democracy as well. This rather abstract work was a fertile soil for notions, theories and dogmatic solutions. The Court searched rather for abstract rules and methods in foreign legal orders than for similar cases or precedents. The judges consulted first of all textbooks and commentaries, and then wrote their opinions in the same style.

The Constitutional Court simply needed the tools for the work; it created and manufactured them for instant use, and made public without delay the measures and methods by which it worked, and the exact meaning of key notions and formulas. The judgments of the first five to six years, even the operative portions, were full of sentences more appropriate for a textbook than a judgment. Of course, a considerable part of those tools were imported goods. Although they were lightly adjusted for domestic use, the Court did not regard them as a foreign element. They harmonised with the Court's policy of acting as if it operated in a fully developed, established democracy. In this 'anticipatory democracy' the European dogmatic arsenal was in the right place.

F. Favourable Domestic Preconditions

The law received from abroad did not arrive in a vacuum. There were traditions of some sort of constitutional review, and knowledge of foreign legal materials was present.

As to constitutional review, in the 1980s constitutional councils or similar bodies were set up in some socialist countries, among others in Hungary.[8] The

[8] Besides the early Yugoslav Constitutional Court, the Constitutional Tribunal in Poland and the Russian Authority for Constitutional Supervision, the Constitutional Council in Hungary can be named.

socialist doctrine of the absolute sovereignty of parliament did not allow for the nullification of acts (or even their review) by such bodies. But the idea of a clear hierarchical order of legal norms without contradictions surely paved the way for an easy acceptance of the abstract review and abstract competences of the Constitutional Court. I think the abstract norm control also fitted well with democratic change. The task was to set up a new system and to confine the other powers within the frame of the Constitution. In a settled democracy individual infringements of basic rights are malfunctions; here the abstract review is a means to create a settled democracy.

From the point of view of knowledge of foreign law and its possible impact, the tradition of comparative law in the socialist époque must be mentioned first. The socialist system was in many respects traditional, that is, not 'modern'. The common European culture of the nineteenth century survived long here. Hungarian law students had obligatory classes on the trends and great personalities of the British, French and most of all German legal history in fine detail. They heard about recent developments, as well. The Hungarian presence in the international comparative law scene, even from the 1960s on, might officially have been aimed at making socialist law known and accepted abroad. But this policy also made possible contacts with the Western legal world (mainly universities). The comparative method prevailed especially in civil law. The role of the civil law in the development of the new constitutional culture was in many respects more important than that of constitutional law.

In the mid-1980s a real freedom fight broke out on the basis of the Civil Code. Its provisions on privacy and other personal rights were suddenly used to secure spheres of personal autonomy and, at that time very importantly, protect personal data and enforce access to public data. The rules about legal entities and especially associations were claimed to legalise civil organisations, too. Some civil courts were very helpful in such cases.[9] Naturally, this trend pointed to the individual protection of human rights.

Considering that in the first Constitutional Court former civil law professors and civil judges had decisive influence, all of whom had a certain skill in German law, it is no miracle that in the first period of the Constitutional Court human dignity, *das allgemeine Persönlichkeitsrecht, die allgemeine Handlungsfreiheit* (the right to free fulfilment of one's personality, the general freedom of action), and 'the right to informational self-determination' played an outstanding role. The Constitutional Court simply continued the domestic tradition and therefore I would be reluctant to speak of an original reception in this field.

[9] For illustration, see a case from the 1980s. To obtain a pass to travel to non-socialist countries the application to the police had to contain the recommendation of the employer (issued by the Director and the Party and union leaders). A county court held that refusal of the recommendation (they simply saw no guarantee that the applicant would return to Hungary) violated the applicant's personality right. For the use of the civil law in the role of a constitutional complaint see L Sólyom, 'Constitutional Privacy in Today's Hungary: A Civil Lawyer's View' in L Swidler (ed), *Human Rights: Christians, Marxists and Others in Dialogue* (New York, Paragon House, 1991) 157.

In sum, German (and partly American)[10] examples were already assimilated into Hungarian legal thinking, not to speak of our own tradition. Personal rights have had a long history in Hungary going back to the beginning of the twentieth century and developed especially under the impact of Swiss law. The dogmatic differences between the German *Grundgesetz* and the jurisprudence of the Hungarian Constitutional Court concerning human dignity and freedom of action are not misinterpretations; they resulted simply from the civil law origins in Hungary.

Besides the cultural impact—or rather, as I would stress, the preserving of the common European heritage under socialism—a further trait of Hungarian civil law might have been beneficial for the carrier of constitutional justice. Until 1960, when the Civil Code came into force, the civil law in Hungary was customary law, which had lived and developed in the judgments of the courts.[11] On this basis, judicial law-making and even judicial activism was quite natural for the Constitutional Court (or at least for its members with civil law backgrounds).[12]

Finally, one must not forget that the International Covenant on Civil and Political Rights was already promulgated in Hungary in 1976. As the possibility of an individual complaint was created in Hungary at the end of 1988, everybody saw it as part of the process of a changing system. In 1989, the chapter on basic rights of the totally amended (ie new) democratic constitution was mostly compiled of rules of both UN Covenants on human rights. Nevertheless the Constitutional Court wanted to set higher requirements than the minimum standards of international conventions.

G. The Force of Ideas: the Process of Integration into European Constitutionality

Now we can turn to the question, in what manner the reception occurred. Hegel said it is the way of implementation that matters. It would be unrealistic to suppose that the new constitutional courts had a thorough or ordered knowledge of foreign constitutional laws, or that the reception was a systematic process. It was based on fragments of information, on impressions, on documents without knowing

[10] In the field of freedom of speech, the leading decision is 30/1992 (V.26) AB határozat (Constitutional Court of Hungary) (Decision 30/1992); Sólyom and Brunner, *Constitutional Judiciary in a New Democracy* (n 2) 229.

[11] The freedom of the judges in interpreting and, by this, determining, the content of the law was held by the Constitutional Court to be the basis of the independence of the judicial power. See 38/1993 (VI.11) AB határozat (Constitutional Court of Hungary); Sólyom and Brunner, *Constitutional Judiciary in a New Democracy* (n 2) 5, 475, 481.

[12] R Procházka, *Mission Accomplished: On Founding Constitutional Adjudication in Central Europe* (Budapest, Central European University Press, 2002) 51, also emphasises the role of the traditional 'fluidity of the law making authority' in Hungary, and that the Constitutional Court with its 'invisible constitution', the review of the 'living law' and determining 'constitutional requirements' reaffirmed the paradigm of polycentric law-making. However, the force of tradition is always a result of a multitude of influences.

their circumstances and setting. The reception worked through accidental events, personal meetings,[13] memories of readings and random new books.

However, this chaos was ordered by a high ideal of a truly working Constitutional Court that fulfils its vocation. Unbelievable as it may sound, at that time ideas did have a real force. The ideology of 'Returning to Europe' after 40 years was powerful; everybody wanted to prove that we had not lost connections to Europe, and even if in secret, we had tried to keep abreast of it. There was no hint of anxiety about loss of national sovereignty or leaving the proper path of national heritage, by contrast to today's Euroscepticism. Raising the question whether a court may cite foreign law, as has been highly debated in the United States,[14] was simply unthinkable. All these facilitated the political and popular acceptance of European standards introduced by the Constitutional Court. And the Constitutional Court wanted to become on a par with the best European courts. What then was received: legal techniques or ideas?

The technical aspect of the reception shows the usual picture of legal transplants, but with peculiarities.

First, the Court handled the fresh knowledge without scruples, or I would say, creatively. In a meeting between the Hungarian and the Italian Constitutional Court the president of the Italian Constitutional Court mentioned in passing the *diritto vivente* (living law). Two weeks later the Hungarian Court pronounced a judgment that introduced review of the 'living law', that is, it reviewed the law not as it has been written but in the meaning as it is applied by the ordinary courts. By this means, the Constitutional Court extended its competence, establishing at least a partial control over ordinary courts (as regards their consolidated interpretation of laws). Review of the living law meant reviewing the judge-made law.

In addition, the Constitutional Court introduced the *verfassungskonforme Auslegung* (interpretation of a law conforming to the Constitution). But the constitutional judges were cautious enough not to mention the word 'interpretation' because the ordinary courts held it to be in their exclusive competence. So the Constitutional Court defined the constitutional requirements that the possible interpretations of the law must meet. Even though 'constitutional interpretation' is not explicit in Hungarian law, it played the same role as in the German model case. For the new courts, the goals were more important than the means to achieve it. The 'classic' competences known and taken over from the previous generations of constitutional courts were freely used for other functions. For instance, an

[13] Personal contacts were of eminent importance in the first years of the third generation courts. It is a pity that the impact and results of these meetings—the frequent mutual visits, small informal conferences etc—cannot be exactly documented. The German Constitutional Court was doubtless the main actor in that movement. Later on the Venice Commission (of the Council of Europe), consisting in a great part of constitutional judges and the documentary services of the Commission, took over a part of this role. But in 1991 it was quite natural that one day the Presidents of the German, Austrian and Italian Constitutional Courts, the Swiss Federal Court and the French Constitutional Council dropped in on the Hungarian Court for a full day talk and mutual exchange of information.

[14] For an overview of the debate over the use of foreign authority in interpreting the US Constitution, see MA Water's review of VC Jackson, 'Constitutional Engagement in a Transitional Era' (2011) 59 *American Journal of Comparative Law* 605.

abstract interpretation of constitutional provisions was regularly used to resolve conflicts between high state organs (ie *Organstreitigkeiten)*; or federal conflicts were cleared by abstract review of norms. There occurred obvious misunderstandings, as well. For instance, the Hungarian Court merged the German *Leitsatz* and the American headnote into a long operative part of the judgment, which was nevertheless *erga omnes* binding.

Secondly, notwithstanding the creativity of the new courts, the common language of the European constitutional law had to be learned. Of the new courts, only those who correctly understood and spoke this language could integrate into the common European constitutional tradition.

Thirdly, the new courts had different attitudes towards reception. Some overplayed the role of the good pupil, others, especially the Hungarian Constitutional Court, sought emancipation. In enigmatic cases the Hungarian Court set higher standards than the European average, for instance, regarding freedom of speech or when it prohibited reducing the level of environmental protection once achieved. The Court often raised in the reasons more radical questions than was usual. The opinion relating to the abolition of the death penalty speaks not of the cruelty of that punishment nor does it question its preventive effect. It is based on a monist idea of man, not differentiating between soul and body and reaches the absolute untouchability of the right to life in conjunction with the right to human dignity.[15]

Fourthly, the individual new courts were not the final stage of the reception. Their judgments with their achievements had further impacts within the third generation and even within the general community of constitutional courts.[16] This mutuality was facilitated by the lucky historical moment caused by the international interest in the system change and the fact that, due to the unification of Germany, the most influential Bundesverfassungsgericht faced the same constitutional questions of transition.

Besides the absolutely necessary mastering of the common European language and alongside a random taking over of solutions of concrete cases, the new constitutional courts wanted above all to achieve the authority, political weight and professional level of the established old constitutional courts.

[15] As regards freedom of speech see n 10 as to access to public data, see 32/1992 (V.29) AB határozat (Constitutional Court of Hungary) and Sólyom and Brunner, *Constitutional Judiciary in a New Democracy* (n 2) 384; as to environmental protection see 28/1994 (V.20) AB határozat (Constitutional Court of Hungary) and Sólyom and Brunner, *Constitutional Judiciary in a New Democracy* (n 2) 298; as to capital punishment see Decision 23/1990 (Sólyom and Brunner, *Constitutional Judiciary in a New Democracy* (n 2) 118).

[16] The influence of the Hungarian decision on capital punishment is clearly shown in Eastern Europe. However, the international publicity of the decision was decisive when the new South African Constitutional Court cited the Hungarian Court in two important respects: the absolute inviolability of the right to life and dignity, and the independence of the Constitutional Court's reasoning from the opinion of the Parliament and public opinion. *S v Makwanyane and another* 1994 (3) SA 868 (A) [83–85], [89]. The integration of the third generation in the common constitutional culture is witnessed by its presence in the legal literature even today, when the grants and programmes for 'transitology' have dried up.

Surely, it was an unhistorical, idealised picture they created for themselves. Forty years of development of European constitutionalism was condensed in that idol. The new courts did not bother with the change of the historical context; they did not ask whether the star courts are still at their zenith. They also did not study the early years of the model courts, although searching for historical lessons might have been useful.

I return here to the immense power of ideas, of metaphors, of wishful thinking when they meet the force of the unique moment of a great historical change. It is astonishing how much from the *acquis* of European constitutionality was not known, and yet how much of its solutions, dogmatic phraseology and ways to resolve hard cases the new courts invented for themselves. For instance, the Hungarian Court did not know that the German Constitutional Court had already in its first months determined the content of the motion independently of the intent of the petitioner, or that the German Court had spelled out the inherent unity (*innere Einheit*) of the Constitution from which a hierarchy of the constitutional rules follows.[17] Still, on the ground of its actual circumstances due to the abstractness of the review and the *actio popularis*, the Hungarian Constitutional Court also freed itself very soon from the bounds of the motion. It also developed a hierarchy of norms within the Constitution and took the unity of the Constitution as a starting point of the review. The Hungarian judges did not read the long story of the *Gutachten-Streit* of 1952 but refused with similar words[18] to deliver an advisory opinion and the preliminary review of a not yet passed law.

The strong aspiration to achieve the quality of the model courts and to fulfil the ideally conceived task of a true constitutional court was apt and able to produce comparable results. However, the timing, that is, the tempo on which the quality of all performances turns, of realising that task was not comparable. The Hungarian Court wanted to deliver interpretations of each provision of the Constitution and to develop a coherent constitutional law within the shortest possible time. In half a decade it wished to be integrated into European constitutionality and within the same time it wanted to establish a firm status in the political system. But as regards the latter, the rapidity of the system change did not allow time to ripen the fruits. Seminal cases in Germany had already lost their concrete and politically sensitive topicality when, after a few years, a judgment set a new direction for constitutional development.[19] By contrast, the Hungarian Court wanted to have instant results

[17] [1951] 1 BVerfGE 14. For Hungary see 48/1991 (IX.26) AB határozat (Constitutional Court of Hungary); Sólyom and Brunner, *Constitutional Judiciary in a New Democracy* (n 2) 159, 170.

[18] It would contradict the judicial function of the Court. See 16/1991 (IV.20) AB határozat (Constitutional Court of Hungary); Sólyom and Brunner, *Constitutional Judiciary in a New Democracy* (n 2) 151, 154.

[19] See the *Lüth* case; Bundesverfassungsgericht, 1 BvR 400/51 of 15 January 1958, [1958] 7 BVerfGE 198. The original case (boycott against a film of a director with Nazi past in 1950) was a long time in the past when the Constitutional Court spoke out about the effect of the basic rights and the value system of the Constitution on the entire legal system.

and allowed no time for getting rid of daily political confrontations, which in turn made the acceptance of principal achievements more troublesome.[20]

What then was received? Most concretely, the new constitutional courts introduced parts of the praxis of the traditional European courts and solutions of cases and doctrines, which had been for the most part commonly used in democratic Europe. Most importantly, they took over the spirit, the ethos of European constitutionality, which is the true role of a constitutional court in a democratic order. By this, the new constitutional courts joined the European constitutional culture and assimilated it creatively, each in its own way. It is not easy to define the 'common European constitutional tradition'. However, if we consider it as the sum or the essence of the constitutional praxis of all EU Members, it is then the ethos of European constitutionality, or, as Pedro Cruz Villalon worded it so aptly, *ein Verfassungswillen* (the will to act constitutionally).[21] I would say the notion of the common constitutional tradition resembles *Weltliteratur*. Thus, reception did not mean simple imitation, but rather gaining education, becoming highly literate. The Hungarian Constitutional Court read a great deal and became well informed, with good taste and a secure *judicium*. The Hungarian constitutional judges and their Central European colleagues received a constitutional culture. And the goal and the real performance of the Hungarian Constitutional Court were to create and maintain constitutional culture in Hungary.

II. AND THE DECLINE

For the second part of my chapter I have to change the tone. On 1 January 2012, a new Constitution and a new Constitutional Court Act entered into force, which brought about fundamental changes in the attitude towards constitutionalism. In fact, the changes had already started in 2010 when the previous opposition had a landslide victory in the 2010 parliamentary elections. It is not exaggerated to say that Parliament and government have abandoned the constitutional culture that had been developed in the last 20 years. I should like to consider the prospects for that constitutional culture under these circumstances.

A. Achievements by 2010

The democratic constitutional reform of 1989 was passed as an amendment of the communist Constitution, so the new content appeared under the old

[20] The beautiful fruits of the 'anticipatory democracy' policy of the Hungarian Constitutional Court must prove their ripeness and durability in today's crisis.

[21] C Villalon, 'Impulse aus der spanischen Verfassungstradition für den europäischen Grundrechtsschutz' in PJ Tettinger and K Stern (eds), *Kölner Gemeinschaftskommentar zur Europäischen Grundrechte-Charta* (Munich, Beck, 2006) 148.

numbering as Act XX of 1949. This contradiction between form and content had little significance at that time.[22] It proved to be the fertile soil from which constitutional culture in Hungary grew strong and fast. This new culture embraced a much wider circle of the population than legal practitioners and people in public administration. Not least due to the *actio popularis*, people had daily experience with the effects and enforceability of the Constitution. With some exaggeration I would state that the *actio popularis* served as a channel for direct democracy. Citizens participated in legislation, even if from the negative (Kelsenian) side; they could achieve amendments or nullification of laws, but all these acts took place under the strict measure of the Constitution and its principles. This was an immense learning process of understanding the essence of constitutionality and experiencing the absolute rule of the Constitution. On the other hand, the population learned that there are limits to political power, and that those barriers are to be found in the Constitution.

The Constitutional Court developed the Constitution into a coherent system in full accordance with the common European traditions. Although the situation was far from being ideal, the Constitution was accepted by the political forces as the ultimate framework of their possibilities. The conflicts between the Constitutional Court and the political branches of the state remained within limits and in the end there was sufficient harmony between the text of the Constitution and 'constitutional reality'.

An aggravated counter-majoritarian difficulty was programmed into the abstract competences, ambitions and activism of the Constitutional Court. However, even the fiercest reactions of the government did not overstep the measures and methods observable in other European countries; these reactions included extended vacancies of seats, manipulative use of competencies by state authorities as petitioners and harsh public criticism from the side of the Parliament or government following certain decisions of the Court.[23]

B. New Government will Return to Absolute Parliamentary Sovereignty

The decline or fall of a constitutional culture is a complex process and cannot be grasped solely by referring to changes in constitutional texts. On the other hand, it is a slippery ground to speak in general terms of changes in the attitude towards constitutionality, especially if these arose from small and in themselves

[22] The Preamble to the Constitution has foreseen the passing of a new Constitution after the transition.

[23] Even the early history of the German Federal Constitutional Court was full of rough interventions of the government. But as Boulanger states, the institution of the Constitutional Court itself never became endangered, C Boulanger, *Hüten, Richten, Gründen: Rollen der Verfassungsgerichte in der Demokratisierung Deutschlands und Ungarns* (epubli, Berlin, 2013).

insignificant steps.[24] Nevertheless, constitutional culture is more than formal legality. It imparts a conceptual unity to the implementation of the basic law. In effect it defines unwritten limits: there are things you would never do even if they were not explicitly prohibited by the Constitution. That is why constitutionalism presupposes an intellectual and emotional culture, a shared interpretation of the meaning of words and participation in an intellectual and political community that keeps reinterpreting the meaning of words as required by changing times. Hence, it follows that constitutional culture is not an internal affair.[25]

In case of a constitution-making majority, acting contrary to the spirit of the constitution goes hand in hand with corruption of the actual text of the constitution. This is what happened in Hungary.

In 2010, the centre-right parties won a two-thirds parliamentary majority. The victory resulted from the deep dissatisfaction with, and protests against, the socialist government of the last eight years. The victor announced a new beginning and declared the 20 years since the democratic change as a failed experiment. Thus, not only the long-lasting previous socialist government was rejected but the 'unsuccessful (since compromise-based) system change' itself had to be remade. From this arises the revolutionary rhetoric of the new government. From this follows the return to the agenda of 1989–90 in many respects. Such a remake has not been limited to 'unsettled', 'unfinished' themes, such as, for instance, punishing political crimes of the communist era.

While the old Constitution was based on the separation of powers and a system of checks and balances, the new *Verfassungswirklichkeit* is grounded on absolute parliamentary sovereignty and the practical weakening of all counterweights to it. This weakening meant personnel changes as well as changes in the organisation and competences of the other powers. If the relation between the Constitutional Court and the legislature could be identified in the former system with the counter-majoritarian difficulty, this has now been replaced by majoritarian arrogance. According to an often-repeated statement from the government side, nothing can halt a two-thirds majority, not even the Constitution.

[24] This has been the difficulty of the European criticism (eg, in the European Parliament but first of all in the press) about the new Constitution and organic laws in Hungary. If the general feeling of discontent about the state of democracy in Hungary searches for evidence in norms, which are certainly not the bearer of the negative changes and can be found in other countries, too, the criticism will be counter-productive. Disproportionate or ill-founded criticism of the country may hurt the citizens. A good example of moderate and professional criticism is the opinions of the Venice Commission.

[25] As the Constitutional Court held in 1992, that Hungary is a state under the rule of law is both a statement of fact and a statement of policy. Not only must the legal provisions and the operation of state organs comply strictly with the Constitution but the Constitution's values and its conceptual culture must permeate the whole of society. This is the rule of law, and this is how the Constitution becomes reality; Decision 11/1992 (n 2); Sólyom and Brunner, *Constitutional Judiciary in a New Democracy* (n 2) 214, 219.

C. Degrading the Constitution to a Tool of Everyday Politics

Indeed, the status of the Constitution has changed in this sense. The new government promised a new constitution as a symbol of the now actualised revolutionary changes. For a revolution one needs an enemy. Hence, all the blame for the failures and disappointments of the previous 20 years was put on the old Constitution. 'The constitution in force does not deserve respect', declared the incoming Prime Minister.[26] And this programme has in fact been realised. Within only a year and a half (from May 2010 up until the coming into force of the new Constitution on 1 January 2012) the new Parliament pushed through 12 amendments to the Constitution containing twice that number of actual changes and most of them serving momentary political interests. The degradation of the Constitution thus began with the treatment of the old one, which was amended like a ministerial decree, mostly by private member's Bills. Thus, the treatment of the Constitution has been out of tune with the existing constitutional culture, in fact in several areas running contrary to it. This disrupted the steadfastness of and respect for the Constitution but did not yet rewrite the very foundations of the constitutional order.

However, continual questioning of the constitutional rules in force will inevitably damage the idea of constitutionality, too. In the last 20 years it was imperative that all political goals be realised exclusively within the framework of the Constitution.[27] That tenet differentiated the then new regime from the communist one, in which those in power used law as a tool at will. Abandoning this basic concept of constitutionality is the essence of the recent changes. The Constitution is used nowadays again merely as a tool of everyday politics.

Constitutional amendments were passed to 'settle' personnel issues, for instance, in the case of the removal of the President of the Supreme Court while he was in the middle of his term. The elevation of topical economic or taxation policies of the present government to constitutional status, thereby making changes by future governments practically impossible, are similar cases.[28]

The most alarming new tenet is, however, that rules and amendments are being put into the Constitution in order to exclude their constitutional review. The constitutionality of many such provisions is doubtful. But this was exactly the reason why they were incorporated into the Constitution. Some of these provisions should under normal circumstances be included in ordinary laws. For instance, a case involving life sentence without parole was pending in the Constitutional Court. Then, this issue appeared in article IV(2) of the new Basic

[26] MTI (National News Agency), 10 November 2009.

[27] Numerous decisions of the Constitutional Court have made it clear that the rule of the Constitution is absolute; exceptions may not be made even under extraordinary circumstances, as for instance the historical circumstances of the system change. 'A state under the rule of law cannot be created by undermining the rule of law': stated by the Court in Decision 11/1992 (n 2).

[28] But it presented no hindrance to amending such rules in the Constitution by the present government when the financial situation of the country changed.

Law. There are examples when a provision found its way into the Constitution after the Constitutional Court had declared the unconstitutionality of an identically worded law; or where after the annulment of a law by the Constitutional Court, newly amended rules, sometimes identical with the original rejected rules, sometimes meeting only partially the requirements of constitutionality as defined by the Court, have appeared in the Constitution, sometimes in detail, in order to avoid new review.[29] The means of 'constitutionalisation' of norms is used in a preventive sense as well. For instance, since the plan to restrict the right to vote to those who have previously registered had been heavily discussed in the public sphere and declared to be unconstitutional, the rules were written into the transitory provisions of the Basic Law in complete detail.[30]

D. The 2012 Basic Law of Hungary

The new Constitution was passed and came into force on 1 January 2012. I do not recite here the politically heated international and domestic discussion about the 'Basic Law of Hungary'[31] as the Constitution was renamed. I would rather refer again to the difference between the words of the Constitution and the praxis (the 'constitutional reality'). Various constitutional realities may develop from the inherent potentials of the text. In our case, a further differentiation is appropriate between the Constitution proper and its Transitory Provisions. This difference was essential until the fourth amendment to the Basic Law of 11 March 2013.

If we only consider the wording of the new Basic Law as it was originally passed, there is no tragic break between the old Constitution and the new one; the foundations of the latter share a common basis with the former Constitution and with the common democratic standards. Through proper interpretation, this text could have been basis for the survival and growth of the constitutional

[29] Such themes appear in the fourth amendment, among others the restrictive definition of 'family relation' found unconstitutional in 43/2012 (XII.20) AB határozat (Constitutional Court of Hungary), but now found in Basic Law, art L(1); the granting of the status of 'church' to religious organisations by the Parliament 6/2013 (III.1) AB határozat (Constitutional Court of Hungary) (Decision 6/2013), now found in Basic Law, art VII(2) and (3); the prohibition of political advertising by parties in commercial media during the electoral campaign 1/2013 (I.7) AB határozat (Constitutional Court of Hungary) (Decision 1/2013), now found in Basic Law, art IX(3); the introduction of collective defamation despite Decision 30/1992 (n 10); 95/2008 (VII.3) AB határozat (Constitutional Court of Hungary) and 96/2008 (VII.3) AB határozat (Constitutional Court of Hungary), now found in Basic Law, art IX (4)–(6).

[30] But the rules of its implementation were held unconstitutional in Decision 1/2013 (n 29). The fourth amendment in turn does not include the registration of voters.

[31] No doubt the new Constitution is a one-party constitution because the opposition did not participate either in the preparation or in the parliamentary debate on it. For criticism of the non-transparent constitution-making and the lack of public discussion see the Opinions of the Venice Commission: European Commission for Democracy through Law (Venice Commission), Opinion on three legal questions arising in the process of drafting the new constitution of Hungary (Opinion No 614/2011, 28 March 2011). The title 'Basic Law of Hungary' will emphasise the difference between the old Constitution and the new one.

culture. One should attach hope to this text itself, for any constitutional culture needs a constitution. One should cherish this hope despite the fact that there are fundamental system errors in the Basic Law, or that it is overloaded by ideological elements.

Why, though, did the text of the new Constitution remain acceptable? The text of the Basic Law was written behind the veil of secrecy; the Parliament, which consistently gave signs of breaking with the previous constitutional culture, did not participate in its framing.[32] The text's high level of abstraction could have been another reason why the Basic Law remained for the most part outside the requirements of day-to-day politicking. And, finally, as the original motivation for a new constitution was symbolic, emphasis was laid on the novelty of the ideological declarations within the Basic Law and not on any novelty of the operative provisions.

Despite the above positive assessment of the text of the new Basic Law proper, there is a fundamental error in it that makes the whole system questionable. This is the restriction of the competences of the Constitutional Court. Now that the Constitutional Court has been barred from reviewing budget and tax laws by a constitutional amendment in November 2010,[33] the door is open to pass and implement unconstitutional laws in key fields of governance. As has been clear since *Marbury v Madison*, if unconstitutional legislation is possible the Constitution makes no sense.[34]

Another system error of the Basic Law is its very easy amendment. Even based on a private member's Bill, the Constitution can be amended by two-thirds of the votes. Consequently, the Constitution is defenceless against all of the anomalies that presently mark the legislature. The Basic Law is not basic at all; it is not a firm frame for the legal and political order but a comfortable means to make rules of daily interest non-reviewable and perpetual, until the next need to change them. The weight and the roots of this error have become clear only today. Constitution-making and amending the Constitution are regulated in the Basic Law in a common procedural rule requiring two-thirds majority for both. Hence, the required majority thinks that there are no substantial limits to constitutional amendments. Besides, the above-mentioned topical political provisions had been incorporated into the so-called Transitory Provisions of the Basic Law. The Transitory Provisions were continuously 'enriched' by new rules, mostly in response to decisions of the Constitutional Court annulling a law, or preventively, in order to exclude a later review by the Constitutional Court. These rules were

[32] The text was written by a Member of the Hungarian Parliament and a Member of the European Parliament entrusted with the task by the Prime Minister. The MPs, like the public, could read the text for the first time less than one month before the final vote. The Basic Law was passed after a very short discussion with a low presence and participation of even the MPs of the government parties.

[33] Act CXIX of 16 November 2010 amending the Constitution (2010. évi CXIX. törvény a Magyar Köztársaság Alkotmányáról szóló 1949. évi XX. törvény módosításáról). The restriction has been maintained by the Basic Law, art 34(4).

[34] *Marbury v Madison* 5 US 137 (1803).

definitely unconstitutional in the light of the very text of the Basic Law, or would with high probability have proved unconstitutional in the case of review. When the Ombudsman challenged the constitutionality of the Transitory Provisions before the Constitutional Court, the Parliament declared them to be part of the Basic Law in order to exclude review.[35]

E. Restrictive Rearrangement of the Constitutional Court

The change of the status of the Constitutional Court, its subordination to the two-thirds parliamentary majority, began immediately. Right after the elections, in mid-2010, the constitutional rules on the nomination of judges were amended. Instead of being based around the parity of seats in the nominations committee of the Parliament, now seats are distributed according to the number of MPs in the factions. Within a year, the number of judges was increased from 11 to 15. Including the vacant seats, the government factions making up the two-thirds majority immediately sent six new judges of their exclusive choice to the Constitutional Court. Also, the right of the judges to elect the Court's President for a three-year term was replaced by election by Parliament for 12 years. It is worth noting that this was the exact approach proposed by the communists at the Round Table that the democratic opposition (which the now ruling parties were part of) rejected.[36]

A parallel to President Roosevelt's 'court packing' is hardly avoidable. But the analogy doesn't hold. The Supreme Court of the *Lochner* era was conservative, opposing necessary social changes. In contrast, the Hungarian Constitutional Court was the pioneer of constitutional democracy in synchronicity with the time. I think it was not the jurisprudence of the Court that had hurt the new majority; the very idea of constitutional review did not fit into the logic of an unconditioned parliamentary supremacy, especially not under the rule of a constituent majority. Compared to the US Supreme Court, the Hungarian Court did not get involved in conflicts of principle with the new government.[37] The government advanced the distrust by the immediate securing of the nomination of judges for itself and then 'packed' the Constitutional Court with the perspective of soon

[35] This was the first amendment to the Basic Law of 4 June 2012.

[36] The Hungarian Round Table talks were a series of formalised, orderly and highly legalistic discussions held in Budapest, Hungary in the summer and autumn of 1989, that ended in the creation of a multiparty constitutional system.

[37] A first clash, which struck down a law that imposed retroactively a 98 per cent tax on severance bonuses, and which in turn led to the restriction of the competences of the Constitutional Court by excluding the review of budgetary laws in November 2010, had only high propagandistic value for the government. This possibility was then written into the Constitution so as to prevent its examination and possible annulment by the Constitutional Court.

having a majority of its own nominees.[38] Nothing could save the nine.[39] However, in Hungary, even with the new judges no sure government majority emerged. Yet the 'time' is coming and 'switches' occur from case to case. Of course, I do not question the impartiality and independence of any member of the Constitutional Court. I speak of the institutional guarantees embodied in their nomination and election. An analysis of the opinions in the politically sensitive recent decisions is outside the reach of this chapter. But in fact, the Court became extremely divided following the 'packing', and the narrow majority finding unconstitutionality of laws in the present legislation is continually growing smaller.[40]

Besides these institutional changes, the Constitutional Court also had to endure the cutting off of its competences soon after the elections.[41]

In addition, in the period of time between the 2010 elections and the passage of the Basic Law, the Constitutional Court's very existence was being endangered. It was unsure whether it would survive under the new Constitution or would be merged with the Supreme Court. In the end, the Constitutional Court remained a separate organ. However, its character was turned more 'judicial'. The *actio popularis* and the role of a negative legislator were unacceptable to the new regime of absolute parliamentary sovereignty. So the Kelsenian path was abandoned, the *actio popularis* ceased and the possibility of abstract norm control was greatly narrowed down.[42] On the other hand, or in exchange, a constitutional complaint against judgments of ordinary courts has been introduced. This change in the character of the Court may not necessarily alter its political weight and performance.[43] Indeed, the future role and significance of the Constitutional Court is in the hands of the judges.

[38] The Parliament maintained the amendment of the Constitution regarding the nomination of judges despite the fact that the President of the Republic declared concerns and sent the amending law back to Parliament for reconsideration in June 2010. The amendment became valid in November 2010. Accordingly the government factions had 10 seats out of 15, the quorum for nomination is eight. Another amendment to the Constitution elevated the number of judges to 15 in June 2011.

[39] Because of vacancies the Court consisted of nine members at that time; hence the parallel to the well known rhyme on Roosevelt's court 'packing' (a switch in time/that saved nine) and hence the arrival of six new judges. By spring 2013 two further judges retired and with the two new judges the government nominees now have a majority.

[40] In a recent important decision on the unconstitutionality of the forced retirement of judges, the votes for and against were equal. In such situation the President's vote decides. With his 'double counting' vote the Court held the law unconstitutional. The new judges, with a single exception, were dissenting; indeed, a clearly identifiable block of the new judges has never voted for unconstitutionality of a law issued by the present majority or the government.

[41] Law CXIX of 2010 amending the Constitution of 16 November 2010.

[42] Originally only the government and one-quarter of the MPs, as well as the Ombudsman, could initiate an abstract review. The Ombudsman obtained this right on the recommendation of the Venice Commission. He remained the only possibility to forward motions from the people to the Court. The Ombudsman was very active in this field and raised his own motions as well. This recalls the legendary role of the Polish Ombudsperson Ewa Letowska in the years of the democratic transition in Poland. Recently, the fourth amendment extended this right to the President of the Kúria (Supreme Court) and the Prosecutor General.

[43] A practical effect of the shift from abstract review to the constitutional complaint may be that the review of recent laws has to wait some years, until a final judgment of an ordinary court is delivered,

F. The Effect of the Changes

Comparing the formative period of the Constitutional Court and the constitutional culture in Hungary with the present crisis, some differences are natural, while others are telling.

In 1990, the Constitutional Court had been armed with the highest status ('constitutional organ'), with all formal guarantees of independence and a long list of nearly all imaginable (abstract) competences. The new Court enjoyed broad freedom to determine its own character and role. It could define its procedural rules, it dropped or formed competences and it confessed and exercised judicial activism. As a 'negative legislator' the Constitutional Court became the counterbalance of the Parliament. The Constitutional Court of the time of democratic transition could claim not only a symbolic role but leadership as well.[44]

Now the circumstances are changing. The status of the Court is clearly weaker. In 1989, the uncertainty as to which party would win the system-changing free elections moved the parties at the Round Table to set up a strong guardian of their rights in the future. This was a unique situation, but the well-guaranteed balance of powers prevailed for the following 20 years. Today, the certainty of the power of the two-thirds governmental majority prevails. In the spirit of unlimited parliamentary sovereignty (and a daily and instrumental use of the constituent power of that majority) the Constitutional Court, like the Constitution itself, was given a subordinate role. The Court had to endure the restriction of its competence of abstract norm control and changes in the nomination of judges. By cutting off the competences of the Court, an essential part of government behaviour has been exempted from constitutional review. The number of the members of the Court was raised and the election of new judges (and the President) was turned over into the hands of the governing majority. The Constitutional Court was once the symbol of the rule of a law-based new constitutional democracy. Now the new Basic Law is intended to symbolise the ideology of the regime.

The first Constitutional Court worked within a rigid constitution using steadfast principles and strived to build up a firm and coherent constitutional law. Now the shape of the Constitution has become uncertain due to frequent amending and the inner contradictions following from this, which question the principled coherence of the Basic Law. Commands of the Constitution lose force when

which can in turn be challenged in the Constitutional Court on the ground that the law applied was unconstitutional. Nevertheless, a constitutional complaint against laws is (exceptionally) also possible if the law immediately contravenes a constitutional provision and there is no judicial remedy against it. This rule enabled the making of the politically important decisions regarding the unconstitutionality of the forced retirement of judges (33/2012 (VII. 17) AB határozat (Constitutional Court of Hungary)) and the parliamentary recognition of churches (Decision 6/2013 (n 29)).

[44] Comparing the role of institutions in the democratic changes at the end of the twentieth century, Arjomand found that in Hungary and South Africa it was the Constitutional Court that facilitated political change. SA Arjomand, 'Law, Political Reconstruction and Constitutional Politics' (2003) 18 *International Sociology* 7.

something other than the law determines behaviour, while the law and even the constitution are adjusted to suit momentary governmental behaviour.

The Constitutional Court was activist in the first period, between 1990 and 1998. It delivered during this period the bulk of its leading judgments, which determined its jurisdiction for 20 years. Now the Court is still cautious after working in 'survival mode' for a time, and in a new personnel setting, with continuing divisions between new and old judges. Nevertheless, it declared the continuity of its jurisprudence and held that the decisions relating to the former Constitution (of 1989–90) would also remain valid in the future (if they do not contradict a provision of the new Basic Law).[45] This attempt to secure constitutional continuity is most important. Still the Constitutional Court faces further challenges. First, it is now enjoying the same liberty to develop procedural and material standards concerning constitutional complains as the first Court had regarding its abstract competences. The first Court was concerned with its relationship with the legislature, while the present Constitutional Court has to develop its behaviour in relation to the ordinary judiciary. Whether the Constitutional Court of the present will have the same will to act as a 'truly working constitutional court' also remains open at this moment. The second and most urgent task for the Constitutional Court was, however, to find a way to review the constitutionality of amendments to the Constitution. In contrast to the first task, it is faced with an unprecedented situation. For 20 years the Court has refused to review constitutional amendments. But today the political status of the Constitution has been profoundly changed in consequence of its instrumental handling by the Parliament and government. Maintaining constitutionality and also the proper functioning of constitutional review today require changing this opinion of the Constitutional Court. If elevating unconstitutional provisions into the Constitution to exclude their review can continue, constitutional justice becomes senseless. The Court has become well aware of this task. However, as discussed below, this attempt was blocked by the fourth amendment of the Basic Law, as was the effort to maintain the continuity of the constitutional jurisprudence.

G. Last Battle Lost: Parliament Overrides the Constitutional Court

Of all the constitutional amendments the fourth, that of 11 March 2013, is the most important. Its significance does not lie in the content. The amendment mainly incorporates provisions from the Transitory Provisions into the actual text of the Basic Law, following the judgment of the Constitutional Court that had annulled a part of the Transitory Provisions for formal reasons.[46] Hence,

[45] 22/2012 (V. 11) AB határozat (Constitutional Court of Hungary).

[46] 45/2012 (XII.29) AB határozat (Constitutional Court of Hungary). The formal ground of unconstitutionality was that the rules concerned were not really of transitional nature and so they were beyond the authorisation provided for by the Basic Law.

the government spoke of a merely technical amendment remedying formal errors and, emphasising that the Constitutional Court did not review the substantive constitutionality of the concerned rules. This reasoning is misleading. I need to point out that just about every single regulation in question had already undergone thorough study by the Constitutional Court while it reviewed the respective laws, and had been declared unconstitutional and therefore annulled. The root of the problem lies precisely in the fact that after the judgments these regulations were included in the Transitional Provisions in order to exclude constitutional review. The real significance of the fourth amendment is that it brings the instrumental handling of the Constitution and the parliamentary overruling of Constitutional Court decisions to a climax; it makes that 'development' irrevocable since it excludes the substantial review of constitutional amendments. It raises further, not less grave questions as well, as it changes the identity of the Constitution by reshaping the relationship between the powers.

However, the amended text of the Basic Law does not show what the essence of the change actually is, for on paper the Constitutional Court remains the supreme guardian of the Constitution. In this respect, therefore, the change in the constitutional system remains invisible. What appears in the text is merely the restriction of the constitutional review of constitutional amendments to procedural rules of their passage. Moreover, the Basic Law contains a great number of concrete provisions that the Constitutional Court had formerly found unconstitutional. These provisions will continue to contradict other rules and principles of the Basic Law. Their incorporation into the Basic Law is the incorporation of contradictions. All these changes are, however, noticed only by people who consistently follow the life of the Constitution as a whole, complete with its practical applications.

As a starting point, we have to recall that Hungary's new democracy and constitutional order, even under the Basic Law-based regime, has rested on the division of power, the separation of the branches of government and on balance and cooperation among them. This was set forth in Hungary's Constitution adopted when the political regime was changed in 1989–90, elaborated in the Constitutional Court's judgments and taken over into the Basic Law. In this configuration, the Constitutional Court is the supreme body protecting the Constitution and Parliament is Hungary's supreme body of popular representation. Each is 'supreme' within its own area. It is important to realise that the Basic Law did not include the role of a 'supreme organ of state power' among the functions of Parliament. The placement of Parliament as legally above all else had been a specific characteristic of the single-party system in communist Hungary where it was in fact called 'the supreme organ of state power'.

There are, of course, democratic regimes in which Parliament really does exercise supreme power on its own. In those places, such as Great Britain or Switzerland, there are, however, traditional political counterbalances. But in Hungarian history, when constitutional democracy was first established the Constitutional Court played a significant role. A regime based on unrestricted parliamentary rule was never thought to be democratic in Hungary or in Central Europe in general, and such regimes have left very unpleasant historical memories in their wake.

Above I described the practice that when a piece of legislation was declared unconstitutional, Parliament simply voted it into the Transitional Provisions to the Basic Law. Using this procedure in a routine way, the government majority in Parliament turned the Hungarian constitutional system inside out, into something that was diametrically opposed to the original setting of checks and balances in the Basic Law itself. Instead of accepting Constitutional Court decisions as binding for one and all, Parliament overrode them, granting itself the right to the final say on matters of constitutionality. Hungarians were well acquainted with this system from the days of socialist government. In that era, Parliament was the absolute supreme body and the Constitutional Council[47] merely delivered advisory opinions on the constitutionality of laws. It did not have the authority to annul legislation, since the final decision was in the hands of Parliament.

In the current extraordinary situation, as Parliament has routinely included legislation declared unconstitutional within the body of the Basic Law itself, and as the weight and stability of the Constitution were essentially changed by the practice of 'permanent constitution-making', the Constitutional Court has still attempted to meet its obligations to protect the Basic Law. Ultimately, the Constitutional Court inevitably had to face the problem of unconstitutional constitutional amendments.

To continue to meet its responsibility in the extraordinary situation that has evolved, it was required to shift away from its former position, which had been normal, for normal conditions, that the Constitutional Court would not review laws that amended the Constitution. We can see the step-by-step evolution of this change in the Court's decisions. It is quite understandable that wherever possible, the Constitutional Court found a law to be unconstitutional for formal reasons, for this option was the generally accepted one and it was more suitable for reaching internal compromises and gaining majority support. The Court went furthest in its most recent relevant decision, in which it scrutinised the Transitional Provisions.[48] Although parts of the Transitional Provisions were annulled on formal grounds, the opinion of the Constitutional Court did not restrict itself to formal criteria. It pronounced in the reasoning of the judgment substantial requirements as regards the constitutionality of the constitutional amendments. It declared that in a democracy governed by the rule of law, there are permanent and undiminishable substantive criteria of constitutionality, and that the Constitutional Court has the right to scrutinise even constitutional amendments so as to uphold these criteria. It stipulated that constitutional amendments may not result in irresolvable contradictions within the Basic Law. It also stood out

[47] Law II of 1983 set up the Constitutional Council, which was intended to oversee the constitutionality of legal rules by internal review, as a sign of moderate political liberalisation.

[48] 45/1992 (IX.26) AB határozat (Constitutional Court of Hungary).

against the practice of amending the Constitution in order to exclude the review of a provision by the Constitutional Court.

This decision follows and even crowns the line in which the Constitutional Court from the beginning had set an order of priority among fundamental rights.[49] By stating the principle cited above, the Court established that there exist criteria that give the Constitution its identity and on which the constitutionality of constitutional amendments will be decided. It is also inherent in the above statement that the right to amend the Constitution is not unlimited.[50] Many constitutions expressly state that there are limits to the powers to amend the constitution. In fact, they specify which provisions may not be altered through constitutional amendments (entrenched or 'eternity' clauses).[51] These are the clauses that guarantee that the Constitution remains true to itself. At the same time, we know of many examples in which the constitution does not contain such an 'eternity' provision. The Basic Law belongs to this category of constitutions. However, in times of constitutional crisis, when amending the constitution runs the risk of altering the identity of the constitution, some Constitutional Courts have taken it upon themselves to sustain the identity of the constitution, thereby declaring the unconstitutionality of some constitutional amendments.[52] In Decision 45/2012, the Hungarian Constitutional Court also spelled out this possibility of establishing the rules that can be the basis of a substantial review of constitutional amendments in future cases.

However, the fourth constitutional amendment reacted to this attempt and effectively blocked this road. It expressly stipulates that the Constitutional Court may only scrutinise the procedural aspects of the drawing up of the Constitution and constitutional amendments. Correspondingly, it restricts the right of the President of the Republic to refer amendments to the Constitutional Court, to procedural matters. This allows the two-thirds majority in Parliament to enact any provision it chooses in amending the Basic Law, even if it directly contradicts any other provision of the Constitution.

This fourth amendment of the Basic Law entrenches the state of affairs in which Parliament may override decisions taken by the Constitutional Court. With this move, which effectively negates the organisational structure of the highest state organs as set forth in the Basic Law, the Constitutional Court is no longer the supreme organ of constitutional protection.

[49] For instance, the right to human dignity and the inviolability of life are to the fore, but it has also defined other paramount rights as so-called 'mother rights' from which other fundamental rights can be derived, eg the freedom of expression.

[50] The Basic Law lists the authorities of Parliament, but it makes no distinction between the powers to enact the Constitution and to pass a constitutional amendment. Parliament, however, issued the amendments to the Constitution in its capacity of 'constituent power'. The commingling of the two types of power might lead to the belief that they are one and the same, and mainly that the right to amend the Constitution is unlimited.

[51] Eg German Grundgesetz, art 79(3).

[52] See Decision of the Austrian Verfassungsgerichtshof of 11 October 2001.

H. Breach of Continuity of Constitutional Jurisprudence?

The fourth amendment also blocked another basic task of the Constitutional Court under the new Basic Law, maintaining the continuity of its jurisprudence and with this, of the constitutional culture. The fourth amendment states that the decisions of the Constitutional Court made before the entry into force of the Basic Law shall cease to be in force. The amendment does not revive laws once declared unconstitutional. However, those rulings contain more than the annulment of Constitutional Court decisions that once declared laws null and void. What the Constitutional Court decisions are comprised of is far more, and far more important to constitutional order, than that. They entail constitutional requirements on future legislation, treatises of principle, interpretations and clarifications of concepts, in other words, an entire system resting on principles. Therefore, voiding the Court's decisions is more than a mere symbolic blow to the two decades of constitutional development of our country's new democracy. The move erases the mandatory power of Hungarian constitutional law, as pronounced in the decisions of the Constitutional Court. In order for these rules of constitutional law to formally regain their validity, they need to be rediscovered and restated by the Constitutional Court. It may be hoped that once a concept has been thought through, it will not be able to be wiped out. Ultimately, the only hope is that the continuity of our constitutional culture will hold out in the longer term.[53] It is remarkable that despite this rule in the Basic Law, the Constitutional Court repeatedly referred to its former decisions and stated that it would consider its previous holdings except they contradict the Basic Law.

I. Chance of Survival

Indeed, this is the question that remains after contrasting the formative period of the constitutional culture in Hungary with the present decline. Is the hope for the survival of constitutional culture pure wishful thinking or does it have a foundation? The events we followed in the second part of this chapter speak for a negative assessment. For the political class and especially the parties in power, constitutionality, as it has developed in the last 20 years, is not a priority.

But constitutional culture is tenacious. It is not possible to annul interiorised needs and measures of constitutionality in the same way as statutes are annulled. Constitutional culture requires a long period to reach organic development but, once that has been accomplished, it has an enormous moment of inertia.

[53] This evaluation draws on my article published on the day of the final voting on the fourth amendment in the Hungarian daily, *Népszabadság*. Versions of that contribution were also published in *Osteuropa*; L Sólyom, 'Ende der Gewaltenteilung. Zur Änderung des Grundgesetzes in Ungarn' (2013) 1 *Osteuropa* 5 and in the *Journal of Parliamentary and Political Law*; L Sólyom, 'The Separation of Powers is Integral to the Fabric of Democracy' (2013) 7(2) *JPPL* 159.

We are facing the paradox that the future of constitutionality in Hungary depends on the past, on the mode and effects of the 'reception'. Now it will come to light which of its features had positive consequences for the long run and which now cause negative repercussions. And above all, how strong is the stamina of a rich though rapidly created 'tradition'? To put down roots and become tradition is not solely a question of time; nevertheless, it should count that Hungary has lived in a (even if developing) constitutional culture for 20 years. That is a generation's time.

The aim of the first Constitutional Court to build up a complete and coherent constitutional law in the shortest possible time, supported by its philosophy of 'anticipatory democracy' and its activism, was a risky undertaking. When, from the first moment on, each case is intended to be a leading case, the whole system becomes rigid too early.[54] More importantly, instant decisions freeze the political conflict inherent in the concrete case. So there is little chance for the wisdom of *Marbury v Madison*, to satisfy the momentary need of the political branches and to establish control over it in the long run.[55] The frozen conflicts accumulate while the concrete situations will be forgotten. Judicial activism still feeds the negative sentiments of the legislature who will assert its supremacy on the first occasion. The opportunity came and the Constitutional Court had to suffer the consequences.

Yet the positive side outweighs the negatives. Due to the extensive efforts of the Court concerning its competences, the interpretation of rights and the enlargement on all possible themes, the Constitution became omnipresent in society. Supported by the experience of the *actio popularis*, the Constitution and the Constitutional Court soon gained the popularity and trust of a wide range of people.[56] The Constitutional Court also reformed legal thinking. The textbook-like decisions proved to be very effective, as being similar to the practice in academia. The flow of decisions of abstract norm control cases was a source of law to be applied. The long operative parts of the judgments were instructive for practitioners. The constitutional culture became the natural environment of the lawyer.

Even more promisingly, constitutional reality and culture have become self-evident for an entire young generation of lawyers. The decisions of the Constitutional Court were ready-made for being used in textbooks, serving at the same time as doctrinal statements and as comments. The students at law schools learned this concept of constitutionality and they heard about similar theses in other European countries. For them, other attitudes were simply examples not to

[54] This is especially so when the Court draws far-reaching conclusions for all respective themes, and enlarges on subjects that may be useful to develop the constitutional system as a whole but which are not decisive in the concrete case. After such judgments, corrections and further development will be even more troublesome. The first Constitutional Court had certainly never heard of Occam's razor.

[55] *Marbury v Madison* (n 34). On Marshall's performance paying heed to the claims raised on both sides of the case, see JE Smith, *John Marshall: Definer of a Nation* (New York, Henry Holt, 1996) 323.

[56] The Court figured permanently at the top of list in polls regarding trust in institutions. In the 1990s it was a common saying in problematic situations: 'Go to the Constitutional Court!'.

follow. What you learn at school and experience around you upon graduation are difficult to refute later.

How enduring are such experiences? I will mention examples from my life. I take first the case of our law professors in the early 1960s. What they had learned from their teachers before communism had a lasting influence on their thinking. Even if during the 1950s their writings suggested otherwise, this continuity was clear to the students. Secondly, I was motivated even at that time by the fact that, despite all the brutality of communist rule and the changes on the surface, the deep-lying strands of the fabric of pre-war society had survived two decades. Between ourselves, we used the old street names. Speaking of people, my mother and everybody of her generation never failed to mention what that person had been in the old regime. This double or shadow society was vivid and influential. When it disappeared in the 1960s, this was not only due to the generational shift. After the failure of the 1956 revolution and with the consolidation, it seemed that communist rule was final.

Of course, a comparison with communism is by definition impossible. Yet the above example shows the enduring force of past experiences and cultural roots even under the worst conditions. The most important difference is, however, that because Hungary is a democratic country, finality of the present decline is out of the question. First of all, constitutional culture does not exist in today's Hungary underground as a shadow culture from the past, rather it has the opportunity and means to demonstrate and assert itself.

Our constitutional culture, then, is expected to last for a long time, at least for the life of a generation. It is not immortal, though, and no one wishes it to remain unchanged. Professional quality (the 'art') is a hallmark of every type of high culture, including constitutional culture. Today we still trust in that 'art'. The trustee of that culture is the legal profession.

Another heritage of the reception is the embedding of the constitutional law and thinking in Europe. Since the beginning, it had provided a protective force against political attacks. By the present day, the common standards have become unquestionable. To abandon the path of constitutional culture in Hungary means not only moving away from the common European constitutional tradition, but in most cases a breach of international obligations as well. As has already been mentioned, using the European or wider international determination of Hungarian constitutionality is part of the legal 'art'.

In sum, due to the history and mode of its development, Hungarian constitutional culture still has considerable legal potential and support to rely on. Beyond the legal profession and institutions such as the Constitutional Court or the Ombudsman, law schools bear special responsibility for it. Yet, at its present stage, the constitutional culture is already living first and foremost in the attitude of the people. Standing up for the Constitution is today a question of personal integrity.

2

The Constitution as an Instrument of Everyday Party Politics: The Basic Law of Hungary

PÁL SONNEVEND, ANDRÁS JAKAB AND LÓRÁNT CSINK*

I. PREFACE

ON 1 JANUARY 2012, a new Constitution entered into force in Hungary. The Constitution, entitled the Basic Law, was adopted solely by the votes of the members of the governing parties, which possessed more than two-thirds of the seats in Parliament, a constitution-making majority according to the previous Constitution. The preparatory work for the Basic Law was short and non-transparent; the actual draft was elaborated within a matter of a few months behind closed doors. The political legitimacy of the Basic Law is built on a fragile foundation given that the opposition either voted against it or was absent from the whole procedure of constitution-making.

It was not only the manner of the adoption of the Basic Law that stirred controversy domestically and abroad. NGOs and the press had already in 2010 and 2011 raised serious questions of constitutionalism with regard to the protection of fundamental rights and the status of independent institutions. Most attention was paid to freedom of the press,[1] but the regulation of the freedom of religion, the status of churches[2] and the protection of property[3] also triggered criticism.

* The authors wish to thank to Johanna Fröhlich, Eszter Bodnár and Sára Hungler for their invaluable advice.

[1] I Traynor, 'Hungary Begins First EU Presidency with Warnings over Press Freedom', *Guardian* (London), 3 January 2011, available at www.guardian.co.uk/world/2011/jan/03/hungary-press-crackdown-eu-presidency.

[2] JK Grieboski, 'The Midnight Adoption of Europe's Most Restrictive Religion Law', *Huffington Post* (London), 21 July 2011, available at www.huffingtonpost.com/joseph-k-grieboski/hungarian-parliament-resu_b_902567.html.

[3] M Smith, 'Protecting Hungary's Freedoms', *Wall Street Journal* (New York), 5 April 2011, available at www.online.wsj.com/news/articles/SB10001424052748703806304576242442777657096.

Equally, an unusual limitation of the competences of the Constitutional Court[4] and a judicial reform that shed a dubious light on the process of appointing judges[5] provoked critical reactions. A peculiar power of the President of the newly established National Office for the Judiciary to reassign cases from one court to another was especially called into question.[6]

The developments also provoked unusual political reactions from the allies of Hungary and from the European Union. Viviane Reding, Vice-President of the European Commission responsible for justice, fundamental rights and citizenship, inquired about a wide range of issues related to the new Basic Law from the Hungarian Minister of Justice in a letter dated 12 December 2011.[7] This letter was followed by another from Jose Manuel Barroso, President of the European Commission, to Prime Minister Orbán, urging him to withdraw two cardinal Acts that contradict European Union law.[8] On 23 December 2011, US Secretary of State Hillary Clinton addressed a letter to Prime Minister Orbán asking for postponement of the entry into force of the so-called cardinal statutes related to the new Basic Law. The Secretary of State specifically requested reconsideration of the provisions on the appointment of judges and the Act on freedom of religion.[9]

The aim of this chapter is to highlight the most significant features of the new Constitution in as detached a manner as possible. We argue that the language of the Basic Law as adopted in 2011 was in general capable of maintaining most of the constitutional traditions of the predecessor Constitution.[10] The adoption of the Transitional Provisions to the Basic Law, as well as five consecutive amendments within a 20-month period after the adoption of the Basic Law, revealed, however, that the separation of powers is seriously flawed if the governing party possesses a constitution-making majority in Parliament. This majority can be used and was used to overrule constitutional concerns or specific Constitutional Court decisions by constitutional amendments. Thus, the Basic Law of Hungary could not provide a solid protection for constitutional values, even if most of the language of the Basic Law still reflects mainstream European constitutionalism.

We will describe Hungary's current constitutional developments from two perspectives. First, we will offer a dynamic view of the constitution-making

[4] C Bryant, 'Hungary Curbs Constitutional Court's Power', *Financial Times* (London), 16 November 2010, available at www.ft.com/cms/s/0/9ac8db2a-f1af-11df-bb5a-00144feab49a.html#axzz1oX9OVUTz.

[5] 'Hungary: Reverse Interference with Courts, Media', *Human Rights Watch* (New York), 6 January 2012, available at www.hrw.org/news/2012/01/06/hungary-reverse-interference-courts-media.

[6] 'Judiciary on Manual Override', *Transparency International Hungary*, 20 February 2012, available at www.transparency.hu/Judiciary_on_Manual_Override?bind_info=page&bind_id=162.

[7] 'Megszereztük: Ezekre várja a választ a Kormánytól az EU pénteken', *HVG* (Budapest), 15 December 2011, available at www.hvg.hu/itthon/20111215_reding_level_biztos.

[8] 'BEU's Barroso Asks Hungary to Withdraw Cbank Law', *Reuters* (New York), 20 December 2011, available at www.reuters.com/article/2011/12/20/uk-hungary-eu-idUSTRE7BJ0J520111220.

[9] 'Hillary Clinton Levele Orbán Viktornak—Itt a Teljes Szöveg', *Népszabadság* (Budapest), 30 December 2011, available at www.nol.hu/kulfold/hillary_clinton_levele_orban_viktornak_-_itt_a_teljes_szoveg.

[10] See A Jakab and P Sonnevend, 'Continuity with Deficiencies: The New Basic Law of Hungary' (2013) 9 *European Constitutional Law Review* 102.

process and of the different constitutional amendments of the past two years. This dynamic view, we hope, will facilitate a better understanding of the functioning of a system in which there is little domestic counterweight to the power of Parliament. Secondly, we choose a static approach and describe the main features of the Basic Law of Hungary, with a special emphasis on issues of concern for constitutionalism.

We cannot describe here every detail of a constitutional system; specifically, we cannot provide a detailed analysis of all so-called cardinal laws, which are, under the Basic Law, Acts of Parliament adopted with a qualified majority and which regulate important areas. The difference between the adoption procedure of the Basic Law (and its amendments) and that of the cardinal laws is that the former has to be consented to by two-thirds of all MPs, whereas the latter need only be consented to by two-thirds of the MPs present. In the hierarchy of laws there is a clear difference between the two; politically, however, they have similar functions. Both limit ordinary everyday politics. Also, the factual presence of MPs is almost complete whenever a cardinal law is voted on, thus the doctrinal difference between 'two-thirds of *all* MPs' and 'two-thirds of MPs *present*' disappears in practice. This is not to deny that the Constitutional Court can annul cardinal laws if they contradict the Basic Law. A fully comprehensive analysis of the Hungarian constitutional situation would require not just an analysis of the Basic Law, but also that of the cardinal laws (especially election laws and media laws). For reasons of length constrains, however, we will restrict ourselves to the analysis of the Basic Law, and we will refer to cardinal laws only if the discussion of a specific question in the Basic Law requires us to do so.

The present chapter is part of a volume that contains specific treatises on the response of different European institutions to the Hungarian developments. Therefore, we do not aim to provide a comprehensive picture of the actions of the Council of Europe and the European Union. Still, we refer to these inasmuch as they contributed to changes in the Basic Law or important cardinal laws. The references are also meant to help the reader to understand the context of the other chapters in this book and to create links to them.

II. BACKGROUND AND ADOPTION OF THE BASIC LAW OF HUNGARY

A. Constitutional History up to 1989: Lack of Living Constitutional Traditions in 1989

Democracy in Hungary emerged in 1989 out of the ruins of a communist dictatorship that prevailed for more than 40 years. For obvious reasons, the communist era could not provide any sort of usable constitutional tradition for the newly established democracy. Ironically, however, the first and, until 1989, only written Constitution of Hungary was adopted in 1949 in the darkest times of communist rule. Before that (ie before the Second World War), the Constitution of Hungary could best be compared to the British Constitution: it comprised a number of important statutes, doctrines and customs, forming together the 'historical constitution'.[11]

This historical constitution was vaguely defined and changed over time. Accordingly, it was not suitable as a starting point for two reasons. First, the transition from dictatorship to democracy required a codified constitution that could serve as a clear reference point for the nation and for all political actors. Secondly, even if the exact scope of the historical constitution was never defined, it clearly contained elements that were no longer valid in a modern, secular democracy. The following section will summarise the major milestones of the development of the constitution until the democratic reforms of 1989.

(i) The Historical Constitution

The central part of the historical constitution was the Holy Crown doctrine, formulated in written form by István Werbőczy in the early sixteenth century.[12] This blend of medieval organic theories and crown-doctrines regarded the Estates and the monarch as 'members of the Holy Crown'. Political power did not derive from the monarch but from the Holy Crown, which was used to crown the King. The monarch became authorised to exert his powers only as a result of the (complete) act of coronation. The territory of the Kingdom was owned by the Holy Crown ('Countries of the Hungarian Holy Crown'). According to this concept, the King only had a mandate to exert public power in the name of the Crown.

The Holy Crown doctrine symbolised the independence and sovereignty of the nation and the continuity of state power. Over the centuries of Hungarian history, the Holy Crown became the supreme institution of state power, including both the legislative and the executive; the Holy Crown embodied the unity of the king and the nation.[13]

Even though the Hungarian historical constitution, based on the Holy Crown doctrine, was fragmented, the doctrine proved to be very flexible. In times when sovereignty was practically absent, the doctrine could serve as a reference point and could represent the independence of the country, such as during the 150 years of Turkish occupation, the reign of the Habsburg monarchs, or the legal background of the Austrian-Hungarian Empire. Under all circumstances the

[11] The historical constitution of Hungary has provoked comparative analyses since early times, see Gy Aranka, *Anglus és Magyar Igazgatásnak Egybenvetése* (Kolozsvár, sn, 1790); B Barits, *Conspectus Regiminis Formae Regnorum Angliae et Hungariae* (Budapest, Srogh Sámuel, 1790). From more recent literature, see B Grosschmid, *Werbőczy és az Angol Jog* (Budapest, Franklin Társulat Nyomdája, 1928). See also Z Szente, 'A Historizáló Alkotmányozás Problémái—A Történeti Alkotmány és a Szent Korona az Új Alaptörvényben' in Z Szente 3 *Közjogi Szemle* (2011) 1.

[12] From recent German publications, see G Máthé, 'Die Lehre der Ungarischen Heiligen Krone' in G Máthé (ed), *Die Problematik der Gewaltentrennung* (Budapest, Gondolat, 2004) 17. The best discussion of the topic remains F Eckhart, *A Szentkorona-eszme Története* (Budapest, Magyar Tudományos Akadémia, 1941).

[13] I Kocsis, *A Szent Korona Tana: Múltja, Jelene, Jövője* (Budapest, Püski, 1995) 91.

doctrine could leave the possibility of returning to the constitutional heritage of the country. Such flexibility enabled the historical constitution to adapt to changing circumstances. As a direct consequence, the exact content of the Hungarian historical constitution can hardly be determined.

Furthermore, it is noteworthy that organic progress and continuity are essential elements of a historical constitution. The notion of a historical constitution is closely connected to customary law; a historical constitution may exist only if constitutional continuity is unbroken. This way the constitution is shaped by minor modifications and long-term reforms, and new elements are based on the old ones. As a result, once continuity is broken, the historical constitution is impossible to restore.

An interesting element of the Basic Law seems to be that article R(3) refers to the 'achievements of the historical constitution' as a basis of constitutional interpretation. We will come back to this provision and the possible modern content of the historical constitution later on.

(ii) First Constitutional Charters

The first attempt to create a written constitution was made during the short period of the Hungarian Soviet Republic after the First World War,[14] yet it cannot be considered a precursor of any further constitutional legislation. On the other hand, Act I of 1946 was an important step towards a constitutional charter, even though it could be amended with simple majority.[15] Even though Act I of 1946 regulated the form of the Hungarian government in the most detailed way to date, it concerned only questions of state organisation and the status of the President, mentioning fundamental rights only in the Preamble without detailing any of them. Nor did the Act contain provisions on the economic or social order.

The aim of the Act was to introduce the republican form of state (until that time, Hungary was a monarchy, even though between the two World Wars the throne was vacant and regent Miklós Horthy headed the state)[16] and to reaffirm Hungary's long-standing parliamentary traditions.[17] Accordingly, most of its

[14] During the short period of post-First World War Soviet time in Hungary, two constitutional charters were adopted: the first one ('interim constitution') as a decree of the Revolutionary Governing Committee on 3 April 1919, and the second one ('constitution') an act of the National Assembly of Soviets on 23 June 1919. See E Schweissgut, 'Das Verfassungsrecht der ungarischen Räterepublik von 1919' (1960) I *Jahrbuch für Ostrecht* 199.

[15] Act I of 1946 (1946. évi I. törvény Magyarország államformájáról).

[16] J Sári, 'A Köztársasági Elnök Alkotmányjogi Státusa' (1990) 7 *Magyar Közigazgatás* 577. This aim can be seen from its Preamble: 'in the name of the Hungarian Nation and upon its authorisation, the National Assembly constructs the form of state that suits the will and interest of the Nation: the Hungarian Republic'. Characteristically, Act I of 1946 contained only one article on the judiciary. Article 18 provided: 'Courts exercise judicial power in the name of the Nation and they return their verdicts and other decisions in the name of the Republic of Hungary'.

[17] *Cf* article 1 of Act I of 1946.

provisions dealt with the election, competences, responsibility and termination of office of the President.

As opposed to the historical constitution, Act I of 1946 did have an important influence on the democratic constitutional reform of 1989. Naturally, this concerned the position and the powers of the President, with one major difference: according to Act I of 1946, executive power was to be exercised by the President via ministers who were responsible to the National Assembly. Thus, the President was not only a possessor of executive power but formally the head of it. This solution was not reintroduced in the 1989 political transition.[18]

(iii) Communist Constitution of 1949

The republican form of state and the parliamentary system of government did not last long after 1946. Under Soviet pressure, Hungary was transformed into what was called 'a people's republic' in 1949. Like those of other Central Eastern European states, Hungary's Constitution of 1949[19] was modelled on the Marxist concept. The Constitution was little more than a mere translation of Stalin's Soviet Constitution of 1936. The 1949 Constitution was promulgated on 20 August 1949, on the day which was traditionally the day of festivities of St Stephen, Founder of the Hungarian state. The new regime renamed the day from 'St Stephen's Day' to the 'Constitution's Day', but it still remained a holiday.

Needless to say, the 1949 Constitution was a clear break with any previous constitutional traditions and was a flat denial of democratic values. It did not separate powers; on the contrary, state power was explicitly united, while there was only a division of labour among the leading persons and institutions of the country. Furthermore, the powers and functions were interlocked under the strong cooperation of their possessors. According to the original text of the Constitution, the Parliament exercised all the rights deriving from the people's sovereignty (article 10(2)).[20] However, the real legislative power was not delegated to the Parliament but to the Presidential Council of the People's Republic (basically a standing committee of the Parliament), which adopted statutory decrees that could derogate from Acts of Parliament.[21] In practice the Presidential Council exercised legislative powers and Parliament played only a minor role.

Nor did the Constitution guarantee fundamental rights. Despite the fact that the Constitution enumerated basic rights, especially social and economic rights,

[18] P Paczolay, 'Prezidenciális vagy Parlamentáris Demokrácia—Választhat-e Közép-Európa?' (1992) 1 *Politikatudományi Szemle* 174.

[19] Act XX of 1949 on the Constitution of the Hungarian People's Republic (1949. évi XX. törvény A Magyar Népköztársaság Alkotmánya).

[20] L Csink, 'Creating Presidential Status in Hungary' (2009) 2 *Studia Iuridica Caroliensia* 9.

[21] The legislative power was nearly unlimited until the adoption of the Act on Legislation in 1987. Statutory decrees could supplement, amend or repeal Acts, with the sole exception being that they could not amend the Constitution.

they were not implemented in the legal order, and people could not refer to their rights in everyday cases.

Later reforms partially liberalised private economic activities, and even introduced a Constitutional Council in 1983.[22] The Constitutional Council, however, was not entitled to declare Acts of Parliament or statutory decrees null and void, nor could it suspend their application.[23] Thus the supremacy of Parliament—and, in practice, of the Presidential Council—was not challenged.[24]

B. Democratic Constitution of 1989

(i) A Fragile Compromise

In Central European states like Hungary, the political transition was more a process than an exact event. On the other hand, the time of the legal transition can be defined more easily; this is the time when political events turn to the form of (constitutional) law and the institutions of the new state order appear in the Constitution. In Hungary, the date of the legal transition was 23 October 1989 (the 33rd anniversary of the 1956 Revolution and Freedom Fight against communist dictatorship and Soviet occupation), when Act XXXI of 1989 on the amendment of the Constitution entered into force.[25] This Act not only modified the Constitution but set a new basis for it, so substantively it was rather a new Constitution than an amendment of the previous one.

The political transition in a narrow sense started in March 1989, when the Round Table of the Opposition was established, gathering all movements opposing the communist regime. The Round Table of the Opposition was a political rather than a legal body; besides, it consisted of members who were mostly not elected in any fashion. This was due to the fact that the first free elections only took place in March and April 1990 after the constitutional reforms had been enacted (by the last Parliament of the dictatorship) in 1989. Accordingly, in 1989 there were only a few Members of Parliament who gained their seat as a result of recall elections, all the others were elected back in 1985.

In spite of the lack of its formal legitimacy and its unclear legal status, the relevance of the Roundtable of the Opposition is undoubted. On 10 June 1989, in the 'Hunting Hall' of the Parliament, the leaders of the Communist Party agreed with

[22] Article 1 of Act No. I of 1983 on the amendment of the Constitution.

[23] Constitution, art 21(3), in force between 1 January 1984 and 23 October 1989.

[24] For instance, the establishment of the Constitutional Council in 1983 to control the constitutionality of legislation, the electoral reform in 1985 or the Act on Legislation in 1987. For further details see L Trócsányi, 'Alaptanok' in L Trócsányi and B Schanda (eds), *Bevezetés az Alkotmányjogba* (Budapest, HVG Orac, 2012) 47.

[25] Act XXXI of 1989 (1989. évi XXXI. törvény az Alkotmány módosításáról).

the opposition to commence political negotiations on a constitutional reform.[26] As a result, on 13 June 1989 the National Round Table was established comprising the participants of the Round Table of the Opposition, the representatives of the Communist Party, and the members of the 'third wing' (trade unions and civil society organisations close to the Communist Party). The National Round Table rarely had plenary sessions, as the main issues were of concern to two committees, one dealing with the political transition, and the other with economic issues.

The legal position and the formal legitimacy of the National Round Table was as questionable as that of the Round Table of the Opposition. The new constitutional order was nevertheless based on the negotiations of the National Round Table to a great extent: the text of 1989 constitutional reform was agreed upon in the National Round Table on 18 September 1989, and was adopted with only slight modifications by Parliament.[27] Yet even the National Round Table was divided; two opposition parties (SZDSZ and Fidesz) refused to sign the agreement because of the manner of the presidential election.[28]

The results of the National Round Table negotiations were criticised in many ways. István Kukorelli stated that the agreement was practically 'the modernisation of Act I of 1946 strengthening the Parliament and the Roundtable itself resulted in a fragile political consent'.[29] Similarly, Péter Paczolay reckoned that short-term aspects, personal ambition, and political battles shaped the status and powers of the President, which resulted in ill-considered constitution-making.[30]

The constitutional reform of 1989, however, was not meant to be the final solution. There were two reasons to regard the newly amended and thus democratic Constitution as a provisional instrument. First, the text of its Preamble stated, similarly to the German Grundgesetz before its amendment of 23 September 1990, that the Constitution would be valid only until a new constitution was adopted.[31] This language was also included in the legislative intent of Act XXXI of

[26] I Kukorelli and I Takács, 'A Magyar Alkotmány Története: Az Alkotmányos Rendszerváltás Jellemzői' in I Kukorelli (ed), *Alkotmánytan I* (Budapest, Osiris, 2003) 62.

[27] Plenary session of the National Roundtable, 18 September 1989, in A Bozóky (ed), *A Rendszerváltás Forgatókönyve, Kerekasztal Tárgyalások 1989-ben* (Budapest, Magvető, 1999) 516. See also the legislative intent to Act XXXI of 1989 (1989. évi XXXI. törvény az Alkotmány módosításáról).

[28] The Communist Party proposed that the President be elected in a direct election before the first parliamentary elections. The Communist Party had confidence that its candidate would have a good chance of winning. Ultimately, almost all members of the National Round Table consented to this, except Fidesz and SZDSZ. Therefore, they launched a referendum (the first national referendum ever held in Hungary) that decided conversely, as a result of which the right to elect the President was reserved for the first freely elected Parliament. See J Elster, 'Bargaining over Presidency' (1993–94) Fall/Winter *East European Constitutional Review* 96.

[29] I Kukorelli, 'A Magyar Kormányzati Rendszer Egyenetlenségei' in A Ádám (ed), *Alkotmányfejlődés és Jogállami Gyakorlat* (Budapest, Hanns Seidel Alapítvány, 1994); I Kukorelli, 'A Magyar Kormányzati Rendszer Egyenetlenségei' (1993) *11 MagyarKözigazgatás* 196.

[30] Paczolay, 'Prezidenciális vagy Parlamentáris Demokrácia' (n 18) 174.

[31] From 23 October 1989, the Preamble to the Constitution stated that 'In order to facilitate a peaceful political transition to a state under the rule of law, realising a multi-party system, a parliamentary democracy and a social market economy, the Parliament hereby establishes the text of the Constitution of our country—until the adoption of the new Constitution of our country—as follows'.

1989 that introduced the constitutional reform. Secondly, the provision concerning constitutional amendments and the adoption of a new constitution in article 24(3) only required a two-thirds majority of all MPs of the unicameral Parliament.[32] This relative flexibility was intended to allow the parties of the former democratic opposition to adopt a formally new constitution after the first free elections to be held in spring 1990.

As in other post-communist countries, in the early years of democracy the political community was anxious to create a new constitution that had no connection with the communist regime. By autumn 1990 it became clear, however, that the parties of the former democratic opposition were divided so strongly that no consensus would emerge that could allow for making a new constitution.[33] Due to the lack of political agreement, all the attempts failed, as there was no chance for a document to receive the required qualified majority. This was so even between 1994 and 1998; although the coalition gained a super-majority, the governing parties were in disagreement concerning constitution-making. Thus, the flexibility of the Constitution only allowed for amendment step by step: between the first free elections (1990) and the last elections before the adoption of the Basic Law (2010), a total of 22 amendments were made.

Despite all the weaknesses of the constitutional system of 1989, both the political community and the theorists of constitutional law accepted the status quo. The constitutional adjudication played a huge part in this process, and as a result of the interpretation of the Constitution by the Constitutional Court, nearly all political powers found the basic principles and values in the text that they identified themselves with.

(ii) Vulnerability of the 1989 Constitution

There are several factors that made the 1989 Constitution fragile. They certainly did not doom the Constitution to failure, but they reduced its chances of surviving a crisis situation.

First, the constitutional reform of 1989 was prepared within just a few months and thus resulted in a text containing gaps as well as contradictions, even after the corrective amendments of 1990. The Constitutional Court did endeavour to deal with most of the (rather minor) substantive imperfections by means of its interpreting activity. The Court used its competence of *ex post* abstract review to fill the gaps in the text, and to make the Constitution effective and a real standard

[32] Z Szente, '24. § Az Országgyűlés működésének szabályai' in A Jakab (ed), *Az Alkotmány Kommentárja* (Budapest, Századvég, 2009) para 59. This interpretation relies on art 24(3) of the Constitution, which used the term 'change' (*megváltoztatás*) rather than 'amendment' (*módosítás*) for constitutional amendments, whereas it was the latter that has been usual in Hungarian legal terminology.

[33] See P Sonnevend, 'Der Verfassungsmäßige Schutz sozialrechtlicher Ansprüche in der jüngeren Rechtsprechung des ungarischen Verfassungsgerichts' (1996) 56 *Heidelberg Journal of International Law* 977.

for law-making. Moreover, the Constitutional Court became known and popular quite quickly among the Hungarian population, not least because of its 1995 decisions concerning a widely unpopular austerity package.[34]

Yet the Constitutional Court could not rely on national constitutional traditions in its case law. Instead, it transplanted Western European solutions, mostly focusing on the practice of the German Bundesverfassungsgericht.[35] In doing so, it certainly implemented mainstream constitutionalism in Hungary and helped to develop the rule of law according to its best traditions.[36] Nevertheless, reference to long-standing Hungarian traditions could not help legitimise the constitutional law developed by the Court.

This lead to the central deficiency of the 1989 Constitution: the lack of political legitimacy. Again, this would not necessarily have been lethal; the way that legitimacy was gradually created by economic, political, and moral success in Germany after the Second World War could serve as an example. In contrast, the lack of legitimacy allowed the political parties in Hungary to blame the Constitution for the economic and moral problems (eg corruption and the lack of transparency concerning the secret police files of the dictatorship), and so to seek exoneration of their own misdeeds.

The fact that the 1989 Constitution fails to symbolise the democratic transition is closely related to the lack of political legitimacy. A sharp cathartic action that could serve as a symbolic discontinuity between the former communist constitutional system and the democratic set-up was missing. That might also explain the lack of emotional attachment in the population towards the 1989 Constitution.

Finally, the relative flexibility of constitutional amendments was coupled with election laws that in certain situations disproportionally benefited the winner of the general elections. This became obvious in the 2010 elections, where less than 53 per cent of the votes cast were sufficient to get more than 67 per cent of the seats in Parliament.[37]

[34] For a rather critical view, see A Sajó, 'Reading the Invisible Constitution: Judicial Review in Hungary' (1995) *Oxford Journal of Legal Studies* 253.

[35] See, inter alia, L Sólyom, 'Aufbau und dogmatische Fundierung der ungarischen Verfassungsgerichtsbarkeit' (2000) *Osteuropa-Recht* 230; C Dupré, *Importing the Law in Post-communist Transitions: The Hungarian Constitutional Court and the Right to Human Dignity* (Oxford, Hart Publishing, 2003).

[36] S Zifcak, 'Hungary's Remarkable Radical Constitutional Court' (1996) 3 *Journal of Constitutional Law in Eastern and Central Europe* 1; R Schaffhauser, 'Zur Verfassungsgerichtsbarkeit in Ungarn: Die angenommene verfassungsstaatliche Herausforderung eines mitteleuropäischen Staates' in B Ehrenzeller *et al* (eds), *Festschrift für Yvo Hangartner* (St Gallen, Dike Verlag, 1998) 313–41; M Bánkúti, G Halmai and KL Scheppele, 'From Separation of Powers to a Government Without Checks: Hungary's Old and New Constitutions' in GA Tóth (ed), *Constitution for a Disunited Nation, on Hungary's 2011 Fundamental Law* (Budapest, CEU Press, 2012) 249. See also László Sólyom, Chapter 1.

[37] Results of the 2010 elections: www.valasztas.hu/hu/parval2010/354/354_0_index.html.

Reference should be made here to the argument according to which the 1989 Constitution allowed for the adoption of a new constitution only by four-fifths of the votes of the MPs.[38] It is argued that:

> [c]ontrary to common belief, the constitution in force in 2011 could not be replaced by a new one with a mere two-thirds majority ... The preparations of the constitution-making work were started by repealing the four-fifth provision—controversially, with a mere two-thirds majority. In this manner, the opposition–representing even in the short run a significant minority of the citizenry and, in the long term, the other half of the country—was deprived of any standing as a party to the process.[39]

This argument is based on article 24(5) of the Constitution which was introduced on 4 June 1995 and stated that '[a] majority of four-fifths of the votes of the Members of Parliament is required to pass the Parliamentary resolution specifying the detailed regulations for the preparation of the new Constitution'.

No doubt, this provision was adopted as a sign of political self-restraint and as a result of political compromise at a time when a socialist-liberal coalition possessed a constitution-making majority in Parliament. It is also true that when Fidesz gained a two-thirds majority in 2010, Parliament decided to remove article 24(5) of the Constitution by a constitutional amendment of 5 July 2010. Yet it is difficult to argue that this amendment was unconstitutional.

Article 24(5) was inserted into the Constitution by section 1 of Act XLIV of 1995, which provided in its section 2 that the entire Act should cease to be in force on the day the mandate of the Parliament elected in 1994 ended. This was a clear expression of the will of the constitution-amending majority in 1995 that the four-fifths rule will only remain in force as long as the 1994 Parliament is sitting. Accordingly, before 2009 there was widespread agreement among Hungarian scholars that article 24(5) of the Constitution had not been part of the Constitution since 1998.[40]

Admittedly, the Constitutional Court ruled in 2006 that amending laws become part of the amended law, and so the *ex nunc* nullification of the amending law does not affect the validity of the amended legislation.[41] Following this logic, one may argue that section 2 of Act XLIV of 1995 may have repealed the Act itself, but this did not affect article 24(5) of the Constitution.

[38] Such a statement is made in the *amicus curiae* brief of some Hungarian scholars to the Venice Commission. See Z Fleck *et al*, *Opinion on the Fundamental Law of Hungary*, available at www.sites.google.com/site/amicusbriefhungary.

[39] J Kis, 'From the 1989 Constitution to the 2011 Fundamental Law' in GA Tóth (ed), *Constitution for a Disunited Nation* (Budapest, CEU Press, 2012) 4.

[40] The leading commentary on the Hungarian Constitution also regarded the provision as one that was no longer in effect. A Jakab (ed), *Az Alkotmány Kommentárja* (Budapest, Századvég, 2009) 64. According to Jakab, the wide, teleological interpretation of the Constitution and the Act together mean that the four-fifths rule was not in force after 1998 (Act XLIV of 1995, art 2). For another standpoint see the criticism of A Arato of the four-fifths rule, www.comparativeconstitutions.org/2011/04/arato-on-constitution-making-in-hungary.html.

[41] Decision 4/2006 (II.15) AB határozat (Constitutional Court of Hungary) paras 101, 115.

It is unclear whether or not codification techniques in 1995 already bore in mind the conclusion which was to be elaborated by the Constitutional Court a decade later. We submit that they did not. The terms of section 2 of Act XLIV of 1995 indicated that the intention of the constitution-amending majority in 1995 was to create provisional regulations for the period of 1994–98. But even if we assume that article 24(5) of the Constitution was in force in 2010, it could certainly be amended or abrogated by a two-thirds majority foreseen for constitutional amendments by article 24(3) of the Constitution, as has actually happened.

C. Constitution-making Process of 2010–2011

(i) Unilateral Process of the Governing Parties

Before the general elections in spring 2010, the polls showed the probability of an overwhelming victory for the right-wing Fidesz party (and its politically subordinated ally, the KDNP), and there was an increasing anxiety that the winning coalition would use its constituent majority for creating a new constitution. Although such intentions were not made explicit before the elections, after realising a constituent majority, Fidesz announced that they were going to make a new constitution.[42] Fidesz used the phrase 'revolution in the polls' to suggest that the constituents actually voted for a revolutionary change. Such revolutionary change logically included the adoption of a new constitution which would not claim any continuity with the constitution of the last two decades. How far this is actually true will be analysed in the following section.

As the governing parties gained more than two-thirds of all seats in Parliament,[43] there were no legal obstacles to introducing changes, and the governing parties felt that they indeed had received sufficient political authorisation from the people to adopt a new constitution. One and a half months after the inaugural sitting of the new Parliament, on 28 June 2010, a new ad hoc committee was set up in the Parliament entrusted with the preparation of the new constitution. Two-thirds of the members belonged to the governing parties while one-third of them came from the opposition.[44] The ad hoc committee's task was to develop by 15 December 2010 the main principles of the new constitutional rules, and to submit it to Parliament in the form of a constitutional document (ie it did not have the

[42] 'A Nemzeti Együttműködés Programja' (the programme of the government led by Viktor Orbán), passed on 29 May 2010, see www.parlament.hu/irom39/00047/00047.pdf.

[43] The distribution of seats after the 2010 elections was as follows: 67.88 per cent Fidesz-KDNP (Conservatives, Christian Democrats); 15.28 per cent MSZP (Socialists); 12.18 per cent Jobbik ('For a Better Hungary', Far-Right); 4.15 per cent LMP ('Politics Can be Different', Green); 0.26 per cent independent.

[44] The committee for elaborating the cornerstones of the new Constitution had 23 members from Fidesz, seven from KDNP, and from the opposition parties seven MSZP members, six members from Jobbik and two from LMP. The committee was headed by István Balsai who, a few months after the adoption of the Basic Law, was elected by the Parliament as a new judge at the Constitutional Court.

task of delivering an actual codified text, but only a report about the ideal content of the new constitution).

The ad hoc committee elaborated the principles of the specific fields in six working groups: 'Fundamental constitutional values'; 'Fundamental rights and obligations'; 'The system of the government and the forms of exercising power'; 'Judiciary, protection of the Constitution and of the rights'; 'Local governments'; and 'Public finances'. By 20 October 2010, the working groups elaborated, with the participation of government representatives as observers, the fields falling into their respective scopes of competence.

Among the opposition parties, MSZP and LMP ceased to participate in the work of the ad hoc committee at the end of October 2010, while the far-right Jobbik party left the committee in mid-November. The left- and the right-wing opposition parties ceased to participate in the committee for significantly different reasons. MSZP and LMP left the committee as a political response to the limiting of the competence of the Constitutional Court, while Jobbik considered it unreasonable to continue participation due to a fundamental difference in views regarding the principles.

Nevertheless, the ad hoc committee elaborated a single concept paper entitled *The Regulatory Principles of the Constitution of Hungary* on 2 December 2010.[45] This concept paper was broadly modelled on the existing Constitution, but would have introduced some novelties, such as a bicameral Parliament, a new Supreme Court, and the absence of an exact definition of what consequences the Constitutional Court may draw from declaring laws null and void.

The concept paper was only considered to be a working document of the process, and the actual draft of the Basic Law mostly did not follow these innovations. What is more, the draft of the Basic Law was elaborated by a committee of three members[46] appointed by the parliamentary faction of Fidesz and KNDP on 10 February 2011. Barely more than a month later, on 14 March 2011, the draft of the new Constitution, named the Basic Law, was submitted to Parliament, and in another month Parliament debated the Basic Law and adopted it on 18 April 2012. It is probably not surprising that none of the opposition parties voted for the Basic Law. MSZP and LMP did not participate in the parliamentary debate at all, while the far-right Jobbik and the independent MPs voted against the draft.

One week after its adoption, on 25 April, the new Basic Law was promulgated by the President of the Republic in the official gazette (*Magyar Közlöny*). That day

[45] 'Magyarország Alkotmányának Szabályozási Elvei', *HVG* (Budapest), 2 December 2010, available at www.hvg.hu/itthon/2010_magyar_alkotmany_koncepcio. In parallel with the Parliament's work there were two private draft constitutions composed by constitutional lawyers. See A Jakab, 'A Magyar Köztársaság Alkotmánya. Magántervezet' in *Az új Alaptörvény keletkezése és gyakorlati következményei* (Budapest, HVG-Orac 2011) 70–173; C Gáli, T Sepsi and C Tordai, *Az Új Alkotmány Egy Tervezete* (Hungary, Tordai Csaba, 2011), available at www.tordaicsaba.hu/newconst/ALK%20I-XIV%20final.pdf. However, these efforts were considered by the Parliament and by the drafters, unfortunately, only in technical detail questions.

[46] The members were MEP József Szájer, MP Gergely Gulyás and MP László Salamon. Salamon was elected almost two years later by the Parliament as a new judge at the Constitutional Court.

was not only Easter Monday, but also the first anniversary of the latest elections won by the conservative governing parties.

(ii) Opinions of the Venice Commission on the Constitution-making Process

During the constitution-making process, the Venice Commission issued two opinions.[47] The first one was issued at the request of the Hungarian Government (more precisely, of its Deputy Prime Minister) before the actual text of the then-draft Basic Law had been published (hereafter, 'First Opinion'),[48] and the second on the request of the Monitoring Committee of the Parliamentary Assembly of the Council of Europe after the adoption of the Basic Law (hereafter, 'Second Opinion').[49]

The First Opinion dealt with three major questions, and some additional ones. The first question was basically whether a 'good domestic charter of fundamental rights' should be identical to the EU Charter of Fundamental Rights. The Venice Commission answered this question in the negative, as according to its view an identical text could lead to concurring (or even conflicting) interpretations while hiding the supranational origin (and the connected supremacy) of the EU Charter; the incorporation of the EU Charter into the text of the Constitution would *not* strengthen the protection of fundamental rights, and consequently it was *not* advisable. Rather, the Constitution should provide for the interpretation of domestic human rights in light of international instruments. The drafters followed this advice (see especially articles E and Q).

The second question of the First Opinion concerned the role of ex ante review. At the beginning of the drafting process, politicians of Fidesz were enthused by the idea that in one of the European countries, namely France (according to their knowledge), there was no ex post review, only ex ante review; thus there was no danger that a Constitutional Court could annul laws once promulgated. However, through interviews, public conference talks, articles in newspapers, and personal conversations with some constitutional lawyers,[50] they must have realised even before submitting the questions to the Venice Commission that ex ante review does not substitute for ex post review and that recently ex post review had also been introduced in France.[51] Thus, the question became how to frame the

[47] See also Joakim Nergelius, Chapter 11.

[48] European Commission for Democracy through Law (Venice Commission), *Opinion on Three Legal Questions Arising in the Process of Drafting the New Constitution of Hungary* (Opinion No 614/2011, 28 March 2011).

[49] European Commission for Democracy through Law (Venice Commission), *Opinion on the New Constitution of Hungary* (Opinion No 618/2011, 17–18 June 2011).

[50] L Szily, 'Jobbos Professzorok Oktatták a Fideszt', *Index* (Budapest), 11 November 2010, available at www.index.hu/belfold/2010/11/11/solyom_alkotmany_salamon/?cp=1; A Jakab, 'Az Alkotmányos Rendszer Aarkhimédeszi Pontja az Alkotmánybíráskodás; Interview by E Babus', *HVG* (Budapest), 15 January 2011, 34. The international conference on the constitutionalisation, organised by the Constitutional Court and the Hungarian Academy of Sciences, Budapest, 4 March 2011, also had the same outcome.

[51] F Fabbrini, 'Kelsen in Paris: France's Constitutional Reform and the Introduction of A Posteriori Constitutional Review of Legislation' (2008) *German Law Journal* 1297.

possibilities of ex ante review. The answer of the Venice Commission was that the competence of ex ante review should be retained and included in the Basic Law. If the Basic Law also gave the right to initiate ex ante review to Parliament (and not just to the President of the Republic), then the control should take place only after adoption in Parliament and before publication of the law, and, in the case of international treaties, before their ratification. The drafters also followed this advice.

The third question of the First Opinion concerned the role of *actio popularis*. The Venice Commission advised that the regime of *actio popularis*, ie the right of everybody to initiate an ex post constitutional review of any law without having to show any personal interest, should be ended, as a German type constitutional complaint (*Verfassungsbeschwerde*) fulfils this function better. It also suggested that the right of the ombudsman (called in the 1989 Constitution 'Commissioner for Citizen's Rights'; renamed in the Basic Law 'Commissioner for Fundamental Rights') to initiate ex post review should be retained. The drafters also followed this advice.

The Venice Commission addressed two further issues that were not contained in the request of the Hungarian Government. One concerned the procedure of drafting, and the Venice Commission emphasised the importance of an open, inclusive and transparent procedure. The other was the issue of the curtailment of the competences of the Constitutional Court in financial, budgetary and tax matters, an issue we will come back to below. The Venice Commission encouraged the drafters to fully restore the competences of the Constitutional Court. Unfortunately, neither of these points were complied with.

The request for the Second Opinion came on 26 March 2011 as part of an ongoing investigation by the Monitoring Committee of the Parliamentary Assembly, launched on 11 March 2011, into whether or not to open a so-called 'monitoring procedure' regarding Hungary after 24 members of the Assembly raised 'serious concerns' about developments in areas related to human rights, the rule of law, and the functioning of democratic institutions.[52] The Second Opinion raised the same objections mentioned in the First Opinion, to which the Venice Commission referred back at several points, especially those concerning the competences of the Constitutional Court. At several places it showed how to interpret (or how *not* to interpret) the provisions of the Basic Law in accordance with international standards (abortion, ethnic Hungarians in neighbouring states, etc). It appositely criticised the fact that the Preamble enshrines a debated political narrative of Hungarian history (instead of leaving it up to the ordinary political

[52] Since the inauguration of the Monitoring Committee in April 1997, applications for opening a monitoring procedure have been tabled regarding Latvia in 1997; Austria in 2000; Liechtenstein in 2003; the United Kingdom in 2006; Italy in 2006; and Hungary in 2011. To date, a monitoring procedure has only been undertaken against Latvia (the Hungarian case is still being examined); all the other cases have been closed without launching a monitoring procedure. There are currently ongoing monitoring procedures (all initiated by bodies other than the Monitoring Committee) against the following states (none of which is an EU Member State): Albania, Armenia, Azerbaijan, Bosnia and Herzegovina, Georgia, Republic of Moldova, Montenegro, the Russian Federation, Serbia and Ukraine. See Parliamentary Assembly of Council Europe, The Monitoring Procedure of the Parliamentary Assembly (7 September 2011) 2.

process and the general public discourse) and thus makes it difficult to gain the emotional attachment of those who disagree with this narrative (paragraph 38). None of the remarks in the Second Opinion have managed to find their way into the Basic Law so far.

(iii) Reactions of the European Parliament

Another resolution was adopted by the Hungarian Basic Law.[53] It seems to be a summary of the two Venice Commission opinions on the Basic Law, with some added broader and rhetorically stronger criticism of the general state of democracy and the rule of law in Hungary. A part of this resolution merits special attention, because it sheds light on the actual mechanism of how it seems to have been prepared. In paragraph (1) item (h) of the resolution, one finds that the Hungarian authorities should 'make sure that the incorporation of the EU Charter of Fundamental Rights into the new Constitution does not cause problems of interpretation and overlapping competences between domestic courts, the new Hungarian Constitutional Court and the European Court of Justice'. In the first Venice Commission opinion there was indeed a recommendation not to incorporate the EU Charter of Fundamental Rights into the new Constitution because according to the Venice Commission this could lead to conflicting interpretations, and the Hungarian Parliament actually did follow this advice (one of the very few pieces of advice that has been followed).[54] Thus, the remark of the European Parliament does not really make sense in the new legal context, because the Charter has *not* been incorporated. It seems that those who prepared the resolution did read the opinions of the Venice Commission carefully, but they failed to read the Basic Law itself. This sadly shows both a lack of actual legal expertise at the European Parliament, and also a lack of curiosity about the real legal situation in Hungary. Many of the remarks of the European Parliament are well justified, but disappointingly such a serious mistake endangers the credibility and honesty of the whole resolution, because it creates the impression that (otherwise sadly existing) legal issues were instrumentalised for party-political purposes.[55]

A few months later, the European Parliament held a debate on Hungary.[56] Several political group leaders raised concerns not only over specific legal and constitutional provisions in Hungary, but also as to what they saw as a wider

[53] European Parliament Resolution of 5 July 2011 on the Revised Hungarian Constitution.

[54] As a matter of fact, the government Bill concerning the judiciary was introduced just a few days before the publication date of the relevant Venice Commission opinion, thus it seems likely that the amendments were prepared on the basis of the draft opinion of the Venice Commission, which had been sent to the Hungarian government before publication.

[55] Paragraph 2 of this Resolution also contains a mandate for the Commission to conduct a 'thorough review and analysis' of the Constitution and the new cardinal laws. It is unclear whether this is supposed to lead to a broader report on which the European Parliament should decide again, or if it is just a vague rhetorical clause with no actual legal consequences.

[56] On 18 January 2012.

undermining of democratic values in the country. Others vigorously opposed this view, warning that such an approach went too far.[57] The Liberal and the Green leaders especially seemed critical of the constitutional developments in Hungary. Obviously implying the possibility of a procedure under Article 7 of the Treaty on European Union (TEU) against Hungary, Liberal leader Guy Verhofstadt said that the conformity of the Hungarian Constitution and cardinal laws should be checked against basic EU values such as freedom, democracy and the rule of law. Rebecca Harms and Daniel Cohn-Bendit, Co-Presidents of the Greens/EFA group, had already demanded initiation of such a procedure in the European Parliament on 5 January 2012.[58] Even if the European Parliament could have proposed an Article 7 TEU procedure, this 'nuclear option', which was obviously considered by at least some of the members of the European Commission as well,[59] was not used, and the European Parliament remained split by political divisions on this matter.

III. TRANSITIONAL PROVISIONS TO THE BASIC LAW: THE SOURCE OF EVIL

The Basic Law applied a unique technique, inasmuch as it provided specifically for the adoption of separate Transitional Provisions to the Basic Law. Point 3 of the Final Provisions of the Basic Law provided that Parliament should pass the Transitional Provisions connected to the Basic Law according to the rules of the previous Constitution on constitutional amendments. Since these provisions are also the legal basis of the Basic Law itself, it seemed reasonable to suppose that the constitution-maker intended to attribute to the Transitional Provisions a rank similar to that of the Basic Law itself (we shall come back to this issue below).

On the basis of this, on 30 December 2011, the Parliament acting *as constituent power* adopted a kind of appendix to the Basic Law, the Transitional Provisions, which entered into force two days later, on 1 January 2012, together with the Basic Law. The Transitional Provisions were heavily charged with political motivation as could be seen already in the Preamble, which stated, inter alia, that 'the Hungarian rule of law cannot be built on the sins of the communist regime'.[60] This sentence was hard to interpret from the point of view of constitutional law. At best, one

[57] 'Orbán Faces Political Group Leaders in Heated Debate on Hungary', *EP News* (Brussels), 18 January 2012, available at www.europarl.europa.eu/news/en/headlines/content/20120113STO35298/html/Orb%C3%A1n-faces-political-group-leaders-in-heated-debate-on-Hungary.

[58] S Geigold, 'Greens/EFA Call for Initiation of Article 7 Procedure against Hungary', *Die Grünen Homepage* (Brussels), 5 January 2012, available at www.sven-giegold.de/2012/hungary-greensefa-call-for-initiation-of-article-7-procedure-against-hungary/.

[59] 'Kroes Threatens Nuclear Option against Hungary', *Euobserver* (Brussels), 9 February 2012, available at www.euobserver.com/9/115209.

[60] The statement that the present Hungarian rule of law is based on the previous regime of communism is misleading. The constitutional continuity was broken in 1989 at the political transition and the Constitution became a new entity upon the statement that 'the Republic of Hungary is an independent and democratic state under the rule of law'.

could argue that the political declarations of Preambles are separated from the legal content and they do not provide binding directives for interpretation.[61]

A. Political Symbolism and Exceptions to Fundamental Rights

The Transitional Provisions consisted of two main parts. First, they contained a political statement condemning the sins of the previous regime and declaring the Hungarian Socialist Party (MSZP) responsible for the actions that were committed during communism.[62] Secondly, the document contained regulations that are said to be necessary for the transition and the application of the Basic Law. Some of the provisions were certainly in connection with the entry into force of the Basic Law. Most importantly, it was the Transitional Provisions (and not the Basic Law itself) that repealed the previous Constitution and contained provisions on the transitional period between the old and the new constitution, etc. However, substantive parts of the Transitional Provisions had no link to the transition whatsoever. Further, some of the provisions seemed to contradict the Basic Law itself.

The fact that the Transitional Provisions contained particular limitations of fundamental rights raised serious issues. Articles 1 and 2 of the Transitional Provisions allowed for such limitations in respect of dealing with the past inasmuch as they allowed for exemptions from the statute of limitations for politically motivated crimes committed but not prosecuted in the communist regime and for the unlimited reduction of the pensions of the leaders of the communist regime. These provisions were clearly designed to overrule the previous case law of the Constitutional Court.[63]

Further, article 11(3) and (4) of the Transitional Provisions were obviously problematic for the right to a lawful judge.[64] In order that judicial procedures are finished within a reasonable time (*cf* article XXVIII(1) of the Basic Law), the head of Hungarian judicial administration (the President of the National Judicial Office) became entitled to reallocate individual cases. Given the internal structure of the Hungarian judiciary system, this could in certain cases result in

[61] Concerning the possible interpretations of Preambles in general see L Orgad, 'The Preamble in Constitutional Interpretation' (2010) 8 *International Journal of Constitutional Law* 417.

[62] The Socialist Party is the formal successor of the communist Hungarian Socialist Workers' Party (MSZMP). This was, legally, especially relevant in property claims.

[63] It should be noted that recent legislation (or rather the lack of it) may be taken to suggest that the anti-communist rhetoric of the Transitional Provisions is not serious but rather just a means of political positioning. Concerning the continuing lack of transparency in issues regarding the communist secret service, especially the list of former domestic secret agents, see K Ungváry, 'Hazugságkényszer', *Komment.hu* (Budapest), 5 March 2012, available at www.komment.hu/tartalom/20120305-velemeny-ungvary-krisztian-ugynokaktak-nyilvanossaga-a-magyar-politika-csodje.html.

[64] A similar conclusion is drawn in the opinion of the Venice Commission on Act CLXII of 2011 on the Legal Status and Remuneration of Judges and Act CLXI of 2011 on the Organisation and Administration of Courts in Hungary, see European Commission for Democracy through Law (Venice Commission), *Opinion on the Act on the Legal Status and Remuneration of Judges and on the Act on the Organisation and Administration of Courts* (Opinion No 663/2012, 19 March 2012).

the President of the National Judicial Office determining, albeit indirectly, which particular judge is going to decide a certain case. A similar power was given to the Chief Prosecutor in criminal cases. A few days before the Transitional Provisions were adopted, on 19 December 2011, the Constitutional Court declared certain provisions of the Act on Criminal Procedure, which had essentially the same content, null and void, as these were contrary to the European Convention on Human Rights (ECHR) and the Constitution (then still in force).[65] It may well be regarded as a response to that, that the constitution-maker added the respective passages to the text of the Transitional Provisions at the last minute before they were passed.

Besides this, articles 12–13 of the Transitional Provisions also affected the judiciary inasmuch as they provided for detailed rules on the reduction of the obligatory retirement age of judges from 70 to the general retirement age, meaning the age of 62. Articles 12–13 of the Transitional Provisions were designed to implement article 26(2) of the Basic Law, which stipulated in general terms that the office of judges, with the exception of the President of the newly named Supreme Court, the Kúria, shall cease at the general retirement age, and allowed for an extremely short transitional period for this radical change.[66]

B. Legal Status of the Transitional Provisions

Whether the Transitional Provisions were on the same level as the Constitution, and whether they were subject to constitutional review were, at first, open questions.[67] The fact that the Transitional Provisions were passed in a procedure provided for constitution-making and that the text of the Transitional Provisions suggested a position equal to that of the Basic Law (article 31(2) declared of the Transitional Provisions that they are part of the Basic Law) suggested regarding it as such. On the other hand, such a status was questionable since the Transitional Provisions were passed as a separate document and their constitutional rank was not declared expressly by the Basic Law itself. Such a declaration would have been possible, as for example in the case of Article 6(1) TEU, which explicitly grants the EU Charter of Fundamental Rights a status equal to that of the Treaty. It was also of importance that from 2012, the basis of the Hungarian legal system has been the Basic Law, as is declared explicitly by article R(3) (in the singular, suggesting one single document). This explicit declaration implied that it was not appropriate under the constitution-making power to make several documents of constitutional rank, which might contradict one another. On the basis of article R(3), it was arguable that the Transitional Provisions may be of constitutional

[65] 1149/C/2011 AB határozat (Constitutional Court of Hungary).

[66] Both questions related to the judiciary are dealt with below.

[67] For a detailed discussion, see L Csink and J Fröhlich, *Az Alaptörvény és az Átmeneti rendelkezések viszonya*, Pázmány Law Working Papers No 2 (2012), www.plwp.jak.ppke.hu/images/files/2012/2012-2.pdf.

rank only insofar as their content deals with *temporary* matters related to the suspension of the previous Constitution and the entering into force of new Constitution (Basic Law).

In light of the practice of the Constitutional Court, an even more radical approach seemed possible, as Decision 1260/B/1997 AB explicitly affirmed the possibility of constitutional review of constitutional amendments if a specific amendment did not become part of the text of the Constitution.[68] According to this logic, all of the Transitional Provisions could have been reviewed for their compatibility with the Basic Law, the latter having unlimited precedence over the former.

The question of the legal status of the Transitional Provisions was probably the most important constitutional question in the first two years after the coming into force of the new Basic Law. In the following section we describe the legal struggle between the Parliament as constitution-maker and the Constitutional Court over this issue.

IV. FIVE AMENDMENTS TO THE BASIC LAW: A STRUGGLE BETWEEN PARLIAMENT AS CONSTITUTION-MAKER AND THE CONSTITUTIONAL COURT

All five amendments of the Basic Law were borne out of immediate political needs and motivations. Some are related to each other (like the First, Fourth and Fifth Amendments) others not, yet all but one have one feature in common: they served to exclude or reduce the possibility of challenging specific legislative projects before the Constitutional Court.[69] The only exception is probably the Fifth Amendment which was adopted partly to respond to the critiques of the Venice Commission.

A. Cementing the Transitional Provisions: First Amendment

Given the problematic nature of many provisions of the Transitional Provisions and the insecurities surrounding its constitutional status, the Commissioner for Fundamental Rights filed a petition with the Constitutional Court arguing that the Transitional Provisions are unconstitutional.[70] Probably to prevent any speculation on the status of the Transitional Provisions and a possible review by the Constitutional Court, Parliament decided to amend the Basic Law less than

[68] Decision 1260/B/1997 AB határozat (Constitutional Court of Hungary) paras 816, 819.

[69] A Vincze, 'Wrestling with Constitutionalism: The Supermajority and the Hungarian Constitutional Court' (2014) 8 *ICL Journal* 86.

[70] For the petition of the Commissioner of Fundamental Rights, see www.public.mkab.hu/dev/dontesek.nsf/0/b139ef59dd213d0bc1257ada00524ec0/$FILE/ATTU2GAV.pdf/2012_2559.pdf.

six months after its entry into force.[71] Article 1(1) of the First Amendment to the Basic Law included a new point in the Final Provisions of the Basic Law which stipulated explicitly that 'the Transitional Provisions adopted according to Point 3 [of the Final Provisions of the Basic Law][72] are part of the Basic Law'. This specific reference to the actual Transitional Provisions seemed to eliminate the possibility of challenging the constitutional rank of the Transitional Provisions.

B. Paving the Way for Voter Registration upon Request: Second Amendment

The next amendment to the Basic Law concerned an issue more limited in scope but with enormous relevance to the functioning of democracy. Already in July 2012 the Prime Minister announced that the existing system of voter registration would be changed. According to the plans, ex officio, automatic registration was to be replaced by registration upon petition by the voters. All those not having registered several weeks before the general elections would not have been eligible to vote.[73] The plans provoked fierce criticism. First among the critics was László Sólyom, former President of the Republic and former President of the Constitutional Court who declared publicly that this move would be clearly unconstitutional.[74]

In order to prevent possible constitutional challenges to the new rules, the Bill on election procedure was submitted to Parliament together with a Bill on the Amendment of the Basic Law. According to its legislative intent, the Amendment was meant to legitimise the exclusion from the elections of those who do not register in advance.[75] The language of the Bill was modified upon the proposal of the Standing Committee on Constitutional Matters of Parliament, probably because the original language turned out not to cover the envisaged legislation.[76] Technically, the Second Amendment was described as an amendment to the Basic Law, but it actually inserted new paragraphs into article 23 of the Transitional Provisions.

Surprisingly, the Second Amendment could not fulfil its mission: the President of the Republic, János Áder, challenged the law on election procedure before the

[71] Magyarország Alaptörvényének első módosítása (8 June 2012) 73/2012 *Magyar Közlöny* 11856.

[72] 31 December 2011.

[73] 'Orbán: Jön a Választási Feliratkozás', *Index* (Budapest), 27 February 2012, available at www.index.hu/belfold/2012/07/27/orban_jon_a_valasztasi_feliratkozas.

[74] 'Sólyom: A Kétharmad Nem Ismer Korlátot Maga Fölött', *Origo* (Budapest), 4 August 2012, available at www.origo.hu/itthon/20120804-solyom-laszlo-kemenyen-biralta-a-kormanypartokat.html.

[75] For the proposed text of the amendment see www.parlament.hu/irom39/08404/08404.pdf.

[76] The Standing Committee on Constitutional Matters submitted its motion to amend the language of the Bill on 3 October 2012. See www.parlament.hu/irom39/08404/08404-0006.pdf. This motion and the Second Amendment were adopted on 15 October 2012. See www.parlament.hu/internet/plsql/ogy_szav.szav_lap_egy?p_szavdatum=2012.10.15.17:34:00&p_szavkepv=I&p_szavkpvcsop=I&p_ckl=39.

Constitutional Court. In his petition[77] of 6 December 2012 for ex ante review[78] (the only one submitted to the Constitutional Court by President Áder to date), he argued that the exclusion from the elections of those who have not registered previously constitutes a disproportionate limitation of the right to vote as protected by article XXIII of the Basic Law, even considering the newly inserted article 23(3)–(5) of the Transitional Provisions. The petition also challenged provisions of the new law on election procedure that limited political campaigning, inter alia, by prohibiting private broadcasting and cinemas from airing political advertisements and prohibiting in general televised political adverts starting 48 hours before the general elections.

The Constitutional Court followed the petition of the President of the Republic in its Decision 1/2013 (I.7) AB,[79] and declared the relevant provisions of the law on election to be in violation of articles XI (freedom of expression and freedom of the press) and XXIII (right to vote) of the Basic Law. As regards voter registration, this decision was made possible by the fact that the Court annulled several parts of the Transitional Provisions, including the newly inserted article 23(3)–(5), just a few days earlier in its Decision 45/2012 (XII.29) AB.[80] Probably because of the disagreement within the governing party over the question of whether or not it would actually benefit them, the issue of voter registration was not raised again in Parliament, and the law on election procedure was adopted accordingly.

C. Creating Special Constitutional Foundations for the New Land Legislation: Third Amendment

The Third Amendment to the Basic Law had a far less controversial subject matter, even if it was adopted in connection with the preparation of a new law on arable land. The Bill for this new law was already submitted to Parliament in July 2012,[81] and was still pending as the Third Amendment entered into force on 22 December 2012.[82] The Third Amendment inserted a new paragraph (2) in article P of the Basic Law dealing with natural resources. The new provision stipulated that the acquisition of ownership of arable land and forests, as well as the organisation of integrated agricultural production, family farms, and other agricultural holdings, should be governed by cardinal law. Article P(2) also referred to the possibility of limitation of property in arable land. Arguably, this possibility is of

[77] For the petition, see www.keh.hu/pic/upload/20121206_ab_inditvany_vej.pdf.

[78] Regarding the power of the Constitutional Court of ex ante review.

[79] Decision 1/2013 (I.7) AB határozat (Constitutional Court of Hungary).

[80] Decision 45/2012 (XII.29) AB határozat (Constitutional Court of Hungary) para 347.

[81] See www.parlament.hu/irom39/07979/07979.pdf.

[82] Magyarország Alaptörvényének harmadik módosítása (21 December 2012) 177/2012 *Magyar Közlöny* 29770.

little relevance, since arable land is considered traditionally a property subject to far-reaching limitations.

D. Undoing the Results of Constitutional Adjudication: Fourth Amendment

In contrast, the Fourth Amendment to the Basic Law had a fundamental effect on constitutionalism in Hungary and also on the perception of the Basic Law. For the time being it seems to be the last substantive act in the struggle to limit the power of Parliament, with the Constitutional Court on the losing side of this struggle.[83]

(i) Origins of the Fourth Amendment

The Fourth Amendment had its origin in an already mentioned petition by the Commissioner for Fundamental Rights to the Constitutional Court concerning the Transitional Provisions. In his petition, the ombudsman argued that several provisions of the Transitional Provisions adopted by the Parliament in December 2011 in a separate document gravely violated the rule of law, and that this might cause problems of interpretation and endanger the unity and operation of the legal system. He also argued that the Transitional Provisions contained, in many instances, rules that were obviously not of a transitional character. According to the ombudsman, there were numerous articles of the Transitional Provisions that do not comply with the requirement of transitionality. The main criterion of transitional provisions is that their adoption is made necessary by the transition from the old regulation into the new one; therefore, they always include specific and temporary, ie transitional, provisions related to the transition itself.[84]

As the Parliament adopted the First Amendment to the Basic Law declaring the Transitional Provisions to be part of the Basic Law, the Constitutional Court asked the Commissioner if he maintained his petition against the new constitutional background. Somewhat surprisingly, the ombudsman replied that the First Amendment to the Basic Law had not answered all the questions on the basis of which he challenged the Transitional Provisions.[85] The Commissioner argued that only provisions of the Transitional Provisions that were necessary for the transition from the former Constitution to the new one were part of the Basic Law.

The Commissioner also referred to article R(1) of the Basic Law which declares the Basic Law to be the foundation of Hungary's legal system. Like any other constitution, so the ombudsman argued, the Basic Law required absolute

[83] For a plausibly worrying analysis of the Fourth Amendment, see PA Collot, 'Difficulté Contre-majoritaire et Usage Impérieux du Pouvoir Constitutant Dérivé au Regard de la Quatrième Révision de la Loi Fondamentale de Hongrie' (2013) 96 *Revue française de Droit constitutionnel* 789.

[84] For the petition, see www.public.mkab.hu/dev/dontesek.nsf/0/b139ef59dd213d0bc1257ada00524ec0/$FILE/ATTU2GAV.pdf/2012_2559.pdf.

[85] For the letter, see www.public.mkab.hu/dev/dontesek.nsf/0/b139ef59dd213d0bc1257ada00524ec0/$FILE/II_2559_3_2012_AJB_valaszlevel.pdf.

implementation in the whole legal order; it was a standard upon which all pieces of legislation should be evaluated. If the Transitional Provisions could make exceptions from the Basic Law, the 'standard' itself would be infringed. Such a situation would question the constitutional status of the Basic Law.

While Point 3 of the Final Provisions of the Basic Law authorised the adoption of the transitional provisions to the Basic Law, the word 'transition' is used in a different context in the first part of the Transitional Provisions (the part entitled 'The Transition from the Communist Dictatorship to Democracy'). However, the second part of the Transitional Provisions, entitled 'Transitional Provisions Pertaining to the Coming into Effect of the Basic Law' contains rules of a non-transitional nature as well (designation of a court other than the courts of general competence; cardinal Acts on churches and nationalities; provisions on constitutional complaints; the right of government officers to apply to a court; the organisation of the National Bank of Hungary, etc).

In its Decision 45/2012 (XII.29) AB, the Constitutional Court found the ombudsman's petition well-founded.[86] The core of the Court's argument was that Parliament had overstepped its constitutional authorisation when it implemented regulations in the Transitional Provisions which had no transitional character.

Interestingly, the Court made efforts to conceal the fact that it had actually declared norms to be unconstitutional that seemed to be covered by Point 5 of the Final Provisions of the Basic Law. As already mentioned, Point 5 of the Final Provisions was inserted by the First Amendment and declared the Transitional Provisions to be part of the Basic Law. Hence the reasoning of the Decision is somewhat blurred and not completely free of contradictions. The Court reaffirmed its previous case law claiming that it does not have the power to review the Constitution, now the Basic Law, but it is entitled to ensure that procedural rules are respected in the course of adopting norms of constitutional rank.[87] It then went on to state that Point 3 of the Final Provisions of the Basic Law is an authorisation for Parliament to adopt transitional provisions in order to ensure the transition from the old legal regime to the new one.[88] In the view of the Court, this authorisation can be deemed a procedural rule, the violation of which results in the nullity of the piece of legislation adopted, even if Parliament acted as a constitution-making power.[89] According to the Court, the authorisation in Point 3 of the Transitional Provisions was overstepped by Parliament because large parts of the Transitional Provisions were not provisional in nature, and this was not changed by the insertion of Point 5 into the Final Provisions by the First Amendment.[90] As a result, the Decision annulled several provisions of the Transitional Provisions, as well as its Preamble.

[86] Decision 45/2012 (XII.29) AB határozat (Constitutional Court of Hungary) para 347.
[87] Decision 45/2012 (XII.29) AB határozat (Constitutional Court of Hungary) para 380.
[88] ibid paras 347, 388.
[89] ibid paras 347, 397.
[90] ibid paras 347, 400.

It was probably to reduce confrontation with Parliament that the Constitutional Court cautiously framed its ruling as the enforcement of formal rules and emphasised that it did not review the merits of the Transitional Provisions. In fact, this claim was wrong, since Decision 45/2012 (XII.29) AB *did* carry out a review of the merits, otherwise it would have not been possibly to distinguish 'real' transitory provisions from non-transitory ones. Nevertheless, the Court explicitly referred to the possibility of including the annulled provisions in the Basic Law, thereby implying that such inclusion would make constitutional review impossible.[91] Still, the Decision also seems to introduce the concept of unconstitutional constitutions in its paragraph 118, which reads as follows:

> Constitutional legality has substantive criteria besides the procedural, formal, public law ones. [These are] [t]he constitutional requirements of the democratic state under the rule of law, constitutional values and principles acknowledged by democratic communities under the rule of law and enshrined in international agreements, as well the so-called *ius cogens,* which partly overlaps with these. Under certain circumstances the Constitutional Court is empowered to review whether the substantive constitutional requirements, guarantees and values of a democratic state under the rule of law are consistently respected and included in the constitution.[92]

It is remarkable that the Court not only claims here the power to carry out a substantive review of norms formally incorporated into the Constitution (Basic Law), but it seems to introduce international law, ultimately international *ius cogens*, as a standard of review of the national constitution.

(ii) Reversing Constitutional Court Decisions by the Fourth Amendment

Barely one month after Decision 45/2012 (XII.29) AB of the Constitutional Court, the Members of Parliament belonging to the governing party submitted a Bill for the Fourth Amendment to the Basic Law. This was passed on 11 March 2013, published on 25 March, and entered into force on 1 April 2013.[93]

The most important part of the Fourth Amendment was that it incorporated those provisions of the Transitional Provisions into the text of the Basic Law that were previously annulled by the Constitutional Court. These reinstated rules included substantive provisions, such as the reallocation of cases by the President of the National Judicial Office (article 27(4)), the possibility to reduce pensions of former communist leaders (article U(5)), and the suspension of the statute of limitations for crimes not prosecuted for political reasons in the communist regime (article U(6)). Besides these, the Fourth Amendment included in article U(1) of the Basic Law the previous Preamble to the Transitional Provisions, which declared, inter alia, that the Hungarian Socialist Workers' Party (the communist

[91] ibid paras 347, 402.

[92] ibid paras 347, 403.

[93] Magyarország Alaptörvényének negyedik módosítása (25 March 2013) 49/2013 *Magyar Közlöny* 6400.

party before 1989) bears responsibility for different wrongdoings, including 'the systematic destruction of European civilisation, legacy and prominence', and for depriving the people or certain groups of citizens of their basic human rights, or grossly curtailing such rights; and in particular for murdering people; for selling them to foreign powers; for their unlawful incarceration, deportation to forced labour camps, torture and inhuman treatment; for indiscriminately depriving the people of their wealth and possessions; for censorship of their property rights; for depriving the people of all freedom, rights and liberties; for exerting central control on political activities such as the freedom of expression of their political will; for the discrimination of people on the basis of race, worldview or political conviction; and for blocking their progression and advancement on the basis of knowledge, diligence and talent; for setting up and maintaining a secret police force for the surveillance of people; for unlawfully invading the people's right to privacy and for asserting influence upon them.

What is more, article U(1) also declares that the successor of the Hungarian Socialist Workers' Party, the Hungarian Socialist Party (which is at the present time the strongest opposition), shares the responsibility of its predecessor.

However, the constitution-making power did not stop at undoing one single Constitutional Court ruling. Rather, the Fourth Amendment basically reversed all politically sensitive decisions handed down by the Constitutional Court after the 2010 elections. This was carried out by including specific exceptions in the Basic Law on the basis of which laws previously annulled by the Constitutional Court can no longer be regarded as unconstitutional.

For example, the Fourth Amendment inserted the following provision into article L(1) of the Basic Law:

> Hungary shall protect the institution of marriage as the union of a man and a woman established by voluntary decision, and the family as the basis of the nation's survival. Family ties shall be based on marriage or the relationship between parents and children.

This is a direct response to Decision 43/2012 (XII.20) AB,[94] in which the Constitutional Court annulled section 7 of the Act on Protection of Families. Section 7 had defined family as a system of relations that generates an emotional and economic community of natural persons, based on the marriage of a man and a woman, next of kinship or adoptive guardianship. The Court found this concept of a family too narrow as the state should also protect long-term emotional and economic partnerships of persons living together (for example, those relationships in which the couples raise and take care of each other's children, or couples who do not have any children or are not able to have any children, grandchildren cared for by grandparents, etc).

Another reaction to one of the recent decisions of the Constitutional Court was the amendment of article VII(2) and (3) of the Basic Law which authorise

[94] Decision 43/2012 (XII.20) AB határozat (Constitutional Court of Hungary) para 296.

Parliament to recognise religious organisations as churches. Just ten days before the adoption of the Fourth Amendment, in its Decision 6/2013 (III.1) AB, the Constitutional Court decided, inter alia, that on the basis of freedom of religion Parliament cannot be authorised to grant church status.[95]

Similarly, to reverse a Constitutional Court Decision, article XXII of the Basic Law introduced an obligation of the state and local governments to strive for the protection of homeless persons but at the same time granted authorisation for the Parliament and the local governments to outlaw the use of certain specific sections of public areas for habitation. This amendment was a reaction to Decision 38/2012 (XI.14) AB,[96] in which the Constitutional Court reviewed the Petty Offence Act and stated that the punishment of homeless people for living in a public area is in violation of the right to human dignity. In the Court's view, homelessness is a social problem which the state must handle within the framework of social administration and social care instead of punishment. Ultimately, therefore, the newly introduced article XXII(3) created an exception to the protection of human dignity concerning homeless people at the level of the Basic Law.

Equally, the Fourth Amendment included a new paragraph in article IX of the Basic Law which explicitly allows for banning political advertisements from private broadcasting in times of political campaign, thereby reversing Decision 45/2012 (XII.29) AB, discussed above. Besides this, the new article IX(3) discourages political advertising in private broadcasting by prohibiting media outlets from charging for broadcasting political adverts, should they decide to air these.

What is more, some provisions of the Fourth Amendment relating to hate speech aim to cut back a 20-year-old case law of the Constitutional Court. Between 1992 and 2008, the Constitutional Court found several laws to be unconstitutional that aimed to penalise hate speech.[97] As an answer to this, article 5(2) of the Basic Law stipulates that:

> [t]he right to freedom of speech may not be exercised with the aim of violating the dignity of the Hungarian nation or of any national, ethnic, racial or religious community. Members of such communities shall be entitled to enforce their claims in court against the expression of an opinion which violates their community, invoking the violation of their human dignity as determined by law.

In general, reversing several decisions of the Constitutional Court by constitutional amendment resulted in a Basic Law packed with specific exceptions to fundamental rights and provisions that are normally at the level of an ordinary law. Not only did this lower the level of protection of fundamental rights, it

[95] Decision 6/2013 (III.1) AB határozat (Constitutional Court of Hungary) para 203.

[96] Decision 38/2012 (XI.14) AB határozat (Constitutional Court of Hungary) para 185.

[97] See Decision 30/1992 (V.26) AB határozat (Constitutional Court of Hungary); Decision 18/2004 (IV.25) AB határozat (Constitutional Court of Hungary); Decision 95/2008 (VII.3) AB határozat (Constitutional Court of Hungary).

also had the aim of reducing the possibility of review by the Constitutional Court.

(iii) Creating Procedural Hurdles for the Constitutional Court

The Parliament also ensured the limitation on constitutional review by another measure: by limiting the power of the Constitutional Court concerning the review of the amendments of the Basic Law. As already mentioned above, the Constitutional Court indicated in its Decision 45/2012 (XII.29) AB a possible competence to review constitutional amendments from the perspective of substantive constitutionality. This possible way of extensive interpretation of competences was basically blocked by the Fourth Amendment. According to the new article 24(5) of the Basic Law, the Constitutional Court may only review the Basic Law and the amendment thereof for conformity with the procedural requirements laid down in the Basic Law with respect to adoption and promulgation.

This amendment has not only affected the Constitutional Court itself. One of the most disputed elements of the Fourth Amendment was the provision that concerns the applicability of the former case law of the Constitutional Court, an issue we will come back later. Here it will suffice to point out that the Fourth Amendment introduced Point 4 of the Closing and Miscellaneous Provisions, which states that 'Constitutional Court rulings given prior to the entry into force of the Basic Law are hereby repealed. This provision is without prejudice to the legal effect produced by those rulings'.

The Fourth Amendment also concerned the procedure of the Constitutional Court. First, an amendment to article 24(2)(e) of the Basic Law enabled the President of the *Kúria* and the Prosecutor General, in addition to the government, one-quarter of the Members of Parliament and the Commissioner for Fundamental Rights, to make abstract requests for review of legislation to the Constitutional Court. Secondly, a newly introduced article 24(6) provided that the Constitutional Court shall make a decision in concrete review cases, originating from any ordinary judge, within a 30-day limit. Thirdly, the Constitutional Court became obliged by the new article 24(7) to hear the legislator, and the initiator of the act or their representative, and to obtain their opinions during its procedure. This stage of the procedure was opened to the public. These amendments can be evaluated, on the one hand, as positive developments, because they aim to make the procedure of the Constitutional Court more speedy and transparent; however, it may be presumed that limiting its power in politically sensitive questions by aggravating its procedural opportunities was also amongst the goals.

Lastly, the Fourth Amendment also tried to take symbolic revenge for Decision 1/2013 (I.7) AB, in which the Constitutional Court reviewed and annulled more provisions of the Act on election procedure than it was asked to by the President of the Republic. In response, article 24(4), as amended, provides that the Constitutional Court may only review or annul a provision not submitted to it for review if its substance is closely related to a provision that was specifically challenged.

E. Venice Commission's Opinion on the Fourth Amendment and Adoption of the Fifth Amendment

(i) Constitutional Court Surrenders and Council of Europe Steps In

The Constitutional Court seems to have accepted the limitations on its power in Decision 12/2013 (V.24) AB that deals with the constitutionality of the Fourth Amendment.[98] The Fourth Amendment was challenged by the Commissioner for Fundamental Rights, first on formal grounds, namely, that the adoption of the proposal was against the procedural rules of the Standing Order of the Parliament, and, secondly, on the grounds that the incorporated rules created incoherence in the text of the Basic Law which is against the rule of law.[99]

In its Decision 12/2013 (V.24) AB, the Constitutional Court dismissed the petition of the Commissioner for Fundamental Rights. According to the Constitutional Court, the procedural rules were not broken, as Members of Parliament had the possibility to take part actively in the debate and propose amendments to the Bill. Concerning the substantive questions, the Constitutional Court emphasised that its power is limited to ensuring the harmony of legal acts with the Constitution, and that it is not authorised to review the Constitution itself or constitutional amendments from the perspective of a substantive constitutionality. The Constitutional Court may only review the Basic Law and the amendments thereof for conformity with the procedural requirements laid down in the Basic Law with respect to its adoption and promulgation. The Constitutional Court thus also dismissed this part of the petition. At the end of the Decision, the Constitutional Court pointed out that in cases of review of acts which implement the rules of the Basic Law, it will interpret and apply the provisions of the Basic Law as a coherent system and in the context of Hungary's commitments under international and European law.

So this time around, help could no longer be expected from the Constitutional Court. Instead, the Venice Commission intervened. After Hungary adopted the Fourth Amendment to the Basic Law, the Secretary General of the Council of Europe requested another opinion from the Venice Commission as to the Fourth Amendment's compatibility with Council of Europe standards.[100]

[98] Decision 12/2013 (V.24) AB határozat (Constitutional Court of Hungary).

[99] For the petition, see www.public.mkab.hu/dev/dontesek.nsf/0/1e09722e15eb5da0c1257b5d001b9851/$FILE/ATTHHCNG.pdf/II_648_0_2013.pdf.

[100] European Commission for Democracy through Law (Venice Commission), *Opinion on the Fourth Amendment of the Fundamental Law of Hungary* (Opinion No 720/2013, 14 June 2013).

The Commission's criticism encompassed almost every part of the Fourth Amendment: the rules on the protection of marriage and family, the communist past, the recognition of churches, media access for political parties, limitation of the freedom of speech, and homelessness. It dealt in a separate chapter with the independence of the judiciary and the amendments concerning the Constitutional Court.

In conclusion, the opinion of the Venice Commission stated that 'the Fourth Amendment itself brings about or perpetuates shortcomings in the constitutional system of Hungary'.[101] The Venice Commission also held that the new provisions contradict the principles of the Basic Law and European standards.[102] According to the opinion, reacting to Constitution Court decisions by 'constitutionalising' provisions declared unconstitutional threatens to deprive the Constitutional Court of its main function as the guardian of constitutionality and as a control organ in the democratic system of checks and balances.[103] The main conclusion of the Venice Commission is unusually forthright:

> The Fourth Amendment is the result of an instrumental view of the Constitution as a political means of the government and is a sign of the essential difference between constitution-making and ordinary politics.

The Fourth Amendment also prompted the Parliamentary Assembly of the Council of Europe to consider initiating a monitoring procedure concerning Hungary. Ultimately, though, on 25 June 2013, the Parliamentary Assembly decided not to open such a monitoring procedure, but resolved to follow the situation closely and to take stock of the progress achieved in the implementation of the adopted text of the resolution.

Nevertheless, the resolution of the Parliamentary Assembly raises serious concerns and seems to condition the lack of monitoring procedure on a number of factors. According to the resolution:

> The Assembly regrets the recent adoption of the so-called fourth amendment to the constitution against the recommendations of many national and international experts and against the explicit advice of Hungary's international partners. The fact that this fourth amendment knowingly contains a number of provisions that had previously been declared unconstitutional by the Constitutional Court of Hungary and/or flagged as being at variance with European principles and norms by the Venice Commission, is unacceptable and raises questions about the willingness of the current authorities to abide by European standards and norms.[104]

The Parliamentary Assembly also urged the Hungarian authorities to fully address the concerns and implement the recommendations contained in the opinion of the Venice Commission on the Fourth Amendment, and called upon Hungary to

[101] ibid para 140.
[102] ibid para 141.
[103] ibid para 144.
[104] Resolution 1941 (2013) para 9, available at www.assembly.coe.int/ASP/Doc/XrefViewPDF.asp?FileID=19933&Language=EN.

amend the Act on Freedom of Religion and the Status of Churches, the Act on Elections of Members of the Parliament, the Act on the Constitutional Court, the Act on the Judiciary, and media legislation, in order to address several concerns.[105]

(ii) Fifth Amendment

Taking into account some critical remarks from the Venice Commission, the Hungarian government decided to submit the Fifth Amendment to the Basic Law. The Fifth Amendment was adopted on 16 September 2013 and entered into force on 1 October 2013.[106] Among other things, it removed the state's option to levy a tax to compensate for any payment obligations incurred as a result of rulings of the Constitutional Court or international courts, as well as the provisions allowing the National Judicial Office to transfer cases from one court to another. It also extended the time allowed for the Constitutional Court to review new legislation upon the request of judges from 30 to 90 days, and softened the rules applicable to the recognition of churches in article 7 of the Basic Law. Many elements of the Fourth Amendment, however, remained untouched.

V. EVALUATION OF THE BASIC LAW

We have argued above and elsewhere that the language of the Basic Law as adopted in 2011—in spite of the circumstances of its adoption and of its flaws—did not represent a real break with the previous Constitution. Later amendments, however, have injected more and more problematic elements and, in general, called into question the supposed separation of powers. After describing the general features of the Basic Law we will focus on the most important structural problems. While we do not agree with the general judgement that Hungary has become a constitutional democracy in name only,[107] we submit that there are flaws in the constitutional system, the most significant of which is the lack of effective control over legislation.

A. Terminology, Structure and Legal Status

An apparent novelty of the new Hungarian Constitution is its name: 'the Basic Law of Hungary'. It is familiar from the German Constitution, called '*Grundgesetz*', which is the borrowed translation of the Hungarian term.

[105] ibid para 12.

[106] Magyarország Alaptörvényének ötödik módosítása (26 September 2013) 158/2013 *Magyar Közlöny* 67822.

[107] M Bánkúti, G Halmai and KL Scheppele, 'From Separation of Powers to a Government without Checks: Hungary's Old and New Constitutions' in GA Tóth, *Constitution for a Disunited Nation, on Hungary's 2011 Fundamental Law* (Budapest, CEU Press, 2012) 238.

The Basic Law consists of three main Parts: 'The National Avowal of Faith'; 'Foundation, Freedom and Responsibility'; and, finally, 'The State'. At the end of the text, there is a fourth unit, the Final Provisions ('Postscript'), which consists of various points regarding the transitory provisions and the implementation of the Basic Law. Every main unit has a capitalised word or expression at the beginning. These expressions are: 'We, the members of the Hungarian nation'; 'our homeland'; 'man';[108] and finally 'Hungary'. Not only the name and the division of the Constitution, but also the numbering has changed. The Basic Law uses three different notations. 'Foundation' contains articles from A to T, 'Freedom and Responsibility' has articles using roman numbers (I, II, III, etc), and, finally, the articles of 'The State' are numbered using Arabic numerals (1, 2, 3, etc). 'The National Avowal of Faith' does not have separate numbering. This kind of notation makes orientation and quotation rather difficult, but it is probably meant as a symbolic gesture to show respect towards the divided acts of the historical constitution.[109]

In general, one of the most striking features of the text is its strongly traditional-symbolic nature. 'The National Avowal of Faith,' ie the Preamble, serves as the best example of that, starting with the first line of the Hungarian national anthem ('God bless the Hungarians'). The historical character also emerges in the Postscript, where one finds the motto from the 12 Points of the 1848 Hungarian Revolution ('Let there be peace, freedom and concord').

The language of the Basic Law raises the question of whether the Basic Law itself is a law. Article T(2) specifies the items of legislation, from which list the Basic Law is missing. Furthermore, article C(3) stipulates that 'the State shall have the right to use coercion in order to enforce the Basic Law and laws'. Article R(2) states that 'the Basic Law and the laws shall be binding on everybody'. The parallel usage of the terms 'Basic Law' and 'laws' suggests that, at least textually, the Basic Law is not a law. Article T(1), as amended by the Fourth Amendment, also follows the same model by stating that 'A generally binding rule of conduct may be laid down by the Fundamental Law and a law made by a body with legislative competence as specified in the Basic Law and which is published in the Official Journal'.[110] One may note, however, that mentioning the Basic Law separately from laws remains irrelevant as long as the binding force and direct applicability of the Basic Law is guaranteed by article R(3) and article T(1).

[108] The word 'man' is gender-neutral in Hungarian.

[109] This opinion appears in the work of András Jakab about the new Hungarian Basic Law; see A Jakab, *Az Új Alaptörvény Keletkezése és Gyakorlati Következményei* (Budapest, HVG Orac, 2011) 176.

[110] Several scholars accept this interpretation in Hungarian legal literature. See T Drinóczi, 'Gondolatok az Alkotmánybíróság 61/2011 (VII. 12.) AB határozatával kapcsolatban' (2012) 1 *Jura* 1; E Bodnár and M Módos, 'A Jogalkotás Normatív Kereteinek Változásai az Új Jogalkotási Törvény Elfogadása Óta' (2012) 1 *Kodifikáció* 31.

B. Continuity or Discontinuity? The Basic Law and the Previous Constitution

(i) Basic Law: Discontinuity in Rhetoric and Continuity in Substance

The constitution-making process, led by Fidesz and rejected by the opposition parties,[111] resulted in a text whose rhetoric suggests a return to the historical roots of the Hungarian state, while its normative content is borrowed from the democratic Constitution of 1989. The name 'Basic Law,' the role of the historical constitution, and a statement in the Preamble according to which '[w]e do not recognise the communist constitution of 1949, since it was the basis of a tyrannical rule; therefore we proclaim it to be invalid', deserve attention from the perspective of continuity.

First of all, the use of the expression 'Basic Law' (*Alaptörvény*) instead of 'Constitution' (*Alkotmány*) needs to be examined. In our opinion, this usage stems from a certain historicising attitude.[112] It is not that the name 'Basic Law' reflects any historical tradition, for the term and concept were unknown to Hungarian positive law. The historicising attitude can be observed in the avoidance of using the word 'constitution,' which would refer to an individual document.

The makers of the 2011 Constitution expressed their respect for pre-Second World War traditions in several ways. The use of the name 'Basic Law' for the Constitution may be understood in this light as well. It suggests that the Basic Law *(Alaptörvény)* is only one of the important 'laws' *(törvények)* forming the historical constitution of the country, a concept expressly referred to in the Preamble and article R(2) of the Basic Law. This could mean that the constitutional rank of the Basic Law as the single highest law of the land is being challenged.[113] Yet such an interpretation is out of the question. The Basic Law declares itself explicitly in its article R(1) to be the foundation of the legal order. This means that laws that contradict the Basic Law are invalid, and will be annulled by the Constitutional Court (with the exception of financial, tax and budgetary statutes). In this sense no discontinuity arose with respect to the hierarchical structure of the legal order.[114]

This is also highlighted by the fact that the Basic Law was adopted on the basis of the provisions of the previous Constitution applicable to amendment of the constitution and the adoption of a new constitution.[115] From a doctrinal point of view it is contradictory to refer to a procedure contained in an earlier constitution

[111] See H Küpper, *Einführung in das ungarische Recht* (Munich, Beck, 2011) 295; A Vincze and M Varju, 'Hungary: The New Fundamental Law' (2012) 18 *European Public Law* 437.

[112] Küpper, *Einführung* (n 111) 296.

[113] Similarly Cs Gáli *et al*, 'Száz Pont az Alkotmánytervezetről', available at www.igyirnankmi.blog.hu/.

[114] The Basic Law is actually not even a 'law' ('*törvény*') according to its own definition, but has a unique legal nature, see the terminology used in arts R(2), S and 6.

[115] Point 2 of the Final Provisions: 'Parliament shall adopt this Basic Law according to point a) of subsection (3) of Section 19 and subsection (3) of Section 24 of Act XX of 1949'.

that is relevant concerning the adoption of a new constitution.[116] The significance of this may be that the text refers to the regularity of the adoption[117] and that it can also be interpreted as setting the common ground relevant from the point of view of formal continuity.[118] Therefore, one may conclude that the source of formal continuity is the Constitution of 1989. Thus, the title pays respect to the pre-Second World War historical constitution in a rhetorical sense, not in a legal sense.

Another discontinuity is suggested by the Preamble to the Basic Law, which declares the Constitution of 1949 'invalid'. In a similar vein (and in order to whitewash the contribution of Hungarian state organs to the Holocaust), it declares that the constitution-making power 'does not recognise the suspension of our historical constitution due to foreign occupation', and also points out the lack of self-determination of Hungary between 19 March 1944 (the Nazi occupation of Hungary) and 2 May 1990 (the first free election in Hungary). By these, the Preamble intends to 'open a door to the past' in order to resurrect the historical constitution.

Even if it were possible to forget about roughly half a century of Hungarian history, this attempt clearly remains a symbolic one. First, the Basic Law blurs the difference between the state and the constitution, notions that are clearly different. Undoubtedly, Hungarian statehood has a history of a thousand years but this does not mean that the formal and material criteria of constitutionalism have always been fulfilled. Constitutionalism following 1990 continues neither socialist state law, nor the public law before the Second World War. The constitutional development after the end of socialism is, therefore, a new beginning even if the constituent power has drawn considerably on earlier legal sources, such as Act I of 1946.

Secondly, Point 2 of the Final Provisions of the Basic Law clearly contradicts the Preamble, as it expressly provides that the Basic Law was passed on the basis of article 19(1)(a) and article 24(3) of the 1989 Constitution it replaced. Thus, the

[116] Originally, the Constitution of 1949 did not state that Parliament would be a constituent power. Such an amendment was introduced in 1972. According to the ministerial reasoning of the amendment of 1972, the 'socialist transition has been completed, the social classes has become stable, therefore it is worth making steps towards the development of democratic socialism'. Although the reasoning did not find it necessary to establish a new constitution, it was worth referring to the possible replacement of the constitution. In the political transition of 1989, the Constitution's reference to the establishment of the new constitution (using the definite article, ie the reference pertained not to constitutions in general but to the one replacing the communist Constitution of 1949) acquired a new meaning. The Preamble stated that the Constitution was an interim one and that it would be replaced by a new one. Article 19 delegated this competence to the Parliament's qualified majority. L Csink and J Fröhlich, '… Az alkotmányjogon innen' (2011) 1 *Alkotmánybírósági Szemle* 68.

[117] Jakab, 'Az Új Alaptörvény' (n 109) 302–3.

[118] According to certain views, the application of the procedural rules of, and the reference to, the previous constitution would not be necessary at all during the establishment of a new constitution. Therefore the Basic Law is just an amendment to the previous Constitution; a new constitution could have been adopted by referendum only. See S Kirste, 'Bekommt Ungarn eine neue Verfassung?', *VSR Europa Blog*, 1 April 2011, available at www.vsr-europa.blogspot.com/2011/04/bekommt-ungarn-eine-neue-verfassung.html.

rhetorically important but normatively weak Preamble signifies a discontinuity, while the legally decisive Final Provisions suggest continuity.

This internal contradiction seems less harsh if one considers that the Basic Law appoints 2 May 1990 as the beginning of the new constitutional order. This means that the 'invalidity' of the 1949 Constitution only refers to its form until 2 May 1990 and says nothing about the Constitution in force until 31 December 2011. This would imply that the constitution of the communist era is declared to be invalid by the Preamble. However, even this would lead to absurd results, as it would question the validity of a number of laws passed between 1949 (the year of the adoption of the communist constitution) and 1990, including the Civil Code and the Criminal Code.

It is, therefore, to be assumed that the declaration of the invalidity of the communist constitution in the Preamble can only be regarded as mere political rhetoric. At the same time, by limiting this political rhetoric to the period before 2 May 1990, the constitution-making power acknowledges the values of the democratic constitution that was in force until the constitution-making in 2010–2011, and does not deny continuity in that sense.

(ii) Continuity in the Case Law of the Constitutional Court

The question of continuity between the 1989 Constitution and the Basic Law has important consequences for the question of how far the democratic Constitution of 1989 and the case law of the Constitutional Court relating thereto informs the interpretation of similarly worded provisions of the Basic Law.

First, the Constitutional Court gave a clear positive answer to the question of continuity in its Decision 22/2012 (V.11) AB of 11 May 2012.[119] In that decision, the Constitutional Court declared that it will continue to use and refer to all of its decisions made under the 1989 Constitution, provided that the relevant provisions of the Basic Law are essentially the same as those in the previous Constitution. The Court even stated that a deviation from the previous practice requires express justification. Surprisingly, however, the decision did not link this result to any specific provision of the Basic Law nor did it elaborate on the possible implications of its language, as discussed above.

Apparently, the constitution-making power was not content with this far-reaching expression of continuity. Article 19 of the Fourth Amendment to the Basic Law introduced a new fifth item into the final and miscellaneous provisions of the Basic Law, declaring that '[d]ecisions of the Constitutional Court delivered prior to the Fundamental Law entering into force shall be repealed. This provision shall be without prejudice to the legal effects of such decisions'. According to the legislative intent of the Fourth Amendment,[120] this provision was adopted to

[119] Decision 22/2012 (V.1.) AB határozat (Constitutional Court of Hungary) 10, 15–16.

[120] Magyarország Alaptörvényének negyedik módosítása (25 March 2013) 49/2013 *Magyar Közlöny* 6400.

ensure that the Basic Law is interpreted in its own context and independent from the previous Constitution. The legislative intent expressly stated that by this provision, the Constitutional Court was 'liberated' from the obligation to interpret the Basic Law in harmony with its previous case law based on the Constitution.

After the Fourth Amendment, the Constitutional Court first interpreted the relevant new provision of the Basic Law on 17 June 2013 in its Decision 13/2013 (VI.17) AB.[121] After this decision, to put it bluntly, the rule is that there is no rule. This is because Decision 13/2013 (VI.17) AB stated that the Constitutional Court is entitled to use the statements of its decisions taken prior to the entry into force of the Basic Law, if the language and the context of the interpreted provision of the Basic Law is essentially the same as that of the 1989 Constitution, and the rules of interpretation of the Basic Law (article R(3)) as well as the facts of the case allow for the same interpretation.[122] It is also stated that the Court will decide on a case-by-case basis whether or not to follow its previous case law.[123]

This means that the Constitutional Court is free to leave its previous case law out of consideration even in cases where the text of the Basic Law corresponds with the rule of the Constitution. What is more, recourse to previous case law requires, on the face of the language of Decision 13/2013 (VI.17) AB, specific justification. Whether continuity in the case law of the Constitutional Court is thus broken is an open question. To date, it seems that the Court has tended to follow its previous case law with respect to such important rights and principles as the right to property[124] or the rule of law.[125] But the continuation of the previous case law obviously depends on the future composition of the Court.

(iii) Selective Continuity of Personnel in Independent Institutions

According to article 8 of the Transitional Provisions, all functionaries elected according to the Constitution were to remain in office.[126] MPs, mayors, the President of the Republic, the cabinet, etc could keep their offices. However, different provisions applied to the Commissioner for Data Protection and the President of the Supreme Court. Both changes had consequences at European level.

The six-year term of the incumbent Data Protection Commissioner was prematurely brought to an end by article 16 of the Transitional Provisions on the day of the entry into force of the Basic Law on 1 January 2012. This came along with the creation of a new National Authority for Data Protection to replace the current Data Protection Commissioner's Office. This move was challenged by

[121] Decision 13/2013 (VI.17) AB határozat (Constitutional Court of Hungary).
[122] ibid para 32.
[123] ibid para 34.
[124] Decision 26/2013 (X.4) AB határozat (Constitutional Court of Hungary) para 160.
[125] Decision 3062/2012 (VII.26) AB határozat (Constitutional Court of Hungary) paras 604, 619.
[126] After the Fourth Amendment it was inserted into the Final and Miscellaneous Provisions of the Basic Law as Point 11.

the European Commission before the Court of Justice of the European Union (CJEU). In its action submitted on 8 June 2012, the Commission relied on article 28(1) of Directive 95/46/EC on the protection of individuals with regard to the processing of personal data and on the free movement of such data and argued that the removal from office before time of the authority responsible for supervising data protection undermines the independence required by the Directive of that authority.[127] The opinion of Advocate General Wathelet of 10 December 2013 followed the action of the Commission and found a violation of article 28 of the Directive.[128] The judgment of the CJEU on 8 April 2014 confirmed this.[129]

An even more grave case was the recall of the President of the Supreme Court, András Baka. Chief Justice Baka had been elected by Parliament President of the Supreme Court for a six-year term on 22 June 2009, after 17 years of service as a judge at the European Court of Human Rights and, subsequently, more than one year of service as a member of the Metropolitan High Court. After the 2010 elections, Chief Justice Baka openly criticised different legislative projects he believed had affected the integrity and independence of the judiciary.

The Basic Law established in its article 25(1) that the highest judicial body would be the Kúria (Hungarian historical name for the Supreme Court), and, as a consequence, article 11(2) of the Transitional Provisions provided, inter alia, that the President of the Supreme Court would have his term of office terminated upon the entry into force of the Basic Law. Further, statutory legislation established a new criterion for the election of the new President, which lead to the ineligibility of the former President of the Supreme Court as President of the Kúria.

Such a move would be acceptable only after the end of an autocratic regime, or if the judge breaks the law. Here, however, neither was the case. It was no surprise that the Venice Commission protested repeatedly.[130] In its Opinion on the New Constitution of Hungary,[131] the Commission had already argued that the adoption of the Transitional Provisions to the Basic Law 'should not be used as a means to put an end to the term of office of persons elected or appointed under the previous Constitution'.[132] This concern was repeated in the Opinion on Act CLXII of 2011 on the Legal Status and Remuneration of Judges and Act CLXI of 2011 on the Organisation and Administration of Courts of Hungary.[133] The Venice Commission also stated that the provisions on the eligibility to become President of the Kúria could operate as a kind of a sanction against the former President of the Supreme Court. The opinion points out that this impression, even if not

[127] Case C-288/12 *Commission v Hungary* [2012] OJ C227/15–16.

[128] ibid, Opinion of AG Melchior Wathelet of 10 December 2013, para 82. See also Hoffmeister, Chapter 7.

[129] Case C-288/12 *Commission v Hungary* (2014, nyr).

[130] See also Nergelius, Chapter 11.

[131] European Commission for Democracy through Law (Venice Commission), *Opinion on the Constitution of Hungary* (Venice Commission) (No 621/2011, 21 June 2011).

[132] ibid para 6.

[133] ibid para 110.

well founded, bears the risk of causing a chilling effect, thus threatening the independence of the judiciary.[134] The issue came up again seven months later in the Opinion on the Cardinal Acts on the Judiciary that were amended following the adoption of Opinion 683/2012 on Hungary. In this opinion, the Venice Commission stated that '[t]he Hungarian Legislator did not address the remarks on the eligibility to become President of the Curia, which should be revised'.[135]

Besides this energetic yet unsuccessful intervention by the Venice Commission, Chief Justice Baka himself filed a complaint with the European Court of Human Rights.[136] Interestingly, the complaint relied on the right to property as regards the remuneration he lost because of the removal. Further, Chief Justice Baka has also complained under Article 6(1) of the ECHR that he has been denied access to a tribunal to defend his rights relating to his premature dismissal, and under Article 10 of the ECHR that he was dismissed in connection with the views and public position he expressed in his capacity as President of the Supreme Court. The case was communicated to the Hungarian government[137] and is still pending.

C. Basic Features of the Political Community as Envisaged by the Basic Law

(i) 'Nation'

Since the fall of communism, there has been an interesting division in the approach to the Hungarian nation taken by Hungarian legal sources: internally, ie within the territory of Hungary, the term 'nation' seems to be understood sometimes as a civic/political and sometimes as an ethnic/cultural nation;[138] externally, ie beyond the territory of Hungary, it seems to be conceived as a clear-cut ethnic/cultural nation.[139] Such logical inconsistency concerning the subject of the Constitution is not unusual.[140]

[134] ibid.

[135] European Commission for Democracy through Law (Venice Commission), *Opinion on the Cardinal Acts on the Judiciary that were Amended following the Adoption of Opinion CDL-AD(2012)001* (Opinion No 683/2012).

[136] *András Baka v Hungary*, Application no 20261/12 (logged on 14 March 2012).

[137] As of 10 March 2014.

[138] In Hungary, the legal order has expressed an ethnic-cultural-Hungarian vision with strong minority protection since 1989 (in a rhetorically more ethnic form since the enactment of the new Basic Law in 2011), although the vision of the political left is the civic (US) model. See A Batory, 'Kin-state Identity in the European Context: Citizenship, Nationalism and Constitutionalism in Hungary' (2010) *Nations and Nationalism* 42. The difference is also expressed when naming the country: the political left prefers 'the Republic of Hungary', whereas the political right prefer simply 'Hungary' (without actually intending to change the state form).

[139] H Hornburg, 'The Concept of Nation in the Hungarian Legal Order' in A Jakab, P Takács and AF Tatham (eds), *The Transformation of the Hungarian Legal Order 1985–2005* (The Hague, Wolters Kluwer, 2007) 507.

[140] For Spain, see E Martínez-Herrera and TJ Miley, 'The Constitution and the Politics of National Identity in Spain' (2010) *Nations and Nationalism* 8.

This fuzzy picture did not change with the approval of the Basic Law in 2011. For internal purposes, the concept is used sometimes in a civic sense, sometimes in an ethnic/cultural sense. Examples of a civic use are found for example in article J of the Basic Law, which mentions '*national* holidays' when it means 'state holidays' (the most important national holiday even bears the name '*official* state holiday'); in article L, 'the family as the basis of the *nation's* survival' refers to the general demographic situation (and not to ethnicity). Similarly, the 'the *nation's* common heritage' in article P also includes the culture of ethnic minorities; and when the President of the Republic 'embodies the unity of the *nation*' according to article 9, it means all citizens of the country. And also when article 38 declares state property as '*national* assets', or when issues of '*national* security' are regulated, then the concept of nation is ethnic-neutral (emphasis added throughout).

The Preamble to the Basic Law begins with the words 'We, the members of the Hungarian *Nation*'.[141] Whether it uses the term 'nation' in an ethnic or cultural sense as the *pouvoir constituant* is not entirely clear, but there are probably stronger arguments for an ethnic/cultural interpretation. An argument for the ethnic nature of the term can be found in the following paragraph of the Preamble:

> We [ie the 'Hungarian Nation'] promise to preserve the intellectual and spiritual unity of our *nation* torn apart in the storms of the past century. The national minorities living with us form part of the Hungarian political community and are constituent parts of the State. (emphasis added)

The first sentence refers to ethnic Hungarians living abroad (note that they are part of the nation), the second to ethnic non-Hungarians living in Hungary (note that the national minorities are not part of the 'Nation' but of the 'State').

On the other hand, the last sentence of the Preamble refers to a civic concept of the nation ('We, the citizens of Hungary' used now as synonymous with 'We, the members of the Hungarian Nation'):

> Our Basic Law ... is a living framework expressing the *nation's* will and the form in which we wish to live. *We, the citizens of Hungary*, are ready to found the order of our country upon the cooperation of the *nation*. (emphasis added)

Thus, the picture about the use of the term 'nation' changes frequently and is possibly even deliberately contradictory. The Preamble confirms, on the one hand, that the concept of nation is an ethnic one ('We promise to preserve the intellectual and spiritual unity of our nation torn apart in the storms of the past

[141] The Preamble is entitled 'The National Avowal of Faith', giving a quasi-religious flavour to the self-description of the nation. For more detail on the English and Hungarian terminology, see F Horkay-Hörcher, 'The National Avowal' in L Csink, B Schanda and ZSA Varga (eds), *The Basic Law of Hungary: A First Commentary* (Dublin, Clarus, 2012) 26. Other religious elements in the new Basic Law are the motto, which is in fact the first line of the national anthem written in 1823 ('*God* bless the Hungarians'), and references to the *Holy* Crown as a symbol of Hungarian historical statehood (though not adopting the doctrine of the Holy Crown). On the quasi-religious nature of nations in general see JR Llobera, *The God of Modernity: The Development of Nationalism in Western Europe* (Bloomsbury Academic, 1994).

century'),[142] but at the same time, right in the next sentence, we find a non-ethnic inclusive definition of the political community conceived as a group of ethnic groups ('The national minorities living with us form part of the Hungarian political community and are constituent parts of the State').

The actual rules about ethnic/national minorities living in Hungary reflect, however, a vision in which a dominant ethnic majority recognises the ethnic minorities. These minorities are recognised as cultural entities with special constitutional privileges (autonomies, language rights and seats in the Parliament to be won with lower thresholds than otherwise).

It seems that the Basic Law of 2011 differs from its predecessor through a stronger rhetorical emphasis on ethnic Hungarians (not only in the Preamble but for example also in a new article H on the state's duty to protect the Hungarian language, which does not seem to carry any concrete legal relevance;[143] and in article D with a more detailed description of the state's responsibility for ethnic Hungarians abroad than in the former Constitution).[144] But it also contains, perhaps as something balancing out the latter, a stronger emphasis on the collective rights of ethnic minorities within Hungary.

(ii) References to Religion and Christianity

Unlike the Constitution, the Basic Law contains several religious references. Preambles in general explicitly contain values but the Preamble to the Basic Law, ie 'The National Avowal of Faith', is strongly emotional and even religious in character. The name of the Preamble ('The National Avowal of Faith') in itself has a devotional character.[145]

Moreover, the first line of the Hungarian national anthem ('God bless the Hungarians') comes before 'The National Avowal of Faith' in the text, so the very first word of the Constitution refers to God.[146] On the one hand, some say that such a reference is a misuse of the name of God and is contrary even to the Bible

[142] The nation 'torn apart' is an implied reference to the Trianon Peace Treaty which meant that territories inhabited by several million ethnic Hungarians became parts of Hungary's neighbouring countries. On this topic, see A Jakab 'Trianon Peace Treaty (1920)' in R Wolfrum (ed), *Max Planck Encyclopedia of Public International Law* (Oxford, Oxford University Press, 2012) vol X, 88–92, available at www.mpepil.com/.

[143] Jakab, 'Az új Alaptörvény' (n 109) 190.

[144] Article D: 'Bearing in mind that there is one single Hungarian nation that belongs together, Hungary shall bear responsibility for the fate of Hungarians living beyond its borders, shall facilitate the survival and development of their communities, shall support their efforts to preserve their Hungarian identity, the application of their individual and collective rights, the establishment of their community self-governments, and their prosperity in their native lands, and shall promote their cooperation with each other and with Hungary'.

[145] Horkay-Hörcher, 'The National Avowal' (n 141) 26–28.

[146] It is an open question whether the reference to God means the supernatural in general, or the god of any religion or, in a narrow sense, only the God of the Christian Bible.

in this regard.[147] On the other hand, it is also argued that the national anthem seems to be neutral in public usage.[148] The first part of the Preamble also states that Hungary is 'part of Christian Europe' and recognises the role of Christianity in preserving the nation. Finally, the Final Provisions mention that the Members of Parliament adopted the Basic Law 'being aware of [their] responsibility before God and man'.

References to God or Christianity are not unknown in European constitutions. The Preamble to the Polish Constitution states: 'Beholden to our ancestors for their labours, their struggle for independence achieved at great sacrifice, for our culture rooted in the Christian heritage of the Nation and in universal human values'. A similar reference to historical-religious heritage can be found in the Slovak Constitution, which was adopted 'in the sense of the spiritual heritage of Cyril and Methodius and the historical legacy of the Great Moravian Empire'. The Constitutions of Greece and Ireland are also well-known examples of Preambles with religious content. According to its Preamble, the Greek Constitution was adopted 'in the name of the Holy and Consubstantial and Indivisible Trinity'.[149] The Irish Constitution was established 'in the Name of the Most Holy Trinity, from Whom is all authority and to Whom, as our final end, all actions both of men and States must be referred'. The Preamble to the Irish Constitution 'humbly acknowledge[s] all our obligations to our Divine Lord, Jesus Christ, Who sustained our fathers through centuries of trial'. Besides this, article 6(1) even acknowledges that 'all powers of government, legislative, executive and judicial, derive, under God, from the people'. Furthermore, the Irish Constitution includes a very strong religious confession in article 44(1): 'The State acknowledges that the homage of public worship is due to Almighty God. It shall hold His Name in reverence, and shall respect and honour religion'.

It is not unique either that the constitution refers to the responsibility of the Members of Parliament who adopted the constitution. The relevant reference in the German Preamble (*Im Bewußtsein seiner Verantwortung vor Gott und den Menschen*) and the Polish Constitution are very similar to the Hungarian phrase that can be found in the Postscript. On the other hand, the Czech Constitution refers to responsibility without mentioning God; according to the Preamble, the Czech Republic is 'home of free citizens who are aware of their obligations towards others and of their responsibility to the community'.

From the examples mentioned above, it can clearly be seen that European constitutions vary as regards the way they refer to the supernatural. Religious references are often mixed with cultural and historical heritage or they refer to the

[147] I Vörös, 'Gondolatok egy Jövőbeli Alkotmány Preambulumához' (2011) 1 *Jogtudományi Közlöny* 25.

[148] B Schanda, 'Considerations on the Place of Religion in Constitutional Law' in Z Csehi, B Schanda and P Sonnevend (eds), *Viva Vox Iuris Civilis* (Budapest, Szent István Társulat, 2012) 280, 285.

[149] The Greek President and Members of Parliament also take their oath 'in the name of the Holy and Consubstantial and Indivisible Trinity' (art 33 s 2 and art 59 s 1).

responsibility of the creators of the constitution. On the other hand, a constitution cannot disregard the social cohesion of the nation. If a constitution neglects the real circumstances (ie it contains deeply religious references when a minority of the population considers itself to be practising a religion) then this fact encumbers integration of the political community. It is also problematic, if religious references are included in the constitution unilaterally by one political side, without an overarching consensus. More specifically, the Basic Law does not consider the views of a considerable part of the population as worthy of rhetorical gestures towards them. This is especially strange and unintelligible in a society in which a large part of the population (presumably including the voters of the governing party and even many of the leaders of the governing party itself) do not consider themselves religious.[150]

D. References to the Historical Constitution

Article R(3) suggests yet another discontinuity with the previous Constitution with its referral to the 'achievements of the historical constitution' as an aid to interpretation. From a rhetorical perspective, this can be regarded as a revival of the historical constitution, yet this provision is practically unusable. On the one hand, it is not quite clear exactly which laws should be regarded as part of the 'historical constitution'.[151] On the other hand, several of the laws that may qualify to be part of the 'historical constitution' are unacceptable by today's standards (eg medieval rules bound to the then-social circumstances), or simply do not conform to a republican form of regime. To avoid absurdities, some scholars recommend use of the word 'achievement' as a filter,[152] in the sense that what is to be regarded as an achievement has to correspond to international treaties on human rights and the modern conception of constitutionalism. Interpreted in this way, the reference to the historical constitution is a mere tautology.

[150] *Cf* M Tomka, 'Religiosity in Central and Eastern Europe: Facts and Interpretations' (2010) 3 *Religion and Society in Central and Eastern Europe* 1.

[151] This is not least because the legal system had a much more primitive doctrine of rules. The reason for compiling the first *Corpus Iuris Hungarici* (a private compilation) in the sixteenth century was that many ancient laws were simply forgotten. In such a legal system (which never had a complete and authoritative list of legal rules) it was impossible to make it clear on the occasion of issuing a new law exactly which rules had to be repealed. Thus, new laws repealed older ones even if they did not provide for their explicit repeal (today we would say that they applied a 'material derogation'). Because of this material derogation, the historical constitution could not create parallel rules that would contradict one another. Thus, even if the provision of the Preamble quoted above could mean that the historical constitution enters into force as positive law (which it cannot mean, as being part of the *Preamble* it cannot have such normative force), only those parts of it that are *not* contrary to the Basic Law of 2011 could be applied today. Consequently (and supposing that the Basic Law covers all problems of constitutional law), that reference is a tautology even according to the inherent logic of the pre-Second World War historical constitution, and can by no means lead to medieval rules being revived. On the various kinds of derogation, see A Jakab, 'Problems of the Stufenbaulehre' (2007) *Canadian Journal of Law and Jurisprudence* 56.

[152] Jakab, 'Az új Alaptörvény' (n 109) 184, 199.

We claimed above that organic development and continuity of constitutionalism are essential elements of a historical constitution. We argued that the legal development after the end of socialism is not a direct continuation of the period before 1944. It follows that article R(3) of the Basic Law cannot revive the Holy Crown doctrine on which the historical constitution was based. As Zoltán Szente says, 'reviving traditions and connecting them with the current Hungarian constitutional principles can only be done by neglecting the Holy Crown Doctrine and the actual content of the historical constitution and by partially changing the Hungarian common law traditions'.[153] The historical constitution embodied in the Holy Crown doctrine is inconsistent with the charter constitution.

This does not mean that historic references were alien to constitutionalism under the 1989 Constitution. The Constitutional Court has repeatedly referred to historic laws. This was the case with the constitutional review of the regulations that forbade the limitation of war crimes, where the Constitutional Court referred to the first Criminal Code of 1878,[154] or with the review of the standing orders of Parliament during which the Constitutional Court referred to Act IV of 1848, which declared the right of Parliament to establish its own rules of procedure.

After the entry into force of the Basic Law, the Constitutional Court may refer to the development of Hungarian constitutionalism and public law to fortify its argument. The Court first used this form of argumentation after the entry into force of the Basic Law in its decision on the retirement age of the judges.[155] According to the decision, the principle of judicial independence is an achievement of the historical constitution that should be considered in the interpretation of the current text of the Basic Law. The Constitutional Court pointed out, however, that it is its own duty to determine which elements of the historical constitution should be regarded as relevant achievements under the Basic Law.[156]

A partly different solution is advocated by László Sólyom. According to his method of interpretation, the historical constitution is a flexible concept which can be adapted to ever-changing circumstances.[157] Sólyom thus argues that nothing forces us to regard the historical constitution as a concept which refers to the period before 1944 rather than one that comprises the achievements of modern constitutionalism. In his view, article R(3) tells us that the constitutional case law as developed by the Constitutional Court over the last two decades forms part of the historical constitution as an aid to interpret the Basic Law.[158]

[153] Szente, 'A Historizáló' (n 11) 1.
[154] Decision 2/1994 (I.14) AB határozat (Constitutional Court of Hungary).
[155] Decision 33/2012 (VII.17) AB határozat (Constitutional Court of Hungary) para 99.
[156] ibid paras 99, 108.
[157] Szente, 'A Historizáló' (n 11) 1.
[158] As László Sólyom, former President of the Constitutional Court, and later President of the Republic, put it in an interview: 'The Invisible Constitution is part of the historical constitution'. See www.hetivalasz.hu/itthon/solyom-laszlo-az-uj-alkotmanyrol-37067.

E. The Organisation of State: Continuity and Programmed Blockades

As for the form of government, the Basic Law brings no change. Hungary remains a unitary (ie not a federal) state, a republic[159] and a parliamentary democracy. At the centre of the structure of political power is the Prime Minister elected by the Parliament (which still works as one chamber), with the general powers of control and guidance of the PM explicitly provided by article 18(1) of the Basic Law. The President of the Republic is, as before, elected by the Parliament according to article 10 of the Basic Law. His or her authority remains essentially limited to protocol, except for the powers related to legislation. Article 6(4) entitles the President to send any law passed by the Parliament to the Constitutional Court for preliminary review before (s)he signs it. Moreover, article 6 (5) grants the President the power to send any law back to the Parliament for further consideration before (s)he signs it, together with his or her comments, in case (s)he disagrees with (part of) it, rather than sending it for preliminary constitutional review (there is nothing new in that, either). There is no real extension of the powers of the President related to the dissolution of the Parliament either. Article 3(3) provides that (s)he may dissolve the Parliament in two cases, setting at the same time a date for the elections: if the Parliament does not, after the mandate of the Cabinet has ended, elect the person recommended for Prime Minister by the President within 40 days after the first recommendation was made; or if the Parliament does not adopt the respective year's central budget by 31 March.[160]

Despite the basic continuity that can be observed in the Part regulating state organisation, a future majority government may face two sorts of massive obstacles allowed for by the Basic Law. First, article 44(3) sets a hard limit by giving the power of approval to the newly established Budget Council;[161] secondly, the scope of the so-called cardinal Acts requiring a two-thirds majority are defined in a way that makes governing without that majority more than difficult.

(i) Powers of the Budget Council

Article 44(3) of the Basic Law provides that before laws on the central budget are passed, the Council has to approve them. The Budget Council is composed

[159] Basic Law, art B(2) makes this explicit. Changing the official name of the country from 'Republic of Hungary' (*Magyar Köztársaság*, lit. Hungarian Republic') to 'Hungary' (*Magyarország*) has no legal consequences.

[160] 1989 Constitution, art 28(3) provided for the following cases of the dissolution of the Parliament: 'The President of the Republic may dissolve the Parliament, simultaneously with the announcement of new elections, if (a) the Parliament expresses its lack of confidence in the Government on no less than four occasions in a period of twelve months during the course of one parliamentary term; or (b) the mandate of the Government terminates, a candidate for Prime Minister nominated by the President of the Republic is not elected by the Parliament within a period of forty days from the day upon which the first candidate was nominated'.

[161] The Budget Council was set up in 2009 by an Act, but only the Basic Law raised it to a constitutional level.

of three persons, whose terms reach beyond the parliamentary term in which they were elected.[162] One might suggest that if a new government is elected, a veto of the Budget Council loyal to the previous majority may prevent a budget being adopted, which may, in turn, lead to the President dissolving the Parliament according to article 3(3).[163]

A right of approval of a non-parliamentary organ does in fact question the discretion of the Parliament in terms of the budget. Yet it is fair to note that according to article 44(3), the Budget Council may only use its power to enforce the limit placed on state debt that was newly introduced by article 36(4) and (5). These articles mean that if the Budget Council abuses its power to deny approval, this would not prevent Parliament from passing the budget. Moreover, even a legitimate refusal to approve a budget would not in itself impede the passing of that budget, nor would it entitle the President to refuse to sign the budget without further grounds. A lack of approval by the Budget Council for the budget is ultimately a constitutional issue, which has to be ruled on by the Constitutional Court, either in the form of a preliminary review, if initiated by the President, or an ex post constitutional review on the basis of a petition from some of those entitled to do so (the relevant possibility is that one-quarter of the MPs may submit such a petition).

It has to be noted, too, that article 3(3)(b) of the Basic Law speaks of the budget not being adopted before 31 March as one of the possible grounds for dissolving Parliament. Implicitly, the adoption of the Act on the state budget is a vote of confidence. In constitutional terms, neither the government nor Parliament questions the confidence, but politically the issue is so essential to the government that it would be unable to govern any longer.[164]

According to one interpretation, this implies that the budget has to be adopted in a legitimate way, ie an illegitimate budget (one passed in spite of a legitimate veto from the Budget Council) cannot be regarded as adopted from the perspective of article 3(3)(b). Yet another interpretation, a textualist one also based on the function of Article 3(3)(b) cannot be excluded either, according to which passing the budget is always a measure to see if the government has a parliamentary majority, and the dissolution of Parliament is the sanction for the lack of a majority. According to this interpretation, if the budget has a parliamentary majority, ie the budget is adopted (as required by article 3(3)(b)), dissolving Parliament is out of the question, even if the budget was otherwise adopted contrary to article 44(3).

[162] According to Basic Law, art 44(4), 'The members of the Budget Council shall be the President of the Budget Council, the Governor of the National Bank of Hungary and the President of the State Audit Office. The President of the Budget Council shall be appointed for six years by the President of the Republic'.

[163] Küpper, *Einführung* (n 111) 300.

[164] P Norton, 'Government Defeats in the House of Commons: Myth and Reality' in *Ministerial Responsibility* (Oxford, Clarendon Press, 1998) 40.

Irrespective of which interpretation one chooses, the final decision on the legality of passing the budget lies with the Constitutional Court rather than the President of the Republic alone. In this sense, refusing to sign the budget without asking for a preliminary preview would clearly be against the Constitution. Thus, a situation allowing for the dissolution of Parliament could only arise if Parliament passed the budget despite the constitutionally grounded veto of the Budget Council, which would then be examined by the Constitutional Court, in the form of either a preliminary or an ex post review and decided to the effect that the passing of the budget is to be regarded as invalid.

The veto power of the Budgetary Council is undoubtedly an undemocratic one, just like the powers of independent institutions (courts, constitutional courts, national banks) in general. The question is rather whether it will try to abuse this power for party-political reasons. As two of the three members have been long-serving former politicians (an MP and a former Minister) of the governing party, many are sceptical about their independence, but the real test will come when the political colour of the government and that of the Budget Council differ.

(ii) Cardinal Acts: Blockades Programmed

The case of the so-called cardinal Acts is, however, a cause for serious concern. The 1989 Constitution already required a two-thirds majority for a wide range of legislative subject matters. These laws are now termed 'cardinal Acts' by article T(4).[165] While the number of subjects requiring a special majority did not increase with the Basic Law (in fact, their number fell from 28 to 26, which means that the regulation of several guarantees of fundamental rights does not require a two-thirds majority),[166] the range of the subject matters covered changed considerably.[167] We submit that several of these should be left to ordinary legislation.

[165] Basic Law, art T(4): 'Cardinal Act shall mean an Act, the adoption or amendment of which requires the votes of two-thirds of the Members of Parliament present'.

[166] See Jakab, 'Az új Alaptörvény' (n 109) 173. Since then, however, the amendments also concerned the introduction of new topics which could only be regulated by cardinal laws, thus today the number of two-thirds majority topics is approximately the same as before the adoption of the Basic Law.

[167] The Basic Law stipulates that the following issues be regulated by cardinal statutes: citizenship; national symbols and decorations; family relations; publishing of laws; authority for the protection of information rights; churches; political parties; freedom of the press; media; minority rights; elections of Members of Parliament; elections of representatives of local governments; status of Members of Parliament; operation of the Parliament and of its committees; the President; autonomous regulatory bodies; the Constitutional Court; the judiciary; prosecution services; local governments; protection of national wealth; the taxation and pension system; the National Bank of Hungary; supervision of financial institutions; the State Audit Office; the Budget Council; police and intelligence; the national army; and special legal orders. Furthermore, issues concerning the European Union also require qualified majority. According to the Constitution, qualified majority was required in the following fields: EU affairs; national symbols; legislation and publishing of laws; special legal orders; status of Members of Parliament; national referendums; the President; the Constitutional Court; the Commissioner for Human Rights; the State Audit Office; the relationship between the Parliament and the government in EU affairs; the National Army; police and intelligence; local governments; the judiciary; public prosecutors; migration; information rights; religious freedom; freedom of the press; the media; freedom

These include the rules on the protection of families;[168] the requirements for preserving and protecting national assets, and for the responsible management thereof;[169] the scope of the exclusive property and of the exclusive economic activities of the state, as well as the limitations and conditions of the alienation of national assets of outstanding importance for the national economy;[170] the basic rules for the sharing of public burdens and for the pension system;[171] and the detailed rules on the operation of the Budget Council.[172]

In the present legislative cycle, the governing parties possess the necessary majority to adopt these cardinal Acts. However, a future government having a simple majority without support from the opposition will be limited in shaping its economic and financial policies. Given the deep cleavages between the different wings of Hungarian politics, this may quickly lead to a stalemate in the case of any future Cabinet that does not have a two-thirds majority in the Parliament. This, in turn, may raise further issues in light of the First Protocol to the European Convention on Human Rights, which guarantees the possibility for the democratic majority to govern.[173]

The scope of cardinal Acts has also been criticised by the Venice Commission in its Opinion on the New Constitution of Hungary. The opinion refers to article 3 of the First Protocol to the ECHR and states that '[t]he more policy issues are transferred beyond the powers of simple majority, the less significance will future elections have and the more possibilities does a two-third majority have of cementing its political preferences and the country's legal order'. Ultimately, argues the Venice Commission, '[e]lections, which, according to Article 3 of the First Protocol to the ECHR, should guarantee the "expression of the opinion of the people in the choice of the legislator", would become meaningless if the legislator would not be able to change important aspects of the legislation that should have been enacted with a simple majority'.[174]

It is noteworthy here that cardinal Acts and 'ordinary' statutes can both equally be subjects of constitutional adjudication.

of assembly; freedom of association; political parties; the right to asylum; minority rights; citizenship; right to strike; elections of Members of Parliament; elections of representatives of local governments; self-governments of the minorities.

[168] Basic Law, art L(3).
[169] ibid art 38(1).
[170] ibid art 38(2).
[171] ibid art 40.
[172] ibid art 44(5).
[173] Venice Commission Op 720/2013 (n 100).
[174] Venice Commission Op 621/2011 (n 131).

F. Fundamental Rights

The substantive continuity between the previous Constitution and the Basic Law as adopted in 2011 could be best observed in the Chapter on fundamental rights. This applied to the tests of the limitation of fundamental rights, the liberty rights, and the ban on negative discrimination. The new classification of social fundamental rights as mere 'state purposes' brought no change in terms of content either, if one looks at the previous interpretation of these rights by the Constitutional Court. However, the Transitional Provisions raised serious concerns in terms of the fundamental rights of the individual, particularly for the principle of *nullum crimen sine lege* and the right to a lawful judge. The Fourth Amendment transplanted these problematic provisions into the Basic Law, and also introduced a number of specific exceptions to different fundamental rights in order to offset the case law of the Constitutional Court. The result of this is a Basic Law with a catalogue of fundamental rights and a limitation clause that in general correspond with European standards. Yet the wide scope of exceptions to several fundamental rights raises the very serious question of whether the Basic Law is based on a coherent set of values, or, rather, if it merely treats the protection of fundamental rights as a technical matter.

(i) Test Applicable to Limitations of Fundamental Rights

The Basic Law does not depart from the tradition of the previous Constitution, as it stipulates the limits of fundamental rights in a single article. Previously, article 8(2) of the Constitution provided for the guarantee of essential content as the sole limit on fundamental rights.[175] On this basis, the Constitutional Court developed the concept of the guarantee of relative essential content,[176] practically equating it with the principle of proportionality.[177] Although there are several references in the decisions of the Constitutional Court to the tripartite principle of 'suitability–necessity–proportionality in the narrow sense' developed by German

[175] 'In the Republic of Hungary rules pertaining to fundamental rights and duties shall be determined by statute, which, however, shall not limit the essential content of any fundamental right'.

[176] It was only on one occasion that the Constitutional Court seemed to use the essential content in an absolute sense. In connection with the proportionality of capital punishment, the Court ruled that capital punishment would lead to the annihilation of the right to life and human dignity, which is contrary to art 8(2) of the Constitution. See Decision 23/1990 (X.31) AB határozat (Constitutional Court of Hungary). The concurring opinion of the President of the Constitutional Court went even further, arguing that the right to life is the absolute essential content in itself, which cannot, therefore, be limited. See Decision 23/1990 (X.31) AB határozat (Constitutional Court of Hungary). It is primarily this concurring opinion that is the basis of scholarly debates on the guarantee of essential content in a relative sense (to be discussed below). G Brunner, 'Vier Jahre ungarische Verfassungsgerichtsbarkeit' in G Brunner and L Sólyom, *Verfassungsgerichtsbarkeit in Ungarn, Analysen und Entscheidungssammlung* (Nomos-Verlag, 1995) 54.

[177] First in Decision 20/1990 (X.) AB határozat (Constitutional Court of Hungary).

constitutional law,[178] this test was normally used by the Constitutional Court in a shorter form. This means that the limitation of a fundamental right is contrary to the Constitution if there is no compelling reason for it, or if it is disproportionate to the aim it serves.[179]

The Constitutional Court applied, at least in its rhetoric, a strict measure to decide what counts as a compelling reason for the purposes of article 8(2) of the Constitution. According to the Constitutional Court, interference with a fundamental right can only be justified by the protection of another fundamental right or a constitutional value.[180] The only exception is the right to property, which may be limited in favour of an unqualified public interest. This strict measure was, however, considerably softened by the Court's broad interpretation of the concept of 'other constitutional values'.[181]

The Basic Law enshrines the guarantee of the essential content in article I(3), and complements it with an explicit formulation of the principle of proportionality. As regards proportionality, the second sentence of article I(3) makes a clear reference to the previous practice of the Constitutional Court:

> A fundamental right may only be restricted in order to allow the exercise of another fundamental right or to protect a constitutional value, to the extent that is absolutely necessary, proportionate to the objective pursued, and respecting the essential content of the fundamental right.

This change, it seems, will not influence the application of the principle of proportionality. A new feature is, however, that the guarantee of essential content and the principle of proportionality are juxtaposed in the text. This necessarily attributes an independent meaning to the guarantee of essential content, which can no longer be interpreted in the usual way. This suggests that the guarantee of the essential content now has to be understood in an absolute sense.[182] According to this analysis, the essential content protects the most important aspects of the exercise of fundamental rights, forming some kind of hard core that is inaccessible to the public power, for each fundamental right. In everyday practice this interpretation may not change much, as it is unlikely that the hard core of a fundamental

[178] First in ibid; then in Decision 7/1991 (II.28) AB határozat (Constitutional Court of Hungary); Decision 30/1992 (V.26) AB határozat (Constitutional Court of Hungary). See also, Brunner, 'Vier Jahre' (n 176) 55; G Halmai and GA Tóth, 'Az Emberi Jogok Korlátozása' in G Halmai (ed), *Emberi Jogok* (Budapest, Osiris, 2003) 130.

[179] First in Decision 8/1991 (III.5) AB határozat (Constitutional Court of Hungary).

[180] See eg, Decision 6/1998 (III.11) AB határozat (Constitutional Court of Hungary).

[181] Therefore the Constitutional Court has referred to concepts such as the 'virtue of public life' ('közélet tisztasága'), Decision 20/1990 (X.4) AB határozat (Constitutional Court of Hungary); the 'public order' (*közrend*), Decision 30/1992 (V.26) AB határozat (Constitutional Court of Hungary)' the 'public morals' (*közerkölcs*), and 'considerable public interest' (*nyomós közérdek*), Decision 56/1994 (XI.10) AB határozat (Constitutional Court of Hungary) as reasons legitimating intervention.

[182] See, in particular, Remmert, Article 19 para 2, in T Maunz and G Dürig, *Grundgesetz Kommentar 63 Suppliment* (Munich, Verlag, 2009) para 28.

right will be violated by a law or its application.[183] Still, the guarantee of an absolute essential content, as an addition to the principle of proportionality, adds a further keystone to the structure of the Basic Law.

(ii) Novelties concerning Fundamental Rights in the Basic Law as Adopted in 2011

As for rights of liberty and equality, the Basic Law in part basically copies the catalogue of fundamental rights contained in the previous Constitution and then supplements it with fundamental rights contained in the EU Charter of Fundamental Rights, as regards, for example, the prohibition of cloning in article III(3).[184] The Basic Law also features the right to self-defence, which is, in fact, rather difficult to interpret.[185]

Article II ensures human dignity, stipulating that it shall be inviolable. It continues by stating that every person shall have the right to life and human dignity, and that the life of the foetus shall be protected from the moment of conception. In the former Constitution, the 'inherent right to life and to human dignity' was protected, which means that the Basic Law aims to distinguish the protection of life from the protection of human dignity.[186] There are serious debates as to whether this article will prohibit abortion or not. Based on the text and the former case law[187] of the Constitutional Court, the fear that this provision will prohibit abortion does not seem to be founded. Under the previous Constitution, the Constitutional Court declared that the life of the foetus needs protection and this constitutionally limits the self-determination of the woman concerned. This is exactly what the Basic Law declares; the 'foetus protection' of article II of the Basic Law already existed in the same legal form, as an obligation of objective institutional protection.[188] Therefore, the wording of the Basic Law cannot lead to prohibition of abortion and does not lead to a further limitation of the right of self-determination.

[183] German commentaries agree in not attributing much relevance to Grundgesetz, art 19 para II, which contains the guarantee of essential content. See Remmert, Article 19 para 47 (n 182) for further references.

[184] The Hungarian term used here for cloning (*egyedmásolás*, literally 'cloning of individuals') may be the result of a mistranslation. It probably refers to the 'prohibition of the reproductive cloning of human beings' in Art 3 of the EU Charter of Fundamental Rights.

[185] Including this fundamental right may follow US patterns, E Volokh, 'State Constitutional Rights of Self-Defense and Defense of Property' (2007) *Texas Review of Law and Politics* 399.

[186] This solution also follows a German example, from Grundgesetz, art 1 para I: 'Human dignity shall be inviolable. To respect and protect it shall be the duty of all state authority'.

[187] See Decision 64/1991 (XII.17) AB határozat (Constitutional Court of Hungary) on the abortion judgment, www.codices.coe.int/NXT/gateway.dll/CODICES/precis/eng/eur/hun/hun-1991-s-003?fn=document-frameset.htm$f=templates$3.0. On later case law of the Constitutional Court see H Küpper, 'Das zweite Abtreibungsurteil des ungarischen Verfassungsgerichts' (1999) *Osteuropa-Recht* 422.

[188] See Jakab, 'Az új Alaptörvény' (n 109) 203–4.

The Basic Law was also criticised for not declaring a prohibition of capital punishment.[189] However, the introduction of capital punishment does not seem to be a real option in Europe and the absence of such a declaration does not seem to constitute a derogation of the level of constitutional protection. Furthermore, article XIV(2) states that '[n]o person shall be expelled or extradited to a state where he or she is threatened to be sentenced to death or to be subjected to torture or to inhuman treatment or punishment'. This rule can be interpreted as an implicit prohibition of capital punishment.[190]

Accordingly, we submit that in these questions constitutional adjudication will not change much. Apart from certain exceptions, the text of the Basic Law does not lower the level of protection provided for fundamental rights by the Constitution. One of these exceptions is the possibility of a sentence of life without parole for 'intentional violent crimes', which is allowed for explicitly by article IV(2). Although similar punishments do exist in Italian (*ergastolo*, article 22 of the Italian Penal Code),[191] English and Welsh (whole life order, Criminal Justice Act 2003),[192] Dutch (*levenslange gevangenisstraf*, article 10 of the Dutch Penal Code)[193] and French law (*réclusion criminelle à perpétuité*, articles 221-3 and 221-4 of the French Penal Code),[194] these examples are harshly criticised in the literature.[195] At the time the Basic Law was passed, it was doubtful that unlimited imprisonment, which was already provided for in the Hungarian Penal Code, was in conformity with Article 3 of the ECHR.[196] Recently, however, the European Court of Human Rights decided in *László Magyar v Hungary*[197] that where domestic law does not provide for the possibility of review of a life sentence with a view to its commutation, remission, termination or the conditional release of the prisoner, a whole life sentence will not measure up to the standards of Article 3 of the ECHR.

[189] Venice Commission Op 621/2011 (n 131) para 68.

[190] Z Balogh and B Hajas, 'Rights and Freedoms' in Csink 'The Basic Law of Hungary' (n 141) 26.

[191] Italian Penal Code, art 176, as a general rule allows for probation *(liberazione condizionale)* after 26 years in cases of life sentence but Act on Penal Execution, art 4*bis* (*legge sull'ordinamento penitenziario, 26 luglio 1975 n. 354)* as a special rule prohibits any mitigation for a range of crimes (eg human trafficking, terrorism, or *associazione mafiosa*, ie, mafia crimes), if the perpetrator does not cooperate with the authorities (ie (s)he shows no repentance). Thus, if life imprisonment is applied by the judge in such a case, because of aggregate sentences and/or aggravated cases, then it means actual life imprisonment.

[192] D van Zyl Smit, *Taking Life Imprisonment Seriously in National and International Law* (The Hague Kluwer International, 2002) 78–133.

[193] C Noorduyn, 'Life is Life in Netherlands' (2008) *IBA Legal Practice Division—Criminal Law Committee Newsletter* 12.

[194] On the debates concerning the latest amendments to French law, see S Enguéléguélé, 'L'Iinstitution de la Perpétuité Réelle' (1997) 1 *Revue de science criminelle et de droit pénal comparé* 59.

[195] A Demetriades, S Bartolini and T Christodoulidou, 'Life Imprisonment as Inhuman and Degrading Treatment' (2008) *European Human Rights Law Review* 656; A Jakab and P Sonnevend, 'Kontinuität mit Mängeln: Das neue ungarische Grundgesetz' (2012) 72 ZaöRV 79.

[196] *Kafkaris v Cyprus*, Application no 21906/04 (2009) 49 EHRR 877, paras 95–99.

[197] *László Magyar v Hungary*, Application no 73593/10, para 50–52.

Another criticism that has arisen is that article XV does not refer expressly to the prohibition of sexual discrimination. As the list in article XV is not exhaustive, the phrase 'or any other ground whatsoever' can be understood to include sexual discrimination. This is also confirmed by the case law of the Constitutional Court.[198]

Similarly, no considerable change has been made to the rules concerning social rights, which were formulated in the previous Constitution as fundamental rights. Some of these are defined by the Basic Law as state goals rather than fundamental rights (eg the right to work[199] and social security).[200] But these were already interpreted as such by the Constitutional Court, which, therefore, constituted constitutional measures that were generally not directly enforceable.[201] Moreover, the Basic Law introduces several new social fundamental rights. Examples of these social provisions include the right to working conditions that respect health, safety and dignity in article XVII(3), which was Article XVIII(1) of the EU Charter of Fundamental Rights.

Problems of protection of fundamental rights arise, however, from the Preamble to the Basic Law. Certain of its passages, if interpreted in a particular way or regarded as standards of interpretation in the light of article R(3), may lead to a lower level of protection for the fundamental rights acknowledged by the Basic Law. Such passages include, for example, the one referring to the nation-preserving role of Christianity, or the one according to which the most important forms of living together are 'the family and the nation' which 'provide the most important framework for our coexistence', and 'our fundamental cohesive values are fidelity, faith and love'. If such interpretations are to be avoided, these parts of the Preamble also have to be interpreted in the light of international treaties on human rights (which is made possible by article Q and treated as merely symbolic statements.[202]

Finally, a formal novelty should be mentioned. Under the previous Constitution, most of the fundamental rights were to be regulated by a qualified majority. The Basic Law maintains the institution of statutes of a qualified majority (the so-called cardinal Acts) but it mostly singles out issues of state organisation and the economic bases of the society to be regulated by cardinal statutes and not the guarantees of human rights.

[198] Decision 20/1999 (VI.25) AB határozat (Constitutional Court of Hungary); Decision 37/2002 (IX.4) AB határozat (Constitutional Court of Hungary).

[199] Constitution, art 70/B, now in Basic Law, art XII(2).

[200] Constitution, art 70/E, now in Basic Law, arts XIX and XXII.

[201] Sonnevend, 'Der Verfassungsmäßige Schutz sozialrechtlicher Ansprüche in der jüngeren Rechtsprechung des ungarischen Verfassungsgerichts' (n 33); P Sonnevend, 'Armut und Verfassung. Die Rechtslage in Ungarn' in R Hofmann *et al* (eds), *Armut und Verfassung, Sozialstaatlichkeit im europäischen Vergleich* (Vienna, Nomos, 1998) 300, 327.

[202] Such an interpretation was suggested, eg, by Jakab, 'Az új Alaptörvény' (n 109) 182.

(iii) *Specific Exceptions to Fundamental Rights Introduced by the Fourth Amendment to the Basic Law*

We have already referred to the number of specific exceptions to different fundamental rights introduced by the Fourth Amendment to the Basic Law. We submit that these exceptions are incompatible with the ideals of protecting fundamental rights as expressions of universal values. In this section of the chapter we will focus on two issues that give rise to specific concerns.

(a) Right to Marry and the Concept of Family under the Basic Law

Article L of the Basic Law as adopted in 2011 became one of the most debated provisions of the Basic Law, stipulating that Hungary 'shall protect the institution of marriage as the union of a man and a woman established by voluntary decision, and the institution of family as the foundation of the subsistence of the nation'. However, no real change is brought about by this reference. This provision, which is not in the Chapter on the fundamental rights but in the Chapter entitled 'Fundamentals', does not change the legal situation, since the previous Constitution also mentioned the protection of marriage among its general provisions.[203] Similarly, the definition of marriage as a life union between a man and a woman does not bring any substantial change either; the Constitutional Court has already defined marriage on the basis of the 1949–89 Constitution as the relationship between a man and a woman.[204] To this extent, the Basic Law only codifies the already existing practice of the Court. Moreover, the explicit reference to the concept of heterosexual marriage in the text of the Basic Law does not preclude the introduction of same-sex marriage, as can be seen by the Spanish example.[205]

In contrast to the definition of marriage, the Fourth Amendment indeed stepped back from the 1989 Constitution as regards the definition of family. The 1989 Constitution stipulated in its article 15 that the Republic of Hungary protects the institution of marriage and family. This provision was interpreted by the Constitutional Court to apply not only to families that were based on marriage, but also to families in the sociological sense.[206] Article L(1) of the Basic Law as adopted in 2011 did not change this. It did refer to the family 'as the basis of the

[203] Constitution, art 15, stated that 'The Republic of Hungary shall protect the institutions of marriage and family'.

[204] Decision 154/2008 (XII.17) AB határozat (Constitutional Court of Hungary).

[205] See Jakab, 'Az új Alaptörvény' (n 109) 194.

[206] Decision 14/1995 (III.13) AB határozat (Constitutional Court of Hungary) paras 82, 83; Decision 154/2008 (XII.17) AB határozat (Constitutional Court of Hungary) paras 1203, 1210. The case law of the Constitutional Court never accepted, though, the right of gay couples to get married, see R Uitz, 'Hungary: Mixed Prospects for the Constitutionalisation of Gay Rights' (2004) 2 *International Journal of Constitutional Law* 705.

nation's survival', but this had no immediate impact on the definition of family under the Basic Law.

Against this background, section 7 of Act CCXI of 2011 on Protection of Families raised concerns, since it defined the concept of the family as a system of relations that generates an emotional and economic community of natural persons, based on the marriage of a man and a woman, next of kinship or adoptive guardianship. In its Decision 43/2012 (XII. 20) AB, the Hungarian Constitutional Court had annulled this section for breach of article L of the Basic Law.[207] According to the Decision, the concept of a family based on the marriage of a man and a woman is too narrow, since the state should also protect long-term emotional and economic partnerships of persons living together. As a result, already existing rights of those couples who are not married cannot be taken away. The Court found it especially important to protect the interests of children who may be affected negatively by a narrow definition of the family.[208]

Parliament, it seems, was not impressed by the reasoning of the Constitutional Court. The Fourth Amendment reversed Decision 43/2012 (XII.20) AB by inserting language in article L(1) of the Basic Law according to which 'family ties are based on marriage or the relationship between parents'. Thus the Basic Law today excludes a number of different forms of families in the sociological sense from the legal definition of family (ie those relationships in which the couples raise and take care of each other's children, or couples who do not have any children or are not able to have any children, grandchildren cared for by grandparents, registered same-sex partnerships, etc). This also raises serious concerns on the basis of the general ideals of the prohibition of discrimination.

(b) Status of Churches

As in the case of the definition of family, the (original) language of article VII of the Basic Law guaranteeing the freedom of religion as adopted in 2011 was in harmony with European standards.[209] Nevertheless, Act CCVI of 2011 on the Right to Freedom of Conscience and Religion and the Legal Status of Churches, Denominations and Religious Communities, a cardinal law, introduced a system of recognition of churches which raised serious concerns. Section 7(1) of the Act reserved the right to recognise churches for Parliament, and section 7(4) provided that churches recognised by Parliament (at the time of the adoption of the Act, 14 churches) are contained in the Annex to the Act. All other organisations that previously enjoyed the status of a church lost this status and were declared to be associations under civil law by section 34(1) of the Act.

[207] Decision 43/2012 (XII.20) AB határozat (Constitutional Court of Hungary) para 296.

[208] Decision 43/2012 (XII.20) AB határozat (Constitutional Court of Hungary) paras 296, 314.

[209] The original version of art VII of the Basic Law had been found to be in line with Art 9 ECHR in the Opinion of the Venice Commission on the new Constitution of Hungary. See Opinion on the new Constitution of Hungary, Venice Commission Op 618/2011 (n 49).

Non-recognised religious organisations could gain recognition by a cardinal law of Parliament amending the Annex to the Act. This indeed occurred in February 2012 when the Act was amended, bringing the list of recognised churches to 27 churches.

Not only was the right to recognise churches reserved for Parliament, its decision was not subject to clear criteria, and remedies were not available. The recognition procedure and the criteria for recognition were foreseen by section 14 of the Act. Religious organisations had to request recognition directly from the Religious Affairs Committee of Parliament. The Committee was supposed to ascertain whether the criteria of recognition are fulfilled, including whether the organisation primarily performs religious activities and it has a confession of faith and rites containing the essence of its teachings. The Committee had to submit a Bill regarding the recognition to Parliament, which was to be adopted by a two-thirds majority. Should Parliament have decided not to recognise an organisation as a church, this negative decision was to be included in a resolution.[210]

The Constitutional Court reviewed the Act in its Decision 6/2013 (III.1) AB.[211] The Decision declared, inter alia, the reference to the power of Parliament to recognise churches in section 7(1) of the Act, as well as section 14(1) and (3)–(5) governing the recognition procedure, to be unconstitutional. The Court criticised the lack of an obligation to provide an appealable reasoned decision in case of a rejection of the request for recognition. The decision by Parliament could thus result in a political decision rather than one based on the applicable criteria.

The Fourth Amendment, adopted hardly more than three weeks after the decision of the Constitutional Court, opened the possibility of disregarding the decision by amending article VII(2) of the Basic Law and inserting a new article VII(4) into the Basic Law. Article VII(2) provided after the amendment that Parliament may recognise, in a cardinal Act, certain organisations engaged in religious activities as churches, with which the state shall cooperate to promote community goals. Article VII(4) read as follows:

> The detailed rules relating to churches shall be laid down in a cardinal act. As a precondition for granting church status to religious organisations, the cardinal act may prescribe that the candidate must have been in existence for a considerable period of time, it must have demonstrable social backing and must be able to collaborate for common objectives.

Obviously, these provisions of the Basic Law were designed to maintain the essence of the rules of recognition of churches despite the decision of the Constitutional Court. They confirmed that Parliament, with a two-thirds majority, is entitled to decide on the recognition of churches. In addition, the new criterion, 'suitability for cooperation to promote community goals', lacked precision and left too much

[210] For a defence of the Act with arguments from comparative law, see B Schanda, 'The Freedom of Religious Association in Hungary: Recent Developments' (2013) 8 *Religion and Human Rights* 1.

[211] Decision 6/2013 (III.1) AB határozat (Constitutional Court of Hungary).

to the discretion of Parliament.[212] An effective remedy was not available either, as article VII(2) as amended merely provided that the parliamentary decision on recognition can only be challenged if it is not legal, ie the substantive discretion about 'suitability for cooperation to promote community goals' still remains with the Parliament unchecked.[213]

Article VII as amended by the Fourth Amendment was strongly criticised by the Venice Commission.[214] In order to mitigate the situation, Parliament amended article VII of the Basic Law in the Fifth Amendment. It appears, however, that this amendment was rather a change in style and tone, but did not affect the essence of the provision introduced by the Fourth Amendment.[215]

G. The Constitutional Court: Still Alive but Severely Impaired

As in the case of the entire Basic Law, the understanding of the position of the Constitutional Court requires both a static and a dynamic view. In other words, it is necessary to see the context of the changes to the competences of the Court in order to assess the reach of constitutional adjudication in times when the constitution of the country can be amended at will by the governing majority.

(i) *Constitutional Adjudication between 1989 and 2012*

The 1989 democratic constitutional reform introduced a highly abstract but powerful form of judicial review. As is well known,[216] the Constitutional Court could only review the constitutionality of laws but had no power to decide on

[212] Venice Commission Op 720/2013 (n 100).

[213] On the need for objective criteria applied or reviewed by courts, according to international human rights law, when registering churches (with further references to and quotes from case law and scholarly literature) see R Uitz, *Freedom of Religion in European Constitutional and International Case Law* (Strasbourg, Council of Europe Publishing, 2007) 87–107.

[214] Venice Commission Op 720/2013 (n 100) 8–10.

[215] Article VII reads after the Fifth Amendment as follows: '(1) Everyone shall have the right to freedom of thought, conscience and religion. This right includes freedom to change religion or belief and freedom, either alone or in community with others and in public or in private, to manifest religion or belief through religious acts or ceremonies, or in any other way, in worship, teaching, practice and observance. (2) People of the same faith or religious belief shall be entitled to establish religious communities in an organisational form provided for in the relevant cardinal act in which to practice their religion. (3) In Hungary the State and religious communities shall be separated. Religious communities shall be independent entities. (4) The State and religious communities may collaborate for the public interest. Such cooperation shall be decided by Parliament, upon the religious community's request. The cooperating religious community shall function as a listed church. The State shall grant special licenses to listed churches having regard to their participation in tasks aiming to achieve certain goals in the public interest. (5) The common rules relating to the religious communities, the conditions of collaboration, listed churches and the detailed regulations pertaining to them shall be laid down in a cardinal act.

[216] G Brunner, 'Structure and Proceedings of the Hungarian Constitutional Judiciary' in L Sólyom and G Brunner (eds), *Constitutional Judiciary in a New Democracy: The Hungarian Constitutional Court* (Ann Arbor, MI, University of Michigan Press, 2001) 65.

court judgments or other forms of individual application of the laws. This pure Kelsenian type of constitutional adjudication was linked with a special sort of class action, the *actio popularis*, within the framework of which anybody could challenge laws in front of the court without a time limit and without any proven individual interest. This broad *locus standi*, exceptional in Europe,[217] enabled the court not only to intervene with any politically debated legislation, but also to do this in a very quick manner. The result was a Constitutional Court pronouncing many important principles in a short time in an abstract manner and at the same time being present in the political arena as a last, neutral instance.

Using this rather broad power, the Constitutional Court proved to be a powerful instrument in safeguarding the text and the spirit of the Constitution; it gained a high level of public esteem. In many sensitive cases of high political impact, it was the Constitutional Court that resolved the issue. Significant cases included the abolition of capital punishment, regulation of abortion, media issues and borderline cases concerning freedom of expression.[218]

In addition to these human rights cases, the Constitutional Court resolved a number of delicate political issues such as the relationship between the President of the Republic and the Prime Minister, the role of referenda and their effect on representative democracy, the independence of the judiciary and the autonomy of local self-governments. The Constitutional Court also played an important role in making fundamental choices during the transition from communism to democracy. It determined how to handle criminal acts committed by former rulers, how to compensate for expropriations and the denial of liberty, and what kind of consequences should ensue for collaboration with the communist secret services.[219]

Especially in the first decade of its existence, the Constitutional Court adopted an activist approach to human rights issues, whereas with regard to state organisation it exercised more self-restraint. These early years of the Court were decisive for the fate and character of democracy after the communist rule. The success of the transition and its constitutional nature, including the Constitution becoming

[217] Venice Commission Op 614/2011 (n 48) para 57. In Europe, *actio popularis* only existed in Bavaria, Serbia, Montenegro and Macedonia. In Croatia, there exists a kind of independent *actio popularis*, which does not compel the Constitutional Court to start the procedure. On these countries, see B Wieser, *Vergleichendes Verfassungsrecht* (Vienna, Springer, 2005) 140.

[218] R Uitz, 'Lessons from the Abolition of Capital Punishment in Hungary: A Fortuitous Constellation Amidst and Beyond Democratic Transition' (2004) 45 *Acta Juridica Hungarica* 1, 67–99; G Halmai, 'Freedom of Expression in Hungary' (1998) 4 *East European Human Rights Review* 2, 127–52.

[219] On the issues of how Hungary dealt with the past, see I Pogany, *Righting Wrongs in Eastern Europe* (Manchester, Manchester University Press, 1997); M Szabó, 'New Constitutionalism Based on an Old Notion: The Rule of Law in the Mirror of the Decisions of Hungarian Constitutional Court' (1995) 26 *Rechtstheorie* 3, 291–303; G Halmai and KL Scheppele, 'Living Well is the Best Revenge: The Hungarian Approach to Judging the Past' in AJ MacAdams (ed), *Transitional Justice and the Rule of Law in New Democracies* (Paris, University of Notre Dame Press, 1997) 155–84; P Sonnevend, 'Verjährung und völkerrechtliche Verbrechen in der Rechtsprechung des ungarischen Verfassungsgerichts' (1996) 57 *Heidelberg Journal of International Law* 195.

a truly living document that determined the political system and value choices of society, are to a great extent achievements of the Constitutional Court.[220]

(ii) Changing Character of Constitutional Adjudication under the Basic Law

The Basic Law has fundamentally changed the character of constitutional adjudication in Hungary. In the early stage of the making of the Basic Law, it was not clear whether or not the role of the Constitutional Court would be altered. The ad hoc committee responsible for preparing the new Constitution did not intend to change the model of constitutional adjudication.[221] Nonetheless, the Constitutional Court itself suggested strengthening the individual complaint, according to the German model.[222]

The Basic Law follows this suggestion and brings the previous rather unique judicial review (which was certainly well justified in the times of the change of the regime from dictatorship to democracy) closer to Western European models. On the one hand, the Basic Law abolished the *actio popularis* by not mentioning it amongst the powers of the Constitutional Court in article 24 of the Basic Law. On the other hand, article 24(2) of the Basic Law introduced constitutional complaint following German patterns.[223]

(a) Constitutional Complaint

Article 24(2) of the Basic Law allows for the review of both legislation and judicial decisions, but generally only if personal involvement can be proved. This way, constitutional review now serves the protection of individuals' rights as its main function, while the possibility of abstract control did not disappear either.

This change in the character of the Constitutional Court, which had already been urged by constitutional lawyers, is a welcome development. For the same reason, the Venice Commission praised the extension of constitutional review to

[220] In general, see L Sólyom 'Introduction to the Decisions of the Constitutional Court of the Republic of Hungary' in L Sólyom and G Brunner (eds), *Constitutional Judiciary in a New Democracy: The Hungarian Constitutional Court* (Ann Arbor, MI, University of Michigan Press, 2001).

[221] For draft decision H/2057, www.parlament.hu/irom39/02057/02057.pdf.

[222] For the latter, see www.parlament.hu/biz/aeb/info/ab.pdf.

[223] According to Basic Law, art 24(2): 'The competence of the Constitutional Court includes: a) the ex ante examination of the constitutionality of Acts of Parliament adopted but not yet promulgated; b) review under priority, in any case within ninety days at the latest, upon judicial initiative, of laws to be applied in a specific case with regard to their conformity with the Basic Law; c) review, on the basis of a constitutional complaint, of laws to be applied in a specific case or of a judicial decision with regard to their conformity with the Basic Law; d) review, on the basis of a constitutional complaint, of court decisions for conformity with the Basic Law; e) review of laws with regard to their conformity with the Basic Law at the initiative of the Government, one-fourth of all Members of Parliament, President of the Kúria, the Prosecutor General, or the Commissioner of Fundamental Rights; f) examination of the conformity of national legislation with international treaties; g) performance of other tasks and exercise of other competencies laid down in the Basic Law and in an implementing act'.

judicial decisions,[224] and made it clear that the suppression of *actio popularis* is not contrary to European constitutional traditions.[225]

Despite its new competence, the Constitutional Court has not become a 'super-court'. It does not examine whether or not the courts applied the laws correctly, but, rather, whether or not they chose a constitution-conforming interpretation of the laws. The Constitutional Court has always been entitled to define the constitutional interpretation of laws (the so-called constitutional requirement).[226] It is a significant difference, however, that under the Basic Law the Constitutional Court does not define in advance the requirements that the application of laws have to meet, but rather decides subsequently whether the judiciary fulfilled these requirements.

As a further consequence, the judiciary might create the 'constitution-conforming' interpretation of the laws. Prior to the Basic Law, courts were only responsible for applying the laws, but from now on, due to the constitutional review process, they also have to pay attention to interpret and apply laws in a way such that fundamental rights can prevail.

(b) Abstract Review of Legislation

Abstract review of legislation still remains possible, although, to a certain extent, in a limited and at the moment problematic fashion. With the abolition of *actio popularis*, an ex post norm control can only be initiated by the Cabinet, the Commissioner for Fundamental Rights, or one-quarter of the MPs. This, in itself, seems acceptable. Yet in the present legislative cycle, none of the opposition parties have one-quarter of the places in the Parliament. Thus, the radical right- and the left-wing factions of the opposition have to cooperate to be able to submit a petition to the Constitutional Court. This gives the impression that the right to make a petition is tailored to the voting proportions of the present legislative cycle, so the constitutive majority can impede the submission of petitions. The only authority on the basis of the Basic Law which is able to initiate abstract ex post review of legislation during the present legislative period against the will of the government is therefore the Commissioner for Fundamental Rights, who has actually filed some petitions in highly important cases.

The Constitutional Court Act somewhat broadens the possibility of abstract norm control allowing for constitutional complaints directly against laws. According to section 26(2) of the Constitutional Court Act:

> By way of derogation from paragraph (1), Constitutional Court proceedings may also be initiated—by exception—based on Article 24 paragraph (2) point c) or Article VII

[224] Venice Commission Op 614/2011 (n 48) para 62.

[225] ibid para 64.

[226] See P Paczolay (ed), *Twenty Years of the Hungarian Constitutional Court* (Budapest, MKAB, 2009) 23–24.

> paragraph (2) of the Fundamental Law, if a) due to the application of a legal provision contrary to the Fundamental Law, or when such legal provision becomes effective, rights were violated directly, without a judicial decision, and b) there is no procedure for legal remedy designed to repair the violation of rights, or the petitioner has already exhausted the possibilities for remedy.

Besides ex post norm control, article 24(2)(a) of the Basic Law provides for ex ante review of Acts of Parliament adopted but not yet promulgated. This is a competence the President already exercised under the 1989 Constitution. The Basic Law not only grants to the President the right to initiate ex ante review, but also to the parliamentary majority, upon the motion of the Speaker, the government or the sponsor of the Bill. However, there is a different approach between the two initiations. The President is the legal balance of the Parliament, who 'guards the democratic operation of the state'. It is the President's constitutional obligation not to sign a statute he or she finds unconstitutional. On the contrary, if Parliament decides to turn to the Constitutional Court then it wishes to verify the constitutionality of the law.

(iii) Changing the Composition of the Constitutional Court

Already in the summer of 2010, Parliament changed the manner of the nomination of justices of the Constitutional Court. Under article 32/A(4) of the 1989 Constitution, justices of the Constitutional Court had been elected by a two-thirds majority in Parliament, upon nomination by a committee of Parliament in which every parliamentary group had one representative. Because there were more parliamentary groups on the side of the opposition, this provision resulted in a need to compromise between the governing party and the opposition.

An amendment to article 32/A(4) of the Constitution adopted on 14 June 2010 changed the composition of the relevant committee, providing only that the committee shall consist of eight members. This enabled Parliament to form a committee reflecting the actual two-thirds majority of the governing party, thus making it possible for the parliamentary supermajority to decide on the justices without the participation of the parties in opposition. The amendment was questioned by László Sólyom, then the President of the Republic,[227] but his concerns did not impress Parliament.[228]

Another amendment to article 32/A(5) of the Constitution that entered into force on 15 June 2011 raised the number of Constitutional Court justices from 11 to 15. Because there was a vacancy in the court at that time, the amendment enabled the governing majority to elect five new justices at one time. Furthermore,

[227] The President used his power of political veto under art 26(2) of the Constitution and sent the constitutional amendment back to Parliament for reconsideration on 21 June 2010, see www.solyomlaszlo.hu/archiv//admin/data/file/6939_20100621_visszakuldo_level_alkotmanybirok_cimerrel.pdf.

[228] Since the political veto of the President could be overridden in Parliament by a simple majority, Parliament easily adopted the same amendment on 5 July 2010.

the same constitutional amendment[229] also changed the way the President of the Constitutional Court is elected. Previously, the President was elected by the members of the Court for three years. According to the amendment, Parliament became entitled to elect the President of the Constitutional Court, and the term of the President expires with his or her mandate.[230]

Needless to say, all these amendments were designed to enhance the influence of the governing majority on the Constitutional Court. The Venice Commission reflected only on the election of the President in its Opinion on the New Constitution of Hungary. The Commission acknowledged that 'the election of the Constitutional Court's president by a political actor, and not by the Court itself, is a widely accepted phenomenon'. It noted, however, that, 'according to the present Constitution of Hungary, the judges have elected the president from their own ranks, a system which is seen, in general, as a stronger safeguard for the independence of the Constitutional Court'.[231]

The Basic Law today contains the same provisions on the election of the members and of the President of the Constitutional Court in its article 24(8). Besides this, the term of office of Constitutional Court justices is prolonged from nine years to 12. The possibility of re-election is not excluded by the Basic Law itself, but by a cardinal Act on the Constitutional Court.[232] This may strengthen the independence of justices, as was requested by the Venice Commission.[233]

(iv) An Institutional-Procedural Loophole: Limitation of the Competences of the Constitutional Court in Article 37(4) of the Basic Law

The restraint on constitutional adjudication is certainly a very serious loophole in the Basic Law, since judicial review becomes limited in an unusual fashion. This is because article 37(4) of the Basic Law excludes a wide range of issues from the competence of the Constitutional Court. According to that provision:

> As long as the level of state debt exceeds half of the Gross Domestic Product,[234] the Constitutional Court may, within its competence pursuant to points b) to e) of paragraph (2) of Article 24, review the Acts on the central budget, on the implementation of the budget, on central taxes, on duties and on contributions, on customs duties, and on the central conditions for local taxes as to their conformity with the Basic Law exclusively in connection

[229] Act LXI of 2011 (2011. évi LXI törvény A Magyar Köztársaság Alkotmányáról szóló 1949. évi XX. törvénynek az Alaptörvénnyel összefüggő egyes átmeneti rendelkezések megalkotása érdekében szükséges módosításáról).

[230] It came as a positive surprise that under the new provisions Parliament re-elected Péter Paczolay, who had been serving as President of the Court since 2008.

[231] Venice Commission Op 621/2011 (n 131) para 94.

[232] Act CLI of 2011 on the Constitutional Court (2011. évi CLI törvény az Alkotmánybíróságról) s 6(3).

[233] Venice Commission Op 621/2011 (n 131) para 95.

[234] The limitation based on temporary austerity is a new one, yet it will not affect the limitation of powers in the near future. Currently, the Hungarian state debt accounts for 80 per cent of GDP, and, according to the most optimistic views, may get below 50 per cent in 20 years.

> with the rights to life and human dignity, to the protection of personal data, to freedom of thought, conscience and religion, or in connection with the rights related to Hungarian citizenship, and it may only annul these Acts for the violation of these rights. The Constitutional Court shall have the right to annul without restriction Acts governing the above matters if the procedural requirements laid down in the Basic Law for the making and publication of such Acts have not been observed.

Article 27 of the Transitional Provisions added to this that the curtailment shall continue to apply to all those laws which were adopted during the (current) high state debt period, and also in the future when state debt sinks under 'half of the Gross Domestic Product'. This provision is now contained in article 37(5) of the Basic Law. Consequently, the competence of the Constitutional Court will *never* cover some of the presently debated economic laws, and once it regains its competences, this will only apply for future laws.

One cannot overestimate the damage to constitutionalism following from article 37(4)–(5) of the Basic Law. A short look into the history of limiting the competences of the Constitutional Court, however, exposes an even graver danger of a constitution-amending majority: the lack of legally sound standards.

(a) Origin and Meaning of Article 37(4) of the Basic Law

On 22 July 2010, the Hungarian Parliament adopted several economic and financial Acts. One Act, inter alia, introduced a new punitive tax on certain payments for employees of the public sector (civil servants, public servants, etc) whose employment was terminated. Accordingly, severance payments and other payments related to the termination of the employment exceeding HUF two million became subject to a 98 per cent tax. Income tax and social security contributions already paid could be deducted from the punitive tax. The proposal of the Act justified the punitive tax by reference to the needs of the society to do justice. Although the Act entered into force on 1 October 2010, the punitive tax was to be applied to the relevant incomes starting from 1 January 2010. In order to ensure the constitutionality of this Act, Parliament also amended article 70/I of the 1989 Constitution by including a new paragraph (2) in the article that allowed for special taxes using the following language:

> In respect of any remuneration received against the good morals from public funds, or from bodies entrusted to manage state assets and state property, including bodies under majority state ownership or control, tax liabilities of a special extent may be introduced on the strength of law, beginning with the given tax year.

The punitive tax was challenged before the Constitutional Court within the framework of an *actio popularis*, and the Court found the relevant provisions of the Act to be unconstitutional in its Decision 184/2010 (X.28) AB.[235] According to the Court, incomes gathered solely on the basis of relevant statutory provisions

[235] Decision 184/2010 (X.28) AB határozat (Constitutional Court of Hungary) para 900.

cannot be regarded as being against good morals, and therefore the new article 70/I(2) of the Constitution did not cover the retroactive 98 per cent tax. As a result, the Court annulled the relevant provisions retroactively effective from the day of the entry into force of the law.

In response, Parliament reintroduced the 98 per cent tax with certain modifications. The new rules entered into force on 30 December 2010. At the same time, Parliament modified article 70/I(2) of the Constitution allowing for retroactive taxation going back five years from the actual tax year. To prevent the Constitutional Court from reviewing the legislation, a limitation was also introduced in article 32/A(2)–(3) of the Constitution. The language of article 32/A(2) of the Constitution was basically identical to article 37(4) of the Basic Law today, as it listed the same subjects of legislation as being exempt from full review and the same rights as possible standards of review with regard to these laws.

The Constitutional Court was confronted with this limitation on its powers in Decision 37/2011 (V.10) AB.[236] This decision also concerned a 98 per cent tax legislation introduced on 30 December 2010, yet this time the tax applied retroactively for five years back to 2005. Within the framework of article 32/A of the Constitution, the central question here was whether the Court would utilise its previous case law on human dignity as a subsidiary fundamental right to circumvent the limitation. According to that case law, human dignity can be invoked as a 'mother of rights' in all situations, where the Constitution does not provide for specific protection.[237] Applying this doctrine here would have meant that the Constitutional Court invoked the right to human dignity to review violations of fundamental rights not mentioned in article 32/A(2) of the Constitution.

Decision 37/2011 (V10) AB ultimately followed a different path. It annulled the language of the relevant Act ordering the five-year retroactive application of the 98 per cent tax. According to the Court's reasoning, the taxation of incomes gathered between 2005 and 2009 was a violation of the right to human dignity, whereas introducing the tax on 30 December 2010 for the current tax year was not.[238] The reasons of the Decision make it clear that the Court could only review the Act on the basis of the right to human dignity itself, and not as a mother right. The Decision provides no reasons on the exact threshold for the violation of human dignity by retroactive tax legislation. It is clear that the Court would use a higher threshold than that used for limitations of specific fundamental rights. In other words, review under the old article 32/A of the Constitution is a limited

[236] Decision 37/2011 (V.10) AB határozat (Constitutional Court of Hungary) para 225.

[237] L Sólyom, 'Introduction to the Decisions of the Constitutional Court of the Republic of Hungary' in L Sólyom and G Brunner (eds), *Constitutional Judiciary in a New Democracy: The Hungarian Constitutional Court* (Ann Arbor, MI, University of Michigan Press, 2001) 6.

[238] Decision 37/2011 (V.10) AB határozat (Constitutional Court of Hungary) paras 225, 234.

one and is reserved for the most serious human rights violations that also conflict with the right to human dignity.

(b) Economics Trump Constitutionalism

Since the language of article 32/A(2) of the Constitution and article 37(4) of the Basic Law are identical, the interpretation developed in Decision 37/2011 (V.10) AB probably governs the understanding of article 37(4) of the Basic Law as well. Thus, article 37(4) of the Basic Law fundamentally questions constitutionalism: without judicial review there is no guarantee that the Basic Law will prevail. It is also unclear why the Basic Law names those four fundamental rights (right to life and human dignity, to the protection of personal data, right to freedom of thought, conscience and religion, and the rights related to Hungarian citizenship) to be the possible bases of review by the Constitutional Court.

In light of this, article 37(4) has created an unacceptable gap in constitutional review, which has been rightly criticised by the Venice Commission.[239] The issue of whether the regulations of the Basic Law are respected or not by the legal acts on budget and taxes depends solely on the goodwill of the legislator.[240] In effect, article 37(4) of the Basic Law expresses that the Basic Law may be violated without any sanction if justified by economic or budgetary considerations. Moreover, this supposition of the constitution-maker is based on an obvious mistake, since the rule of law does not impede the success of economic policy. Quite the contrary, the perfect functioning of the rule of law is the basis of an economic life based on trust and it allows for the creation of a positive atmosphere for investments.

H. Changes to the Ombudsman System

The former Constitution designated the ombudsmen as the independent organs of parliamentary control. Due to the nature of the institution, ombudsmen are external to the executive branch. Their task is not to grant remedies in a strict legal sense for infringements of human rights. They only investigate anomalies that have come to their attention and recommend particular or general measures for redress.

Before the entry into force of the Basic Law, four ombudsmen were active: the Parliamentary Commissioner for Civil Rights, the Commissioner for the Rights of Minorities, the Commissioner for Future Generations (dealing with issues concerning environment protection)[241] and the Commissioner for Data Protection

[239] Venice Commission Op 614/2011 (n 48).

[240] E Kirs, 'Freedom and Responsibility in the New Constitutional System of Hungary' (2012) 1 *Revue Est Europa* 82.

[241] The office of the Commissioner for Future Generations was established in 2007 and started its operations in 2008. Its name is somewhat misleading, as many countries in Europe and throughout the

and Freedom of Information. The latter two institutions had a dual nature; they were ombudsman-like institutions, on the one hand, and authorities on the other, as they could use direct administrative measures to protect the rights and interests of their specific field.

The Basic Law left the role of the ombudsman intact but introduced significant changes to the structure of the institution. First, as we noted above, a new National Authority for Data Protection replaced the current Data Protection Commissioner's Office. At the same time, the six-year term of the incumbent Data Protection Commissioner was prematurely brought to an end by article 16 of the Transitional Provisions on the day of the entry into force of the Basic Law on 1 January 2012. As we also noted, the removal of the Data Protection Commissioner was found to be in violation of article 28(1) of Directive 95/46/EC by the CJEU.[242] This will have serious implications for the newly created National Authority for Data Protection.

Besides this, the institutions of the other three Commissioners were unified by the Basic Law and the name of the institution changed to Commissioner for Fundamental Rights. According to article 30(3) of the Basic Law, the Commissioner for Fundamental Rights has two deputies who 'ensure the protection of the interests of future generations and the rights of national minorities residing in Hungary'. As opposed to the Data Protection Commissioner, under article 6 of the Transitional Provisions, the Commissioner for Civil Rights could continue his mandate as Commissioner for Fundamental Rights, and the two other independent commissioners became his deputies.

Interestingly, there is an administrative hierarchy between the Commissioner for Fundamental Rights and his or her deputies, but the deputies have their own competence. The legitimacy of the Commissioner and his deputies is the same, too, as all of them are elected by Parliament by a two-thirds majority for six years.[243] Further, the deputies have their own tasks and operate according to the Acts on minorities and environment protection, their procedures being stipulated by the Ombudsman Act (Act CXI of 2011 on the Commissioner for Human Rights), just like the general ombudsman's.[244]

Similarly to other institutions of public law and human rights, the new Basic Law retained the institution of ombudsman in a fundamentally unaltered form; the ombudsman still pursues disclosure of the anomalies concerning fundamental rights and issues recommendations to the government, the public administration

world operate an autonomous ombudsman to protect the rights of children, and the general meaning of 'future generations' refers to this function. However, the protection of the rights of children has always been the competence of the general ombudsman, and the 'rights of future generations' has meant the rights stipulated in the Act on environment protection.

242 Case C-288/12 *Commission v Hungary* (2014, nyr).

243 L Csink and J Fröhlich, 'Topics of Hungarian Constitutionalism' (2012) 4 *Tijdschrfit voor Constitutioneel Recht* 437.

244 M Szabó, 'Main Directions of the New Ombudsman System' (2011) *Report of the Parliamentary Commissioner for Civil Rights* 33.

or Parliament for redress. The ombudsman's control does not pertain to courts or the prosecutor's office, nor can he or she enquire about private law entities, unless their operation concerns the rights of many citizens.[245] Further, its competence under article 24(2)(e) to turn to the Constitutional Court for ex post review has gained heightened importance, as the possibility of *actio popularis* was terminated.

I. The Judiciary

The Basic Law left the system of the courts basically unchanged, even if it changed the name of the Supreme Court to Kúria. There have been, however, three issues that have raised concern: the administration of the court system by the newly created National Judicial Office in general, and specifically the appointment procedure for judges; the forced early retirement of judges; and the reallocation of cases by the President of the National Judicial Office. These concerns were partly based directly on the language of the Basic Law and the Transitional Provisions, and partly rooted in cardinal Acts on the judiciary. All three issues also provoked reactions from European institutions.

(i) Appointment of Judges

From 1997, the administration of the courts in Hungary was entrusted with a strong National Council of Justice, an organ specifically mentioned in article 50(4) of the Constitution. The National Council of Justice was regarded as an institution of self-government of the judiciary, and as such, its majority consisted of judges, even though Parliament, the Ministry of Justice, state prosecutors and attorneys were also represented amongst its members. The President of the Supreme Court was ex officio President of the National Council of Justice.

Whereas this form of self-government did shield the judiciary from the influence of the executive, it could not contribute to the reduction of the substantial backlog of cases in some courts. Besides, the National Council of Justice was supposed to control the leaders of the different courts, but its members were mostly judges in leading positions, who thus controlled their own activity. This gave a disproportionately large influence to the presidents of the different courts, which possibly had an impact on judicial independence.[246] Still, the procedure for the appointment of judges secured an overwhelming role for judicial self-government: judges were appointed by the President of the Republic upon proposals by the National Council of Justice.

[245] ibid 34.

[246] For a general overview of the self-government of the judiciary before 2012 see Z Fleck, 'Judicial Independence in Hungary' in A Seibert-Fohr (ed), *Judicial Independence in Transition* (Hedielberg, Springer, 2012) 793.

The Basic Law first made no mention of a specific body of self-government of the judiciary, it merely stipulated in its article 25(5) that the bodies of judicial self-government shall participate in the administration of the courts. This gave Parliament a broad discretion to reshuffle the administration of courts by a cardinal Act, Act CLXI of 2011 on the Organisation and Administration of Courts, which was published in the official gazette on 2 December 2011. The Act established a National Judicial Office and a National Judicial Council, the latter being a body of self-government solely consisting of judges elected by their peers. As a result, article 11(2) of the Transitional Provisions, which was adopted after the Act, declared that the National Council of Justice would cease to exist, and referred to the President of National Judicial Office in its article 11(1). As the Fourth Amendment annulled the whole of the Transitional Provisions, it added a new article 25(5) to the Basic Law with the following language:

> The President of the National Judicial Office manages the central administrative affairs of the courts. The bodies of judicial self-government shall participate in the administration of the courts.

Section 76 of Act CLXI of 2011 on the Organisation and Administration of Courts equipped the President of the National Judicial Office, elected for nine years by a two-thirds majority in Parliament, with an unusually wide range of powers, including, inter alia, the adoption of normative instructions binding on courts; administering the activity of the National Judicial Council; drafting the budget of the court system (which will become part of the Act on the central budget); managing the internal audit of courts; transferring judges between different courts; and appointing certain judicial leaders. Section 76(5)(b) also entitled the President of the National Judicial Office to put forward a proposal to the President of the Republic concerning the appointment and removal of judges.

The procedure leading to the appointment of judges is described in Act CLXII of 2011 on the Legal Status and Remuneration of Judges. At the time of its adoption, the Act provided for a procedure in which a panel of judges hears all possible candidates and ranks them, but the President of the National Judicial Office is not bound by this ranking and can propose to the President of the Republic the appointment of a candidate who was not ranked first by the panel.[247] This power of the President of the National Judicial Office was not limited by any criteria.

It is no surprise then that the Venice Commission heavily criticised the unusually broad powers of the President of the National Judicial Office, and specifically the procedure applicable to the appointment of judges. The first opinion on the judiciary stated that the National Judicial Council is designed as an organ of judicial self-government, but:

[247] The original language of Act CLXII of 2011 on the Legal Status and Remuneration of Judges, s 18(3), provided that the 'President of the National Judicial Office may decide to deviate from the shortlist and propose the second or the third on the list to fill the position'.

> it has scarcely any significant powers and its role in the administration of the judiciary can be regarded as negligible. In contrast, the President of the National Judicial Office has abundant competences and, hence, is the main actor in judicial administration ... Since the President of the NJO is elected by Parliament, ie, an external actor from the viewpoint of the judiciary, it cannot be regarded as an organ of judicial self-government.[248]

On the new system of appointment of judges the opinion notes that this 'results in a reduction of the guarantees for an objective candidate selection' and demands that the discretion of the President of the National Judicial Office be limited by legal criteria, and his or her decision to change the ranking of candidates be subjected to judicial review.[249]

The opinion of the Venice Commission was taken seriously and most (but not all) of its recommendations were implemented into Hungarian law.[250] The changes included the transfer of certain powers from the President of the National Judicial Office to the National Judicial Council.[251] The Fifth Amendment to the Basic Law even included a reference to the National Judicial Council in the language of article 25(5) of the Basic Law, which now reads:

> The President of the National Judicial Office shall manage the central administrative affairs of the courts. The National Judicial Council shall oversee the central administration of courts. The National Judicial Council and other bodies of judicial self-government shall participate in the administration of the courts.

Specifically in relation to the appointment of judges, the power of the President of the National Judicial Office to change the ranking of candidates became limited by the general principles to be established by the National Judicial Council and by the need to have the consent of the National Judicial Council for the change.[252]

It is difficult to guess the actual reasons of Parliament for taking some of the criticism of the Venice Commission of the Acts on the judiciary seriously, since other opinions, such as the one on the freedom of religion, mostly went unheard. One possible explanation is that the independence of the judiciary was apparently also mentioned as a precondition for the beginning of negotiations to borrow money by Hungary from the International Monetary Fund (IMF) and the European Union in desperate times of economic crisis; although unpublished, this was orally and informally confirmed, according to information later leaked to the press by Hungarian politicians.[253]

248 Venice Commission Op 663/2012 (n 64).

249 ibid.

250 Act CXI of 2012 (2012. évi CXI. törvény a bíróságok szervezetéről és igazgatásáról szóló 2011. évi CLXI. törvény, valamint a bírák jogállásáról és javadalmazásáról szóló 2011. évi CLXII. törvény módosításáról).

251 Venice Commission Op 683/2012 (n 135).

252 Act CLXII of 2011 on the Legal Status and Remuneration of Judges, s 103(3)(b) and (c).

253 'Kövér: Botrányosak az IMF-tárgyalás Politikai Előfeltételei', *Mandiner* (Budapest), 3 April 2012, available at www.mandiner.hu/cikk/20120403_kover_botranyosak_az_imf_targyalas_politikai_elofeltetelei.

(ii) Reallocation of Cases by the National Judicial Office

One of the most debated powers of the President of the National Judicial Office was the ability to transfer cases from the court with statutory jurisdiction to another court. This power was first included in section 76(4)(b) of Act CLXI of 2011 on the Organisation and Administration of Courts, and was based on the criterion of 'adjudicating cases within a reasonable period of time'. This, of course, raised serious concerns from the perspective of the right to a lawful judge, especially because of the lack of legally sound criteria for the transfer and because in some cases the designation of a small court would automatically have led to the designation of a single judge or chamber.[254] What is more, not only did the President of the National Judicial Office have the power to transfer cases: an amendment to Act XIX of 1998 on rules of criminal procedure created a similar power for the Prosecutor General in July 2011.

The Constitutional Court reacted rather swiftly to this legislation and on 20 December 2011 gave Decision 166/2011 (XII.20), stating that the transfer of cases by the Prosecutor General was in violation of Article 6(1) of the ECHR and article 57(1) of the Constitution guaranteeing a fair trial before an independent and impartial tribunal. According to the Decision, the fair trial guarantee also requires that no reasonable doubt may arise regarding the impartiality of the tribunal. The possibility of transferring a criminal case between courts by the prosecution may lead to such doubts, and is therefore unacceptable.[255]

Decision 166/2011 (XII.20) of the Constitutional Court did not rule directly on the powers of the President of the National Judicial Office. Still, it made it clear that the reassignment of cases between courts without strict and 'blind' criteria is in general unconstitutional. In response, no later than ten days after the Decision, Parliament inserted article 11(3) and (4) into the Transitional Provisions, which specifically provided for the possibility of transfer by the President of the National Judicial Council and the Prosecutor General. These provisions rested upon two vague criteria for the exercise of the relevant powers: the purpose of adjudicating cases within a reasonable time and the balanced distribution of the workload between courts.

Needless to say, the Transitional Provisions did not eliminate the substantive concerns regarding the right to a lawful judge and to the impartiality of the courts. These concerns were articulated by the Venice Commission in its first opinion on the judiciary. The opinion stated that solutions to the heavy workload of certain courts 'by means of arbitrary designation of another court cannot be justified at all'.[256] The Venice Commission recommended that the Hungarian authorities use other mechanisms for the distribution of cases 'in order to prevent the risk of an

[254] Venice Commission Op 663/2012 (n 64).
[255] Decision 166/2011 (XII.20) AB határozat (Constitutional Court of Hungary) paras 545, 559.
[256] Venice Commission Op 663/2012 (n 64).

abuse of the power to allocate and to bring the provisions in line with Article 6 ECHR'.[257]

At first, the Hungarian Parliament tried to save the disputed measures by setting up some criteria relating to the transfer of cases.[258] The National Judicial Council became entitled by section 103(2)(a) and (b) of Act CLXI of 2011 on the Organisation and Administration of Courts to 'determine the principles to be applied by the President of the National Judicial Office when appointing a proceeding court in the context of the use of the power to appoint a different proceeding court in the interest of adjudicating cases within a reasonable period of time'. At the same time, an amendment to section 76(4)(b) of the Act obliged the President of the National Judicial Office to 'take into account the principle laid down by the National Judicial Council'.

Obviously, taking into account certain principles, not having the rank of a statute, could not be regarded as a sufficient guarantee, especially given that judicial review against the decisions of the President of the National Judicial Office was restricted to compliance with legal provisions. Also it remained unclear how cases are selected to be transferred. Apparently, the legislation only referred to the principles of finding the appropriate court, but not on identifying the cases to be transferred. All of these aspects led the Venice Commission to strongly disagree with the system of transferring cases, because 'it is not in compliance with the principle of the lawful judge, which is an essential component of the rule of law'.

Irrespective of these concerns, relevant laws remained at first unchanged. What is more, after the annulment of article 11(3) and (4) of the Transitional Provisions by the Constitutional Court, the Fourth Amendment inserted the power of the President of the National Judicial Office to transfer cases into article 27(4) of the Basic Law.[259] A similar power of the Prosecutor General was removed from the Basic Law. Only after the Venice Commission repeated its criticism in its opinion on the Fourth Amendment[260] did the Hungarian Parliament eliminate the power of transfer by article 7(1) of the Fifth Amendment, which abrogated article 27(4) of the Basic Law as a whole. Subsequent legislation also amended Act CLXI of 2011 on the Organisation and Administration of Courts accordingly.[261]

[257] ibid.

[258] Venice Commission Op 683/2012 (n 135).

[259] Basic Law, art 27(4), as amended by art 14 of the Transitional Provisions reads as follows 'In the interest of the enforcement of the fundamental right to a court decision within a reasonable time and a balanced distribution of caseload between the courts, the President of the National Judicial Office may designate a court, for cases defined in a cardinal Act and in a manner defined also in a cardinal Act, other than the court of general competence but with the same jurisdiction to adjudicate any case'.

[260] Venice Commission Op 720/2013 (n 100).

[261] Act CXXXI of 2013 (2013. évi CXXXI törvény egyes törvényeknek az Alaptörvény negyedik módosításával összefüggő módosításáról), s 16.

(iii) Forced Retirement of Judges

(a) Relevant Provisions of the Basic Law and of the Transitional Provisions

Until the entry into force of the Basic Law, relevant legislation essentially allowed judges to remain in office until the age of 70. The Basic Law provided in its article 26(2) that 'with the exception of the President of the Kúria, judges may remain in office until the general retirement age'. This provision was supplemented by article 12(1) of the Transitional Provisions, which provided that:

> [i]f a judge reaches the general age of eligibility for a retirement pension referred to in Article 26 paragraph (2) of the Basic Law before 1 January 2012, he shall retire on 30 June 2012. If he reaches the general age of eligibility for a retirement pension referred to in Article 26 paragraph (2) of the Basic Law between 1 January 2012 and 31 December 2012, he shall retire on 31 December 2012.

With these provisions, applied together with the relevant pension legislation, the constitution-maker tied the cessation of the mandate of the judges to the general retirement age, which in 2012 was 62 years and would progressively increase up until 2022, when it will be 65 years. As a result, around 10 per cent of all judges, including many in leading positions, were forced to leave office within a year.

Obviously, protection against removal from office is one of the most important aspects of judicial independence. This has been recognised by the Constitutional Court in its case law under article 46(3) of the Constitution.[262] Equally, the European Court of Human Rights also made it clear that 'the irremovability of judges by the executive during their term of office must in general be considered as a corollary of their independence and thus included in the guarantees of Article 6 paragraph 1'.[263] This does not necessarily mean that this irremovability must under all circumstances be formally declared in law. It suffices that the irremovability is recognised in fact and that the other necessary guarantees are present.[264] From this it follows that independence presupposes a general protection from removal from office except in cases clearly and narrowly defined by law relating to the misconduct or lack of capabilities of the person bearing the office. Irremovability is also considered an important guarantee of independence under EU law.[265]

[262] Decision 1/2008 (I.11) AB határozat (Constitutional Court of Hungary) paras 51, 72; Decision 21/2010 (II.25) AB határozat (Constitutional Court of Hungary) paras 85, 91.

[263] *Campbell and Fell v United Kingdom*, Application no 7819/77 *et al* (ECtHR, 28 June 1984) Series A 80, para 80.

[264] ibid, with reference to *Engel and others*, Application no 5100/71 *et al* (ECtHR, 8 June 1976) Series A 28, para 68.

[265] With regard to the CJEU, Art 19 TEU and Art 254 TFEU stipulate the independence of the Justices of the Court. This is supplemented by several provisions of the Statute of the Court of Justice of the European Union. Amongst these, art 5(1) provides that '[a]part from normal replacement, or death, the duties of a Judge shall end when he resigns'. Article 6 of the Statute only allows for removal from office if a Justice 'no longer fulfils the requisite conditions or meets the obligations arising from his office'. As a procedural safeguard, decision on the removal is reserved for a unanimous Court and Advocates General. Similar rules apply to members of the European Commission. Article 17(3) III

The Constitutional Court was confronted with the forced retirement of judges in its Decision 33/2012 (VII.17) AB.[266] The Court declared the sudden reduction of the upper age limit for judges unconstitutional on the grounds that it was a breach of judicial independence protected by article 26(1) of the Basic Law. Interestingly, the Court largely bypassed the fact that the new age limit was contained in both the Basic Law and the Transitional Provisions, which were still in force at the time of this decision. According to the decision, no provision of the Basic Law can be interpreted in a way that would make another provision meaningless.[267] Specifically, the reference to the retirement age of judges in article 26(2) of the Basic Law 'cannot lead to the violation of essential elements of judicial independence' as protected by article 26(1) of the Basic Law.[268] As a result, the Court did not claim that removal for reason of age is completely unacceptable. Rather, the Decision set up a flexible rule indicating that judges close to the age of 70 may be forced to retire, whereas younger ones would not.[269] Ultimately, the Decision annulled the statutory provisions on early retirement with *ex tunc* effect.

The implementation of this judgment has resulted in considerable legal uncertainty. The legal basis of forced retirement was declared null and void, but this did not directly affect the individual resolutions of the President of Hungary, which actually dismissed the judges. What is more, the President of the National Judicial Office did not initiate a procedure to reinstate those who had been removed, and without an appropriate proposal the President of the Republic could not repeal the previous decisions. Thus the judges concerned were forced to file a suit before the labour courts to have their dismissal reversed. In cases where these suits were successful, even final judgments did not result in an automatic reinstatement of the judges concerned in their previous position. Rather, they had to go through a new appointment process. What is more, by the time of the reinstatement, the leading positions were already filled.

(b) Reactions of the Venice Commission and the EU

The Venice Commission addressed the forced early retirement of judges in both of its opinions on the judiciary.[270] The first relevant opinion referred to the future

TEU declares that 'in carrying out its responsibilities, the Commission shall be completely independent'. The Commission being a political organ with political responsibility, a motion of censure of the Commission in the European Parliament is possible under Art 18(8) TEU. But the independence of individual commissioners is protected by Art 247 TFEU which only allows for the removal of individual commissioners if he or she 'no longer fulfils the conditions required for the performance of his duties or if he has been guilty of serious misconduct'. Decision on this matter is reserved for the CJEU.

[266] M Kocsis, 'Hungarian Constitutional Court: The Mandatory Retirement of Judges' (2013–14) 7 *ICL Journal* 556.

[267] Decision 33/2012 (VII.17) AB határozat (Constitutional Court of Hungary) paras 99, 113.

[268] ibid 99, 114.

[269] Decision 33/2012 (VII.17) AB határozat (Constitutional Court of Hungary) paras 99, 114.

[270] See also Joakim Nergelius, Chapter 11.

possibility of removal, but it stated in clear terms that the Commission regards the issue as a matter of the independence of the judiciary.[271] The second referred to Decision 33/2012 (VII.17) AB of the Constitutional Court, pointed out that the situation of the dismissed judges was unsatisfactory, and urged the Hungarian legislator to adopt appropriate provisions to reinstate them without a lengthy reappointment procedure.[272]

The European Commission and the CJEU also reacted to the issue of early retirement, but in a different context. In a letter dated 12 December 2011,[273] Viviane Reding, Vice-President of the European Commission, raised two issues relating to independent institutions, the sudden reduction of the retirement age of judges from 70 to 62 and the independence of the Data Protection Supervisor. It took barely three weeks for the Commission to take the next step. On 17 January 2012, three Letters of Formal Notice to Hungary were sent as the first stage in an infringement procedure. The letters concerned the independence of the Central Bank and data protection authorities, and certain measures affecting the judiciary.[274]

The lowering of the mandatory retirement age of judges from 70 to 62 was addressed by the European Commission as discrimination in the workplace on grounds of age in the light of the rules on equal treatment in employment (Directive 2000/78/EC). It is probably due to concerns relating to the competence of the European Union in this field that the Commission did not argue the case on the basis of the independence of the judiciary. These concerns were implicitly admitted by the President of the European Commission in a plenary debate at the European Parliament on the situation in Hungary.[275]

In January 2012, the Commission gained more persuasive force as the government of Hungary applied for balance of payments aid from the EU and for precautionary financial assistance ('Stand-by Arrangement') from the IMF. As the IMF made it clear that it would not negotiate with Hungary without the European Union,[276] the European Commission seemed to be in a strong negotiating

[271] Venice Commission Op 663/2012 (n 64).

[272] Venice Commission Op 683/2012 (n 135).

[273] Letter from Vice-President Viviane Reding to Vice-Prime Minister Tibor Navracsics (Brussels, 12 December 2011), available at www.lapa.princeton.edu/hosteddocs/hungary/letter_from_vp_of_the_european_commission.pdf.

[274] European Commission Press Release, 'European Commission Launches Accelerated Infringement Proceedings against Hungary over the Independence of its Central Bank and Data Protection Authorities as well as over Measures affecting the Judiciary' (Strasbourg, 17 January 2012), available at www.europa.eu/rapid/pressReleasesAction.do?reference=IP/12/24.

[275] Editorial Comments, 'Fundamental Rights and EU Membership: Do as I Say, Not as I Do' (2012) 49 *CMLRev* 481, 486, with further references.

[276] International Monetary Fund Managing Director Christine Lagarde's Statement on Hungary, Press Release No 12/7 (12 January 2012): 'I indicated that, before the Fund can determine when and whether to start negotiations for a Stand-By Arrangement, it will need to see tangible steps that show the authorities' strong commitment to engage on all the policy issues that are relevant to macroeconomic stability. Support of the European authorities and institutions would also be critical for successful discussions of a new program', see www.imf.org/external/np/sec/pr/2012/pr1207.htm.

position. From an outside perspective, it even seemed possible that the Commission would demand that Hungary complied with the reports of the Venice Commission in exchange for the initiation of negotiations on financial aid, even if those reports also affected areas clearly beyond the scope of EU law.[277] This would have meant a large-scale attempt to enforce European standards of the rule of law beyond the actual competences of the EU.

However, following Hungary's replies to the letters of formal notice on 17 February 2012, the Commission decided to narrow the focus, inasmuch as it issued only two reasoned opinions on 7 March, on the compulsory retirement of judges and on the independence of the data protection authority.[278] Accordingly, Hungary was referred to the CJEU for two infringement cases concerning the independence of the data protection authority and the retirement age of judges, prosecutors and public notaries. Having taken these legal steps, the Commission put no further pressure on Hungary by delaying the start of the talks on financial aid, and announced that it was ready to begin negotiations.[279] The following day the IMF declared that it was ready to start negotiations as soon as adequate steps were taken to ensure the independence of the Central Bank, as had been discussed with the Hungarian government.[280]

In the infringement procedure on the compulsory retirement of judges, the CJEU acceded to the position of the European Commission. On 6 November 2012, the CJEU ruled that the relevant national legislation gives rise to a difference in treatment on grounds of age which is neither appropriate nor necessary to attain the objectives pursued and therefore does not comply with the principle of proportionality. Thus, according to the ruling, Hungary had failed to fulfil its obligations under Council Directive 2000/78/EC.[281]

In response, Hungary, taking into account the previous decision of the Hungarian Constitutional Court as well, amended the legislation on the legal status of the judges, and it introduced a new method of calculation, setting the

[277] As President Barroso put it in a statement before the European Parliament, 'the Council of Europe is currently considering other points of the Hungarian legislation which are under its remit. The Council of Europe Venice Commission could play an important role in this respect'. See Editorial Comments, 'Fundamental Rights and EU Membership' (n 275) 486, with further references.

[278] Regarding the independence of the Central Bank and further aspects concerning the independence of the judiciary, the Commission sent two administrative letters demanding further clarifications: 'Commission takes further legal steps on measures affecting the judiciary and the independence of the data protection authority, notes some progress on central bank independence, but further evidence and clarification needed' (European Commission MEMO/12/165, 7 March 2012), available at http://europa.eu/rapid/pressReleasesAction.do?reference=MEMO/12/165&format=HTML&aged=1&language=EN&guiLanguage=en. Ultimately, on 25 April 2012, the European Commission noted that the Hungarian government promised to take into account the Commission's legal concerns on the independence of the Central Bank and to amend its national legislation.

[279] 'UPDATE 3-EU Gives Green Light to Hungary Aid Talks', *Reuters* (Brussels), 25 April 2012), available at www.reuters.com/article/2012/04/25/eu-hungary-aid-idUSL6E8FP50L20120425.

[280] 'IMF to Talk to Hungary Once Bank Autonomy Assured', *Reuters* (Washington), 26 April 2012), available at www.reuters.com/article/2012/04/26/us-imf-hungary-idUSBRE83P13Y20120426.

[281] Case C-286/12 *Commission v Hungary* (2012, nyr).

retirement age to between 65 and 70, depending on the date of birth of the judge. The law also set forth a unified retirement age calculation method for judges, prosecutors and notaries.[282]

VI. CONCLUSIONS

The constitutional developments of the last few years in Hungary have been marked by three crisis symptoms: permanent constitution-making, a gradual deterioration of the guarantees of fundamental rights, and a lack of effective checks and balances.

After the 2010 elections and before the Basic Law entered into force on 1 January 2012, the 1989 Constitution was amended no less than eight times. The Basic Law, the product of unilateral constitution-making by the governing parties, went through five amendments by the very same parties in less than two years. The amendments served everyday political needs, either by reacting to Constitutional Court decisions or by neutralising possible constitutional concerns relating to specific legislative projects. Thus, the constitution of Hungary has lacked the stability and reliability that is necessary for a constitution to fulfil its role as the paramount law of the land.

This is not to say that guarantees of fundamental rights in the Basic Law are in general missing or insufficient. The Basic Law as adopted in 2011 was in line with mainstream European constitutionalism. Yet the specific exceptions to fundamental rights, first in the Transitional Provisions and later in more amendments to the Basic Law, especially in the Fourth Amendment, led to the gradual deterioration of the level of fundamental rights protection. Freedom of religion relating to the recognition of churches, free speech relating to the protection of personality rights and political campaigning, and the right to property in relation to retroactive taxation are all examples of fundamental rights where the previous level of protection was lowered, sometimes below the obligatory minimum of the ECHR.

This negative process is a result of a lack of effective checks and balances. Again, we do not argue that the judiciary is no longer independent in Hungary. In fact, in spite of the problematic organisational changes in the administration of courts, the independence of the judiciary is the area where negative changes (ie the forced retirement of judges and the reallocation of cases) could somewhat be reversed. Yet in a parliamentary democracy, the single most important counterweight to Parliament is the constitutional court, and the Hungarian Constitutional Court is seriously impaired. Limitations to the competence of the Court, changes to the composition and the election of judges, and, most of all, the permanent

[282] Act XX of 2013 (2013. évi XX. törvény az egyes igazságügyi jogviszonyokban alkalmazandó felső korhatárral kapcsolatos törvénymódosításokról).

constitution-making, made it extraordinarily difficult for the Court to maintain the general European ideals of constitutionalism.

In this respect, it does not seem that there are ideological motives behind the changes to the constitutional system: the different emerging ideological elements are too contradictory and too eclectic (liberal catalogue of fundamental rights with ad hoc exceptions; conservative Preamble; anti-Marxist rhetoric; parliamentary sovereignty in justifying the curtailment of the competences of the Constitutional Court; limiting the budgetary powers of the Parliament by the veto power of the Budget Council). The constitution-making was most likely motivated simply by short-term party political interests, and pragmatism was probably stronger than any of the ideological components. The constitution was basically considered just as an *instrument* in the political struggle for power. The 'winner takes it all' and the Schmittian 'us versus them' (where these terms are not defined by principles but only by personal connections) are most characteristic of this mentality. The government is basically using the Basic Law in order to cement its own position and policies which seem to support its position.[283]

This also means that reasoning is ineffective in healing Hungary's constitutional problems. Where there are no principles behind the changes, or rather where the principles are only motivated by party political interests and also change from time to time, the old wisdom becomes most evident: power can only be controlled by power. The present chapter illustrated that the governing parties in Hungary mostly retreated if European institutions intervened. Even then, the possible economic implications looked more threatening than any denouncement about breaches of certain values. The lesson is that the lack of domestic checks and balances can partly be compensated for by European institutions, yet these institutions can only address a small portion of the problems that arise.

That being said, the last words will be devoted to the stability of the Basic Law. We cannot of course predict with certainty what is going to happen in Hungary, but there are empirical studies on cases similar to the present Hungarian one. According to these, the longevity of constitutions depends on three factors: flexibility, an integrating character, and a sufficiently detailed constitution.[284] The Basic Law is sufficiently (or perhaps even more) flexible, as article S(2) only requires (similarly to the previous Constitution) a two-thirds majority for constitutional amendments, and the electoral system is even more disproportionate than before. The text of the Basic Law cannot be said to be insufficiently detailed,

[283] See D Landau, 'Abusive Constitutionalism' (2013) 47 *UC Davis Law Review* 189, referring explicitly to the Hungarian Basic Law of 2011 as an example of abusive constitutionalism. On legal self-restraint and on the symbolic integrating functions of constitutions (none of them followed by the drafters of the Basic Law) see A Jakab, 'The Two Functions of a Constitution' in E Bos and K Pócza (eds), *Verfassunggebung in konsolidierten Demokratien: Neubeginn oder Verfall eines Systems?* (Baden-Baden, Nomos, 2014) 78–104.

[284] Z Elkins, T Ginsburg and J Melton, *The Endurance of National Constitutions* (Cambridge, Cambridge University Press, 2009) 65.

either (the Basic Law was some 15 per cent longer than the previous Constitution in its 2011 form, and now it is about 50 per cent longer). It is, in turn, questionable whether or not the Basic Law has an integrating character.[285] Currently, one of the openly purported main goals of the opposition is to adopt a new constitution. Once they have the power (even if not a constitution-making majority in the Parliament), it will be difficult to stop their project. Many constitutions in history were adopted illegally (quite a few of them were democratic ones),[286] and according to what we know about the life prospects of constitutions in general, there is a chance that the 2011 Basic Law of Hungary will end in a similarly dramatic way. We, however, still hope that the mistakes of the Basic Law which drove Hungary further from the European constitutional mainstream can be corrected in a legal and peaceful way.

[285] For a more general outlook on this problem, see A Jakab, 'On the Legitimacy of a New Constitution: Remarks on the Occasion of the New Hungarian Basic Law of 2011' in MA Jovanović and Đ Pavićević (eds), *Crisis and Quality of Democracy in Eastern Europe* (The Hague, Eleven Publishing, 2012) 61–76, available at www.papers.ssrn.com/sol3/papers.cfm?abstract_id=2033624. We do not agree with Gábor Halmai who requires a constitution to be ideologically neutral, see G Halmai, 'Hochproblematisch: Ungarns neue Grundgesetz' (2011) 12 *Osteuropa* 147. In our view, no constitution is ideologically neutral and no constitution should be (rule of law and democracy are important ideological elements themselves, just like 'neutrality' itself). It is not neutrality, but *inclusion* that is missing. The problem is, namely, that the Basic Law does not consider the political views of a considerable part of the population as worthy enough to make rhetorical gestures towards them (as opposed to the Preamble to the Polish Constitution where we do find a more inclusive rhetoric towards atheists); see the criticism by B Schanda, 'Considerations on the Place of Religion in Constitutional Law' in Z Csehi *et al* (eds), *Viva Vox Iuris Civilis. Festschrift László Sólyom* (Budapest, HVG Orac, 2012) 285. It is especially strange and unintelligible in a society in which the population (including the voters and supposedly even the leaders of Fidesz) is much less religious than most European countries.

[286] Elkins, Ginsburg and Melton, *The Endurance of National Constitutions* (n 284) 225, with statistical data on 'extra constitutional leadership change' in the context of constitution-making. An illegal adoption, however, makes the life prospects of any new constitution shorter as well, see ibid 132.

3

Understanding Hungary's Constitutional Revolution

KIM LANE SCHEPPELE*

SINCE ITS ELECTION in 2010, the Fidesz government in Hungary has created a constitutional frenzy. It won two-thirds of the seats in the Parliament in a system where a single two-thirds vote is enough to change the constitution. Twelve times in its first year in office, it amended the Constitution it inherited. Those amendments removed most of the institutional checks that could have stopped what the government did next—which was to install a new constitution. The new Fidesz Constitution was drafted in secret, presented to the Parliament with only one month for debate, passed by the votes of only the Fidesz parliamentary bloc, and signed by a President that Fidesz had named. Neither the opposition parties nor civil society organisations nor the general public had any influence in the constitutional process. There was no popular ratification. The Fidesz Constitution went into effect on 1 January 2012.

With this new Constitution, the current Hungarian government felled the tree of democratic constitutionalism that Hungary planted in 1989.

While the government claims it was given a mandate to make major changes, the general Hungarian public thinks otherwise. During the election campaign in 2010, Fidesz never said it would change the whole constitutional system, so it is difficult to claim that the election was a referendum on a new constitution. Once the Fidesz governing programme became clear after the party came to power, the popularity of Fidesz plummeted, even more so after the government undertook to replace the Constitution. In the year when the constitutional plan was announced and enacted, the governing party's popularity fell to only 15 per cent in the opinion polls.

Even though the government pushed through a one-party constitution without support from any other political fraction, except its own party list partner, the Christian Democrats, this didn't stop the constitutional juggernaut. The

* Testimony, US Commission on Security and Cooperation in Europe (Helsinki Commission), hearing on 'The Trajectory of Democracy: Why Hungary Matters', presentation held at Capitol Visitor Center, Room SVC 210 (Senate Side), 19 March 2013, 3 pm.

government amended its new Constitution four times in the first 15 months of the new Constitution's life. Each time, the government did so with the votes of only its own political bloc, rejecting all proposals from the political opposition or from civil society groups. The current Hungarian Constitution remains a one-party constitution.

In March 2013, the Fidesz government passed a 15-page amendment to the new 45-page Constitution. László Sólyom, the Conservative former President of both the Constitutional Court and the Republic of Hungary, said in a public statement at the time that the 'Fourth Amendment' removed the last traces of separation of powers from the Hungarian constitutional system. Under the Constitution as amended, no institution has the legal right to check many of the key powers of the one-party government.

The Fourth Amendment nullified more than 20 years of rights-protecting case law that the Hungarian Constitutional Court had developed before the new Constitution went into effect. This left a giant gap where firm legal protection of basic rights once stood. The Fourth Amendment specifically overturned nearly all of the decisions that the Constitutional Court made in the previous year striking down controversial new laws the Fidesz government had passed. The Fourth Amendment removed the Court's power to evaluate on substantive grounds any new constitutional amendments, a move which allowed the government to escape review by inserting any controversial new proposal directly into the Constitution. The Fourth Amendment entrenched political control of the judiciary and gave the government new tools to prevent the opposition from coming to power. The Fourth Amendment reversed many of the concessions Hungary made in the first year of the new Constitution when the European Union, the Council of Europe and the US State Department criticised fundamental aspects of that Constitution.

Under cover of constitutional reform, the Fidesz government gave itself a practically unlimited power. It now has discretion to do virtually anything it wants, even if civil society, the general public and all other political parties are opposed.

How could Hungary have fallen so far so fast from the family of stable constitutional democracies? The answer lies in the Achilles' heel of the old constitutional system: a disproportionate election law combined with an easy constitutional amendment rule.

Hungary's 1990 election law gave disproportionate numbers of seats to the winner of an election, a feature that was designed to help plurality parties form stable governments. When Fidesz got 53 per cent of the vote in the 2010 election, the election law converted this victory into 68 per cent of the seats in the Parliament. While Fidesz won this vote in a joint party list with the Christian Democrats (KDNP), the Christian Democrats barely have an independent existence apart from Fidesz and its members vote in a bloc with Fidesz on every issue.

Armed with its two-thirds supermajority, the Fidesz government has been able to make use of the old Constitution's amendment rule, dating to the communist

Constitution of 1949, which permitted the Constitution to be changed with a single two-thirds vote of the Parliament. This 'magic two-thirds' has enabled Fidesz to make all of its constitutional changes in a formally legal manner. Only one barrier remained: in 1995, under a prior two-thirds government, the old Constitution was amended to require a four-fifths vote of the Parliament before any new constitutional drafting process could begin. One month into its term, Fidesz used its two-thirds vote to amend the Constitution to remove the four-fifths requirement.

Many of the laws, including the Constitution itself, many of the constitutional amendments and most of the cardinal laws, were introduced through the parliamentary procedure of a 'private member's Bill', which bypasses the stage of public consultation required of all government Bills. That, combined with the fact that the Parliament instituted a new rule through which a two-thirds vote could cut off parliamentary debate on any topic, meant that most of these new laws received very little public discussion. It has not been uncommon for a constitutional amendment go from first proposal to final enactment in just a few weeks.

Taken over the first three years of the Fidesz government, the constitutional changes are complicated, detailed and spread out across a new Constitution, four major constitutional amendments, dozens of 'cardinal' (supermajority) laws, and thousands of pages of ordinary laws that were all passed in a giant legislative blur, sometimes in the middle of the night. I strongly suspect that most Hungarians do not understand the details of this new constitutional system. Even Hungarian lawyers are not able to keep up with the total revolution in the law. In what follows, I will try to explain how the new system of Hungarian government is structured (as of March 2013) taking all of this new law into account.

I will call this whole new legal structure the 'Fidesz Constitution' even though not everything is in the single constitutional text or its amendments. Many elements of the system I describe are in two-thirds 'cardinal' laws that are almost as entrenched as the Constitution itself, which is why I don't make fine distinctions here except where they are crucial for understanding how the system works.

In this testimony, I will focus on the system of divided and checked powers necessary for a government to remain both constitutional and democratic. History tells us that a government that has no limits on what it can do and that concentrates all powers in a single party will soon cease to be either constitutional or democratic.

The importance of checked and limited powers was an insight very familiar to the American constitutional framers. The Philadelphia Convention did not even include a Bill of Rights in the US Constitution because the framers believed that the most effective protection for rights was a government that was limited by law. While American history has taught us that a Bill of Rights matters—and the ratification process of the US Constitution insisted on including one—we have also learned much from James Madison, who wrote: 'The accumulation of all powers, legislative, executive, and judiciary, in the same hands, whether of one, a few, or many, and whether hereditary, self-appointed, or elective, may justly be pronounced the very definition of tyranny'.[1]

By James Madison's definition, Hungary is on the verge of tyranny. In what follows, I will show that the Fidesz political party has gathered all of the powers of the Hungarian government into its own hands, without checks from any other political quarter and without any limits on what it can do.

We should start with the basics: Hungary has a unicameral parliamentary system of government. A unicameral Parliament has no upper house to check what the lower house does, no 'Senate' to complicate life for the 'House of Representatives' and vice versa. A parliamentary system means that the most powerful executive, the Prime Minister, is elected by the Parliament rather than directly by the people. As a result, the Prime Minister in Hungary is virtually guaranteed a majority for all of his legislative initiatives because that legislative majority put him into his job. Not surprisingly, the legislative-executive cooperation guaranteed in Hungary's unicameral parliamentary system dates back to the communist Constitution of 1949.[2]

In 1989, however, major constitutional changes in Hungary added a number of checks to this basic framework. A Constitutional Court was created as the primary watchdog on the majoritarian dangers of a unicameral parliamentary system. Unlike a Supreme Court, which is the highest court of appeal in the legal system (something we are familiar with in the United States), a Constitutional Court is the only court that is allowed to hear and decide constitutional questions—and it does nothing else besides rule on constitutional matters. Because the Hungarian Constitutional Court conducts the primary oversight in a system that has little formal separation of legislative and executive power, it is even more important than the Supreme Court in the American separation-of-powers system.

Given such weighty responsibility in the 1989 constitutional design, the Constitutional Court was made highly accessible to the new democratic public in Hungary. Literally, anyone could ask the Constitutional Court to review a law for constitutionality using a so-called *actio popularis* petition. As a result, virtually every law was challenged. From the time it opened in January 1990, the active Constitutional Court kept each new government under constitutional constraint regardless of the political leanings of the government. Opinion polls showed that the Constitutional Court was consistently the most highly respected political institution in Hungary.

The procedure for electing judges to the Constitutional Court before 2010 prevented the Court from being captured by any one political fraction. Because each judicial nominee to the Constitutional Court had first to be approved by a majority of parliamentary parties before then being elected to the Court by a two-thirds

[1] J Madison, 'Separation of Powers' *Federalist No 47* (30 January 1788) 323–31.

[2] From the mid-nineteenth to the mid-twentieth centuries, Hungary had a bicameral Parliament.

vote of the Parliament, the Court always had a balance of different political views represented on the bench.

Other changes made to the constitutional system in 1989 provided more checks on Hungary's unicameral parliamentary government. Revamped parliamentary procedure required extensive consultation with both civil society and opposition parties before government Bills could be put to a vote. Important issues of constitutional concern required a two-thirds vote of the Parliament. As we have seen, however, the private member's Bill procedure allowed the consultation stage for legislation to be bypassed and the two-thirds laws could cease to be a real check on power when the government had two-thirds of the parliamentary seats, something the disproportionate election law made quite likely.

Four ombudsmen added after 1989 to the system of rights protection. Other independent institutions (the Central Bank, State Audit Office, Prosecutor General's Office, National Election Commission and Media Council) provided both expertise and additional checkpoints. For example, both the National Election Commission and the Media Council were structured to ensure representation from across the political spectrum. An independent self-governing judiciary ensured that the laws were fairly applied.

There were so many different checks instituted after 1989 on the power of the Prime Minister and his parliamentary majority that the post-1989 constitutional system worked reliably to ensure that the operation of majoritarian political power guaranteed by the unicameral parliamentary system didn't ride roughshod over democratic guarantees and constitutional limitations.

By contrast with this robust system of complementary powers, the new Fidesz Constitution removes virtually all of the checks added to the prior communist Constitution after 1989. I will detail the major reversals here.

Under the Fidesz Constitution, the Constitutional Court's power and independence have been compromised in multiple ways. The system for electing constitutional judges was changed so that now a single two-thirds vote of the Parliament is sufficient to put a judge on the Court, abolishing the multiparty agreement that was once necessary for nomination. The Fidesz Constitution also expanded the number of judges on the Court from 11 to 15, giving the governing party four more judges to name immediately.

Between changing the process for electing judges and expanding the number of judges to be elected, the Fidesz government has been able to select nine of the 15 judges on the Court in its first three years in office. The Fidesz parliamentary bloc, voting in unison as it always does, put these judges onto the Court without multiparty support, though a few of the new judges were able to garner some votes from the far-right Jobbik party. The new constitutional judges have almost always voted for the Fidesz government position in each case. Some of the new judges have just voted for the government's position without even giving reasons.

Even if the Court is in Fidesz-friendly hands, however, a powerful Court might still be dangerous to a government that shuns checks on its freedom of action. This may explain why the jurisdiction of the Court has been cut. The Court no longer has the power to review laws based on *actio popularis* petitions, which are petitions that anyone can file. Now, the only individuals who can challenge laws must show that they have been concretely injured by the application of a potentially unconstitutional law and that they have exhausted their remedies in the ordinary courts. If the Constitutional Court can only hear cases that have concrete victims, it is hard for the Court to rule on matters pertaining to separation of powers and the structure of democratic institutions. Individuals rarely get 'standing' to challenge a law that creates a new system for judicial appointments or a law that gives a government agency the power to issue decrees without parliamentary oversight, both laws that have been passed since Fidesz came to power. Some elements of 'abstract review' remain with the Constitutional Court, but these, too, have been restricted.

Abstract review allows the Court to hear challenges to laws without a concrete dispute before it. With the exception of the Parliamentary Commissioner for Human Rights,[3] the Constitution gives the power to challenge laws abstractly only to particular offices that are currently occupied by people affiliated with Fidesz. One might guess that Fidesz appointees do not have a strong incentive to limit the power of their own government. While one-quarter of the Parliament is also given the power to challenge a law at the Constitutional Court, the one-third of the seats in the current Parliament that are not held by the governing party are divided between parties of the centre-left and a party of the far-right, who would have to agree on a challenge, something that is not very likely. As a result, many laws have been effectively insulated from constitutional challenge by the way that abstract review power has been designed.

Even with the limitations on access to the Constitutional Court that were built into the Fidesz Constitution, the system of judicial review in Hungary may seem broader than the system in the United States. Therefore, the dangers of the new system in Hungary may not be apparent to an American eye. Limiting the power to initiate judicial review only to those who have been directly injured and only to officials who owe their jobs to this government limits the ability of the Court to reach constitutional violations that it used to be able to reach. The US Supreme Court cannot reach all constitutional violations either, but the United States has a bicameral Congress, a separately elected President, a vigilant and active civil society, and federalism, which adds state governments and state courts as additional checks on the power of temporary majorities. Hungary has none of those checking institutions and so relies on the Constitutional Court to carry more weight in the constitutional system. Making it difficult for this Court to reach all constitutional violations creates blind spots in which unconstrained political discretion can override constitutional values.

[3] The Parliamentary Commissioner for Human Rights, inherited when the Fidesz government came to power, was replaced later in 2013. The new ombudsman has not actively challenged Fidesz legislation before the Constitutional Court for review as the prior ombudsman did.

In addition to limiting access to the Court, the Fidesz Constitution restricted the jurisdiction of the Court in other ways as well. The Court may no longer review any law that deals with taxes or budgets when those laws are passed at a time when the national debt is more than 50 per cent of GDP. Under the Fourth Amendment passed in March 2013, the Court will never have the power to review budget and tax laws that were passed under these circumstances. As a result, if a tax law passed in 2013 infringes an individual's constitutionally guaranteed property rights or if such a tax is applied selectively to particular minority groups, there is nothing that the Constitutional Court can do—in perpetuity. This opens up a space for the government to violate many personal rights without any constitutional oversight.

The Fourth Amendment has also banned the Court from reviewing constitutional amendments for substantive conflicts with constitutional principles. As a result, if the Constitution promises freedom of religion but a constitutional amendment requires a two-thirds parliamentary vote before a church is officially recognised (a provision that was added to the Constitution with the Fourth Amendment), the Court can do nothing about this. Or if the Constitution says anyone may freely express her opinion but an amendment says that no one may defame the Hungarian nation (a provision that was also added to the Constitution with the Fourth Amendment), there is nothing the Court can do. These examples show that the government can now directly amend the Constitution any time it thinks the Constitutional Court might strike down some policy that the government wants to enact, regardless of how much these new amendments violate principles that have been guaranteed elsewhere in the Constitution. In fact, the Fourth Amendment already inserted into the Constitution all but one of the laws that the Constitutional Court had already struck down as unconstitutional once before under the new Constitution.

To make matters worse, the Fourth Amendment also nullified all decisions made by the Constitutional Court before the new Constitution took effect. At one level, this makes sense: old Constitution/old decisions and new Constitution/new decisions. But the Constitutional Court had already worked out a sensible new rule for the constitutional transition by deciding that 'in those cases where the language of the old and new constitutions was substantially the same', the opinions of the prior Court would still be valid and could still be applied. Otherwise, where the new Constitution was substantially different from the old one, the previous decisions would no longer be used. Constitutional rights are key provisions that are the same in the old and new Constitutions—which means that, practically speaking, the Fourth Amendment annulled primarily the cases that defined and protected constitutional rights. With those decisions gone, no one can say for certain whether Hungarian law protects free speech, freedom of religion, equality of all Hungarians before the law, property rights, and virtually every other right in precisely the way that everyone in Hungary had come to take for granted.

What other checks on Fidesz's untrammelled power were also removed in the Fidesz Constitution? The independence of the ordinary judicial system has taken a big hit. In 2011, the Fidesz government suddenly lowered the judicial retirement age from 70 to 62, thus removing the most senior 10 per cent of the judiciary, including 20 per cent of the Supreme Court judges and more than half of the appeals court Presidents. Both the Hungarian Constitutional Court and the Court of Justice of the European Union (CJEU) found that the sudden change in the judicial retirement age was illegal.

The government's first reaction was to defy both courts' judgments, before finally agreeing at the end of 2012 to reinstate fired judges who wanted to return to their jobs. Few of them actually returned, however, because the government offered them generous compensation packages if they did not return to work. In the meantime, however, all of the court leadership positions were filled with new judges, so the old judges who wanted to be reinstated were returned to much less important positions. Through this move, the government was able to replace much of the top leadership of the judiciary in a single year. One court leader who could not have been replaced in this manner (because he was too young) was the then-President of the Supreme Court, András Baka. He was removed from office formally by a transitional law, but in practice by a new requirement, effective immediately, that judges must have five years of judicial experience in Hungary before being named to the Supreme Court (newly renamed the Kúria). President Baka's 16 years of experience as a judge on the European Court of Human Rights did not count and he therefore became ineligible to remain a judge on the highest ordinary court in Hungary.

How were the new judges named? The new President of the Supreme Court (Kúria) was elected by a two-thirds vote of the Fidesz Parliament. Beyond that, a new institution was created to oversee the appointment of all other judges as well as the administration of the judiciary: the National Judicial Office (NJO). This office replaced a system of judicial self-government. The President of the NJO, elected by two-thirds of the Parliament, received the power to hire, fire, promote, demote and discipline all judges in the system without any substantive oversight from any other institution. The national President must countersign in cases where a judge is appointed for the first time in the system, but it is not clear that he could refuse to do so. The new leadership of the ordinary courts has thus been replaced by judges who owe their careers to an official elected by the 'magic two-thirds' of the Fidesz Parliament.

The Council of Europe's Commission on Democracy through Law (Venice Commission) sharply criticised the extraordinary powers of and general lack of legal standards governing the President of the National Judicial Office. The US State Department has also raised questions about the independence of the judiciary under this system. In a concession to criticism, the Fidesz government agreed to limit the powers of the President of the NJO in legislation passed in summer 2012. But the Fourth Amendment reinstated these outsized powers of the President of the NJO without constitutionalising the checks included in the legislation. The Constitution therefore entrenched the NJO, whose President has the constitutional power to 'manage the central administrative affairs of the courts', a set of responsibilities in which the judges merely 'participate'. None of the other constraints that the Fidesz government agreed to under international pressure—requiring a significant role for the judges in their own self-government, establishing legal standards for the President of the NJO to use in managing the judiciary, and no longer allowing the President of the NJO to stay in office until her successor was elected—were introduced into the Constitution itself, they were only included in a cardinal law governing the judiciary that might have been determined to be unconstitutional because absolute powers were given to the President of the NJO in the Constitution.[4]

In another move that has attracted universal criticism, the Fidesz government gave the President of the NJO the power to take any case in the entire court system and move it to a court different from the one to which normal procedure would assign it. So, for example, if a political corruption case against members of the main opposition party would normally be assigned to the trial-level court in Pest, the President of the NJO can move the case to Kecskemét. In fact, this is not a hypothetical; that very example happened. The rationale given for this extraordinary power to move cases is that the courts are overcrowded and case resolution can be speeded up by moving cases to less crowded courts.[5]

But the rationale for the President of the NJO to have this power was belied by the facts: from public sources, I kept track of the movement of cases in the first year that the President of the NJO had this power. She moved only a few dozen cases away from courts that had thousands of backlogged cases. And she moved the cases not to the least crowded courts in the countryside but to other courts that also had backlogs. She moved some of the highest-profile political cases in which the political opposition had a stake, leading the opposition to charge the government with picking the judges, particularly in cases that have strong political overtones. While my statistics cannot reveal the motivation of the government, they can show that the government was not moving a substantial enough number of cases to make a difference in waiting times and it was not moving cases from the most to the least crowded courts.

The Constitutional Court and the ordinary judiciary have suffered a severe blow under the Fidesz Constitution. Other independent institutions have fared no better.

The ombudsman system, which once comprised four independent ombudsmen with independent jurisdictions, has now been folded into one office with a much smaller staff. The former data protection ombudsman was fired and the office has been absorbed directly into the government, something that has generated an

[4] After the international outcry, a Fifth Amendment to the Constitution, passed in September 2013 after this testimony was given, reinserted into the constitutional text some role for judicial councils to participate in the selection of judges.

[5] The Fifth Amendment to the Constitution also removed this power from the President of the NJO but did not restore the cases already moved to the courts to which they had been assigned by law.

infringement action launched by the European Commission against Hungary at the CJEU because EU law requires an independent data privacy officer.

In March 2013, after many public battles with the governor of the Central Bank that the Fidesz government had inherited, the government was finally able to replace him with one of their own ministers. Before he moved to the Bank, however, he used his ministerial power to unilaterally change the rules in the Charter of the Central Bank. Without the need for parliamentary approval or Court review, then, György Matolcsy, as the Fidesz Economics Minister, gave the office of György Matolcsy, the new Central Bank governor, dramatically increased powers just before he moved from one job to the next.

The new Media Council has a chair appointed directly by the Prime Minister and a membership that consists exclusively of members elected by the Fidesz parliamentary two-thirds, all for nine-year terms. The Media Council has draconian powers to levy bankrupting fines based on a review of the content of both public and private media, including broadcast, print and Internet. A Constitutional Court decision freed the print media from some of these constraints, but the Fidesz government could still easily amend the Constitution to bring the print media back under control and the Constitutional Court could say nothing further about it.

The Election Commission has been revamped and now consists exclusively of members who have been elected by the Fidesz parliamentary two-thirds majority, all for terms of nine years. While each party with a national list in the next election, scheduled for April 2014, will have a temporary member on the Commission during the campaign, opposition parties will easily be outvoted by the Fidesz majority.

The legal framework for the 2014 election was still in flux one year before the polling was to occur.[6] Early on, however, the Fidesz parliamentary two-thirds enacted two election laws over vociferous protest from opposition parties, creating an even more disproportionate system than the one it replaced. One law gerrymandered the districts for the next election in such a way that it would be very difficult for the opposition to win. The law even fixed the exact boundaries of election districts in a cardinal law that requires a two-thirds vote of the Parliament to change. This law also eliminated the second round of voting for single-member districts so that someone without majority support in a district can enter Parliament, which was not previously the case.

The government passed a second cardinal law on elections that instituted a system of voter registration, even though the country had conducted more than 20 years of elections with an excellent 'civil list' that never produced any complaints of irregularity. The Constitutional Court struck down voter registration as

[6] Effective 18 April 2013, Law XXXVI of 2013 (2013. évi XXXVI. törvény a választási eljárásról) regulated many features of the election, but changes in the election framework were still occurring through 2014. There is no guarantee, as I update this testimony in January 2014, that the election rules will not be changed again before the spring election. In fact, the government pledged in January 2014 that it would legislate to alter the way that minority voters can register to vote for nationality parties.

unconstitutional, and the governing party seems to have given up on this idea. But with its parliamentary two-thirds vote, the government has the power to override the Constitutional Court by simply adding voter registration to the Constitution at any point. The government may also change other important features of the election system right up until the election takes place. For example, one year before the election, no rules had yet been devised for making and verifying voter lists for ethnic Hungarians in the neighbouring states who recently became eligible for citizenship as the result of constitutional changes.

The Fourth Amendment added new electoral rules in March 2013. The amendment created a constitutional ban on political advertising during the election campaign in any venue other than in the public broadcast media, which is controlled by the all-Fidesz media board. Moreover, only parties with national party lists could advertise at all in the national media, which potentially excluded smaller and newer parties. These restrictions had been previously declared unconstitutional by the Constitutional Court, so the government amended the Constitution to override that decision. And since these provisions are now in the Constitution itself, the Constitutional Court cannot review them again.

But suppose that, despite all of the obstacles that the current governing party put in the way of the political opposition, an opposition coalition manages to win an election anyway. The Fidesz Constitution created a trap that can be snapped shut in just such a case. The Constitution created a National Budget Council with the power to veto any future budget that adds to the national debt, which any foreseeable budget will do. The members of the Budget Council have been chosen by the Fidesz two-thirds majority for terms of six or 12 years and can be replaced only if two-thirds of the Parliament can agree on their successors when their terms are over. Not only does this mean that, for three election cycles out, any future government must follow a budgetary course agreed on by a council where all of the members were elected by the Fidesz government, but this Budget Council has even more power than that.

The Constitution requires the Parliament to pass a budget by 31 March of each year. If the Parliament fails to do so, the President of the country can dissolve the Parliament and call new elections. When this provision is put together with the powers of the budgetary council, the constraints on any future government are clear. If a new non-Fidesz government passes a budget that adds to the debt, that budget can be vetoed by the all-Fidesz Budgetary Council at any time, including on the eve of the budget deadline given in the Constitution. The Parliament would then miss the deadline and the President (also named by Fidesz and serving through 2017) could call new elections. And this process can be repeated until an acceptable government is voted back into power.

The Fidesz government may have created this unfortunate interaction of constitutional provisions inadvertently in an earnest attempt to create a binding mechanism to achieve budget discipline. But it would be easy for the Fidesz government to achieve fiscal discipline without creating this anti-democratic trap. The Fidesz government could amend the Constitution to require that the Budget

Council veto the budget by a deadline that would give the Parliament time to pass a new budget before the President gains the power to dissolve it. I have personally suggested this to high-level members of Fidesz, but an amendment to this effect has so far not appeared.

There is more that could be said about the new Fidesz Constitution. I have only mentioned what I take to be the biggest obstacles posed to constitutionalism and democracy by this new constitutional framework.

What can be done about the Fidesz consolidation of power by the United States, the US Helsinki Commission, and by the Organization for Security and Cooperation in Europe?

First, of course, Hungarian democracy must be created and maintained by Hungarians themselves. But a democratic public must be an educated public and Hungarians themselves need to learn what has happened to their own Constitution over the last three years. Most have no idea, and not because they could not or would not understand.

The government celebrated its new Constitution with great fanfare. They set up 'constitutional tables' at every town hall where people could sign up to receive their very own copy of the Constitution. In June 2012, the government presented to every secondary school graduate a coffee-table book with the words of the new Constitution illustrated with historic and specially commissioned paintings. But much of what I have mentioned above is not contained in the text that the government has distributed.

Hungary's friends, including the United States, could assist financially with a programme to educate citizens, lawyers and judges in Hungary about the new constitutional framework in Hungary. A public education campaign about the new constitutional structure, conducted by Hungarian constitutional experts from the government, from the opposition and from academia, may assist in giving Hungarians better information about their new constitutional system. Such a campaign would be especially effective if it could be conducted through the broadcast media in Hungary, though since the government functionally controls the broadcast media through its Media Council, some monitoring system would have to be put in place to ensure that both the government and opposition voices are heard. Having read thousands of petitions that ordinary Hungarians sent to the Constitutional Court in the 1990s, I am confident that Hungarians themselves will rise to the defence of both democracy and constitutionalism once they see the dangers of a flawed constitutional design.

Secondly, the Hungarian government vociferously claims that it is still a democracy because political parties may still freely organize and contest the election. But its critics are concerned that the government presently controls the media landscape, has enacted a number of legal provisions that disadvantage opposition parties, and continues to change the electoral rules. In fact, nothing prohibits the government from changing important elements of the electoral framework at the last minute. With the election coming up, it is important to get the rules of the game fixed—fairly—as soon as possible.

The Organization for Security and Cooperation in Europe (OSCE) has expertise in monitoring elections to ensure that they are free and fair. The OSCE should insist that the electoral rules be settled far enough ahead of the election so that all who want to contest the election have a reasonable amount of time to organise themselves accordingly.

Enough questions have been raised about the willingness of the current Hungarian government to recognise the political opposition that the OSCE/Office for Democratic Institutions and Human Rights (ODIHR) should also fully monitor the 2014 Hungarian parliamentary elections. This should include not just an election-day mission. The comprehensively changed new constitutional framework warrants an early Assessment Mission from OSCE/ODIHR, one that can fully review the effects of all the new provisions. It should focus on the ability of political parties to organise and to get their message out, access to the media, and the fairness of the basic election framework including the creation of electoral districts and the compatibility of both the content and timing of the new electoral rules with the principles of free and fair elections.

Thirdly, the US government should press the Hungarian government to live up to its international commitments to democracy, constitutionalism, the rule of law and robust rights protection. The United States should be vigilant in monitoring backsliding from the high level of constitutional democratic protections that Hungary had achieved after 1989, and the United States should cooperate with the Venice Commission, the Council of Europe Parliamentary Assembly Monitoring Committee, and the European Union (for example, the LIBE Committee of the European Parliament), all of which have ongoing monitoring processes in place.

But the US government should also be aware that, under pressure, the Fidesz government has in the past promised minor changes to its comprehensive framework and then has discarded those changes when the pressure lifted. Moreover, the changes that the Fidesz government has previously offered to make do not really address the key problems of the system. The Fidesz constitutional framework is a highly redundant system that must be understood as a whole. Each individual legal rule cannot be evaluated by itself because one must understand the function of that rule in the larger system. Changing a number of small features of this constitutional order may not in fact address the most serious problem, which is the concentration of political power in the hands of one party. In deciding whether the Hungarian government has been responsive to international and domestic criticism, Hungary's allies need to examine whether proposed changes really alter the way this complex and integrated system works as a whole.

The United States should resist entering the battle of competing checklists of constitutional features. The Hungarian government often insists that some other European country has the same individual rule that its friends criticise. Perhaps we should remember Frankenstein's monster, who was stitched together from perfectly normal bits of other once-living things, but who was, nonetheless, a monster. No other constitutional democracy in the world, let alone in Europe, has the combination of constitutional features that Hungary now has. In evaluating

Hungary for its compliance with international standards, its international friends must look at the whole constitutional system and not just at individual pieces as it assesses whether Hungary still belongs to the family of constitutional democracies.

Finally, Hungary is a small country in Europe. It may be hard to see why the United States should spend any of its political capital to address what former Secretary of State Hillary Clinton called Hungary's backsliding from constitutional democracy. There are two main reasons why the United States should care, apart from the fact that it is painful to see any country retreat from democracy and one should always be concerned about the people adversely affected.

Hungary is a partner with the United States not only in the OSCE, but also in NATO. OSCE commits its member states to the protection of human rights as defined under the Helsinki Final Act of 1975, and long experience shows that human rights receive their best protection from the maintenance of a constitutional and democratic government, both of which are now in doubt in Hungary. The NATO Charter creates a union of states 'determined to safeguard the freedom, common heritage and civilisation of their peoples, founded on the principles of democracy, individual liberty and the rule of law'. But these commitments are also being challenged by the concentration of power in Hungary under its new constitutional framework. Both the OSCE and NATO commit its member states to good behaviour and good government, which these organisations should be able to monitor.

In addition, other countries in Hungary's neighbourhood are looking with great interest at what Hungary is doing. They can see that the European Union, the Council of Europe, the OSCE, NATO and the United States have limited influence and ability to induce a national government to change its domestic laws. Hungary's neighbours understand that Hungary is getting away with consolidating all political power in the hands of one party, and many find that enticing. Troubling recent developments in Romania, Bulgaria and Slovenia show that the Hungarian problem of overly concentrated power could spread if the United States and its European allies do not stand up for their values in the Hungarian case. The United States should therefore treat constitutional problems in Hungary with a sense of urgency, both because of the speed with which this system is being locked in and because of the likelihood that the Hungarian constitutional disease could spread around the neighbourhood.

In closing then, I strongly urge the United States, the US Helsinki Commission and the OSCE to take Hungary seriously, engage with the Hungarian government on matters of constitutional reform, and work toward ensuring that the channels of democratic participation remain open in Hungary so that the Hungarian people retain the capacity to determine the sort of government under which they will live. The legal changes I have described pose a real danger to fundamental democratic and constitutional values, and Hungary's friends need to sound the alarm.

4

Context, Rules and Praxis of the New Hungarian Media Laws

How Does the Media Law Affect the Structure and Functioning of Publicity?

GÁBOR POLYÁK

THE ADOPTION OF the new media laws in 2010 not only laid the foundation for the complete overhaul of the Hungarian media system but at the same time represented one of the current administration's first measures to scale back constitutional democracy. Fitting in comfortably with the broader arsenal of media policy, the new regulation provides a clear-cut picture of the government's conception of democracy. First and foremost, the new regulation is aimed at a structural revamping of the media system that will cement for the long haul the dominance of the current ruling parties in the public domain, at the very least via the channels of telecommunication that reach most people in the country. Enterprises and editorial boards forced into compromise; single-party supervisory agencies; media businesses with close ties to the parties in power gaining ground—these are some of the main consequences of the media policy enabled by the new regulatory framework.

At the same time, the adoption of the new media laws has directed the attention of Europe and the world at large to the ongoing marginalisation of constitutional democracy in Hungary. From the Organization for Security and Cooperation in Europe (OSCE) to the United Nations and the European Council, virtually all organisations concerned with fundamental rights have voiced severe criticism of the regulations, and their objections have been seconded by journalist forums and other non-governmental organisations (NGOs). The present chapter does not undertake to provide a synopsis of the criticisms articulated to date.[1] The

[1] See generally 'Forced Maneuver: Proposals and Expectations toward the Amendment of the Media Act', *Mérték Media Monitor*, 11 June 2012, available at www.mertek.eu/en/article/forced-maneuver-proposals-and-expectations-toward-the-amendment-of-the-media-act. The author of this chapter is the professional leader of *Mérték Media Monitor* and co-author of its reports.

most comprehensive among them is certainly the expert opinion of the European Council, which essentially recommends a revision of the media laws across the board. Instead of such a summary, then, our aim here is to describe certain idiosyncratic, even eccentric solutions, now aided by the benefit of experience with the application of the new provisions.

Following an analysis of the constitutional underpinnings of the media regulation, we will provide a brief introduction to the specific features of the Hungarian media system that exert a profound influence on the operation of the new provisions. In our account, we focus on the two most prominent risks that follow from the language of the law, namely, the chilling effect of excessive content restrictions and the structural revisions threatening the pluralism of media in Hungary.

I. CONSTITUTIONAL FRAMEWORK FOR MEDIA REGULATION

A. Freedom of Expression and Freedom of the Press in the Basic Law of Hungary

The previous Hungarian Constitution, which was effective until 2011, ensured the freedom of the press between 1989 and 2010 using phrasing unrevised from the version effective in communist times. It was evident even in the phrasing of the provision in the Constitution that 'protection' of the freedom of the press presupposes active cooperation on the part of the state as opposed to the passive provision of freedom of thought.[2]

At the end of 2010, two Acts were adopted on the freedom of press and the fundamental rules of media content,[3] and on media services and mass media.[4] Subsequently, the constitutional approach was modified by the Basic Law in 2012.

In line with the EU Charter of Fundamental Rights and the practices of the Constitutional Court, the Basic Law of Hungary provides for freedom of expression and the press.[5] Changes in the text of the Constitution do not in themselves necessarily mean changes in the content of freedom of expression and the media.

[2] 1989 Constitution, art 61(1): 'In the Republic of Hungary everyone has the right to freely express his opinion, and furthermore to access and distribute information of public interest. (2) The Republic of Hungary recognizes and respects the freedom of the press. (3) A majority of two-thirds of the votes of the Members of Parliament present is required to pass the law on the public access to information of public interest and the law on the freedom of the press. (4) A majority of two-thirds of the votes of the Members of Parliament present is required to pass the law on the supervision of public radio, television and the public news agency, as well as the appointment of the directors thereof, on the licensing of commercial radio and television, and on the prevention of monopolies in the media sector'.

[3] Act CIV of 2010 (2010. évi CIV. törvény a sajtószabadságról és a médiatartalmak alapvető szabályairól).

[4] Act CLXXXV of 2010 (2010. évi CLXXXV. törvény a médiaszolgáltatásokról és a tömegkommunikációról).

[5] Basic Law, art IX(1): 'Everyone shall have the right to freedom of expression. (2) Hungary shall recognize and protect the freedom and diversity of the press, and shall ensure the conditions for the freedom to receive and impart information as is necessary in a democratic society. (3) The detailed

The content of the already laconic laws and the framework of the constitutional regulation of the media have been formed by the Constitutional Court, as to which revision is enabled but is certainly not required by the modification of the text.[6]

B. Most Significant Statements of the Constitutional Court regarding Media Regulation

The first Decision on freedom of the media was issued in 1992,[7] in which the Constitutional Court established the framework and objectives in line with European constitutional traditions. It set out the constitutional conditions for the operation and place of public broadcasting and at the same time it opened up the possibility of the development of a liberalised media market as well. Practice concerning freedom of the media became more established after the adoption of the first media law in the second half of the 1990s, although overall there were no more than ten decisions relating to issues about media regulation.[8] The Constitutional Court found decisive parts of the 1996 media law unconstitutional in 2007[9] and in 2008.[10] Practically the entire frequency tendering system was qualified as unconstitutional and the Court also examined fundamental issues concerning the regulation of media content. It examined particular provisions of the new media laws in December 2011.[11] The Court cannot deal with such submissions in the future. Thus, in its Decisions it annulled provisions relating to the regulation of media content and concerning the scope and procedures of media authorities but it did not assess a number of submissions relating to media laws. It did not pay particular attention to the composition and independence of the media authority and the concerns about the independence of public broadcasting.

Hereinafter we summarise the important and general principles of media regulation that can be deduced from the practice of the Constitutional Court.

rules relating to the freedom of the press and to the supervision of media services, press products and the communications market shall be laid down in an implementing act'.

6 L Majtényi and G Polyák, 'A Szabadság Hazai Hagyományának Megtagadása—Új Médiatörvények Magyarországon' (2011) 1 *Közjogi Szemle* 1.

7 Decision 37/1992 (VI.10) AB határozat (Constitutional Court of Hungary).

8 The most important Decisions: ibid; 47/1994 (X.21) AB határozat (Constitutional Court of Hungary); 61/1995 (X.6) AB határozat (Constitutional Court of Hungary); 22/1999 (VI.30) AB határozat (Constitutional Court of Hungary); 1006/B/2001 AB határozat (Constitutional Court of Hungary); 766/B/2002 AB határozat (Constitutional Court of Hungary); 1/2005 (II.4) AB határozat (Constitutional Court of Hungary); 46/2007 (VI.27) AB határozat (Constitutional Court of Hungary); 37/2008 (V.8) AB határozat (Constitutional Court of Hungary); 165/2011 (XII.20) AB határozat (Constitutional Court of Hungary). There are significantly more decisions dealing with the general issues of the freedom of expression, from hate speech to the protection of public figures and the regulation of election campaigning.

9 Decision 46/2007 (VI.27) AB határozat (Constitutional Court of Hungary).

10 Decision 37/2008 (V.8) AB határozat (Constitutional Court of Hungary).

11 Decision 165/2011 (XII.20) AB határozat (Constitutional Court of Hungary).

(i) Development of a Pluralistic Media System

The fundamental purpose of media regulation in Hungarian constitutional practice, as well as in the practice of international and national authorities protecting fundamental rights, is the development of a pluralistic media system.

The constitutional role of the media is defined by the constitutional standard of democratic public opinion. The Constitutional Court stated that the freedom of the media 'serves the constitutional right of expression' by 'magnifying the effect of individual expression of opinion and supporting the information of the democratic public opinion about public affairs and the expression of opinion about public affairs'.[12] Later it explained that 'by exercising the right to freedom of the press the individual retaining fundamental rights is an active former of democratic public opinion', while its 'public watchdog role' facilitates 'the disclosure of statements vital for individual expression of opinion, complete public information and the prevention of the emergence of a "correct official view" based on monopolistic public opinion'.[13]

Regarding media regulation, it follows that in its interpretation of freedom of expression the Constitutional Court has stated that 'the right of information essential for the expression of opinion is believed to be a limit to the freedom of the press but only to a necessarily small extent'.[14] The interpretation of the 'necessary extent' is helped by the most significant but not consistently applied constitutional statement regarding freedom of expression, according to which freedom of expression 'protects free expression of opinion regardless of its value and truth content'.[15] Consequently, democratic public opinion cannot merely be the summary of valuable or correct points of view. In public discourse 'there is a place for all kinds of points of view whether good or harmful, pleasant or offensive especially because the classification of opinions is in itself the product of this very process'.[16]

Consequently, democratic public opinion can be subject only to a kind of restriction that still makes it possible to disclose all the relevant information and points of view. Ultimately the Hungarian Constitutional Court formulated the obligation of the state as to develop a pluralistic media system via the concept of democratic public opinion, which is widely known in foreign and international fundamental rights courts.[17] Democratic public opinion does not, in addition, mean an expectation of the quality of the public sphere and if the legislature intends to exclude particular information from this public sphere to protect certain other fundamental rights or constitutional values, then it has to find a different constitutional basis.

[12] Decision 37/1992 (VI.10) AB határozat (Constitutional Court of Hungary).
[13] Decision 165/2011 (XII.20) AB határozat (Constitutional Court of Hungary).
[14] Decision 37/1992 (VI.10) AB határozat (Constitutional Court of Hungary).
[15] Decision 30/1992 (V.26) AB határozat (Constitutional Court of Hungary).
[16] ibid.
[17] See generally G Polyák, 'Pluralizmus és Médiaszabályozás' (2009) 5 *Jogtudományi Közlöny* 208.

On the other hand, it is controversial that the Constitutional Court's interpretation concerning the new media laws imposed the following restriction:

> by definition, any media content denying the institutional and basic values connected to the fundamental rights of democracy is excluded from the development and implementation of democratic public opinion.

Instead of the former content-neutral approach, this particular interpretation at least opens up the way to a democratic public opinion being defined as raising expectations of quality and precluding certain information based on their content. This interpretation would make restrictions imposed on freedom of the press futile and it would serve as a basis for interventions in the operation of the media that would not be justified either by the protection of individual or community interests or the demand for varied information.[18]

(ii) Independence of Media Supervisory Bodies

The implementation of freedom of expression is significantly influenced by decisions about entering the market, sanctions and the accountability for public service remedy. The independence of institutions accountable for these decisions, such as media authorities and media supervisory bodies, is an essential condition for freedom of the media. The independence of media authorities appeared as a community legislation requirement in the Committee Proposal for the Modification of the Community Television Directive.[19] Ultimately, however, the relevant Directive refers to the politically sensitive requirement in the Preamble,[20] and includes an indirect reference to this.[21] Similarly, the Hungarian Constitution requires radio and television broadcasting to be independent from the state and certain social groups. These cannot be entitled to make broadcasting one-sided or exercise considerable influence upon its content. This restriction includes indirect influence and the possibility of influence as well.

As early as 1992, the Constitutional Court laid out the concept and essence of independence according to which regulations 'must exclude the possibility that any state organization or social group could influence the content of programmes in a way that compromises the integrity and presentation of existing opinions

[18] See for this interpretation A Koltay and G Polyák 'Az Alkotmánybíróság Határozata a Médiaszabályozás Egyes Kérdéseiről' (2012) 1 *Jogesetek Magyarázata* 11.

[19] According to the proposed art 23b 'member states guarantee the independence of national regulatory authorities and ensure that these authorities operate within their scope in an impartial and transparent way'.

[20] European Council and Parliament Directive 2007/65/EC of 11 December 2007 amending Council Directive 89/552/EEC on the coordination of certain provisions laid down by law, regulation or administrative action in Member States concerning the pursuit of television broadcasting activities [2007] OJ L332, Preamble, para 65.

[21] ibid art 23b: 'Member states take measures to—especially through their independent competent regulatory authorities—provide the Committee with all the information necessary for this particular directive regarding in particular article 2, 2a and 3'.

in the society, the balance of their proportions, their realistic expression and impartial information'.[22] It was emphasised that 'it is foreign to a special representative body guaranteeing the freedom of expression to have an exclusive or decisive political representation of the society in them'. The consensus of political parties, much less the consensus of parliamentary parties, does not guarantee the integrity of freedom of expression.

In its later practice the Constitutional Court found formal legislative guarantees of independence sufficient and it did not evaluate the possibility of informal influence. In a 2007 decision,[23] the Constitutional Court considered the guarantee of independence to be found primarily in the regulation on operation exclusively subordinate to the law, in the absence of instruction and repeal, in rules of incompatibility, in the mandate of bodies separate from the parliamentary term and in the possibility for a court revision regarding the decisions of the media authority. Consequently, it stated that legislative provisions are, in theory, capable of ensuring the independence of the members of the National Radio and Television Commission and ruled out the possibility for parliamentary parties to exert formally their influence.[24]

Regarding the new media law, the Constitutional Court has not examined issues about the independence of the new media authority and the public service institution system even though the European Council, the OSCE, the UN expert on press freedom and several international NGOs objected to the politically one-sided composition and the substantially broad scope of the media authority.

(iii) Indispensable Public Service Broadcasting

The Constitutional Court has assigned particularly strong constitutional positions to public service, a vital element of the Hungarian media system. The Constitutional Court stated[25] that 'providing fundamental constitutional rights to learn of public interest data makes it the constitutional obligation of the state to facilitate a smooth public service and news service operation',[26] including the obligation to provide full and proportionally balanced and accurate information in accordance with the principles of internal pluralism.[27]

[22] Decision 37/1992 (VI.20) AB Határozat (Constitutional Court).

[23] Decision 22/1999 (VI.30) AB Határozat (Constitutional Court).

[24] In ibid, the Court emphasised that political representation cannot be decisive regarding the supervision of public service media. At the same time, it failed to examine the necessity of validating civil, professional, etc, interests by way of the media authority.

[25] ibid.

[26] This argument is not in line with the widely accepted interpretation of the accessibility of public interest data. According to the Constitutional Court, gaining information about public interest is 'an open, transparent and controllable public authority task, as a rule before state bodies and executive power' and as a guarantee it is an independent fundamental right which everyone is entitled to retain. Freedom of information is not the privilege of journalists and especially not of public service media.

[27] Decision 37/1992 (VI.10) AB határozat (Constitutional Court of Hungary).

The Constitutional Court has examined the financial and organisational conditions of independent public service media in several of its decisions. Concerning institutional independence it confirmed that the law must exclude the possibility that either state institutions or certain groups of the society could exert a decisive influence on the content of programmes on public service radio and television, while these institutions and groups cannot be licensed to make a broadcasting offer that is one-sided.[28] In its later decisions it was satisfied with 'the balance between the representatives of government and opposition groups' that 'could prevent representative groups from being predominant on either side of the Parliament'.[29] Ultimately, however, the Constitutional Court believed that 'the establishment of the one-sided supervisory body of public service broadcasting poses a "less serious constitutional threat" against the freedom of expression than the non-functional public service media advisory boards in the absence of the presidency'.[30]

Regarding financing, there is no decision that specifically states that in order to enable the media to perform public service tasks the state is obliged to provide suitable financial sources, while the Constitutional Court has not stated that sustainment of public service broadcasting is a state function as to which the provision of the required funds (including the determination of taxes) as well as their allocation are public authority functions deriving from the Constitution and other legislation.[31] Nevertheless, the Constitutional Court has stated that every resolution that authorises the government to perform tasks requiring funds beyond the fulfilment of public service duties compromises the financial independence of public service broadcasting.[32]

(iv) Stricter Regulation of Media Content

It has been a particular characteristic of the Hungarian media regulation since 1996, that regarding media content it imposes stricter requirements than the provisions in civil and criminal law, the Privacy Act, etc, while providing that it must not compromise freedom of expression. The most significant but most of all disconcerting current feature of the 2010 media laws was the extension of legal restrictions on public communications, which affected every on-demand print and online medium.

In the case of printed and online media, the Constitutional Court limited the effectiveness of imposing media law sanctions as a result of its examination of the new media law. However, relating to these media, it did not find media

[28] ibid.

[29] Decision 22/1999 (VI.30) AB határozat (Constitutional Court of Hungary). This was complemented by an expectation according to which 'the number of presidency members elected by the Parliament cannot exceed the number of curators delegated by non-governmental organizations'.

[30] ibid.

[31] Decision 1/2005 (II.4) AB határozat (Constitutional Court of Hungary).

[32] Decision 47/1994 (X.21) AB határozat (Constitutional Court of Hungary).

law sanctions and the possibility of using media authority sanctions inherently against the Constitution.

One example of media law restrictions beyond the general provisions of the legal system is the regulation of hate speech. Both the previous and the current media law facilitates imposition of media law sanctions against media contents inciting hatred, and the Constitutional Court found two reasons to support this point of view. Media law sanctions are less severe than those of criminal law; therefore, they can be used even in cases when a criminal law restriction would qualify as disproportionate. Furthermore, as the Constitutional Court stated it, 'compared to other manifestations of the freedom of speech, opinions voiced in the media have a cumulative effect and have a powerful influence over what the people think and the formation of public opinion'.[33]

In 2007, the Constitutional Court approved the power of the media authority according to which it is entitled to use a kind of abstract procedure relating to personality protection rights, stating that the media authority is entitled to 'decide whether the operation of the broadcaster respects human rights and whether the subject, style and point of view of its particular programmes harm fundamental values present in human rights'.[34]

However, the extension of this particular power relating to printed and online media was considered unconstitutional by the Constitutional Court in 2011, stating that 'proceedings instituted by a public authority in the interest of the viewers and listeners qualifies as a necessary and proportionate procedure with regard to a particularly significant influence over the public', 'in the case of printed and online media, dissimilar in their effects, the possibility for such action ... qualifies as a disproportionate restriction'.[35] Ultimately, it is the presumed effect of the media that determines the limits of the intervention in this case as well.

II. RISKS INVOLVED IN THE APPLICATION OF MEDIA REGULATION AND THE FREEDOM OF THE MEDIA

Two years after the adoption of the new media laws, it is often stated that criticism of the laws has proved unjustified; the Media Council did not search editorial offices and did not impose fines on journals, while criticism of the government did not diminish. This, however, is nothing more than the minimum level of freedom of the press. The real risk of the adoption of the laws was not that the media authority might make the operation of the media impossible by imposing huge fines. It was rather that editorial offices might adapt and make compromises to avoid conflicts relating to the regulation or the authority, and that themedia policy might aim to manipulate the less politically active and less politically conscious

[33] Decision 1006/B/2001 AB határozat (Constitutional Court of Hungary).

[34] Decision 1/2007 (I.18) AB határozat (Constitutional Court of Hungary).

[35] Decision 165/2011 (XII.20) AB határozat (Constitutional Court of Hungary).

media consumers of the public with one-sided information. Most of these risks have indeed been realised.

A. Restrictions on Media Content and the Chilling Effect

Since the adoption of the 2010 laws, the most contested rules have been modified according to the expectations of the European Commission and the Constitutional Court. Perhaps due to the intense international attention paid to the regulation, the practice of the media authority has proved to be moderate, although in many cases inconsistent. On the other hand, it is important to mention that the laws passed in 2010 have not been considerably changed as to their concept and the regulatory pressure exerted on editorial offices.

(i) Necessity and Proportionality of Media Law Regulation

The most significant result of the decision of the Constitutional Court regarding the new media laws was the reduction of the scope of media content regulations that are to be applied to the non-audio-visual media as well. However, the Constitutional Court 'did not categorically exclude the possibility of a regulation which is content based or might induce state action in the case of printed press media either' and it stated that 'a retrospective, systematic and ex officio control and the possibility of sanctioning means, without doubt, a restriction on the freedom of the press but the mere possibility—along with an efficient and substantive judiciary control as a guarantee—cannot be considered unconstitutional'.[36]

In its decision regarding the proportionality of media law restrictions, however, it failed to consider that media law sanctioning relating to the protection of particular rights and values was merely one of its instruments. Parallel proceedings and sanctions that can be simultaneously imposed in particular proceedings impose a considerable additional restraint on the freedom of expression.[37]

The Constitutional Court also did not examine the possible extent and character of the media law sanctions. Sanctions that can be used against products of the press and the prospective fines are still factors capable of making the operation of a certain press product impossible.[38] The severity of the sanction is influenced

[36] ibid.

[37] In its Decision 57/2001 (XII.5) AB határozat (Constitutional Court of Hungary), the Constitutional Court referred to the disproportionality of the combined effects of the particular restrictions in connection with freedom of expression itself.

[38] The most serious sanction against daily newspapers and online press products is a fine in the amount of HUF 25 million. An audio-visual service provider can be punished by the withdrawal of its licence; the highest amount of the fine against these providers is HUF 200 million in the case of a broadcaster with significant powers of influence, and HUF 50 million in other cases. Act CLXXXV of 2010 (2010. évi CLXXXV. törvény a médiaszolgáltatásokról és a tömegkommunikációról) (Mttv), paras 185–87.

by other conditions too. The laws include weak guarantees, such as the principles of gradualism and proportionality, but the detailed rules are, in several points, unfinished and unrefined. The Media Council introduced a practice according to which it strictly applies the principle of gradualism so that it imposes the mildest sanction against every media service provider the first time, while it has largely ignored other aspects of sanctioning, especially the seriousness of the infringement.

As the law defines neither the concept of periodicals nor that of online papers or news portals, and in spite of the modifications having been carried out since the adoption of the law, it does not clarify the extent of the scope of media regulation—the requirements of clarity of norms are not met. Although the Constitutional Court stated that 'private communication, web pages, blogs, community sites, etc, cannot be managed together with online journals and news portals serving to inform or entertain the public', it did not examine, by taking the aspects of the application of the law into consideration, whether the effective provision complies with the conditions laid down by the determination of the subject of the regulation. The Constitutional Court has also failed to examine whether the institutional framework regulating implementation guarantees that all operators of the media system are assessed according to the same aspects when their behaviour is appraised. The political and economic independence of the media authority responsible for the implementation is a fundamental guarantee of the imposition of the same media law requirements on all the operators of the media system and that infringement of regulations is followed by the same sanctions without discrimination.

The combined chilling effect of the above-mentioned factors can still lead to the disappearance of certain subjects or critical voices, in the form of self-censorship, even if the reasonableness of each and every proceeding could be justified. This chilling effect is entirely independent from the question of whether the media authority will ever impose the media law sanctions or not.[39]

(ii) Media Content Regulations Applicable to All Media

Constitutional order, according to the Constitutional Court, is disrupted by 'press products circulating and identifying with notions which ignore democratic order, the enforcement of human rights and human dignity which forms the basis of constitutional order'.[40] A previous decision considered the application of the provision only under certain 'special circumstances' considered acceptable; 'an

[39] It poses a serious danger especially in a social environment where 36 per cent of journalists believe that there is an enormous, and 44 per cent believe there is a considerable, political pressure on the media and where 22 per cent of journalists have already withheld or distorted political or economic facts in order to avoid some disadvantageous consequences. See 'Press Freedom Index 2012', *Mérték Media Monitor*, available at www.mertek.eu/en/reports/press-freedom-index-2012.

[40] Decision 165/2011 (XII.20) AB határozat (Constitutional Court of Hungary).

example of which would be a case if a broadcaster operated continuously by advertising an ideology which ignores equal human dignity forming the basis of constitutional order'.[41] These messages would not fail to have legal consequences and the extreme cases outlined by the Constitutional Court would encounter criminal law barriers as well.[42]

As described above, the Constitutional Court did not find either the sanctioning of incitement to hatred by the media law or its extension to printed and online media unconstitutional. The effective text of the law prohibits incitement to hatred against and the disassociation of any social groups, whether majority or minority. The provision has previously been modified according to the expectations of the European Commission: the prohibition of open or implied offence of social groups has been removed. After the decision of the Constitutional Court, the law was amended by the legislature, making it clear that apart from offences against any member of a group, it does not extend to any offence given to individuals.

The interpretation of the Constitutional Court as regards the prohibition of incitement to hatred by the media law has changed. In a previous decision, the extension of this prohibition to a wider range of communications was considered acceptable, such as the prohibition of hate speech in criminal law. According to the new decision, however, the scope of the application of the prohibition by the media law is exactly the same as that of the criminal law regarding the incitement to hatred. This regulation considerably restricts the application of the provision by the media law[43] which, from the point of view of the freedom of the press, is, beyond doubt, a favourable interpretation. On the other hand, in case of parallel proceedings at the criminal court and the media authority regarding the assessment of the same behaviour, different conclusions might be reached, undermining legal certainty.[44]

Surprisingly, criticism of the practice of the authority has been directed against the lack of intervention by the authority in certain cases. The Media Council has

[41] Decision 46/2007 (VI.27) AB határozat (Constitutional Court of Hungary).

[42] The application to such cases of media law views by the media authority did not take place in either the previous or the current regulatory environments.

[43] According to the consequent interpretation of the Constitutional Court, criminal law sanctions against hate speech can be applied in the case of 'clear and present danger'. In its Decision 30/1992 (V.26) AB határozat (Constitutional Court of Hungary), the Constitutional Court stated: 'The disturbance of the social order and peace—or public peace, to use the Criminal Code terminology—also contains the danger of a large-scale violation of individual rights: emotions whipped-up against a group threaten the honour and dignity (and in more extreme cases, also the lives) of the individuals comprising the group, and by intimidation restrict them in the exercise of their other rights as well (including the right to the freedom of expression) … Although the actual outcome of the examination is the same, this reasoning considers not only the intensity of the disruption of public peace which—above and beyond a certain threshold (clear and present danger)—justifies the restriction of the right to the freedom of expression'. The Court in its Decision 165/2011 (XII.20) AB határozatmade it unambiguous that these standards are also applicable to media law.

[44] At present, there is no experience available regarding the practical consequences of the constitutional decision.

ruled against media contents inciting hatred in four cases altogether,[45] three of which were related to incitement of hatred against the Roma minority. The Media Council did not find it reasonable to impose a sanction against a programme on public service television featuring the gypsy community in a negative way, which sparked off a heated debate. The Commissioner for Fundamental Rights, who also examined the programme, did not find the decision of the Media Council reasonable and called on the authority to act 'with increased professional care' in the future.

(iii) Regulations concerning Audio-visual Media Services

Extending the scope of media regulation to printed and online media products does not, of course, created an undifferentiated regulation. The legislature continues to impose the heaviest regulatory burden on linear media services, namely, radio and television content services. The Constitutional Court has contributed to a further differentiation of the regulation.[46]

A frequently criticised element of the laws is concerning the obligation to provide balanced, unbiased information.[47] This obligation was also originally extended to on-demand media services by the legislature, on the recommendation of the European Commission, but without consideration of the difficulties of implementation; however, its application was limited to radio and television media services. This obligation, in a similar form, was part of the previous media law as well. The extension of the regulation is still a cause for concern. The Constitutional Court stated in its justification of a decision in 2007 that balanced and unbiased information can exclusively be required from public service channels, radio and television companies, as to which the 'power of opinion formation becomes significant'.[48]

According to the media laws, linear media services engaged in the pursuit of information activities are required to ensure that the newscast and news programmes they provide concerning local and national events of interest to the public, as well as European events and public debates that are of interest to the people of Hungary and to members of the Hungarian nation, are diverse, factual, timely, objective and balanced. Among the rules concerning media content, regulations relating to service providers with so-called significant powers of influence must be highlighted as good examples of establishing differentiated regulations and taking economic reality into consideration.[49] Having an annual 15 per cent

[45] 'Content Regulation in the Practice of the Media Council', *Mérték Media Monitor* (2012), available at www.mertek.eu/en/reports/content-regulation-in-the-practice-of-the-media-council.

[46] The differentiation applied by the different Constitutional Court decisions regarding human rights infringement was already introduced above.

[47] Act CIV of 2010 (2010. évi CIV. törvény a sajtószabadságról és a médiatartalmak alapvető szabályairól), para 13; Mttv (n 38) paras 12, 181.

[48] Decision 1/2007 (I.18) AB határozat (Constitutional Court of Hungary).

[49] Mttv (n 38) para38.

average viewer rating qualifies a media service provider as one with significant powers of influence, provided that at least one of its media services reaches an annual 3 per cent viewer rating; in the domestic media market, only national commercial television and radio broadcasters are likely to meet this criterion. The imposition of content obligations based on viewer ratings is, without doubt, a more proportionate and effective regulatory solution compared to obligations based on the area of transmission required by the previous law. The law stipulates three obligations concerning media service providers with significant powers of influence: they are required to broadcast news programmes, broadcast a specified proportion of cinematographic works in their original language with Hungarian subtitles, and provide subtitles or sign language interpretation for a gradually increasing proportion of programmes. Compared to the previous regulation, this places a significantly smaller and more realistic burden on commercial television broadcasters.

On the other hand, the imposition of the obligation to broadcast newscasts poses serious legal interpretational problems. According to the law, news content or reporting on crime not serving to provide information for the public cannot be longer in duration on an annual average than 20 per cent of the duration of the news programme. After the introduction of this restriction the proportion of crime reports in commercial television newscasts decreased but at the same time the proportion of reports on accidents increased. In spite of the intention of limiting tabloid news (in line, however, with media policy endeavours to restructure the media system discussed below), the proportion of public news has decreased in the newscasts of commercial television since the adoption of the laws; this reveals the failure of the regulation.[50]

(iv) Co-regulation

The media law has established a specific co-regulation system as an alternative to official control. Except in the case of television and radio media services, the law made it possible for the operators of the media market to implement the regulations concerning media content within the framework of self-regulatory bodies with an exclusive legal power.[51] According to the law, the Media Council has the authority to conclude administrative agreements with the self-regulatory bodies. Based on the agreement, the self-regulatory body performs specific tasks related to the scope of official authority, media administration and media policy. The official scope of the self-regulatory bodies extends to assessment of complaints concerning the activities of the service providers, settlement of debates between media enterprises and supervision of the operation of the service providers. The procedure on the part of the self-regulatory body has priority over the administra-

[50] Mérték Media Monitor, 'Content Regulation' (n 45).

[51] Mttv (n 38) paras 190–202/A.

tive procedure of the Media Council. The law emphasises that the self-regulatory body does not have administrative authority.

Since summer 2011, four organisations have been part of the established co-regulation system, including the Hungarian Publishers Association, the Association of Hungarian Content Providers, the Association of Hungarian Electronic Broadcasters and the Advertising Self-Regulatory Board.[52]

Part of the administrative agreement is a professional Code of Conduct devised by the self-regulatory body, the adoption of which requires the approval of the Media Council. These would have been the most significant result of the co-regulation system if the Codes had elaborated on legal facts in a more detailed and clear way, making them easier to interpret during the course of editorial work. In essence, media law views and facts have been adopted by the Codes without modification and with some minor supplements. Thus, the law has an ambiguous content; its directly restrictive provisions affecting freedom of expression are being interpreted by lay dispute resolution forums. Real self-regulation is not realised in the system; it could more accurately be interpreted as the outsourcing of official administrative tasks.

Issues concerning regulation of procedures, including what sanctions can be imposed and how these are to be executed, are entrusted to the self-regulatory bodies by the law without defining the guarantee framework. This is worrying because in practice the Codes regard the rights of the complainant as defined according to the law; in fact they even restrict those who were excluded from establishment and implementation of the Codes. The complainant is obliged to contact the media service provider within a specified period of time and confer with them. After an unsuccessful attempt at conferring with the service provider a written petition must be submitted in compliance with strict content conditions and accompanied by a fee for the procedure; this is not implied by the law itself. The most significant advantage of co-regulation for the providers is that the co-regulatory bodies do not apply fines against their members. The most substantial sanction that can be imposed according to the Codes is exclusion from the co-regulation system for a specific period of time. Further sanctions serve to ascertain, stop and publicise norm violation and to provide moral reparation. However, the Codes do not include provisions for implementation of decisions made within the framework of the co-regulation system at all.

According to the law, the Media Council is obliged to review all the decisions of the self-regulatory body. The authority also acts as a forum for legal remedies; if any of the parties requests revision of the decision, the Media Council is obliged to review such decision within 30 days. If the Media Council finds that the decision of the self-regulatory body does not comply with the administrative agreement concluded with the self-regulatory body, in particular with the provisions of the Code of Conduct, or that it violates the provisions of the relevant legislation, or if

[52] For a summary see www.mediajogfigyelo.hu/index.php?do=a&id=1575.

the self-regulatory body is unable to enforce its decision, the Media Council must establish a procedure concerning the subject of the petition. This opens up the possibility of judicial review as well. On the other hand, because of the ambiguous content of media law facts and the possibility of a wide range of interpretation, the Media Council has a rather broad scope of revisionary authority. Furthermore, the Media Council has the authority to oversee all activities performed by the self-regulatory body under the administrative agreement, supervise procedures and decisions extensively and, as a last resort, terminate the administrative agreement.

The co-regulation system established in the media law is not in line with certain important European expectations regarding co-regulation systems.[53] One of the most significant concerns relating to financial independence is that the Media Council provides the co-regulatory bodies with financial support, which is not in accordance with the principles of the media law, while at the same time including it in the administrative agreement. Independence from market operators is threatened by the fact that experts acting in the course of complaints procedures are exclusively delegated by the enterprises concerned, who in the majority of the cases have a permanent legal relationship with the particular establishment. Although this does not endanger the impartiality of the particular procedures, since there are appropriate rules for avoidance of conflicts of interests concerning the acting committees, the process is clearly dominated by the views and interests of the service providers.

There have been only a few complaints procedures so far. This is probably partly because of the procedural difficulties, although it is more likely to be caused by the low level of awareness of the co-regulation system. The co-regulation system undoubtedly places a less severe restriction on freedom of the press than the control of the authorities. In its present form, however, it ignores all voluntary initiatives and is not more than an alternative sanctioning system that service providers apply to themselves. Joining the co-regulation system is, in itself, a difficult compromise on the part of the editorial offices. By joining the co-regulation system, they accept and conform to the strict rules concerning media content so as not be forced to pay substantial fees stipulated by the law. This is how co-regulation becomes a spectacular expression of self-censorship. Furthermore, not every service in question participates in co-regulation and the current low number of complaints does not guarantee that they will not increase.

B. Structural Transformation of the Media System

The most severe and longest-lasting damage to democratic journalism is caused by structural interventions that follow from the letter of the law only in part,

[53] See especially European Commission, *European Governance: A White Paper*, COM(2001)428 final.

many of them implemented through informal measures of media policy. The latter type of intervention has led to the dramatic market expansion of media businesses nurturing close ties with the main ruling party Fidesz, including their attempts, so far frustrated by the market itself on two separate occasions, to take over part or all of the nationwide commercial television stations, as well as the successful buy-out of the free daily with the largest circulation in the country.

Among the various regulatory tools serving to restructure the media system and threatening the pluralism of media selection on offer, we will single out the transformation of the institutional system supervising the media, along with the means of regulating the media market, and recent experiences with their application.

(i) *Institutional Threats to Pluralism*

(a) Independence of the Media Council

The independence of the media authority is a cardinal point of Hungarian media regulation. A politically lopsided media authority, like the one ushered in by the new provisions, presents a serious threat to the pluralism of the media system, notwithstanding any other safeguards as may be set forth by law. Considering that 'pluralism' is not something that can be precisely defined and enshrined as a requirement in the abstract, as to which entities could be held accountable, it is inevitably predicated on the condition that the institutions supervising commercial and public service media themselves be sufficiently pluralistic and autonomous in making their decisions.[54] Hungary's media laws fail to create adequate safeguards for a pluralistic and autonomous oversight of either the commercial or public service media.

The rules governing the election of the President and members of the Media Council, an authority vested with broad regulatory powers, are incapable of barring one-sided political influence from decisions concerning media market management and control over media content. The Media Council is part of the National Media and Info-communications Authority (NMHH) but is vested with autonomous discretionary powers within that authority. NMHH is a convergent communications authority responsible for both telecommunications and media. According to the original rules of the Media Act, the NMHH's President, who was appointed by the Prime Minister, became automatically nominated for the office of chairperson of the Media Council at the time of appointment.[55] In fact, these rules locked in the majority of ruling-party delegates to the media authority.

[54] KH Ladeur, 'Einspeisung digitaler Fernsehprogramme—Zur Rechtsstellung von Kabelnetzbetreiber und Programmveranstalter: Zugleich ein Beitrag Verhältnis von Medien—und Telekommunikationsrecht unter Multimediabedingungen' (2001) 10 *Kommunikation und Recht* 496.

[55] Mttv (n 38) para 125(1). Because the two posts are indeed filled by one and the same person, for the sake of simplicity hereafter we will refer to both as 'President', whether the President of the media authority or the chairperson of the Media Council is meant.

Direct instruction is not the only form of this unilateral influence, which can be exercised, as the Constitutional Court has suggested, 'by any means at will'.[56] For instance, indirect influence can be accomplished if the mechanism for nominating and electing members fails to guarantee participation in the Media Council by social groups and political forces other than the ruling parties.

The four members of the Media Council are nominated by an ad hoc parliamentary committee[57] composed of members with a voting power commensurable with the number of members in the respective parliamentary faction that elected them in turn. In the first round, members are nominated to the Media Council by a unanimous vote of the nominations committee. If a unanimous decision is unavailable, candidates are nominated by a two-thirds majority of the weighted votes in the second round. The President of the Media Council was originally nominated by the Prime Minister.[58] The members and the President were elected by a two-thirds majority of Parliament.

This goes to show that, whenever the ruling parties hold a two-thirds majority in Parliament, which is the case at present, the nomination and election of members to the Media Council can be accomplished without any contribution by the political opposition or any other social group. A two-thirds majority in Parliament is obviously an exception to the general rule,[59] however, the media laws were passed by the same parliamentary majority that became the beneficiary of its application.[60] Yet even if Parliament succeeded in agreeing on nominees by a unanimous vote, the fact should be borne in mind that the Media Council always remains free to make its own discretionary decisions by a simple majority.[61] For all intents and purposes, no nomination procedure is conceivable today without the ruling parties nominating at least two out of the four members. Together with the President of the Media Council, who is nominated by the Prime Minister, ruling-party delegates are guaranteed to hold a majority. This represents a major setback compared to the former regulations, which ensured the right of each parliamentary faction to independently nominate a member, while the votes by the members of the authority were always distributed evenly among ruling-party and

[56] Decision 37/1992 (VI.10) AB határozat (Constitutional Court of Hungary).

[57] Mttv (n 38) para 124.

[58] ibid para 125.

[59] In the specific case at hand, there was very little chance that the four members of the nominations committee, delegated by five parties in Parliament, would be able to agree on nominations by a unanimous vote. As expected, the ruling party went on to support exclusively its own nominees in the second round, who were then duly voted into office by the same two-thirds majority. Another example of abusing the two-thirds majority is the provision which, whenever Parliament fails to elect a new President to the helm of the Media Council, automatically extends the mandate of the incumbent President until such time as a new President is elected. Mttv (n 38) para 216(8).

[60] The European Council has more than once pointed out that the stipulation of the two-thirds majority vote in itself is insufficient to ensure that the freedom of the media will be upheld, either in the enactment of media laws or in the process of electing members to the relevant bodies. Instead, the European Council recommends that Hungary develop solutions that presuppose a genuine cooperation and consensus between the ruling parties and the opposition.

[61] Mttv (n 38) para 144(4).

opposition nominees, regardless of the number of the members. The President of the predecessor authority would be nominated jointly by the Prime Minister and the President of the Republic. This arrangement alone meant a more solid protection of autonomy, not to mention the fact that the President did not previously have a voting right on the most important matters pertaining to market entry.

Another reason why the nomination of the President of the Media Council by the Prime Minister is a cause for concern has to do with the rather broad scope of powers which are vested in the President. Being single-handedly in charge of appointing and relieving of duty, without explanation, the organisation of the Media Council and the executive director of the Media Support and Asset Management Fund (MTVA), the President holds direct sway over the entire process of preparing decisions.[62]

Equally problematic from the point of view of media freedom is the nine-year term for which members of the media supervisory agencies are appointed. The constitutional mission of these agencies is to represent social diversity in their decisions pertaining to the media. Social diversity, however, is not a static fact but a dynamic attribute in constant flux. The excessively long term of appointment increases the risk of perpetuating in media-related decisions a momentary stratification of society that will not reflect actual conditions of diversity in the more distant future.

All these practical concerns could hardly be dispelled by formal safeguards.[63] Even if the Constitutional Court's pertinent opinion, as quoted above, cannot be controverted in academic terms, it can be said with certainty that a solution must exist allowing nomination and election of council members in such a way as to remove them out of reach of any political party affiliation.[64]

In March 2013, the Parliament modified the rules on nominating the NMHH's President. The objective of the March amendment was to enshrine into law the terms of the agreement between the Council of Europe and the Hungarian government. The said agreement aimed to bring some critical aspects of the Hungarian media laws in line with the expectations of the Council of Europe. A crucial element of the agreement and the resulting March amendment was the adoption of more rigorous professional selection criteria vis-à-vis potential candidates for the NMHH presidency. The amendment, which had been drafted in consultation with the Council of Europe, formulated strict criteria regarding the authority's President. In addition to a higher education degree in either law, economics or the social sciences, a candidate must also have at least five years of experience 'connected to the public oversight of media services or press products

[62] ibid para 115.

[63] ibid 123.

[64] For example, extending the right of nomination to more organisations could be instrumental in reducing the direct influence of Parliament and the government on media content, as proposed by the expertise of the European Council. See E Salomon and J Barata, *Council of Europe Experts on Hungarian Media Legislation: Act CIV of 2010 on the Freedom of the Press and the Fundamental Rules on Media Content and Act CLXXXV of 2010 on Media Services and Mass Media* (Strasburg, 11 May 2012).

or the public oversight of info-communications', or, alternatively, must have a scientific degree related to media or info-communications and at least ten years of experience in higher education.

In July 2013, the Hungarian Parliament again adopted an amendment of the rules for nominating and appointing the President of the NMHH. The amendment softened the professional criteria applicable to the selection of the NMHH's President. This has significantly expanded the range of potential candidates.

(b) Public Service Broadcasting

One of the most obvious fiascos of recent media regulation in Hungary has been the transformation of the public service system. Despite massive increases in funding, public service media are losing audiences rapidly, and routinely feature in reports on news doctoring, severely prejudiced journalistic practices, mass lay-offs based on non-transparent criteria, internal power struggles and attempts to thwart demonstrations protesting abuses in the public service media. In this chapter, we will confine ourselves to identifying some of the structural and institutional problems that have directly contributed to the disfunctionality of public service media in Hungary.

The laws assign the task of providing public media services to four private limited companies, all of them owned exclusively by the Public Service Foundation and supervised by its Board of Trustees (Board). At present, the Board is the only body within the system of media supervision that has one member delegated by the opposition. Also elected for a term of nine years under the law, half of the members are delegated by the ruling parties, and half by factions of the opposition. They are elected by a two-thirds majority vote of Parliament.[65] However, even in this body, majority is guaranteed for the ruling parties, since another two members and the chair are delegated by the Media Council.

The Board is vested with general regulatory powers in connection with public service provision and management, most notably including the appointment of executive directors of the public media service providers.[66] Here we have another procedure that is left wide open to political influence. The executive directors and the terms of their future employment contracts are proposed by the President of the Media Council for approval by the Media Council. The provision on the selection process makes no mention of application, professional qualifications or presentation of a professional concept. In the next step, the Board decides between the candidates by a two-thirds majority vote in the first round and, in the event of an unsuccessful first round, by a simple majority in a second round—which is to say, relying on the votes of members delegated by the ruling party and the Media Council.

[65] Mttv (n 38) para 86.
[66] ibid para 102.

The key entity in the entire system of public service institutions is the Media Service Support and Asset Management Fund ('the Fund'). Pursuant to the Media Act, the Fund exercises all ownership rights and obligations associated with public service media assets, including the production and support of public service programmes.[67] What this means in practice is that all the assets and the majority of the employees of public media service providers have been transferred to the Fund. With no independent capacities of their own, the providers are essentially confined to placing orders with the Fund for certain programmes. The Fund is headed by an executive director appointed and relieved from office without explanation by the President of the Media Council. This executive director does not report to the Board or to any other external body.[68] Even the members of the Fund's Supervisory Board are appointed by the President of the Media Council.

The Media Council's already massive influence on public service is aggravated by the fact that it is solely authorised to adopt the so-called Public Service Code ('the Code'),[69] which sets forth the basic principles of public service media provision and fine-tunes the public service objectives established by the Media Act. In practice, however, this document serves as a sort of ethical code rather than providing an in-depth definition of the law's generic public service objectives in the form of specific tasks for which providers could be held accountable. The Code is revised and compliance therewith monitored by the Public Service Board (PSB), which comprises members delegated by organisations defined by the Media Act.[70] Even though the PSB is supposed to implement broad-based social control, journalists and human rights organisations are absent from the list of entities delegating members to it. The Media Act authorises the body to propose that the executive director be removed from office if it refuses to accept his/her annual report. The law fails to articulate the criteria for making such a proposal, while the PSB does not possess the professional competence to make such a judgement.

The failure of the Code to spell out specific public service tasks, the performance of which could be enforced in practice, should impart special significance to the Public Service Fiscal Council, the last entity of the institutional system.[71] It is this body that makes decisions on how to allocate the available funds among the various public media service providers. The amount of the total budget is determined by the Media Act itself. The job of the Fiscal Council is to make sure that the financing is tailored to public service responsibilities as expected by the European state aid law. Under the circumstances, it seems rather odd that neither the Fiscal Council's own rules of procedure nor its resolutions have been disclosed to the public. As the Fiscal Council does not include any member delegated by the Board of Trustees or the Public Service Board, there is simply no external control

[67] ibid paras 100, 136.
[68] ibid para 136.
[69] ibid para 95.
[70] ibid para 97.
[71] ibid para 108.

whatsoever over the allocation of resources, and the law fails to spell out the criteria for making such allocation decisions. Not only does this lack of transparency hinder the fulfilment of EU expectations regarding task-based spending, but it downright jeopardises the independent, professionally well-founded performance of public service functions.

The system of public service institutions set up as the result of the new regulation is centrally managed, stripped of all professional independence, exempt from any meaningful external control and inscrutable in its finances. The intricate organisational structure casts a glaze of ambiguity over individual responsibilities, frustrating the work of journalists and attempts to hold individuals and entities accountable for the performance of specific tasks, while the intertwining with the Media Council precludes unbiased regulatory oversight. That these threats and limitations are very real has been borne out by experience in the field to date, as we have suggested in the context of content regulation. Finally, the vague definition of public service tasks further hampers accountability.

C. Transformation of the Media Market

One of the major legislative objectives was to satisfy the economic needs of the major actors in the media industry, particularly including the largest television stations, as an indispensable condition for halting the migration out of Hungary's media market. Accordingly, the Media Act permits the broadest possible manoeuvring space in the acquisition of funds, for instance by relaxing the ceiling on airtime devoted to advertising, streamlining sponsorship rules and allowing product placements.[72]

The extent of regulatory penetration into the Hungarian media market has been significantly constrained by certain previous policy measures that may effectively afford economic leeway to the largest market actors, but they are nevertheless unable to offset the damage caused by the intervention in local markets.

(i) *Restructuring of the Media Market*

(a) Regulation of Market Entry

The Preamble to the Audiovisual Media Services Directive expressly states that '[N]o provision of this Directive should require or encourage Member States to impose new systems of licensing or administrative authorisation on any type of audiovisual media service'.[73] Contravening this provision, the Media Act has made it mandatory to register not only downloadable audio-visual media services but print and online press products as well. One of the concerns the

[72] ibid paras 23–35.
[73] Directive 2007/65, recital 20.

European Commission voiced over the regulation in Hungary had to do with this excessively broad registration requirement, which it said imposed an unreasonable restriction on the freedom of service provision and opinion. Consequently, the Hungarian legislature revised the registration provisions soon after the Media Act had entered into force.

Press products must be reported at the time of commencing the activity. There is no requirement to report content in the course of subsequent operations, but failure to comply with the registration obligation carries a fine of up to HUF 1 million. In the case of press products, the media authority is not allowed to use deletion from the records as a sanction. In December 2011, the Constitutional Court upheld the mandatory registration of press products as being constitutionally acceptable, pointing out that, 'beyond the obvious bureaucratic burden, the reporting obligation and the keeping of such records do not hinder or restrict the release of a press product, let alone prevent it'.[74] At the same time, the Constitutional Court did not address the accuracy of the criteria defining the services subject to the registration obligation or the deterrent power of the contemplated sanctions, nor did it examine whether there was any regulatory objective that could not be accomplished by any means other than mandatory registration. Apart from these concerns, the expertise of the Council of Europe warns that the mandatory registration of print and Internet-based media is incompatible with the principles followed in the practice of the European Court of Human Rights.[75]

The registration of television services involves the reporting of detailed information regarding programming. The commencement of broadcasting is subject to obtaining a resolution confirming the registration. The failure to register carries general media law sanctions. Subsequent violations may result in the deletion of the service from the records by the Media Council.

Tendering as a method of licensing services is now limited to radio frequencies, including local stations. The rules for bidding for analogue terrestrial frequencies essentially follow the logic of the country's 1996 media law. The media authority continues to select the winner in the outcome of a rather convoluted and costly process even today, when virtually all the bids concern local radio frequencies.

In its Decision 46/2007 (VI.27) AB,[76] the Constitutional Court found that the former media law 'failed to implement a transparent tendering mechanism'. Among other objections, the Constitutional Court pointed out that 'the evaluation criteria to be applied to bids for a media service licence are not regulated by the law, and the entire decision-making process remains impossible to follow for the bidders and the public at large'. Ironically, the new media laws do not contain such rules either. Formerly, the industry authority would be obliged to set forth and publish the evaluation criteria as part of the general tender terms. The new law neglects to provide for this responsibility. In fact, the outlines for defining the

[74] Decision 165/2011 (XII.20) AB határozat (Constitutional Court of Hungary).
[75] Salamon and Barata, *Council of Europe Experts* (n 64) 14.
[76] Decision 46/2007 (VI.27) AB határozat (Constitutional Court of Hungary).

evaluation criteria are nowhere to be found in writing, leaving the authority free to define those criteria arbitrarily. This oversight alone would be sufficient to call into question the fairness of any bidding process. There are two illustrative cases to show the problems of the tender praxis, the case of Lánchíd Rádió, and the case of Klubrádió.[77]

Lánchíd Radio has been available to listeners since 2006 on the Budapest 100.3 MHz frequency. It is owned by Infocenter Zrt, which can be tied to the political right-wing (Fidesz), with national weekly *Heti Válasz* and Class FM national commercial radio also under its umbrella. At the start of the tendering process, Lánchíd Rádió possessed a Budapest regional radio broadcast right. The obvious intent to expand was apparent from the fact that they bid on one-third of the announced licences. Wherever they bid, they won. Where they did not win, they did not lose against the other candidates but either withdrew their proposal or the Media Council did not consider their bid because in the event of winning they would have exceeded the ownership limitations set forth by the rules under the Media Act. According to the justification of the decisions, the radio was awarded the frequencies based on its intent to provide local content.

A few months after selecting Lánchíd Rádió as the winner, the Media Council as responsible authority for frequency tendering and managing of contracts approved the amendment of the contracts pertaining to the four newly-acquired frequencies. In each case, these amendments resulted in the expansion of the Budapest broadcast coverage area and, consequently, what is broadcast on the new frequencies is not the local content committed to in the proposals but the Budapest central programme. The programmes of Lánchíd Rádió with the expanded frequencies essentially cover most of Western Hungary; moreover, Lánchíd Rádió reaches this region with a single licence. This clearly circumvents the regulations in force pertaining to the restriction of media concentration, because it allows for obtaining further licences due to those merged into one coverage area. In addition to the above, the radio operates as a public service provider, without paying a media service fee.[78]

Klubrádió, an opposition radio in Budapest and some other towns, had to take two lawsuits with seven decisions to retain its service in Budapest and its programme structure. The first suit had to do with the tender announced for the 92.9 MHz frequency in Budapest. Although Klubrádió won the tender in April 2010 (a tender arranged by the former media authority), the Media Council refused

[77] On the new tendencies see further 'Media Council Redraws the Radio Market: Report on the Frequency Tendering by the Media Council', *Mérték Media Monitor*, Budapest, 18 September 2013 available at www.mertek.eu/en/reports/media-council-redraws-the-radio-market-report-on-the-frequency-tendering-by-the-media.

[78] See K Nagy 'Selective Publicity', *Mérték* (Budapest), 9 January 2013, available at www.mertek.eu/en/article/selective-publicity; K Nagy 'A Map of Community Media', *Mérték* (Budapest), 9 January 2013, available at www.mertek.eu/en/article/a-map-of-community-media; P Gábor, 'The Radio Market as a Political Playground', *Mérték* (Budapest), 14 November 2013, available at www.mertek.eu/en/article/the-radio-market-as-a-political-playground.

to sign a contract with the station. The other process reviewed the results of the tender for the 95.3 MHz frequency, in which Klubrádió finished as a close second bidder. In both litigations, the court ruled in all decisions, that the Media Council had violated the law. It clearly follows from these judgments that Klubrádió actually won both tenders.

In the case of the 92.9 MHz frequency, the Media Council sought to justify its refusal to sign a contract with the station by saying that Klubrádió had not been eligible to file a bid in the first place, because it was airing broadcasts at the time using another frequency in Budapest. However, the station had made the commitment, pursuant to the requirement set forth in the tender announcement, to resign that other frequency if it won. Ultimately, the Court not only declared that the Media Council had acted against the law by refusing to sign the contract, but in effect produced that contract itself by virtue of this very judgment. After a repeated proceeding the Court decided in a judgment with legal force that the Media Council did not have the right to refuse the signing of contract. In April 2013, the Media Council and the provider contracted on the use of frequency as a community radio with the original programme structure of Klubrádió.

In the case of the 95.3 MHz frequency, Klubrádió appealed the Media Council's resolution after it had lost to a competitor by a few points. Finally, the Court annulled the result of the tender citing formal errors, noting that the winning bid did not have properly authorised signatures affixed. According to the Media Council's interpretation of the decision (which was not a necessary consequence of the judgment in my opinion), all bidders should sign all of the pages of the bid documents even if they do not contain any information. So the Media Council voided all bids, including Klubrádió's. After three court decisions in this case, the Media Council contracted with Klubrádió as the winner of the tender. Klubrádió used the 95.3 MHz frequency as a commercial radio with more music in its programme up to February 2014, when the radio could continue broadcasting its service on the frequency 92.9 MHz. In the meantime, the Klubrádió lost the majority of its rural broadcasting network and got into an uncertain financial position. Overall, the tendering practices of the Media Council have been subsumed by and made subservient to a media policy primarily aimed at further bolstering the market dominance of businesses close to the government while weakening the position of enterprises critical of the status quo or simply mounting a competition to the favoured entities. Apart from this, the tender announcements do not reveal any other concept of media policy or any effort to take into account the specific features of local markets. The arbitrary element in all these processes is compounded by the rather broad opportunity that the law allows for obtaining a media service provision licence without a tender process. Such authorisation may be granted, for a period of up to three months, to media providers capable of discharging a public function in times of a state of emergency, natural catastrophe or industrial disaster, and of serving a certain community's 'special educational, cultural, information needs, or needs associated with a specific event affecting the given community'.[79]

(b) Media Concentration

One thing that can be said with certainty about the regulatory concept for curbing industry concentration is that it is much better attuned to the realities of the market than the previous media law. It is more proportionate in delimiting the manoeuvring space of media providers, and more attentive to the real constitutional motive of curtailing market concentration, which is the promotion of diversity in the media selection on offer. Even so, this field is no different in that, here too, the specific details of the regulation incorporate loopholes for arbitrary interpretation in practice. The law does not in any way restrict cross-ownership between diverse types of media. The constitutional risk this implies is particularly severe in light of the market processes arising in Hungary. Under the circumstances, the threat is not just theoretical but very much real-world, and this lends weight to the constitutional concerns over the legislative failure to hold back cross-ownership.

The very lenient rules of media concentration are compounded by the decision of the legislature to require the Media Council to participate as contributing specialised authority in processes conducted by the Hungarian Competition Authority,[80] whenever a merger involves 'enterprises or the affiliates of two groups of companies ... bearing editorial responsibility'. However, the Media Council is not allowed to withhold endorsement 'when the level of merger between independent sources of opinion after the merger will ensure the right for diversity of information within the relevant market for the media content service'. Obviously, this caveat leaves much latitude for arbitrary interpretation in practice without fear of accountability, not least because the courts are not in a position to overrule a deliberated decision by the Media Council in this regard.

By requiring the approval of the specialised authority to be applied to ongoing official processes,[81] the law effectively enabled the Media Council to step in and interfere with the proposed Axel-Springer/Ringier merger,[82] which had been under scrutiny by the Competition Authority quite some time before the adoption of the Media Act. The two ventures involved in the contemplated merger are among the largest enterprises in Hungary's print media market. Apart from major interests in the magazine segment, Axel-Springer holds a dominant stake in the regional daily market, while Ringier is the majority owner of *Népszabadság*, the leading political daily, and *Blikk*, the largest-circulation tabloid paper, among

[79] Mttv (n 38) para 48(4).
[80] ibid para 171.
[81] ibid para 216(5).
[82] At the end of the day, however, Ringier decided not to sell.

other publications. The proposed merger of the two would have been a reasonable response to the economic woes of the print media market, notwithstanding the fact that it would have undoubtedly created an overriding market force. Consequently, it is not so much because of the end result itself that the Media Council could be called to task for its refusal to approve the merger, but because of the low professional standards of the explanation attached to the resolution.[83]

III. CONCLUDING THOUGHTS

While pluralism features prominently among the fundamental principles embraced by the Media Act, the regulatory details and the practices while applying its provisions tend to work precisely against a free and pluralistic media system. Two years after the laws entered into force, it seems safe to declare that it has impaired the healthy operation of public discourse in Hungary, even if the damage is not always as extreme as could possibly be inferred from a first glance at the text of the law.

Any change in the media regulations in Hungary should entail consequences on the European level. Despite the fact, however, that the European Union, notably its Parliament and Council, has attentively followed and frowned on these developments from the start, the measures posing a clear danger to the freedom of the media in Hungary have failed to elicit a legally binding response from Europe so far. This goes to show that EU-level media regulation, particularly the Audiovisual Media Services Directive (2010/13/EU), was adopted as a result of political compromises that continue to prevent the European harmonisation of media policy issues regarded as sensitive by certain Member States. The European Commission has found nothing to criticise in terms of fundamental rights; its recommendations expressed in 2011 exclusively concern narrow fields of regulation under the Audiovisual Media Services Directive.

In the absence of the appropriate legal underpinnings, the ongoing exercise of political pressure from the European Union remains ineffectual, lending support to the argument that the unredeemed threats of sanctions only demonstrate the feebleness of the European Union. In the long term, then, Hungarian media regulation could prove most profitable by fermenting a revision at the European level of the arsenal we have at our disposal to defend the freedom of the media and fundamental rights.

[83] See especially M Gálik and A Vogl, 'Az Új Médiakoncentráció-szabályozás Első Vizsgája: Az Axel Springer és a Ringier Kiadói Csoport Meghiúsult Összeolvadása a Magyar Piacon' (2011) 3 *Médiakutató* 83.

Issues of Constitutionality in Romania

5

Separation of Powers and the Rule of Law in Romania: The Crisis in Concepts and Contexts

BOGDAN IANCU

I. INTRODUCTION: THE CRISIS IN CONTEXT

AT THE BEGINNING of summer 2012, a constitutional crisis erupted in Romania and trod along an increasingly tortuous course during that entire season. Although to many foreign observers this recent upheaval appeared precipitous and unexpected, it had been anticipated by a number of social and political milestones. In the preceding winter, street protests had violently broken out in the capital. Demonstrations subsequently brought together hundreds and sometimes thousands of people to the University Square of Bucharest as well as in cities across the country. The initial trigger of the winter 2011 outburst was a widely-considered abuse of power by President Băsescu who, in an impromptu televised intervention, openly supported the planned healthcare privatisation measures and threatened the removal of a Secretary of State in the Ministry of Health, Dr Raed Arafat. The latter, a respected professional who had made a name for himself by building from scratch an efficient emergency rescue service, had publicly opposed the proposed privatisation measures. The attempt to push through the health reform package in an aggressive manner and the intervention of the President against Dr Arafat provoked the immediate backlash on the streets.[1] Even though the protesters' anger had primarily been directed against the government in power and the incumbent President, and although the opposition had identified itself with the discontent, the demonstrators themselves took no definitive political stand. In fact, many slogans shouted on the streets were aimed indiscriminately at the political class as a whole.

[1] The Western press portrayed the protests as determined by the economic crisis and the austerity package of the government but drastic cuts in the pensions and the salaries of state employees in 2010 had elicited almost no significant popular reaction. See, eg, KP Schwarz, 'Absurdes Theater in Bukarest' *FAZ* (Frankfurt), 7 February 2012, available at www.faz.net/aktuell/politik/ausland/rumaenien-absurdes-theater-in-bukarest-11641321.html.

In the aftermath of the street revolts, the centre-right Cabinet led by Emil Boc (supported by the Democratic Liberal Party (PDL), the party representing the Hungarian minority in Romania (UDMR), and a splinter faction (UNPR)) resigned in early February 2012. A new Cabinet, chaired by the former director of the External Intelligence Services (SIE), Mihai Răzvan Ungureanu, took over the Executive. This latter government, the youngest and the briefest post-communist Romanian executive until now, was itself swiftly ousted by a vote of no confidence. Subsequently, the opposition, a centre-left political alliance (Social Liberal Union (Uniunea Social Liberală, USL)) initially composed of the Social Democratic Party and the National Liberal Party,[2] came to power and formed a new government in spring 2012. In the Romanian political landscape, the general ideological labels of left/centre/right have become increasingly nominal. They mean relatively little in a context where internal politics is characterised by variable geometry alliances and, moreover, endemic and uncontrollable parliamentary migration. The National Union for the Progress of Romania (UNPR) is the epitome of these phenomena; composed primarily of defectors from the Social Democratic Party, the faction first sided with the centre-right government, then supported the centre-left government headed by Victor Viorel Ponta, and is now in the process of coming full circle by dissolving once again into the Social Democratic Party. Ideology as such also matters less nowadays as a result of EU membership (many policy-making areas have shifted to Brussels) and due to the constraints imposed on the country by EU/IMF structural adjustment programmes. To wit, the new government (although dominated by social democrats and national liberals) will continue the budget cuts and massive privatisation programmes it had vociferously railed against while in opposition. At the behest of the IMF, Poşta Română SA, the national mail services, and CFR Marfă, the freight transportation section of the national railroad company, are already scheduled for privatisation.

Once the new government came to power, its supporting parliamentary majority profited from a massive negative vote (a characteristic of post-communist Romanian democracy) and won a landslide victory in the local elections. Immediately after this boost in legitimacy, the agenda of the executive was fully captured by an attempt to sack the incumbent President whose candidacy had been endorsed by the PDL, the strongest party in the former governing coalition. In this process, the speakers of both Houses of Parliament and the ombudsman

[2] The USL is a political alliance, formed in accordance with the Political Parties Law 14 of 2003 (Legea no 14/2003 'a partidelor politice') Ch V, 'The Association of Political Parties'. Unlike coalitions, political alliances (albeit the parties composing them preserve their separate legal personalities and structures) are subject to relatively restrictive procedural and substantive requirements, partly analogous to those provided for in the case of parties. Nowadays the formation is composed of four parties, grouped in two alliances, Centre-Left (PSD and UNPR) and Centre-Right (PNL and the Conservative Party).

were removed from office with little ceremony, the Referendum Law[3] and the Constitutional Court Law[4] were both amended in a cavalier fashion, and bitter, albeit somewhat petty, bickering ensued between the Prime Minister and the President over representation of the country at European Council summits. All this took place amid protracted plagiarism scandals[5] and a cascade of challenges of unconstitutionality that raised the Constitutional Court to a position of influence and public visibility that it had never before enjoyed.

All these events brought Romania, an otherwise peripheral area of the European Union, to the foreground of international attention. Accusations of rule of law abuse and a litany of boilerplate constitutional commands to the government found their way into the formerly tame and tepid biannual monitoring reports of the European Commission within the Cooperation and Verification Mechanism.[6] Alarmed press statements were issued by the Justice Commissioner (and Vice-President of the EU Commission) Viviane Reding.[7] The President of the Venice Commission, Gianni Buquicchio, took public stands in defence of the allegedly beleaguered Romanian Constitutional Court.[8] Even the US Department of State sent a special envoy to discuss with the parties involved and report on the unfolding crisis. Respectable newspapers across Europe covered the developments extensively, while reputed academics wrote editorials against the abuses of the Ponta government and its supporting majority in Parliament.[9] The common tenor of all these eminent positions was that the rule of law and the separation of powers in Romania were in grave danger.

This chapter will not engage directly with the external reactions to the crisis, other than by noting in passing that the accusations of lawlessness, albeit in the larger context unduly Manichean, were in principle justified. My argument will try to place the summer crisis in its broader Romanian constitutional environment. In what follows, I will first review the main features and inherent tensions of Romanian constitutionalism, proceeding afterwards to a forensic chronology of the summer developments, and concluding with a note on the current conditions for the possibility of constitutionalism in the country.

[3] Referendum Law 3/2000 (Legea no 3/2000 'privind organizarea si desfasurarea referendumului').

[4] Law 47/1992 (Legea no 47/1992 'privind organizarea si functionarea Curtii Constitutionale').

[5] Prime Minister Ponta and one of his appointees to the Education Ministry were accused of having plagiarised a doctoral dissertation and scientific articles, respectively. The Minister was replaced, whereas Ponta refused to resign, while the scandal eventually died down in a labyrinth of contradictory committee findings.

[6] European Commission, *Report from the Commission to the European Parliament and the Council on Progress in Romania under the Cooperation and Verification Mechanism*, COM(2012)410 final.

[7] See www.europolitics.info/sectoral-policies/reding-on-romania-art339838-16.html.

[8] See www.venice.coe.int/webforms/events/?id=1544.

[9] P Krugman, 'The Conscience of a Liberal', *New York Times*, 5 July 2012, available at www.krugman.blogs.nytimes.com/2012/07/05/guest-post-romania-unravels-the-rule-of-law/.

II. METAMORPHOSES OF ROMANIAN CONSTITUTIONALISM: CONCEPTS AND CONTEXTS

Romania started its modernisation relatively late. In legal terms, progress consisted in a massive overnight importation of Western forms, including the adoption in 1866 of a slightly modified version of the 1831 Belgian Constitution. The disconnect between the transplanted form and the realities of the Romanian principalities (later, the Kingdom) was, up until the close of the nineteenth century, so great that even an arch-Westerniser such as IC Brătianu, an iconic Liberal Party figure, Prime Minister between 1876 and 1888, remarked in a political speech:

> It was not enough that they translated laws word for word from French into Romanian, they now had to dress after the French fashion too. This is how we see our judges and barristers, clad in borrowed cloaks that in France might signify something according to their traditions but here, with us, only look ridiculous.[10]

This bitter irony was fully validated by practices which Brătianu should have known only too well. For a conspicuous example, instead of appointing the Prime Minister from the midst of the party or coalition which had won the elections, as Western parliamentary orthodoxy dictated, the king established the tradition of dismissing the incumbent, dissolving the Parliament, and charging a favoured political leader with the organisation of new, in practice usually rigged, elections. The three royal decrees, to deal with this process, were issued simultaneously.[11] As P.P. Carp, a prominent nineteenth-century conservative politician and Prime Minister tellingly quipped: 'Give me the power and I shall give you a Parliament'. Nonetheless, until the beginning of the twentieth century, the juridical and political practices had started to evince a steady degree of reflexive rapprochement to the ideal-typical features of liberal constitutionalism.[12] The process of drafting the 1923 Constitution was a local development, informed by thorough debates and determined by a conscious national choice for a clear constitutional form.[13] This inchoate tendency towards normalisation was, however, short-lived; it ended abruptly with the installation of the 'royal dictatorship' under Carol II in 1938, followed by the Iron Guard, military, and lastly communist forms of authoritarianism.

[10] T Drăganu, *Începuturile şi Dezvoltarea Regimului Parlamentar în România Până în 1916* (Cluj-Napoca, Editura Dacia, 1991) 354.

[11] See M Gutan, 'Reflectii în Legătură cu Începuturile Regimului Parlamentar în România Modernă, între Transplant Constituţional şi Autoritarism Regal (1866–1914)' (2011) 8 *Dreptul* 131.

[12] See Drăganu, *Începuturile* (n 10) and B Iancu, 'Constitutionalism between Transplant and Irritation: The Case of Nineteenth-Century Romanian Modernization' in J Kirov and M Stolleis (eds), *Establishment of National Legal Systems in Post-ottoman South Eastern Europe: Deconstruction, Formation and Transfer of Normativity* (Frankfurt am Main, Vittorio Klostermann, forthcoming 2014). See for analogous findings of rapprochement in terms of economic and socio-cultural development, B Murgescu, *România şi Europa-acumularea Decalajelor Economice (1500–2010)* (Iasi, Polirom, 2010) and L Boia, *De Ce Este România Altfel?* (Bucharest, Humanitas, 2012).

[13] A Stroe, *Constituţia din 1923 în Dezbaterea Contemporanilor* (Bucharest, Humanitas, 1990).

The only relatively successful and coherent liberal-constitutional tradition to which Romania could have looked for a model after the demise of the communist regime in 1989 was thus arguably the brief reign of the 1923 Constitution. But such a choice was at the time fused at the hip with the restoration of the monarchy, an option supported in the early 1990s by only a thin layer of public intellectuals and academic eccentrics.[14] Since the possibility of building upon tradition under the circumstances was foreclosed, post-communist constitutionalisation was bound to be an exercise in selective imitation, conditioned by 'generational preferences'[15] and the professional limitation of the experts at hand. Due to the violent nature of the overthrow of communism in Romania, which both obscured and legitimated a massive degree of continuity in personnel and network structures, the overall quality of the available elites, including legal elites, had a determining influence on the process of drafting the 1991 Constitution.[16] A few clear political options, partly informed by status quo preferences and biases, predetermined the broader features of the new fundamental law (republican form of government, bicameralism, semi-presidentialism, a limited role for the Constitutional Court, rigid amendment rules, emphasis on national and territorial unity, etc). The proverbial constitutional devil lies, however, in the details. The many more technical decisions, including the crucial choices on the actual institutional settings and the checks-and-balances configuration, were the result of a rather haphazard form of bricolage,[17] a jigsaw puzzle of Western constitutional templates, originally rearranged and tailored to the framers' ideological proclivities and theoretical worldview perspectives.

The option for bicameralism, for example, was not accompanied by a clear delineation of the houses' competences: the Chamber of Deputies and the Senate were designed to be in practically all respects (mode of election, terms of office, structure and attributions) almost identical. This original duplication of the mandates, together with the cumbersome procedural hurdles entailed by the subject matter normative division between ordinary and 'organic' legislation, rendered the work of the legislature cumbersome and placed that branch at an evident relative disadvantage to the executive. The situation was, from the outset, further complicated by the possibility of the executive to bypass Parliament by emergency ordinances.[18] Whereas ordinary 'delegations' are authorised by the Parliament within a certain time limit and solely within the domain of ordinary

[14] See E Focseneanu, *Istoria Constituţională a României (1859–1991)* (Bucharest, Humanitas, 1992) arguing that, due to its illegal suspension, the Constitution of 1923 re-entered into force automatically after the demise of the communist regime.

[15] For the notion of foundational 'generational preferences' in constitutionalism, A Sajó, 'Preferred Generations: A Paradox of Restoration Constitutions' in M Rosenfeld (ed), *Constitutionalism, Identity, Difference, and Legitimacy: Theoretical Perspectives* (Durham, NC, Duke University Press, 1994).

[16] See A Sajó, 'Comment: Socialist Law Unaccounted' in B Iancu (ed), *The Law/Politics Distinction in Contemporary Law Adjudication* (Utrecht, Eleven International Publishing, 2009).

[17] M Tushnet, 'The Possibilities of Comparative Constitutional Law' (1999) 108 *Yale LJ* 1225.

[18] Constitution of Romania, art 115 (as revised in 2003).

legislation, so-called 'constitutional delegations' by emergency ordinance are in effect a loosely-fettered prerogative of the executive which can routinely bypass Parliament and place it in a perpetual state of normative *fait accompli*, on the basis of a practically unreviewable plea of necessity. The possibility to adopt 'motorised legislation' provides governments with a formidable instrument which, due to time limitations and an ossified law-making process, is seldom subject to effective parliamentary scrutiny. An emergency ordinance can amend legislation, including organic laws, needs no enabling law as a legal basis, takes effect immediately (it must only be 'laid before Parliament') and is automatically adopted if neither of the legislative chambers takes action within a 30-day period.[19] The only somewhat effective substantive limitations set forth by article 115(6) of the Constitution are that emergency ordinances cannot amend the Constitution, affect the regime of 'fundamental state institutions', infringe upon fundamental rights, liberties and duties, or give effect to takings (eg nationalisations). Moreover, due to the fact that the current constitutional regime immunises such measures from timely review, ordinances are also a useful political weapon. Unlike ordinary laws, whose validity can be challenged before promulgation, ordinances can, as a rule, be reviewed only by way of exceptions raised by the parties in the course of ordinary litigation and referred to the Constitutional Court by the ordinary judge or court. This means in practice that it could take months before the dispute is submitted to constitutional review; until that time, the political context would have changed considerably.

Another fundamental mistake of the original post-communist framers was to transplant the French semi-presidential model to Romania in a partial and distorted transposition. The Romanian President, just like his French counterpart after de Gaulle's 1961 amendment, is directly elected on a national basis and therefore enjoys the benefit of a strong legitimacy. Unlike a French President, the Romanian office-holder has almost no effective powers since only the broadly symbolic and decorative functions have been borrowed in full. The attributions which could have given their user actual political clout were severely circumscribed or stripped of binding legal effect: the President can thus initiate a consultative referendum on 'matters of national concern'. Likewise, parliamentary dissolution is not an effective prerogative since it can only take place, according to article 89 of the Constitution (as revised in 2003), after consultation with the speakers and parliamentary groups, if at least two consecutive requests for a vote of confidence at the formation of the government have been rejected within 60 days of the failure of the first request to form a government. These are, as one

[19] The procedure is partially similar to that provided by the Italian Constitution in art 77. Unlike in the Italian case, where emergency decrees lose effect if they are not transposed into law by Parliament within 60 days, Romanian emergency ordinances are considered adopted if the Houses of Parliament do not act on them within two months.

author justly noted, 'conditions that are almost impossible to meet in practice'.[20] The same author, in an otherwise elegant analysis of the Romanian President's constitutional powers, concluded that the numerous attributions either devoid of legal effect or fettered by onerous conditions create, in constitutional terms, 'a colossus with clay feet'.[21] The statement, true in strictly positivistic terms, ignores the destabilising tendency induced by this interplay of high legitimacy located in the office with the vague attributions provided by the Constitution. In political reality, the constitutional tension between legal and political forms has induced a state of perpetual ambivalence regarding the place of the presidency in the constitutional architecture and, more particularly, never-ending disputes regarding the proper division of attributions between the President and the Prime Minister.

An opportunity to remedy the initial shortcomings presented itself in 2003 when the Constitution was revised, in view of the pending Euro-Atlantic integration. The changes, dubbed by some 'Euro-amendments', were drafted in haste, without a thorough, fundamental public discussion and certainly without much popular or civic enthusiasm as to the matters concerned. Further, the Romanian Constitution is particularly rigid in its form of amendment: two-thirds majorities are required to pass the Bill through each house. Three-quarters are needed in case of disagreement, when the mediation procedure fails in conference committee and a common draft is voted on in a joint sitting. The amendments must be subsequently approved by a popular referendum, convened within 30 days after the revision proposal or draft has passed through Parliament.[22] Since the 2003 revision was presented to the political class and the public as indispensable to EU integration—a desire universally supported—passage through Parliament was relatively unproblematic. By the same token, since this presentation was hardly conducive to a 'constitutional moment' (the citizenry understood and warmly supported the general objective but took little interest in such matters),[23] the poll had to be extended by the government at the last moment, through an emergency ordinance, so that the requisite quorum could be met. Eventually, the referendum was validated, with 55.7 per cent of registered voters turning out and 89.7 per cent voting in favour of the proposed amendments. This discrepancy and the entire story of the 2003 amendment process are revealing of another structural deficiency of the Romanian Constitution. The problem is all the more important nowadays, in the context of a constitutionally-induced path dependency: accelerated

[20] ES Tănăsescu, 'The President of Romania, or: The Slippery Slope of a Political System' (2008) 4(1) *European Constitutional Law Review* 64, 84.

[21] ibid 76.

[22] Constitution of Romania, art 151 (as revised in 2003).

[23] See for insightful general analyses of the constitutional implications of European and Europe-induced constitutionalism in the newer, formerly communist, EU Member States, A Sajó, 'Constitution without the Constitutional Moment: A View from the New Member States' (2005) 3(2–3) *International Journal of Constitutional Law* 243; W Sadurski *et al*, *Spreading Democracy and the Rule of Law: The Impact of EU Enlargement on the Rule of Law, Democracy, and Constitutionalism in Post-communist Legal Orders* (Dordrecht, Springer, 2006).

institutional and political fragmentation. Remedial amendments in the public interest are the changes least likely to be supported by the political coalitions that could secure the required parliamentary supermajorities. By the same token, once the opportunity presented by the last grand project, EU integration, had been missed, in a climate now dominated by power grabs and diluted forms of politicking with minor factional stakes, broad political and popular consensus around principled debates is much more difficult to build.

Not all the 2003 changes were Europe-related but those modifications that did take place under the sway of EU institutions were not necessarily auspicious. For instance, the Superior Council of the Magistracy (CSM), the representative body of the Romanian judiciary, was rendered fully autonomous from direct political influences. This change (undertaken primarily at the behest of the EU Commission) created, within a short period of time, both a countervailing problem and a constitutional antinomy. The Commission's requests, in its pre-accession monitoring reports, for increased judicial autonomy had been justified by an excess of authority by the Ministry of Justice over the judiciary and contextual abuses arising from it. Such autonomy was, however, taken to the other extreme, tilting the balance in the opposite direction, without consideration of any intermediate arrangements that could have reconciled the need for social responsiveness and democratic accountability with the values of judicial independence. The Romanian response to the Commission turned the problem upside down and created the perfect institutional setting for equally nefarious corporatist corruption and occult forms of politicisation within the judiciary.[24] The antinomy results from the structure of the Council, under whose institutional umbrella stand both judges and prosecutors. The weaker institutional form of the CSM provided by the initial version of the Constitution impliedly took into account the distinction between those two categories: unlike judges, prosecutors form a hierarchical structure with executive features and attributions, recognised as such by the fundamental and judicial organisation laws. The entity is designated as a 'Public Ministry' (article 131) and the activity of prosecutors is placed 'under the authority of the Minister of Justice' (article 132).[25] Once the Council gained full, insular autonomy from the political branches and thus from majoritarian democracy, a constitutionally unanswerable tension inevitably ensued as to the proper degree and precise procedural articulation of ministerial and CSM influence, for

[24] B Iancu, 'Post-Accession Constitutionalism with a Human Face: Judicial Reform and Lustration in Romania' (2010) 6(1) *European Constitutional Law Review* 28; ES Tănăsescu, 'Reforma Consiliului Superior al Magistraturii între Analogia Dreptului şi Nimicuri Etice' (2011) 2 *Pandectele Române* 19.

[25] According to Law regarding the Judicial Organisation 304/2004 (republished) (Legea no 304/2004 'privind organizarea judiciara republicata, cu modificarile si completarile ulterioare'), art 63(h), (i), prosecutors 'act for the prevention and combating of criminality under the coordination of the Minister of Justice, for the realisation of the unitary penal policy of the state' and 'study the causes generating and favouring criminality, elaborate and propose to the Minister of Justice measures to eliminate such'.

instance, with respect to control over the Inspectorate of the Judiciary or over the appointment of higher-ranking prosecutorial positions.

Related structural changes were undertaken without taking into account problems of constitutionally-systemic coordination and coherence. For instance, in Romania, the exponential multiplication of politically autonomous institutions, with attributions in crucial fields of social and economic regulation but also in domains related to the functioning of the state under the rule of law, directly resulted from the process of EU accession. Autonomous agencies were sometimes established (eg the National Integrity Agency) or pre-existing structures gained a much higher degree of autonomy (CSM or the National Anticorruption Directorate) as a direct result of specific requests by the Commission, related to the transposition of the *acquis*. The term, as such, of 'autonomous administrative authority' appeared in the 1991 Constitution but was mentioned in passing and in a somewhat oxymoronic formulation: autonomy was to exist 'in the subordination of the Government and the ministries' (article 115(2)). The structure of the provision was radically changed in 2003 and autonomous administrative authorities were now expressly detached from the executive structure and placed alongside the hierarchical edifice of the Government (article 116(2)).[26] The majority of such institutions, across constitutional systems, have quasi-jurisdictional attributions and features. These functions are akin to adjudication or at least can be (mis)described as such in the course of constitutional review. Since an odd provision taken over from the 1991 Constitution was preserved (article 21(4) (2003)), according to which special administrative jurisdictions must be 'optional and free of charge', the mandates of Romanian 'independent agencies' were from the very outset vulnerable to future findings of unconstitutionality.[27]

Some of the alterations resulting from domestic initiatives on constitutional engineering proved to be equally detrimental. The legislative process, for example, was rationalised, so that now each House was granted a final say (as a 'decisional Chamber') with respect to specific legislative competences, whereas the mediation procedure in conference committee was abandoned with respect to organic and ordinary legislation. Due to the general difficulties entailed by attempts to coordinate the legislative process along normative divisions of competence, especially in view of the fact that the same bill might contain provisions which fall into the

[26] Other specialised agencies may be organised in subordination to the government or Ministries, or as autonomous administrative authorities.

[27] Decizia No 415 of 14 April 2010 (Constitutional Court of Romania), whose holding, with reference to this provision, severely curbed the attributions of the National Integrity Agency with respect to the procedure for confiscation of unjustified assets. The National Integrity Agency was established in fulfilment of Romania's obligations under the Treaty of Accession to accept and heed post-accession monitoring by the EU Commission, within the framework of the Cooperation and Verification Mechanism.

decision-making competences of both Houses, the general benefits of this change are, to say the least, not yet apparent.[28]

Last but not least, the revision overhauled and greatly altered the position of the Constitutional Court in the constitutional architecture. Some changes could at the time be perceived as unimportant: the new possibility of vesting the Court with ex post ('concrete') review competence by means of an exception raised by the Ombudsman directly before the constitutional tribunal passed relatively unobserved until recently. The abolition of the 1991 procedure by virtue of which a two-thirds majority vote in Parliament could override a judicial finding of unconstitutionality was, however, on its face important, as were some of the new attributions included in the amendment package. The Court was charged with the competence to review the constitutionality of treaties and other international agreements upon the notification by the parliamentary speakers, parliamentary groups, or at least 50 deputies or at least 25 senators (article 146(b)) and, more importantly, granted the power 'to solve legal disputes of a constitutional nature between public authorities, at the request of the President of Romania, one of the presidents of the two Chambers, the Prime Minister, or of the president of the Superior Council of Magistracy' (article 146(e)).[29] In the abstract and on the presupposition of a healthy constitutional culture and generally accepted normative standards, a strong constitutional court is a guarantee of the supremacy of the constitution and consequently of the rule of law. In a context such as the one described above, an increase in the power of the constitutional tribunal is not necessarily conducive to the legal integration and normalisation of the political order. Judicial power without accountability may just as easily lead to perverse forms of politicisation under the guise of constitutional principle. Gaps in the constitutional structure, such as the vague and overlapping attributions which characterise the separation of powers framework, as well as the systemic malfunctions ensuing from a lack of proper foundations, allow the justices a considerable amount of discretion. As we shall see in the following section, the Constitutional Court has not often raised itself to the height of its new responsibilities. By the same token, this newer configuration has created political incentives for encroaching upon constitutional case law, for instance in the course of the judicial appointments procedure. Moreover, according to a new section added in 2003 to the article which enumerates the Court's attributions, the competence of the tribunal can be increased by amending its organic law, Law 47/1992.[30] Article 146(l) of the Constitution now reads: '[The Constitutional Court] exercises other attributions, as provided in its organic law'. Analogous provisions can, of course, be found

[28] See in the French context, the partly analogous (normative separation between the legislative and the regulatory domains) and generally apposite considerations by J Boulouis, 'L'Influence des Articles 34 et 37 sur l'Équilibre Politique entre les Pouvoirs' in J Boulouis and L Favoreu, *Le Domaine de la Loi et du Règlement* (Paris, Presses Universitaires d'Aix-Marseille, 1981).

[29] See generally on the matter B Dima, 'Conflictele Juridice de Natură Constituţională dintre Legislativ, Executiv şi Puterea Judecătorească' (2009) 141(2) *Sfera Politicii* 3.

[30] Law 47/1992 (n 4).

in other jurisdictions.[31] In the local context, this possibility opened up another avenue for manipulation.

III. THE SUMMER CRISIS

Once the initiative to remove the incumbent President was placed on the parliamentary agenda, seven articles of impeachment were drafted. Traian Băsescu was accused of infringing fundamental rights and transgressing his powers repeatedly by encroaching on the constitutional attributions of the government and the Constitutional Court and by breaching his constitutional duty of political impartiality.[32] According to the Constitution (article 95), the Romanian President can be impeached for 'committing grave acts infringing upon constitutional provisions'. One-third of the MPs (deputies and senators) can initiate the procedure. Following the receipt of an advisory opinion by the Constitutional Court, an absolute majority must vote on the articles of impeachment, in a joint sitting of the two Houses, for the suspension from office to take effect. A popular referendum is subsequently held, within 30 days of the adoption of the parliamentary impeachment resolution. During this period, the Speaker of the Senate (or, in this order of succession, that of the House of Representatives) serves as acting President (article 98). The acting President exercises almost the full gamut of presidential attributions (with the exception of parliamentary dissolution, addressing the legislature, and initiating a consultative referendum). The acting President can also be impeached for the same reasons and following the same procedure (article 99). If the impeachment is confirmed by popular referendum, the President is removed from office.

The Constitution entrenches neither a validity condition (quorum) nor a clear decisional rule (majority) for the procedure; and article 10 (impeachment referendum) of Referendum Law 3/2000[33] was thus, over the years, repeatedly amended, for everyday needs, by all governing coalitions. In 2007, during the first attempt to impeach Traian Băsescu, Parliament amended the law, providing for a relative majority (and thus absence of a quorum condition) to confirm the impeachment of a President elected in the second ballot (ie Băsescu's case). The amendment was declared unconstitutional at the time, based on the reasoning that the mandate was the same in both situations and, besides, an acting (unelected) President could also be impeached. Nonetheless, the Constitutional Court noted in 2007 that nothing prevented Parliament from opting for the same

[31] See, eg, German Basic Law, art 99(3): 'Das Bundesverfassungsgericht wird ferner in den ihm sonst durch Bundesgesetz zugewiesenen Fällen tätig'.

[32] For an earlier version of this constitutional chronology of the crisis, analysed in the context of the European Commission's July 2012 reactions, see B Iancu, 'Romania under EU Influence: Note on the Constitutive Limits of External Constitutional Interventions' (2012) 12(2) *Romanian Journal of Political Science* 53.

[33] Referendum Law (n 3).

solution (absolute or relative majority) in all hypotheses.[34] Upon a change in the political configuration, the law was again modified by a government politically close to the President. Emergency Ordinance 103/2009[35] amended article 10, so that a quorum (the majority of registered voters) was set again as the precondition of validity for all constitutional referenda, including impeachment. Subsequently, the law that approved the ordinance (Law 62/2012)[36] modified the article yet again, this time raising the procedural bar to a practically unattainable height. The new form of the article read: 'The impeachment of the President is approved if the proposal is affirmed by a majority of the citizens registered on the electoral lists'.

The Speakers of the two Houses had been appointed by the former party in power. According to two Constitutional Court decisions of 2005, the symmetrical removal provisions of the Standing Orders of the Houses had been declared unconstitutional. According to the two holdings, removal as a sanction for breaches of constitutional provisions or for 'repeated and serious infringements' of the Standing Orders contravened the 'rights to defence' of the accused speaker. Conversely, a purely political removal was also deemed unconstitutional since it contradicted 'the principle of [electing the Speakers in conformity with] the political configuration resulting from the parliamentary elections'. The Court held that only the parliamentary group that had initially sponsored the nominations to these offices could require the removal of the incumbents before the end of their terms.[37] The reasoning in both proceedings was unusual as the dissenting opinions had indicated. Removal as a political sanction could not be analogised to the rigours of a criminal prosecution and thus the analogy with the judicial requirements under article 24 of the Constitution, concerning the defence rights of the criminally accused, was—according to the dissenters—untenable. Moreover, as practice and common sense dictate, the political configuration that forms a parliamentary and by consequence a governmental majority does not result from poll results but from post-electoral negotiations among parliamentary groups within the new Parliament. In spite of all these contradictions, this was still the established principle, in constitutional law and parliamentary practice, as of 2012.

The removal of a parliamentary Speaker, as well as the vote to suspend the President, are effected by parliamentary decisions. According to the text of the Constitution, such decisions are not subject to constitutional review but article 27 in the Constitutional Court Law was amended in 2010, adding the constitutional review of such decisions to the competence of the Court. The amendment, initially sponsored by a social democratic senator, passed, following a change

[34] Decizia No 147 of 21 February 2007 (Constitutional Court of Romania). This obiter appreciation was restated in Decizia No 420 of 3 May 2007 (Constitutional Court of Romania).

[35] Emergency Ordinance 103/2009 of 31 September 2009 (*Ordonanta* de urgenta nr 103/*2009* pentru modificarea si completarea Legii nr 3/2000 privind organizarea si desfasurarea referendumului).

[36] Law 62/2012 (Legea no 62/2012 'privind aprobarea OUG 103/2009').

[37] Decizia No 601 of 14 November 2005 (Constitutional Court of Romania); Decizia No 602 of 14 November 2005 (Constitutional Court of Romania).

in the Court membership, with the vote of the centre-right coalition in power (PDL-UDMR-UNPR).

Against this constitutional and legislative background, Parliament removed the speakers of both Houses and the ombudsman on the same day (3 July 2012). As noted above, the ombudsman can bring an exception of unconstitutionality against provisions in an ordinance directly before the Constitutional Court (article 146(d)). Formally, the ombudsman was accused of challenging the constitutionality of a number of ordinances that regulated purely administrative matters and thus of exceeding the constitutional competence of the institution (that of safeguarding the fundamental rights and liberties of natural persons).[38] The accusation was formally valid, even though the most likely circumstantial motive for the action was to replace the incumbent with an office-holder more sympathetic to the new government and thus to prevent further constitutional challenges to emergency governmental ordinances. At the same time, amendments to the Constitutional Court Law and the Referendum Law were made, in the simultaneous form of parliamentary Bills and emergency ordinances, in order to remove parliamentary decisions from the jurisdiction of the Court and to provide for a relative majority rule applicable to the impeachment referendum. The probable rationale of this duplication was that, in the event that the Bill would be declared unconstitutional, the analogous provisions in the ordinances would remain in force due to the lack of a legal remedy against them. The Constitutional Court was subsequently asked to state its position on the impeachment within 24 hours. Following the receipt of a rather ambiguous advisory opinion,[39] the President was suspended on 6 July 2012.

The objections of unconstitutionality regarding the legislative proposals to amend Law 47/1992 and Law 3/2000 and the constitutional complaints against the removals reached the Court. Decisions were rendered in quick succession, during early July 2012. The Court held the Referendum Law as amended 'constitutional … insofar as it ensures the participation in the referendum of 50 per cent plus one of the number of citizens registered on the electoral lists'.[40] The holding was strangely formulated; it stands to reason that a normative proposition cannot ensure a physical outcome. More unusual still was the departure

[38] According to the Constitution (art 58(1)), the ombudsman ('Advocate of the People') is appointed for a term of office of five years 'to defend the natural persons' rights and freedoms'. One example regarded the reorganisation by emergency ordinance of the Romanian Cultural Institute, taken from the institutional custody of the presidency and placed under the authority of the Senate. The measure was in reality an act of retaliation against the President and against public intellectuals perceived by the new majority as sympathetic to or affiliated with Băsescu.

[39] Aviz consultative No 1 of 6 July 2012 (Constitutional Court of Romania). The Court rejected most of the articles of impeachment, upon a consistent general reasoning (excluding the expression of political opinions as not covered by the constitutional impeachment provision, which sanctions actual deeds that contravene the constitutional provisions). A number of arguments in the impeachment proposal were, however, albeit very cautiously and partially, validated, and insofar the appreciation of their seriousness was left at the political discretion of the legislature.

[40] Decizia No 731 of 10 July 2012 (Constitutional Court of Romania).

from the pre-2007 case law which, as we have seen, had expressly left the matter of an impeachment referendum quorum to determination by the legislature. The reasoning extemporised on the constitutional need for an effective exercise of popular sovereignty and the civic duties of the citizens but such considerations were in any event irrelevant and, even on the assumption that one accepted their validity, could have applied just as forcefully in 2007. The primary argument in support of the holding was electoral stability and the primary reference made in support of this argument was to a Code of Good Practice in Referenda adopted by the Venice Commission, sensibly recommending that electoral legislation should not be changed within a time-frame of less than one year prior to elections.[41] Nonetheless, the authors of the Venice report also warned against quorum provisions in referenda which would open the possibility of politically manipulating the results, for instance by equating actual negative votes with the purported motives of absentee electors.

The decision on the constitutionality of the Constitutional Court Law amendments was also unusual in the broader context. The amendment was declared unconstitutional with the persuasive argument that the Court's jurisdiction cannot be removed at will while cases are pending on the docket. Yet the justices hastened to add that not all parliamentary decisions were to be reviewed since such an extension of jurisdiction would constitute an encroachment by the Court upon the autonomy of the legislative branch. The Court emphasised the assertion that only parliamentary decisions that affect 'constitutional values, rules, and principles' would be subjected to judicial scrutiny.[42] Yet, in the cases that followed, those regarding the constitutionality of the actual parliamentary decisions removing the two speakers, the justices did not find a breach of constitutional principles or values.[43] But this position contradicted the 2005 constitutional case law declaring the majority resulting from elections as the paramount principle governing the speakers' elections.

In the month of August, the constitutionality of the impeachment referendum came under scrutiny. The permanent electoral lists for presidential elections comprised at the time the figure of 18,292,464 registered voters. Eventually 8,459, 053 citizens (46.24 per cent of the baseline figure) took part in the referendum on 29 July 2012. Among these, over 87 per cent voted in favour of dismissal. The vote was influenced by a strategic volte-face by the impeached President who, while initially supporting participation, changed tactics once opinion polls indicated

[41] See European Commission for Democracy through Law (Venice Commission), *Code of Good Practice in Referendums* (19 March 2007), CDL-AD (2007)008rev 23, available at www.venice.coe.int/webforms/documents/?pdf=CDL-AD(2007)008-e; European Commission for Democracy through Law (Venice Commission), *Opinion on the Act on the Legal Status and Remuneration of Judges and on the Act on the Organisation and Administration of Courts* (Opinion No 663/2012, 19 March 2012) para 117.

[42] Decizia No 727 of 9 July 2012 (Constitutional Court of Romania).

[43] Decizia No 728 of 9 July 2012 (Constitutional Court of Romania); Decizia 729 of 9 July 2012 (Constitutional Court of Romania).

a massive affirmative vote and campaigned for a boycott of the procedure by his supporters. This action was challenged before the Court which, in a ruling of early August, declared the boycott fully in conformity with the Constitution and equally expressive of sovereignty and civic duty. This was the case, as the Court observed, especially when 'the applicable legislation requires participation'. Hence, the civic duty to participate in the referendum, in the name of which the Court had imposed a quorum in July (in contradiction to the 2007 case law), became in August a political right to subvert participation, equally expressive of sovereignty and furthering of civic duties and values. Ironically, the prior action of the Court was presented in this reasoning as a precondition independent of the Court's volition.[44]

What remained unsettled for a few more weeks was whether the validity of the referendum was to be measured in terms of the permanent electoral lists applicable by virtue of the Law on the Election of the President (370/2004)[45] or of the general electoral laws. The difference is that, whereas the permanent electoral list for presidential elections comprises all Romanian citizens over the age of 18, only citizens whose residence is registered in their respective constituencies are on the general permanent electoral lists. The reference to the Presidential Election Law was, prior to the referendum, not contested by the political actors but, in view of the results, the focus of the political contention shifted to the figures. While the Court initially awarded the government time to update the lists prior to a final ruling on the validity, neither the text of the Referendum Law nor the Court's 2 August 2012 ruling gave guidance as to what the recount would actually have to bear on. A reference in the text intimated, however, that Romanian citizens residing abroad vote on 'supplementary electoral lists' and a reasonable implication could have been that the constitutional justices were in favour of a reassessment of the baseline. In view of massive emigration from Romania over the past decades, subtracting the diaspora (1,101,809) registered voters from the recount figure would have decisively tilted the balance in favour of dismissal.

On 6 August 2012, however, while the Court was not in session, an 'erratum', making express reference to Law 370/2004, was sent by the constitutional justice on duty to the *Official Journal*, published and inserted retroactively in the original text, immediately below the paragraph referred to above. Three of the constitutional justices, who had taken part in the initial ruling, were not informed by the Court President of this alteration. After a few more weeks, the Court invalidated the referendum for lack of quorum. But this was a decision that could just as well

[44] Hotărârea no 3 of 2 August 2012 (Constitutional Court of Romania). See, for a chronology of the events and an analysis of the contradictions in the referendum-related case law of the Court, Bianca Selejan-Gutan, 'The Illusion of the Romanian Constitution?', I-*CONnect*, 7 December 2012, www.iconnectblog.com/2012/12/the-illusion-of-the-romanian-constitution/.

[45] Law 370/2004 (Legea no 370/2004 'pentru alegerea Presedintelui Romaniei').

have been taken in July, immediately after the poll results had been made public by the Central Electoral Office.[46]

IV. CONCLUSION: THE CONSTITUTIONAL CRISIS IN CONTEXTS AND CONCEPTS

The political and judicial orgy described above is, of course, incongruous with any theory on the separation of powers or the rule of law, however fluid and contested these notions are in the abstract. But accusations about breaches of the rule of law, the separation of powers and, alas, constitutionalism are more credible in contexts where such elated concepts have already crystallised into stable, broadly accepted meanings or frameworks of reference. It should be apparent from the prior articulations of this argument that separation of powers, rule of law and constitutionality have acquired surprisingly pliable and unstable meanings in the current Romanian climate. The lack of a political or public sphere capable of fostering a meaningful 'constitutional moment' at the beginning of the 1990s, the lack of a body of competent constitutional experts able to flesh out the technicalities of a workable constitutional setting, and the vagaries of the syncopated amendment process of 2003, have all contributed to creating a system characterised by increasing fragmentation, normative antinomies and pathological path dependencies. The 'guarantor of constitutional supremacy', the Romanian Constitutional Court, has thus far not proven able to alleviate by means of interpretation some of the drafting blunders. Even though the Court is not subject to the rigours of a common law-style *stare decisis* doctrine, a measure of rationality and consistency in case law is indispensable to any form of credible mechanism of adjudication. The current record, marked rather by opportunistic twists and turns in the case law, leaves much to be desired. One can certainly hope for a rational process of amendment that would remedy these dysfunctions[47] but such expectations are, under the current circumstances, primarily nourished by an optimistic leap of faith.

It might also be possible to hope that membership in the Union and the 'European constitutional space' evoked by the title of the present volume would be conducive to a process of normalisation. Improvements could theoretically be produced by formal systemic interactions within the current European

[46] Hotărârea no 6 of 21 August 2012 (Constitutional Court of Romania). See the dissenting opinion by Justices Toader, Gaspar, and Predescu: 'Our disagreement with the ruling … rests on the fact that it has been adopted by reference to the provisions of Art 2(1) of Law 370/2004 on the election of the President of Romania, a solution anticipated through the "errata" of August 6, 2012, referring to the Ruling of the Constitutional Court No 3 of 2 August 2012, an "errata" regarding the adoption of which we were not consulted, a procedure unprecedented in constitutional case law'.

[47] A parliamentary commission has been recently convened to discuss the revision of the Constitution and the current coalition in power, USL, can muster the required majorities in both chambers. At this stage only broad guidelines and desiderata (streamlining the parliamentary process, clarification of the executive attributions, etc) have been announced. Hence, it is too early to speculate on the substance of the envisioned changes.

constitutional structure (eg European Commission country reports or the incentive provided by the postponement of accession to the Schengen Area) or result from informal nudges coming from germane international structures (such as the Venice Commission). *Pace* the overhanging assumptions in the Lisbon decision of the Bundesverfassungsgericht, the assertion of the editors, that 'in Europe constitution-making is not solely a national matter', is averred not only by the increasingly cosmopolitan way in which constitutional courts interact with the European project but also by the reality of overlapping attributions and interdependencies, challenging the normative monopoly of nation-states and the underpinning conceptual dichotomies of nation-state constitutionalism.[48] Indeed, even the German Constitutional Court, traditionally reluctant to cede its interpretive supremacy over the national constitution, found it hard, in the said decision, clearly to articulate the contours of an inalienable German constitutional core. External pressures bear even more heavily on Romania whose political system has been directly impacted on by the pre-accession scrutiny in accordance with the 'political *acquis*' and is still under monitoring within the framework of the Mechanism for Cooperation and Verification. That such influences exist and are relevant to constitutional evolution does not answer the crucial question regarding their benefits. Thus far, the jury is still out on the particular effect such processes have on constitutional justice in a state in transition such as my own. The European Commission, the primary institutional interface between the worlds of EU and Romanian constitutionalism, has not been very successful in promoting beneficial changes; this has partly been a consequence of the Commission's own institutional limitations and its lack of capacity to handle systemic problems of politics and values. A positive conclusion to the general, deeper crisis whose epiphenomenon was the constitutional-political turmoil during the summer of 2012 would presuppose the anticipation of a propitious window of opportunity for change, but all such predictions are now hypothetical.

[48] D Grimm, *Souveränität: Herkunft und Zukunft eines Schlüsselbegriffs* (Berlin, Berlin University Press, 2011); see also D Grimm, 'The Achievement of Constitutionalism and its Prospects in a Changed World' in P Dobner and M Loughlin (eds), *The Twilight of Constitutionalism?* (Oxford, Oxford University Press, 2010).

6

Romania in the European Union: Political Developments and the Rule of Law after Accession

COSMINA TANASOIU

I. INTRODUCTION

THE POST-ACCESSION RECORD in new Member States, including Romania, is a mix of progress (ie structural and formal progress including institution building, transposition of EU laws and energising anti-corruption mechanisms) and shortcomings (ie backtracking, delays and deficiencies in implementing EU laws). Post-accession, EU pressure manifested itself through a host of formal and discursive mechanisms (the negative-positive assessment model). Relying upon a mix of strongly worded public declarations carrying the threat of penalties (from activating the safeguard mechanisms and withdrawing EU funds to delaying Schengen accession), the actual imposition of penalties (freezing or withholding funds) and the Cooperation and Verification Mechanism (CVM), Brussels limited the scope and range of derailments but was unable to prevent them entirely. Romanian political elites show little restraint in breaching laws for the purpose of advancing or protecting individual or clan interests. The rule of law is often subordinated to accommodate the interests of the incumbents and progress is largely defined by the agenda of political elites rather than structural change. The political elites also appear to have mastered the technique of double discourse (one for Brussels stressing commitment to membership obligations and another for national audiences where political gameship takes priority over the rule of law). Reforms pursued under EU pressure, pre- and post-accession, are rolled back whenever they threaten to expose networks of influence, or endanger personal and clan interests.

Over the past two years concerns over democracy backsliding across Central and Eastern Europe increased following political developments in Hungary that threatened freedom of expression and raised the level of concentration of power and politicisation of public institutions. In Romania, the arrival in office in April 2012 of a Social Democrat-Liberal coalition government led to a flurry of measures (from restraining the powers of the Constitutional Court to the impeachment of the President), covered and debated by both national and international media, and worrying Western politicians as well as academics.[1] Brussels expressed serious concerns (by way of Commissioner Reding, President Barroso, President von Rompuy and selected MEPs) over the rule of law and the independence of the judiciary, and summoned the Prime Minister for explanations. German Chancellor Angela Merkel classified breaches of the rule of law as 'unacceptable', German Foreign Minister Guido Westerwelle found that the political conflicts threatened 'fundamental European values', the French government's spokesperson and the US ambassador to Romania voiced their respective administrations' 'deep concerns', and Christian Democrat German politicians considered that the changes endanger the rule of law and the democratic principles even more than in Hungary. The Romanian political and public arena split between those making accusations that a *coup d'état* had taken place and those denouncing Brussels for treating the country as 'a colony', rather than praising the democratic pursuit of removing a dictator from office.

II. FRAGILITY OF THE RULE OF LAW

Even by the standards of Romanian post-communist politics, the period 2007–12 has been marked by political instability and polarisation of political forces, pitching political camps against each other and Parliament against President. Since 2007, the political arena has been split between pro- and anti-President Traian Băsescu (in office since 2004) factions. Impeachment procedures were initiated twice against the sitting President for overstretching constitutional powers. Both went all the way to a referendum (in 2007 won by the President with over 70 per cent of the votes cast; in 2012 invalidated by a lower than required turnout, although 83 per cent of the votes favoured impeachment). Post-election coalition governments were recipes for instability and stagnation. The 'Justice and Truth' coalition broke months after EU accession and the liberal minority government faced numerous motions of censure. The grand coalition brokered by President Băsescu between the first two ranked parties (the Social Democrats and the Liberal Democrats) after the 2008 elections, despite securing a parliamentary majority of around 70 per cent, looked more like a minority government as both party leaders pursued their own agendas in view of the upcoming presidential elections. This coalition collapsed three months ahead of the elections, and was followed by a minority caretaker government whose legitimacy was challenged by the opposition and which spent most of the time battling motions of censure.

[1] KL Scheppele and V Perju, 'Guest Post: Separating Law and Politics in Romania' in P Krugman, *New York Times* blog, 12 July 2012, www.krugman.blogs.nytimes.com/2012/07/12/guest-post-separating-law-and-politics-in-romania/; T Gallagher and A Mungiu-Pippidi, opinion pieces in *România Liberă* (Bucharest), in 2012.

In such a belligerent environment, the rule of law becomes subject to appropriation by incumbents and its abuse is justified by previous abuses. The generalised practice of ethical minimalism dilutes individual responsibility, deflecting calls for sanctions by pointing to collective failures and shared culpability ('everyone does it'). Intra-elite conflict is fuelled by the determination to secure access and control over public institutions and resources whether political, legal (eg suspicions about the use of anti-corruption bodies to weaken opponents) or financial (eg EU funds). Each side accuses the other of breaches of law, endangering the rule of law and breaching democratic principles. The record of both pro- (consolidated around the Liberal Democrats (PDL)) and anti- (consolidated around the Social Liberal Union between the Social Democrats and the liberals) Băsescu camps that have dominated the political arena since 2007 is chequered. While in government, the Liberal Democrats merged local elections with parliamentary elections through a government decree in 2012 (claimed to be motivated as an austerity measure but suspected as a strategy to manipulate the vote as well as limit the build-up of a negative momentum ahead of parliamentary elections), passed legislation through parliament under dubious circumstances (ie the 2011 Pension Law[2] was passed in the Chamber of Deputies with more votes in favour than the number of MPs present) and modified legislation after it had been passed through Parliament but before it had been published in the Official Journal, thus effectively legislating by bypassing the legislature. The actions of the anti-corruption prosecutors have often been questioned over their target choices, which tend to disfavour the President's opponents.

In 2012, following the resignation of the Democrat Liberal (PDL) led coalition government (in power since 2008) amid popular protests against the austerity measures pursued to secure IMF financial assistance and the successful motion of censure against the short-lived replacement government in April 2012, the social democrat-liberal (Social-Liberal Union (USL)) coalition[3] entered office. United by its determination to remove the President from office, the coalition brought together the main political protagonists of the anti-Băsescu movement (the liberals and the social democrats) supported by the financial and media power of the former leader of the tiny Conservative Party. The coalition pursued a governing programme essentially geared towards impeaching President Băsescu in the name of parliamentary sovereignty, defence of the Constitution and popular discontent. The coalition claimed both a popular and a legal mandate, prompting some observers to call this either a 'people's coup'[4] or a 'legal putsch'. Decisions

[2] Law 187/2011 (Legea no 187/2011 'privind înfiinţarea, organizarea şi funcţionarea Fondului de garantare a drepturilor din sistemul de pensii private').

[3] Formed in February 2011 between the Social Democratic Party (PSD), and the Centre Right Alliance (the National Liberal Party and the Conservative Party) with the purpose of removing President Băsescu. The Union won the 2012 local elections, formed a parliamentary majority since 2007 and won a landslide victory in the December 2012 parliamentary elections.

[4] Interview with CT Popescu, Journalist (RTV, 3 July 2012), available at www.rtv.net/ctp-nu-asistam-la-o-lovitura-de-stat-ci-la-o-lovitura-de-popor_34787.html.

(often through government decrees) and measures taken in succession and with remarkable efficiency by the new government caused worries as to the degree of concentration of power, the same sin for which the new government had previously criticised the President.

The sharing of quasi-undemocratic practices across political parties, coalition governments and ruling elites validates a defence that points to previous breaches of laws and norms to justify and exonerate further breaches of law. In 2012, some civil society organisations and intellectual and cultural elites were unfazed by the coalition actions, minimising current misbehaviour by comparing these with their predecessors. Consequently, the value system is in perpetual motion, and the legal framework constantly moulded to accommodate incumbents. Amendments are justified as improving democratic control and/or efficiency, while actually increasing political control. Subsequently, institutions, mechanisms and procedures are subject to continuous change, adjustment and readjustment. Public institutions are quickly politicised to secure a subservient behaviour towards the new ruling elites through the enactment of government decrees. While ruling through governmental decrees is not in itself illegal, the abuse of such a practice is a recipe for executive overreach. In 2012, this practice allowed the government to speed up the pursuit of its agenda, securing the institutional framework that would facilitate the impeachment of the President and transferring control over state institutions from one camp to another (see below), leading to accusations of a *coup d'état*.

Scholars have warned about post-accession problems of compliance in terms of political conditionality,[5] partly because during the pre-accession period the framework of political conditionality did not rely upon a clear substantive distinction between democracy and the rule of law.[6] However, five years after accession, the events of 2012 were surprising because of the intensity, efficiency, relative disregard towards EU reactions, level of amateurism (public statements' blunders and contradictory messages across members of government) and professional (in)competence. The new government spent less time on its governing agenda and more on fending off accusations of plagiarism, which exposed a culture of copy-paste nursed by the collusion between politics and academia that reduced the distribution of academic credentials (both degrees and titles) to administrative paperwork and challenges over the incompatibility of its appointed ministers (some of whom were forced to resign).[7] Over a relatively short period of time

[5] See, eg G Pridham, 'Romania and EU Membership in Comparative Perspective: A Post-accession Compliance Problem? The Case of Political Conditionality' (2007) 8 *Perspectives on European Politics and Society* 168, 188.

[6] D Kochenov, *EU Enlargement and the Failure of Conditionality in the Fields of Democracy and the Rule of Law* (The Hague, Kluwer Law International, 2008).

[7] Two nominees were declared incompatible with the office either by the High Court of Justice and Cassation or by the Supreme Council of Magistrates (CSM) (the appointee for Minister of Culture was at the time of his appointment investigated for misuse of funds and nepotism; the nominee for Minister of Justice for combining a CSM position with a public office breaching the provisions of

(less than two months), through either government decrees or parliamentary enactments, the ruling coalition replaced the ombudsman (who tended to challenge government decrees in the Constitutional Court) on grounds of constitutional breaches;[8] restricted the power of the Constitutional Court to review Acts of Parliament on grounds of reducing workload; amended the referendum law; changed the status of the official gazette (a government decree transferred authority from the Chamber of Deputies to the government effectively allowing the government to determine when a law or a Constitutional Court ruling will come into force);[9] and changed the status of the Romanian Cultural Institute (ICR) from the presidential administration to the Senate by governmental decree.[10] The speakers of both Chambers of Parliament were sacked and replaced with representatives of the ruling coalition securing in the process the position of the President of the Senate for the leader of the National Liberal Party and thus granting him the opportunity to become interim President following a successful impeachment vote in the Parliament (the USL agreement distributes the balance of power between the main partners in the event of electoral victory and as such the presidential office is promised to the liberal leader). The Parliament decided by 256 to 114 votes in favour of impeachment.

During the 29 July 2012 referendum campaign, each camp accused the other of breaching democratic norms by calling for a boycott of the vote, thus

Law 317/2004 (Legea no 317/2004 'privind Consiliul Superior al Magistraturii') and two successive Ministers of Education were forced to resign (one for misrepresenting academic credentials by misappropriating degrees and for combining functions incompatible with each other by being simultaneously the chair of a body representing private universities who were suing the Ministry of Education over a ranking system, creating the absurd situation of being simultaneously accuser and defendant in a trial; one following accusations of plagiarism in academic publications). The Prime Minister's PhD thesis was exposed as plagiarised by the scientific journal, *Nature*. This triggered a flurry of political and academic debates over the norms of plagiarism, and led to the politicisation of investigative bodies and arbitrary decisions by the interim Minister of Education.

[8] Decision No 32 of 3 July 2012 for the dismissal of Mr Gheorghe Iancu from the office of Ombudsperson.

[9] The decree came at a time when the Prime Minister was challenging the President over representing Romania at European Council meetings. The Constitutional Court ruled, on the basis of art 146(e) of the Constitution, that representation at the European Council falls among the attributes of the President (27 July 2012). The ruling was published after the June 2012 European Council, allowing the Prime Minister to represent the country.

[10] Emergency Ordinance 27/2012 of 14 June 2012 (Ordonanta de urgenta no *27/2012* 'privind unele masuri in domeniul cultural'). Created in 2003, ICR was placed under the authority of the President, who was its honorary President (at the time, President Ion Iliescu). Its purpose is to promote Romanian culture and civilisation both nationally and abroad. The government justified the measure on democratic grounds (shifting control from one person to representatives) and expressed worries over the institute's policy to minimise the 'attachment to the Romanian nation'. Following the decree, a silent protest called the Black Tie Protest (in reference to then ICR President Horia-Roman Patapievici's habit of wearing black tie attire) challenged the government's justifications, claiming the decree had little to do with the institutional record and more with pursuit of depleting the current President's control over public institutions and transforming ICR into an instrument of propaganda. Occasionally the subject of controversies, the ICR record is on average praised by the cultural elite. The ICR leadership announced their resignation following the Constitutional Court validation of the decree on 31 July 2012.

relinquishing civic duty (the presidential camp), and by electoral fraud (the USL coalition). The government urged voters to impeach a dictator. This narrative was developed, as during the 2009 presidential campaign, through references to Ceauşescu[11] and the 1989 revolution. As in 2009, a large pre-referendum rally was held in Timişoara, the city where it all began in December 1989, including the chants from December 1989 'today in Timişoara, tomorrow throughout the country'. Both sides threatened the other with jail terms in the event of its victory (the leaders of the coalition for engineering the *coup d'état*; the President and his clan for illegal financial transactions and defrauding *poporul* (the nation). The referendum campaign was framed as a choice between a likely onslaught on the rule of law by a coalition motivated by securing control over the judiciary, and an incumbent presented as a 'rascal', head of a clan that had enriched itself to the detriment of average Romanians. His powers allegedly ranged from commanding prosecutors as personal janissaries, manipulating the West, and controlling the Constitutional Court. Against such mighty forces, the parliamentary majority and the government supported by their respective partisan media outlets (some of which were rating leaders, eg Antena 3) posed as powerless defenders of democracy and future victims of prosecution. While the result of the vote was largely in favour of impeachment (around 87 per cent), a turnout of 46 per cent could not offer an outright victory. Both sides, however, called the result a victory for democracy. The President talked about reconciliation and demanded an investigation of those responsible for the *coup d'état*. The government claimed morality demanded resignation and maintained that the President was effectively impeached given the results.

Following the invalidation of the referendum, the battle continues against either 'the Băsescu regime' or the 'horsemen of the Apocalypse' (a metaphor used by the novelist Mircea Cartarescu in reference to Victor Ponta, Crin Antonescu and Dan Voiculescu). Both camps seek legitimacy from the people, for the people, by the people through regular references to being *pentru popor* (for the people), *al poporului* (of the people). The government and the coalition parliamentary leaders claim a mandate from the over 7 million voters supporting impeachment, the President from the 10 million absentees, though not all 7 million or so were pro-USL, nor were all absentees pro-Băsescu. Opponents, portrayed as enemies (*duşmani*), are demonised. President Băsescu is portrayed as a dictator and as such compared to Ceauşescu, Stalin, Putin and his supporters dismissed as lackeys (eg the Prime Minister dismissed the possibility of cooperating with 'Băsescu's waiters'). The USL tactics are compared to miners' violent interventions (*mineriade)* against the rule of law. Such Leninist logic (us versus them) prevents compromise

[11] Eg, on 29 July 2012, the Prime Minister opened the doors at Villa Dante to ordinary citizens. One of the residences for the use of high level officials, the villa was presented as a potential future residence for President Băsescu post-mandate. Its luxury was expected to resonate badly in times of economic hardship as well as serve as a reminder of the discovery of Ceausescus' villas in December 1989. Random interviews among visitors by journalists showed that the strategy was not without success.

and fosters conflict. Both sides ground their credibility in the constitutionality of their positions. President Băsescu continues to pose as the defender of an independent justice, USL claims popular mandate, representing a parliamentary majority, and parliamentary sovereignty above all other institutions, including the Constitutional Court.

III. (IN)DEPENDENCE OF THE JUDICIARY AND THE CONSTITUTIONAL COURT

At the time of its accession, Romania had yet to meet the membership criteria for judicial reforms and anti-corruption measures. Worries over the European Union's ability to influence domestic change in the absence of leverage mechanisms (conditionality of membership) led to a host of formal (the CVM, the safeguard clauses and cutting of funds) and discursive (the negative-positive assessment model) mechanisms as substitute incentives for the pursuit of reforms post-accession. The CVM was aimed at monitoring progress through reports assessing the standards on justice and home affairs by meeting specific benchmarks (four for Romania, six for Bulgaria). They reinforced the EU orthodox deterrence mechanisms (ie the infringement procedure and the use of Article 7 of the Lisbon Treaty granting the EU power to sanction and even exclude countries violating its fundamental democratic rules) and the development of new mechanisms (ie benchmarking, the OMC and annual 'scoreboards' on implementation records with internal market regulation).

Established de jure by the 1991 Constitution and reinforced by the 1992 Law on the Organization of the Judiciary,[12] the independence of the judiciary remains a matter of concern. Investigative media reports often point to connections between officers of the court and political circles. Political allegiance is often credited as the explanation for professional success and breaching norms is not an impediment to one's career. Control over the judicial branch has often led to open political warfare. Nominations of Ministers of Justice, public prosecutors or anti-corruption prosecutors are subject to debates that have more to do with their perceived allegiance and less with their competence. In 2007, then Minister of Justice Monica Macovei, largely credited with jump-starting the judicial reforms, including the judicial pursuit of public officials, was impeached by the Senate six months after accession (the only minister to be impeached since 1990).

In 2012, the government and its allies challenged the legitimacy of the Constitutional Court every time the rulings were not favourable. The Constitutional Court ruled the amendments to the referendum law unconstitutional and required a quorum of 50 per cent + 1 of registered voters for a referendum to be valid, prompting declarations such as 'nine unelected judges cannot rank higher

[12] Law 92/1992 (Legea no 92/1992 'pentru organizarea judecătorească').

than a directly elected legislature' from the sitting Prime Minister. The government eventually bowed to pressure from Brussels (which demanded respect for the Constitutional Court rulings) and accepted the quorum. While in Brussels, the Prime Minister gave assurances that the government would abide by the rulings of the Constitutional Court. However, on 26 July 2012, Romanian media (both written and broadcast) made public a document carrying the signatures of the sitting Prime Minister, the interim President and the new Presidents of the Chambers of Parliament, by which they committed to dismantle the Constitutional Court and shut down the National Agency for Integrity (ANI)[13] and the Anti-Corruption Prosecutorial Office (DNA),[14] both part of the conditionality criteria for EU accession. At the peak of the conflict, some judges complained of pressure and one reported death threats.[15] The European Commission's report of July 2012 blasted these actions as effectively jeopardising the independence of the judiciary.

Established as a authority distinct from the judiciary by the 1991 Constitution (article 144), the Romanian Constitutional Court is a political-judicial hybrid, which despite the independence of the judiciary remains vulnerable directly or indirectly to political factors.[16] Initially appointed by a Parliament in which one party held a 70 per cent majority, its judges have often come under criticisms for political affiliation. In time, the Court has emerged as a conservative actor, its rulings often defending the status quo and stalling reformist agendas. Between 2007 and 2012, the Romanian Constitutional Court has effectively refereed between political factions as well as influenced the pace and scope of judicial reforms. Its rulings have been hailed or dismissed depending upon how they rate in reference to a party's interests.

In July 2007, the Court ruled unconstitutional the laws allowing the prosecution of former high level government officials as private citizens in a corruption case involving former Prime Minister Adrian Năstase. The Court established that former government officials can only be investigated for corruption upon approval by the President and Parliament. Following President Băsescu's refusal to accept the government nominee for Minister of Justice, the Court ruled that

[13] Responsible for vetting public officials' declared assets, ANI was created in May 2007 as part of the membership pre-accession commitments.

[14] Created in 2002 as the Anticorruption Prosecution Office, DNA is headed by a chief prosecutor and two deputies, nominated by the Minister of Justice and appointed by the President. DNA is subordinated to the General Prosecutor's Office attached to the High Court of Cassation and Justice. Its tasks are to prevent, investigate and prosecute corruption-related offences (eg bribery, graft, patronage and embezzlement) causing a material damage higher than 200,000 euros or whose value of involved amounts or goods is higher than 10,000 euros.

[15] The judge Aspasia Cojocaru, largely seen as the swing vote during the deliberations on the validity of the referendum, reported receiving death threats. The police investigation identified a former inmate as the source of the threats. It remains unclear whether this was the action of a disgruntled defendant or of a pawn in a political game.

[16] For an overview see R Weber, 'The Romanian Constitutional Court: In Search of Its Own Identity' in W Sadurski (ed), *Constitutional Justice, East and West: Democratic Legitimacy and Constitutional Courts in Post-Communist Europe in a Comparative Perspective* (The Hague, Kluwer Law International, 2002).

the President can only refuse a nomination once despite the absence of such a constitutional limitation. Incidentally, the next appointment was responsible for backtracking on several previously introduced reforms. The rulings of the Court were often criticised for being grounded in short-term considerations rather than constitutional jurisprudence. The Court found that the law creating the National Council for the Study of Securitate Archives (CNSAS), the institution responsible for screening public officials, was unconstitutional, a month before it was expected to start screening magistrates for former links to the secret police. In 2010, the Court declared ANI, an anti-corruption institution praised in European Commission reports, as unconstitutional (removing its mandate of investigating the wealth of political figures), a decision widely criticised as political and even personal in nature (seven of its nine judges were being investigated by ANI at the time of the verdict).[17]

In 2012, the Constitutional Court was at the centre of the unfolding political theatre. As both sides sought legitimacy through the law, much of the political conflict was channelled through the Constitutional Court. Both the President and his opponents (whether the government or the new parliamentary majority) posed as guarantors of the constitutional order. The Constitutional Court validated the procedure by which the President was impeached (the incumbent himself in his address to Parliament during the impeachment debates acknowledged the right of the Parliament to attempt his impeachment), although stating that the examples of constitutional breaches provided (eg statements in relation to retirees, the economic crisis or calling for doctors to emigrate) do not constitute 'grave breaches of constitutional attributions' (as per article 95 of the Constitution) and fall within the limits of freedom of expression allowed for public, including presidential, office (as per previous Court Decision No 53 of 28 January 2005).[18] Called upon to rule on the validity of the referendum, while pressed by both sides for a favourable resolution and presented with conflicting documents by the Minister of Home Affairs over the numbers of eligible voters and census irregularities,[19] the Constitutional Court chose initially to postpone its decision (being both

[17] 'CCR: ANI Law is Unconstitutional', *Ziare* (Bucharest), 29 April 2010, available at www.ziare.com/articole/legea+ani+neconstitutionala.

[18] Decizia No 53 of 28 January 2005 (Constitutional Court of Romania).

[19] The government found itself challenging the organisation of its own referendum on grounds that the electoral lists were not updated to reflect the demographic decrease that would have reduced the necessary quorum. The Minister of Home Affairs was unable to provide clear numbers. The Court asked for electoral lists, its request allegedly falsified by a clerk to read 'updated electoral lists' thus substantiating the government's argument for a post-referendum 'mini census'. The debacle led to the resignation of the Minister of Home Affairs and the Secretary of State for population census. Taped phone calls conversations between these officials revealed their reluctance to alter electoral lists, fearing having 'to spend retirement in jail' (published in *România Liberă* (Bucharest), 10 August 2012, available at www.romanialibera.ro/actualitate/educatie/titularizare-2012-rezultate-finale-dupa-contestatii-jumatate-dintre-profesori-au-luat-note-mai-mici-de-7-273391.html). Civil servants were also taped while discussing absurd census data (eg 400,000 deaths in one county over one month).

praised for thoughtfulness and criticised for lacking guts) and finally ruled the referendum invalid on 21 August 2012.[20]

Prior to accession, EU political conditionality determined formal and institutional changes in the fight against corruption, which in Romania led to the creation of bodies, agencies and institutions.[21] Their number served to account for progress in annual EU reports, but failed to deliver, due to constant overlapping in functions, the absence of a clear distribution of responsibilities and the continuous reshuffling they underwent following government changes. Although public perception of corruption levels changed little between 1993 and 2007 (according to the Transparency International Index),[22] due to EU pressure (and the work of certain civic organisations, such as the Romanian Academic Society Campaign for a Clean Parliament) progress was noticeable in terms of the institutionalisation of public declarations of assets by public officials, investigations of these assets when discrepancies were present and even occasional resignations of ministers accused of mismanagement of public funds and illegal allocation of public procurement contracts (eg the case of Romanian Minister of Sports Monica Iacob Ridzi in 2009) or EU funds, bribery or traffic in influence. Yet, the post-2007 European Commission country reports consistently point out shortcomings in meeting the benchmarks and foot-dragging in addressing systemic corruption, but also the lack of administrative capacities and non-transparency in dealing with EU funds, particularly agricultural subsidies. If accession introduced a number of treaty obligations to fight corruption, it also multiplied the opportunities for corruption, through the privatisation of national enterprises and access to EU funds (which resulted in scandals over misappropriation of EU funds and preferential awarding of public procurement contracts).

The dilution of the external incentive motive credited with triggering reforms prior to accession[23] from reward for reform to penalty for non-reform appears to have succeeded in preventing a complete halt to reforms. Meanwhile, the conventional EU mechanism to address infringements seems to infuse no sense of urgency. The CVM and its biannual progress reports were the most visible tools in monitoring and pursuing achievements. While their direct impact

[20] The political allegiance of the judges renders a two-thirds majority required for such a decision all but impossible: four appointed by the Social Democrats, four by liberal democrats, and one representative of the ethnic Hungarian minority. A first vote counted five out of nine judges in favour of invalidating the referendum. The representative of the ethnic minority worried that the Prime Minister would blame the Hungarian minority for the results (post referendum both the Prime Minister and the interim President made statements, on the fringe of xenophobia, blaming the Hungarian minority for the low turnout).

[21] Eg, the National Council for Action Against Corruption and Organized Crime (1997), the Anti-Corruption Criminal Investigation and Criminology Section (1998), the Special Anti-corruption and Organized Crime Unit within the General Prosecutor's Office (2000), National Anti-Corruption Prosecutor's Office (2002), the National Anti-Corruption Directorate (DNA) (2002), the Directorate General for Anti-corruption answering to the Minister of Interior (2005).

[22] See www.transparency.org.ro/politici_si_studii/indici/ipc/2007/index_en.html.

[23] See, eg F Schimmelfenning and U Sedelmeier (eds), *The Europeanization of Central and Eastern Europe* (Ithaca, NY, Cornell University Press, 2005).

is hard to estimate, the CVM reports have been called into question over their methodology for tracking progress, data collection strategies and sampling methods when deciding which high corruption cases are monitored and included in the final report. Although envisioned as precursors to the activation of safeguard clauses should progress be less than expected, the CVM reports have so far contributed to the political narrative, signalling the mood in Brussels and delivering warnings or praise, rather than announcing measures to come. After 2010 and the disappearance of the looming threat of safeguard clauses, the Schengen accession became a new carrot/stick. The refusal by a core of EU countries (France, Germany, the Netherlands, Belgium, Sweden and Finland) to admit Romania and Bulgaria to the Schengen area in June 2011 despite their meeting the technical requirements (both the European Parliament and the Commission recommended accession) was publicly linked to their failure to tackle corruption and organised crime and uneven progress towards judicial reforms.[24] It constituted the first effective sanction grounded in the CVM mechanism.

At the preliminary stage of the reform, there appeared to be progress regarding the depoliticisation of the judiciary (eg changing the procedure for appointing prosecutors) and energising the anti-corruption mechanisms, but subsequent amendments to the legal framework often diluted developments. According to a report issued by a Romanian coalition of non-governmental organisations, the Initiative for a Clean Justice (IJC), the amendments to Law 144/2007[25] (which among others politicised the ANI's structure, at the level of the Secretary of State, placed immediately under the director) rendered ANI 'toothless'. As a result, passing a law promises little in terms of future implementation.

Despite the growing number of anti-corruption investigations and trials involving high level officials, both high and low level corruption remain rampant. National political elites show a remarkable consensus across party lines in resisting pressure from Brussels to reform those areas where personal costs trump national benefits, ie judicial reforms and anti-corruption measures. Anti-corruption investigations involving MPs often stop at the doors of the Parliament, which more often than not tends to uphold parliamentary immunity. The 2008 European Commission report criticised the Romanian Parliament's measures aimed at 'sheltering high level officials from prosecution on corruption charges'.[26] The 2009 proposed amendments to the Romanian penal and civil codes minimised the scope of corruption trials (ie classifying frauds below 9 million euros as misdemeanours, subject to a maximum five-year sentence, which prompted a public statement by the 25 ambassadors of EU Member States).

[24] 'Bulgaria, Romania, Denied Schengen Entry', *EurActiv* (Brussels), 9 June 2011, available at www.euractiv.com/future-eu/bulgaria-romania-denied-schengen-news-505471.

[25] Law 144/2007 (Legea no 144/2007 'privind infiintarea, organizarea si functionarea Agentiei Nationale de Integritate').

[26] European Commission, *Report from the Commission to the European Parliament and the Council on Progress in Romania under the Cooperation and Verification Mechanism*, COM(2012)410 final.

In the aftermath, an EU delegation was dispatched to hold closed-door meetings with the Parliamentary Committee for Judicial Affairs.

The judiciary itself is not above corruption scandals, whether due to abuse of function, bribery or incompatibility with office. The Superior Council of the Magistrates (CSM), known for its opaque structure and whose membership is largely decided by political actors (the Parliament, President) as well as courts, is responsible for the code of conduct of all members of the judiciary and has been blamed for shielding members of the judiciary from public or judicial scrutiny. Following accession, CSM enacted a new strategy for human resources in response to criticisms of non-transparent personnel practices but continues to be a factor of regress rather than progress. In October 2008, the Romanian CSM appointed as President of the High Court of Cassation and Justice someone who, while CSM President, campaigned to prevent the publication of a magistrate's income and faced accusations of nepotism for having facilitated his daughter's bar exam and securing her a position as a CSM consultant. Similar to the Parliament's upholding of parliamentary immunity and thus preventing the initiation of anti-corruption investigations, CSM has dismissed requests for an investigation. In December 2012, the government amended Law 317/2004[27] through a government decree (No 23/2012)[28] to allow the appointment of a new CSM member declared incompatible with the position by ANI in accordance with the provisions of the 2004 Law. The amendment removed the interdiction of combination of mandates (the nominee held a university rector position) for CSM members.

The fight against corruption energised under pressure from Brussels has become a battle ground for political actors seeking to use it against opponents. The legitimacy of anti-corruption bodies is called into question and they are accused of becoming tools in the hands of the incumbent. Plans by the current coalition to replace the anti-corruption prosecutor and even dismantle the anti-corruption body (DNA) are regularly exposed in the media. In 2012, following the conviction of former Prime Minister Adrian Năstase in one of the four trials commenced against him in January 2012, both Năstase and the new leader of the Social Democrats, Victor Ponta, labelled the verdict 'political' and criticised the DNA for political partisanship.[29] What followed resembled a political soap opera involving a botched suicide attempt, and the Ministry of Home Affairs relaxed

[27] Law 317/2004 (n 7).

[28] Decree 23/2012 of June 2012 (Ordonanţă Guvernului no 23/2012). OG 23/2012 primarily modifies the law on the status of magistrates (Law 303/2004 of 27 September 2004 (Legea no 303/2004 'privind statutul judecătorilor şi procurorilor')) but also Law 247/2005 of 22 July 2005 (Legea no 247/2005 'privind reforma în domeniile proprietăţii şi justiţiei, precum şi unele măsuri adiacente') and art 54 of the law on the accumulation of functions and their 'dignitary' status (Law 317/2004 of 1 July 2004 (Legea no 317/2004 'privind Consiliul Superior al Magistraturii')). President Băsescu asked that it be re-examined in December 2012.

[29] In an Euronews interview in July 2012, he denied any previous friendship with the former Prime Minister, despite common knowledge that his whole political career has been effectively mentored by Năstase, who also acted as his PhD supervisor.

the application of the law by postponing the former Prime Minister's transfer to the penitentiary system on grounds of emergency medical treatment. His party colleagues were quick to lament his fate, praising his service to the country and dismissing the corruption charges as political vendetta. He was compared with Prime Ministers and inter-war political elites imprisoned as political prisoners by the communist regime, effectively equating fraud with political repression.

However, by contrast to the 1990s when the judiciary failed to prosecute often blatantly corrupt behaviour of some ministers, closer to accession and after accession corruption trials were initiated and prosecuted involving both political and economic heavyweights (eg former Romanian Prime Minister Adrian Năstase; oil magnate and National Liberal Party financier Dinu Patriciu; media magnate and leader of the Conservative Party Dan Voiculescu; media magnates Sorin Ovidiu Vântu and Dan Diaconescu) and these occasionally secured convictions (as mentioned, in January 2012, former Prime Minister Adrian Năstase was sentenced to two years in prison for fraud in one of the four trials initiated against him and the verdict was confirmed by the High Court of Justice and Cassation, rendering it permanent). These trials exposed deep and intricate links between the political elites and business circles. The work of the prosecution (praised repeatedly by the European Commission), possibly regenerated by the recruitment of new, younger personnel who are less anchored in the informal networks, rarely translates into indictments. Trials drag on in court, and are often dismissed or suspended. In the few cases where prosecution of high level officials (ministers, former ministers or former Prime Ministers) for corruption, bribery, abuse of public office or traffic in influence got under way, they were either rebuffed by Parliament, which refused to strip defendants of immunity, or stalled in front of judges.[30] The nomination and appointment of DNA personnel has been the subject of intense political conflict over the years. In summer 2008, debates over the appointment of the Romanian anti-corruption chief prosecutor, Daniel Morar, led to political warfare between the President-government camp and the opposition. Though in the end, Morar was reappointed (not least due to pressure from Brussels), the issue was not settled. During the 2009 presidential campaign, the Social Democrat candidate hinted at the possibility of replacing the prosecutor general as well as the DNA prosecutor. In 2012, following initial indications of the government intent to replace the general prosecutor and the anti-corruption prosecutor with allies, the

[30] Attempts by anti-corruption prosecutors to indict former Prime Minister Adrian Năstase (ie Afacerea Tamara, Afacerea Zambaccian, Trofeul Calităţii) were initially rebuffed by Parliament, which refused to revoke his parliamentary immunity. Investigations of ministers for misuse of public money also stalled. Sport Minister Monica Iacob-Ritzi (rumoured to have financed President Băsescu's daughter's campaign for the European Parliament as an independent), resigned under pressure, and the prosecutor general asked Parliament for permission to prosecute. Minister of Tourism Elena Udrea was investigated by a parliamentary commission, which complained of restricted access to documents, and the Minister's refusal to testify. In December the prosecutors closed the case. She was appointed Minister for Development and Tourism (the ministry with the largest budget, including managing EU funds).

government initially postponed the plans in the face of EU unease and exposure of behind closed doors deals.[31] The initial nominees were rejected by the parliamentary committee after hearings. Rumours abound that the impeachment of the President was partly fuelled by the need to roll back the power of anti-corruption prosecutors, whether to secure the former Social Democrat Prime Minister a pardon from a more willing President or to avoid Dan Voiculescu's prosecution by anti-corruption prosecutors.[32]

IV. BALANCING MEMBERSHIP COMMITMENTS AND DOMESTIC POLITICS

The dynamic of pre-accession and conditionality has functioned with the assumption that Europeanisation[33] is a one-way process, and that conditionality criteria would secure the irreversibility of reforms. In practice, clientelistic politics and the overriding of public policy by private interests means that Europeanisation is contained by network politics and that it has been incorporated in domestic politics mainly as a strategy/mechanism to score points against opponents rather than structural change. Pre-accession, Brussels has been outfoxed by this type of pretence politics masterminded by predatory elites[34] seeking the benefits of membership (especially access to EU funds) while ducking commitments. Post-accession, Brussels' strategy of limiting criticisms to language rather than sanctions has taught national politicians that the European Union's scrutiny is limited in scope (in 2012 a member of government dismissed the possibility of sanctions on the grounds that Brussels has other things to worry about). Progress is dependent upon those in a position to govern, enforce policy, prosecute or judge. The Romanian political elite increasingly challenge Brussels' assessment and the CVM monitoring mechanism for practising double standards, and for trampling on Romanian sovereignty. In 2012, Romanian ruling elites perfected the practice of double narrative: one in Brussels (appeasing and reassuring over

[31] Phone conversations intercepted by anti-corruption bodies and made public by the media exposed the attempt of two CSM members (currently under investigation by DNA prosecutors) to lobby the Prime Minister for these positions, promising in return obedience.

[32] Daily newspaper *Evenimentul Zilei* ('Dan Voiculescu Announces the Return to the Mafia State', *Evenimentul Zilei* (Bucharest), 26 June 2012, available at www.evz.ro/detalii/stiri/dan-voiculescu-nu-moare-parlamentul-fara-mine-si-nici-eu-fara-parlament-988786.html), attributed the following remark to the sponsor, founder and former leader of the Conservative Party (junior partner of the coalition in power), Dan Voiculescu (a media magnate and a politician with an informer past for the communist secret police, the Securitate): 'we do not have the whole power, until we get the judiciary'. His party denied the quote and charged the newspaper with inventing news.

[33] Europeanisation is understood here as the process by which Member States' domestic polities, politics and policies are influenced by EU policy outcomes and structures of governance (for overviews see, eg K Featherstone and C Radaelli (eds), *The Politics of Europeanization* (Oxford, Oxford University Press, 2003).

[34] T Gallagher, *Romania and the European Union: How the Weak Vanquished the Strong* (Manchester, Manchester University Press, 2009).

Romanian commitments) and one at home (flexing muscles against '*diktats*' from the European Commission and pursuing the same measures they committed in Brussels not to seek).

Optimistic readings of the Romanian post-accession record have noted the success of political conditionality, the compliance record[35] and the use of 'forceful language' by the Commission when pressing for anti-corruption measures.[36] Structural developments (eg legal framework and institution building) and apparent compliance (ie the relatively small number of infringement procedures compared with old Member States) are moderated when read in reference to parliamentary records (eg the parliamentary Committee on European Affairs) showing that speedy transposition is largely due to lack of parliamentary discussion of EU legislation such as Directives that require the national Parliament's approval, and the difficulties of implementation.[37] The succession of events in 2012 confirm that Romanian political elites released from the pressure of conditionality and accession show a rather cavalier attitude towards EU rules and regulations and EU commitments when personal and clan interests are at stake. Institution building and legal frameworks developed under EU pressure appear as forms without substance, a facade Europeanisation rather than systemic change.[38]

While for the period 2007–11, Romania boasted an almost spotless record of transposition of EU legislation, the Commission has opened several infringement procedures (at different stages, ie warning, formal notice or reasoned opinion) for discriminatory taxation, breaching EU legislation on energy, telecommunication (lack of availability and lack of caller location for '112' calls) and environment (failing to implement nature law protection and insufficient environmental protection of the Black Sea coast). The breach of EU environmental legislation confirms that post-accession, pre-accession problems persist: environmental legislation during the pre-accession period had the worst chance of transposition regardless of government capacity or political preferences.[39]

[35] U Sedelmeier, 'After Conditionality: Post-accession Compliance with EU Law in East Central Europe' (2008) 15 *Journal of European Public Policy* 806, 825; B Steunenberg and D Toshkov, 'Comparing Transposition in the 27 Member States of the European Union: The Impact of Discretion and Legal Fit' (2009) 16 *Journal of European Public Policy* 951, 970; MA Vachudova and AB Spenzharova, 'Consolidating Liberal Democracy in Bulgaria and Romania after EU Accession' (2012) 35 *West European Politics* 39, 58.

[36] MA Vachudova, 'Corruption and Compliance in the EU's Post-Communist Members and Candidates' (2009) 47 *Journal of Common Market Studies* 43, 62.

[37] See, eg C Knill and J Tosun, 'Post-Accession Transposition of EU Law in New Member States: A Cross-country Comparison' (2009) 13 *European Integration Online Papers*, para 18, www.papers.ssrn.com/sol3/papers.cfm?abstract_id=1562666; F Trauner, 'Post-Accession Compliance with EU Law in Bulgaria and Romania: A Comparative Perspective' (2009) 13 *European Integration Online Papers*, para 21, www.papers.ssrn.com/sol3/papers.cfm?abstract_id=1562666.

[38] See, eg SA Andreev, 'The Unbearable Lightness of Membership: Romania and Bulgaria after the 2007 EU Accession' (2009) 42 *Communist and Post-communist Studies* 375, 393; C Tanasoiu, 'Europeanization Post-accession: Rule Adoption and National Political Elites in Romania and Bulgaria' (2012) 12 *Journal of Southeast European and Black Sea Studies* 173, 193.

[39] D Toshkov, 'Embracing European Law: Compliance with EU Directives in Central and Eastern Europe' (2008) 9 *European Union Politics* 379, 402.

In May 2011, Romania risked infringement procedures over failing to adopt new EU portability regulations and online gaming regulations.[40] It has to be pointed out, however, that as of 2011, Romania (and Bulgaria) has one of the lowest numbers of infringement cases among Member States (Italy boasting 135 cases in 2011, followed by Greece with 123 and Belgium with 117 cases).[41] Problems over implementation can be partly explained by national politicians' focus upon avoiding activation of the safeguard clause (following the 2009 country report, the Romanian Minister of Justice declared that 'the good thing is that we avoided the safeguard clause'), and partly because implementation of EU law ranks behind vested interests in national politics.[42] Both the number of infringement procedures and the governments' unresponsiveness in addressing these problems verify scholars' expectations that conventional EU mechanisms will have limited results post-accession.

Brussels appears ill-equipped to deal with breaches of political conditionality. The suspension clause (Article 7 of the Lisbon Treaty) foresees the suspension of some of a Member State's rights, while its obligations remain binding, when the Union's fundamental values (liberty, democracy, respect for human rights and fundamental freedoms and the rule of law) are endangered. However, the suspension of voting rights is an extreme measure requiring a complicated decision-making process (Article 354 TFEU) and while previously mentioned in reference to the developments in Hungary in 2011 and Greece in 2010, it has not yet been applied. It also seems to be unprepared for backsliding, functioning with a similar linear logic, expecting acquired standards to remain permanent. While in 2012 Brussels acknowledged in the 11 points included in the CVM's July 2012 report that achievements are not irreversible, Brussels' involvement in national politics is vulnerable to national political elites reverting towards a narrative of national sovereignty. This discourse has gained force since 2008 following the EU reports critical towards the Parliament, identified as a veto player in terms of pursuing an anti-corruption agenda, sheltering MPs from prosecution by not revoking their parliamentary immunity and amending legislation curbing the power of investigative bodies. At the time, former Prime Minister Adrian Năstase (as already mentioned, currently serving a two-year term in jail for bribery), the Social Democrat MEP Adrian Severin (currently investigated for bribery and one of the three MEPs entrapped by British journalists to accept money in exchange for

[40] 'Romania Risks Iinfringement If It Fails to Adopt New EU Portability Stipulations', *Business Review* (Bucharest), 24 May 2011, available at www.business-review.eu/news/romania-risks-infringement-if-it-fails-to-adopt-new-eu-portability-stipulations-11604/.

[41] European Commission, *29th Annual Report on Monitoring the Application of EU Law 2011*, COM (2012)714 final.

[42] In 2007, the Romanian parliamentary Committee for European Affairs never met. The chair dismissed a consultant inquiry over the pace of adopting EU Directives. By December 2007, the committee had discussed no EU legislation, an activity dismissed as irrelevant in May ('we have no time for peanuts now', on the referendum to impeach the President) and as secondary in the autumn (time of local elections). (This author's informal gathering of information).

lobbying, and the only one not to resign in the aftermath), and current Prime Minister Victor Ponta accused the European Commission of being undemocratic and undermining the rule of law by criticising the Parliament, and referred to the CVM as irrelevant to Romanian reality and over-focused on high level officials' corruption. In 2012, Romanian ruling elites accused Brussels of treating the country as a 'colony', with 'second class membership', over-stepping its authority, allowing itself to be manipulated by opponents' propaganda and lacking knowledge of the Romanian context.

Since 2007, while the European Commission expressed 'concerns', delivered 'warnings' and waived the prospect of penalties, Brussels' written language has been consistently less tough than expected, choosing pressure over punishment. Common to all country reports is the Commission's negative-positive assessment model (ie 'genuine efforts and some progress made but more needed', 'fundamentals are in place but the bases are still fragile'). The EU country reports noted the 'uneven commitment' between state institutions (2008) and the 'unwillingness of the leadership or the judiciary to cooperate' (2010), placed responsibility on the Parliament for stalling reforms and interfering with the judicial process (2008, 2009, 2011), and acknowledged the work of the prosecutor general and the DNA despite the limited success in courts (2009, 2011). The July 2012 CVM report was expected to be extremely critical and, as usual, observers raised the spectre of sanctions. While the July 2012 report reflected the European Commission's concerns over political developments, including the EU's 11 points presented to the Prime Minister earlier in the month, it did not carry any sanctions. In the face of blatant derailments, the EU dispatches delegations to Bucharest reminding the Romanian elites of their commitments, Member State ambassadors make public declarations or hold meetings, or as in 2012, government representatives are called to Brussels to provide explanations. On 12 July 2012, Prime Minister Victor Ponta was called to Brussels amid growing concerns over the rule of law and the independence of the judiciary. The EU President presented the Prime Minister with 11 points (later included in the EU report), among which the independence of the Constitutional Court and the application of the referendum law, as to which it required answers. On 16 July, the Commission confirmed receipt of the Romanian response and declared itself satisfied 'if followed accordingly', but also stated that the EU will continue to monitor the evolution in the country, in addition to the CVM mechanism.

The reluctance of the European Union to apply sanctions has validated the political elites' strategy to 'talk the talk, without walking the walk'[43] perfected under years of communist rule when pretence was internalised as survival technique. By 2012, national elites have also learned to use their allies in Brussels. The European Parliament political groups positioned themselves along the lines

[43] W Jacoby, 'Talking the Talk and Walking the Walk: The Cultural and Institutional Effects of Western Models' in KF Bönker *et al* (eds), *Postcommunist Transformation and the Social Sciences: Cross-Disciplinary Approaches* (Bouldner, Rowman & Littlefield, 2002).

of their Romanian members,[44] though at times their positions converged with the comparatively critical line taken by the European Commission, particularly Commissioner Reding. Former European Parliament President Hans-Gert Pőttering declared that Romania was not ready to become an EU Member State, echoing similar declarations made by then Commissioner for Enlargement Oli Rehn, Commissioner Reding calling the Romanian government to order several times. Meetings between Romanian representatives (Prime Minister, Minister of Foreign Affairs and Romanian ambassador to Berlin) and European counterparts became PR exercises, prompting public declarations by European counterparts forced to counter the often distorted presentations of their Romanian partners who downplay these as 'friendly', 'regular' consultations rather than calls to order.

Since 2007, national politicians (regardless of political party affiliation) have found their voice in challenging the EU reports' findings, the relevance of the monitoring system and the Commission's obsession with personnel rather than procedure. In 2012, given the high stakes of the national political games, the ruling elites were not shy of rebuffing criticism from Brussels officials as well as EU heads of government. Interim President Crin Antonescu dismissed any external attempts to 'tell the Romanian president what to do', and the 11 points demands by Brussels as being outside the framework of the CVM monitoring mechanism and therefore irrelevant (former President Constantinescu claimed such demands would not have been made of any other Member State). Prime Minister Victor Ponta dismissed the relevance of Chancellor Merkel's statements given that she 'does not vote in the referendum'. Brussels' criticisms were minimised as being the result of manipulation and propaganda by the incumbent camp and of a lack of understanding of Romanian political progress, prompting the EU spokesperson to stress that the EU opinion is not based on open letters,[45] rumours or individual sympathy for one politician or another.[46] Summoned by President Barroso to deliver the electoral lists requested by the Constitutional Court in view of its ruling over the referendum, the Prime Minister replied that the government is working within the deadlines set by the Court, not by Brussels.

[44] For example, the debate over suspending Romania's vote in the European Council sponsored by Romanian social democrat-liberal MEPs (among them former Minister of Justice Monica Macovei, who relentlessly points out breaches of the law) was refused by the PES and Liberal group in the European Parliament.

[45] Highly popular methods of communication are used during these times. Former President Constantinescu lectured President Barroso on treating Romania as a second class Member State. The academic and political journalist Stelian Tănase wrote a point by point explanation on why this was not a *coup d'état* but an expression of democracy (in a letter signed by other academics). In the aftermath of the Prime Minister's PhD plagiarism exposure, the philosopher and former Minister of Culture and Foreign Minister Andrei Pleşu, the philosopher Gabriel Liiceanu and the director Andrei Şerban, among others, addressed a letter to all EU heads of government expressing their worries as to the government and some media outlets' attempts to minimise the significance of plagiarism and their concerns about the long lasting impact upon the Romanian scientific community.

[46] The government often referred to the alleged influence in Brussels of MEP Monica Macovei.

Despite institution building and legal frameworks aimed at increasing transparency and penalising public officials for abuse of office and breach of norms, the political arena is populated by political characters with significant legal baggage, relying upon support from *baroni locali* (local barons) (financial powerhouses in particular counties) and media moguls (new class owners of dubiously acquired media empires, some of which are currently under investigation by DNA prosecutors). Though ministers, MPs or public officials are repeatedly embroiled in corruption scandals, their careers are rarely compromised as a result. Neither EU accession, nor the CVM mechanism, the prospect of sanctions or Brussels' forceful language have changed this pattern. National elites learn to use EU membership as an additional escape path. European elections became opportunities to exempt businessmen and politicians from corruption charges. During the 2009 campaign and after their elections, these candidates enjoy immunity from prosecution.[47] Successive Romanian governments since 2007, whether liberal, liberal democrat or social democrat, have included several political figures previously investigated for corruption and misuse of public money, who were either exonerated prior to their appointments or confirmed by Parliament on the basis of partisan votes. In 2012, the government included ministers incompatible with the office given that they were (some resigned) or are under investigation for abuse of office at the time of their appointment. In Parliament, MPs already indicted for fraud, traffic in influence and/or abuse of office (referred to in jargon as *puşcăriabili* (potential inmates)) pursue their parliamentary responsibilities, and enjoy the privileges that come with the office pending resolution of their appeals. While 2012 registered the most high profile successes in terms of anti-corruption verdicts, it also witnessed the legitimation of dubious practices through popular vote. The parliamentary elections in December 2012 produced the most legally indictable Parliament of the post-communist era. Among the 588 newly elected MPs, 27 had been previously sentenced, arrested or declared incompatible with the office of a parliamentarian, or are currently under investigation for breaches of law such as money laundering, embezzlement and/or fraud. One candidate ran, and was elected, while under arrest. Hence, neither are the political elites restraining from such practices, nor is the electorate willing or interested in sanctioning them.

V. CONCLUSION

Since 2007, political developments in Romanian national politics show that while political conditionality helped secure reforms prior to accession, EU accession

[47] Gigi Becali, owner of the football club Steaua and leader of the New Generation Party (PNG), under investigation for corruption and bribery of public officials, entered the European elections in coalition with the nationalists of Romania Mare Party. Both parties' leaders were elected MEPs. Following several appeals, he was granted the right to exit the country and assume his mandate.

provides little guarantee against breaches of the rule of law. The 2012 events are a crisis only in relation to the intensity and the scope of the measures undertaken in a relatively short period of time (previous ruling elites pursued similar goals but over a longer time span, masking the intent as well as the impact). Rather, they are a symptom of a political environment inhabited by elites pursuing personal and clan benefits rather than policy agendas. The generalised practice of quasi-illegal political manoeuvres validates further breaches of law. Brussels, while an engaged spectator, is relegated by national political elites to refereeing from a distance through public declarations and annual reports. The EU leverage over national political elites is moderated by clientelist interests (eg access to structural funds are motivating, anti-corruption measures are not). The European Union's attempts to counter the reversibility of political conditionality (criticisms, demands, summons and threats of sanctions) are rebuffed by a discourse of national sovereignty and popular mandate.

Part II

Instruments for Maintaining Constitutionalism in Europe

Systemic Deficiencies in the Rule of Law and the European Union

7

Enforcing the EU Charter of Fundamental Rights in Member States: How Far are Rome, Budapest and Bucharest from Brussels?

FRANK HOFFMEISTER

I. INTRODUCTION

ACCORDING TO ITS fifth recital, the Charter of Fundamental Rights of the European Union (CFREU) reaffirms, 'with due regard to the powers and tasks of the Union and the principle of subsidiarity, the rights as they result, in particular, from the constitutional traditions and international obligations common to the Member States'. The Charter is hence, on the one hand, part and parcel of the European Constitutional Area, and can even be regarded as the most comprehensive and modern human rights catalogue in Europe. On the other hand, it does not enact standards that EU Member States must observe in all situations. Rather, in line with the principles of conferred powers and subsidiarity, the Charter primarily applies to the institutions of the Union. Member States are only bound to respect the Charter 'when they are implementing Union law' (Article 51(1), first sentence CFREU).

The line between purely national situations (where the Charter does not apply) and situations falling within the scope of Union law (where the Charter applies) is not easy to draw, in particular when horizontal issues of a constitutional nature in a Member State are at stake. Against that backdrop, this chapter will analyse how the Charter can be enforced in the Member States. Two levels will be distinguished. First we look at national constitutional law and the interplay between a constitutional human rights catalogue and the Charter. Then we concentrate on the existing enforcement mechanisms at EU level. Recent practice with respect to infringement procedures and Article 7 TEU will be reviewed with a particular emphasis on Italy, Hungary and Romania.

II. NATIONAL ENFORCEMENT

A. EU Charter as an Inspiration for Designing a National Human Rights Catalogue

A Member State's human rights catalogue usually predates the adoption of the EU Charter in 2001. Only exceptionally has a constitution in an EU Member State been newly designed since 2001. A case in point is Hungary's new Constitution of April 2011. Here, the question may be asked whether modelling the human rights catalogue along the lines of the EU Charter would be advisable. After all, the Charter builds on the European Convention on Human Rights (ECHR), adds a couple of liberal rights (such as the respect for human dignity and the protection of personal data) and gives expression to a number of social rights in Title IV on 'solidarity'.

There are a few downsides, though, if one were to use the Charter too literally as a blueprint or even incorporate it into the national constitution. First, Title V on 'citizens' rights' is clearly not apt for reproduction at national level as it enshrines rights that are, by definition, vested in citizens through European rather than national law. Secondly, within Title IV on solidarity, a number of provisions are formulated from a predominantly European perspective, eg Article 34(3) CFREU speaks of the Union's recognition of the right to social and housing assistance 'in accordance with the rules laid down by Union law and national law and practices'. Such a renvoi makes little sense in a national context since it is for the national constitution to decide the degree to which a right to social and housing assistance is to be enshrined in the supreme law of the land. And thirdly, the Charter is silent about appropriate constitutional enforcement mechanisms. If a Member State establishes a Constitutional Court then that court has to apply the Charter as national law. It might even enjoy the monopoly to declare national laws unconstitutional under the Charter. At the same time, the Charter remains European law, serving as a yardstick for EU compatibility of national laws falling within the scope of EU law. The principle of supremacy empowers and even requires ordinary courts of a Member State to set aside national laws,[1] without having to resort to the Constitutional Court. Accordingly, the double-character of the Charter could create jurisdictional tensions between the Constitutional Court and the ordinary courts with regard to their respective powers in applying the Charter vis-à-vis national legislation.

Against that backdrop, the Hungarian experience is of interest. Responding to a request made by Hungary, the Council of Europe's Venice Commission elaborated its opinion in March 2011 on the question as to whether it was advisable to

[1] On the power of national courts to set aside national law and the need to ask for a preliminary reference to the CJEU, see Joined Cases C-188 and 189/10 *Azizi Melki and Selim Abdeli v France* [2010] ECR I-5667, paras 40–45.

incorporate provisions of the EU Charter into the new Constitution.[2] This expert body pointed out that the most recent developments in the field of human rights were indeed articulated in the Charter. Reflecting it in the national constitution would be a legitimate aim and signal loyalty towards European values.[3] However, given the Charter's restricted scope of application and the potential judicial conflicts in its interpretation, the Venice Commission counselled against incorporation. Rather it advised Hungary to 'consider the EU Charter as a starting point or a point of reference and source of inspiration in drafting the human rights and fundamental freedoms chapter of the new Constitution'.[4] Indeed, that approach seems like the best way forward. To a large degree, it is reflected in the April 2011 text of the Hungarian Constitution (Basic Law).[5]

B. Interpreting the Constitution in Line with the EU Charter

Absent a full incorporation into the national constitution, how can it then be ensured that the EU Charter is fully respected at national level? As part of primary EU law, the Charter enjoys supremacy over domestic constitutional law from an EU perspective.[6] Seen from a national perspective, though, the rank of EU law is defined by the Constitution which may not grant unlimited precedence to European norms. In this respect, a great variety of solutions can be found in Member States, ranging from 'opening' the national constitution to EU supremacy to granting EU law constitutional or infra-constitutional rank.[7]

The Romanian case is a typical example of EU supremacy being expressly granted over national legislation. In 2003, Romania inserted a specific EU integration clause into the 1991 Constitution. Supported by a popular referendum, article 148(1) of the Romanian Constitution (RC) foresees that a two-thirds majority in both Chambers of Parliament are needed to consent to EU accession. As a result thereof, 'the provisions of the constituent treaties of the European Union as well as the other mandatory Community legal rules shall take precedence over the conflicting provisions of national laws, in compliance with the provisions of the Accession Act' (article 148(2) RC). Romania hence possesses a powerful tool according to which EU rights can be enforced directly not only against administrative but also against legislative action. But what is the situation with respect

[2] European Commission for Democracy through Law (Venice Commission), *Opinion on Three Legal Questions arising in the Process of Drafting the New Constitution of Hungary* (Opinion No 614/2011, 28 March 2011) para 11.

[3] ibid para 21.

[4] ibid para 32.

[5] For details see further below.

[6] Case 11/70 *Internationale Handelsgesellschaft* [1970] ECR 1125, para 3; Case C-473/93 *Commission v Luxembourg* [1996] ECR I-3207, paras 37–38.

[7] See in detail F Hoffmeister, 'Constitutional Implications of EU Membership: A View from the Commission' (2007) 3 *Croatian Yearbook of European Law and Policy* 59.

to the Constitution itself? Would article 148(2) RC favour European law in case of conflict between a constitutional norm and EU law? The answer is probably negative. According to the text, supremacy of EU law is granted over provisions of the national laws. That term refers to ordinary laws and not to the Constitution itself. On the other hand, the provision also refers to 'compliance with provisions of the Accession Act', enshrining the will of the constitutional legislator to avoid clashes with EU law as much as possible. Accordingly, where there is interpretative freedom under the Romanian Constitution, a domestic court would probably be justified in using the Charter to ensure interpretative conformity of the Romanian Constitution with European law.

This technique has already been used elsewhere. For example, in 2011 the German Federal Constitutional Court (BVerfG) enlarged the personal scope of the fundamental freedoms of the German Constitution by referring to EU law.[8] Although article 19(3) of the Grundgesetz (GG) explicitly reserves fundamental human rights under the GG to domestic legal persons only, the judges in Karlsruhe found that a company incorporated in Italy could also make a valid claim under the right to property (article 14(1) GG). The Court overcame the restrictive wording of the constitutional norm with reference to the obligations flowing from Articles 26(2) and 18 TFEU so as not to discriminate against economic operators on the basis of nationality within the scope of EU law.[9] It thus applied the doctrine of an 'EU-friendly' interpretation of national law to a norm of constitutional value, arguing that this was necessary to 'avoid a collision with Union law'. The basis for this technique is, again, the German EU integration clause, namely article 23(1) and (2) GG.[10] This doctrine would only reach its limits were an EU-friendly interpretation to touch upon the 'identity' of the Constitution[11] (which was evidently not an issue in the case at hand). Although this judgment does not refer to the EU Charter strictly speaking, it could well have done so. Article 18 TFEU and Article 21(2) CFREU are basically identical in outlawing discrimination on the basis of nationality within the scope of EU law.

For Hungary, the situation under the new Constitution (Basic Law) seems less clear. Article E(1) now combines the constitutional objective to contribute to European unity (the former article 6(4)) with a rather restrictive clause on the joint exercise of competences 'arising from the Basic Law' and only 'to the extent required' for the fulfilment of EU obligations (article E(2), the former article 2A). Strikingly, and in contrast with Romania, Article E does not even enshrine the supremacy of EU law over ordinary Hungarian law. Two government proposals of October and November 2002 to that effect had already been opposed by (the then opposition party) Fidesz and were consequently not introduced into the 2011 Basic Law either. Therefore, all hope has to be put on the interpretation of article

[8] Bundesverfassungsgericht, 1 BvR 1916/09 of 19 July 2011 Absatz-Nr (1-100), [2011] *EuGRZ* 637.
[9] ibid paras 75–80.
[10] ibid para 81.
[11] ibid para 82.

E(1). As already argued in doctrine on the predecessor provision,[12] Hungary's wish to contribute to European unity allows for the interpretation of its human rights provisions in an EU-friendly way.

That could mean, on the one hand, that the Hungarian Constitution does not demand that EU law abide precisely by every Hungarian fundamental right in order to be applicable in Hungary. In this reading, an objective and general protection of human rights by the Court of Justice of the European Union (CJEU) would be sufficient. On the other hand, I would submit that article E(1) of the Basic Law could also be read as bringing potentially problematic provisions of the Hungarian Constitution into line with European standards, as far as this would be permitted by interpretation. That would be similar to the operation of article Q(2) with respect to international law. Under that provision, Hungary is to ensure harmony between international law and Hungarian law in order to fulfil its obligations under international law. For example, when it comes to defining the object, purpose and limits of article D on the protection of Hungarians living outside Hungary, the international law principle of non-interference with the domestic jurisdiction of neighbouring EU Member States could well become important.[13] Similarly, article E(1) of the Basic Law could lend itself to the doctrine of an EU-friendly interpretation of Hungarian law, including the Constitution: as Hungary is to contribute to European unity, an EU-friendly interpretation of its Constitution would surely further this aim. In a clear-cut conflict which cannot be solved through interpretation, however, the Hungarian Constitution would prevail over EU law, including the Charter. It remains to be seen whether national courts could then bring such situations to the attention of the CJEU by invoking a breach of the fundamental status of Union citizenship in conjunction with core human rights protected under Article 2 TEU, as argued elsewhere.[14]

C. Using the EU Charter as a Constitutional Yardstick

Finally, the EU Charter may even be elevated to serve as a yardstick for constitutional complaints. In the specific situation of Austria, where the Constitutional Court has the power to receive complaints concerning alleged violations of either the European Convention (which has constitutional rank in Austria) or a national

[12] P Sonnevend, 'Offene Staatlichkeit: Ungarn' in A von Bogdandy (ed), *Ius Publicum Europaeum, Tome II 'Offene Staatlichkeit—Wissenschaft des Verfassungsrecht'* (Heidelberg, Müller, 2012) para 29.

[13] For the importance of this principle in the previous dispute between Hungary and Slovakia/ Romania on the Hungarian 'Status law' during accession negotiations see F Hoffmeister, 'Monitoring Minority Rights in an Enlarged European Union' in G Toggenburg (ed), *Minority Rights and the Enlarged European Union: The Way Forward* (Budapest, LGI Books, 2004) 96–100.

[14] A von Bogdandy *et al*, 'Ein Rettungsschirm für europäische Grundrechte—Grundlagen einer unionsrechtlichen Solange Doktrin gegenüber Mitgliedstaaten' (2012) 72 *ZaöRV* 45; A von Bogdandy, 'An Individual Right to Challenge a Domestic Constitution on the Basis of Article 2 TEU' (2000) 37 *CML Rev* 1307.

human right, the principle of coherence demands that the Court can also review alleged violations based on the Charter. In its landmark case of March 2012, the Court thus admitted a complaint by an asylum seeker in Austria who had argued that Article 47 CFREU gave him a right to a hearing before a national asylum court. A condition for allowing an EU Charter complaint before the Austrian Constitutional Court is, however, that the Charter right is similar to a national human right under the Austrian Constitution.[15] Reassuringly, the Court also held that it would follow the case law of the CJEU, which in turn is inspired by rulings of the European Court of Human Rights.[16] The Charter thus plays a very powerful role in Austria as a constitutional yardstick for ordinary law which can be declared null and void in case of incompatibility.[17]

III. EUROPEAN ENFORCEMENT

What is the situation when the mechanisms to enforce the EU Charter at national level are not properly used or otherwise put in jeopardy? Are there possibilities for the European institutions to intervene and protect the common standards of the European constitutional area? Under the founding Treaties, two main tools exist: the European Commission can launch an infringement procedure under Article 258 TFEU, or the remedies under Article 7 TEU against a risk of a breach or an actual breach of the basic Union values can be activated.

A. Infringement Procedure

(i) Respecting the Charter as a Treaty Obligation

If the Commission considers that a Member State has failed to fulfil an obligation under the Treaty on European Union, it may bring a case to the CJEU after having delivered a reasoned opinion to the Member State in question (Article 258 TFEU). This is the classical central enforcement tool, basically used to bring Member States in line with specific obligations under secondary law. If a Member State does not implement a Directive or Regulation correctly, an infringement case is the likely response from Brussels. But is this tool also apt to counter breaches of the Charter? No doubt, respecting the Charter constitutes an obligation of Member States under Article 6(1) TEU. Hence, violations thereof can be brought to the attention of the Court as failures to fulfil an obligation 'under the Treaty', as required by Article 258(1) TFEU. However, as noted in the introduction, Article

[15] Verfassungsgerichtshof, VfGH *U 466/11-18, U 1836/11-13* (14 March 2012) para 35, [2012] *EuGRZ* 331.

[16] ibid para 39.

[17] ibid para 43.

51 CFREU does not apply to purely domestic situations but only when a Member State implements European law. Accordingly, a Charter-based case must always show that the problem falls within the scope of European law. This may lead to roughly three different scenarios.

(ii) Three Scenarios

In the first scenario, a Charter right is further specified by EU secondary law. For example, Article 8 CFREU on the protection of personal data lies at the heart of Directive 95/46/EC which largely harmonises the rules on data protection in Europe. If a Member State were to breach specific obligations under the Directive spelling out details of the Charter, an infringement case based on the incorrect transposition or application of the Directive could be seen as an enforcement action of the Charter itself.

In the second scenario, a Charter right is not underpinned by specific EU legislation. That is the case, for example, with Article 10(1) CFREU on the freedom of thought, conscience and religion. Using Article 258 TFEU against any national practice or law which would seem to infringe that freedom, would therefore be problematic unless a situation falls within the scope of European law. Such is the case when the measure would also restrict a fundamental freedom and would therefore have to be justified under EU law.[18] This is the *cas de figure* referred to in the explanations to the Charter,[19] which are themselves binding according to Article 6(1) TEU. If, hypothetically, a national law would require a foreign TV station to give at least one hour's airtime every day to the national church, that would constitute a restriction to the freedom to provide services. If the Member State were to justify this measure by reference to the national constitution privileging Christianity over other beliefs, the question whether such discrimination was in line with the neutrality principle enshrined in Article 10(1) CFREU could be put before the CJEU.

The third scenario relates to horizontal guarantees on the rule of law and due process, such as the right to good administration under Article 41 CFREU or the right to an effective remedy and to a fair trial under Article 47 CFREU. Again, the observance of these rights constitutes an obligation on a Member State, when a case has an EU dimension. This could range from such different topics as applying an EU internal market Directive up to treating an application for asylum in line with Directive 2004/83/EC on the minimum standards for asylum seekers. Interestingly though, these horizontal guarantees may also come into play when institutional questions arise about the proper administration of justice in general.

[18] Case C-260/89 *ERT* [1991] ECR I-2925, holding that the derogation to the freedom of services on the grounds of public policy, public security or public health could only be accepted if the national provision in derogation of the Treaty was compatible with the fundamental rights the observance of which is ensured by the Court.

[19] [2007] OJ C303/1.

If, for example, there were doubts about the independence of the civil branch of the judiciary *tel quel* because it would, hypothetically, be under the command of the government, any decision of such a tribunal could not live up to the right to an independent tribunal under Article 47(2) CFREU. If such an improperly functioning court had jurisdiction over ordinary civil law cases, it might well be asked to decide not just purely national cases but also cases with an EU dimension. This, again, would open up the scope for an infringement case based on Article 47 CFREU, as there is a clear European interest to prevent the misapplication of EU law through improperly constituted national courts. It follows that the horizontal guarantees on the rule of law and due process under the Charter may well become an important part of CJEU case law with respect to the set-up of the national judiciary and administration.

B. Article 7 Procedure

(i) Genesis

Whereas the infringement procedure has existed since the inception of the European Communities, the Article 7 TEU procedure only came into being in the Treaties at a much later stage. In the 1980s, the question was asked as to how the Union could react if a Member State were breaching fundamental rules on democracy or human rights. As a legal basis was lacking in the Treaty, some authors suggested resorting to the then existing Articles 224 and 225 EEC by analogy[20] or to general principles of law.[21] For its part, the European Parliament called for a treaty-based sanction procedure.[22] While this point did not create traction in Maastricht in 1991, the Irish Presidency took up the idea in the preparations of the next treaty revision in 1996.[23] It was accepted at the Intergovernmental Conference and, with some changes,[24] found its way into the final text of the Amsterdam Treaty 1997 as Article 7 TEU. Under the provision, the Council, meeting in the composition of the Heads of State or Government, and acting by unanimity on a proposal by one-third of the Member States or by the European

[20] JA Frowein, 'Die rechtliche Bedeutung des Verfassungsprinzips der parlamentarischen Demokratie für den europäischen Integrationsprozess' (1983) 18 *Europarecht* 301, 313.

[21] J Schwarze, 'Das allgemeine Völkerrecht in den innergemeinschaftlichen Rechtsbeziehungen' (1983) 18 *EuR* 1 and European Commission, Response of 5 June 1985 to Written Question No 1895/84 [1985] OJ C208/3.

[22] European Parliament Resolution of 14 February 1984 on the Draft Treaty establishing the European Union [1984] OJ C77/55. Articles 4(4) and 44 of the Draft Constitution foresaw sanctions in case of serious and persistent breaches of the principles of democracy and human rights by a Member State. The determination would have had to be made by the CJEU.

[23] EU IGC, Conference of the Representatives of the Governments of Member States CONF/3879/96/ LIMITE, Annex A.

[24] EU IGC, Conference of the Representatives of the Governments of Member States CONF/3940/96/ LIMITE, Annex B.

Commission and after obtaining the assent of the European Parliament, might determine the existence of a serious and persistent breach by a Member State of principles mentioned in Article 6(1) TEU.

The Treaty of Nice (2000) introduced a second layer into the procedure, namely, a possibility to react not only to a breach, but also to a 'clear risk' thereof. Such a determination could be made by the Council on a reasoned proposal by the Commission, one-third of the Member States or the European Parliament. Before doing so, the Council should hear the Member State in question and 'may call on an independent person to submit within a reasonable time limit a report on the situation in the Member State in question' (Article 6(1), second sentence TEU, Nice version). Evidently, this new layer was the consequence of the *causa Austria*, which had created a constitutional crisis in the Union from spring to autumn 2000. In that case, it will be remembered, the other 14 Member States sanctioned the participation of Jörg Haider's far-right Austrian Freedom Party (FPÖ) in federal coalition government under the conservative Chancellor Schüssel, by freezing contacts at bilateral level and by refusing to support Austrian candidates in international organisations. There was no formal decision of an EU institution, but only a statement of the Portuguese Presidency of 31 January 2000[25] that was applied after the formation of the government on 4 February 2000. In particular, some Member State ministers boycotted informal Council meetings when the Austrian representative was speaking.[26] Late June, three 'wise men' (Frowein (Germany), Oreja (Spain) and Ahtisaari (Finland)) were asked to report on whether the Austrian government was actually threatening EU fundamental principles. In their opinion of 8 September 2000,[27] the independent experts concluded that the party programme of the FPÖ and certain statements from party officials were not in line with EU standards on non-discrimination and minority protection, but that no actual government action had been affected. In addition, FPÖ politicians in the federal government had not used insulting language. Upon their recommendation, the sanctions were lifted by a declaration from French President Chirac on 12 September 2000.[28]

(ii) Lisbon Procedure

The Treaty of Lisbon has retained this two-stage approach but no longer mentions the report of independent experts in Article 7(1) TEU. In return, it broadened the scope of the protection. Whereas Article 6 TEU (Nice version) referred to liberty,

[25] The statement is cited in T Brune, *Der Fall Österreich* (Government Education Program Thesis, Frankfurt am Main, 2004) 9.

[26] See examples given by W Hummer and W Oberwexer, 'Die Wirkung der Verfassungsgrundsätze der EU—zu den Österreich-Sanktionen' (2000) 16 *EuZW* 485, 486.

[27] 'Bericht von Ahtisaari, Frowein und Oreja' [2000] *EuGRZ* 404.

[28] F Schorkop, *Die Maßnahmen der XIV EU Mitgliedstaaten gegen Österreich* (Berlin, Springer, 2002) 53.

democracy, respect for human rights and fundamental freedoms, and the rule of law, the new Article 2 TEU (Lisbon version) encompasses a number of 'values'.

Consequently, the following set of rules applies: according to Article 2, first sentence TEU, the Union is founded on the values of respect for human dignity, freedom, democracy, equality, the rule of law and respect for human rights, including the rights of persons belonging to minorities. The notion of 'human' rights slightly differs from the 'fundamental' rights of the EU Charter. However, this nuance can be explained by the fact that 'human rights' are broader and all-encompassing, whereas the term 'fundamental rights' allows for a distinction between rights that belong to 'everybody' (human rights) or only to 'EU citizens'. Moreover, in the previous Article 6 TEU (Nice version), reference was also made to fundamental freedoms. It can thus be assumed that the term 'human rights' in today's Article 2 TEU is used as a 'shortcut' for what is further specified later on in Article 6(1) TEU.[29] Accordingly, the Charter may serve as the first reference point when interpreting what is covered by the corpus of human rights under Article 2 TEU. The fact that the Charter has a limited scope for national measures is not decisive for this purpose.[30] Under Articles 2 and 7 TEU, the Charter is not applied *à la lettre* to individual cases but rather serves as a yardstick to identify a European standard in the field of human rights. And that is precisely one of its proclaimed purposes: rendering visible rights which form part of the Union's values.[31]

While the Charter thus enjoys a strong status under Article 2 TEU, the respective enforcement procedure is considerably more cumbersome than an ordinary infringement procedure. In the first phase, under Article 7(1) TEU, an application can be made by either one-third of the Member States, the European Parliament or the European Commission. Any applicant must present a 'reasoned proposal' evidencing a 'clear risk of a serious breach' of the values referred to in Article 2 TEU. As the Commission observed in its Communication of 2003, these words imply a certain gravity in the violation, touching upon the basic functioning of the Member State in question.[32] On the other hand, not all of the values enshrined in Article 2 must be in danger. The plural 'values' simply denotes that any of the values mentioned could be at stake. As any serious breach of a single fundamental value touches upon the mutual trust between Member States, action can be triggered in case of serious human rights concerns without a threat to democracy or the rule of law.[33] Any such application is handled by

[29] Similarly F Schorkopf, *Homogenität in der Europäischen Union—Ausgestaltung und Gewährleistung durch Art. 6 und 7 EUV* (Berlin, Duncker & Humblot, 2000) 93, who argued that the notion of human rights in Art 6(1) TEU was specified by the then Art 6(2) TEU.

[30] But see K Serini, *Sanktionen der Europäischen Union bei Verstoß eines Mitgliedstaates gegen das Demorkatie- oder Rechtsstaatsprinzip* (Berlin, Duncker & Humblot, 2009) 117–18, claiming that the Charter would be irrelevant for the interpretation of Art 2 TEU (former Art 6(1) TEU, Nice version).

[31] Charter of Fundamental Rights of the European Union [2000] OJ C364/1 (CFREU), recitals 2–4.

[32] European Commission, Communication from the Commission to the Council and the European Parliament on Article 7 of the Treaty on European Union, COM(2003)606 final 7–9.

[33] Schorkopf, *Homogenität* (n 29) 157.

the Council instead of the Court. The Council is to hear the Member State in question and make an assessment, the case being complemented by a recommendation, by a four-fifths majority vote after obtaining the consent of the European Parliament.

In the second phase, under Article 7(2) TEU, the European Council may determine 'the existence of a serious and persistent breach' by a Member State of Union values. In comparison to the Article 7(1) TEU determination, the additional element of a 'persistent' breach points to structural deficits or a pattern of violation and would exclude action based on individual wrongdoings. Such a determination needs unanimity among the Heads of State and Governments (excluding the representative of the Member State in question) and the prior consent of the Parliament. It may subsequently lead to the suspension of Treaty-based rights, including voting rights (Article 7(3) TEU). The procedural and substantive threshold for such a sanction is particularly high. Again, the CJEU is not involved—it may only scrutinise later on whether the procedural rules have been properly followed (Article 269 TFEU).

C. Relationship between the Two Procedures

There is nothing in the Treaty which informs us about the relationship between the two procedures. Article 7 TEU is found in the common provisions established under the Treaty on European Union, whereas Article 258 TFEU has its place in the Chapter on the jurisdiction of the CJEU. Does this give us a systematic hint about their proper interaction?

One argument could be made in favour of exhaustion. As Article 7 TEU is designed to tackle 'serious' (and persistent) breaches of 'values' (only), it might be seen as *ultima ratio* when infringement procedures have not remedied the situation. In other words, the European Commission should first use all means available under Article 258 TFEU before considering Article 7 TEU. The downside of this argument is, however, that not all worrying developments in a Member State could be caught under Article 258 TFEU. A number of issues might not fall within the scope of secondary law and thus escape normal infringement logic.

Another argument would be to stress the different context of the two procedures. Under Article 258 TFEU the Commission acts as the guardian of the treaty. The legal watchdog should quasi-automatically respond to infringements in order to safeguard the correct application of Union law. Bringing an application under Article 7(1) or (2) TEU would, in return, be much more political. Here, the Commission should exercise much more restraint as only one of several potential applicants. From a legal point of view, there is, however, no requirement to exercise political constraint. The Commission is not confined to act as a legal, technocratic guardian of the Treaties. Rather the opposite: the nomination procedure of Commissioners (including hearings at the European Parliament) shows that the College of Commissioners is intended to act as a political force in Europe.[34] Moreover, the cross-party composition of the College and its practice to decide by consensus are a safeguard against politically one-sided action against Member States. Given its particular expertise and function, one should evidently expect more from the Commission than from the European Parliament or one-third of Member States to take the initiative in bringing an Article 7(1) application when the conditions are satisfied.

In sum, neither infringement exhaustion nor political restraint is warranted in a legal sense before activating Article 7 TEU. There may well be cases where infringement cases and Article 7 proceedings might have to be brought at the same time. Whether such a step would be wise would be for the political consideration of the College.

IV. PRACTICE

A. Italy

Leaving aside the special circumstances of the Austrian case reported above, the first practical test of enforcing fundamental EU human rights with respect to a problematic government policy in a Member State occurred vis-à-vis Italy under the second government of Prime Minister Silvio Berlusconi from 2001–06. Prior to assuming office, he had been confronted with a number of criminal charges, including false accounting and bribery. He was also controlling the private media sector in Italy, through running the conglomerate Mediaset. Having been sworn in, two patterns of action caused concern.

(i) Laws ad Personam

First, Berlusconi's parliamentary majority started adopting a number of laws that seemed to have the purpose of helping the Prime Minister *ad personam* in his ongoing trials. Among those were:

- a reduction of penalties for falsification of books;
- a change of location of trials in exceptional circumstances;
- a revision of the statute of limitations; and
- the establishment of absolute immunity for the highest officials of the state during office. Fortunately, though, these four self-serving laws did not go unnoticed.

[34] F Schorkopf, 'Die Kommission im institutionellen Rahmen der Verträge' in U Immenga and T Körber (eds), *Die Kommission zwischen Gestaltungsmacht und Rechtsbindung* (Baden-Baden, Nomos, 2012) 53 identifies 'two bodies' of the Commission: one body related to administrative execution and the other body acting as 'politische Gemeinwohlbürokratie' (political bureaucracy for the public good).

The revision of the Company Law Code[35] apparently served the Prime Minister's interest insofar as it reduced the penalty for publishing false documents from an indictable offence (a so-called *delitto*), with a term of imprisonment of up to five years, to a summary offence (a so-called *contravvenzione*) with a term of imprisonment of less than two years. Correspondingly, the limitation periods shrank from ten years to a maximum of four and a half years.[36] Several Italian courts asked the CJEU whether the sanctions introduced by the new legislation could be considered as effective, proportionate and dissuasive sanctions for breaching EU law, as laid down in several company law Directives. The Court did not find a ground to question the Italian law. Rather, it stressed that the retroactive application of the more lenient penalty forms part of the constitutional traditions common to the Member States.[37] Indeed, nowadays, Article 49(1), third sentence CFREU expressly says so. Against this yardstick, no breach of European law was found and, in September 2005, Berlusconi was acquitted since the date of the acts which underlay the alleged crimes was before the expiry of the shortened limitation period.[38]

Less successful was Berlusconi's attempted transfer of a court case to another local tribunal under the Legge Cirami of November 2002.[39] Here, the interest of the Prime Minister was to 'avoid' certain trial judges whom he considered to be biased against him by applying to relocate the case to another city. This violates the determination of the trial judge on the basis of objective criteria. Accordingly, the Italian Constitutional Court interpreted the notion 'exceptional circumstances' narrowly.[40] Such circumstances could only be accepted if there were extraneous reasons questioning the independence and impartiality of a local court. After this useful clarification, Berlusconi's trial was not transferred from Milan to Brescia.

With respect to the amendment of the statute of limitations, the Prime Minister did not even manage to harness support from his parliamentary majority. Critics from the Christian Democrat coalition party UDC ensured that the new rules in the Salva Previti[41] Act would not apply to pending cases, so as to avoid the public perception that Parliament was trying to ensure the acquittal of the Prime Minister.[42]

[35] Law 366/2001 (Legge no 366/2001 'Delega al Governo per la riforma del diritto societario'); Decree 61/2002 of 11 April 2002 (Decreto no 61/2002 concernente gli illeciti societari).

[36] F Tacconi, 'Casenote: Berlusconi at the European Court of Justice, C-387/02' (2006) 7 *German Law Journal* 313, 314.

[37] Case C-387/02 *Berlusconi and others* [2005] ECR I-3565, paras 68–69.

[38] Serini, *Sanktionen* (n 30) 209.

[39] Law 248/2002 (Legge no 248/2002 'Modifica degli articoli 45, 47, 48 e 49 del codice di procedura penale').

[40] Corte costituzionale, sentenza no 1/2003 (Constitutional Court of Italy), reported by J Luther, 'Das Gesetz als Mittel der Prozessverschleppung, die Politisierung der italienischen Justiz und die Grenzen der europäischen Rechtsstaatlichkeit' [2005] *EuGRZ* 350, 351.

[41] Law 251/2005 (Legge no 251/2005 'Modifiche al codice penale e alla legge 26 luglio 1975, n 354, in materia di attenuanti generiche, di recidiva, di giudizio di comparazione delle circostanze di reato per i recidivi, di usura e di prescrizione').

[42] Serini, *Sanktionen* (n 30) 221–22.

Finally, the Constitutional Court intervened three times on highly controversial immunity laws. Faced with the Lodo Schifano[43] of 2003, the Italian judges underlined the principle of equality before the law of all citizens under article 3 of the Constitution. Absolute immunity from criminal prosecution for the five highest state officials in office was unconstitutional. The law was annulled in January 2004.[44] Astonishingly, when he came to power a second time, Berlusconi pushed through another form of the law, the Lodo Alfano, in 2008.[45] The Constitutional Court also declared this law unconstitutional in October 2009. As a reaction, the legislator then proceeded to adopt the 'legitimate impediment' Act.[46] Under that new statute, any government minister had the right to refuse to appear before a court because of their government function. Again, the Constitutional Court brushed aside such a blanket exception, in January 2011, ruling that the trial judge could assess on a case-by-case basis whether a minister had a legitimate reason not to appear. The Court also held that the law should be amended to allow an impediment to last only for up to six months rather than 18.

In sum, on the first front of doubtful government action designed to obstruct justice, the checks and balances within the Italian constitutional system worked well.[47] Attempts to escape criminal prosecution by changing the judge, reducing the statute of limitations or proclaiming immunity largely failed. At the time of writing, the clearest sign that in Italy the rule of law is upheld against great odds is the news that, in October 2012, a Milan tribunal convicted the ex-Prime Minister for tax fraud and sentenced him to four years' imprisonment.

(ii) Media Pluralism

The same can probably not be said on the second big issue of the second Berlusconi government, namely, attempts to curb media pluralism. Upon his election, Berlusconi requested the dismissal of three RAI reporters in April 2002 and even pressurised the written media, inter alia, leading to the resignation of the editor of the *Corriere della Sera* in May 2003. Moreover, a November 2002 Constitutional Court judgment calling for the adoption of new broadcasting legislation by the end of 2003[48] was largely ignored. Following consistent prior case law, Berlusconi would be required to give up one of his three national channels.[49]

[43] Law 140/2003 (Legge no 140/2003 'Disposizioni per l'attuazione dell'articolo 68 della Costituzione nonché in materia di processi penali nei confronti delle alte cariche dello Stato').

[44] Corte costituzionale, sentenza no 24/2004 (Constitutional Court of Italy), reproduced in [2005] *EuGRZ* 385.

[45] Law 124/2008 (Legge no 124/2008 'Disposizioni in materia di sospensione del processo penale nei confronti delle alte cariche dello Stato').

[46] Law 51/ 2010 (Legge no 51/ 2010 'Disposizioni in materia di impedimento a comparire in udienza').

[47] Serini, *Sanktionen* (n 30) 254–55.

[48] Corte costituzionale, sentenza no 466/2002 (Constitutional Court of Italy).

[49] That had already been the conclusion from the previous Constitutional Court ruling (Corte costituzionale, sentenza no 420/1994), which had not been implemented either. On this see Serini, *Sanktionen* (n 30) 233.

Criteria for frequency attribution, however, remained unclear, thereby allowing the Prime Minister to exert maximum power in this sector.

The Prime Minister's interference with individual media and his inaction with respect to the implementation of Court judgments triggered a harsh reaction from the European Parliament. In its resolution of 22 April 2004,[50] it noted that a free and pluralist media reinforces the principle of democracy on which the Union is founded (Article 6 TEU, Nice version). It linked the EU Charter on Fundamental Rights to Articles 6 and 7 TEU and stressed that pluralism was a fundamental value of the European Union (enshrined in the then draft Constitution).[51] The European Parliament also regretted the lack of specific EU legislation to 'specify the minimum conditions to be respected by Member States to ensure an adequate level of pluralism'.[52] More specifically with respect to Italy, the European Parliament noted that the level of concentration in the television market was the highest in Europe, with a duopoly of RAI and Mediaset sharing 90 per cent of the total audience.[53] The Parliament highlighted:

> its deep concern in relation to the non-application of the law and the non-implementation of judgments of the Constitutional Court, in violation of the principle of legality and the rule of law, and at the incapacity to reform the audiovisual sector, as a result of which the right of its citizens to pluralist information has been considerably weakened for decades; a right which is also recognised in the Charter of Fundamental Rights.[54]

Operationally, the Parliament then called upon the European Commission to submit a proposal for a Directive to safeguard media pluralism[55] and to consider using its right of initiative under Article 7(1) TEU as a last resort when it has political misgivings regarding media diversity and pluralism in one of the Member States.[56]

After this hard shot, the Italian Parliament adopted the Lodo Gaspari[57] in May 2004. It replaced the provisions on media concentration of the previous Laws 112/2004 and 223/1990. However, rather than introducing tougher disciplines, it confirmed the 20 per cent rule for digital frequencies. Only with respect to income through publicity, the limit was lowered from 30 per cent to 20 per cent. The effect of the law was that Berlusconi could keep his third channel (Rete 4), which he was supposed to give up according to the case law of the Constitutional Court. In other words, the law legalised a situation which had hitherto been regarded as unconstitutional because

[50] European Parliament Resolution of 22 April 2004 on the risks of violation, in the EU and especially in Italy, of freedom of expression and information (EU Charter of Fundamental Rights, art 11(2)) [2004] OJ C104E.

[51] ibid recitals D, F and G.

[52] ibid para 2.

[53] ibid para 55.

[54] ibid para 66.

[55] ibid para 76.

[56] ibid paras 83–84.

[57] Law 112/2004 (Legge no 112/2004 'Norme di principio in materia di assetto del sistema radiotelevisivo e della RAI-Radiotelevisione italiana Spa, nonché delega al Governo per l'emanazione del testo unico della radiotelevisione').

of its negative effect on media pluralism.[58] In the subsequent discussions neither the European Parliament nor the European Commission exercised their right to bring a reasoned proposal under Article 7(1) TEU.

B. Hungary

After the landslide victory of the conservative party Fidesz in parliamentary elections in April 2010, the newly-formed government enjoyed the unusually large majority of 269 seats, compared with 59 seats for the former governing Socialist party MSZP and 47 seats for the extreme nationalists of Gabor Vona's Jobbik. Endowed with this strong democratic legitimacy, the new Prime Minister Viktor Orbán introduced a government policy to review the legal and institutional landscape of the country. These changes included dismissals, changes in a number of laws and, finally, also the adoption of a new Constitution (Basic Law) in April 2011, complemented by so-called cardinal laws which require a qualified two-thirds majority of the MPs present for their adoption and amendment. A number of those executive, legislative or even constitutional measures sparked huge controversies in Europe, in particular in the area of media freedom, data protection, central bank independence, reform of the judiciary and other constitutional issues. These will be presented one by one in some detail.

(i) Media Pluralism

The first confrontation related to the Hungarian Media Law adopted in 2010.[59] This gave the newly-founded State Media Commission unprecedented powers to control the content of media reports, which had to be in line with vaguely defined concepts of dignity and privacy. The President of the Commission was to be appointed for the unusually long term of nine years (more than two legislative periods) by the President of the Republic. The Acts also foresaw high levels of fines for breaches and abolished the protection of informants. However, all these issues were outside the reach of secondary EU law. Based on the Audiovisual Services Directive 2010/13/EU, Commissioner Kroes could only argue that Hungary had violated its *acquis* obligations:

— to offer balanced coverage to all audio-visual media service providers;
— to respect the country of origin principle; and
— to comply with registration requirements.

[58] Serini, *Sanktionen* (n 30) 242.

[59] These included the Press and Media Act 2010 (2010. évi CIV. törvény a sajtószabadságról és a médiatartalmak alapvető szabályairól) and the Mass Media Act 2010 (2010. évi CLXXXV. törvény a médiaszolgáltatásokról és a tömegkommunikációról).

Since Hungary adopted relevant amendments on 7 March 2011, the case was discontinued, much to the dissatisfaction of the European Parliament which, in a resolution of 10 March 2011, called upon the European Commission to assess the media law also on the basis of the Charter.[60]

In December 2011, the Hungarian Constitutional Court handed down a landmark case on the Media Law. It found several limitations for the written press unconstitutional (eg on disclosure of sources and on the control of content). It also annulled the entire section on the media ombudsman/Commissioner's powers. Despite this positive development, concerns over the state of media freedom remained. Under the EU Authorisation Directive 2002/20/EC, there is a general condition that the award procedure must be objective, transparent and proportionate. At the end of 2011, the main radio station critical towards the government (Klubrádió) had been unsuccessful in bidding for a radio licence. As the fact could not be excluded that the decision had been based on subjective political rather than objective administrative grounds, Commissioner Kroes contacted the Hungarian authorities by letter of 18 January 2012. Since then, the Budapest Appeals Court has delivered four judgments in favour of Klubrádió concerning the bidding procedure for the radio licence. The first annulled the Media Council's decision to allocate Klubrádió's current frequency to a competitor on the grounds that the competitor's bid had been inadmissible. The second invalidated the Council's order to exclude Klubrádió from the bidding procedure, arguing that such an act should have been adopted by way of a decision and not an order. The third Court decision reinstated Klubrádió in the bidding procedure, and after the fourth ruling the Media Council finally awarded it the long-term frequency in March 2013.

Importantly, Commissioner Kroes also referred in her letter to a comparative study showing that the Hungarian law would go beyond or against European standards in a number of other aspects. She asked the government to seek advice from the Council of Europe and fully follow it when revising the media laws. At a hearing of 9 February 2012 in the European Parliament, the Commissioner repeated that line forcefully, even mentioning the possibility of an Article 7 TEU procedure.[61] In May 2012, the Council of Europe's media expert body adopted a report with no less than 61 recommendations on how to align the media laws with European standards and the case law of the European Court of Human Rights.[62] The three most important points were the lack of independence of the media authority from political influence, the vague terminology regulating the boundaries of admissible media content which has a chilling effect on journalists,

[60] European Parliament Resolution of 10 March 2011 on media law in Hungary [2011] OJ C309E, para 3.

[61] J Croft, 'Neelie Kroes Ups Pressure on Budapest' (4362) *Europolitique* (Brussels), 13 February 2012, available at www.europolitics.info/pdf/Europolitics_en/eure4362.pdf.

[62] Council of Europe Secretariat-General, *Council of Europe Experts on Hungarian Media Legislation: Act CIV of 2010 on the Freedom of the Press and the Fundamental Rules on Media Content and ACT CLXXXV of 2010 on Media Services and Mass Media* (Strasburg, 11 May 2012) 36.

and the potential erosion of protection of their sources. However, as of the time of writing, only a part of the recommendations seems to have actually been implemented. Other than promised improvements on the protection of sources, relevant exchanges between Hungarian authorities and the Council of Europe in August and October 2012 did not yield many results.

(ii) Human Rights and the Protection of Hungarians Abroad Under the Constitution

Prior to the adoption of the new Constitution in April 2011, the European Parliament had already organised a hearing on the latest draft in late March of that year. Few criticisms were put forward during that meeting, chaired by MEP József Szájer, one of the architects of the text. For example, the Chair ignored opposition MEP Bokros for quite some time, before giving him the floor for only a short period.[63] Social Democrat MEPs were largely absent (holding an internal meeting on Athens that day), and liberal MEP Ludford focused on three side issues. She pointed out that the prohibition of discrimination did not contain the category of sexual orientation and that the definition of the family as a union between a man and a woman did not represent modern life. Moreover, she found that the provision on the protection of Hungarians abroad was 'irredentist'.

Those attacks, however, were hardly convincing from the perspective of the European legal order. There is no European principle suggesting that all grounds of discrimination, listed in Article 21 CFREU, need to be reproduced in a national constitution: what counts is that the Charter is correctly applied when European law is implemented. Similarly, the definition of a family is certainly left to the constitutional autonomy of every Member State, and the current formulation codifies previous judgments of the Hungarian Constitutional Court.[64] With respect to protection of Hungarians abroad, President Barroso admitted in his letter of 26 May 2011 to Martin Schulz, the President of the SPE faction in the European Parliament, that article D of the Basic Law could lead to questions under international law. However, article Q(2) of the Basic Law would also oblige Hungary to act in harmony with international legal principles. In his view, the conditions for triggering Article 7(1) TEU were thus not met. This line was repeated in the plenary debate on 1 June 2011. Vice-President Šefčovič added that the Commission would not pass political judgement on the fundamental constitutional and institutional choices of a Member State, as long as they were in line with the values under Article 2 TEU. He also noted that the Constitution required adoption of a number of cardinal laws down the line. Therefore, the Commission did not see

[63] 'New Hungarian Constitution Slithers through EU Hearing' *EurActiv* (Brussels), 1 April 2011, available at www.euractiv.com/future-eu/new-hungarian-constitution-slith-news-503641.

[64] Decision 154/2008 (XII.17) AB határozat (Constitutional Court of Hungary).

any provision in the Hungarian Constitution that would justify taking steps in its capacity as guardian of Union law.[65]

On 20 June 2011, the Venice Commission adopted its report on the Constitution, finding that the human rights catalogue followed closely the technique and the contents of the ECHR and 'to some extent' the EU Charter.[66] Indeed, if one compares the structure of the Chapter on 'Freedoms and Responsibility' of the Hungarian Basic Law with the EU Charter, a number of similarities are striking. Both catalogues start with human dignity.[67] 'New' issues related to medicine, biology and human trafficking are mentioned as well.[68] The Hungarian Basic Law then enshrines a number of fundamental freedoms, as they are recognised in the ECHR and, to a certain degree, refined in Title II of the Charter. Remarkably, it then also reflects the set of rights which can only be found in the Charter, such as the freedom of the arts and sciences, the right to education, and the right freely to choose one's work.[69] The same goes for the Chapters in the Charter on equality and solidarity: again, the Hungarian Basic Law follows the structure rather closely in articles XV–XXII. We can also find traces from the Charter, Chapters V and VI, on citizen rights and justice in articles XXIII–XXVIII of the Basic Law. Very importantly, the clause on limitations in article I(3) seems to relate to Article 52(1) CFREU insofar as it requires limitations to be proportional and to respect the essential content of a right.[70]

On the other hand, the text contains a number of concepts rather alien to the Charter. First, in stark contrast to the latter's secular approach,[71] 'The National Avowal of Faith' sets a strong Christian tone. The Hungarian human rights catalogue is entitled 'Freedom and Responsibility', with article XXX articulating a basic duty that every person shall contribute to satisfying community needs to the best of his or her capabilities. The concept of a 'human duty towards to the community' does not form part of European human rights discourse. The legislator can lay down duties when restricting human rights, but without any legal precision, establishing a constitutional duty acting as an inherent restriction to a number of other individual rights is doubtful. Similarly, to write into a fundamental rights catalogue the right of every person 'to repel any unlawful attack against his

[65] Intervention of Vice-President Sefcovic in the European Parliament plenary meeting on Hungary (1 June 2011).

[66] European Commission for Democracy through Law (Venice Commission), *Opinion on the New Constitution of Hungary* (Opinion No 621/2011, 20 June 2011) para 18.

[67] Constitution of Hungary (Magyarország Alaptörvénye) (Basic Law, 25 April 2011), art II; Art 1 CFREU.

[68] Basic Law, art III(2), (3); Arts 3(2), 5(3) CFREU.

[69] Basic Law, arts X–XII; Arts 13–15 CFREU.

[70] On the interpretation of these two important principles by the Hungarian Constitutional Court to date see A Jakab and P Sonnevend, 'Kontinuität mit Mängeln: Das neue ungarische Grundgesetz' (2012) 72 *ZaöRV* 79, 86–88.

[71] Compare the first recital of the CFREU, which refers to the 'spiritual and moral heritage of Europe'.

or her person or property, or one that poses a direct threat to the same' (article V HC) does not find its place within the European tradition.

None of these points, however, featured in the discussions between Budapest and Brussels. Rather, on 5 July 2011, the European Parliament adopted its first resolution on the Hungarian Constitution[72] which was basically a shortcut to the two opinions from the Venice Commission. Unfortunately, it also wrongly asserted that the Charter had been incorporated into the new Constitution, creating problems of interpretation and overlapping competences between domestic courts, the Hungarian Constitutional Court and the CJEU.[73] Such incorporation was discussed in the first opinion of the Venice Commission but did not actually take place.

It seems that at that stage the European institutions were not fully prepared to put forward an informed critique of the human rights part of the constitutional text. The real debate only took off later when, in late 2011, Hungary adopted a number of cardinal laws and transitional provisions with great speed and without adequate consultation of the opposition and civil society.

(iii) The Judiciary

Brussels initially became worried by article 12 of the Transitional Provisions on the judiciary and the corresponding provisions of Act CLXII of 2011 on the status and remuneration of judges. These norms lowered the retirement age from 70 years to the general statutory pensionable age (currently 62, rising to 65 years) as of 1 January 2012. In her letter of 12 December 2011, Vice-President Reding objected to this move, raising arguments based on age discrimination under article 2(1) and (2)(a) of Directive 2000/78/EC and Article 21 CFREU and the right of citizens to a lawful judge. In this she was joined by US Secretary of State, Hillary Clinton, who expressed a similar concern in a letter of 23 December that year. Absent a meaningful reply, the European Commission sent a letter of formal notice to Hungary on 17 January 2012. A month later, the Hungarian authorities pointed out that the retirement age would be applied to all officials in the public sector. Moreover, they proposed to give judges the right to request an individual extension of their retirement age, based on an annual quota and on a test of the applicants' professional and medical aptitude.[74] While the Venice Commission rather cautiously asked for a 'less intrusive and not so hasty solution',[75] EU Commission Vice-President Reding considered this system incompatible with the European prohibition on age discrimination. In particular, the aim of the measure

[72] European Parliament Resolution of 5 July 2011 on the Revised Hungarian Constitution [2013] OJ C33E.

[73] ibid para 1(h).

[74] The content of the letter is reproduced by the Venice Commission in its opinion on the judiciary, European Commission for Democracy through Law (Venice Commission), *Opinion on the Judicial System of Hungary* (Opinion No 663/2012, 19 March 2002) para 108.

[75] ibid para 110.

was not properly explained in the law. Moreover, the right to request an extension did not render proportional the sudden drop in the mandatory retirement age in 2012 and its slow rise as from 2014. The EU Commission therefore issued a reasoned opinion on 7 March 2012, with the infringement case reaching its final stage in April when the CJEU was seized of a violation of Directive 2000/78/EC.

Importantly, while the case was pending in Luxemburg, the Hungarian Constitutional Court handed down a landmark ruling on the issue on 16 July 2012.[76] It found that the sudden lowering of the age from 70 to 62 breached the independence of the judiciary from both a formal and a substantive point of view. Such a change could only have been introduced gradually and in the form of a cardinal law. Importantly, the judges also invoked the 'historical constitution' of Hungary to annul those provisions of Act CLXII of 2011 on the status and remuneration of judges. On the other hand, it remained unclear whether the dismissed judges were 'ipso facto' re-established in their previous function. According to the head of the National Judicial Office, every single judge would first have to apply for reinstatement before the labour courts.[77] Those who did so, would even then face an appeal from the National Judicial Office.[78] Moreover, in September 2012, the legislator introduced a new pension age of 65 years in the Transitional Provisions.

In its judgment of 6 November 2012,[79] the CJEU found that the compulsory retirement infringed Directive 2000/78/EC because it gave rise to a difference in treatment on grounds of age which was not proportionate as regards the objectives pursued. Importantly, the Court found that the judgment of the Constitutional Court only annulled part of the contentious rules. This is a clear, but not explicit, finding that the Transitional Provisions of the Basic Law (which the Constitutional Court had no power to assess) also needed to be amended in order to be brought into line with Directive 2000/78/EC. This further had the effect of preventing the Hungarian government from circumventing the judgment of the Constitutional Court by including more expressly the rules on early retirement in the Basic Law, thereby excluding any constitutional review. The Court left open, though, how Hungary should comply with its findings. However, under its general case law it was clear that Hungary had to reinstate the illegally dismissed judges. For example, in *Commission v Germany*,[80] the CJEU had found that 'the aim of the Treaty is to achieve the practical elimination of infringements and the

[76] Decision 33/2012 (VII.17) AB határozat (Constitutional Court of Hungary). Note that the judgment was decided by votes 8:7. Six of the seven judges who handed down a dissenting opinion had been appointed by Fidesz in 2010/2011.

[77] See discussion on the practical consequences of the judgment by KL Scheppele at www.verfassungsblog.de/author/kim-lane-scheppele.

[78] European Commission for Democracy through Law (Venice Commission), *Opinion on the Cardinal Acts on the Judiciary that were Amended Following the Adoption of Opinion CDL-AD(2012)001* (Opinion No 683/2012, 13 October 2012) para 76.

[79] Case 286/12 *Commission v Hungary* (2012, nyr).

[80] Case 70/72 *Commission v Germany* [1973] ECR 813, para 13.

consequences thereof, past and future'. Similarly, in *Humblet*,[81] the Court had said that in case of infringements of EU law, Member States are obliged 'to rescind the measure in question and to make reparation for any unlawful consequences which may have ensued'. Against that backdrop, the Hungarian Parliament adopted on 11 March 2013 a new law which lowered the retiring age for judges and public prosecutors to 65 years over a period of ten years.[82] This aligned with the general retirement age of 65 in Hungary. The new law also granted all judges and prosecutors who had been forced to retire to be reinstated in their posts, with no need to bring a case in court. While reinstatement in the post did not necessarily imply that the previously dismissed judge would also get his management position, the law nevertheless remedied the crucial point, namely, the unjustified dismissal. It also provided for compensation for lost remuneration during the period a dismissed judge or prosecutor was not working. The adoption and proper implementation of this law convinced the European Commission to close the infringement case in November 2013.[83]

Finally, the Commission also sent administrative letters on the independence of the judiciary. A particular problematic point was the concentration of very large powers in the hands of the President of the National Judicial Office (NJO), appointed for nine years and not democratically accountable. No other European state has established such a powerful post.[84] The Venice Commission warned that the powers of the President of the NJO would have to be cut and their decisions reasoned and subject to judicial control.[85] In particular, the power to assign cases to other courts on the vague criterion of 'adjudicating cases within a reasonable time' (articles 11.3 and 11.4 of the Transitional Provisions) was seen as undermining the guarantee of a lawful judge.[86]

Following a first request for information in January 2013, the European Commission inquired about the powers of the President of the NJO to designate a court and to transfer judges without their consent. With a clear reference to Article 47 CFREU, the Commission also reminded Hungary in March that its courts would act as 'Union courts' whenever they would apply Union law and would therefore need to satisfy minimum standards of independence and effective judicial redress.[87] Subsequently, the Secretary-General of the Council of Europe pushed in the same direction, asking Hungary, as a matter of urgency, to subject the powers of the President of the NJO to judicial review, prevent an indefinite prolongation of their term by a blocking minority of one-third of

[81] Case 6/60 *Jean-E Humblet v Belgian State* [1961] ECR 559, 569.

[82] Act XX of 2013 amending Act CLXII of 2011.

[83] European Commission Press Release, 20 November 2013, available at www.europa.eu/rapid/press-release_IP-13-1112_en.htm.

[84] Venice Commission Op 663/2012 (n 74) para 26.

[85] ibid para 43.

[86] ibid para 90; Jakab and Sonnevend, 'Kontinuität mit Mängeln' (n 70) 93.

[87] European Commission Press Release, 7 March 2012, para 4, available at www.europa.eu/rapid/press-release_MEMO-12-165_en.htm.

Members of Parliament and to do away with the President's power to transfer cases.[88] The amendments of 2 July 2013 did, indeed, address these points to a large extent. Henceforth, such Presidents cannot be re-elected and will lose office automatically upon expiry of their nine-year mandate.[89] Accountability has been strengthened by the motivation obligation, by additional reporting obligations, by the possibility for Members of Parliament to question the President on their activities, and by the right of judges to appeal against decisions and rules of the President.[90] Finally, the transfer of cases is to remain the exception, based on objective criteria to be adopted by the National Judicial Council.[91] Nevertheless, the Venice Commission continued to object to the system on a point of principle, finding that transferring cases was not in compliance with the principle of the lawful judge.[92]

(iv) Data Protection

The second issue triggering a Commission infringement case related to data protection. Once again, in her letter of 12 December 2011, Vice-President Reding had already voiced her concern about two points. First, the former Data Protection Commissioner, appointed in 2008 for six years and a staunch opponent of Prime Minister Orbán, had been dismissed apparently without his prior consultation and without a proper reason, as the legislature had created a new National Agency for Data Protection as of 1 January 2012. Secondly, section 45(1)(f) of the Cardinal Law on Data Protection, Act CXII of 2011, contained a vague clause on dismissal which seemed to compromise the independence of any Hungarian data protection authority in the future. This would run contrary to the relevant obligation under article 28 of the Data Protection Directive 1995/46/EC and Article 8(3) CFREU. The College of Commissioners launched an infringement case with a letter of formal notice adopted on 17 January 2012.

In its reply, Hungary showed evidence that the 'former' Data Protection Commissioner had been consulted and had himself issued an oral and a written opinion. This point was thus dropped. Hungary also declared its willingness to make the legal requirements for future dismissals stricter. On the other hand, on the most political point—the sudden dismissal of the 'former' Data Protection Commissioner—the government still did not give any valid reason. The Commission hence continued the case with a reasoned opinion of 7 March 2012 stressing this latter point and keeping its criticism of the dismissal grounds in the law as long as the law had not been formally amended.[93] On 25 April 2012,

[88] Venice Commission Op 683/2012 (n 78) para 9.
[89] ibid para 15.
[90] ibid para 29.
[91] ibid paras 61–68.
[92] ibid para 74.
[93] European Commission Press Release, 7 March 2012, para 3, available at www.europa.eu/rapid/press-release_MEMO-12-165_en.htm.

the Commission seized the CJEU, claiming a breach of article 28 of Directive 1995/46/EC.[94] Subsequent amendments of the Act in 2012 removed the discretionary elements in the dismissal procedure to the satisfaction of the Venice Commission.[95]

(v) Independence of the Central Bank

Another serious irritation was caused by government's treatment of the Hungarian National Bank. Under article 41 of the Basic Law, the Governor of the Central Bank is appointed by the President of the Republic for six years and the competences are regulated by a cardinal law. Ignoring a written warning from President Barroso to Prime Minister Orbán in late December 2011, the cardinal law[96] allowed for political interference. In particular, it foresaw that the Prime Minister could nominate all bank deputies without consulting the governor, thereby curtailing the latter's function. Under section 34 of the 2011 Act, the Bank even had to submit the agenda of the meetings of its Monetary Council to the government, which had the right to be present at those meetings through a minister or a representative. The Act also allowed the dismissal of the Bank's Monetary Council in cases of 'serious misconduct' which appears to be an overly vague concept. Finally, the government had cut the salary of the governor from HUF 8 million to HUF 2 million in a clear move to pressurise him. This ceiling was kept in the new Act.

Against that background, and upon a proposal from Economic and Finance Commissioner Rehn, the European Commission decided to launch an infringement case on 17 January 2012. Its legal basis was Article 130 TFEU which contains a clear Treaty obligation to ensure the independence of the central bank not only in euro-zone members but in all EU Member States (Article 130 TFEU). Moreover, the Commission (and the IMF) suspended talks with Hungary about granting macro-economic assistance. The latter lever seemed to work. In the memorandum setting out its defence, circulated on 9 February 2012,[97] the government was able to explain the policy reasons for the above-mentioned interferences only in most general of terms ('in forming policies in times of financial crisis all governments work closely with their central banks') and had conceded that it would have to make the necessary amendments were

[94] European Commission Press Release, 25 April 2012, available at www.europa.eu/rapid/press-release_IP-12-395_en.htm.

[95] European Commission for Democracy through Law (Venice Commission), *Opinion on Act CXII of 2011 on Informational Self-determination and Freedom of Information of Hungary of 13 October 2012* (Opinion No 672/2012, 18 October 2012) paras 37–38.

[96] Act CCVIII of 2011, in force as of 1 January 2012, available at www.english.mnb.hu/Root/Dokumentumtar/MNB/A_jegybank/kozerdeku_informaciok/tevekenysegre_mukodesre_adatok/mnbhu_szerv_alaptevekenyseg_hataskor/arh_jegybanktorv_en_20120101.pdf.

[97] Communication from the Cabinet of the State Secretariat for Government Communication, 'Hungary: Myths and Facts' (9 February 2012).

the CJEU to find fault. Indeed, based on assurances received in response to his second administrative letter of 7 March 2012, Vice-President Rehn proposed to close his case on the independence of the Central Bank in April.[98] The government declared to remove some of the possibilities of the executive to interfere with the Bank's decision-making, such as the presence of the Finance Minister at sessions of the Bank. The government also promised to stop its practice of systematically criticising the Bank's monetary decisions. Moreover, the European Central Bank from now on would have to be consulted on draft laws within the field of its competence. In return, the Commission announced its willingness to re-enter negotiations on precautionary financial assistance.[99] On 21 June 2012, the government introduced the changes to Parliament, and after the actual adoption of the Bill on 6 July 2012,[100] the talks eventually started in the second half of that month through a joint Commission/IMF/ECB mission to Hungary.[101]

(vi) Remaining Constitutional Issues

Equipped with the College of Commissioners' decision of 17 January 2012 on the above-mentioned infringement cases, President Barroso addressed the Plenary of the European Parliament on 18 January 2012. In his speech, he stressed that the Commission would treat the situation in Hungary 'mainly as an issue of application of European Union law', acknowledging at the same time that they 'may go beyond the European Union law matters that have been raised'.[102] However, rather than hinting at EU remedies, he was then referring to the role of the Council of Europe and the Venice Commission.[103]

President Barroso was thereby responding to different sentiments. Whereas conservative MEPs had been content if the Commission were to remedy 'issues on some pieces of legislation',[104] the rest of the House articulated much broader

[98] European Commission Press Release, 25 April 2012, available at www.europa.eu/rapid/press-release_IP-12-395_en.htm.

[99] European Commission Press Release, 25 April 2012, available at www.europa.eu/rapid/press-release_IP-12-407_en.htm.

[100] Act CCVIII of 2011, as amended on 6 July 2012, available at www.english.mnb.hu/Root/Dokumentumtar/MNB/A_jegybank/kozerdeku_informaciok/tevekenysegre_mukodesre_adatok/mnbhu_szerv_alaptevekenyseg_hataskor/arh_jegybanktorv_en_20120714.pdf.

[101] European Commission Press Release, 26 July 2012, available at www.europa.eu/rapid/press-release_MEMO-12-604_en.htm.

[102] JM Barroso, 'A Europe of Values and Principles', Plenary debate at the European Parliament on the situation in Hungary, Strasburg, 18 January 2012, available at www.europa.eu/rapid/press-release_SPEECH-12-16_en.htm.

[103] For a discussion of the President's intervention see Editorial Comment, 'Fundamental Rights and EU Membership: Do as I Say, Not as I Do!' (2012) 49 *CML Rev* 481.

[104] EPP Press Release, 6 January 2012, www.arc.eppgroup.eu/press/showpr.asp?prcontroldoctypeid=1&prcontrolid=10888&prcontentid=18278&prcontentlg=en.

concerns about the risks to civil liberties,[105] 'highly controversial legislative acts'[106] and a perceived 'dangerous slide towards an authoritarian regime'.[107] After a hearing in the European Parliament's Committee on Civil Liberties on 9 February, to which the Hungarian government was also invited, the European Parliament adopted a resolution on Hungary on 16 February 2012. A liberal-left-green majority called on the Conference of Presidents to consider necessary measures on the basis of the LIBE Committee report. Next to the issues of media pluralism, the Data Protection Commissioner[108] and the judiciary,[109] already addressed by the Commission, the European Parliament was also displeased with a number of other constitutional issues.

Among those were that further concerns were raised by the cardinal laws as regards 'fair competition and political alteration', as well as by the 'so-called stability law subjecting the income tax system to a two-thirds majority' and by the cardinal laws giving an exclusive right to appoint officials for an unusually long time, 'thus affecting the ability of future government to govern'.[110] The European Parliament noted 'the significant number of matters relegated, for detailed regulation, to cardinal laws requiring a two-thirds majority, including issues which should be left to the ordinary political process'.[111] This criticism attacked the peculiar Hungarian approach to cardinal laws. Such organic laws (which category also exists, eg, in Albania, Austria, Croatia and France)[112] are not per se questionable; indeed, they were used in the previous Hungarian Constitution and their absolute number was even reduced from 28 to 26.[113] However, their scope had been drastically enlarged under the 2011 Basic Law to cover areas of economic and social policy which were normally left to ordinary legislation. In addition, the Venice Commission criticised this too broad use of cardinal laws[114] and repeated that point with respect to the overregulation of the judiciary through two Acts whose detailed provisions had largely been defined as cardinal.[115] There was thus a perception that Fidesz, the ruling party, used that concept so as to ensure that

[105] ALDE Press Release, 4 January 2012, available at www.alde.eu/press/press-and-release-news/press-release/article/alde-calls-on-commission-to-apply-fundamental-rights-check-to-hungary-37815/ and ALDE Press Release, 6 January 2012, available at www.alde.eu/press/press-and-release-news/press-release/article/ladle-demande-au-parlement-europeen-denqueter-sur-les-risques-de-violation-des-droits-fondamenta/.

[106] S & D Press Release, 5 January 2012, available at www.socialistsanddemocrats.eu/gpes/public/detail.htm?id=136487&section=NER&category=NEWS&startpos=699&topicid=-1&request_locale=EN.

[107] Green Press Release, 5 January 2012, available at www.greens-efa.eu/democracy-in-hungary-5109.html.

[108] European Parliament Resolution of 16 February 2012 on the recent political developments in Hungary [2012] OJ C127E/79 (European Parliament Resolution 16 February 2012) recital H.

[109] ibid recitals E, G.

[110] ibid recital D.

[111] ibid recital L.

[112] Venice Commission Op 621/2011 (n 66) para 23.

[113] Jakab and Sonnevend, 'Kontinuität mit Mängeln' (n 70) 96.

[114] Venice Commission Op 621/2011 (n 66) para 24.

[115] ibid paras 19–20.

some economic, social or institutional issues could only be revised in the future by a political opponent which had secured the necessary two-thirds majority in the Hungarian Parliament through a comparable landslide victory at the polls. As this would be unlikely to happen, the content of any cardinal law could consequently become untouchable for a long time, putting a hurdle in the way of the exercise of the principle of political alteration, as the European Parliament had formulated.

Secondly, the European Parliament noted that article 11 of the Transitional Provisions foresaw that all sitting judges of the Supreme Court (renamed 'Kúria' under the new Constitution) could continue with the exception of its President. That meant de facto shortening the six-year term of Dr András Baka, formerly Hungarian judge at the European Court of Human Rights, to two years.[116] As the Venice Commission found, such singling out of the President as well as defining criteria for appointing the Kúria President (seemingly designed to exclude Dr Baka's eligibility) threatened the independence of the judiciary.[117] Previous media attacks on Dr Baka by government representatives[118] reinforced the impression that this measure was nothing other than a political dismissal of one of the highest judges of the country and as such incompatible with the EU principle of tenure of judges.

Thirdly, the European Parliament found that the adoption of several retroactive laws contravened one of the most basic principles of European law, namely, that of not adopting retroactive laws.[119] This reproach referred probably to the imposition of retroactive 'crisis taxes' imposed on the telecoms, energy and retail sectors in 2010 and to the most unusual law Act XCCI of 2011 on mortgages, passed in September 2011, which interfered with subsisting contracts by allowing Hungarian mortgage borrowers with mortgages denominated in Swiss francs and euros to repay their loans by the year-end at exchange rates about 25 per cent below current market rates. As the latter issue had been raised by Internal Market Commissioner Barnier and led to a settled compromise in December 2012 between the banks and the Hungarian government, according to which the government covered 30 per cent of the losses incurred by the banks, the point was not pursued any further.

Fourthly, the European Parliament addressed the 'unusually restrictive rules' in the cardinal law on churches and religious denominations.[120] Indeed, this law

[116] European Parliament Resolution of 16 February 2012 (n 108) recital F.

[117] Venice Commission Op 663/2012 (n 74) paras 111–15.

[118] Jakab and Sonnevend, 'Kontinuität mit Mängeln' (n 70) 100.

[119] European Parliament Resolution of 16 February 2012 (n 108) recital I.

[120] ibid recital J. This referred to Act CCVI of 2011 (2011. évi CCVI. törvény a lelkiismereti és vallásszabadság jogáról, valamint az egyházak, vallásfelekezetek és vallási közösségek jogállásáról) which replaced the earlier cardinal law Act C of 2011 (2011. évi C. törvény a lelkiismereti és vallásszabadság jogáról, valamint az egyházak, vallásfelekezetek és vallási közösségek jogállásáról) which was about to be annulled by the Constitutional Court on procedural grounds (European Commission for Democracy through Law (Venice Commission), *Opinion on Act CCVI of 2011 on the Right to Freedom of Conscience and Religion and the Legal Status of Churches, Denominations and Religious Communities* (Opinion No 664/2012, 17 March 2012) para 10.

had reduced from over 300 to 14 the notion of 'recognised churches' in the list included in the Act. The non-listed communities lost their privileged status for tax breaks and financial support on 1 January 2012. The Act also gave the Hungarian Parliament the power to amend this list and, after a hearing of 29 February 2012, the Parliament finally recognised 32 churches in total in Hungary. As it is most uncommon that the legislature defines what belief is 'recognised' or not, criticism was voiced by the United States in a letter of 23 December 2011 from Secretary of State Clinton and the Venice Commission. The latter held that recognition could not be a prerequisite to establish a church under Article 9 ECHR.[121] Moreover, the recognition criteria (such as the duration requirement of 100 years internationally or 20 years in Hungary)[122] were clearly excessive. (Non-)recognition by the Hungarian Parliament also begged questions of procedural due process.

Finally, the European Parliament noted that the powers of the Hungarian Constitutional Court to review budget-related laws had been substantially reduced.[123] That criticism might look at first sight somewhat surprising as it lies in the constitutional autonomy of every Member State to define the powers of its Constitutional Court. However, in this particular case, cutting the Court's powers served the purpose of defying the Court's judgments of the past and of getting rid of one uneasy check on government economic policy. In response to the Constitutional Court striking down a retroactive punitive tax on certain payments for employees in the public sector in 2010,[124] the Fidesz-led parliamentary majority had introduced the predecessor provision in November 2011 into the former Constitution as article 32/A(2) and (3).[125] This was probably done to avoid implementing the Court judgment, as the impugned law was reintroduced with certain modifications at the same time as Act CXXIV of 2010. Despite the newly-reduced review standard, the Court again annulled parts of the Act in May 2011, finding that retroactive application of a tax for five years violated human dignity.[126] In the light of this history, it is clear that article 37(4) of the 2011 Basic Law is anything but a 'normal' definition of Court powers. Article 27 of the Transitional Provisions enacted on 30 December 2011 (ie after the second Court ruling on the matter) re-enforced this anti-Court trend even further. The proviso under article 37(4) of the Basic Law that jurisdiction is only limited to the standards of human dignity as long as the state budget is higher than 50 per cent of GDP was simply dropped. This turned a transitional provision into a permanent one, which is highly problematic in itself.[127] In its reply of 19 June 2012 to the Venice

[121] ibid paras 28–34.

[122] ibid paras 57–64.

[123] European Parliament Resolution of 16 February 2012 (n 108) recital K.

[124] Decision 184/2010 (X.28) AB határozat (Constitutional Court of Hungary).

[125] Jakab and Sonnevend, 'Kontinuität mit Mängeln' (n 70) 98.

[126] Decision 184/2010 (X.28) AB határozat (Constitutional Court of Hungary).

[127] European Commission for Democracy through Law (Venice Commission), *Opinion on Act CLI of 2011 on the Constitutional Court of Hungary* (No 665/2012, 19 June 2012) para 38; Jakob and Sonnevend, 'Kontinuität mit Mängeln' (n 70) 98–99.

Commission, however, the Hungarian government showed no understanding of this point. It simply recalled that the objective of economic stability should also be pursued in better economic times.[128] Unfortunately, the government did not explain why such objective should also justify the breach of constitutional rights and disarm the Constitutional Court. Seen from an EU perspective, the effective protection of human rights by strong courts provides the basis for a reliable investment and business climate rather than blowing a hole in the rule of law.

The European Parliament then formulated a number of demands to remedy these shortcomings and instructed its LIBE Committee to present its findings on the follow-up in a report, on the basis of which it would then consider whether it would be necessary to activate the Article 7(1) TEU mechanism.[129] After a fact-finding mission of a committee delegation in Budapest in September 2012 and with over a year's preparation on a cross-party basis, LIBE actually voted for the 'Tavares Report' on 19 June 2013 (with 31 votes in favour, 19 against and 8 abstentions).[130] The Committee defeated the majority of over 500 amendments, mainly brought by Fidesz members who tried to take out critical statements or recommendations.

On the one hand, the majority remained critical of the above-mentioned points on media pluralism,[131] but acknowledged at the same time the overall satisfactory outcome on the reinstatement of judges.[132] Its recommendation thus centred on the establishment of objective criteria for the transfer of cases.[133] On the respect for human rights, the Committee switched its attention to the rights of persons belonging to minorities, making some general recommendations to adopt positive action and strengthen social dialogue.[134] Also the data protection issue became rather low key, grouped as a sub-point under the heading 'democratic system of checks and balances'.[135] The independence of the National Bank was not even raised any further. Hence, those point where the Commission had become active were more or less regarded as solved.

On the other hand, the report came out very strong on the remaining constitutional issues which the Commission had not tackled with infringement procedures. First and foremost, the Committee was highly irritated by the Fourth Amendment of the Basic Law of 11 March 2013. That Amendment not only integrated into the Basic Law previously annulled parts of the Transitional Provisions, but also stripped the Constitutional Court of its power to control the substantive

[128] Response of the Hungarian Government to the Venice Commission on the Opinion of the Venice Commission on the Constitutional Court (13 June 2012).

[129] European Parliament Resolution of 16 February 2012 (n 108) paras 4–7.

[130] European Parliament, *Report on the Situation of Fundamental Rights: Standards and Practices in Hungary (pursuant to the European Parliament Resolution of 16 February 2012)*, A-70229/2013 (24 June 2013) ('Tavares Report').

[131] ibid 42–50, 71 (recommendations).

[132] ibid 31–35.

[133] ibid 71.

[134] ibid 51–54, 71 (recommendation).

[135] ibid 22–24, 71 (recommendation).

legality of new constitutional amendments. For the Committee that amendment undermined the supremacy of the Constitution and seriously disturbed the checks and balances in Hungary.[136] The Strasburg representatives also recalled their concern that the extensive use of cardinal laws reduced the powers of any newly elected Parliament even in such fields as family, social, fiscal and budgetary matters.[137] Moreover, the European Parliament's Committee also made remarks and recommendations on electoral reform.[138] Finally, it disapproved another part of the Fourth Amendment to the Basic Law, namely, the decision to give the power to Parliament to recognise by way of cardinal laws, and without a constitutional duty to justify a refusal of recognition, certain organisations engaged in religious activities as churches.[139] In conclusion, the Committee held that:

> the systematic and general trend of repeatedly modifying the constitutional and legal framework in very short time frames, and the content of such modifications, are incompatible with the values referred to in Article 2 TEU, Article 3(1) and Article 6 TEU, and deviate from the principles referred to in Article 4(3) TUE.

It considered that 'unless corrected in a timely and adequate manner, this trend will result in a clear risk of a serious breach of the values referred to in Article 2 TEU'.[140] However, rather than invoking Article 7(1) TEU right away, the Committee preferred to call for a future mechanism below that threshold to enforce Article 2 effectively.[141] Only if a new dialogue between Parliament, Council, Commission and Hungary should not bear fruit, would the Conference of Party Presidents in the European Parliament reconsider resorting to Article 7 TEU.[142]

C. Romania

Another constitutional crisis occurred very soon thereafter in neighbouring Romania. Here, a bitter conflict was fought between Prime Minister Ponta and President Băsescu. Before going into the role of the European Union, it is useful to recall the constitutional background and political developments first.

(i) The 'Cohabitation'

Under its 1991 Constitution, Romania is a semi-presidential Republic. The President is elected by popular vote for a five-year term. He designates a candidate as Prime Minister, after consultation with the strongest party in the Romanian

[136] ibid 5, 17, 71 (recommendation).
[137] ibid 8, 71 (recommendation).
[138] ibid 38–41, 71 (recommendation).
[139] ibid 55, 71 (recommendation).
[140] ibid 57.
[141] ibid 72–83.
[142] ibid 86.

Parliament. The Prime Minister in turn forms the government which is then appointed by the President, based on the Parliament's vote of confidence. The government as a whole is responsible to the two-chamber parliament (composed of House of Deputies and Senate), elected every four years under a system of proportionate voting for party lists. The system is inspired by the French model and may lead to 'cohabitation', ie President and Prime Minister belonging to different political families. Romania also has an unusual system of impeachment. A President, who severely violates the Constitution, may be suspended from office by a joint session of both parliamentary Chambers, after having received an advisory opinion of the Constitutional Court. If the suspension is passed, a national referendum has to be called within 30 days. In the interim period, the President of the Senate is acting President.

In December 2004, Traian Băsescu was elected President. He is a leading figure of the PDL (Democrat Liberal Party, affiliated to the European People's Party (conservative) in the European Parliament). In April 2007, the Romanian Parliament suspended his duties but he reassumed office on 23 May after a referendum of 19 May had confirmed his popular support. Parliamentary elections were held in November 2008. The conservative PDL won (37 per cent of seats), followed by the alliance of social democrats and conservatives (PSD and PC) (31 per cent of seats) and liberals (16 per cent of seats). The remaining deputies represented the Hungarian minority, other minorities or independent forces. Against that background, Băsescu appointed Emil Boc as Prime Minister. He was supported by a 'grand coalition' from PDL and the alliance of social democrats (PSD: European Parliament affiliation to Social Democrats (centre-left)) and conservatives (PC: no European Parliament affiliation), which eventually broke down, triggering the dismissal of the government in October 2009.

At the presidential elections of 6 December 2009, Băsescu won in the second round with the very slight margin of 50.33 per cent against his main social democrat challenger Geoana. On 23 December 2009, the President confirmed PDL leader Emil Boc as Prime Minister (second Boc government) who was also supported by the Hungarian minority, some other minority representatives and certain independent MPs (who later on, in 2010, formed the National Union for Progress in Romania (UNPR)). A number of PDL MPs switched sides, being deeply unhappy with the austerity course of Băsescu as well as about the week-long public protests against the most severe measures (eg 25 per cent cut in public sector wages and freezes on pensions). In February 2012, Boc stepped down in view of such prolonged public dissatisfaction and Băsescu then appointed the independent Ungureanu as Prime Minister. The former head of the Foreign Intelligence Service only stayed in office for three months, as his slim majority (five votes) ended after the defection of the non-Hungarian minority representatives.

On 7 May 2012, a new government took office. It was a coalition consisting of social democrats (PSD), liberals (PNL: European Parliament affiliation to the Alliance of Liberal and Democrats (centre)) and conservatives (PC). This new formation is called the Social Liberal Union (USL) and is co-chaired by the social democrat Ponta and the liberal Antonescu. The new coalition forced Băsescu to appoint Victor Ponta as the new Prime Minister. Soon after, the new Prime Minister received the green light from the international financial institutions to upgrade public sector wages and pensions towards the levels they had been in June 2010, before the austerity cuts. This cost is estimated at 0.35 per cent GDP but keeps the overall deficit around 2.3 per cent, ie clearly below 3 per cent. After that, tensions between Ponta and Băsescu escalated, reaching a pinnacle after a huge ULS electoral victory at local elections in mid-June 2012.

(ii) The Crisis

On 27 June 2012, the Constitutional Court ruled in the inter-institutional case whether the President or the Prime Minister was entitled to represent Romania at European Council meetings. The Court ruled in favour of the President, who might delegate his authority to the Prime Minister. Irrespective of this finding, Prime Minister Ponta travelled to the European summit of 28–29 June, relying on the formalistic point that the judgment had not been published at the material time. Indeed, the said judgment was only published in the Official Journal on 11 July 2012, when the reasoning was also published. However, what 'smacked' of dubious legitimacy was the fact that the government had also issued an Emergency Ordinance in the meantime,[143] under which it took away from Parliament its power over the Official Journal. The timing of this move, at a period where a ruling against the Prime Minister was about to be published, looked rather suspicious.

On the same day (27 June 2012), the Court also found the modification of the electoral law to be unconstitutional. That law would have altered electoral districts based on current voters' preferences, allegedly securing a clear victory for the ruling coalition (up to 65–70 per cent of mandates). Representatives of the coalition publicly criticised the Court in strong terms.

On 3 July 2012, the Justice Minister asked the National Integrity Agency (ANI) to open investigations against some judges at the Constitutional Court. In reaction, the Court made a public request to the Venice Commission, asking for protection against what it called 'unprecedented attacks'. The next day the ruling coalition issued a press release denying any intention to remove judges of the Constitutional Court. Prime Minister Ponta stated that the Justice Minister withdrew his request, which is remarkable as he had previously stated as a matter of public record that five out of the nine judges were 'marionettes' of Băsescu.[144] The same day, in an extraordinary joint session, the Parliament replaced the

[143] Emergency Ordinance 36/2012 of 30 June 2012 (*Ordonanta* de urgenta nr *36/2012* privind unele masuri de reorganizare si pentru modificarea Legii nr 202/1998 privind organizarea Monitorului Oficial al Romaniei).

[144] C Stieger, 'Miese Manöver in Rumänien', *Neue Zürcher Zeitung* (Zürich), 5 July 2012, available at www.nzz.ch/meinung/kommentare/miese-manoever-in-rumaenien-1.17323723.

leadership of a number of other institutions with its new majority. It approved a new chairman to public television and radio networks and replaced ombudsman Gheorge Iancu, a position holding the unique power to attack emergency ordinances of the government directly before the Constitutional Court. Senate President Blaga (PDL) was replaced by Antonescu (PNL), while the Chamber President (Anastase, PDL) had to give her place to Zgonea (PSD). The President reacted by stating that 'EU fundamental values are seriously violated'. However, on 9 July 2012, the Constitutional Court found the opposition's challenge against the revocation of the chairpersons of the two Chambers of Parliament inadmissible.[145] The Court also refused to look into the dismissal of the ombudsman, a power reserved to Parliament.[146]

The Court was less lenient with respect to its own powers. Most dramatically, on 4 July 2012, the government had adopted Emergency Ordinance 38/2012 taking away the powers of the Constitutional Court to check resolutions of either Chamber of Parliament or jointly taken by both Chambers. An identical provision was put in an amending law to the Constitutional Court Act of 1992. In a ruling of 9 July 2012, the Court also found this modification to section 27(1) of the 1992 Act to be unconstitutional as it violated the principle of constitutional justice, one of the backbones of the Romanian state under article 1(3) and (4) of the Constitution. Interestingly, its line of argumentation also pointed to the Venice Commission's criticism of the reduction of powers of the Hungarian Constitutional Court.[147]

The crisis finally culminated in a second impeachment proceeding against the President. Although in its consultative opinion of 6 July 2012, the Constitutional Court had not found that the President had 'committed a serious offence in violation of the Constitution',[148] the Parliament suspended Băsescu that very day. It argued that he had overstepped his competences and failed to respect the separation of powers and independence of the judiciary. Only his own party supported him in a 256:114 vote. The President of the Senate and leader of the liberal party, Antonescu (PNL), temporarily assumed office.

[145] Decision No 728 of 9 July 2012 on the rejection of a claim of inconsistency with the Constitution of the Decision of the Senate No 24 of 3 July 2012 for the dismissal of Mr Vasile Blaga from the office of President of the Senate, 34–42; Decision No 729 of 9 July 2012 on the rejection of a claim of inconsistency with the Constitution of the Decision of the Chamber of Deputies No 25 of 3 July 2012 for the dismissal of Mrs Roberta Alma Anastase from the office of President and member of the Bureau of the Chamber of Deputies, 43–51.

[146] Decision No 730 of 9 July 2012 (Constitutional Court of Romania) on the rejection of a claim of inconsistency with the Constitution of the Decision of the Parliament No 32 of 30 July 2012 for the dismissal of Mr Gheorge Inacu from the office of Ombudsperson, 52–62.

[147] Decision No 727 of 9 July 2012 (Constitutional Court of Romania) on the referral of unconstitutionality of the Law amending Art 2(1) of Law No 47/1992 on the Organisation and Operation of the Constitutional Court, 25–33.

[148] Aviz consultative No 1 of 6 July 2012 (Constitutional Court of Romania) concerning the proposal to suspend from office the President of Romania, Mr Traian Băsescu, reprinted in European Commission for Democracy through Law (Venice Commission), *Opinion on Constitutional Issues in Romania* (Opinion No 685/2012, 5 September 2012) 3–20.

Moreover, considerable confusion arose with respect to the necessary thresholds for the referendum. By adopting Emergency Ordinance 41/2012 of 5 July 2012, the new ruling coalition did away with the 50 per cent participatory threshold in the referendum law. An impeachment referendum would be valid if a majority of voters casting their ballot were to support it.[149] That was done at a time when the constitutionality of a parliamentary amendment to the referendum law was already pending before the Constitutional Court for *ab a priori* review. That amendment (in contrast to the Emergency Ordinance) had confirmed the 50 per cent participation threshold for dismissal of the President.[150] On 10 July, the Constitutional Court upheld the constitutionality of the amendment to the law, insofar as the minimum threshold under the referendum law also applied to dismissal referenda.[151] The same day, the government announced it would carry out the 29 July referendum according to the Emergency Ordinance, arguing that the legal rules governing the impeachment process could not be changed when it was already under way.

(iii) Commission Decision of 18 July 2012

On 6 July 2012, a number of Romanian NGOs and intellectuals had already written an open letter to Commission President Barroso, complaining about attacks on Romania's institutions. On the same day, the Commission expressed public concern, especially about measures curbing the powers of independent institutions like the Constitutional Court.[152] On 11–12 July 2012, Prime Minister Ponta visited Brussels, meeting the Presidents of three EU institutions, Martin Schulz (European Parliament), José-Manuel Barroso (Commission) and Herman Van Rompuy (European Council).

This time, the right-wing parties were more critical towards the Romanian government than the left side of the house. European Parliament President Schulz (SPE) said that government policies 'looked legal but remained very dubious from a political point of view'. ELDR President Graham Watson (ALDE) intervened on Romanian television stating that the 50 per cent plus 1 quorum of the total number of electors is one of the highest in Europe; whereas Chair of the European Parliament's Foreign Relations Committee Brok and former Justice Minister of Romania Macovei (both EPP), argued that the Romanian case called for an Article 7

[149] The Ordinance said: 'By derogation from Article 5(2) the dismissal of the President of Romania is approved if it meets the majority of valid votes of the citizens that took part in the referendum'.

[150] That amendment provided: 'The dismissal of the President of Romania is approved if, following the conduct of the referendum, the proposal meets the majority of the votes validly expressed'. Since art 5(2), which contains the 50 per cent threshold, remains applicable, the amendment thus consolidated the 50 per cent rule to be applicable in all instances where the Romanian Constitution foresaw a referendum.

[151] Decision No 731 of 10 July 2012 (Constitutional Court of Romania) on the rejection of the claim of inconsistency with the Constitution of the Law amending Art 10 of Law No 3/2000 concerning the organisation of the referendum, 65–70.

[152] European Commission Press Release, 6 July 2012, available at www.europa.eu/rapid/pressReleasesAction.do?reference=IP/12/799.

TEU intervention.[153] In return, the President of the European Council wished to see 'respect for both the letter and the spirit of the Constitution', a principle he deemed at the heart of the European project.[154] He asked Prime Minister Ponta to pursue a constructive dialogue with the Commission and follow its recommendations.

The blunt messages were left for Commission President Barroso, who expressed serious concerns about the rule of law, the independence of the judiciary and the role of the Constitutional Court to the Prime Minister. He underlined the need to guarantee the necessary checks and balances in a democratic system. President Barroso made clear that the Romanian government had to respect the full independence of the judiciary; restore the powers of the Constitutional Court and ensure that its decisions were observed; appoint an ombudsman enjoying cross-party support; ensure a new open and transparent procedure for appointing a general prosecutor and Director of the Anti-Corruption Directorate; and make integrity a political priority.[155] He also recommended that all MPs with final rulings on incompatibility or conflict of interests ought to resign. The Prime Minister should avoid appointing any ministers who had had rulings censuring their integrity made against them.[156]

Interestingly, those points were later formally incorporated into the Commission's Cooperation and Verification Mechanism Report on Romania, adopted on 18 July 2012.[157] Based on the two safeguard clauses in the Accession Treaty with Romania and Bulgaria, this report listed shortcomings in judicial reform and in the fight against corruption. Designed to give a five-year overview, it was due on that date and coincided with Romania's political and constitutional crisis. In particular, the Commission invited the government to repeal the Emergency Ordinances on the referendum process and on curbing the powers of the Constitutional Court; to 'implement all the decisions of the Constitutional Court'; to 'ensure the immediate publication of all acts in the Official Journal, including decisions of the Constitutional Court'; and to 'require all political parties and government authorities to respect the independence of the judiciary with a commitment to discipline any government or party member who undermines the credibility of judges or puts pressure on judicial institutions'.[158] In the meantime, in a letter of 16 July 2012, updated on 17 July, Prime Minister Ponta had informed Barroso of his acceptance to carry out the latter's recommendations. Indeed, a joint session of the two Chambers of the Romanian Parliament on 17–18 July 2012 amended

[153] M Macovei, 'The Romanian Coup d'Etat', *European Voice*, 12 July 2012, available at www.europeanvoice.com/article/imported/the-romanian-coup-d-etat/74831.aspx.

[154] A Gardner and T Vogel, 'Van Rompuy "Deeply Concerned" about Romania', *European Voice*, 12 July 2012, available at www.europeanvoice.com/article/2012/july/van-rompuy-deeply-concerned-about-romania/74850.aspx.

[155] JM Barroso, Press Release, 12 July 2012, available at www.europa.eu/rapid/press-release_MEMO-12-553_en.htm.

[156] Gardner and Vogel, 'Van Rompuy' (n 154).

[157] European Commission, *Report from the Commission to the European Parliament and the Council on Progress in Romania under the Cooperation and Verification Mechanism*, COM(2012)410 final.

[158] ibid 20.

Emergency Ordinance No 38/2012 on the reduced powers of the Constitutional Court in an attempt to bring it into line with the Court's ruling of 9 July. In the same session, Parliament also repealed the relevant provisions of Emergency Ordinance 41/2012 by Law 153/2012. In the meantime, the 50 per cent turnout condition required by the Constitutional Court decision of 9 July had been reinstated by the publication, on 17 July 2012, of Law 131/2012 (for the amendment of article 10 of Law 3/2000).[159] This proved a decisive factor for the impeachment referendum on 29 July 2012. While a large majority (87.5 per cent) of voters actually voted for impeachment, less than half of the voters (46 per cent) participated in it. Due to this low turnout, after a heated dispute about the accuracy of the voters' lists used,[160] the Constitutional Court confirmed the referendum's invalidity on 21 August 2012. Accordingly, President Băsescu remained in office, though politically weakened since he had asked his supporters to boycott the referendum rather than to cast a negative vote, which can hardly be seen as democratic behaviour.

It is worth mentioning that Prime Minister Ponta also formally committed himself to ensuring immediate publication of all Acts in the Official Journal and to implement all Constitutional Court judgments.[161] The interim President of Romania and the Prime Minister reiterated adherence to the independence of the judiciary, asking political parties to refrain from criticising judicial decisions.[162] Ponta's letter fully addressed points made with respect to the appointment of the new ombudsman, dismissal of MPs or ministers with rulings against them censuring their integrity, and also the need not to grant any pardon during the interim mandate of the President.[163] However, to date a new ombudsman has not yet been appointed, and the first integrity rulings are still awaited.

(iv) Comparison

In my view, all three cases were legally ripe for triggering the Article 7(1) TEU procedure. All of them contained a risk of serious breach of at least one of the fundamental values of the Union. However, in none of them was the procedure actually triggered.

In Italy, Berlusconi's *ad personam* laws were neutralised by the Italian judiciary and by parliamentary process before becoming a systematic rule of law problem. Unusually high media concentration, combined with non-implementation of Constitutional Court judgments and biased media reporting in favour of the government, created a clear risk for the operation of a pluralist democracy and the rule of law.[164] As the European Parliament rightly observed, these elements

[159] *Official Journal of Romania* I, No 489 of 17 July 2012.

[160] For details see Decision No 3 of 2 August 2012 and Decision No 6 of 21 August 2012 (Constitutional Court of Romania).

[161] Letter from Prime Minister Ponta to President Barroso, 16 July 2012, paras 5, 6.

[162] ibid para 6.

[163] ibid paras 7–11.

[164] Serini, *Sanktionen* (n 30) 269–70.

fell within the scope of Article 6 TEU (Nice), and would certainly be covered by Article 2 TEU (Lisbon), expressly referring to a pluralist society. Nevertheless, the time was not ripe for a formal intervention by the EU institutions. Brussels relied on national political remedies instead. Indeed, in the parliamentary elections of April 2006, Berlusconi lost his majority to a centre-left government. In this respect, the democratic principles worked in Italy.

In Hungary, by January 2012, a number of values under Article 2 TEU were endangered at a systematic level. The new Constitution together with cardinal laws and Transitional Provisions, negatively affected the functioning of the judiciary. When, in March, the Venice Commission deemed judicial reform in Hungary to threaten the independence of the judiciary,[165] this added an important element to an interpretation of the rule of law criterion under Article 2 TEU. Moreover, the principle of democracy was, and continues to be, threatened by over-use of cardinal laws, making it impossible for any future government to govern without a two-thirds majority. As correctly observed by the Venice Commission, this threatens the principle of political alteration enshrined in Article 3 of the First Additional Protocol to the ECHR.[166] Moreover, there was a threat to the separation of powers through interference with the independence of the central bank, and severe shortcomings in handling media pluralism, both falling foul of the value of a pluralistic society enshrined in Article 2 TEU. Those risks also related to 'serious' breaches of Union values as the proper functioning of those institutions was important for the entire population of Hungary.

And yet, the European Commission did not activate Article 7(1) TEU. As a warning shot, it preferred a piecemeal approach of infringement cases coupled with conditioning macro-economic financial assistance. These tactics brought some success, such as to the thorny issue of central bank independence which was restored shortly thereafter. Moreover, the Commission's action encouraged the Hungarian judiciary to become more active. In particular, the courageous decisions of the Hungarian Constitutional Court of July 2012 on the retirement age of judges would have been inconceivable without the prior infringement case from Brussels. EU pressure also helped the Council of Europe to bring home some important points on the judiciary. On the other hand, Europe's influence was very limited in the area of media freedom: the recommendations of the Council of Europe were largely ignored once the 'hot phase' of the Commission versus Hungary debate was over. Here, as in the Italian case, a lack of a proper EU Directive on media pluralism constitutes a weakness in the European system, as this greatly reduces the possibility to bring proper infringement cases. Finally, a big question mark remains over why the Commission failed officially to criticise the government's curbing of the Constitutional Court's powers in the new

165 Venice Commission Op 663/2012 (n 74) para 117.

166 European Commission for Democracy through Law (Venice Commission), *Opinion on the New Constitution of Hungary* (Opinion No 618/2001, 18 March 2011) para 24.

Constitution and the excessive use of cardinal laws in areas which are better left to ordinary legislation. As these points cannot be raised under the *acquis* and Article 258 TFEU, and Commissioner Reding never took them to the College of Commissioners, they simply fell through the enforcement net. It is, however, heartening to note that the European Parliament included them in its very important resolution of 16 February 2012.

Very soon thereafter, the screws were tightened in the case of Romania. In summer 2012, questions of constitutional justice and institutional balance of powers were at the heart of Brussels' enforcement action. While the attempt to impeach President Băsescu and the substitution of parliamentary chairpersons was in line with the Romanian Constitution, a number of highly doubtful accompanying measures had called into question the respect of the government for the rule of law and the balance of powers. This included the ignorance of the delivered, but not yet published, Constitutional Court judgment on the representation of Romania at European Councils, the narrowing down of the Court's competences and the elimination of the 50 per cent threshold for the impeachment referendum. Moreover, the European Commission went a long way to create a 'European link' to the other institutional issues, including the appointment procedures of the ombudsman and the dismissals of ministers or MPs subject to pending cases challenging their integrity. The CVM report was the 'hook' for tackling these points. As observed above, however, this is only a particular feature for Romania and Bulgaria.

In its reaction towards Bucharest, the European Commission for the first time went into considerable detail with respect to questions of constitutional justice. There is a certain degree of contrast with the Hungarian case here. Besides possible political factors, open defiance of concrete Constitutional Court judgments in Romania could not be tolerated, whereas general and abstract cuts in jurisprudential competences in Hungary could at least be defended as there is no European requirement to operate a constitutional court with wide-ranging powers. However, a closer look reveals that the rule of law is also threatened when existing Constitutional Court judgments are overturned by subsequent constitutional amendments, as was the case in Hungary several times, and at the latest with the scandalous Fourth Amendment to the Basic Law of March 2013. In an important development, President Barroso then took action for the Commission, writing of his concerns on the rule of law to Prime Minister Orbán on 8 March 2013 and making them public in a joint statement with the Council of Europe Secretary General Jagland on 11 March 2013. Again, the most convincing analysis on this point came, however, subsequently from the European Parliament in the Tavares Report of June 2013 which, however, also fell short of activating the Article 7(1) TEU procedure in the absence of a sufficient political majority for such a move.

V. CONCLUSION

Enforcement of the EU Charter of Fundamental Rights is entrusted to national and European institutions, which can either act upon application of EU citizens or *ex officio*. Clearly, calibrating a human rights catalogue on Charter rights, interpreting the national human rights catalogue in line with the Charter where interpretative margins exist, or even elevating the Charter to a constitutional yardstick for constitutional complaints constitute effective means to ensure proper application.

Tougher questions arise when systematic Member State government policy seems to defy fundamental values of the Charter, also enshrined under the notion of human rights in Article 2 TEU. Here, the European Commission can launch *acquis*-related infringement cases, as in the case of Hungary. However, this approach faces inherent restrictions given the piecemeal nature of the *acquis*. In such a case, only Article 7 TEU provides for a legal basis to act. I submit that in the cases of Italy, Hungary and Romania the legal requirements for action under Article 7 TEU were met. However, cross-party political majorities to trigger this heavy instrument were present neither in the European Parliament nor in the European Commission. Nevertheless, intense discussions and public peer pressure did not go unnoticed.

Arguably, European dissatisfaction with Berlusconi's policies was arguably picked up by Italian voters. With respect to Hungary, European Commission action lent substantial support to efforts of the Council of Europe, albeit with certain limits. Subsequent revisions in the fields of media pluralism, the judiciary and independence of the data protection authority are clearly indirect results of pressure from Brussels. *En revanche*, points noted only by the European Parliament in its February 2012 and June 2013 resolutions (excessive use of cardinal laws, cutting Constitutional Court competences and issues of religious freedom) were not pursued by the Commission. In the case of Romania, the Commission did not exercise restraint and went into the details of constitutional justice and balance of powers. Had Romania not promptly complied with the direct demands from Brussels, we would quite likely have seen the initiation of a first Article 7(1) TEU case.

Is the European enforcement machinery too weak to handle these struggles? Probably not. Raising an issue in Brussels with ever-intensive degrees of scrutiny had positive effects on subsequent events in Rome, Budapest and Bucharest. On the other hand, it is clear that more work needs to done to define clearer criteria and thresholds for triggering an Article 7(1) TEU procedure.[167] This could allow both the Parliament and the Commission to better live up to one aspect of the rule of law principle enshrined in Article 2 TEU: equal treatment of equally serious problems, irrespective of the size, political colour or historical merits of a particular EU Member State.

[167] Compare European Parliament Resolution of 15 December 2010 on the situation of fundamental rights in the European Union [2012] OJ C169E/7, in which it called for a follow-up to the 2003 Communication from the Commission on Article 7 TEU, and the very precise ideas in the Tavares Report (n 130) 72–83. Such a mechanism has also been requested in a letter of 6 March 2013 from the Ministers of Foreign Affairs of Germany, the Netherlands, Denmark and Finland to Commission President Barroso.

8

A European Response to Domestic Constitutional Crisis: Advancing the Reverse-Solange *Doctrine*

ARMIN VON BOGDANDY, CARLINO ANTPÖHLER, JOHANNA DICKSCHEN, SIMON HENTREI, MATTHIAS KOTTMANN AND MAJA SMRKOLJ*

I. INTRODUCTION

EUROPEAN SCHOLARSHIP AND practice have recently experienced a lively debate on the European Union's duty to react to domestic constitutional crises in Member States. Detrimental developments, particularly in Hungary and Romania, have spurred an intense debate on the inadequacies of the existing European instruments. On the one hand, the European institutions have been reluctant to use Article 7 of the Treaty on European Union (TEU).[1] On the other hand, the piecemeal approach of the European Commission, using a number of technical infringement procedures,[2] has rightly been described as insufficient. Some of the European institutions,[3] as well as a group of Foreign Ministers[4] and many scholars[5] share the conviction that a third way to react in a

* The chapter is based on and develops an article published by the authors in (2012) 49 *CML Rev* 489.

[1] Vice-President of the Commission V Reding even described the Art 7 mechanism as a 'nuclear option' in a speech at the General Affairs Council of 22 April 2013, 'Safeguarding the Rule of Law and Solving the "Copenhagen Dilemma": Towards a New EU-Mechanism', SPEECH/13/348, available at www.europa.eu/rapid/press-release_SPEECH-13-348_en.htm.

[2] Case C-288/12 *European Commission v Hungary* (not yet decided); Case C-286/12 *European Commission v Hungary* (2012, nyr). A third case regarding the independence of the Central Bank of Hungary was settled out of court, IP/12/222, see www.europa.eu/rapid/press-release_IP-12-222_en.htm.

[3] Reding speech (n 1); C McCrudden, speech at a conference of the Irish Presidency, 'Mapping the Landscape: Institutions, Problems, Ideas', 9 May 2013.

[4] The Foreign Ministers of Germany, the Netherlands, Denmark and Finland sent a letter to the President of the Commission on 6 March 2013 asking for 'a new and more effective mechanism to safeguard fundamental values in Member States', available at www.rijksoverheid.nl/bestanden/documenten-en-publicaties/brieven/2013/03/13/brief-aan-europese-commissie-over-opzetten-rechtsstatelijkheidsmechanisme/brief-aan-europese-commissie-over-opzetten-rechtsstatelijkheidsmechanisme.pdf.

[5] The overall agreement on the insufficiency of the current mechanisms was one remarkable outcome of two online symposia held on the Verfassungsblog, 'A Rescue Package for EU Fundamental Rights, Illustrated with reference to the Example of Media Freedom', verfassungsblog.de/de/category/

more comprehensive manner needs to be found while avoiding the deficiencies of the Article 7 TEU[6] mechanism. The reverse-*Solange* doctrine offers one such novel instrument, combining the strengths of legal enforceability and respect for the constitutional identities of Member States. The mechanism can be developed based on the Treaties and relies on a premise that has already been found valuable in *van Gend en Loos*, 'the vigilance of individuals concerned to protect their rights'.[7] The doctrine also mitigates the gap between strict pre-accession control and scant post-accession action in fundamental rights matters.[8] This chapter will recap the approach, adapt it to novel developments, respond to criticism and further advance it.

The conviction that a massive deterioration of fundamental rights protection in some Member States ought to be of concern to the European institutions has been undisputed in the debate. Such constitutional crises might threaten a foundation of European integration, namely, the principle that the Union can rely on the functioning democratic polities of the Member States.[9] Seriously detrimental developments in Member States might rock the EU to its very roots and might even call the system itself into question.

The rights protected by the reverse-*Solange* doctrine are not those of a transnational *homo oeconomicus* but of citizens. Our proposal, therefore, aims at linking the discourse of fundamental rights with the rapidly evolving status of Union citizenship. In section II below, we build upon recent jurisprudence according to which 'Article 20 TFEU precludes national measures which have the effect of depriving citizens of the Union of the genuine enjoyment of the substance of the rights conferred by virtue of their status as citizens of the Union'.[10] We claim

schwerpunkte/rescue-english/page/2 and 'Hungary: Taking Action', verfassungsblog.de/en/category/schwerpunkte/antworten-auf-ungarn/.

[6] See S Greer and A Williams, 'Human Rights and the Council of Europe and the EU: Towards "Individual", "Constitutional" or "Institutional" Justice?' (2009) 15 *European Law Journal* 462, 474; O De Schutter, 'Les droits fondamentaux dans le traité d'Amsterdam' in Y Lejeune (ed), *Le traité d'Amsterdam* (Bruxelles, Bruylant, 1998) 153, 179 ff; T Stein, 'Die rechtlichen Reaktionsmöglichkeiten der Europäischen Union bei schwerwiegender und anhaltender Verletzung der demokratischen und rechtsstaatlichen Grundsätze in einem Mitgliedstaat' in V Götz, P Selmer, and R Wolfrum (eds), *Liber amicorum Günther Jaenicke—zum 85. Geburtstag* (Berlin, Springer, 1998) 871, 898; J Crawford, 'Democracy and the Body of International Law' in GH Fox and BR Roth (eds), *Democratic Governance and International Law* (Cambridge, Cambridge University Press, 2000) 91, 112 note 85.

[7] Case C-26/62 *Van Gend en Loos* [1963] ECR 1, para 24.

[8] A Albi, 'Ironies in Human Rights Protection in the EU: Pre-Accession Conditionality and Post-Accession Conundrums' (2009) 15 *European Law Journal* 46, 48 ff; C Hillion, 'Enlargement of the European Union:

The Discrepancy between Membership Obligations and Accession Conditions as Regards the Protection of Minorities' (2004) 27 *Fordham International Law Journal* 715; A Williams, *EU Human Rights Policies: A Study in Irony* (Oxford, Oxford University Press, 2004) 97; K Nicolaidis, '"What" versus "Who": Europe's Rule of Law Agenda Revisited' in Verfassungsblog, 'Hungary: Taking Action' (n 5).

[9] In detail A von Bogdandy, 'The European Union as Situation, Executive, and Promoter of the International Law of Cultural Diversity: Elements of a Beautiful Friendship' (2008) 19 *European Journal of International Law* 241.

[10] Case C-34/09 *Ruiz Zambrano* (2011, nyr) para 42.

that this 'substance' basically consists of the essence of fundamental rights, which is enshrined in Article 2 TEU and applies to public authority *throughout* the European legal space. In order to preserve the constitutional pluralism protected by Article 4(2) TEU, we propose to frame this as a 'reverse' *Solange* doctrine, applied at the European level to the Member States; beyond the scope of Article 51(1) of the EU Charter of Fundamental Rights (CFREU), Member States remain autonomous in fundamental rights protection and in drafting and amending a constitution *as long as* they generally safeguard the essence of the fundamental rights enshrined in Article 2 TEU. However, should this presumption be rebutted, individuals can rely on their status as Union citizens to seek redress before national courts, as discussed in section III below. Section IV below further elucidates this doctrine. Insights from the debate are taken up and we react to the latest jurisprudence. Additionally, one particular field of application, domestic constitutional law, is sketched.

II. TOWARDS A MUTUALLY REINFORCING RELATIONSHIP OF CITIZENSHIP AND FUNDAMENTAL RIGHTS

Our proposal is to anchor the essence of European fundamental rights in Union citizenship in order to make them available for individual legal actions. But is it doctrinally convincing to link these two concepts, which normally are treated separately? In our view, it is not only plausible but necessary to do so as there is a pronounced historical and teleological connection between them. Both discourses developed around the same period in reaction to the pressing question of the democratic legitimacy of the European Union. Citizenship and fundamental rights are, therefore, two mutually reinforcing concepts that essentially pursue the same objective, namely, to bring the Union closer to the individual.[11] This is also reflected in today's positive law. With the Treaty of Lisbon, Union citizenship has become the core of an emerging European democratic theory. According to Title II of the TEU, democracy in the Union consists of two strands, one leading to political processes at the Union level, namely, to the European Parliament, and one, mediated by the national governments, originating in the political processes of the Member States (see Article 10(2) TEU).[12] Both strands eventually lead back to the individuals who are simultaneously citizens of the Union and of Member States.[13] In addition, fundamental rights protection can foster democratic legitimacy by enabling individual participation in the political processes at the Union

[11] See further S O'Leary, *The Evolving Concept of Community Citizenship* (The Hague, Kluwer Law International, 1996) 549.

[12] A Peters, *Elemente einer Theorie der Verfassung Europas* (Berlin, Duncker & Humblot, 2001) 556.

[13] See S Dellavalle, 'Between Citizens and Peoples' (2004/2005) II/III *Annual of German and European Law* 171; I Pernice, 'Europäisches und nationales Verfassungsrecht' (2001) 60 *Veröffentlichungen der Vereinigung der Deutschen Staatsrechtslehrer* 148, 160; A Levade, 'Citoyenneté de l'Union européenne et identité constitutionelle' (2011) 18 *Revue des Affaires Européennes* 98.

or Member State level.[14] A fine example of this is provided by media freedom: obviously democracy in the Union would be seriously affected if Union citizens were hampered in expressing their opinions in or informing themselves via independent media.[15]

In light of the foregoing, it is not surprising that the Court of Justice of the European Union (CJEU) has continuously expanded and partially converged the two concepts in a rapidly evolving jurisprudence without fully grasping their combined potential. Of particular importance for our proposal are two lines of case law, the development of a 'substance' of Union citizenship that even covers so-called 'internal situations' (as described in section A) and the inclusion of concerns for fundamental rights protection in the meaning of Union citizenship (as discussed in section B).

A. 'Substance' of Union Citizenship

In its famous *Grzelczyk* judgment, the CJEU proclaimed that 'the Union Citizenship is destined to be the fundamental status of nationals of the Member States'.[16] Advocate General Sharpston rightly points out that this development is 'potentially of similar significance to [the Court's] seminal statement in *Van Gend en Loos*'.[17] In this regard it is important to recall that the CJEU has construed the right to move and to reside freely (now in Article 21 TFEU) as a directly effective individual right that may not be inhibited by any unjustified burden or 'serious inconvenience' and that can also be invoked against the Union citizen's Member State of origin.[18] While most of the cases involved physical movement from one Member State to another, this element was increasingly blurred over time.[19] Eventually, this led to the seminal decision in *Ruiz Zambrano*, which provided the protection of a 'substance' of Union citizenship rights by virtue of Article 20 TFEU absent any cross-border element whatsoever.

[14] J Habermas, *Die postnationale Konstellation* (Frankfurt am Main, Suhrkamp, 1998) 175.

[15] S Kadelbach, 'Union Citizenship' in A von Bogdandy and J Bast (eds), *Principles of European Constitutional Law*, 2nd edn (Oxford, Hart Publishing, 2010) 466.

[16] Case C-184/99 *Grzelczyk* [2001] ECR I-6193, para 31. This formula has been used in the case law ever since, *cf* Case C-413/99 *Baumbast and R* [2002] ECR I-7091, para 82; *Ruiz Zambrano* (n 10) para 41.

[17] *Ruiz Zambrano* (n 10) (AG Sharpston) para 68.

[18] Case C-406/04 *De Cuyper* [2006] ECR I-6947, para 39; Case C-208/09 *Sayn-Wittgenstein* [2010] ECR I-13693, para 67. See in detail E Spaventa, 'Seeing the Wood Despite the Trees? On the Scope of Union Citizenship and its Constitutional Effects' (2008) 45 *CML Rev* 13, 22 ff; F Wollenschläger, 'A New Fundamental Freedom Beyond the Market' (2011) 17 *European Law Journal* 1, 25 ff.

[19] See Case C-148/02 *Garcia Avello* [2003] ECR I-11613, para 26; Case C-200/02 *Zhu and Chen* [2004] ECR I-9925, para 26; Case C-135/08 *Rottmann* [2010] ECR I-01449, para 42. See in detail D Kochenov, 'A Real European Citizenship: The Court of Justice Opening a New Chapter in the Development of the Union in Europe' (2011/2012) 18 *Columbia Journal of European Law* 55.

Mr Ruiz Zambrano and his wife had taken refuge in Belgium due to the civil war in their home country Colombia. His applications to have his residence status regularised were rejected by Belgian authorities. In the meantime, his wife had given birth to two children who had, according to Belgian law, acquired Belgian nationality and consequently the status of Union citizens. However, as they had never moved beyond Belgium's borders, according to the conventional rules one would have described the situation as 'purely internal' and thus outside the ambit of Union law.[20] This constellation of facts led the CJEU to adopt a new concept in its jurisprudence on Union citizenship. It held categorically that 'Article 20 TFEU preclude[d] national measures which have the effect of depriving citizens of the Union of the genuine enjoyment of the substance of the rights conferred by virtue of their status as citizens of the Union'.[21] The Ruiz Zambrano children being dependent on their father, the judges argued, they eventually would have to leave the Union's territory, should he be denied residence. Yet, this would mean that they were 'unable to exercise the substance of the rights' conferred by Union citizenship.[22] Later case law has refined this principle, which is so far applicable merely with regard to the residence of family members. It is understood narrowly: a right of residence to relatives is granted only if refusal would result in the Union citizen being *factually obliged* to leave the Union's territory. Practice shows that the threshold is difficult to cross.[23]

No doubt, *Ruiz Zambrano* is a groundbreaking step of judicial law-making. Given its importance, it is unfortunate, although easy to understand, that the CJEU has failed to provide a comprehensive doctrinal justification.[24] Yet, what

[20] This was indeed argued by the European Commission and all of the nine Member States which submitted observations in that case (*Ruiz Zambrano* (n 10) para 37).

[21] ibid para 42.

[22] ibid para 44.

[23] Case C-434/09 *McCarthy* [2011] ECR I-03375, para 49; Case C-256/11 *Dereci* (2011, nyr) para 66; Case C-40/11 *Iida* (2012, nyr) para 71; Case C-87/12 *Ymeranga* (2013, nyr) para 36.

[24] See for a critique K Hailbronner and D Thym, 'Annotation' (2011) 48 *CML Rev* 1253, 1259 ff; A Lansbergen and N Miller, 'European Citizenship Rights in Internal Situations: An Ambiguous Revolution?' (2011) 7 *European Constitutional Law Review* 287, 306 ff; N Nic Shuibhne, 'Seven Questions for Seven Paragraphs' (2011) 36 *EL Rev* 161; A Tryfonidou, 'Redefining the Outer Boundaries of EU Law: The *Zambrano*, *McCarthy* and *Dereci* Trilogy' (2012) 18 *European Public Law* 493; L Manigrassi, 'Vers une citoyenneté européenne fédérale? Quelques réflexions sur l'arrêt "Zambrano"' (2011) *Revue du Droit de l'Union Européenne* 411; S Platon, 'Le champ d'application des droits du citoyen européen après les arrêts *Zambrano*, *McCarthy* et *Dereci*' (2012) 48 *Revue trimestrielle de droit européen* 23; for a more positive appraisal Kochenov, 'A Real European Citizenship' (n 19); M Nettesheim, 'Der ‚Kernbereich' der Unionsbürgerschaft' (2011) 66 *JuristenZeitung* 1030, 1031 ff; M del Rosario Carmona Luque, 'El disfrute efectivo de la esencia de los derechos de ciudadanía da la Unión' (2011) 15 *Revista de Derecho Communitario Europeo* 185; L Montanari, 'Una nuova tappa nella definizione della portata della cittadinanza europea: Alcune riflessioni sulle sentenze *Ruiz Zambrano* e *McCarthy*' (2011) 66 *La Comunità Internazionale* 433; S Mantu, 'European Union Citizenship Anno 2011: *Zambrano*, *McCarthy* and *Dereci*' (2012) 26 *Journal of Immigration, Asylum and Nationality Law* 40; W Frenz, 'Reichweite des unionsrechtlichen Aufenthaltsrechts nach den Urteilen Zambrano und McCarthy' (2011) 31 *Zeitschrift für Ausländerrecht und Ausländerpolitik* 221; P Hamernik, 'The Case C-34/09 Ruiz Zambrano v. Onem' (2012) 2 *The Lawyer Quarterly* 216; I Solanke, 'Using the Citizen to Bring the Refugee in' (2012) 75 *MLR* 101.

emerges from the Court's reasoning is that it views Union citizenship as entailing more than transnational citizenship. The 'fundamental status' has a domestic dimension. The Union emerges to protect its citizens against violations even by their Member States of origin if such violations would deprive their Union citizenship of its practical meaning.[25] This almost inevitably leads to the question what role fundamental rights play in such a construct.

B. 'Fundamental Status' and Fundamental Rights

Linking Union citizenship with EU fundamental rights is an established project.[26] Within the CJEU, the idea was first voiced by Advocate General Jacobs in his famous conclusions in *Konstantinidis*. He argued that a Union citizen exercising his right to movement was, by virtue of his status, entitled to say '*civis europaeus sum*' and to invoke European fundamental rights.[27] In this initial phase, the CJEU did not follow that approach and decided the case on the basis of the freedom of establishment.[28] Today, in many of its citizenship cases the CJEU seems to be driven by a fundamental rights discourse in all but name.[29] Often, this can be traced back to conclusions by the Court's Advocates General that exposed the fundamental rights background of what sometimes seemed to be rather technical cases,[30] or to references by national courts pointing in that direction.[31] As a consequence, European Court of Human Rights (ECtHR) jurisprudence, inter alia, on the right to family life or the right to a name, openly or covertly found its way into the CJEU's case law on Union citizenship.[32] The *Ruiz Zambrano* case also

[25] D Dittert, 'Les droits des citoyens de l'Union: vers un statut détaché de tout élément transfrontalier?' (2011) 18 *Revue des affaires européennes* 223, 226; P Van Elsuwege, 'European Union Citizenship and the Purely Internal Rule Revisited' (2011) 7 *European Constitutional Law Review* 308, 313 ff.

[26] For the development of such concepts see M Benlolo Carabot, *Les fondements juridiques de la Citoyenneté Européenne* (Bruxelles, Bruylant, 2008) 606, 614 ff; Kadelbach, 'Union Citizenship' (n 15) 464; Case C-228/07 *Petersen* [2008] ECR I-6989 (Opinion of AG Colomer) para 25.

[27] Case C-168/91 *Konstantinidis* [1993] ECR I-1191 (Opinion of AG Jacobs) para 46. This has met with divided reactions. See for an affirmation N Reich and S Harbacevica, 'Citizenship and Family on Trial: A Fairly Optimistic Overview of Recent Court Practice with regard to Free Movement of Persons' (2003) 40 *CML Rev* 615, 634 ff; DH Scheuing, 'Zur Grundrechtsbindung der EU-Mitgliedstaaten' (2005) 40 *Europarecht* 162, 179; for a critique U Haltern, *Europarecht und das Politische* (Tübingen, Mohr Siebeck, 2005) 372; F Wollenschläger, *Grundfreiheit ohne Markt* (Tübingen, Mohr Siebeck, 2007) 353.

[28] *Konstantinidis* (n 27).

[29] But see *Baumbast and R* (n 16) para 91, where the Court held that limitations of rights granted by Union citizenship must be applied in conformity with the general principles of Community law.

[30] See, eg *Garcia Avello* (n 19) (AG Jacobs) para 27, who assessed the dispute about the composition of a surname in light of the right to a personal identity; *cf* further *Baumbast and R* (n 16) (AG Geelhoed) para 58; *Zhu and Chen* (n 19) (AG Tizzano) para 94; *Sayn-Wittgenstein* (n 18) (AG Sharpston) para 3.

[31] See for a recent example the reference in *Iida* (n 23) para 23.

[32] A fine example is *Sayn-Wittgenstein* (n 18), which explicitly relies on ECtHR case law pertaining to Art 8 ECHR.

was centred on fundamental rights questions although the CJEU avoided making this explicit.[33]

However, one has to resist the temptation to reformulate any fundamental rights issue as a 'serious inconvenience' with regard to movement and residence or as an infringement upon the 'substance' of Union citizenship. This would ultimately induce general fundamental rights review of Member State action, thus contravening Article 51 CFREU.[34] As recent case law shows, the CJEU is well aware of the problem but refrains from taking an unambiguous position. In *Ruiz Zambrano* and *McCarthy*, the Court, in contrast to the respective Advocates General, did not address fundamental rights at all.[35] In *Dereci*, it declared that the 'substance' of Union citizenship was not activated 'by the mere fact that it might appear desirable' for a Union citizen to live with his family in the territory of the Union. It continued, however, by stating that this finding was 'without prejudice' to the question whether the claimants could rely on the right to family life. The Court held that the referring court had to verify whether the case fell under EU law and, if in the affirmative, apply Article 7 CFREU, or, if in the negative, consider Article 8 of the European Convention on Human Rights (ECHR).[36] It is unusual for the CJEU to raise a question concerning EU fundamental rights and then to refrain from deciding whether they in fact apply. This seems to be a sign of a deeper discomfort about the question of the relationship between citizenship and fundamental rights.[37]

One could even draw the conclusion from some recent cases that the CJEU prefers to separate strictly Union citizenship and fundamental rights and to adopt an extensive interpretation of Article 51(1) CFREU instead. In *Ymeranga* and *Iida*, the Court, having decided that the 'substance' of Union citizenship was not at stake, went on to hold that EU fundamental rights did not apply because the national measures at hand did not involve any 'implementation' of EU law in the sense of Article 51(1) CFREU.[38]

We claim, however, that there is a doctrinally more convincing way to resolve the tension between the effectiveness of Union citizenship and respect for the limited scope of EU fundamental rights: in principle, the 'substance' of Union citizenship does not trigger fundamental rights protection by the Union. Outside

[33] See *Ruiz Zambrano* (n 10) (AG Sharpston) paras 54, 81 ff. But see for a reading limited to the right of residence Hailbronner and Thym, 'Annotation' (n 24).

[34] See N Graf Vitzthum, 'Die Entdeckung der Heimat der Unionsbürger' (2011) 46 *Europarecht* 550, 557 ff. This might be the effect of the *Åkerberg Fransson* jurisprudence, Case C-617/10 *Åkerberg Fransson* (2013, nyr). The Court equated the 'implementation of Union law' in Art 51 CFREU and the scope of Union law. A Union citizenship case, apart from the *Ruiz Zambrano* constellation, comes within EU law's scope if there is a cross-border element. In such a situation now fundamental rights apply in their entirety. We deal with the *Åkerberg Fransson* jurisprudence explicitly in the conclusion.

[35] See *Ruiz Zambrano* (n 10) (AG Sharpston) para 54; *McCarthy* (n 23) (AG Kokott) para 59.

[36] *Dereci* (n 23) paras 68–72.

[37] See also S Adam and P Van Elsuwege, 'Citizenship Rights and the Federal Balance between the European Union and Its Member States: Comment on *Dereci*' (2012) 37 *EL Rev* 176, 184 ff.

[38] *Iida* (n 23) para 76; *Ymeranga* (n 23) para 39.

the boundaries of Article 51(1) CFREU, such issues are left to national law and the ECHR.[39] However, a domestic fundamental rights violation falls under Union law and the 'substance' of citizenship if it amounts to emptying Union citizenship of its practical meaning.[40] This is our doctrinal starting point. In the following section we argue that it should be generalised and framed within the reverse-*Solange* doctrine.

III. OUR PROPOSAL: REVERSE-*SOLANGE* DOCTRINE

In the previous section we have shown that the Treaties and related jurisprudence of the CJEU offer a basis for providing Union citizens with a remedy to challenge fundamental rights deficits that threaten their 'fundamental status'.[41] In the following, we propose to frame this argument in terms inspired by the German Federal Constitutional Court's *Solange* doctrine. As is well known, the Karlsruhe Court no longer exercises its competence to control EU secondary law as long as the Union ensures 'essentially similar' fundamental rights protection as the German Basic Law, meaning that it 'generally safeguard[s] the essential content of fundamental rights'.[42] We argue that this should be taken up by the CJEU and directed towards the Member States.[43] Outside the Charter's scope of application, a Union citizen cannot rely on EU fundamental rights as long as their respective *essence* is *generally* safeguarded in the Member State concerned. However, should this presumption be rebutted, the 'substance' of Union citizenship—within the meaning of *Ruiz Zambrano*—is infringed.

The essence of fundamental rights (we argue in section A) is set out in Article 2 TEU as a basic condition for the exercise of public authority in the European legal space and can be drawn inductively from the jurisprudence of the ECtHR, the CJEU

39 With regard to Art 7 CFREU: *Dereci* (n 23) (AG Mengozzi) para 37; this is important in order to avoid conflicts given that the ECtHR's jurisprudence on Art 8 ECHR seems noticeably less generous than the corresponding case law of the CJEU on citizenship. See in this regard Lansbergen and Miller, 'European Citizenship Rights in Internal Situations' (n 24) 303.

40 See also H van Eijken and SA de Vries, 'A New Route into the Promised Land? Being a European Citizen after *Ruiz Zambrano*' (2011) 36 *EL Rev* 704, 718; Van Elsuwege, 'European Union Citizenship and the Purely Internal Rule Revisited' (n 25) 323.

41 The German Federal Constitutional Court follows a similar idea on the national level by interpreting the right to vote in art 38(1) of the Basic Law to give the individual a right to challenge 'the relevant deficits in the democratic legitimation of the European Union' (Decision of the German Federal Constitutional Court (BVerfGE) 123, 267, 331 (2009) *Lisbon*, English translation available at www.bverfg.de/en/decisions/es20090630_2bve000208en.html).

42 See BVerfGE 73, 339, 376 (1986) *Solange II*; BVerfGE 89, 155, 174 ff (1993) *Maastricht*; BVerfGE 102, 147, 164 (2000) *Banana*; BVerfGE 125, 260, 306 (2010) *Data Retention*. A different formula is used only in *Lisbon* (n 41) 335. As is equally well known, the Court had initially claimed that competence as long as fundamental rights protection in the EU had not reached such a level. See BVerfGE 37, 271, 280 (1974) *Solange I*.

43 Similar proposals are made by Advocate General Maduro in Case C-380/05 *Centro Europa 7* [2008] ECR I-349, para 17; P Cruz Villalón, 'All the Guidance', ERT and Wachauf' in MP Maduro and L Azoulai (eds), *The Past and Future of EU Law: The Classics of EU Law Revisited on the 50th Anniversary of the Rome Treaty* (Oxford, Hart Publishing, 2010) 162, 168.

and national Constitutional Courts. The bases for the second prong of our reverse-*Solange* doctrine are the principles of subsidiarity and respect for national identities (Articles 4(2) and 5(1) TEU). In general, it should be assumed that national law and institutions comply with Article 2 TEU. However, this presumption can be rebutted. Union citizenship consequently comes into play if it can be shown that there is a systemic violation of that standard (as is discussed in section B).

A. Article 2 TEU and the Essence of Fundamental Rights

In the words of Article 2 TEU, the Union 'is founded on', inter alia, 'respect for human rights'. This standard not only binds the Union itself, but also candidate countries (*cf* Article 49 TEU) and actual Member States (*cf* Article 7 TEU). With regard to the latter, Article 2 TEU is not limited to measures 'implementing Union law', in contrast to Article 51(1) CFREU.[44] But what does 'respect for human rights' entail? Obviously, as concrete legal consequences are attached to the failure to respect it, it cannot simply command adherence to an abstract *idea* of human rights protection.[45] On the other hand, this cannot mean that the Member States are comprehensively bound by the full *acquis* of EU fundamental rights, which, according to Article 51(1) CFREU, is binding on the Member States '*only* when they are implementing Union law' (emphasis added).

In order to define the content of 'essence of fundamental rights', a first hint can be drawn from the wording itself. While the specific mode of fundamental rights protection is conditioned by the different legal, political and cultural characteristics of each Member State, the principles protected by Article 2 TEU are said to be 'common to the Member States'. In our view, the best way to find such a common denominator is to rely on the concept of the *essence of fundamental rights*. This premise is grounded in a long-standing tradition and enjoys widespread recognition.[46] Not only is it laid down in Article 52(1) CFREU and numerous

[44] Declaration of the Presidency of the Convention, 6 February 2003, CONV 528/03, 11; European Commission, COM(2003)606, 5. See also M Hilf and F Schorkopf in E Grabitz and M Hilf (eds), *Das Recht der EU* (Munich, CH Beck, looseleaf) Art 2 TEU para 18; M Ruffert, in C Calliess and M Ruffert (eds), *EUV/AEUV Das Verfassungsrecht der Europäischen Union mit Europäischer Grundrechtecharta* (Munich, CH Beck, 2011) Art 7 TEU para 4; S Schmahl, 'Die Reaktion auf den Einzug der Freiheitlichen Partei Österreichs in das österreichische Regierungskabinett—Eine europa- und völkerrechtliche Analyse' (2000) 5 *Europarecht* 819, 822; F Schorkopf, *Homogenität in der Europäischen Union—Ausgestaltung und Gewährleistung durch Art 6 Abs. 1 und Art 7 EUV* (Berlin, Duncker & Humblot, 2000) 69, 99 ff; A Verhoeven, 'How Democratic Need European Union Members Be?' (1998) 23 *EL Rev* 217, 222–24, 234.

[45] Hilf and Schorkopf (n 44) Art 2 TEU para 36.

[46] By this we do not claim that there is a fixed or universally valid essence which can be defined *a priori*. However, a 'European essence' can be approached inductively in that certain infringements upon certain rights cannot be justified. See in detail J von Bernstorff, 'Kerngehaltsschutz durch den UN-Menschenrechtsausschuss und den EGMR: Vom Wert kategorialer Argumentationsformen' (2011) 50 *Der Staat* 165, 167 ff.

Constitutions of EU Member States,[47] it is also used by several Constitutional Courts as a yardstick for European integration. As such, it has become part of an *ordre public* in the European legal space.[48] It also underlies the jurisprudence of the ECtHR.[49]

There are various methods to determine the content of this 'essence'. With regard to the ECtHR's jurisprudence it should be safe to assume that the rights that are non-derogable solely by virtue of Article 15(2) ECHR are 'essential'.[50] This is a very small group of rights indeed. But the concept is applied by the ECtHR to other rights as well, although not in a fully consistent manner.[51] For our purpose, two patterns can be pointed out that can help to identify in a concrete situation whether Article 2 TEU is infringed. First, sometimes the Court refers to the notion of essence as an absolute limit to balancing, that is, in order to underline that a certain interference actually destroys a certain right or strips it of any content.[52] Secondly, if a question of essence is at stake, a Member State's margin of appreciation is reduced.[53] Finally, even where the term is not explicitly used, an implicit differentiation between the 'essence' and the 'periphery' of a right can be drawn from the ECtHR's jurisprudence. Originally we developed the approach to this issue using the example of media freedom. In that field, the Court constantly holds that 'there is little scope … for restrictions on political speech or on debate

[47] Czech Fundamental Rights Charter, art 4(4); German Basic Law, art 19(2); Hungarian Constitution (Basic Law), art 8(2); Polish Constitution, art 30(3); Portuguese Constitution, art 18(3); Rumanian Constitution, art 49(2); Slovakian Constitution, art 13(4); Spanish Constitution, art 53(1).

[48] *Solange I* (n 42) 280; BVerfGE 58, 1, 40 (1981) *Eurocontrol*; *Solange II* (n 42) 376; Czech Constitutional Court Case Pl ÚS 19/08 Judgment of 22 November 2008, paras 110, 196; Danish Supreme Court Case I 361/1997 Judgment of 6 April 1998, (1999) 26 *Europäische Grundrechte-Zeitschrift* 49, 50; Italian Constitutional Court Case 183/1973 Judgment of 18 December 1973, (1975) 1/2 *Europäische Grundrechte-Zeitschrift* 311, 315; Italian Constitutional Court Case 170/84 Judgment of 8 June 1984 *Granital*, in A Oppenheimer (ed), *The Relationship between European Community Law and National Law* (Cambridge, Cambridge University Press, 1994) vol 1, 643, 651; Italian Constitutional Court Case 232/1989 Judgment of 13/21 April 1989 *Fragd*, in Oppenheimer, ibid 653, 657; Polish Constitutional Court Case K 18/04 Judgment of 11 May 2005, (2006) 41 *Europarecht* 236, 239 ff; Polish Constitutional Court Case SK 45/09 Judgment of 16 November 2011, trybunal.gov.pl/eng/summaries/documents/SK_45_09_EN.pdf; Spanish Constitutional Court Case 1/2004 Judgment of 13 December 2004, (2005) 40 *Europarecht* 339, 343; for an example where a court actually declared a judgment *ultra vires* see *Landtová*, Czech Constitutional Court Case Pl ÚS 5/12 Judgment of 14 February 2012.

[49] See in detail von Bernstorff, 'Kerngehaltsschutz durch den UN-Menschenrechtsausschuss und den EGMR' (n 46) 169.

[50] See with regard to Art 3 ECHR, *Gäfgen v Germany*, Application no 22978/05 (ECtHR, 1 June 2010) para 87.

[51] In some cases the concept is devoid of self-standing content and used as a mere rhetorical device or equated with proportionality balancing. Yet, since this kind of use is not fruitful for our purpose, it is not further addressed here. See in detail von Bernstorff, 'Kerngehaltsschutz durch den UN-Menschenrechtsausschuss und den EGMR' (n 46) 171.

[52] See *Brogan v United Kingdom*, Application no 11209/84 (ECtHR, 29 November 1988) para 55; *Hutten-Czapska v Poland*, Application no 35014/97 (ECtHR, 19 June 2006) para 202. This approach can also be found in the jurisprudence of the UN Human Rights Committee, see M Nowak, *UN Covenant on Civil and Political Rights*, 2nd edn (Kehl, Engel, 2005) Art 5 para 6.

[53] See *F v Switzerland*, Application no 11329/85 (ECtHR, 18 December 1987) para 32.

on questions of public interest'.[54] This means that in such cases the Member States' margin of appreciation is severely limited unless there is a public 'incitement to violence'.[55] On this basis, the Court, without employing a balancing test, has repeatedly held that a 'blanket ban' on certain media or 'draconian' measures that dissuaded reporting on certain topics could not be justified.[56] Outside that 'political' sphere it is much easier to justify interferences in media freedom.[57] This jurisprudence of the ECtHR informs that of the CJEU.[58] A contextual assessment in the field of media freedom also confirms the appropriateness of applying such a differentiating approach to Article 2 TEU. First, freedom of political expression falls under Article 2 TEU not only because it enters in the category of 'respect for human rights' but also because it is indispensable for another European 'value'; it is a 'fundamental pillar of a democratic society'.[59] Secondly, the practice of the European Commission, which actually applies Article 2 TEU in accession procedures, points in the same direction in that it focuses on deficits threatening the democratic function of the media.[60] A similar argument can be made as to access to independent courts or the right to free elections. To sum up the first prong of our proposal, it is possible to designate an EU-specific essence of fundamental rights enshrined in Article 2 TEU.

One could further think of this as encompassing all the Union's foundational values, as enshrined in the first sentence of Article 2 TEU. The German Federal Constitutional Court indeed follows an analogous logic by giving German voters the right to 'challenge the constitutionally relevant deficits in the democratic legitimation of the European Union'.[61] However, individual legal actions to enforce abstract principles like democracy (beyond political rights) or the rule of law (beyond civil rights) are more difficult to defend, as critiques of the Constitutional Court's approach have shown.[62] In any case, on the European level

[54] *Sürek and Özdemir v Turkey*, Joined Applications nos 23927/94 and 24277/94 (ECtHR, 8 July 1999) para 46; *Wingrove v United Kingdom*, Application no 17419/90 (ECtHR, 26 November 1996) para 58.

[55] *Sürek and Özdemir v Turkey* (n 54) para 46; *Ürper v Turkey*, Application no 14526/07 (ECtHR, 20 October 2009) para 35; *Demirel v Turkey*, Application no 11976/03 (ECtHR, 9 December 2008) para 27.

[56] *Demirel v Turkey* (n 55); *Ürper v Turkey* (n 55) para 38.

[57] See *Scharsach v Austria*, Application no 39394/98 (ECtHR, 13 November 2003) para 30; in detail JA Frowein and W Peukert, *Europäische Menschenrechtskonvention*, 3rd edn (Kehl, Engel, 2009) Art 10 para 27.

[58] See Case C-71/02 *Karner* [2004] ECR I-3025, para 51; Case C-380/03 *Germany v Parliament and Council* [2006] ECR I-11573, para 155, which distinguish between a 'political' essence and an 'economic' periphery of media freedom.

[59] *Germany v Parliament and Council* (n 58) para 154; similarly already *Handyside v United Kingdom*, Application no 5493/72 (ECtHR, 7 December 1976) para 49.

[60] See European Commission, *Turkey 2010 Progress Report*, COM(2010)660, 20; European Commission, *FYROM 2010 Progress Report*, COM(2010)660, 17; both expressing 'serious concern' about intimidation and pressure on the media.

[61] See *Lisbon* (n 41) 331.

[62] For an account see HH Klein, in T Maunz and G Dürig (eds), *Grundgesetz*, 62th edn (Munich, CH Beck, 2011) Art 38 para 146.

such a step seems even more far-reaching than the one we propose, given the lack of relevant case law of the CJEU.[63] We thus at this point limit the reverse-*Solange* doctrine to only one value of Article 2 TEU, namely, 'respect for human rights'.[64] This application of the doctrine is supported by the fact that there is a long-standing tradition in Europe that courts play an important role in that context.

B. General Compliance with Article 2 TEU: A Presumption

The second prong of our proposal is based on the presumption that in the fields autonomous from EU law, the Member States respect the essence of fundamental rights enshrined in Article 2 TEU. Therefore, a Union citizen cannot rely on Article 20 TFEU to invoke a violation of Article 2 TEU unless this presumption is rebutted.

Such a presumption is crucial to the German Federal Constitutional Court's *Solange* doctrine.[65] The ECtHR and several national Constitutional Courts have adopted similar stances.[66] It has, therefore, played a pivotal role in European integration in both its rationale and its consequences. On the one hand, it has held off the threat that the CJEU would review EU legislation on fundamental rights grounds. This might arguably have pushed the CJEU to refine its related jurisprudence and even to resist great political pressure on the part of EU institutions and Member States governments in the *Kadi* case.[67] On the other hand, the Constitutional Court's presumption has made clear that no review of EU acts would take place on a day-to-day basis. This has enabled the EU to develop an autonomous standard of fundamental rights protection that, for good reasons, might differ in individual cases from the one adopted by the German Basic Law.[68] Thereby, the *Solange* doctrine is a cornerstone of European constitutional pluralism.[69]

[63] See, however, K Lenaerts, 'The Principle of Democracy in the Case Law of the European Court of Justice' (2013) 62 *International and Comparative Law Quarterly* 271.

[64] We understand the other values of 'human dignity', 'freedom' and 'equality' to form part of 'human rights'.

[65] See n 42 above.

[66] See *Bosphorus v Ireland*, Application no 45036/98 (ECtHR, 30 June 2005) para 149; for an overview over national jurisprudence see PM Huber, 'Offene Staatlichkeit: Vergleich' in A von Bogdandy, P Cruz Villalón and PM Huber (eds), *Handbuch Ius Publicum Europaeum* (Heidelberg, CF Müller, 2008) vol 2, § 26 para 34; W Sadurski, '"Solange, Chapter 3": Constitutional Courts in Central Europe—Democracy-European Union' (2008) 14 *European Law Journal* 1.

[67] See D Halberstam and E Stein, 'The UN, the EU and the King of Sweden: Economic Sanctions and Individual Rights in a Plural World Order' (2009) 46 *CML Rev* 13, 63.

[68] This is expressly underlined by the Federal Constitutional Court. See *Solange II* (n 42) 116.

[69] See for this concept according to which the relationship between national and European constitutional law is not to be understood in hierarchical terms: N MacCormick, 'Beyond the Sovereign State' (1993) 56 *MLR* 1, 6, 9; MP Maduro, 'Contrapunctual Law: Europe's Constitutional Pluralism in Action' in N Walker (ed), *Sovereignty in Transition* (Oxford, Hart Publishing, 2003) 501; N Walker, 'The Idea of Constitutional Pluralism' (2002) 65 *MLR* 317; M Kumm, 'Who is the Final Arbiter of Constitutionality in Europe?: Three Conceptions of the Relationship between the German Federal

This approach finds support in the decision in *NS and others v SSHD*.[70] In that case, the CJEU was essentially called to rule on the legal significance of the structural deficiencies of Greece in processing asylum applications in a way respectful to fundamental rights. The Court explicitly ruled that there might be occasions in which the presumption that EU Member States are by and large capable of protecting fundamental rights does not hold.[71] This has been dubbed appropriately as *horizontal Solange*.[72]

This makes the presumption of compliance an ideal component of our proposal. Respect for national identities (Article 4(2) TEU) requires that, other than within the scope of the CFREU, the EU refrain from individually superseding the delicate balance between fundamental rights and general interests enshrined in national constitutions. In light of the subsidiarity principle (Article 5(1) TEU), EU law must limit itself in this respect to protecting a basic safety net and leave the main part to national law and (constitutional) courts. Finally, such restraint is also in line with a concept of Union citizenship, which 'shall be additional to and not replace national citizenship' (Article 20(1) TFEU).[73]

How then could the presumption of compliance be rebutted? In light of what has just been said, it cannot be rebutted by simple and isolated fundamental rights infringements. Instead, there must be a violation of the essence of fundamental rights that in number or seriousness constitutes *systemic* failure and is not remedied by an adequate response within the relevant national system.[74] Such deficiencies would not only put into question the basics of the European legal space, they also would pose a direct threat to the idea of Union citizenship.[75] In this respect, inspiration can be drawn from the interpretation given to the criterion of a 'serious and persistent breach' in Article 7(2) TEU. Conceivable examples therefore include refusal to abide by a final judgment of the ECtHR in a domain that

Constitutional Court and the European Court of Justice' (1999) 36 *CML Rev* 351. From a comparative perspective with the constitutional order of the United States see D Halberstam, 'Constitutional Hierarchy: The Centrality of Conflict in the European Union and the United States' in JL Dunoff and JP Trachtman (eds), *Ruling the World? Constitutionalism, International Law, and Global Governance* (Cambridge, Cambridge University Press, 2009) 326.

[70] Joined Cases C-411/10 and C-493/10 *NS v Secretary of State for Home Department* and *ME v Refugee Applications Commissioner, Minister for Justice, Equality and Law Reform* (2011, nyr). See for a commentary on the judgment M den Heijer, 'Joined Cases C-411 & 493/10, *N.S. v. Secretary of State for the Home Department and M.E. and Others* v. *Refugee Applications Commissioner, Minister for Justice, Equality and Law Reform*, Judgment of the Court (Grand Chamber) of 21 December 2011' (2012) 49 *CML Rev* 1735. For an analysis of the importance of that decision for EU constitutional law, see I Canor, 'Am I My Brother's Keeper? Horizontal Solange: "An Ever Closer Distrust among the Peoples of Europe"' (2013) 50 *CML Rev* 383. See also S Lieven, 'Case Report on C-411/10, N.S. and C-493/10, M.E. and Others, 21 December 2011' (2012) 14 *European Journal of Migration and Law* 223.

[71] *NS v Secretary of State for Home Department* and *ME v Refugee Applications Commissioner, Minister for Justice, Equality and Law Reform* (n 70) paras 84–86.

[72] Canor, 'Am I My Brother's Keeper?' (n 70).

[73] Similarly *Ruiz Zambrano* (n 10) (AG Sharpston) para 148.

[74] See also *NS v Secretary of State for Home Department* and *ME v Refugee Applications Commissioner, Minister for Justice, Equality and Law Reform* (n 70) para 86.

[75] See in the same vein *Centro Europa 7* (n 43) (AG Maduro) para 22.

touches upon the essence of fundamental rights;[76] defiance, bypassing or intimidating of domestic courts in such cases;[77] or intentional, reckless or evidently illicit conduct of the highest state authorities, such as the enactment of measures that clearly fall short of the requirements of Article 2 TEU.[78]

Put into practice, our proposal could then work as follows: if a national of a Member State felt that her rights have been violated she would turn to the national judge. In that court, she could rely on the domestic (and possibly ECHR) standard of fundamental rights protection. Outside the scope of the CFREU she could not invoke EU fundamental rights, nor could she rely on Union citizenship to claim a violation of Article 2 TEU unless the presumption of compliance was rebutted. However, in case of systemic violation of the essence of fundamental rights, the 'substance' of Union citizenship, within the meaning of *Ruiz Zambrano*, would be activated as a basis for her redress. First of all, it would be up to the national court to establish the facts and to apply the respective provisions of Union law. Yet, according to Article 267 TFEU the national court would be enabled and, in a case of last instance, obliged to refer to the CJEU for a preliminary ruling on the interpretation of Articles 2 TEU and 20 TFEU. This mechanism not only has the well-known advantage of combining the interpretative rulings of the CJEU with the authority and enforceability of domestic court decisions.[79] Arguably, it can also provide national judges with some backing from the side of Union law and the voice of the CJEU speaking on behalf of a Union founded on respect for human rights.[80] Hence, it could be said that our proposal ultimately aims at strengthening domestic courts in critical situations.

IV. ADVANCING THE REVERSE-*SOLANGE* DOCTRINE

The reverse-*Solange* doctrine has spurred a lively debate among scholars. The following section advances the approach by drawing on insights from the scholarly debate (elucidated in section A), and by applying it to constitutional law (as discussed in section B).

[76] See European Commission, COM(2003)606, 9; Ruffert (n 44) Art 7 TEU para 6.

[77] In both cases the violation of the rule of law principle in Art 2 TEU would aggravate the fundamental rights infringement. See for this interdependence also European Commission, COM(2003)606, 9.

[78] See with regard to this and to further categories H Schmitt von Sydow, in H von der Groeben and J Schwarze (eds), *Kommentar zum EUV und EGV*, 6th edn (Baden-Baden, Nomos, 2003) Art 7 TEU para 20.

[79] See JHH Weiler, 'The Least Dangerous Branch' in JHH Weiler, *The Constitution of Europe* (Cambridge, Cambridge University Press, 1999) 188, 192 ff; KJ Alter, *Establishing the Supremacy of European Law* (Oxford, Oxford University Press, 2001).

[80] Here the example of the Hungarian Constitutional Court, which has recently been stripped of some competences and packed with judges appointed by the government's majority, comes into mind. See European Commission for Democracy through law (Venice Commission), *Opinion on the New Constitution of Hungary* (Opinion No 618/2011, 20 June 2011, CDL-AD(2011)016) para 91.

A. Insights from the Debate so Far

In the first presentation of our proposal, we discussed and rebutted three possible rejoinders, the *ultra vires* objection, the approach's failure to include third-country nationals and its detrimental effects on the ECtHR.[81] The reverse-*Solange* and the Copenhagen Commission proposals were also presented and discussed on the Verfassungsblog.[82] From that discussion, some important points can be taken.

It is noteworthy that all of the commenting scholars seem to share a sense of dissatisfaction with the current state of affairs, including the problem of double standards and the lack of sufficient legal instruments. The common ground is the need for change in order to have better and broader fundamental rights protection under EU law. This in itself is a remarkable outcome.[83] The comments, however, differ on how such change should best be implemented. Our response points towards deeper (and probably more 'legal') integration.[84] The alternative favours a more 'politicised' route,[85] which, however, as Mattias Kumm rightly stresses, eventually means secret bargaining among national executives.[86] The proponents of a more politicised approach argue that we rely on the CJEU whereas the problem needs to be solved in the political realm.

We are not, however, proposing to provide a substitute for the political process, but rather to complement it. Demands to strengthen the procedure of Article 7 TEU[87] are thus not in contradiction to our approach. But even with improved political processes there remains a role for domestic courts and the CJEU.[88] It is the very business of courts to protect individual rights. Arguably, this is one task they fulfil more satisfactorily than the political branches of government.[89] Even

[81] A von Bogdandy, C Antpöhler, J Dickschen, S Hentrei, M Kottmann, and M Smrkolj, 'Protecting the Essence of Fundamental Rights against EU Member States' (2012) 49 *CML Rev* 489, 514–18.

[82] Verfassungsblog, 'A Rescue Package for EU Fundamental Rights' (n 5) and 'Hungary: Taking Action' (n 5).

[83] E Kanterian made a similar observation regarding a conference on the topic 'Legality and Legitimacy: From Weimar 1932 to Bucharest 2012', E Kanterian, 'The Crisis of Democracy in Hungary and Romania: Learning from Weimar?' in Verfassungsblog, 'Hungary: Taking Action' (n 5).

[84] An idea shared in the discussion on the Verfassungsblog in the online symposium, 'A Rescue Package for EU Fundamental Rights' (n 5) in the respective comments of D Halberstam, D Kochenov, M Kumm and A Wiener, and C Franzius 'The Sense and Nonsense of a Copenhagen Commission' in the online symposium, 'Hungary: Taking Action' (n 5).

[85] P Lindseth, AK Mangold, W Sadurski, P Sonnevend, D Thym and R Uitz advocated the politicised approach in Verfassungsblog, 'A Rescue Package for EU Fundamental Rights' (n 5).

[86] M Kumm in Verfassungsblog, 'A Rescue Package for EU Fundamental Rights' (n 5).

[87] Emphasised by W Sadurski and M Kumm in Verfassungsblog, 'A Rescue Package for EU Fundamental Rights' (n 5). Not all of these proposals, however, seem convincing. It remains unclear why a European Citizen's Initiative to initiate Art 7 TEU should be less populist or opportunistic than the institution's approach, see M Dani, 'Opening the Enforcement of EU Fundamental Values to European Citizens' in Verfassungsblog, 'Hungary: Taking Action' (n 5).

[88] Franzius, 'The Sense and Nonsense of a Copenhagen Commission' (n 84).

[89] JH Ely, *Democracy and Distrust: A Theory of Judicial Review* (Cambridge, MA, Harvard University Press, 1980) 105; Halberstam, 'Constitutional Hierarchy' (n 69) 338; *cf* U Haltern, *Verfassungsgerichtsbarkeit, Demokratie und Mißtrauen. Das Bundesverfassungsgericht in einer Verfassungstheorie zwischen Populismus und Progressivismus* (Berlin, Duncker & Humblot, 1998) 204.

if sanctions under Article 7 TEU could be imposed more easily, there would still be incentives not to use the procedure. To be sure, the reverse-*Solange* doctrine does not offer a full-fledged response to all human rights issues (in particular as concerns nationals from third countries) and all EU legitimacy concerns.[90] The reverse-*Solange* doctrine does, however, empower citizens and in that way sets the conditions for the enhancement of domestic political processes.[91] A constitutional crisis can never be solved by the CJEU on its own,[92] but the Court might contribute to its resolution. That is, the judgment might trigger domestic political discourses anew while effectively addressing the grievances of the affected individual.

The proposal by Jan-Werner Müller of a Copenhagen Commission as a more 'politicised' option has gained prominence.[93] It is telling that an approach deemed to be more politicised rests on a quasi-judicial independent body.[94] Furthermore, it remains highly questionable whether the new institution would indeed increase enforceability. The CJEU's generally accepted authority rests on the direct effect of Union law and the strong domestic enforceability of its judgments. This, precisely, is one of the benefits of our approach. While doubts concerning the affected state's willingness to comply with a judgment[95] are not entirely unfounded, none of the proposals seems more capable of dealing with these concerns than ours.

A second widespread objection concerns the practical implementation of our proposal.[96] The *essence* of fundamental rights, it is argued, is too vague a concept to be applied judicially. The decline of the notion in German constitutional law is used as an illustration. We are not convinced by this line of argument. First, the example is ill-suited. The rare use of the 'essence clause' of the German Basic Law is not the consequence of practical impossibility but rather due to the Constitutional Court's proclivity for balancing.[97] Furthermore, the concept of human dignity has largely replaced this idea of an essence of fundamental rights, thereby depriving it of much of its presumed scope.[98] Secondly, more general

See the critique of C Möllers, 'Legalität, Legitimität und Legitimation des Bundesverfassungsgerichts' in C Schoenberger *et al*, *Das entgrenzte Gericht. Eine kritische Bilanz nach sechzig Jahren Bundesverfassungsgericht* (Berlin, Suhrkamp, 2011) 281, 406 ff.

[90] This is rightly pointed out by Dani, 'Opening the Enforcement of EU Fundamental Values to European Citizens' (n 87).

[91] Franzius, 'The Sense and Nonsense of a Copenhagen Commission' (n 84).

[92] Mangold in Verfassungsblog, 'A Rescue Package for EU Fundamental Rights' (n 5).

[93] JW Müller, 'Protecting Democracy and the Rule of Law Inside the EU, or: Why Europe Needs a Copenhagen Commission' in Verfassungsblog, 'Hungary: Taking Action' (n 5).

[94] Franzius, 'The Sense and Nonsense of a Copenhagen Commission' (n 84).

[95] J Komarek, 'The EU is More than a Constraint on Populist Democracy' in Verfassungsblog, 'Hungary: Taking Action' (n 5); Müller, 'Protecting Democracy and the Rule of Law Inside the EU' (n 93).

[96] See eg Sadurski, Sonnevend and Thym in Verfassungsblog, 'A Rescue Package for EU Fundamental Rights' (n 5).

[97] H Dreier, in H Dreier (ed), *Grundgesetz Kommentar*, 2nd edn (Tübingen, Mohr Siebeck, 2004) Art 19(2) paras 14, 16; B Schlink, *Abwägung im Verfassungsrecht* (Berlin, Duncker & Humblot, 1976) 80; R Alexy, *Theorie der Grundrechte*, 2nd edn (Frankfurt am Main, Suhrkamp, 1985) 269.

[98] PM Huber, in H von Mangoldt, F Klein and C Starck (eds), *Kommentar zum Grundgesetz* (Munich, Franz Vahlen, 2010) Art 19(2) para 123.

observations call for a stronger role for the essence guarantee. Experiences with the UN Human Rights Committee, where the essence of fundamental rights plays a prominent role, suggest that it can indeed serve as a useful concept to deal with systemic violations. Jochen von Bernstorff has put forward a powerful argument for a revival of that concept in other jurisdictions, showing that it offers both more legal security and a better means to counter political pressure than ad hoc balancing.[99] Thirdly, Dimitry Kochenov is right in arguing that establishing a culture of justification is more important than focusing solely on a few big cases.[100] This is exactly what we hope for. Even if our proposal is very rarely applied, its continuing presence will encourage national judges in their everyday control of public action.

B. Constitutional Revisions Violating Article 2 TEU

In light of this discussion, we take our proposal one step further and explicitly argue for its application to constitutional law.[101] As Article 2 TEU applies to any exercise of public authority, there is no reason why drafting or changing a constitution should be outside the scope of application of the reverse-*Solange* doctrine. We wish to stress that in this chapter we only develop the doctrine for application, but do not actually apply it. Any utilisation needs a very careful analysis of the specific provision in its political and legal context, a complex task we do not engage in here. Of course, constitutional law is a specific case of application of the reverse-*Solange* doctrine because of its close link to the idea of national self-determination. However, to see constitutional acts as a '*domaine réservé*' where foreign, supranational and international institutions have no role to play is an outdated vision that is supported neither by contemporary law nor practice. Rather, as many contributions in this book show, constitutional law and its elaboration and enactment are deeply embedded in broader political and legal frameworks, in particular in Europe. A critique of this development easily comes with Schmittian overtones.[102]

Moreover, excluding constitutions from the scope of application of EU law would mean potentially allowing national authorities to reject primacy. A violation

[99] von Bernstorff, 'Kerngehaltsschutz durch den UN-Menschenrechtsausschuss und den EGMR' (n 46) 165.

[100] Comment by D Kochenov in Verfassungsblog, 'A Rescue Package for EU Fundamental Rights' (n 5).

[101] This extends to laws with similar forms of entrenchment such as Hungarian cardinal laws or the constitutional statute that accompanies the new Hungarian Constitution, see A Jakab and P Sonnevend, 'Kontinuität mit Mängeln: Das neue ungarische Grundgesetz' (2012) 72 *Zeitschrift für ausländisches öffentliches Recht und Völkerrecht* 79; see further contributions in this book as well as the debate on the Verfassungsblog, 'Hungary: Taking Action' (n 5).

[102] See J Rubenfeld, 'The Two World Orders' and, for a critique, A von Bogdandy, 'Comment on "The Two World Orders" from Jed Rubenfeld', both in G Nolte (ed), *European and US Constitutionalism* (Cambridge, Cambridge University Press, 2005) 280–96, 297–300.

of the essence of fundamental rights by a constitution is even worse than violations by ordinary legislation as it complicates the return to a lawful state. The CJEU has held repeatedly that the primacy of EU law imposes a duty upon national courts to refrain from applying national law, even constitutional law, if it conflicts with the former.[103] National Constitutional Courts recognise that EU law enjoys primacy over domestic constitutional law, albeit with some limits.[104] The concern to protect the domestic constitutional process is addressed by the safeguards: only the essence itself is protected and the reverse-*Solange* threshold must be met. National courts that have so far refrained from allowing challenges to constitutional changes or acts of similar importance might then be encouraged to do so, with the support of the CJEU in cases where fundamental rights are violated in their essence. If some commentators doubt that such courageous judges exist in Europe, the Hungarian Constitutional Court has, for example, lately proven its strength in resisting strong political pressure.[105]

V. CONCLUSION: BETWEEN SCYLLA AND CHARYBDIS

Any approach to fundamental rights protection in the European Union has to find a way between the Scylla of a dysfunctional Union and the Charybdis of fundamental rights based centralisation.[106] The ship of integration is navigating towards Charybdis. In *Åkerberg Fransson*, the CJEU gave an extremely broad reading to the concept of 'implementation' of Article 51(1) CFREU by equating the concept with the 'scope of Union law'.[107] The matter of Union citizenship is, apart from the *Ruiz Zambrano* fact pattern, within the scope of EU law if it has a cross-border dimension.[108] The CJEU's interpretation in *Åkerberg Fransson* seems too broad because it is hardly reconcilable with the respect for national identities required by Article 4(2) TEU and the purpose of Article 51(1) CFREU.[109] It is also

[103] Case 106/77 *Simmenthal* [1978] ECR 629, para 24; Case C-314/08 *Filipiak* [2009] ECR I-11049, para 81.

[104] See n 48 above.

[105] Decision 45/2012 (XII.29) AB határozat (Constitutional Court of Hungary, 28 December 2012), see mkab.hu/letoltesek/en_0045_2012.pdf and Decision 1/2013 (I.7) AB határozat (Constitutional Court of Hungary, 7 January 2013), see europeanrights.eu/public/sentenze/Ungheria_copy_1.pdf; for a review of practice see S Ragone, *I controlli giurisdizionali sulle revisioni costituzionali. Profili teorici e comparativi* (Bologna, Bologna University Press, 2011) 125–50.

[106] For the centralising potential of fundamental rights, see JA Frowein, S Schulhofer and M Shapiro, 'The Protection of Fundamental Human Rights as a Vehicle of Integration' in M Cappelleti, M Seccombe and JHH Weiler (eds), *Integration Through Law* (Berlin, de Gruyter, 1986) vol 1, 231; PM Huber, 'Auslegung und Anwendung der Charta der Grundrechte' (2011) 64 *Neue Juristische Wochenschrift* 2385, 2386.

[107] *Åkerberg Fransson* (n 34) para 16.

[108] See eg Case C-274/96 *Bickel and Franz* [1998] ECR I-7637; Case C-85/96 *Martínez Sala* [1998] ECR I-2591; Case C-209/03 *Bidar* [2005] ECR I-2119.

[109] *Cf* German Federal Constitutional Court, *Antiterrordatei* Judgment of 24 April 2013, para 88, see www.bundesverfassungsgericht.de/entscheidungen/rs20130424_1bvr121507.html.

adverse to harmonious court relations in light of constitutional pluralism.[110] At the same time, the *Åkerberg Fransson* approach fails where European interference is truly needed. Cases that neither have a cross-border element nor come within the scope of Union law[111] have to meet the post-*Ruiz Zambrano* threshold of requiring the concerned party to be factually obliged to leave the Union's territory. The CJEU's jurisprudence merely benefits a mobile minority and those who happen to be within its scope. However, it fails to address the existential fundamental rights problems of many citizens. The reverse-*Solange* doctrine offers a doctrinally more convincing way out. It is independent of the contingent criterion of cross-border mobility[112] and focuses on those violations where protection is really needed. The day-to-day fundamental rights business is then left to the national courts, while the CJEU can intervene in case of systemic violations. Our proposal, thus, leads to a pluralist conception of Constitutional Courts, including the CJEU, in the European legal space.

[110] For a pluralist conception see also M Avbelj, 'The Hungarian Dilemma from a Pluralist Perspective' in Verfassungsblog, 'Hungary: Taking Action' (n 5).

[111] In the original article we have, for example, shown that the press fails to be covered by the scope of Union law in contrast to television. It fails to be convincing to apply fundamental rights merely to the latter; see von Bogdandy *et al*, 'Protecting the Essence of Fundamental Rights against EU Member States' (n 81) 497–500. A similar argument could be made for taxes other than VAT.

[112] Advocate General Sharpston has shown convincingly in her opinion on *Ruiz Zambrano* (n 10) paras 69, 75 ff how the existence of a cross-border element is a question of mere chance rather than of a coherent interpretation of Union law. A similar argument can be made for the 'scope of Union law'.

The Role of the European Convention on Human Rights

9

The European Convention on Human Rights: Inherent Constitutional Tendencies and the Role of the European Court of Human Rights

CHRISTOPH GRABENWARTER

I. INTRODUCTION

THE EUROPEAN COURT of Human Rights (ECtHR) is a remarkable institution. Over the past 50 years, it has shown that the protection of human rights is no longer an exclusive matter for national constitutions and national courts. Human rights, as guaranteed under the European Convention on Human Rights (ECHR), have become an issue in European law and public international law.

This process has advanced considerably and has not yet come to an end. The practice under the ECHR of more than 60 years and the thousands of decisions of both the former European Commission on Human Rights and the ECtHR, clearly show that it is a success story without comparison in the history of public law. Established and ratified by the states of Western Europe against the background of the ruins of the Second World War and the horrors of Nazism, the ECHR, as a charter of human rights, became a necessary element of a democratic society. Twenty years ago, after having influenced the legal orders of two dozen of more or less 'old' democracies, and after their people had torn down the Iron Curtain, this remarkable instrument of European law started conquering the countries of the old communist regimes in Central and Eastern Europe. Within less than a decade, the ECHR became an undisputed legal instrument in these states too and started influencing constitutional law as well as legislation and the judiciary. At about the same time, in 1998, the new—permanent—Court began to work with higher capacity, leaving behind the former system of a Commission and a non-permanent Court.

As a direct consequence of its success, particularly in Eastern Europe but also in the 'old' Member States, the ECtHR was flooded with applications. By the beginning of 2012, for instance, the ECtHR was faced with some 150,000 pending applications.[1] Individual applications have been increasing constantly in number ever since the right to individual application was introduced and led to the ECtHR's case overload. While the 'old' Court delivered fewer than 1,000 judgments in 38 years from 1959 to 1998, the number of judgments delivered by the 'new' Court since 1998 exceeds 14,000.[2]

At the same time, the ECtHR's case law and its institutional background have changed enormously. What is its approach to interpreting fundamental rights today? What is its relationship with domestic courts and above all constitutional courts?

II. ECHR: A CONSTITUTIONAL INSTRUMENT ON HUMAN RIGHTS

A. ECHR as an Instrument of 'European Public Order'

The ECHR is the oldest international treaty in the field of regional human rights protection. Its development is closely linked to the end of the Second World War and was the response to the systematic human rights violations, in particular in the Third Reich. In the aftermath of the war, great effort was put into the development of international human rights documents with legally-binding effect. Following the Universal Declaration of Human Rights of the United Nations General Assembly of 10 December 1948, and in the face of the atrocities of Nazism, it was in Europe where the first international instrument of human rights protection was established. This was, on the one hand, a consequence of the realisation that a purely national mechanism to protect fundamental freedoms and human rights had proved woefully inadequate. On the other hand, it was an expression of the will of the democratic states of Europe for self-determination against the totalitarian communism of the Soviet regime.[3]

The ECHR as a multilateral treaty enjoys an exceptional position among international treaties in several respects. As regards their content, human rights treaties contrast with other sources of international law in that their object is not the relationship between states but generally the relationship between individuals, who rely on human rights, and states that are obliged under international law to conform to the guarantees. Since the entry into force of Protocol No 11, the ECHR itself provides for a system of legal protection authorising the ECtHR to review judicially whether member states have complied with the guarantees, and obliges

[1] ECtHR, *Annual Report 2011 of the European Court of Human Rights, Council of Europe*, available at www.echr.coe.int/NR/rdonlyres/77FF4249-96E5-4D1F-BE71-42867A469225/0/2011_Rapport_Annuel_EN.pdf 152ff.

[2] ibid 14.

[3] R Grote in R Grote and T Marauhn (eds), *EMRK/GG Konkordanzkommentar zum europäischen und deutschen Grundrechtsschutz* (Tübingen, Mohr Siebeck, 2006) ch 1, para 10; E Bates, *The Evolution of the European Convention on Human Rights: From Its Inception to the Creation of a Permanent Court of Human Rights* (Oxford, Oxford University Press, 2010).

the member states to grant a right to individual application to the permanent ECtHR.[4]

In the course of time, the ECHR liberated itself from a purely international context. Through manifold influences on the legal orders and the process of implementation into the constitutions of European states, a close link between the ECHR, national constitutions and European Union (EU) law has been established. Nowadays, in Europe, fundamental guarantees form an essential, indispensable part of the constitutional structure and are spread across different legal systems. The ECHR, apart from the member states' constitutions, constitutes one of these legal systems. The member states, aligned with each other through the ECHR, have outsourced part of their substantive constitutional law to the 'complementary constitution' or 'ancillary constitution', the ECHR. It therefore seems appropriate to describe the ECHR, by reference to the ECtHR, as a 'constitutional instrument of European public order' and, by reference to literature, as part of the *ordre public européen*, as a 'European constitution of human rights', a 'substantive common European constitution', a 'constitution of human rights' or as a 'process of constitutionalisation'.[5] Especially since the entry into force of Protocol No 11 to the ECHR and in the light of 50 years of decision-making of the ECtHR, the ECHR may be described as a European constitutional instrument of human rights and thus as a partial constitution in the field of human rights; the ECtHR may be referred to as a 'European constitutional court' for human rights.[6]

B. Protocols to the ECHR: From '*à la Carte*' to 'All Inclusive'

One of the characteristics which distinguish the ECHR from national constitutions is that only certain core human rights are legally-binding upon all member states. New human rights guarantees contained in Additional Protocols to the ECHR are binding only upon those states who have ratified the respective Protocols. The number of ratifications in respect of the Protocols varies with the Protocol concerned. Protocol No 1, which comprises three very different human rights (protection of property, the right to education, the right to free elections), and Protocol No 6 concerning the abolition of the death penalty were ratified by almost all member states,[7] including all EU Member States. Protocols No 4 and No 7 have not

[4] C Tomuschat, *Human Rights Between Idealism and Realism* (Oxford, Oxford University Press, 2003) 198.

[5] C Grabenwarter and K Pabel, *Europäische Menschenrechtskonvention* (Basel, Beck, 2012) Art 2, para 3 with further references.

[6] ibid.

[7] Protocol No 1 to the Convention for the Protection of Human Rights and Fundamental Freedoms CETS No 009, available at www.conventions.coe.int/Treaty/Commun/ChercheSig.asp?NT=009&CM=&DF=&CL=ENG; Protocol No 6 to the Convention for the Protection of Human Rights and Fundamental Freedoms concerning the Abolition of the Death Penalty CETS No 114, available at www.conventions.coe.int/Treaty/Commun/ChercheSig.asp?NT=114&CM=&DF=&CL=ENG.

been ratified by a large number of member states.[8] There is even greater reluctance to ratify Protocol No 12 concerning equality of treatment of all persons, which is still open to signature. So far, Protocol No 12 has been ratified by 18 states and entered into force on 1 April 2005.[9] Among the signatory states are only seven EU Member States (Finland, the Netherlands, Croatia, Cyprus, Luxembourg, Romania, Spain and Slovenia) have ratified it. Protocol No 13, which contains a general prohibition on the death penalty, entered into force on 1 July 2003. So far, 42 of the 45 states who have acceded have ratified the Protocol.[10]

When considering the dates of accession, it becomes obvious that almost all Central and Eastern European states that acceded to the ECHR in the 1990s have ratified all Additional Protocols which had then already existed.

C. Case Law Strengthening the Rule of Law and Democracy

For more than 30 years the ECtHR has delivered numerous judgments that have considerably strengthened the rule of law and democracy. Beginning with a right of access to court, the case law focused on the rights of the accused. In the course of time, the ECtHR gave a legal basis to core guarantees under the rule of law, such as the right to remain silent,[11] clarity of the law,[12] legal effect or the principle of *non bis in idem*.[13] Today, it can be said without exaggeration that the judicial guarantees of the ECHR contain a European principle of the rule of law.[14] What is more, the ECtHR has constantly expanded the scope of political rights, in particular the freedom of expression. Beginning with cases concerning the freedom of press and defamation,[15] there is a differentiated case law on the

[8] Protocol No 4 to the Convention for the Protection of Human Rights and Fundamental Freedoms, securing certain rights and freedoms other than those already included in the Convention and in the first Protocol thereto CETS No 046, available at www.conventions.coe.int/Treaty/Commun/ChercheSig.asp?NT=046&CM=&DF=&CL=ENG; Protocol No 7 to the Convention for the Protection of Human Rights and Fundamental Freedoms CETS No 117, available at www.conventions.coe.int/Treaty/Commun/ChercheSig.asp?NT=117&CM=&DF=&CL=ENG.

[9] Protocol No 12 to the Convention for the Protection of Human Rights and Fundamental Freedoms CETS No 177, available at www.conventions.coe.int/Treaty/Commun/ChercheSig.asp?NT=177&CM=&DF=&CL=ENG.

[10] Protocol No 13 to the Convention for the Protection of Human Rights and Fundamental Freedoms, concerning the abolition of the death penalty in all circumstances CETS No 187, available at www.conventions.coe.int/Treaty/Commun/ChercheSig.asp?NT=187&CM=&DF=&CL=ENG.

[11] *John Murray v United Kingdom*, Application no 18731/91 (ECtHR, 2 February 1996) 22 EHRR 29, para 45; *Saunders v United Kingdom*, Application no 19187/91 (ECtHR, 17 December 1996) 23 EHRR 313, para 68; *Heaney and McGuiness v Ireland*, Application no 34720/97 (ECtHR, 21 December 2000) 33 EHRR 264, para 40.

[12] See, eg *Kokkinakis v Greece*, Application no 14307/88 (ECtHR, 25 May 1993) 17 EHRR 397, para 52.

[13] See, eg *Franz Fischer v Austria*, Application no 37950/97 (ECtHR, 29 May 2001) para 25.

[14] See, eg *Lavents v Latvia*, Application no 58442/00 (ECtHR, 28 November 2002) para 114.

[15] *Steel and Morris v United Kingdom*, Application no 68416/01 (ECtHR, 15 February 2005) 41 EHRR 22.

rights of journalists;[16] the electronic media, including the Internet;[17] access to information;[18] and the freedoms of civil servants[19] and judges.[20] This 'essential foundation of a democratic society' has become a backbone of all member states in Europe, notwithstanding their respective judicial traditions. Various member states were affected by the new case law on the role of investigative journalism and on the conflicts with the interests in the protection and confidentiality of journalistic sources and, above all, the protection of private life. A rough analysis shows that the ECtHR has strengthened the rights of the journalist as regards reports on topics in the public sphere or on public figures in public debates. On the other hand, it has become more sensitive as regards the protection of private life, in particular the protection of personal data.[21]

A second development has occurred through the case law on voting rights under Article 3 of Protocol No 1. Within this ambit, the required 'European standards' are clearly influenced by soft law. This may best be illustrated by giving three examples.

In the Turkish electoral case of *Yumak and Sadak*, the ECtHR quoted a 2007 Resolution of the Council of Europe according to which 'in well established democracies, there should be no thresholds higher than 3 per cent during the parliamentary election'. An even more political statement is drawn from two further Resolutions and a report on elections in Turkey in which the organs of the Council of Europe urge the country to lower the 10 per cent threshold.[22]

In the *Tanase* case concerning the ban on candidates of dual nationality standing for parliamentary elections in Moldova, the ECtHR quoted a report of the Council of Europe's Commission against Racism and Intolerance of 2007 and two Resolutions of the Parliamentary Assembly of the Council of Europe, criticising not only the raising of the threshold from 4 per cent to 6 per cent but also the

[16] As to the right to confidentiality of journalistic sources, see, eg *Goodwin v United Kingdom*, Application no 17488/90 (ECtHR, 27 March 1996) 22 EHRR 123, para 39; *Sanoma Uitgevers BV v Netherlands*, Application no 38224/03 (ECtHR, 14 September 2010) para 54; the right to divulge information on issues of general interest provided that they are acting in good faith and on an accurate factual basis and provide 'reliable and precise' information in accordance with the ethics of journalism: *Fressoz and Roire v France*, Application no 29183/95 (ECtHR, 21 January 1999) 31 EHRR 28, para 54.

[17] As to electronic media see, eg *Jersild v Denmark*, Application no 15890/89 (ECtHR, 23 September 1994) 19 EHRR 1, para 31; *Radio France and others v France*, Application no 53984/00 (ECtHR, 30 March 2004) 40 EHRR 29, para 39; as to Internet media see, eg *Editorial Board of Pravoye Delo and Shtekel v Ukraine*, Application no 33014/05 (ECtHR, 5 May 2011) para 63 ff.

[18] *Observer and Guardian v United Kingdom*, Application no 13585/88 (ECtHR, 26 November 1991) 14 EHRR 153, para 59; *Thorgeir Thorgeirson v Iceland*, Application no 13778/88 (ECtHR 25 June 1992) 14 EHRR 843, para 63; *Guerra and others v Italy*, Application no 14967/89 (ECtHR, 19 February 1998) 26 EHRR 357, para 53.

[19] See, eg *Vogt v Germany*, Application no 17851/91 (ECtHR, 26 September 1995) 21 EHRR 205.

[20] See, eg *Kudeshkina v Russia*, Application no 29492/05 (ECtHR, 26 February 2009).

[21] See, eg *Leander v Sweden*, Application no 9248/81 (ECtHR, 26 March 1987) 9 EHRR 433, para 48; *Amann v Switzerland*, Application no 27798/95 (ECtHR, 16 February 2000) 30 EHRR 843, paras 69, 80; *Rotaru v Romania*, Application no 28341/95 (ECtHR, 4 May 2000) para 46; *Wasmuth v Germany*, Application no 12884/03 (ECtHR, 17 February 2011) para 74.

[22] *Yumak and Sadak v Turkey*, Application no 10226/03 (ECtHR, 8 July 2008) paras 52, 58.

ban on dual nationality candidates. In addition, the ECtHR quoted an opinion of the Venice Commission and its Code of Good Conduct in Electoral Matters concerning particular amendments to the Moldovan Electoral Code. In this judgment, as in other recent judgments, there is a separate section entitled 'Relevant Instruments of the Council of Europe'.[23]

In *Sejdić and Finci*, the ECtHR had to deal with the ineligibility of candidates of Roma and Jewish origin and not belonging to one of the constituent peoples. In this case, the ECtHR again quoted opinions of the Venice Commission and even admitted the Commission as a third party in the proceedings. Not surprisingly, the ECtHR followed the Opinion of the Venice Commission.[24]

In conclusion: the ECtHR is establishing principles of the rule of law and democracy. In doing so, it uses the experience not only of the member states or the European Union but also, and above all, of other Council of Europe organs.

III. ECtHR: AN EMERGING EUROPEAN CONSTITUTIONAL COURT

A. From the 'Old' Court to the Permanent Court

For more than 40 years, until the entry into force of Protocol No 11, the system of legal protection of the ECHR consisted of three organs, namely, the European Commission on Human Rights (EComHR), the 'old' European Court of Human Rights ('old Court') and the Committee of Ministers of the Council of Europe ('Committee of Ministers').[25] In a first stage of procedure, the EComHR had to examine the admissibility of an application. In case it determined an application to be admissible, it drew up a 'report' (*rapport*) on the question of whether a violation of the ECHR had occurred. Thereafter, the case could be brought before the old Court. If the case was not referred to the Court within a period of three months, the Committee of Ministers decided on whether there had been a violation of the ECHR. In such way, and contrary to the system, it was up to a political organ to make the legal assessment in a dispute on individual rights carried out before the Court.

Protocols Nos 11 and 14 have brought important changes to the organisational framework of the ECtHR. Today, the ECtHR functions on a permanent basis (Article 19). Its judges are independent; they are elected by the Parliamentary Assembly on the basis of a list of three candidates nominated by each member state for a period of nine years without the possibility of re-election. There are no rules securing the candidate's professional suitability comparable to Articles 253

[23] *Tanase v Moldova*, Application no 7/08 (ECtHR, 27 April 2010) paras 45, 48, 51 ff.

[24] *Sejdić and Finci v Bosnia and Herzegovina*, Application no 27996/06 *et al* (ECtHR, 22 December 2009) paras 22, 48 ff.

[25] V Schlette, 'Das neue Rechtsschutzsystem der Europäischen Menschenrechtskonvention: Zur Reform des Kontrollmechanismus durch dass 11. Protokoll' (1996) 56 *ZaöRV* 905, 906 ff.

and 255 TFEU. However, in 2010, a panel comprising seven experts was established, which gives its opinion on the candidates' suitability to the Parliamentary Assembly.

The cases brought to the ECtHR are considered in a single-judge formation, in Committees of three judges, in Chambers of seven judges or in the Grand Chamber of 17 judges (Article 26). The competence of single judges is enshrined in Article 27, the competence of the Committees and of the Chambers in Articles 27–31 ECHR. Other important organs that fulfil organisational tasks are the President and the plenary court (Article 25).[26]

Recently, there have been discussions about the enactment of a statute of the ECtHR which would simplify the revision procedure, just like the Group of Wise Persons recommended to the Committee of Ministers in 2006.[27] Based on the existing legal protection regime, a draft statute consisting of 65 Articles was published on behalf of the Swiss Federal Department of Foreign Affairs for the Interlaken Conference in 2010.[28]

B. Right to Individual Application

The right to individual application is one of the cornerstones of the ECHR system as it is a procedural instrument guaranteeing the effective enforcement of the most essential human rights as part of European values. In other words, ECHR rights are given true practical relevance by virtue of individual application. Since the entry into force of Protocol No 11, the granting of the right to individual application is no longer optional for the states but compulsory (Article 34). The possibility of individuals being able to defend their rights against the state before a judge of an international court and to obtain a legally-binding judgment is a peculiarity of the ECHR system compared to other international treaties on human rights protection.[29]

C. Legal Effects of Judgments

According to Article 46(1) ECHR, the member states 'undertake to abide by the final judgment of the ECtHR in any case to which they are parties'. Final judgments of the ECtHR may not be appealed against and have formal legal force; a

[26] For further details see Grabenwarter and Pabel, *Europäische Menschenrechtskonvention* (n 5), Art 8, paras 1ff.

[27] Council of Europe, *Report of the Group of Wise Persons to the Committee of Ministers of 15 November 2006* CM(2006)203.

[28] H Keller, D Kühne, A Fischer, 'Statut-Entwurf für den Europäischen Gerichtshof für Menschenrechte/Ein Beitrag zur Reform des Konventionssystems' [2011] *EuGRZ* 341.

[29] For further details see Grabenwarter and Pabel, *Europäische Menschenrechtskonvention* (n 5) Art 9, para 1 ff.

judgment of formal legal force has, at the same time, substantive legal force. Thus, the parties to a case are bound by the elements of a judgment. The personal scope of a judgment is limited to the parties to a case (an effect *inter partes*). It is only the member state being a party to a case who is, under Article 46, obliged to abide by the judgment. However, the judgment has an 'indicative effect' for other member states.[30] The material scope of protection only encompasses the facts of the case and the content of the application.

The scope of the obligation under Article 46 differs as to how the situation contravening the ECHR may be remedied. Thus, the ECtHR's competence is limited to finding a violation of ECHR rights; it may not quash laws or other acts of member states.[31] If the ECtHR holds that a state has violated the ECHR, Article 46 imposes upon this state the obligation to put an end to the breach and to make reparation for its consequences in such a way as to restore, as far as possible, the situation existing before the breach.[32]

In order to end human rights violations, a state has to take general and/or (if appropriate) individual measures which have to be adopted into domestic law.[33] In cases of continuing human rights violations, states are obliged to put an end to these breaches.[34] However, the member states enjoy a freedom of choice as to the means of implementing the judgment. In the light of the declaratory nature of the judgments of the ECtHR, it is generally for the states to choose the measures to be taken under national law to fulfil the obligation pursuant to Article 46, provided that the measures are compatible with the judgment's conclusion.[35]

Apart from the obligation to end human rights violations, member states have a duty under Article 46 to make reparation for the consequences of the violation. This requires that the state restores the situation existing before the breach (*restitutio in integrum*).[36] Therefore, in case of a violation of the right to property, states have to retransfer property of which a citizen was unlawfully deprived as *restitutio in integrum*.[37] In the context of Article 1 of Protocol No 1, the ECtHR concluded

[30] C Grabenwarter, 'Grundrechtsvielfalt und Grundrechtskonflikte im europäischen Mehrebenensystem—Wirkungen von EGMR-Urteilen und der Beurteilungsspielraum der Mitgliedstaaten (2011)' (2001) 38 *EuGRZ Jg Heft 8-9* 193, available at www.d-nb.info/1013588320/04.

[31] J Polakiewicz, *Die Verpflichtungen der Staaten aus den Urteilen des Europäischen Gerichtshofs für Menschenrechte* (Heidelberg, Springer, 1993) 223; W Okresek, in K Korinek and M Holoubek (eds), *Österreichisches Bundesverfassungsrecht—Kommentar* (Vienna, Springer, 2007) Art 46 EMRK, paras 1, 4, 8.

[32] See also the case law in this respect, eg *Papamichalopoulos and others v Greece*, Application no 14556/89 (ECtHR, 31 October 1995) 16 EHRR 440, para 34.

[33] *Scozzari and Giunta v Italy*, Application no 39221/98 *et al* (ECtHR, 13 July 1999) 25 EHRR 12 para 249.

[34] *Assanidze v Georgia*, Application no 71503/01 (ECtHR, 8 April 2004) 59 EHRR 52, para 198; Polakiewicz, *Die Verpflichtungen* (n 31) 63, 355; J Frowein and W Peukert, *Europäische Menschenrechtskonvention* (Kehl am Rein, Engel, 2009) Art 46, para 6.

[35] *Scozzari and Giunta* (n 33) para 249; *Goodwin* (n 16) para 120; *Gluhaković v Croatia*, Application no 21188/09 (ECtHR, 12 April 2011) para 85.

[36] G Ress, 'Wirkung und Beachtung der Urteile und Entscheidungen der Straßburger Konventionsorgane' [1996] *EuGRZ* 350, 351.

[37] *Hentrich v France*, Application no 13616/88 (ECtHR, 22 September 1994) 18 EHRR 440, para 71.

that, by ratifying, states do not only undertake to comply with the legal situation under the ECHR but also to remove all obstacles in their domestic legal system that might prevent an adequate redress of the applicant's situation.[38]

It is a purely national matter to determine what national authority is competent to implement judgments of the ECtHR. Article 46 does not distinguish between state functions but equally binds the legislature, the executive and the judiciary. From the ECtHR's point of view, it is decisive that an end is put to the breach of the ECHR.[39]

According to Article 46(2), it is for the Committee of Ministers to supervise the execution of final judgments. Therefore, final judgments of the ECtHR have to be transmitted to the Committee of Ministers.

D. Pilot Judgment Procedure

In order to cope with the excessive workload pressure and to facilitate the way applicants obtain redress more speedily with a relevant national remedy, the ECtHR has gradually expanded its powers over the years. Since 2004, with the express approval of the Committee of Ministers,[40] the ECtHR applies, in repetitive cases rooted in the same structural or systematic problem or other similar dysfunction in a member state, the so-called 'Pilot Judgment Procedure' (PJP). This instrument does not allow for the delivery of more judgments each year. Instead, the ECtHR is able to examine more applications while deciding fewer cases. From a general perspective, the PJP aims at reconciling the interests of every 'party' involved (individuals, national authorities, the ECtHR) and it displays features of a constitutional court.[41]

The PJP enables the ECtHR to single out certain applications for priority treatment while it formally adjourns all similar applications (until it finds that a member state has failed to comply with the operative provisions of the judgment or where the interests of the proper administration of justice require a resumption of the examination) if it concludes that all these cases are rooted in the same structural or systematic problem or other similar dysfunction in a member state.[42] The PJP of the 'original type' (eg *Broniowski*;[43] *Hutten-Czapska*)[44] requires the Grand Chamber to decide on a possible violation of ECHR rights and a connected conclusion that the underlying problem is systemic and that it has caused or may

[38] *Maestri v Italy*, Application no 39748/98 (ECtHR, 17 February 2004) 3 EHRR 38, para 47.

[39] Grabenwarter and Pabel, *Europäische Menschenrechtskonvention* (n 5) Art 16, para 4.

[40] Committee of Ministers, Resolution of the Committee of Ministers of 12 May 2004 on judgments revealing an underlying systematic problem, Res(2004)3.

[41] C Grabenwarter, 'The European Convention on Human Rights and its Monitoring Mechanism' in M Nowak *et al* (eds), *Vienna Manual on Human Rights* (Vienna, NWV, 2012) 128.

[42] E Fribergh, 'Pilot Judgments from the Court's Perspective', Stockholm Colloquy, Stockholm, 9–10 June 2008, available at www.coe.int/t/dghl/standardsetting/cddh/Publications/Stockholm_Proceedings.pdf 87.

[43] *Broniowski v Poland*, Application no 31443/96 (ECtHR, 22 June 2004) 40 EHRR 21.

[44] *Hutten-Czapska v Poland*, Application no 35014/97 (ECtHR, 19 June 2006) 42 EHRR 15.

cause a multitude of individual applications. The ECtHR provides the state with guidance on the type of remedial measure to end the human rights violations and to eliminate, as far as possible, their consequences. It demands that these measures are retroactive and implemented within a set period of time. It reinforces the state's obligation to take legal and administrative measures by virtue of the operative provisions of the judgment.[45]

Independent of the type of a pilot judgment, the execution stage remains under the authority of the Committee of Ministers. Article 4(1) of the Rules of the Committee of Ministers stipulates that priority treatment must be given to the supervision of pilot judgments. The ECtHR additionally assesses the implementation of the indicated general measures so as to be able to strike out the respective pending cases as soon as the measures have been complied with.[46]

The PJP forms another element which brings the competences of the ECtHR closer to that of a constitutional court. However, its legal basis is still subject to debate[47] and execution by the Committee of Ministers is something unusual for an established 'constitutional court'.

It is a unanimous opinion among experts that the PJP does not constitute customary international law as it does not meet the requisite requirements.[48] Therefore, its legal basis has to be found in the ECHR itself. The demand of the ECtHR expressly to include the PJP in Protocol No 14 was rejected by the Steering Committee for Human Rights on the grounds that it considered such procedure covered by the ECHR in its Protocol No 11 configuration.[49] Therefore, the ECtHR now grounds the procedure on Article 46, which is supplemented by Rule 61 of the Rules of Court. The new rule provides for a stronger legal basis of the PJP.

IV. MARGIN OF APPRECIATION: A FLEXIBLE INSTRUMENT OF EUROPEAN CONSTITUTIONAL JUSTICE

A. Doctrine of the Margin of Appreciation

(i) Margin of Appreciation and Conflicting Rights: A Corridor for National Solutions

There will always be cases in which, from a national point of view, the scrutiny exercised by the ECtHR will appear to be either of a high or a low degree.

[45] Grabenwarter, 'The European Convention' (n 41) 128.

[46] ibid.

[47] C Paraskeva, 'Returning the Protection of Human Rights to Where They Belong, at Home' (2011) 12 *International Journal of Human Rights* 433.

[48] D Milner, 'Codification of the Pilot Judgment Procedure', ECtHR Seminar on Responding to Systematic Human Rights Violations, Strasbourg, 14 June 2010, available at www.londonmet.ac.uk/fms/MRSite/Research/HRSJ/Events/Pilot%20Strasbourg/David%20Milner%20paper.pdf.

[49] Steering Committee for Human Rights, *Interim Activity Report of 26 November 2003*, CDDH(2003)026, para 21.

Especially the Grand Chamber, which has existed since Protocol No 11, shows that the different composition of the ECtHR in a certain case can lead to a different degree of scrutiny being exercised.[50] If the ECtHR, as it does in various cases, corrects national authorities at the expense of subjects of fundamental rights, it is possible—indeed, necessary—to demand a comprehensive approach as to the degree of scrutiny exercised in respect of particular fundamental rights or comparable case groups.

The ECtHR does not review compliance of a particular legal situation on a general basis, but only the compatibility of its application in particular cases to the individual applicant.[51] However, in its recent practice on the calculation of damages according to Article 41 ECHR, the Court increasingly makes general statements about national legal situations,[52] a practice which also shows its tendency towards being a constitutional court.

(ii) Margin of Appreciation and Judicial Guarantees

In this context, two cases may be distinguished: the first case concerns the weighing of interests which is required for the access to a court or which influences the extent to which a public hearing must be held. This case applies to the situations just described. The second case concerns the conceptual side. When deciding on the scope of civil rights, the effectiveness of a remedy or on cases of double jeopardy, specific concepts must be interpreted; the interpretation is, naturally, influenced by the concepts of national law. In this context it is to be determined whether a uniform practice exists all over Europe or whether the systems are quite different. If great differences exist among the member states, a wider margin of appreciation is appropriate.

B. Scope of the Margin of Appreciation

In national discussions about separation of powers and the degree of scrutiny exercised by the ECtHR, the democratic legitimacy of the legislator is considered decisive for its margin of appreciation. This is particularly true in respect of cases where a constitutional court decides on a measure of the national legislator. As

[50] See, eg *Sommerfeld v Germany*, Application no 31871/96 (ECtHR, 11 October 2001) para 41; *Sommerfeld v Germany*, Application no 31871/96 (ECtHR, 8 July 2003) para 68; *Jahn and others v Germany*, Application no 46720/99 *et al* (ECtHR, 22 January 2004) 42 EHRR 49, para 89; *Jahn and others v Germany*, Application no 46720/99 *et al* (ECtHR, 30 June 2005) paras 106, 112 ff, 116.

[51] *Sommerfeld* (2003) (n 50) para 68.

[52] See, eg the pilot judgments *Broniowski v Poland*, Application no 31443/96 (ECtHR, 22 June 2004) 40 EHRR 21, para 189 and *Assanidze v Georgia*, Application no 71503/01 (ECtHR, 8 April 2004) 59 EHRR 52, para 202; critical in this respect M Breuer, Urteilsfolgen bei strukturellen Problemen—Das erste 'Piloturteil' des EGMR [2004] *EuGRZ* 445, 451; Grabenwarter and Pabel, *Europäische Menschenrechtskonvention* (n 5) Art 16, para 7.

long as the legislator in a democratic society is legitimised through elections and stays within the boundaries of national fundamental rights, when enacting laws, the constitutional court must not become active.[53] In this context, an international court might argue with the international principle of subsidiarity. However, this does not mean that the separation of powers between the national courts and the legislator dissolves. The international judge will also respect comprehensible legislative opinions which stay within the boundaries of the ECHR as long as the legislator draws upon comprehensive judgments, assumptions and forecasts.[54]

The following criteria are relevant for determining the scope of the margin of appreciation:[55]

- diversity of national solutions: if there is no common European standard on a matter, the margin of appreciation is wider than in cases of uniform legislation throughout Europe;
- the quality and character of guarantees: a margin of appreciation is granted in respect of core guarantees as well as in respect of most of the judicial guarantees;
- conflicting ECHR rights: in cases of conflicting ECHR rights, the balance struck will affect the various groups of persons concerned;
- the quality of the national authorities that have decided: if decisions were made by independent tribunals or a court or constitutional court, the ECtHR will more likely accept the limits of the margin of appreciation applied;
- the quality of proceedings and, in particular, the reasoning: the more detailed a reasoning is and the better the right to be heard has been respected in the proceedings, the more the ECtHR is willing to accept particular national solutions.

From a constitutional perspective, the margin of appreciation is an instrument dealing with the separation of powers. The margin of the legislature under domestic law corresponds to the 'international' margin of appreciation. They both influence the control exercised by the constitutional court. While lowering the degree of scrutiny exercised, the ECHR affords a margin for different national solutions. Such plurality is not in itself incompatible with the idea of uniform human rights standards or, in other words, with constitutional standards.[56]

[53] K Korinek, 'Die Verfassungsgerichtsbarkeit im Gefüge der Staatsfunktionen' (1981) 39 *VVDStRL* 7, 45 ff.

[54] *Jahn* (2005) (n 50) Art 116: 'In that connection the FRG parliament cannot be deemed to have been unreasonable in considering that it had a duty to correct the effects of the Modrow Law for reasons of social justice'.

[55] C Grabenwarter, 'Kontrolldichte des Grund- und Menschenrechtsschutzes in mehrpoligen Rechtsverhältnissen aus der Sicht des österreichischen Verfassungsgerichtshofs' [2006] *EuGRZ* 487, 489 ff.

[56] Grabenwarter, 'Grundrechtsvielfalt' (n 30) 231.

V. ROLE OF COMPARATIVE LAW

If we look at the case law of the ECtHR, we find a considerable number of cases where references to the legal situation of various member states constitute one of the decisive, if not the decisive, argument of the ECtHR for finding a violation or a non-violation of ECHR rights. Three examples will illustrate this point.

A. References to 'European Standards' in the ECtHR's Case Law

A first example concerns voting rights. In its recent case law on Article 3 of Protocol No 1, the ECtHR established the unwritten principle of proportionality.[57] Against this background, the ECtHR, in *Yumak v Sadak*, decided that a 10 per cent threshold imposed for the Turkish Parliament elections complied with the ECHR.[58] The decisive argument put forward in the proportionality test was drawn from comparative law. The ECtHR pointed out that there were a few states with high thresholds of 7 per cent or 8 per cent, that one-third of the states had a threshold of 5 per cent and that another 13 states had even lower thresholds; the remainder of some ten states did not have a threshold at all. On that basis, the ECtHR found that no violation had occurred. It stressed that the great variety of national standards and the electoral and political background of each state, which had to be taken into account, warranted a wider margin of appreciation. While it found that a 10 per cent threshold appeared excessive, it concluded that the correctives and other safeguards in the Turkish system and especially the role of the constitutional court in enforcing these safeguards, led to its finding of a non-violation.[59]

A second example concerns the freedom of the press and TV advertising, more specifically a general ban on political advertising on Norwegian TV.[60] The proportionality test under Article 10(2) is too influenced by a comparative analysis of the law. It showed that a vast majority of Western European countries had a ban on political advertising; many Eastern European countries, on the other hand, allowed paid political advertising. The ECtHR stated the figures: 13 countries had a ban, ten allowed advertising, 11 provided for free airtime for political parties and/or candidates, and several states had no system of free airtime. The ECtHR found that there was no European consensus and was therefore (although somewhat reluctantly) prepared to accept that the analysis peaked in favour of allowing a somewhat wider margin of appreciation than the one usually granted with

[57] *Ždanoka v Latvia*, Application no 58278/00 (ECtHR, 16 March 2006) 46 EHRR 17, para 115; *Paksas v Lithuania*, Application no 34932/04 (ECtHR, 6 January 2011) para 101.

[58] *Yumak and Sadak* (n 22) para 147.

[59] ibid para 126.

[60] *TV Vest As and Rogaland Pensjonistparti v Norway*, Application no 21132/05 (ECtHR, 11 December 2008) 48 EHRR 51.

respect to restrictions on political speech. However, the reasoning following this statement shows that this is not much more than paying lip service. The ECtHR began a critical examination of all arguments in favour of a ban but rejected them all, in particular the position of the government that there was no viable alternative to a blanket ban.[61]

An example of European consensus concerns the freedom of religion and conscientious objectors.

On 7 July 2011, the ECtHR departed from the case law of the former EComHR, according to which there was no right to alternative service for conscientious objectors.[62] In the case of *Bayatyan*, a young Jehovah's Witness, the Grand Chamber of the ECtHR found a violation of Article 9 of the ECHR as there was no alternative service under Armenian law. The ECtHR referred to the fact that almost all member states of the Council of Europe with compulsory military service had implemented the right to conscientious objection. In particular, it referred to an obvious trend in the late 1980s and the 1990s to recognise the right to conscientious objection. It counted 19 countries that had introduced such a right after the last decision of the EComHR on the matter.[63] Lastly, the ECtHR referred to the fact that Azerbaijan and Turkey were the only states not having introduced the right to conscientious objection, and that Armenia itself had recognised the very right.[64] In a German metaphor, this situation could be referred to as a '*Hornberger Schießen*' (ie coming to nothing); it was an argument which would not have been worthwhile mentioning if it were not for Article 4(3)(b). Article 4(3)(b) contains an exception to the ban on forced labour, *inter alia*, for service exacted instead of compulsory military service 'in case of conscientious objectors in countries where they are recognised'. The Chamber judgment of 2009 was based on that argument and thus concluded that no violation of the ECHR had occurred.[65]

B. References to Soft Law in the Council of Europe

One main function of comparative law concerns the distribution of competences between national legislators and courts, on the one side, and the competence to review of the ECtHR, on the other side. We can draw two lessons from the case law that are reflected by the examples chosen: if there is a uniform practice in the member states, there is little room for a wide margin of appreciation. If, however, national solutions vary considerably, the margin of appreciation is generally

[61] ibid para 63.

[62] *Grandrath v Germany*, Application no 2299/64 (EComHR Decision, 12 December 1966) 8 YB 324.

[63] *Bayatyan v Armenia*, Application no 23459/03 (ECtHR, 7 July 2011) paras 46, 103.

[64] ibid para 104.

[65] ibid para 56.

wider. If the ECtHR holds (for other reasons) that the national discretion is narrower, it is ready to restrict the margin of appreciation even if there is no common European standard. One of these reasons is the soft law generated within the framework of the Council of Europe.[66] Other arguments are drawn from international law and EU law.[67] The latter, from the point of view of democratic legitimacy, are less problematic. Consequently, focus will be put on the role of the soft law of the Council of Europe. There are three main sources of soft law, that is non-binding instruments which have some influence on the practice of the organs of the Council of Europe, including the ECtHR and the organs of the member states:

(1) Resolutions of the Parliamentary Assembly of the Council of Europe;
(2) Recommendations of the Committee of Ministers of the Council of Europe;
(3) Documents of the Venice Commission.

In an increasing number of judgments, the ECtHR refers to Resolutions of the Parliamentary Assembly; this either in combination with an argument of comparative law or, in the absence of such an argument, alone. A good example for the 'combination approach' is the *Üner* case, where the ECtHR quoted a Recommendation of 2001, in which the Parliamentary Assembly recommended that the Committee of Ministers invite member states to guarantee that long-term migrants who were born or raised in the host country could not be expelled under any circumstances.[68]

C. Methods of Interpretation

Comparative law serves as a flexible tool for the ECtHR to regulate the extent of its scrutiny. It serves as a basis for the interpretation of specific words that are typical of constitutions and, above all, human rights,[69] or as an instrument to assess the weight of the interest of the respondent government in a particular national solution. This is part of the proportionality test. While constitutional courts draw their arguments from constitutional law, the ECtHR refers to the democratic legal systems of other member states.

From a methodological standpoint, it is, in both cases, an argument of systematic interpretation, with the difference being that its content is influenced by the practice of other states and their democratic decisions. At first glance, this practice

[66] See, eg *Üner v Netherlands*, Application no 46410/99 (ECtHR, 18 October 2006) para 37; *Bayatyan* (n 63) para 107.

[67] See, eg *Zolotukhin v Russia*, Application no 14939/03 (ECtHR, 10 February 2009) para 79; *Scoppola v Italy (No 2)*, Application no 10249/03 (ECtHR, 17 September 2009) 51 EHRR 323, para 105; *Bayatyan* (n 63) para 106.

[68] *Üner* (n 66) para 37.

[69] Grabenwarter, 'Grundrechtsvielfalt' (n 30) 231.

seems to deserve to be favoured as in most cases it helps to improve the standard of protection of human rights. However, this approach may raise problems in cases of conflicting rights or if a widely criticised change in the fundamental rights protection (as in Hungary) is followed by the other states, which may ultimately even constitute a trend.

The last example shows that we are talking not only about systematic interpretation but also about an *effetutile* interpretation in the light of present-day conditions. The historical-systematic interpretation would lead to the opposite result, as Article 4(3) contains a clear statement that it is for the member states to decide whether conscientious objection is allowed or not.

VI. CONCLUSION

While the above analysis focuses only on some aspects of the constitutional character of the ECHR and the ECtHR, a more detailed analysis would not show different results. After 60 years of the ECHR and 50 years of decision-making of the ECtHR, the conclusion would not change: the role of the ECHR for the development of national legal systems cannot be appreciated enough. The ECtHR is the last 'conscience' in human rights questions, a last legal instance or decision-making body similar to a constitutional court. It has, in many cases, given guidelines to the national courts, just as a national constitutional court does. Sometimes it even uncovers structural problems that can only be solved by adaptation and amendment of the legal system. The amendment of the legal system is influenced by European best practice or at least a better practice elsewhere.

The fact that the ECtHR, due to this role, is constantly faced with challenges and objections seems obvious. The tremendous workload, but also the ECtHR's jurisdiction that has lately become volatile in some areas, should not be concealed; one feature of the ECtHR's jurisdiction, its item-centred view, fuels this problem. Today, it is important for the member states and those inside the ECtHR to be aware of these dangers and constantly to face them. However, even critics and state reformers have to admit that the ECHR has become indispensable to all legal systems in Europe, not least to those of the Central European states.

The ECHR rights and the case law generated by the ECtHR stimulate the system of protection under constitutional law. Besides that, it increasingly supplements national guarantees. Both functions are of utmost importance and lead to better results for citizens but ultimately also for democratic states based on the rule of law. While these functions are in principle undisputed, the extent to which they are exercised has to be constantly questioned, especially in the light of recent case law. The margin of appreciation doctrine has for a long time proved to be a consistent and flexible concept. It must be shaped further in order to strike a balance between the needs of effective control by the ECtHR, consistency in the case law and internal practice in the field of human rights. 'Consensus' is drawn from more or less in-depth comparative analyses, whereas Council of Europe soft law cannot substitute for 'democratic legitimacy'.

Lastly, the question of democratic legitimacy of constitutional functions of an international court is also open for discussion, especially with a view to the soft law in the Council of Europe. But this is a separate topic.

10

Central and Eastern European Member States of the EU and the European Convention on Human Rights

MAHULENA HOFMANN

I. INTRODUCTION

THE TASK TO report on the Central and Eastern European Member States of the European Union and their relation to the European Convention on Human Rights ('the Convention' (ECHR)) can be approached from various angles: from the perspective of the position of the Convention in the respective domestic legal orders or from the way national courts deal with the Convention, with a specific focus on the complaints before the European Court of Human Rights ('the Court' (ECtHR)) or the implementation of its decisions.[1] This chapter concentrates on the first approach: can Bulgaria, the Czech Republic, Estonia, Hungary, Latvia, Lithuania, Poland, Romania, Slovakia and Slovenia be treated in their relation to the Convention as a specific category that differs from other ECHR member states, whether or not they are (present) EU Member States.

These countries had belonged for more than 40 years to the communist system, with its legal regime based on the concentrated and leading power of the Communist Party guaranteed by the respective constitutions, a unified system of state power and a planned economy. Human rights were principally confined to economic rights guaranteed by the state and implemented from the state budget. The ratification of international treaties on fundamental and political rights that were domestically not directly applicable was seen as an expression of goodwill on the international scene; their implementation—without any judicial control—was strictly in the hands of a state that did not allow any formation of opposition or deviation from the ideals defined by Communist Party congresses. Consequently, neither the legal system nor legal theory recognised individuals as subjects of international law, not even in the field of international humanitarian

[1] For detail see A Buyse and M Hamilton, *Transitional Jurisprudence and the ECHR: Justice, Politics and Rights* (Cambridge, Cambridge University Press, 2012).

law. Any access of any individual to any supranational structure for the protection of human rights was excluded. This situation changed quite substantially after 1989 with the entry into force of the new Constitutions.[2]

In the course of their initial transformations, all countries dealt with in this chapter adopted ambitious constitutional rules, of which the overwhelming majority enabled international provisions on human rights to be directly applicable in their legal systems.[3] This process turned the provisions of the Convention into a supplementary source of legal rules that was incorporated in the light of its dynamic interpretation by both the (then) European Commission and the European Court of Human Rights.[4] As a consequence, the practice of the national courts, especially of the Constitutional Courts, developed in such a way as to reflect and align their decisions with the applicable decisions of the ECtHR. With some exceptions, the sovereignty discourse dealt and deals with the European Union and its Charter of Fundamental Rights rather than the Convention.[5]

In contrast to the majority of successor states of the former Soviet Union, the group of states willing to become a member of both the Council of Europe and the European Union came under the influence of two regional legal structures. In the course of their accession to the Council of Europe, all candidates faced conditions that aimed at, and resulted in, substantial changes in their legislation (eg the abolition of the death penalty), as well as the ratification, in addition to the Convention, of several regional treaties, eg the Convention for the Prevention of Torture,[6] or the Framework Convention for the Protection of National Minorities or the European Charter for Regional or Minority Languages.[7] Additional conditions aiming at the harmonisation, or even unification, of certain areas of legislation were formulated in the course of their accession to the European Union, based on the Copenhagen Criteria[8] and the *acquis communautaire*. This means that in those specific areas covered by the EU *acquis*, such as data protection, the contents of their legal orders correspond basically to the provisions of other contracting parties of the Council of Europe that are also EU Member States.

[2] A Nußberger, 'Die "Zweite Wende": Zur Verfassungsentwicklung in den Ländern Mittel- und Osteuropas im Zuge der EU-Erweiterung' (2005) 58 *Die öffentliche Verwaltung* 357; A Albi, 'East European Countries' in P Popelier *et al* (eds), *Human Rights Protection in the European Legal Order* (Cambridge, Intersentia, 2011) 173.

[3] E Stein, 'International Law and Internal Law in the New Constitutions of Central-Eastern Europe' in R Bernhardt and U Beyerlin, *Recht zwischen Umbruch und Bewahrung* (Heidelberg, Springer, 1995) 865.

[4] M Hofmann, *Von der Transformation zur Kooperationsoffenheit?* (Berlin, Springer, 2009).

[5] M Hofmann, 'Zum zweiten "Lissabon-Urteil" des Tschechischen Verfassungsgerichts' (2010) 37 *EuGRZ* 153.

[6] European Convention for the Prevention of Torture and Inhuman or Degrading Treatment or Punishment (Strasbourg, 26 November 1987) ETS 26.

[7] Framework Convention for the Protection of National Minorities (Strasbourg, 1 February 1995) ETS 157; European Charter for Regional or Minority Languages (Strasbourg, 5 November 1992) ETS 148.

[8] In this regard see www.europa.eu/legislation_summaries/glossary/accession_criteria_copenhague_en.htm.

II. RATIFICATION OF THE EUROPEAN CONVENTION ON HUMAN RIGHTS

The European Convention on Human Rights was ratified by the Central and Eastern European countries in the 1990s,[9] immediately after the collapse of the communist system.[10] By doing so, the new contracting parties obliged themselves to secure to everyone within their jurisdictions their rights and freedoms contained in the Convention (Article 1 ECHR) and its Protocols; moreover, they became part of the system of the European Court of Human Rights providing for judges elected on their behalf (Article 20 ECHR), the right to use its mechanism for inter-state cases (Article 33 ECHR), and, most significantly, the right of any person, non-governmental organisation or group of individuals claiming to be the victim of a violation by the contracting party of Convention rights to submit applications to the ECtHR (Article 34 ECHR).

This system proved to be more successful than originally expected. Over the past 20 years, the Court has delivered more than 12,000 judgments[11] and influenced substantially the legal order of the Central and Eastern European countries. The judges found at least one violation of the ECHR in 395 cases against Bulgaria, 161 against the Czech Republic, 22 against Estonia, 233 against Hungary, 47 against Latvia, 61 against Lithuania, 815 against Poland, 777 against Romania, 237 against Slovakia and 231 against Slovenia. Although this is less than in cases against Italy (1,651), Russia (1,140) or Turkey (2,404),[12] the expectations of applicants from Eastern European countries remain quite high. Between 1 January and 31 October 2012, the Court decided about 71,802 applications, 1,283 by judgment and 70,519 by other decisions.[13] During this period, Romania (7.9 per cent), Bulgaria (2.9 per cent) and Poland (3.0 per cent) were among the ten contracting parties with the highest number of applications.[14]

III. TYPE OF JUDGMENT AND GENERAL SUBJECT MATTER OF VIOLATION CASES

From the perspective of the type of judgments rendered by the ECtHR, that is (in the terminology of the Court) violation, no violation, friendly settlement or striking out and other judgments, the group of Central and Eastern European EU Member States does not show any apparent differences from other groups

[9] Seewww.conventions.coe.int/Treaty/Commun/ChercheSig.asp?NT=005&CM=&DF=&CL=ENG.

[10] L Hammer and F Emmert (eds), *The European Convention on Human Rights and Fundamental Freedoms in Central and Eastern Europe* (The Hague, Eleven International Publishing, 2012).

[11] ECtHR, '50 Years of Activity: The European Court of Human Rights', 3, www.echr.coe.int/Documents/Facts_Figures_1959_2009_ENG.pdf.

[12] ECtHR, 'Violation by Article and by State 1959–2011', www.echr.coe.int/Documents/Stats_violation_1959_2011_ENG.pdf.

[13] See www.echr.coe.int/Documents/Stats_analysis_2012_ENG.pdf.

[14] See ibid.

of states. The statistics reveal that in 83 per cent of judgments concerning all 47 Member States, the Court held that there was a violation of Convention rights. While all states in our group show 80 per cent or more of such violation judgments (ranging from Lithuania with 80 per cent to Hungary with 95 per cent), in the category of 'old democracies' this number varies between 100 per cent (Liechtenstein, Monaco) and 38 per cent (Denmark). In other groups, 'violation judgments' represent up to 100 per cent (Bosnia and Herzegovina, Montenegro), the lowest being the share of violation decisions concerning Croatia (81 per cent).[15] It should be mentioned, however, that these statistics do not take into account the absolute number of 'violation judgments'.

Let us have a closer look at the general subject matter of violation cases. However, the statistics provided by the Court on the absolute numbers of violation cases[16] during its existence cannot offer any reliable answer specific to Eastern and Central European EU Member States because the number of violations of Convention rights increases in relation to the duration of the country's membership in the Court system.

Moreover, and perhaps at first sight surprisingly, the statistics on the subject matter of violation judgments do not provide any data that would allow establishment of any substantial differences among the various categories of states. The majority of all cases deal with violations of Article 6 ECHR (right to a fair trial), without substantial differences in relation to our group of states. The percentage of this subject matter is 42 per cent of the judgments concerning the Czech Republic, 82 per cent Hungary, 44 per cent Poland, 63 per cent Slovakia and 50 per cent Slovenia. In comparison, the highest percentage of this subject matter in the 'old democracies' shows Italy (57 per cent), followed by Germany and Portugal, both with 51 per cent.

Also surprisingly, the issue of property protection is not specific to the group of European transition countries. Only Romania shows a significant percentage of such violation judgments (38 per cent) whereas in all other states of our group such cases do not belong to the most relevant categories. In contrast, property issues belong to the most relevant categories in France (4 per cent), Greece (8 per cent), Iceland (11 per cent), Italy (15 per cent), Malta (17 per cent) and Portugal (21 per cent), as well as in Serbia (14 per cent), Russia (17 per cent) and Turkey (17 per cent).[17]

The conclusion of this comparison is that the Central and Eastern European EU Member States do not show any apparent differences concerning either the type of violation judgments or the general subject matter of Court decisions as compared to other contracting parties.

[15] ECtHR, 'Statistics on Judgments by State 1959–2010, European Court of Human Rights', 9, www.echr.coe.int/Documents/Stats_violation_1959_2010_ENG.pdf.

[16] ECtHR, 'Violation' (n 12).

[17] ECtHR, 'Statistics' (n 15) 2.

IV. SPECIFIC SUBJECT MATTER

Differences are more visible after a closer look at the subject matter of decisions delivered by the ECtHR. It has already been mentioned that Article 6(1) ECHR is the provision most often held by the Court to have been violated, without any differences in relation to the groups of states concerned. There are, however, several specific issues that are, for obvious reasons, typical of the Central and Eastern European Member States of the EU.[18]

A. Compensation for Property Nationalised by the Communist Regime

These cases deal with failure to enforce judgments recognising the right to restitution or compensation for nationalised land (*Bulves v Bulgaria*);[19] deprivation of property in restitution proceedings (*Pinc v Czech Republic*);[20] lack of legislation regulating the principles of compensation under a law of 1946 for property nationalised under the communist regime (*Ogórek v Poland*);[21] restoration of rights to property nationalised by Soviet authorities in the 1960s (*Jasiuniene v Lithuania*, admissibility decision);[22] a restrictive system of rent control originated in laws passed under the communist regime (*Hutten Czapska v Poland*, pilot judgment);[23] a rent control scheme imposing important restrictions on landlord rights (*Jan Vomocil v Czech Republic and Article 38, AS v Czech Republic*);[24] restitution of properties nationalised under communism (*Atanasiu v Romania*, pilot judgment);[25] or claims for restitution or compensation in respect of property expropriated by the communist authorities (*Sirc v Slovenia*).[26]

B. Punishment for Crimes in the Communist Period

This rather heterogenous group of cases is connected with the retrospective punishment of crimes committed in the communist period. In connection with the application of Article 7 ECHR prohibiting punishment for crimes that did not constitute a crime in the time of the offence, the ECtHR dealt with several crucial cases in which the conditions for retrospective application of criminal law

[18] See Press Country Profiles of ECHR.

[19] *Bulves v Bulgaria*, Application no 3991/03 (ECtHR, 22 January 2009).

[20] *Pincová and Pinc v Czech Republic*, Application no 36548/97 (ECtHR, 5 November 2002).

[21] *Ogórek v Poland*, Application no 28490/03 (ECtHR, 18 September 2012).

[22] *Jasiuniene v Lithuania*, Application no 41510/98 (ECtHR, 6 March 2003).

[23] *Hutten Czapska v Poland*, Application no 35014/97 (ECtHR, 28 April 2008) 45 EHRR 4.

[24] *Jan Vomocil v Czech Republic and Article 38, AS v Czech Republic*, Applications nos 38817/04 and 1458/07 (ECtHR, 5 March 2013).

[25] *Maria Atanasiu and others v Romania*, Application nos 30767/05 and 33800/06 (ECtHR, 12 October 2010).

[26] *Sirc v Slovenia*, Application no 44580/98 (ECtHR, 16 May 2002).

to the detriment of the accused in the transformation countries were specified[27] (eg *Korbely v Hungary*).[28]

C. Affiliation with the Communist Secret Services

These cases deal with the loss of a job as a consequence of being denounced as a former secret KGB collaborator (eg *Zickus v Lithuania*);[29] the ban on applicants from employment in the public sector because of their former membership in the KGB (eg *Rainys v Lithuania*);[30] fairness of lustration proceedings (eg *Matyjek v Poland*);[31] and allegations that the applicant was a member of the former Secret Service 'Securitate' and obstacles to accessing the personal file created on the applicant (eg *Haralambie v Romania*).[32]

D. Pensions and Retirement

Pensions and retirement cases dealt with the existence of a statutory limit on state pensions (eg *Valkov v Bulgaria*);[33] and retirement pensions of former members of the Yugoslav armed forces (eg *Predojevic v Slovenia*).[34] On 11 January 2012, the registrar of the ECtHR announced a further 'thousands of Hungarian applications dealing with retirement pensions'[35] although it should be stressed that these cases do not originate in any measure dealing with the communist past.

E. Specific Situation of Roma

The specific situation of Roma is dealt with in cases on the placement of pupils in special classes (eg *Horváth v Hungary*)[36] or schools (eg *DH v Czech Republic*);[37] Roma settlements and plans to remove a Roma settlement (eg *Yordanova v Bulgaria*);[38] ill-treatment of a 14-year-old Roma by the police (eg *Stoica v Romania*);[39] incidents

[27] See also *K-HW v Germany*, Application no 37201/97 (ECtHR, 22 March 2001) 36 EHRR 59.
[28] *Korbely v Hungary*, Application no 9174/02 (ECtHR, 19 September 2008) 50 EHRR 48.
[29] *Zickus v Lithuania*, Application no 26652/02 (ECtHR, 7 April 2009).
[30] *Rainys and Gasparavicius v Lithuania*, Applications nos 70665/01 and 74345/01 (ECtHR, 7 April 2005).
[31] *Matyjek v Poland*, Application no 38184/03 (ECtHR, 30 May 2006) 50 EHRR 10.
[32] *Haralambie v Romania*, Application no 21737/03 (ECtHR, 27 October 2009).
[33] *Valkov v Bulgaria*, Applications nos 2033/04 *et al* (ECtHR, 25 October 2011).
[34] *Predojević and others v Slovenia*, Applications nos 43445/98 *et al* (ECtHR, 7 June 2011).
[35] Press Country Profile: Hungary (January 2012) 4.
[36] *Horváth and Kiss v Hungary*, Application no 11146/11 (ECtHR, 29 April 2013).
[37] *DH and others v Czech Republic*, Application no 57325/00 (ECtHR, 13 November 2007) 47 EHRR 3.
[38] *Yordanova and others v Bulgaria*, Application no 25446/06 (ECtHR, 24 September 2012).
[39] *Stoica v Romania*, Application no 42722/02 (ECtHR, 4 March 2008).

between Roma and non-Roma villagers (eg *Moldovan v Romania*);[40] sterilisation of Roma women without their express consent (eg *KH v Slovakia*);[41] and failure to carry out an appropriate investigation into a fatal injury that the applicant's father of Roma origin suffered at a police station (eg *Mizigarova v Slovakia*).[42]

F. Russian Speakers in the Baltic States

The cases concerning the situation of Russian speakers in the Baltic states deal with the bar to receiving a pension as a former Russian/Soviet army serviceman (eg *Tarkoev v Estonia*);[43] deportation of the family of a former Soviet army officer in accordance with the inter-state treaty between Russia and Latvia (*Slivenko v Latvia*);[44] disqualification of a Russian-speaking candidate from parliamentary election because of her lack of command of the official language (Latvian) (*Podkolzina v Latvia*);[45] and the order to deport a Russian national from Lithuania as he was considered to constitute a threat to national security (*Borisov v Lithuania*).[46]

V. EUROPEAN CONVENTION ON HUMAN RIGHTS IN HUNGARY

In order to take the situation of Hungary as an example of the relation of a post-communist Central European country with the ECHR, the position of the Convention in the Hungarian legal order must be detailed as a first step.

The Hungarian Constitution of 1949,[47] as substantially amended in 1989–90 to correspond to the new political and legal order, stated in its article 7(1) that Hungary's legal system accepts the generally recognised rules of international law; furthermore, it shall ensure the consistency of Hungary's international legal obligations and its domestic law. This means that with respect to international treaties, the Constitution applied the dualist doctrine: they were not regarded as directly applicable in the domestic legal order and had to be 'incorporated' individually into the domestic law.[48] The constitutional catalogue of fundamental rights adopted the core of the main international human rights instruments.

[40] *Moldovan and others v Romania*, Applications nos 41138/98 and 64320/01 (ECtHR, 5 July 2005) 44 *EHRR* 302.

[41] *KH and others v Slovakia*, Application no 32881/04 (ECtHR, 6 November 2009) 49 *EHRR* 34.

[42] *Mizigarova v Slovakia*, Application no 74832/01 (ECtHR, 14 December 2010).

[43] *Tarkoev and others v Estonia*, Applications nos 14480/08 and 47916/08 (ECtHR, 4 November 2011).

[44] *Slivenko v Latvia*, Application no 48321/99 (ECtHR, 9 October 2003) 39 *EHRR* 24.

[45] *Podkolzina v Latvia*, Application no 46726/99 (ECtHR, 9 April 2002).

[46] *Borisov v Lithuania*, Application no 9958/04) (ECtHR, 14 June 2011).

[47] Act XX of 1949 (1949. évi XX. törvény A Magyar Köztársaság Alkotmánya), as amended.

[48] H Bokor-Szegő and M Weller, 'Hungary' in R Blackburn and J Polakiewicz (eds), *Fundamental Rights in Europe: The ECHR and its Member States 1950–2000* (Oxford, Oxford University Press, 2001) 384.

The decisive role in protecting human rights in Hungary was vested in the Constitutional Court.[49]

The path for ratification of the European Convention on Human Rights was opened by Resolution 76/1990 of the Hungarian Parliament[50] on the signature of the Convention. At the same time, in the Explanatory Report to the Resolution, the Parliament expounded in detail that during the signature and ratification of the Convention it should be assessed whether the Hungarian legal order was in harmony with all provisions of the Convention. The Convention and its Additional Protocols were ratified on 5 November 1992 and promulgated by Act XXXI of 1993.[51] The Convention had a considerable impact on the Hungarian legal order. Several Acts touching upon human rights contain explicit references to the Convention.[52] Importantly, the 2000 Code on Criminal Procedure[53] allows for reopening a domestic procedure following a decision of the European Court of Human Rights.

On 18 April 2011, the Parliament passed the new Basic Law of Hungary;[54] it entered into force on 1 January 2012,[55] together with the Act on Transitional Provisions to the Basic Law.[56] As concerns the relation between the domestic legal order and international law, the new Constitution follows the logic of the 1949 Constitution; article Q of the Basic Law states that Hungary shall ensure harmony between international law and Hungarian law in order to fulfil its obligations under international law (article Q(2)); Hungary shall accept generally recognised rules of international law (article Q(3)), and other binding sources of international law, especially treaties, become part of the Hungarian legal system only by 'publication in the form of legislation' (article Q(3)).

The Venice Commission, which evaluated the text of the new Constitution, stated in its report that neither the constitutional provision dealing with sources of law (article R), nor article 28 dealing with the courts' interpretative obligations mention Hungary's international law obligations, nor does the Chapter

[49] SI Pogány, 'Human Rights in Hungary' (1992) 41 *International and Comparative Law Quarterly* 676.

[50] Resolution 76/1990 (76/1990. (XI. 2.) OGY határozat az Európa Tanács Alapszabályához és az Európa Tanács kiváltságairól és mentességeir ől szóló Általános Egyezményhez való csatlakozásról, valamint az Európai Emberi Jogi egyezmény aláírásáról).

[51] Act XXXI of 1993 (1993. évi XXXI. törvény az emberi jogok és az alapvető szabadságok védelméről szóló, Rómában, 1950. november 4-én kelt Egyezmény és az ahhoz tartozó nyolc kiegészítő jegyzőkönyv kihirdetéséről).

[52] Eg Act LXXXVI of 1993 concerning entry and immigration (1993. évi LXXXVI. törvény a külföldiek beutazásáról, magyarországi tartózkodásáról és bevándorlásáról; Act LXXVII of 1994 on the rights of national and ethnic minorities (1994. évi LXXVII. törvény a nemzeti és etnikai kisebbségek jogairól).

[53] Act XIX of 1998 (1998. évi XIX. törvény a büntetőeljárásról).

[54] In this respect see www.kormany.hu/download/2/ab/30000/Alap_angol.pdf.

[55] K Kovács and GA Tóth, 'Hungary's Constitutional Transformation' (2011) 7 *European Constitutional Law Review* 183.

[56] For an unofficial translation see Annex to G Halmai *et al*, *Amicus Brief for the Venice Commission on the Transitional Provisions of the Fundamental Law and the Key Cardinal Laws* (February 2012), available at lapa.princeton.edu/hosteddocs/hungary/Amicus_Cardinal_Laws_final.pdf.

on 'Freedom and Responsibility' include any reference to international human rights instruments (paragraph 30). The Venice Commission observed the effort to follow closely the technique and contents of the Convention in formulating the constitutional provisions (paragraph 18), but expressed its concern about the risk that the constitutional provisions may be eroded by sub-constitutional acts (paragraph 148).[57] In this situation, the Venice Commission stressed the importance of article Q(2), which states that Hungary shall ensure harmony between international law and Hungarian law in order to fulfil its obligations under international law, as it may acquire a particularly important role guaranteeing that not only the substantive rights, but their limitations as well, will be interpreted in harmony with international human rights instruments, especially the European Convention on Human Rights. The Venice Commission also underlined that it will be no less significant that the decisions of the European Court of Human Rights are executed in the national order. It must be stressed that there is considerable scepticism in the legal literature as to whether these demands will be respected and implemented.[58]

As of the end of 2012,[59] the European Court of Human Rights had delivered altogether 271 judgments concerning Hungary, of which 257 found at least one violation of the Convention, primarily (198) of Article 6 ECHR (length of proceedings).[60]

The only Grand Chamber case, *Korbely*,[61] held that there had been a violation of Article 7 ECHR (no punishment without law). The applicant was found guilty of a crime against humanity and sentenced to five years' imprisonment on the basis of common Article 3 of the Geneva Conventions[62] for a lethal shooting during the quelling of a riot in Tata during the 1956 revolution. In analysing the meaning of 'crime against humanity' in 1956, the Court concentrated on whether the victims of the shooting were protected by their character as part of the 'civilian population'. According to the opinion of the Court, this was not the case. The Court concluded that it was not foreseeable that the applicant's acts had constituted a crime against humanity under international law in 1956 and, as a result, there had been a violation of Article 7.

Another significant case, *Kmetty*,[63] dealt with the failure to carry out an effective investigation into the applicant's allegations of ill-treatment. The applicant had refused to comply with a police order to evacuate a market after a bomb alert. Apparently, he had been ill-treated by the police. Subsequently, the Hungarian authorities did not carry out an effective investigation capable of leading to the

[57] European Commission for Democracy through Law (Venice Commission), *Opinion on the New Constitution of Hungary* (Opinion No 621/2011, 20 June 2011).

[58] See Kovács and Tóth, 'Hungary's Constitutional Transformation' (n 55) 202.

[59] Bokor-Szegő and Weller, 'Hungary' (n 48) 384.

[60] ECtHR, 'Violation' (n 12).

[61] *Korbely v Hungary*, Application no 9174/02 (ECtHR, 19 September 2008) 50 EHRR 48.

[62] Geneva Conventions of 12 August 1949.

[63] *Kmetty v Hungary*, Application no 57967/00 (ECtHR, 16 December 2003) 40 EHRR 6.

identification and punishment of those responsible. In such an absence of a thorough and effective investigation, the Court concluded that there had been a violation of Article 3 ECHR.

Several important cases concern the protection of freedom of expression (Article 10 ECHR). The cases of *Vajnai*[64] and *Fratanoló*[65] dealt with convictions for wearing a five-pointed red star during a demonstration. The convictions were based on a provision of the Hungarian Criminal Code (section 269/B), the constitutionality of which had been confirmed by a 2000 decision of the Constitutional Court.[66] The European Court of Human Rights found that the convictions violated Article 10 ECHR. Even if the measures were based on valid legislation and might have aimed at the prevention of disorder and the protection of the rights of others, in the current Hungarian political context they did not fulfil the condition of 'being necessary in a democratic society'. The symbols were worn by members of a registered political party and during a lawful demonstration. Because there was no real and present danger of any political movement or party restoring the communist dictatorship at present, the convictions were not proportionate to the aim pursued.

A unanimous decision of a violation of Article 10 ECHR was taken in *Uj*.[67] The applicant, a journalist, had published an article criticising the quality of a well-known Hungarian wine variety produced by a state-owned corporation. He was convinced of defamation by a criminal court. In analysing the proportionality of this measure, the ECtHR found that the article was not a defamatory statement of facts but a value judgement or opinion that was expressed with reference to governmental policies concerning the protection of national values and the role of private enterprise and foreign investment. It dealt, therefore, with a matter of public interest. Since the domestic courts had failed to have regard to these considerations, Hungary as the respondent state could not establish that the restriction had been proportionate.

The Hungarian authorities violated Article 11 ECHR (freedom of assembly) in *Bukta*.[68] The applicant had organised, together with others, a spontaneous demonstration protesting against the participation of a high state official in a disputed reception. Because they had not given prior notice of their demonstration, it was disbanded. The Court based its reasoning on the violation of the principle of proportionality. A peaceful demonstration did not present any danger to public order beyond the level of the minor disturbance that is inevitably caused by an assembly in a public place; the public authorities should show a certain degree of tolerance towards peaceful gatherings, if the freedom of assembly guaranteed by Article 11 is not to be deprived of all substance.

[64] *Vajnai v Hungary*, Application no 33629/06 (ECtHR, 8 July 2008) 50 EHRR 44.

[65] *Fratanoló v Hungary*, Application no 29459/10 (ECtHR, 3 November 2011).

[66] Decision 14/2000 (V.12) AB határozat (Constitutional Court of Hungary).

[67] *Uj v Hungary*, Application no 23954/10 (ECtHR, 19 July 2011).

[68] *Bukta v Hungary*, Application no 25691/04 (ECtHR, 17 July 2007) 51 EHRR 25.

Although the Court did not find any violation of Article 11 ECHR, the *Rekvényi* case[69] was important from the perspective of the right of assembly of state officials. The applicant was a police officer who had complained against the effects of the 1993 amendment to the 1949 Hungarian Constitution[70] that prohibited political activities of, inter alia, members of the police forces. The Court stated that Article 11(2) ECHR entitles states to impose lawful restrictions on the right to freedom of association by members of the police. This contested restriction, neither ambiguous nor unclear or unforeseeable, was considered as lawful within the meaning of Article 11(2).

The case of *Metalco Bt*[71] originated in an application by that Hungarian limited partnership under liquidation on account of the unfairness and excessive length of litigation with the Hungarian tax authorities concerning its outstanding taxes. To secure its claim, the Tax Authority attached a 100 per cent share the applicant had in another company. Aware that the applicant intended to sell its share, the Tax Authority forbade the transaction. In the course of a lengthy administrative procedure, the share lost its value. The applicant complained against the loss of the value of its share under Article 1 of Protocol No 1. According to the ECtHR, the Convention allows the state to enforce laws as it deems necessary to secure the payment of taxes. However, the Hungarian law required it to hold an auction in order to sell the attached asset. This obligation formed an integral part of the lawfulness of the interference in proprietary rights in question. This unlawful omission on the part of the state amounted to a violation of Article 1 of Protocol No 1.

Since the adoption and entering into force of the new Basic Law of Hungary and the new cardinal laws, no judgments have been released by the ECtHR in connection with the new regulation of the constitutional system. The reason for this may be the average length of the procedures before the Court. As the new Constitution entered into force only on 1 January 2012, cases complaining about elements of the new rules have not yet been finalised.

However, two judgments should be mentioned as they are strongly related to some of the very first measures taken by the current governmental parties.

The applicant in the first case was a civil servant who was dismissed from service without receiving any reasons for dismissal, which was made possible by an Act adopted after the establishment of the new government in 2010. Considering that in the absence of reasons for her dismissal, she could not sue her former employer with any prospect of success, the applicant did not challenge this measure in Hungarian courts. The ECtHR took the view that it was inconceivable for the applicant to have brought a meaningful action, so this legal configuration deprived her of the right of access to a court (Article 6(1) ECHR).[72] Meanwhile, the Hungarian Constitutional Court annulled the relevant regulation

[69] *Rekvényi v Hungary*, Application no 25390/94 (ECtHR, 20 May 1999) 30 EHRR 519.
[70] Act CVII of 1993 (1993. évi CVII. törvény az Alkotmány módosításáról).
[71] *Metalco Bt v Hungary*, Application no 34976/05 (ECtHR, 1 February 2011).
[72] *KMC v Hungary*, Application no 19554/11 (ECtHR, 10 July 2012).

as unconstitutional and issued a decision concerning the non-applicability of laws, declared unconstitutional also in cases still pending before an ordinary court.[73]

In July 2010, the Hungarian Parliament adopted a law that introduced a new tax on certain payments to employees of the public sector whose employment was terminated. Consequently, severance pay and other payments related to the termination of employment exceeding HUF 2 million became subject to a 98 per cent tax. In *NKM*, the Court held that this measure could not be justified by the legitimate public interest the government relied on (namely, satisfying society's sense of justice and protecting the public purse). Those who act in good faith on the basis of the law (like the applicant) should not be frustrated in their statute-based expectations without specific and compelling reasons. Therefore, the measure could not be held reasonably proportionate to the aim sought to be realised and there had been a violation of Article 1 of Protocol No 1 (protection of property).[74]

One of the points on these judgments worth mentioning is that the Court interpreted the requirement of the exhaustion of all effective domestic remedies in a very flexible way. In *KMC*, the Court was satisfied that the application could not be rejected for non-exhaustion of domestic remedies. According to the judgment, the applicant could not be expected to file a labour action, as such an action, in which she would have had to challenge her dismissal the grounds for which were entirely unknown to her, could only have been a formal motion.[75]

Moreover, in *NKM*, the Court did not mention the requirement of the exhaustion of domestic remedies, despite the fact that the applicant did not file any action in Hungary.[76]

However, in another decision on the same day as *NKM*, the Court declared the application inadmissible and noted that the constitutional complaint that was declared inadmissible without an examination on the merits did not qualify as an effective remedy and did not interrupt the running of the six-month time limit. This is because that complaint (rejected partly since it did not fall within the Constitutional Court's jurisdiction and partly because it concerned matters that were essentially the same as in previously adjudged cases) could not possibly extend the six-month time limit.[77]

Since 1 January 2012, according to the Basic Law and the new Act on the Constitutional Court,[78] constitutional complaints may also be submitted to the Constitutional Court if a right of the petitioner guaranteed by the Basic Law has

[73] Decision 8/2011 (II.18) AB határozat (Constitutional Court of Hungary); Decision 35/2011 (V.6) AB határozat (Constitutional Court of Hungary).

[74] *NKM v Hungary*, Application no 66529/11 (ECtHR, 14 May 2013). In a few months, two more judgments were issued by the Court on the same topic with the same results (and almost the same text). See *Gáll v Hungary*, Application no 49570/11 (ECtHR, 25 June 2013); *RSZ v Hungary*, App no 41838/11 (ECtHR, 2 July 2013).

[75] *KMC v Hungary*, Application no 19554/11 (ECtHR, 10 July 2012) para 28.

[76] *NKM v Hungary*, Application no 66529/11 (ECtHR, 14 May 2013) para 25.

[77] *Hálózati Gyógyszertárak and others v Hungary*, Application no 66925/12 (ECtHR, 14 May 2013).

[78] Act CLI of 2011 (2011. évi CLI. *törvény* az *Alkotmánybíróságról*).

been allegedly violated by a final and binding court decision or by the application of an unconstitutional law in judicial proceedings. If the Constitutional Court declares that the court decision is contrary to the Basic Law, it must annul the decision. However, there is no procedure available for a legal remedy designed to remedy the violation of rights and no pecuniary compensation is available in these proceedings.

In the near future, the Court should also deal with the question whether this new form of constitutional complaint has any relevance for the exhaustion of all effective domestic remedies.[79]

At present, there are 18 cases communicated to the Hungarian government registered on the Court's website.[80] They cover practically the whole spectrum of substantive provisions of the Convention, from Article 3 ECHR prohibiting degrading treatment in detention (*ZH v Hungary*),[81] to Article 8 dealing with the registration of churches (*Magyar Keresztény Mennonita Egyház v Hungary*),[82] to Article 1 of Protocol No 1 dealing with the segregation of Roma children in remedial schools (*Horváth v Hungary*).[83] Moreover, the Court has been addressed by 'thousands of Hungarian applications dealing with retirement pensions'.[84] Two of these cases correspond to the constitutional changes of 2011–12 in Hungary.

In *Baka v Hungary*,[85] the applicant is a former judge at the European Court of Human Rights and later President of the Supreme Court of Hungary, who was dismissed from this later position by the effect of the Transitional Provisions to the Basic Law of Hungary. He complains in particular under Article 6(1) ECHR (right to fair trial) that he has been denied access to a tribunal to defend his rights relating to his premature dismissal. Under Article 10 (freedom of expression), he alleges that he was dismissed in connection with his views and public position expressed in his capacity as President of the Supreme Court and the National Council of Justice. The loss of their church status, and in conjunction with that the loss of state subsidies, is the subject of the case of *Magyar Keresztény Mennonita*

[79] This question came up in one of the cases communicated to the Hungarian government; *KÖNYV-TÁR Kft and others v Hungary*, Application no 21623/13 (ECtHR), lodged on 26 March 2013.

[80] These cases can be found at the following link by searching with the keyword 'Hungary', www.hudoc.echr.coe.int/sites/eng/Pages/search.aspx#{"respondent":["HUN"],"documentcollectionid":["JUDGMENTS","DECISIONS","CLIN","ADVISORYOPINIONS","REPORTS","RESOLUTIONS"]}.

[81] *ZH v Hungary*, Application no 28973/11 (ECtHR, 8 November 2012).

[82] *Magyar Keresztény Mennonita Egyház and Jeremias Izsák-Bács v Hungary and eight other applications*, Application no 70945/11 (ECtHR, 27 September 2012).

[83] *Horváth and Kiss v Hungary*, Application no 11146/11 (ECtHR, 29 April 2013).

[84] Press Country Profile: Hungary (January 2012) 4. Since mid-December 2011, the Court has received almost 8,000 individual applications against Hungary relating to the pension rights of former law enforcement officers who benefited from early retirement. These cases raise essentially identical issues, primarily the replacement of the applicants' retirement pensions, which were not subject to income tax, by an allowance that is taxable at 16 per cent. The Registrar of the Court issued a statement about special measures to deal with the influx of Hungarian pension cases. According to the statement, the Court will identify one or more applications that it will examine as a priority as leading cases and, pending the outcome of those cases, it will not take any procedural steps in relation to the other applications.

[85] *Baka v Hungary*, Application no 20261/12 (ECtHR), lodged on 14 March 2012.

Egyház and eight other applicants. That is a result of the new Act on the Right to Freedom of Conscience and Religion and the Legal Status of Churches adopted by the Hungarian Parliament following the Basic Law. The applicants complain under Article 11 ECHR of violation of their right to freedom of religion and under Articles 6 and 13 of lack of an effective remedy.[86]

VI. CONCLUSION

This chapter tried to find an answer to the question as to whether Bulgaria, the Czech Republic, Estonia, Hungary, Latvia, Lithuania, Poland, Romania, Slovakia and Slovenia can be treated in their relation to the European Convention on Human Rights as a specific category which differs from other contracting parties to the Convention, whether or not (present) EU Member States. This short overview cannot compete with such thorough and far-reaching analyses as those produced by Buyse and Hamilton in their recent publication *Transnational Jurisprudence and the ECHR*, who raise the question whether the cases dealing with transition countries reflect a special, *sui generis* jurisprudence of the European Court of Human Rights.[87] I can only agree with these authors in observing that the transitional context can be seen as an exceptional situation comparable to other exceptional situations. In analysing the jurisprudence of the Court in relation to transition countries, the authors observe that while the Court does take arguments of transition seriously, its approach sometimes lacks consistency. 'In general, the Court applies the normal tools and interpretation methods and does not simply give way to state discretion as soon as a complaint relates to issues of transition.'[88] Can this analysis be a result of the fact that the Court simply does not see any basic distinction between the group of Central and Eastern European states and the applications against acts committed under their jurisdiction, on the one hand, and other categories of contracting parties to the Convention, on the other hand?

This brief overview does, however, provide some additional arguments supporting the thesis that there are not any general issues in which the Central and Eastern European Member States of the EU differ, in their relation to the Convention, from other contracting parties which are also Member States of the EU. The differences that could be traced in the specific subject matters of violation judgments of the Court seem to be issues 'inherited' from the recent communist history. They deal with compensation for property nationalised by the communist regime; punishment of crimes committed during the communist

[86] *Magyar Keresztény Mennonita Egyház and Jeremias Izsák-Bács v Hungary and eight other applications*, Application no 70945/11 (ECtHR, 27 September 2012).

[87] A Buyse and M Hamilton, *Transnational Jurisprudence and the ECHR* (Cambridge, Cambridge University Press, 2011) 289.

[88] ibid 293.

period; consequences of the affiliation to the communist secret service, the specific situation of Roma, typically in the context of the education system, which also has its roots in the communist period; and the situation of Russian speakers in the Baltic countries resulting from the dissolution of the former Soviet Union.

However, there are already some categories of cases that can no longer be described as being of typically transition-related character. Rather, examples such as the problems of pensions as a result of the present economic crisis or of compliance with the freedom of expression or freedom of association are issues that belong to the typical workload of the Court. Whether this means that the mentioned period of the transition of the legislation has been, with the support of the jurisprudence of the ECtHR, successfully completed, and that after the process of transition only new categories of serious problems will occur, is another question.

11

The Role of the Venice Commission in Maintaining the Rule of Law in Hungary and in Romania

JOAKIM NERGELIUS

I. INTRODUCTION

THE PURPOSE OF this chapter is to describe and analyse the role of the Venice Commission, as one part of the human rights protection in Europe offered today by the Council of Europe, with particular regard to the recently very troubled situations in Hungary and Romania. While the European Court of Human Rights is the judicial part of this protection and the Parliamentary Assembly may be said to represent the political part, the Venice Commission may be seen as an advisory part, with 'soft' rather than binding power.

Particular emphasis will be given here to the reactions of the European Union in 2011, 2012 and 2013 to opinions of the Venice Commission regarding the situation in those two states. In other words, may the Venice Commission influence EU decision-making in these most sensitive matters? And what is the general role of the Venice Commission in times of constitutional crisis in Europe?

After a short presentation of the history and organisation of the Venice Commission, this chapter will provide a background description of the recent, controversial developments in Hungary and (although more briefly) Romania. Then, it will analyse the response of the different, relevant EU institutions to the opinions of the Venice Commission. Finally, it will draw some conclusions, though it should be emphasised from the beginning that these are not easy to formulate, because the decisions the EU eventually made are based on a vast number of factors. Regardless of its influence, prestige or whatever more or less important factors, the Venice Commission, thus, is but one of many contributors of information to the EU.

II. HISTORY AND GENERAL ROLE OF THE VENICE COMMISSION

The general historical development of Europe since the end of the 1980s is probably well-known to the reader. The birth of the Venice Commission may also be traced back to the end of communism and the fall of the Berlin Wall. The need to provide guidance to the many new democracies, and after 1991–92 new states, in Central and Eastern Europe led the Council of Europe to establish the Venice Commission, or the European Commission for Democracy through Law as it is formally called.[1]

As its full name indicates, the idea behind the Venice Commission was to strengthen democracy in those states mainly by strengthening their legal institutions and the rule of law. Initially, only 18 of the then 23 member states of the Council of Europe participated in its work, but when the Council of Europe gradually grew, so did the Venice Commission.

Today, all 47 member states of the Council of Europe are also members of the Venice Commission.[2] It may be mentioned that 12 states that are not members of the Council of Europe also have joined the Commission, among them Algeria, Brazil, Chile, Israel, Mexico, Republic of Korea, Tunisia and the United States.

The purpose of the Venice Commission is described in Article 1 of its Statute as being an advisory body for members and non-members of the Council of Europe, with a special focus on Central and Eastern Europe. Its objectives are there described as 'strengthening the understanding of the legal systems of the participating states, with a view to bringing these systems closer, promoting the rule of law and democracy and examining the problems raised by the working of democratic institutions and their reinforcement and development'.[3] In order to achieve this, 'the Commission shall give priority to work concerning the constitutional, legislative and administrative principles and techniques which serve the efficiency of democratic institutions and their strengthening, as well as the principle of the rule of law, fundamental rights and freedoms, notably those that involve the participation of citizens in public life, and the contribution of local and regional self-government to the enhancement of democracy'.[4] As follows from Article 2 of the Statute, the Commission is composed of independent experts in law or political science, one member and one substitute from each state, who hold office for four years and may be reappointed. A special Bureau is composed of the President, three Vice-Presidents and four other members. The seat of the Commission is Venice (Article 8), but the Commission is assisted by the Secretariat General of the Council of Europe, which is located in Strasbourg.

Once a year, the Venice Commission will present a report on its activities to the Committee of Ministers of the Council of Europe. Within the mandate described above, the Commission may, under Article 3.2 of its Statute, supply opinions

[1] The fact that it came to have its premises in Venice seems to be due mainly to the influence of some of its 'Founding Fathers', notably Antonio La Pergola.

[2] Those states have a joint responsibility for financing the work of the Commission, as well as the work of the Council of Europe, and do so basically in relation to the size of their population and net growth income.

[3] Council of Europe, Resolution(2002)3 on the Revised Statute of the European Commission for Democracy through Law, art 1 point 1.

[4] ibid art 1 point 2.

upon request from the Committee of Ministers, the Parliamentary Assembly of the Council of Europe, its Secretary General, the Congress of Local and Regional Authorities of Europe or by any state or international organisation that participates in the work of the Commission (the Commission may also carry out research on its own initiative). Of those different bodies, the Parliamentary Assembly and in particular its so-called Monitoring Committee (officially the Committee on the Honouring of Obligations and Commitments by Member States of the Council of Europe) seems to be the most active initiator of new opinions, having asked for not less than 26 opinions from 2007 until 2011.

Generally speaking, the work of the Venice Commission seems to have become much more important in the last five or six years than was previously the case. Unfortunately, that has a lot to do with the 'constitutional crisis' that some European states are now facing, which has made the activities of the Commission and its focus on human rights, constitutional change, democratic development, free elections and referenda as well as other urgent constitutional matters more crucial than ever. In this respect, the normal working method of the Commission, when an opinion is required, seems to be to establish a special task force, with three or four experts accompanied by some of its own administrative staff, which travels to a given country and meets important persons there. After that, an opinion is written. Once the Commission has approved this opinion in one of its regular meetings (which take place every third month), it will be published, made available on the webpage and sent to the government of the country concerned.

Having this in mind, this chapter will focus on the opinions in 2011–13 dealing with Hungary and Romania and their impact, notably on the EU level.

III. GENERAL REMARKS ON THE POLITICAL AND CONSTITUTIONAL SITUATION IN HUNGARY

On 1 January 2012, a new Constitution entered into force in Hungary.[5] The Constitution, entitled the Basic Law, was adopted only by votes of the members of Fidesz and KDNP, the two governing parties that possess more than two-thirds of seats in Parliament, which made up a 'constitution-making majority' according to the previous 1989 Constitution. The preparatory works for the Basic Law were extremely short and non-transparent; the actual draft was elaborated within a matter of a few months behind closed doors. The political legitimacy of the Basic Law is thus built on fragile soil, since the opposition either voted against it or was absent in the whole procedure of constitution-making.

However, this debate must be seen in the light of the controversial events that had already taken place in 2010 and 2011, in particular with regard to the Press and Media Act of June 2010, followed by the new Media Law adopted by

[5] For a detailed discussion see Pál Sonnevend, András Jakab and Lóránt Csink, Chapter 2.

the Hungarian Parliament on 20 December 2010.[6] This extensive legal text, with some 230 articles divided into seven Chapters, caused widespread reaction and, for instance, prompted EU Commissioner Nellie Kroes, who is responsible among other things for media concentration and freedom, to write expressing her worries in a letter to the Hungarian Government on 23 December 2010.

From the point of view of EU law, the demands for so-called 'balanced coverage' in all media and for registration in advance of any kind of media company (including blogs and other Internet-related activities) were particularly sensitive. So too were the parts of the law that made it also applicable to media companies that were registered and active in other EU states than Hungary. This was said to violate the EU Audiovisual Media Services Directive,[7] and the Green Party Group of the European Parliament already urged at the beginning of 2011 that sanctions should be issued against Hungary, in line with Article 7 of the Treaty on European Union (TEU). It is, however, worth noting that from a more general 'freedom of speech' perspective, the establishment of a special, powerful National Media and Infocommunications Authority (articles 109–202 of the Mass Media Act), to which only sympathisers of the Fidesz party were nominated, was even more controversial.[8] This authority had the power, among other things, to impose fines on media companies that were considered to be 'politically unbalanced' or generally unbalanced in their reporting of news. It could also order journalists to reveal the names of their sources whenever this was considered necessary due to national security or public order, which is undoubtedly far-reaching and very open to the authority's own interpretation.[9] Interestingly enough, the Constitutional Court in December 2011 held that the Media Law violated the former Constitution.[10]

Having received the worried letter from EU Commissioner Nellie Kroes, Deputy Prime Minister Tibor Navracsics, on behalf of the Hungarian government, stated on 31 January 2011 that the government wanted to start a dialogue with the European Commission, aiming at certain changes to the law. On 16 February, the law was subsequently changed as to the very points the Commission addressed, such that it would not apply to foreign media companies, the requirement of 'balanced coverage' would only apply for radio and TV transmissions (which is also the case in many other EU states and thus considered acceptable) and finally the requirement for registration would only occur 60 days after the

[6] Press and Media Act 2010 (2010. évi CIV. törvény a sajtószabadságról és a médiatartalmak alapvető szabályairól); Mass Media Act 2010 (2010. évi CLXXXV. törvény a médiaszolgáltatásokról és a tömegkommunikációról).

[7] Council and Parliament Directive 2010/13/EU on the coordination of certain provisions laid down by law, regulation or administrative action in Member States concerning the provision of audiovisual media services (Audiovisual Media Services Directive) [2010] OJ L95/1.

[8] The same could be said for the alleged lack of protection for media sources ('whistleblowers') under s 6 of the Press and Media Act, a problem that caused the Parliamentary Assembly of the Council of Europe to issue a special recommendation (Council of Europe Parliamentary Assembly, Recommendation No 1950 (2011) (25 January 2011).

[9] ibid.

[10] Decision 165/2011 (XII.20) AB határozat (Constitutional Court of Hungary).

start of any new media activities. Although the role of the National Media and Infocommunications Authority was not affected, the European Parliament nevertheless decided, on 17 February, to suspend a vote on a resolution intended as a protest against the law.

With regard to the new Constitution, it was not only the way in which it was adopted that stirred controversy, both domestically and abroad.[11] NGOs and the press raised serious questions of constitutionalism both with regard to the protection of fundamental rights and the status of independent institutions in 2010 and 2011.[12] Most attention was paid to the freedom of the press,[13] but the regulation of freedom of religion and the status of churches[14] and retroactive legislation also triggered criticism. Equally, an unusual limitation of the competences of the Constitutional Court[15] and judicial reform that included a dubious process of appointing judges[16] provoked critical reactions. An unusual power of the President of the newly established National Office for the Judiciary to reassign cases from the lawful court to another court was especially called into question.[17]

The developments also provoked unusual political reactions from the allies of Hungary and the European Union. For instance, on 23 December 2011, Secretary of State Hillary Clinton addressed a letter to Prime Minister Viktor Orbán asking him to postpone the entry into force of the so-called cardinal laws (ie laws on the basic institutions of the constitutional system that require a two-thirds vote of Members of Parliament present) related to the new Basic Law. The Secretary of State specifically asked for reconsideration of the provisions on the appointment of judges and the law on freedom of religion.[18] Earlier, Viviane Reding, Vice-President of the European Commission responsible for justice, fundamental rights and citizenship, inquired about a wide range of issues related to the new Basic Law from the Hungarian Minister of Justice in a letter dated 12 December 2011.[19]

[11] For the detailed analysis of the new Hungarian Constitution see Pál Sonnevend, András Jakab and Lóránt Csink, Chapter 2.

[12] See, eg J Nergelius, 'The Hungarian Constitution of 2012 and its Protection of Fundamental Rights' (2012) 3 *Swedish Institute for European Policy Studies (European Policy Analysis)* 1.

[13] See, eg I Traynor, 'Hungary Begins First EU Presidency with Warnings over Press Freedom', *Guardian* (London), 3 January 2011, available at www.guardian.co.uk/world/2011/jan/03/hungary-press-crackdown-eu-presidency.

[14] JK Grieboski, 'The Midnight Adoption of Europe's Most Restrictive Religion Law', *Huffington Post* (London), 21 July 2011, available at www.huffingtonpost.com/joseph-k-grieboski/hungarian-parliament-resu_b_902567.html.

[15] C Bryant, 'Hungary Curbs Constitutional Court's Powers', *Financial Times* (London), 16 November 2010, available at www.ft.com/cms/s/0/9ac8db2a-f1af-11df-bb5a-00144feab49a.html#axzz1oX9OVUTz.

[16] 'Hungary: Reverse Interference with Courts, Media', *Human Rights Watch* (London), 6 January 2012, available at www.hrw.org/news/2012/01/06/hungary-reverse-interference-courts-media.

[17] 'Judiciary on Manual Override', *Transparency International Hungary* (Budapest), 20 February 2012, available at www.transparency.hu/Judiciary_on_Manual_Override?bind_info=page&bind_id=162.

[18] 'Hillary Clinton levele Orbán Viktornak—itt a teljes szöveg', *Népszabadság* (Budapest), 30 December 2011, available at www.nol.hu/kulfold/hillary_clinton_levele_orban_viktornak_-_itt_a_teljes_szoveg.

[19] 'Megszereztük: Ezekre Várja a Választ a Kormánytól az EU Pénteken', *HVG* (Budapest), 15 December 2011, available at www.hvg.hu/itthon/20111215_reding_level_biztos.

This letter was followed by one from Jose Manuel Barroso, President of the European Commission, to Prime Minister Orbán, urging him to withdraw two cardinal laws that allegedly contradicted European Union law.[20]

IV. VENICE COMMISSION ON HUNGARY

A. Opinions

Since 2010, the Venice Commission has published several opinions concerning Hungary, including three opinions evaluating the new Basic Law and its Fourth Amendment, and seven opinions evaluating certain 'cardinal laws'.

The Hungarian government requested the first opinion on the new Basic Law before the text of the then-draft new Basic Law was finalised.[21] This opinion addressed the possible implications of the incorporation of the EU Charter of Fundamental Rights in the new Basic Law, the role of the preliminary (ex ante) review of Acts of Parliament by the Constitutional Court, and of the right of every individual to initiate an abstract ex post constitutional review of laws, the so-called '*actio popularis*'. While the European Commission embraced Hungary's legitimate aim and indication of loyalty to European values, it came to the conclusion that a new national constitution should not include one-by-one the provisions of the EU Charter of Fundamental Rights.[22] It also concluded that the Parliament should not have the power to ask for an ex ante review of its acts and that it is compatible with European constitutional traditions to abolish the *actio popularis*.[23]

The request for a further opinion on the new Basic Law from the Venice Commission came on 26 March 2011 from the Monitoring Committee of the Parliamentary Assembly of the Council of Europe after the adoption of the Basic Law.[24]

Concerning the procedural matters, the Venice Commission in its second opinion held it regrettable that the constitution-making process, including the drafting and final adoption of the new Basic Law, had been affected by a lack of transparency, shortcomings in the dialogue between the majority and the opposition, insufficient opportunities for adequate public debate and a very tight time frame.[25]

[20] M Dunai and J Stonestreet (eds), 'EU's Barroso Asks Hungary to Withdraw Cbank Law: Website', *Reuters* (Budapest), 20 December 2011, available at www.reuters.com/article/2011/12/20/uk-hungary-eu-idUSTRE7BJ0J520111220.

[21] European Commission for Democracy through Law (Venice Commission), *Opinion on Three Legal Questions Arising in the Process of Drafting the New Constitution of Hungary* (No 614/2011, 28 March 2011).

[22] ibid paras 21, 75.

[23] ibid para 75.

[24] European Commission for Democracy through Law (Venice Commission), *Opinion on the New Constitution of Hungary* (No 621/2011, 20 June 2011).

[25] ibid para 144.

The main concerns were related to the limitation of powers of the Constitutional Court on taxation and budgetary matters and the prominent role given to the Budget Council in the state budget.[26]

This second opinion also advised how to interpret certain provisions of the Basic Law, and called for adequate clarification by the Hungarian authorities of certain potentially problematic statements and terms contained therein, especially in the Preamble.[27] It noted that the adoption of cardinal and other implementing laws was an opportunity in this respect.[28]

After Hungary adopted the Fourth Amendment to the new Basic Law on 11 March 2013, the Secretary General of the Council of Europe requested another opinion from the Venice Commission as to the Fourth Amendment's compatibility with Council of Europe standards.[29] The Commission's criticism focused on the unchanged position of the President of the National Judicial Office, issues of constitutional review and the endangered constitutional system of checks and balances.[30] The opinion, however, expressly welcomed Hungary's announcement on the planned Fifth Amendment, removing the system of transfer of cases.[31] Consequently, the Fifth Amendment of the Basic Law entered into force on 1 October 2013 and repealed the paragraph of the Basic Law that enabled transferring of cases.

Beside the three opinions concerning the new Basic Law and its amendments, the Venice Commission dealt with some of the cardinal laws of Hungary. Significantly, and in a demonstration of its commitment to European constitutional standards, the Hungarian government requested the opinion of the Venice Commission on three cardinal laws (Laws on the Judiciary, Freedom of Religion and Parliamentary Elections). In January 2012, the Monitoring Committee of the Parliamentary Assembly of the Council of Europe requested an opinion from the Venice Commission on whether five further Hungarian laws were in line with the Council of Europe's standards (Laws on Freedom of Information, the Constitutional Court, Prosecution, Nationalities and Family Protection). In March 2012, the Monitoring Committee of the Parliamentary Assembly filed yet another request, asking the Venice Commission for a review of certain Transitional Provisions.

Of these nine requested laws, the Venice Commission evaluated seven. There were no opinions on the Law on Family Protection and Transitional Provisions. This was because both Acts were examined by the Hungarian Constitutional Court and declared partly unconstitutional. The most disputed articles of the Law on Family Protection, which excluded from the definition of the family relationships

[26] ibid para 146.
[27] ibid para 149.
[28] ibid para 150.
[29] European Commission for Democracy through Law (Venice Commission), *Opinion on the Fourth Amendment of the Basic Law of Hungary* (No 720/2013, 14 June 2013).
[30] ibid para 147.
[31] ibid paras 75, 142.

between same-sex partners and excluded them from intestate succession, were annulled by the Constitutional Court.[32] The Constitutional Court also annulled those parts of the Transitional Provisions of the Basic Law that had no transitional nature. According to the Court, to become part of the Basic Law these regulations should be incorporated into the text of the Basic Law; there is no possibility to include them in a separate document.[33]

The first opinion on the new Hungarian cardinal laws dealt with the judiciary system.[34] This opinion criticised several points of the regulation. Amendment of the examined Acts followed immediately, when the government submitted amendments taking into account the recommendations of the Venice Commission and the Hungarian Parliament adopted these on 2 July 2012.[35]

The second opinion of the Venice Commission about the judiciary examined the effects of this amendment.[36] In this opinion, the Commission found, among other things, that the wide powers of the President of the National Judicial Office had been much limited and would no longer be discretionary, but that the system for appointment and dismissal of judges was still very unsatisfactory, with insufficient legal guarantees against dismissal or removal of a judge. Also the problem concerning transfers of cases from one court to another was unfortunately still unresolved. There were still no objective criteria determining when and how this may occur, which may be seen as one of the main problems in this area.[37]

In the opinion dealing with the Act on the Constitutional Court (issued between the two opinions on the judiciary), the Venice Commission noticed numerous positive aspects of the new regulation.[38] A remaining problem, however, in particular given the current political and parliamentary situation, was the fact that justices of the Constitutional Court are elected by the Parliament with a two-thirds majority. Furthermore, the Commission would have liked to see clearer constitutional guarantees of the legal independence and autonomy of the court, as well as guarantees against premature removal of its judges.[39] Concerning the competencies of the Constitutional Court, the Commission awaited more precise distinction between the two forms of constitutional complaints and transfer of the right to initiate a process in case of the violation of rights affecting

[32] Decision 43/2012 (XII.20) AB határozat (Constitutional Court of Hungary).

[33] Decision 45/2012 (XII.29) AB határozat (Constitutional Court of Hungary).

[34] European Commission for Democracy through Law (Venice Commission), *Opinion on the Act on the Legal Status and Remuneration of Judges and on the Act on the Organisation and Administration of Courts* (Opinion No 663/2012, 19 March 2012).

[35] Act CXI of 2012 (2012. évi CXI. törvény a bíróságok szervezetéről és igazgatásáról szóló 2011. évi CLXI. törvény, valamint a bírák jogállásáról és javadalmazásáról szóló 2011. évi CLXII. törvény módosításáról).

[36] European Commission for Democracy through Law (Venice Commission), *Opinion on the Cardinal Acts on the Judiciary that were Amended following Adoption of Opinion CDL-AD(2012)001 on Hungary* (No 683/2012, 15 October 2012).

[37] ibid paras 90–93.

[38] European Commission for Democracy through Law (Venice Commission), *Opinion on Act CLI of 2011 on the Constitutional Court of Hungary* (No 665/2012, 19 June 2012) para 53.

[39] ibid para 54.

a larger group of people from the competency of the Prosecutor General to that of the Commissioner for Fundamental Rights.[40] The opinion also urged the legislature to make legal aid also available for proceedings before the Constitutional Court because legal representation is mandatory in constitutional complaint proceedings.[41]

In addition to the Acts on the Judiciary and on the Constitutional Court, another opinion on Acts regulating state organs considered the laws on the prosecution service.[42] The Venice Commission took into account the variety of possible models for the organisation of prosecutorial systems in Europe, and stated that the principles of the Hungarian Acts for the operations of prosecutors are in line with applicable standards for prosecutors in a democratic society, as they provide for an autonomous body with a hierarchical organisation, enable non-political activity of prosecutors and contain important anti-corruption rules.[43] After highlighting numerous positive aspects of the regulation,[44] the Commission made recommendations for the revision of the examined acts. Most of these recommendations concern the strong hierarchical control of the Prosecutor General over all other prosecutors. According to the opinion, this wide independence of the Prosecutor General and the hierarchical model should be complemented by sufficient checks and balances.[45] It is important to emphasise that according to the Venice Commission, most issues raised in the opinion do not threaten the rule of law but the Commission made its recommendations in order to propose ways to improve the prosecution service that may be below that threshold.[46] The two relevant Acts were not amended after the issuance of the opinion.

Both fundamental rights and the system of state organs were dealt with in the opinion on the Act on Informational Self-determination and Freedom of Information.[47] In this opinion, the Venice Commission found the Act, as a whole, in compliance with the applicable European and international standards.[48] However, there were several concerns, mainly about the part of the Act that guarantees the protection of personal data and the right to access data of public

[40] ibid paras 28–29.

[41] ibid para 43. Instead of making legal aid available for the initiators of constitutional complaints, the Hungarian Parliament cancelled the rule that required mandatory legal representation. See s 13 of Act CXXXI of 2013 (2013. évi CXXXI. törvény egyes törvényeknek az Alaptörvény negyedik módosításával összefüggő módosításáról).

[42] European Commission for Democracy through Law (Venice Commission), *Opinion on Act CLXIII of 2011 on the Prosecution Service and Act CLXIV of 2011 on the Status of the Prosecutor General, Prosecutors and Other Prosecution Employees and the Prosecution Career of Hungary* (Opinion No 666/2012, 19 June 2012).

[43] ibid para 85.

[44] ibid para 86.

[45] ibid paras 87, 89–90.

[46] ibid para 88.

[47] European Commission for Democracy through Law (Venice Commission), *Opinion on Act CXII of 2011 on Informational Self-determination and Freedom of Information of Hungary* (Opinion No 672/2012, 18 October 2012).

[48] ibid para 79.

interest. The Venice Commission objected among other things to the unclear regulation regarding including personal data in the scope of the general right to information, the scope and purpose of key concepts for the right to access data of public interest, the provision of the remedial mechanism and the protection of media sources.[49] As the opinion came out only after the infringement proceedings launched by the European Commission and the amendment of the Act in answer to that by the Hungarian Parliament, the Venice Commission held that the guarantees of the independence of the National Authority for Data Protection and Freedom of Information, the new state organ with the task to enforce the two above-mentioned fundamental rights, were sufficiently detailed.[50] However, there remained one point that concerned the Commission, the mode of designation of the President of the Authority, which excludes Parliament and does not include sufficient guarantees of independence.[51]

Another examined act in the field of human rights was the Act on the Right to Freedom of Conscience and Religion.[52] In the view of the Commission, as a whole, the Act constituted a liberal and generous framework for the freedom of religion; however, some important issues remained problematic and fell short of international standards.[53] These include arbitrary criteria with regard to the recognition of a church; the deregistration process of hundreds of previously lawfully recognised churches; lack of effective remedies; and discriminatory treatment of religious beliefs and communities depending on their recognition.[54] Nine months after the opinion, the Hungarian Constitutional Court annulled several rules of the Act that had been criticised by the Venice Commission, and following the decision the Parliament amended the Act.[55]

As is usual in these issues, the Venice Commission cooperated with the OSCE Office for Democratic Institutions and Human Rights when examining the Parliamentary Election Act of Hungary and they adopted a joint opinion.[56] According to the concluding remarks, the Act was a good basis for conducting genuine and democratic parliamentary elections and there were several beneficial developments, such as specific provisions favouring better participation of national minorities in Parliament.[57] However, the Commission criticised the lack

[49] ibid paras 44–47, 52–56, 63–66, 77–78.
[50] ibid paras 30–34.
[51] ibid para 36.
[52] European Commission for Democracy through Law (Venice Commission), *Opinion on Act CCVI of 2011 on the Right to Freedom of Conscience and Religion and the Legal Status of Churches, Denominations and Religious Communities* (Opinion No 664/2012, 17 March 2012).
[53] ibid para 107.
[54] ibid paras 64, 70, 79, 86, 92, 104.
[55] Decision 6/2013 (III.1) AB határozat (Constitutional Court of Hungary); Act CXXXIII of 2013 (2013. évi CXXXIII. törvény a vallási közösségek jogállásával és működésével kapcsolatos törvényeknek az Alaptörvény negyedik módosításával összefüggő módosításáról).
[56] European Commission for Democracy through Law (Venice Commission), *Opinion on Act CCIII of 2011 on the Elections of Members of Parliament of Hungary* (Opinion No 662/2012, 15 March 2012).
[57] ibid para 49.

of cross-party consultations during the preparation process[58] and recommended some changes in the Act concerning delimitation of electoral constituencies, secrecy of voting, candidate nominations, voting of citizens abroad and the voting method of persons belonging to national minorities.[59] Some of these problems were solved in the new Electoral Procedure Act adopted in April 2013.[60] Compared to the above-mentioned opinions, the opinion on the Act on Nationalities is less critical.[61] This was due to the fact that according to the Commission, Hungary has continued to pay particular attention to the promotion and protection of minority rights and to makes specific efforts to ensure protection and preservation of the ethnic, cultural and linguistic identity, traditions and cultural heritage of its nationalities. The new Act as part of the process of implementation of the new Basic Law confirms Hungary's internationally recognised commitment to minority protection.[62] The main criticism about the Act was that the regulation was particularly complex and at times excessively detailed and sometimes lacked legal clarity that might result in difficulties in implementation.[63]

B. Evaluation Concerning Hungary

To conclude, the general impression that is gained by the interested reader who studies the new Basic Law and the many heated debates that have surrounded it, is in many ways the same as the impression gained when reading the Media Law of 2010. That is, the main idea behind it is not to limit freedom of speech or other basic rights as such. Nor is it intended to make life difficult for certain ethnic or other weak minorities. Rather, its purpose is to enforce and strengthen the powers of the governing party, in a way that will make it more difficult for other political parties or groups to be taken into account and really be able to influence Hungarian society in the future. The new Basic Law concentrates political power in the hands of Parliament and gives the current, strong political majority the chance to appoint important persons in such a way that, because it is based on qualified parliamentary majority, it will be very difficult for other political parties to win back the initiative and thus influence or control future development.

The constitutional text also has many authoritarian features and must be described as extremely nationalistic, given the values that it stresses. In the Preamble, for example, it is stated, among many other things, that: 'We hold

[58] ibid para 30.

[59] ibid paras 18, 19, 36, 39, 44, 48.

[60] Act XXXVI of 2013 on Electoral Procedure (2013. évi XXXVI. törvény a választási eljárásról). For example, voters belonging to a minority can decide on their registration as a minority voter until the second day before election day (s 94(2)).

[61] European Commission for Democracy through Law (Venice Commission), *Opinion on the Act on the Rights of Nationalities of Hungary* (Opinion No 671/2012, 19 June 2012).

[62] ibid paras 81–83.

[63] ibid para 84.

that the family and the nation provide the most important framework for our coexistence, and that our fundamental cohesive values are fidelity, faith and love'. Even the rule on membership of the European Union, Article E, stresses national sovereignty to the utmost, stating in section 2 that:

> With a view to participating in the European Union as a member state, Hungary may exercise some of its competences arising from the Basic Law jointly with other member states through the institutions of the European Union under an international agreement, to the extent required for the exercise of the rights and the fulfilment of the obligations arising from the Founding Treaties.[64]

In reality, that is hardly a correct description of how EU membership works or how its effects take place; even if an individual Member State does prefer to see things that way, the European Union is not just another international organisation in which all Member States retain their former sovereignty (a fact that is indeed also very present and evident in the current row between the EU and Hungary).

To be more precise, actions by the state against judges in general, and against the former President of the Supreme Court in particular, may threaten judicial independence and thus, ultimately, the right to a fair trial under Article 6 of the European Convention on Human Rights, or Article 47 of the EU Charter of Fundamental Rights. Actions against the National Bank and other public authorities clearly might violate the new right to 'good administration' that is guaranteed in Article 41 of that Charter.

For the future and against this background, the position the Constitutional Court has taken on the legal status of the Transitional Provisions seems to be a very important issue. Also, of course, the position and strategy chosen by the European Commission in relation to possible future legal proceedings, and the response to these future actions from the Hungarian government, will be of the utmost importance, and not only for Hungary. In reality, this matter is likely to have a wider importance for future relations between the EU and other Member States that might, once having been accepted as EU Members with all the legal and political obligations that such a change requires,[65] for some reason lower their standards concerning vital democratic principles or legal and other administrative standards. While it is well known and generally recognised that the EU action against Austria in 2000 (which did not amount to sanctions in the formal sense) was inefficient and lacking legal basis, since Austria had in fact not violated any of the core values mentioned in Articles 2 and 6 TEU (or in any other binding human rights documents), the situation is in fact quite different this time, when we are

[64] In this respect, it is also slightly odd for an EU Member State that is, at least theoretically, aiming for future euro membership despite the current economic crisis, to state that 'The official currency of Hungary shall be the forint' (Basic Law, Art K).

[65] These are often referred to as the so-called 'Copenhagen criteria' for EU membership, after an EU summit meeting that took place in Copenhagen in 1993. They include democracy, rule of law and respect for human rights as well as independent courts and public administration.

dealing with what seems to amount to a series of real violations of human rights and the rule of law.

Thus, the moment for the European Commission to act may now have come. But what will come from such an initiative? Well, that will, of course, depend on the reactions and reasoning of both the Hungarian government and the Court of Justice of the European Union (CJEU). A formal decision of the European Council on real sanctions against Hungary under Article 7 TEU may still be far away—but for the first time ever, such a move is now at least possible to imagine.

V. SITUATION IN ROMANIA

In Romania, power struggles between the Prime Minister and the President have led to constitutional developments that attracted the attention of the European public in the summer of 2012 (though the roots of the conflict are probably much older). Many of the conflicts have concerned the widespread use of emergency ordinances or decrees instead of laws, which seems to be a general constitutional problem. The crisis grew deeper when a new law approved in late June 2012 allowed a simple majority of voters to approve Parliament's removal of the President (while the previous law required an absolute majority of the electorate). On 4 July 2012, the government approved an emergency decree that curbed the powers of the Constitutional Court,[66] barring it from ruling on parliamentary decisions and allowing it only a consultative role in impeachment proceedings. On 3 and 4 July, Parliament also dismissed the speakers of the Senate and Chamber of Deputies, both members of the opposition party PDL, and the country's ombudsman (the so-called 'Advocate of the People'), replacing them with members of the ruling coalition. All of these measures the Constitutional Court later considered to be unconstitutional.

Significantly, the President of the Senate is first in line to succeed the country's President, Mr Traian Băsescu, who was suspended from office by Parliament on 6 July. In other words, the conservative President was simply dismissed by the socialist government. Between this date, 6 July, and the referendum on the impeachment of President Băsescu on 29 July, having been given 24 hours to consider the question, the Constitutional Court rejected the law that would have allowed Băsescu to be removed from office with the vote of a simple majority of those who cast ballots in the national referendum. On 29 July 2012, about 80 per cent of the votes cast were in favour of impeachment, but the threshold of the majority of all voters was not reached. Consequently, and after a decision from the Supreme Court that was confirmed by the Constitutional Court, President Băsescu was reinstalled. Shortly afterwards, the Venice Commission was asked to

[66] Emergency Ordinance 38/2012 of 4 July 2012 amending Law no 47/1992 concerning the Organization and Functioning of the Constitutional Court (*Ordonanta* de urgenta nr 38/2012 pentru modificarea Legii nr 47/1992 privind organizarea si functionarea Curtii Constitutionale).

intervene; one of the reasons the Venice Commission sent a task force to Romania, in addition to general worries about the situation, was in fact a number of threats addressed to the judges of the Constitutional Court.

Reactions by the European Commission against these events were strong. In a statement published on 6 July 2012, the Commission expressed its concerns about current developments in Romania, especially regarding actions that appear to reduce the effective powers of independent institutions such as the Constitutional Court.[67] On 18 July, the Commission adopted a report under the so-called Cooperation and Verification Mechanism in which it expressed a requirement that Romania ensure respect for the rule of law and judicial independence in order to win back the trust of its partners in the EU. In the light of recent challenges to the rule of law and judicial independence, the Commission decided to adopt a further report under the Cooperation and Verification Mechanism before the end of 2012, in order to assess whether its concerns had been addressed and democratic checks and balances restored.[68] However, by the end of 2012 this report had not been published.

Also, the Venice Commission issued a new opinion, no 685/2012, which was adopted at the Commission's 93rd Plenary Session in Venice, 14–15 December 2012.[69] In this opinion, the Commission criticised all the controversial steps previously taken by the government and the Parliament, though with slightly different legal arguments. Concerning the use of governmental emergency ordinances, which had been used no less than 140 times in 2011, it was stated that the government seemed to use them in a way that actually circumvented the restrictions laid down in article 115 of the Romanian Constitution. Thus, the Parliament was told instead to make more use of the instrument of delegated legislation and empower the government to adopt urgent legislation whenever legislation has to be adopted quickly. As far as the 'attacks' on the Constitutional Court intended to curb its powers were concerned, it was established that the Court must also have the possibility to review internal acts (resolutions) of the Parliament, since these may also affect human rights such as the right to vote. Further emergency ordinances should never be adopted in the field of constitutional law, for example, concerning the Constitutional Court (a fact that is actually stated in the Constitution itself

[67] European Commission, Statement by the European Commission on Romania, www.europa.eu/rapid/pressReleasesAction.do?reference=MEMO/12/529&format=HTML&aged=0&language=EN&guiLanguage=en.

[68] European Commission, 'Romania: Urgent Action Needed to Demonstrate Commitment to Rule of Law and Judicial Independence', www.europa.eu/rapid/pressReleasesAction.do?reference=IP/12/799.

[69] European Commission for Democracy through Law (Venice Commission*), Opinion on the Compatibility with Constitutional Principles and the Rule of Law of Actions taken by the Government and the Parliament of Romania in respect of Other State Institutions and on the Government Emergency Ordinance on Amendment to Law no 47/1992 regarding the Organisation and Functioning of the Constitutional Court and on the Government Emergency Ordinance on Amending and Completing Law no 3/2000 regarding the Organisation of a Referendum of Romania* (Opinion No 685/2012, 17 December 2012).

in article 115 section 6). Furthermore, no urgency to undertake the measure taken here had been proven.[70]

The most controversial part of the opinion is probably the one that deals with the referendum on the dismissal or suspension of President Băsescu. Here, it was found that attempts had been made, through ordinances, to change the rules concerning the quorum required for adoption of a referendum after the referendum had been called, which was not acceptable. The Commission then stated that 'the use of government emergency ordinances to immediately bring into force a Law which is being examined by the Constitutional Court amounts to an abuse of the instrument of government emergency ordinances and is not in conformity with basic principles of correctness derived from the rule of law and the separation of powers'.[71] Also, the suspension of the President as such was illegal, but since the participation quorum had not been met, this was in the end less important. Nevertheless, the constitutional rule regulating those matters (article 95) should be made clearer, according to the Venice Commission.

Finally, the Commission also dealt with the dismissals of the ombudsman and the speakers of both Chambers of the Parliament. Here, it was found that the dismissal of the People's Advocate had strictly speaking not been unconstitutional as such, but this was mainly due to the fact that the mechanisms of protection for this institution were insufficient. Concerning the two speakers, the Constitutional Court came to the conclusion that it lacked competence to review these issues, which was mainly due to some of the emergency ordinances mentioned above. The Venice Commission then refrained from commenting further on this particular issue.

As mentioned above, one of the main reasons the Venice Commission went to Bucharest in the first place was the alleged threats and pressure against the judiciary, notably the Constitutional Court. Here, the Commission found that certain statements from public officials that showed disrespect for the Constitutional Court were unacceptable and stated, as a general remark, that '[t]he independence and neutrality of the Constitutional Court is at risk when other state institutions or their members attack it publicly'.[72] Similar remarks were made concerning attacks on prosecutors who had tried to investigate alleged corruption among government officials.

In total, the opinion is a clear and bold statement that makes it clear that the events that took place in Romania in the summer of 2012, initiated by the Romanian government, were not in line with a general and acceptable European standard of rule of law and democracy.

[70] ibid paras 84–87.
[71] ibid para 36.
[72] ibid para 64.

VI. EU RESPONSE TO OPINIONS FROM THE VENICE COMMISSION

As mentioned above, the European Commission finally brought a case against Hungary before the CJEU concerning the forced retirement of judges. This case was settled on 6 November 2012, when the CJEU found that the Hungarian rules violated EU Directive 2000/78,[73] which prohibits discrimination based on age.[74] Hungary has stated that it intends to comply with this judgment.

It should, however, be noted that the Court, as the Commission had done before, preferred to deal with this matter in a rather technical way, while avoiding more difficult and crucial issues concerning the rule of law and similar matters. Here, the Court was obviously not inspired by the previous opinion of the Venice Commission in October 2012,[75] in which clearer steps enabling dismissed judges to be reinstalled in their previous positions were requested. Furthermore, so far no votes have taken place in the European Council concerning possible legal actions based on Article 7 TEU. The EU thus seems to be waiting and watching what will happen in Hungary and Romania, before deciding how to act.

However, the history of the relations, contacts and discussions between Hungary and the EU institutions in 2011 and 2012 is complicated. Some of the contacts have concerned purely economic matters; in early 2012, as already mentioned, the European Commission decided to suspend certain economic commitments to Hungary (of no less than 495 million euros) from the EU Cohesion Fund from January 2013, due to Hungarian non-compliance with recommendations of the ECOFIN Council of 24 January 2012 on how to correct the allegedly excessive budget deficit. The decision referred to previous shortcomings and repeated failure to address the deficit. And later on, in October 2012, Hungary announced, after pressure from the Commission, that some highly controversial so-called 'crisis taxes' on the retail and telecommunications sectors were to be abolished as of January 2013 (while strongly denying that this was due to any kind of pressure from the EU).[76]

Needless to say, though, there have also been a number of important statements and opinions in the human rights area. For instance, on 12 February 2012, the European Parliament adopted a resolution on the recent political developments in Hungary.[77] This text is interesting for a number of reasons, including the fact that it explicitly referred to two opinions on Hungary from the Venice Commission (Opinions no 663/2012 and 621/2011). Expressing its worries regarding and condemning much of the recent developments in Hungary, and noting 'the commitment of the European Commission, the Council of Europe

[73] Council Directive 2000/78/EC establishing a general framework for equal treatment in employment and occupation [2000] OJ L303.

[74] Case C-286/12 *Commission v Hungary* (2012, nyr).

[75] Venice Commission Op 683/2012 (n 36) paras 77–80.

[76] See also pending Case C-462/12 (not yet decided).

[77] European Parliament, Resolution 2012/2511 on the recent political developments in Hungary.

and the Venice Commission thoroughly to examine the compliance of Hungarian legislation with not only the letter but also the spirit of European law', it calls on the European Commission to request the opinion of the Venice Commission, once again, on the whole legislative package consisting of the new Basic Law, Transitional Provisions and cardinal laws.

After a heated debate, the European Parliament adopted a resolution on the situation of fundamental rights in Hungary on 3 July 2013.[78] The resolution is very detailed, and deals with the recent changes in Hungary's constitutional system, among others in the field of extensive use of cardinal laws; accelerated legislative procedures; weakening of checks and balances by changes concerning the Constitutional Court and the Data Protection Authority; judicial independence; electoral reform; media legislation; rights of persons belonging to minorities; freedom of religion or belief; and recognition of churches.

The resolution, which makes several recommendations to the Hungarian authorities, echoes the recommendations of the Venice Commission's above-mentioned opinions on Hungary, especially the one on the Basic Law and the Fourth Amendment of the Basic Law.[79]

According to the European Parliament, the procedure is not only about Hungary but also about European fundamental values, therefore it called for a rethink of the European Union's Fundamental Rights Agency's role, suggesting that it could be used to monitor Member States' compliance with Article 2 TEU, and that there could be a 'Copenhagen Commission' to monitor compliance with these values and the Copenhagen Criteria before and after accession to the European Union.[80]

The resolution leaves open the possibility that it might try to trigger an Article 7 TEU sanction against Hungary, tasking the Parliament's Conference of Presidents with considering the move.[81]

VII. CONCLUSIONS

A general impression, as stated above, is that the influence and importance of the Venice Commission has grown significantly in the last five years, due to a number of reasons.[82] Its opinions not least on Hungary and Romania are now widely quoted, both by legal experts and in the general, public and political debate in a way that they seldom were before.

One of these reasons, undoubtedly, is the current constitutional crisis in Europe, of which the events in Hungary and Romania are perhaps the clearest

[78] European Parliament Resolution 2012/2130 on the situation of fundamental rights standards and practices in Hungary (pursuant to the European Parliament Resolution of 16 February 2012).

[79] Venice Commission Op 621/2011 (n 24); Venice Commission Op 720/2013 (n 29).

[80] European Parliament Resolution 2012/2130 (n 78) para 79.

[81] ibid para 87.

[82] For a perspective from 2001, compare with S Bartole, 'Final Remarks: The Role of the Venice Commission' (2000) 26 *Review of Central and East European Law* 351.

example. These events remind us of the importance of maintaining the 'European Constitutional Heritage', to borrow the title of a book that the Venice Commission published in 1996[83] (and an expression that is quite often used in more recent opinions from the Commission).[84] And quite clearly, precisely those values that we associate with such an expression are at the moment jeopardised in these same countries.

The question then, of course, is which role the Venice Commission may be expected to play in the near future. To a certain extent, this depends on how the European Commission, the European Council and other EU institutions will deal with Hungary, Romania and possibly also other troubled Member States in the next few years. If the EU continues its cautious policy of the last few years, hoping that the problems that we have recently seen will disappear, this influence is likely to be very limited. But on the other hand, if real legal, economic or political sanctions will be on the agenda, decisions from the EU are unlikely to be made without taking opinions of the Venice Commission into account, in much the same way that the somewhat misguided 'sanctions' against Austria in 2000 were lifted upon the advice of three so-called 'wise men'. Such decisions would mean something substantially new in the history of European contemporary politics and are thus unlikely to be made without strong support from leading legal expertise. Needless to say, the Venice Commission is not the only body or institution in Europe that possesses such expertise, but at the same time, its international and multinational composition, together with its official status as an integrated part of the Council of Europe, give it a prestige and weight that few other bodies in Europe may today claim.

Thus, the Venice Commission is a force to be reckoned with in the future, but its real influence will much depend on the depth and seriousness of the current constitutional crisis. The deeper it gets itself into trouble over rule of law-related issues in individual Member States, the more the EU will rely upon the Venice Commission in order to set things right. But the opposite is also true. Should the future of Europe be generally sunny, the Venice Commission may soon return to its early, peaceful existence.

[83] European Commission for Democracy through Law (Venice Commission), 'The Constitutional Heritage of Europe' (1996) 18 *Science and Technique of Democracy* 1.

[84] For instance in Venice Commission Op 685/2012 (n 69).

Theories of Limits of the Constitution-making Power

12

What Legitimises a National Constitution?

On the Importance of International Embedding

MATTHIAS HARTWIG

I. CONSTITUTIONAL LEGITIMACY: A NORMATIVE CONCEPT OR A DESCRIPTION OF THE EXERCISE OF POWER?

THE QUESTION OF legitimacy of constitutions has been ever present since political philosophy began to analyse what is a good government. Today, it is generally agreed that a good government needs to be legitimate.[1] But what does that mean? Is it that the government promotes good and avoids evil, as even modern thinkers up to John Stuart Mill declared.[2] However, the idea of a metaphysical definition of legitimacy was lost in major parts of constitutional scholarship in the late nineteenth century. The focus was shifted from intrinsic principles to a sociological depiction of what makes a constitution legitimate.[3] Legitimacy was not conceived as a result of values but as a description of relations. The constitutional scholarship of the twentieth century conceives of legitimacy as an expectation that a norm or an action is accepted. Carl Schmitt defined the concept in the *Verfassungslehre* of 1928. 'A constitution is legitimate not only as a factual condition. It is also recognized as a just order, when the power and authority of the constitution-making power, on whose decision it rests, is acknowledged'.[4] In this definition, all ethical questions are excluded; legitimacy is reduced to the corollary concepts of power and recognition. In this sense, Schmitt turns the classical discourse on legitimacy

[1] U Scheuner, 'Die Legitimitätsgrundlage des modernen Staates' (1981) 15 *Archiv für Rechts- und Sozialphilosophie* 1, 8.

[2] JS Mill, *On Representative Government* (London, Longmans, Green and Co, 1919) 7.

[3] It was the famous German sociologist Max Weber who derived legitimacy of power from three different sources, ie tradition, charisma and legality in a technical sense, prescinding from any tentative of a substantial evaluation. M Weber, *Wirtschaft und Gesellschaft: Grundriss der verstehenden Soziologie* (Köln, Kiepenheuer und Witsch, 1964) 157.

[4] C Schmitt, *Verfassungslehre* (Berlin, Duncker & Humblot, 1989) 87; for the English translation, see C Schmitt, *Constitutional Theory* (Durham, NC, Duke University Press, 2008).

upside down. A constitution is not recognised because it is legitimate, but it is legitimate because it is recognised, ie the constitution-making power must be recognised. Kelsen, commonly regarded as holding opposite opinions from Carl Schmitt, shares his approach of excluding all metaphysical references. To Kelsen, legality (Kelsen tries to avoid the concept of legitimacy) is constructed in a similar way as in Schmitt's analysis, the difference being that Kelsen derives legality from higher ranking norms, not from authorities and power. As the construction of justification is linear, there is an end of the chain of legitimacy, and it is exactly here where the famous *Grundnorm* is located. As a result the *Grundnorm* itself cannot be legitimated for lack of a superior norm. Here Kelsen meets Schmitt's thinking.

The understanding of legitimacy as a purely mechanical process without any content led to well known results. Schmitt's theoretical voluntarism has led him to support the National Socialist Government. Even after the Second World War, Kelsen wrote: 'Whatever content can be law'.[5] And he confessed that from his point of view the law of the Third Reich must be considered as legal, in as far as it had been developed within a coherent hierarchy of norms.[6] Why would the authorisation of power to make the constitution and the legal hierarchy be of such an importance if the content of the norms does not matter? Will not this approach result in a pure justification of power as a '*factum brutum*'?

Schmitt's sociological twist in the discussion on legitimacy and Kelsen's infinite regress, which only comes to an end with a *Grundnorm*, frustrate any meaningful discussion on the legitimacy of a constitution in a normative sense. Schmitt's approach will not help in shaping a constitution, as whether a constitution is legitimate can be decided only ex post, ie if the constitution is recognised, yet the constitution may lose its legitimacy at any time, when the recognition is withdrawn. Kelsen's concept allows us to set up whatever nature of constitution, with the constitution being considered to be derived from a fictive *Grundnorm*. Legitimacy in a normative sense requires other forms of justification. Another famous constitutional scholar of the early twentieth century declared this clearly. 'Only a judgment on the rightness of the established law may answer the question whether the State authority based on a legitimacy in a social sense only serves the normal legal certainty and maintains an unjust legal order for the sake of the order.'[7]

The following will not develop a theory of material legitimacy of a constitution, that would overstretch the frame of this contribution. More modestly, it will

[5] H Kelsen, *Reine Rechtslehre* (Vienna, Deuticke, 1960) 201.

[6] ibid 42: 'Nach dem Recht totalitärer Staaten ist die Regierung ermächtigt, Personen unerwünschter Gesinnung, Religion oder Rasse in Konzentrationslager zu sperren und zu beliebigen Arbeiten zu zwingen, ja zu töten. Solche Maßnahmen mag man moralisch auf das schärfste verurteilen; aber man kann sie nicht als außerhalb der Rechtsordnung dieser Staaten stehend ansehen' [According to the law of totalitarian States the government is authorised to jail persons having an undesirable conviction, religion or race in a concentration camp and to force them to whatever labour, even to kill them. One may condemn such measures very harshly from the moral point of view; but one cannot consider them as being outside the legal order of these States].

[7] H Heller, *Staatslehre* (Leiden, Mohr Siebeck, 1983) 334.

describe in what way constitutionalism today tries to establish the legitimacy of a constitution. Four main approaches to establish the legitimacy of a constitution will be looked at here. First, religion is one of the oldest sources of legitimacy of constitutions. It incapsulates values which are beyond the reach of men and therefore may grant a stable and recognised basis. Secondly, the will of the people supplements or replaces the reference to religion; the consent to the constitution means that the people has to respect what was agreed on. Thirdly, the pure will as a source of legitimacy of a constitution does not predetermine its content, therefore some substantive minimum requirements have been established which a constitution has to fulfil in order to be legitimate. Fourthly, certainly the most innovative form of establishing the legitimacy of a constitution lies in the orientation towards standards developed on the international level.

II. THE CONSTITUTION: SOURCE AND OBJECT OF LEGITIMACY

In modern times constitutions have become a source of legitimacy. Actions of state organs are qualified as legitimate if they are taken within the frame set up by the constitution. The constitution authorises the exercise of state power, it distributes the competences and establishes the limits of the exercise of power. The compatibility of actions with the constitution implies their legitimacy, whereby legitimacy and constitutional legality are tacitly identified.

Raising the question of legitimacy of the constitution shifts the perspective. The constitution is not the source, but the object, of legitimacy. Creating legitimacy does not mean having legitimacy. The question transcends the constitutional frame within which the legal discourse takes place. It cannot be answered inherently with reference to the constitution.

Legitimacy always implies a justification that an act or a norm is of such nature. The justification must be found beyond the act or the norm to be justified. Otherwise the legitimacy would end up in an ontological affirmation of the existing constitution or circular question-begging reasoning. The norm to be legitimised needs a legitimising reference, a ground from which legitimacy is derived. The legitimacy of a constitution may derive from various sources that, depending on historical, cultural and political circumstances, are of different importance. Legitimacy may be created, for instance, by references to extra-legal norms, by the application of a certain procedure for the adoption of the norms or with respect to certain standards that have been developed beyond the constitutional law.

III. SOURCES OF LEGITIMACY

A. Religion as a Source

When looking for a higher justification of the supreme secular norm, traditional constitution-makers somehow automatically ended up with religion. The constitutional provisions were said to be derived from divine commandments. This gives a quasi-religious aura to the state organs, specifically to the king: '*Wir Kaiser von Gottes Gnaden*—We king by grace of God'.

It corresponds with the line of this understanding that constitutions were not conceived as treaties between the king and his subjects but were imposed, as were the Charte constitutionnelle of France of 1814[8] or the Prussian Constitution of 1848[9] or the Italian Constitution of 1848, the Statuto Albertino.[10]

References to religion are not found only in past constitutions, but are also laid down in many current basic laws. The dependence of the constitution on religious values is sometimes declared by a provision requiring the compatibility of state law including constitutional law with the norms established by a religion. Article 3 of the Afghan Constitution or article 7 of the Iraqi Constitution require that the law of the land must be in line with the sacred religion of Islam. In this way the question is not whether religious commandments and practice are in line with the requirements of the constitution, but, on the contrary, whether the constitution is in line with the religious norms. A constitution that responds to the religious requirements has to be considered legitimate, because the religious norms are not subject to a secular review. In Saudi Arabia, the link between religion and the constitution is even more outspoken; article 1 reads: 'God's book and the *Sunnah* of His Prophet are its [ie the state's] constitution'. And further in article 7: 'Government in Saudi Arabia derives power from the Holy Koran and the Prophet's tradition'. The constitution is identical with the religion. In this understanding its legitimacy is beyond doubt.

The *invocatio dei* constitutes a more modest form of justification, while still being a reference to a superior power whose recognition may endow some legitimacy on the constitution. The German Constitution of 1949 starts with such an *invocatio dei*: 'Conscious of their responsibility before God and men'.[11] The

[8] The Preamble to the Charte constitutionnelle starts with the words: 'Louis, par la grâce de Dieu …' and it continues: 'La divine Providence, en nous rappelant dans nos États après une longue absence, nous a imposé de grandes obligations' ['Louis, by the grace of God king of France and Navarre, to all those to whom these presents come, salutation: Divine Providence, in recalling us to our estates after a long absence, has imposed grave responsibilities upon us.' Quoted from http://personal.ashland.edu/~jmoser1/constitutionalcharter.htm].

[9] The Preamble to the Constitution describes the source of the legitimacy: 'Wir Friedrich Wilhelm, von Gottes Gnaden, König von Preußen usw. usw. thun kund und fügen zu wissen: daß Wir … die nachfolgende Verfassungs-Urkunde zu erlassen beschlossen haben' [We, Frederick William, by grace of God, King of Prussia, etc, hereby declare and make known that … we have finally established the provisions of that constitution].

[10] In the Preamble to the Statuto Albertino: 'Perciò di Nostra certa scienza, Regia autorità, … abbiamo ordinato ed ordinamiamo in forza di Statuto Legge fondamentale' ['For this reason, by Our certain Royal authority, having had the opinion of Our Council, We have ordered and We do order with the force of Constitution and fundamental Law, perpetual and irrevocable from the Monarchy, that which follows' quoted from http://users.dickinson.edu/~rhyne/232/Four/Statuto.html].

[11] Similar provisions may be found in some of the Constitutions of the German federated states, see, eg the Preamble to the Constitution of Baden-Württemberg, Rhineland-Palatina, Saxony-Anhalt. The Preamble to the Bavarian Constitution declares that the disaster of the Third Reich was caused by a system deprived of God.

Preamble to the Irish Constitution reads: 'In the Name of the Most Holy Trinity, from Whom is all authority and to Whom, as our final end, all actions both of men and States must be referred'.

Religious values will convey legitimacy only insofar as they themselves are not disputed but generally recognised and accepted by the people. Otherwise they could provoke exactly the contrary effect, ie the delegitimation of the constitution. Proposals to incorporate an *invocatio dei* in the Treaty on the Constitution of the European Union were rejected because of the great variety of positions of the European states towards religion. Having lost its religious unanimity at the latest with the termination of socialism, Poland introduced a formula that would serve everybody: 'We, the Polish Nation—all citizens of the Republic, Both those who believe in God as the source of truth, justice, good and beauty, as well as those not sharing such faith but respecting those universal values as arising from other sources'.[12] This duality or ambiguity in the reference is repeated in another part of the Preamble: 'Recognising our responsibility before God or own consciences'. In this way, the language neutralises the reference to religion, whose value consists in the claim to universality, not in its capacity to accept the contrary.

In a pure form, religious legitimacy is hostile to constitutional reforms, God's will not being subject to human manipulations. In this way the stability of the system is significantly strengthened as long as this form of legitimacy is maintained. On the other hand, to the extent that the constitution receives a strong substantive justification by reference to religion, it is deprived of its role as supreme law of the land in as far as it incorporates religious values and contents.

B. Consent as Source: A Legitimacy by Procedure

The most common form of legitimising a constitution in modern times lies in the consent of the people. Consent is one of the constituting principles of law, as has been developing for a long time in private law. The binding force of a contract is not conceivable without consent. In the relationship between a king and his subjects, which is constructed as a hierarchy, there is no place for the idea of a treaty that presupposes equality of the partners. Only when the subjects of the king became subjects under law could the contractual idea, with all its legitimising force, be imported into public law. However, once the transformation from a monarchical system with a sort of hereditary legitimacy to a system that involved the people in the creation of legitimacy was accomplished, consent of the people became the most important source of the constitution. Constitutions not only establish this principle through provisions such as 'all power derives from the people', which can be found in many constitutions.[13] But constitutions found their

[12] A similar provision can be found in the Preamble to the Albanian Constitution.

[13] See, eg German Basic Law, art 20(2); French Constitution, art 3; Italian Constitution, art 1; Spanish Constitution, art 1(2).

own legitimacy on the will of the people.[14] The principle that it pronounces also forms its own basis. In this sense, democracy is not only a constitutional choice or a constitutionally established regime, but is a preconstitutional principle. The German Constitutional Court held in its famous decision on the Lisbon Treaty that when the transfer of powers by German state organs to the European Union reaches a point that the Federal Republic can no longer be qualified as a sovereign state for lack of powers, it could become necessary to obtain the consent of the people.[15] In its reasoning the Constitutional Court implied that loss of statehood has to be treated like a complete change of the constitutional system. The new legitimacy would have to be derived from the will of the people. The loss of statehood would take place beyond the constitutional order. Here, decisions which concern the constitutional fate of a state require a specific legitimacy through the direct participation of the people.

Almost all modern constitutions, even those strongly impacted by religion, derive their legitimacy through the consent of the people.[16] More often than not constitutions are adopted by way of a referendum, ie are adopted by way of special procedures by constitutional assemblies, a Parliament or the territorial entities of a composed state.[17] Today, an imposed constitution will never be considered as legitimate.[18]

Defining how the will of the people can be expressed is not easy. Rousseau sketched the concept of the *volonté générale*. This, however, remained abstract, in a way more defined than expressed and predetermined by the notion of the common interest, which does not always coincide with the expressed will of the people, as the people do not always recognise what is their common interest. The *volonté de tous* is a more concrete concept, which, however, still may not serve as an instrument to establish the will of the people as the source of legitimacy, for both a practical and a theoretical reason. The practical reason is evident, because unanimity in a political process can hardly be reached. The Polish-Lithuanian Commonwealth of the eighteenth century conveyed on every nobleman member of the Diet the *sejm*, a so-called *liberum veto*. This led to political deadlock and to the end of the Polish state, as it became impossible to take decisions under such circumstances. In a theoretical perspective, the requirement of unanimity or even of a qualified majority may result in a situation where the minority dominates the majority, as a small group can impose its will on the bigger group and impede the will of the majority from being transformed into a binding decision. Such a

[14] See the Preamble to the US Constitution: 'We the people of the United States … ordain and establish this Constitution of the United States of America'; the Preamble to the Spanish Constitution; and the Preamble to the German Basic Law.

[15] Bundesverfassungsgericht, 2 BvE 2/08 of 30 June 2009 para 263.

[16] An exception is the Constitution of Saudi Arabia, which was imposed and never subject to any form of the people's consent.

[17] The German Basic Law was adopted by the Diets of the *Länder*.

[18] See the Constitution of Bosnia-Hercegovina. See below p 319.

situation is certainly more distant from the concept of the will of the people than a simple majority system.

The constitutionalism of the nineteenth century in many cases vested a simple majority of the Parliament with the power to amend the Constitution, as in the case of the Italian Constitution of 1848, the Statuto Albertino[19] or even with slight modifications the Constitution of the German Empire of 1871[20] or the Constitution of the French Republic of 1875 demonstrate.[21] The legitimacy derived from a majority vote seemed to be sufficient, as the conflict at this time was not so much located between different parts of the population as between the monarch and the people. The Parliament was considered as the natural defender of the people's rights and interests, so specific protection of minorities did not seem to be necessary.[22] The Constitution did not enjoy a more specific protection than ordinary laws.

The idea that a simple majority creates sufficient legitimacy is still reflected in all systems where a constitutional amendment can be achieved by referendum, for more often than not a simple majority is qualified to adopt a constitutional reform.[23] The lower threshold, in comparison with the majority requirements of a constitutional convention or in Parliament when deciding on constitutional amendments, is justified by the more direct expression of the people's will. The logic behind this is that the more direct the people's participation, the stronger the legitimacy it creates.[24]

[19] The Statuto Albertino did not provide for an amendment procedure, however, in practice it was subsequently amended by ordinary laws, therefore, it was qualified as a 'costituzione flessibile'.

[20] German Constitution of 1871, art 78: 'Veränderungen der Verfassung erfolgen im Wege der Gesetzgebung. Sie gelten als abgelehnt, wenn sie im Bundesrat 14 Stimmen gegen sich haben'. Amendments are introduced by legislation (ie ordinary legislation). They are considered to be rejected, if they have in the Federal Council 14 votes against.

[21] Article VIII provided for an amendment by an absolute majority vote in the two Chambers of the Parliament and an absolute majority vote in the Assembly composed by the two Chambers.

[22] Conflicting interests in the society were considered by the electoral system, such as the famous *Drei-Klassen-Wahlrecht* of Prussia or by the structure of the legislative body as in the United Kingdom, where the nobility had a special representation in the House of Lords.

[23] See, eg France; in some countries at least 50 per cent of the voters must participate in the referendum, but as a rule the simple majority is sufficient. Article 76(1)(4) of the Weimarian Constitution required in case of a constitutional amendment by referendum a majority of all citizens. The rule for the adoption of the Russian Constitution of 1993 required the minimum participation of 50 per cent of the voters, and the project would be adopted if 50 per cent of the participants voted in favour of the project. See JF Aubert, 'Classification des referendums' (2007) 1:21 *Documents d'Études* 3, 6.

[24] It must also be taken into consideration that such referenda lead to very close results, eg the Spanish Constitution was adopted by a referendum in 1978, where 52 per cent of the citizens eligible for participation in the referendum voted in favour of the Constitution (participation 67 per cent, 88 per cent of them in favour), KP Sommermann, *Der Schutz der Grundrechte in Spanien nach der Verfassung von 1978* (Berlin, Duncker & Humblot, 1984) 87. The Russian Constitution of 1993 was adopted by 31 per cent of the citizens eligible for participation in the referendum (participation 54 per cent, in favour 58 per cent), VD Karpovic (ed), *Kommentarij k Konstitucii Rossijskoj Federacii, Moskau* (Izdat Beek, 2002) 948.

Consent is reached in different ways, either through elected representative organs such as a Parliament or a constitutional assembly or, as just mentioned, by a referendum of the people.

The will of the people in this sense is equivalent to the will of the majority. States with a federal structure sometimes have a more difficult amendment procedure, as for instance in the United States,[25] Australia[26] or Russia.[27] Here, the notion of majority does not refer only to the whole population but also to the populations of each composing entity. A federal system also gains legitimacy through the consent of the federated parts. In this way, democratic legitimacy by the consent of the people as a whole is supplemented by the consent of the composing parts.

Establishment of the will of the people as the basis of the constitution entails far-reaching consequences. First, it replaces other sources of legitimacy. The will of God and the will of the people cannot compete with each other. Even if the reference to God is upheld in the constitution, the will of the people will become the prevailing principle of legitimacy. When amending a constitution or adopting a new constitution, the people may set aside God,[28] whereas God in a positivistic legal environment cannot set aside the will of the people.

Secondly, if the constitution is based on the will of the people it can be changed by the will of the people. Norm-making, including constitution-making, comes under the dominance of the people. As the will of the people changes more quickly than the truth of religion, constitutional amendments become much easier. Legitimacy is at the disposal of the people as it depends only on their will.

Thirdly, the procedural character of legitimacy is the most important change stemming from the will of the people as the basis of legitimacy. Free will by definition having no substantial predetermination, it is a carrier of whatever nature of content. Neither value nor truth but only numbers matter. A constitution is legitimate in as far as the majority consented to it. The purely procedural character of justification simplifies the affirmation of legitimacy, as it is easier to count numbers than to affirm what is right in a substantial sense.

As there is no need for substantive legitimacy, any outcome of a decision can be legitimised in as far as it can be perceived as an expression of the will of the people. A purely formal approach towards legitimacy contains even the possibility of introducing constitutional norms that authorise an undemocratic government, ie to base further decisions on something other than on the principle of consent. This is the product of the democratic paradox. This is not a purely academic question. The famous 'Ermächtigungsgesetz' of 1933 in Germany, which was adopted

[25] See art V of the US Constitution which requires the ratification of an amendment by the legislature of three-quarters of the states or by conventions in three-quarters thereof.

[26] An amendment project must be submitted to the electors of each state and territory according to s 128 of the Commonwealth of Australia Constitutional Act 1900.

[27] Constitution of the Russian Federation, art 136.

[28] Therefore, any reference to God may be struck out from the constitution.

by a parliamentarian majority,[29] empowered in a democratic way the exercise of undemocratic powers by suspending important parts of the Constitution relating to the separation of powers.

The people's will is the strongest and nowadays an indispensable source of legitimacy; almost all constitutions are based on this form of legitimacy. Where such a consent is missing, the constitution may lose its legitimacy. A striking example is the Constitution of Bosnia-Herzegovina, which was never really accepted. Although part of a treaty signed by representatives of the three ethnicities of the country, it never received a real legitimacy from the people. The treaty was in a certain sense imposed, and never ratified by the respective Parliaments, let alone by way of a referendum. It is telling that the Constitution of Bosnia-Herzegovina remained a document in a foreign language, never officially translated into the three state languages.

Even if a constitution is not immune against change—and it would indeed be strange if a constitution adopted by consent could not be changed by consent—the higher obstacles to an amendment in comparison with the amendment of ordinary laws shows that a specific importance is attached to the constitutional provisions. It serves to stabilise the political system, by exempting the most important legislation that lays the ground for the state from an ordinary amendment. This is the functional aspect of the heightened amending procedure. Moreover, it becomes clear that the more important certain norms are for a political system the more comprehensive the consent must be, ie the more qualified the legitimacy by consent. It also means that a minority may block an amendment, maintaining the existing order, which as a result gains a certain protection against change. The protection against an easily approved change does not create legitimacy, but is the result of the higher legitimacy vested in these norms. However, all norms that are created by the application of the amendment procedure will enjoy a higher form of legitimacy as they are based on a broader consent.

C. Substantive Elements of Legitimacy

(i) Legitimacy ex Negativo: *Historical Experience as Legitimacy*

Constitutions are very often answers to a historical change in a political system, for instance after the end of a war, a revolution or the end of a dictatorship. This is reflected in those Preambles which express the rejection of the previous situation, thereby justifying the new legal order. Certainly, fundamental rights and freedoms have a justification of their own. However, put in the perspective of a historical experience these values gain a specific weight. A norm has a specific importance and legitimacy when it protects values that have been violated in the

[29] There is still some discussion about the constitutionality of the Ermächtigungsgesetz, as it was voted only after the communist deputies had been excluded from Parliament.

past. Freedom and equality became so prominent after the French revolution not only for their intrinsic values, but because of the 'systemic' violation of these principles in the preceding monarchical society, which by definition could not admit equality. The principle of territorial integrity is emphasised in constitutions of states that have undergone periods of occupation and foreign rule. Other examples of constitutional approaches generated by history include the specific sensitivity of Germany with regard to fundamental rights that had not always met with sympathy of the international community[30] or Germany's restriction of the executive power with respect to regulatory power or the use of armed forces abroad. In all these cases bad experiences with other norms serve as justification for the existing constitutional legislation. It facilitates the argumentation by hinting at the negative example. However, in the long run and especially in light of the vanishing influence of the past on the ongoing constitutional discourse, a purely history-bound derivation of legitimacy will not suffice.[31]

(ii) Systematic Identification of the Substantive Elements

The democratic paradox[32] could not only result in a situation that is not in line with democratic principles, but, moreover, means that the principle of consent loses its legitimising force if it could be set aside by consent. A principle that carries in itself the possibility of self-destruction cannot create a sustainable legitimacy. The legitimising power must survive the legitimising act.

These considerations, apart from historical experience, indicate the necessity of a substantive legitimacy. Legitimacy cannot be limited to a formal aspect, but rather must live up to minimal substantive criteria, such that the procedural mechanism of legitimacy obtains a substantive value. This idea, by the way, is not completely new. Article 16 of the French Declaration on Human Rights already established: 'A society in which human rights are not guaranteed nor the sphere of powers delineated lacks a constitution'. In his essay about the permanent peace Kant posited that a republican constitution presupposes human rights and equality before the law.[33] However, the concept of a firm guarantee of constitutional values that must be an indispensable part of a constitution originally was not transformed into positivistic law. This idea lost its significance with the stern belief of the nineteenth century in the effective guarantee of human rights by a democratic regime. The famous French declaration of Human and Civic Rights

[30] One has only to mention the criticism of the Constitutional Court decisions in which it declared its willingness to defend the fundamental rights also against infringements by the European Union, see, eg decisions of the German Constitutional Court: BVerfGE 37, 271 of 29 May 1974, BVerfGE 73, 339 of 22 October 1986 (so called *Solange-Entscheidungen*); BVerfGE 89, 155 of 19 November 2013 (*Maastricht-Entscheidung*); 2 BvE 2/08 of 30 June2009 ('Lisbon decision').

[31] It would even be ironical if, eg, Hitler were the supreme explanation of the so-being of the German Constitution.

[32] See above.

[33] E Kant, *Zum ewigen Frieden: Sämtliche Werke* (Berlin, Vorländer, 1922) 126.

of 1789 became operational only in 1971[34] and the German Constitution of 1871 did not encompass a Bill of Rights,[35] which were implemented only on the level of ordinary law. It was beyond imagination that the great achievement of a democratic rule could be used for its own abolition. The necessity of specifically protected principles was rediscovered with the possibility of an anti-democratic exercise of democratic powers.

A legitimate constitution must contain guarantees of the conditions on which it is founded. It must not only be based on the consent of the people, but it must also undertake the obligation that the free will of the people can be exercised in the future. Democracy shall not encompass a right to commit a democratic suicide. There must be a safeguard, because democracy implies the possibility of a change of the government. The free competition in an electoral campaign that forms an essential part of the democracy would lose its character if there were a risk that the election could be the last, ie if the party in power could amend the constitution in such a way that elections would not take place in the future. An open-ended political struggle is the core of democracy, so that each victory lasts only a legislative period. The possibility to perpetuate the victory would mark an end to democratic change.[36]

The rule of law (corresponding in the continental European terminology with the state of law) is the second substantive element of a legitimate state. It implies the binding force of the legal norms for all state organs. This is already an inherent element of a constitutional system. It would be contradictory if the constitution established legal rules and permitted disrespect of these rules. The state of law also implies a judiciary, because the legal provisions would remain paper law if there were no organs established for enforcement of the rules. The judicial organs must be independent, because otherwise they could not fulfil their function.[37] In this sense the separation of powers forms part of the state of law concept, and constitutes the legitimacy of the constitution.

Thirdly, the constitution derives its legitimacy from the Bill of Rights. Almost all of today's constitutions (with some famous exceptions such as Great Britain or Australia) contain a Bill of Rights, this being considered as constituting a guarantee to protect individuals in their private spheres against infringements by the state. The free and independent citizen is a 'prerequisite' of a democratic order, based on the free will of the citizens. Sometimes the state's supreme purpose is

[34] Conseil Constitutionnel, Decision no 71–44 of 16 July 1971.

[35] However, this is also due to the fact that the fundamental rights were protected by most of the constitutions of the composing Länder, ie territorial entities.

[36] It is therefore strange that even democracies allow the amendment of the electoral law by a simple majority for the next elections. Electoral results depend not only on the majorities in a social sense, but also the way in which these majorities are transformed into parliamentarian representation by the electoral law are of utmost importance. Therefore, it seems somehow strange that the actual parliamentarian majority may change the electoral law in its favour, thereby facilitating the perpetuation of the actual exercise of power (Italy, Germany).

[37] See the comprehensive study by A Seibert-Fohr (ed), *Judicial Independence in Transition* (Berlin, Springer, 2012).

identified as the protection of its citizens.[38] The fundamental rights draw the line that must not be trespassed by the state except under certain conditions. The core of fundamental rights, such as human dignity, right to life, freedom of speech and equality, are prerequisites for the conceptualisation of a real citizen who is a necessary element of a democratic state and the object of its protection.

(iii) Delegitimation by the Dismantlement of Legitimising Elements

Even if specific institutions are not indispensable for a legitimate constitution, the abolition of existing guarantees that serve as specific controls over state power could mean a creeping delegitimation of the constitution. There are states without a constitutional Bill of Rights, as the above-mentioned United Kingdom or Australia. Nobody would doubt that the Constitutions of both countries are legitimate, as they guarantee fundamental rights in other ways. A constitutional court empowered to receive individual constitutional complaints is not indispensable for a state in order to qualify its constitutional regime as legitimate. Although the number of constitutional judiciaries that provide for such an individual constitutional complaint is increasing, this process cannot be considered as a necessary part of legitimacy. However, if a state, having once introduced such a remedy then abolished it, it would have to give a specific explanation. Of course, constitutional amendments are not prohibited, and in as far as they remain in the frame of what is indispensable, they may be undertaken. Existing institutions that have the objective to strengthen the protection of the individuals or to control the exercise of the state power contribute to the legitimacy of the constitution even if they cannot be considered indispensable elements of that legitimacy. Their integration into the constitutional system means that they are legitimate. A regression or deterioration of a standard that once has been reached may not proceed without proper justification. Even if the constitution could still be considered to be legitimate after such an amendment, the amending act in as far as it is not justified would lack legitimacy.

(iv) Immunisation Against Change

The substantive guarantees constituting the legitimacy of a constitution, meanwhile, have gained such an importance that they not only must become part of the constitution, but have somehow obtained immunity against change. The German Constitution delivers an extreme example, excluding any amendment to structural principles of the Constitution such as the guarantee of democracy, the rule

[38] The original proposal of art 1 of the draft of the Constitution of the Federal Republic of Germany in 1949 was: 'The State exists for the well-being of the people, and not the people for the well-being of the State'. However, as far as the protection by the fundamental rights is conceived as a protection against the state, this norm does not make sense, as the supreme objective of a state cannot be the limitation of its powers; the supreme objective of a watchdog is not to carry a muzzle.

of law or the guarantee of human dignity.[39] The Czech Constitution also forbids change of a basic attribute of the democratic law-observing state.[40] In France, the form of the republic will not be subject to an amendment,[41] while in Russia the Constitution requires the convocation of a constituent assembly for reform of the basic principles and fundamental rights.[42] This implies that a change of these principles cannot be carried out within the confines of the existing constitution but rather leads to a completely new constitution. The Ukrainian Constitution prohibits any constitutional amendment that eliminates or restricts fundamental rights or aims at abolition of independence or territorial integrity.[43] The Spanish Constitution provides that the amendment of the fundamental principles or the human rights Bill requires a specific procedure, including adoption by two succeeding Parliaments and a referendum.[44] An analysis of the constitutional provisions shows that two types of matters are protected against constitutional amendments. The first constitutes a specific form of government, the republican form, or territorial integrity, which results from political events of a certain importance. A historical achievement must constitutionally be protected. Basic principles of a democratic and social state of law and core elements (or even the entirety of) fundamental rights constitute the second type of values not subject to constitutional revision. The absolute protection of these principles expresses the conviction that there is no constitution without these elements. The *pouvoir constituant constitué* does not extend to these principles.

The fixation of such non-revisable norms in the constitution supplements it with a content that is somehow beyond the constitution, because it is not subject to the constitutional amendment procedure and, further, all constitutional amendments must be in line with these non-revisable principles. In this sense, the constitutional legitimacy of constitutional norms is derived from these non-revisable norms. The constitution must live up to norms that form part of it. The constitution is not only the object of the legitimacy, but also its source.

(v) Functionality as Source of Legitimacy

Legitimacy may be derived from higher values of sacral or secular nature, or it may be founded on the procedures by which it is adopted. However, a constitution will be legitimate only insofar as it is shaped in such a way that it fulfils its function. A constitutional instrument that misses this goal will never be able to prove its own legitimacy. The functionality is part of its output legitimacy, ie the legitimacy created by the results that flow from the constitution.

[39] German Basic Law, art 79(3).
[40] Czech Constitution, art 9(2).
[41] French Constitution, art 89(5).
[42] Russian Constitution, art 135.
[43] Ukrainian Constitution, art 157.
[44] Spanish Constitution, art 168.

Dealing with all matters that are relevant for the exercise of power is a prerequisite of the functionality of a constitution. This embraces specifically the distribution of powers among the relevant state organs, the distribution of powers between the federation and the composing territorial entities in a federal state, and the relation between the citizens and the state.

However, it is not sufficient to deal with the relevant topics concerning the exercise of power, for beyond this the legitimacy of a constitution grows with each success in finding good solutions that contribute to the stability of a political regime. For example, the famous constructive vote of no confidence that was introduced into the German Basic Law in 1949 was a response to the instability of the governments during the Weimar period, and it safeguards the stability of the government.[45] Establishment of a constitutional jurisdiction providing for judicial control of the respect and application of the constitution will raise the juridical force of the constitution by providing a further guarantor. The direct applicability and supremacy of the constitution are implemented if the judiciary has the power to control it. Multiple experiences of constitutional jurisdiction have proven that constitutional jurisdiction contributes substantially to the stability of a political system by its decisions, which are to be recognised by all participants in a political conflict. Whether a specialised constitutional court or ordinary courts will be better for this task is a question of expediency.

The expediency of a given constitutional solution may depend on the political circumstances and the sociological background, history and culture of a country. Whether a state is better constituted as a monarchy or as a presidential system cannot be answered in a purely legal frame. More than 1,000 years of monarchy (with a very short interruption) give a legitimacy of its own to the British monarchy, whereas the conversion of the US presidential system into a monarchy would lack such historical and sociological support. A 5 per cent clause that establishes an obstacle to entering Parliament to parties that do not get more than 5 per cent of the vote may serve the stability of the system. However, in a country where a large proportion of the population vote for parties that do not overcome the 5 per cent barrier, the provision could endanger the democratic principle.

IV. INTERNATIONAL STANDARDS AS CRITERIA OF LEGITIMACY: STANDARDISATION OF CONSTITUTIONS

In recent times, the question is raised more and more often whether basic principles of constitutions have become universal such that a national constitution can be legitimate only if it lives up to these standards. The point of reference is not the internal will of the people. These criteria may be found in two different sources,

[45] The constructive vote of no confidence, art 67 of the Basic Law, requires the election of a new Chancellor in order to topple the actual government; therefore it is not sufficient to be in opposition against the government, but there must be a majority in favour of a new one.

on the one hand, in international law, and on the other hand, in a comparative constitutional law approach.

It has to be taken into consideration that the principles that would legitimise a constitution are very generic. They do not reflect all different characters of these concepts as they have developed in national law. It has been pointed out, for instance, that the British rule of law concept is not identical with the state of law principle as laid down in many continental European Constitutions.[46] The concept of the presidential democracy of the United States differs quite obviously from the parliamentarian democracy of the British type, and even with respect to human rights there is not full conformity among the various catalogues; one must only remember the different approaches to abortion.[47] However, notwithstanding all the differences that can be found in the implementation of these concepts, they share a common denominator. Democracy means that the exercise of state power is based on the will of the people; the people must have the possibility to express their will in periodic free elections. According to the rule of law, the state organs must be subject to legal norms that define and limit their power. Human rights contain guarantees for the protection of the private sphere of individuals. Although these explanations over-simplify the content they make it possible to describe common values in an increasing number of constitutions and in international documents. Insofar as national constitutions refer to these concepts as they might be found by way of a comparative constitutional law approach or with reference to international documents, they refer to the common denominator inherent in the different concretisations.

A. International Law as Source of Legitimacy

The classical international law deals with the relation between states, excluding all questions regarding internal affairs from its field of competence.[48] The internal structure of a state, including the choice of the political regime, is left to the state and its people. On an international level, there are no norms about a state of law or democracy that establish requirements for the internal structure of a state. However, in the last decades the position of international law has changed, and more and more problems of internal law have been dealt with by international law. The UN Security Council considers grave violations of human rights

[46] H Hofmann, 'Geschichtlichkeit und Universalitätsanspruch des Rechtsstaats' (1995) 34 *Der Staat* 1; U Meyer, 'Idealität, Interessen, Ignoranz: Zur schwierigen Gemengelage der internationalen Rechtsstaatsförderung' (2012) 51 *Der Staat* 35.

[47] Even within Europe there is no unanimity on this point. The CJEU did not apply the protection of life according to Art 2 of the European Convention on Human Rights to the '*nasciturus*', as the Member States have too many different positions, *Vo v France,* Application no 53924/00 (ECtHR, 8 July 2004) paras 82, 84.

[48] Article 2(7) of the UN Charter lays this principle down with respect to the competencies of the United Nations.

as a threat to peace in the sense of Article 39 of the UN Charter, and it qualified unconstitutional manners of seizing power in a few cases in the same way.[49] This development shows that the concept of internal affairs has undergone a change; it is interpreted today in a more restrictive sense. Meanwhile, international law does not react only to violations of basic principles of human rights, but is establishing standards with regard to principles that are considered cornerstones of modern constitutions, ie in the realm of human rights, the democratic principle and the rule of law.

In some international organisations, the national political system has to fulfil some substantive prerequisites in order to make a state eligible for membership in the organisation. The Treaty on European Union (TEU) obliges its Member States to respect human dignity, freedom, democracy, equality, the rule of law and human rights (Articles 2, 7), presupposing that these values have a universal character and no constitution may deviate from these.

Human rights nowadays receive a specific form of protection in international law, both on a universal level and on a regional level. The international human rights instruments not only list substantive human rights but, further, they provide for mechanisms for the implementation of these rights, thereby not only establishing points of orientation but also binding legal norms subject to application by national authorities and courts. Not only ordinary law, but also constitutional provisions have to comply with the requirements of international human rights instruments. In as far as the international norm is considered to be on a higher hierarchical level, national legislation in line with this norm will receive legitimacy.

Democracy is referred to in the human rights instruments that guarantee via electoral rights the participation of citizens in the exercise of state power.[50] Regional organisations such as the Council of Europe try to enhance democracy by strengthening the rule of law.[51] Disrespect of this principle can be sanctioned in international relations, for instance, by cutting off economic support for a country.[52] Some international organisations require their members to respect their own constitutions, that is, implicitly the principles of democracy and the rule of law, and provide for the suspension of membership rights if member states do not respect these rights.[53] The European Union makes respect for the principles of democracy, the state of law and protection of human rights a prerequisite for membership; if a Member State violates these rules a sophisticated

[49] See, eg UN Security Council Resolutions S/RES/917 (Haiti); S/RES/1962 (Ivory Coast); S/RES/2085 (Mali).

[50] Covenant on Civil and Political Rights, Art 25(b); First Additional Protocol to the European Convention on Human Rights, Art 3; American Convention on Human Rights, Art 23(b).

[51] See the Democracy through Law programme implemented by the Venice Commission.

[52] See F Hoffmeister, *Menschenrechts- und Demokratieklauseln in den vertraglichen Außenbeziehungen der Europäischen Gemeinschaft* (Berlin, Springer, 1998) 452.

[53] See, eg Charter of the African Union, Art 30 or the reaction of the ECOWAS to the coup d'état in Mali in March 2012.

system of sanctions can be initiated.[54] Scholars have concluded from an analysis of developments in this area that a 'right to a democratic government' is emerging.[55] Even if it is not yet established as a binding norm, it is clear that international law treats it as a positive concept that at least serves as a point of orientation, and even if a state is not directly bound to grant a right to a democratic government, it has to take steps towards this.

The rule of law also has come into the focus of the international community. The Council of Europe established the Venice Commission, which is dedicated to promoting democratic development through law. The United Nations began to promote the rule of law by the establishment of a Rule of Law Unit in 2006, which will enhance the rule of law in the Member States, thereby identifying the rule of law as a core value of the United Nations.[56] The UN General Assembly expressed full support for the Rule of Law Unit.[57] The Unit does not establish binding norms that if respected would grant legitimacy, however it proves that the rule of law is an internationally recognised principle.

National constitutions refer to these international documents in different ways. Some constitutions incorporate international human rights documents into the constitution itself.[58] Other constitutions require that the fundamental rights as laid down in the constitution be interpreted in conformity with the international human rights instruments ratified by the respective state.[59] Such references to international instruments borrow some legitimacy from the international realm for the constitution, relying on the consensus of the international community as to the validity of the respective norms.

B. Comparative Law Approach

The second way to create legitimacy is through a comparative approach. If certain constitutional guarantees or principles are common to a great number of states that are beyond doubt with regard to the legitimacy of their regimes, orientation with these examples will add to the legitimacy of other regimes. Thereby, foreign legal orders become criteria for the application of constitutional law, which implies

[54] See Art 7 and Art 2 TEU [2012] OJ C326.

[55] See TM Franck, 'The Emerging Right to Democratic Governance' (1992) 86 *American Journal of International Law* 46; GH Fox, 'The Right to Political Participation in International Law' (1992) 17 *Yale Journal of International Law* 539.

[56] See www.unrol.org/article.aspx?article_id=7.

[57] UN General Assembly Resolutions A/RES/63/128; A/RES/64/116; A/RES/65/32, A/RES/66/102.

[58] Eg, the European Convention on Human Rights forms part of the Austrian Constitution. In the Constitution of Bosnia-Hercegovina, which is closely linked to the Dayton Agreements of 1995, the fundamental rights set forth in the European Convention on Human Rights apply directly and have priority over all other law (art II(2)). Article 17(1) of the Russian Constitution protects the fundamental rights according to generally recognised principles and norms of international law, art 5(2) of the Chilean Constitution likewise.

[59] See, eg Spanish Constitution, art 10(2).

that these provisions may transfer some legitimacy. Norms that are laid down in many constitutions are qualified as indispensable for a constitutional basis. They do not result from a particular national will but seem to be shared values of a great part of the states. The frequency of their existence in constitutional documents attaches to them a sort of universal character. Thereby, they become ontological prerequisites of states and implicitly are seen as part of all constitutional foundations of states. The comparative constitutional law approach becomes more and more common in the constitutional jurisprudence of constitutional courts, thereby recognising that norms of other legal orders and their interpretation may help to interpret that court's own legal order. Article 39 of the Constitution of South Africa expressly allows for such an approach. An analysis of constitutional jurisprudence shows that the constitution is more and more construed with reference to the case law of other constitutional courts. Specifically, constitutional courts of so-called new democracies that still are looking for legitimacy quote the decisions of other constitutional courts in similar matters.[60] In as far as the country's own constitution can be interpreted in the same manner as the constitutions of recognised democratic states of law, it participates in their legitimacy.

An analysis of the recent constitutional history in Europe shows a sort of standardisation of basic constitutional principles. A Bill of Rights forms part of all constitutions. Even within the European Union the argument that the Charter of Fundamental Rights should be binding was raised in the context of the then ongoing constitutionalisation process. The discussion implied that there could be no constitution without a guarantee of fundamental rights. All new constitutions in the former socialist countries contain a catalogue of fundamental rights with all the classical fundamental rights and sometimes extending beyond these to social rights and recently developed constitutional rights, such as the right to a healthy environment.

Likewise, all incorporated the notions of democracy, the social welfare state and the state of law. A constitution without these elements would be considered to be deficient in the international community.

V. CONCLUSION

The question of what creates legitimacy of a constitution does not find an easy answer. The times when it can be derived from a single source, be it God, the will of the people or fundamental principles, are over. Legitimacy has various roots. It is of an eclectic nature and not all of its characteristics are in harmony with each other. Specifically, the more the substantive preconditions for the legitimacy of a constitution are established, the less a margin remains for the free

[60] See, eg the decision of the Constitutional Chamber of the Supreme Court of Estonia on the European Stabilization Mecanism (Constitutional Judgment no 3-4-1-6-12 of 12 July 2012), where it indirectly refers to the respective decisions of the German Constitutional Court.

will of the people; the bigger the bunch of universally predetermined values, the fewer flowers will be left for the field where national consent farms its form of legitimacy.

The reference to international law, as well as the comparative constitutional law approach, in a way combines both methods. Both international law and comparative constitutional law offer a substantive form of legitimacy, but it is based on principles that are commonly shared either by the international community or by a majority of states. Thereby, an element of voluntarism comes into play, in the case of international law by the will of the states that participate in the establishment of standards relevant to national constitutions in international law, for example, by concluding treaties on human rights, or by the sum of the people's will expressed in many states. In this way legitimacy remains in a positivistic frame. It does not originate in supra-legal principles but in law that is set within other legal orders.

The problem with this approach is that the principles that can be found either in international law or by a comparative approach are of a general character, in a way the least common denominator. The democratic principle requires, for example, 'genuine periodic elections which shall be by universal and equal suffrage and shall be held by secret ballot, guaranteeing the free expression of the will of the electors'.[61] However, it does not predetermine the form of elections, be they proportional or majoritarian ('first past the post'). The rule of law principle does not precisely predetermine the extent of legislative power of the executive.[62] In as far as national tribunals take foreign constitutional orders into consideration when construing the constitution, they may pick and choose the foreign rule that gives support to the result that the tribunal wishes. This may lead to a certain degree of arbitrariness, as a valid methodology of the use of comparative constitutional law has not yet developed.

This does not mean that the reference to international law is unsuitable for finding legitimacy, but this approach still has to be further developed. In the end it may reflect that states are embedded in the international community. Even if the sovereign will of the states plays a role in forming international and transnational standards, as shown above, legitimacy no longer derives exclusively from the will of a single people biased by political struggles and historical contingency. It is not sovereignty, in the sense of a *suprema potestas*, that expresses the supreme will, but values that are shared over time and beyond national borders.

The question of what legitimises a constitution does not always attract much attention. In as far as the constitution and the political order that it establishes work, this question is left to philosophers of law. Constitutional lawyers focus on the constitutional case law taking legitimacy tacitly for granted. Certainly, the

[61] Covenant on Civil and Political Rights, Art 25.

[62] Whereas in Germany the executive needs an express authorisation by Parliament for the exercise of legislative power (Basic Law, art 80), the French Parliament has legislative power only where the Constitution conveys it, otherwise the government may adopt regulations.

success of a political system does not create legitimacy in a philosophical or legal sense. But it makes us forget about this problem. The German writings about the legitimacy of the constitution during the period of stability in the Federal Republic of Germany seem quite boring compared to the highly exciting essays on the same topic written during the Weimar Republic. In times like ours, when we witness globalisation, economic crises and transition in the form of regional integration, the coordinates of the existing system are dramatically moved to new positions and we lose the traditional certainties. Thus, the question of legitimacy of a constitution is newly raised. In such periods, one should be aware of the importance of the question of legitimacy, but—above all—one should take care to know where the right answer may be found.

13

Convention Rights as Minimum Constitutional Guarantees?

The Conflict between Domestic Constitutional Law and the European Convention on Human Rights

TILMANN ALTWICKER*

I. CONSTITUTIONAL LAW AS AN INTERNATIONAL CONCERN

CONSTITUTIONS AND CONSTITUTIONAL law are not immune to international criticism. Recently, this became obvious when the international community criticised in harsh words the new Hungarian Basic Law that entered into force in 2012.[1] International criticism concerning constitutions is a new phenomenon and it certainly needs justification. A democratic constitution can be conceptualised as being endowed with the highest level of legitimacy possible for a domestic legal norm.[2] To challenge a constitution by reference to international law is a demanding task. It relies on assumptions concerning the nature and functioning of international law that cannot easily be made.

Constitutional law has become an international concern.[3] It is clear that matters of constitutional law do not per se belong to the *domaine reservé*. From a

* The author wishes to thank Anne Peters, Johan Rochel and Pál Sonnevend for helpful comments on an earlier version. Any errors are the author's alone.

[1] See European Commission for Democracy through Law (Venice Commission), *Opinion on the New Constitution of Hungary* (Opinion No 621/2011, 20 June 2011); European Commission, Statement of the European Commission on the Situation in Hungary on 11 January 2012, available at www.europa.eu/rapid/press-release_MEMO-12-9_en.htm.

[2] JE Fossum and AJ Menéndez, *The Constitution's Gift: A Constitutional Theory for a Democratic European Union* (Lanham, Rowman & Littlefield, 2011) 26.

[3] See D Thürer, 'Vom paradigmatischen Einfluss des Völkerrechts auf das Staatsrecht' in K Weber and N Wimmer (eds), *Vom Verfassungsstaat am Scheideweg, Festschrift für Peter Pernthaler* (Vienna, Springer, 2005) 387, arguing that the influence of the international community on 'constitutional engineering' processes in states is a novel phenomenon.

purely legalistic perspective, arguing that international law is relevant to domestic constitutional law is, therefore, not surprising. Certainly, the label 'constitutional law' does not immunise domestic rules against international legal criticism. States have to comply with their international legal obligations no matter what status a rule assumes in the domestic hierarchy of norms.[4] While from the perspective of international law constitutional law as such was never immune from international legal criticism, it was nevertheless left untouched for a long time.

The preoccupation of international law with constitutional law is a recent phenomenon. Two developments are primarily responsible for turning constitutional law into an international concern. First, international law has become more ambitious. As Christian Tomuschat has argued, the international legal order today is not only an international order of cooperation, but it also provides a 'comprehensive blueprint for social life'.[5] International law is increasingly relevant for the 'interior design' of states. This new ambition of international law has led to an increasing overlap regarding the content of domestic constitutional norms and international norms.[6] There is an increasing number of 'mirror' norms on the international level regarding fundamental rights, as well as 'mirror' norms that pertain to standards of democracy and to the rule of law.[7] There is a second development that has accelerated the development of constitutional law into an international concern. For almost a decade now, we have witnessed a marked new self-assuredness of parts of the international judiciary.[8] Some international human rights courts, most notably the European Court of Human Rights (ECtHR), have in recent years embarked on a more assertive path towards the contracting states. It is no wonder, then, that constitutional law and design are also gaining more attention from the international judiciary.

There are different ways to operationalise the new preoccupation of international law with constitutional law. For example, international expert groups such as the Venice Commission advise governments on issues of constitutional design.[9]

[4] As a matter of customary international law, reflected in Art 27 of the Vienna Convention on the Law of Treaties, a state cannot absolve itself from its international legal obligations by reference to its domestic constitutional law. See also Art 32 of the ILC Draft Articles on Responsibility of States for Internationally Wrongful Acts of 2001, UN Doc A/CN.4/L.602, Rev 1.

[5] C Tomuschat, 'International Law: Ensuring the Survival of Mankind on the Eve of a New Century' (1999) 281 *RdC* 13, 63.

[6] See A Peters, 'Supremacy Lost: International Law Meets Domestic Constitutional Law' (2009) 3 *Vienna Online Journal on International Constitutional Law* 170, 173–77, arguing that international law and domestic constitutional law are increasingly converging.

[7] See A Peters, 'The Globalization of State Constitutions' in J Nijman and A Nollkaemper (eds), *New Perspectives on the Divide Between National and International Law* (Oxford, Oxford University Press, 2007) 270–93, referring to rule of law, democracy, social security and the organisation of territory as ingredients of a 'good State constitution'.

[8] Y Shany, 'No Longer a Weak Department of Power? Reflections on the Emergence of a New International Judiciary' (2009) 20 *EJIL* 73, arguing that there is a new 'ethos' of the international judiciary emerging, shifting away from that of conflict resolution to that of 'norm-advancement' and 'regime maintenance'.

[9] Recent examples of review of constitutional provisions by the Venice Commission include: European Commission for Democracy through Law (Venice Commission), *Principales questions juridiques discutées au sein de l'Assemblée Nationale Constituante de Tunisie (ANC) en vue de la nouvelle constitution* (6 September 2013); European Commission for Democracy through Law (Venice

Similarly, non-state domestic institutions and independent national human rights institutions have begun to play a key role in the dissemination of best practices regarding standards on institutional constitutionality.[10]

Another way to operationalise the international concern for constitutional law is to scrutinise domestic constitutional norms in international judicial proceedings. This raises some intriguing questions. In which ways can domestic constitutional law come into conflict with international law? Are there binding international guarantees on the separation of powers and democratic governance that could serve as standards of international constitutionality? Within what procedure could the international constitutionality of domestic constitutional norms be scrutinised? Is intrusion of an international court into issues of domestic constitutional law legitimate? As this is a new and largely unexplored field of international law, only tentative answers to these questions can be given here.[11] Additionally, this chapter limits the analysis, with a few exceptions, to the context of the European Convention on Human Rights ('the Convention' (ECHR)). This seems promising as, at present, the Convention is the most advanced legal tool to constrain domestic power by international human rights.[12]

The main argument of this chapter is that the Convention rights not only embody fundamental rights of individuals but also have an institutional dimension that pertains to an international standard on separation of powers and democratic governance. Both dimensions together allow Convention rights to function as 'minimum constitutional guarantees' safeguarding a minimum standard of constitutionality in the Council of Europe (CoE) states. As will be shown, the ECtHR has started to cautiously operationalise this understanding of Convention rights as 'minimum constitutional guarantees' in its case law. Ultimately, the ECtHR may engage in reviewing domestic constitutional norms on a larger scale.

The argument is presented as follows: in section II, two scenarios of conflict between domestic constitutional norms and the Convention are distinguished, ie on the one hand, a conflict between constitutional norms and international fundamental rights, and on the other hand, a conflict between constitutional norms and international standards on separation of powers and democratic governance.

Commission), *Opinion on the Revision of the Constitution of Belgium* (Opinion No 679/2012, 20 June 2012). On the work of the Venice Commission see generally JL Jowell, 'The Venice Commission: Disseminating Democracy Through Law' (2001) *Public Law* 675. See Joakim Nergelius, Chapter 11.

[10] R Carver, 'A New Answer to an Old Question: National Human Rights Institutions and the Domestication of International Law' (2010) 10 *Human Rights Law Review* 1.

[11] See, for recent literature on this topic, L Garlicki and ZA Garlicka, 'External Review of Constitutional Amendments? International Law as a Norm of Reference' (2011) 44 *Israel Law Review* 343, arguing that international law is capable of functioning as a 'norm of reference' in reviewing constitutional norms. See also Y Roznai, 'The Theory and Practice of "Supra-Constitutional" Limits on Constitutional Amendments' (2013) 62 *ICLQ* 557, 595–97, who, based on state practice arguments, holds that international law should not per se be regarded as a limit to domestic constitutional law, but that it should be considered as an explicit or implicit limitation within the constitution itself.

[12] See LR Helfer, 'Redesigning the European Court of Human Rights: Embeddedness as a Deep Structural Principle of the European Human Rights Regime' (2008) 19 *EJIL* 125, referring to the Convention as the 'world's most advanced international system for protecting civil and political liberties'.

Section III analyses how the ECtHR deals with the two scenarios of conflict and outlines recent developments in its jurisprudence suggesting the reinterpretation of Convention rights as 'minimum constitutional guarantees'. Section IV discusses three potential objections to this reinterpretation of Convention rights. Section V addresses the question whether Convention rights should function as 'minimum constitutional guarantees' at all.

II. TWO SCENARIOS OF CONFLICT

In this section, I explain two scenarios of conflict between constitutional law and international law. The first scenario relates to the conflict of domestic constitutional law and international fundamental rights. Examples of this conflict scenario are rare. However, constitutions that draw from religious norms may come into conflict with international non-discrimination provisions or even the prohibition of torture.[13] In the European context, a scenario of such a conflict would, for example, arise if a provision was introduced in a domestic constitution that would allow the death penalty.[14]

The second scenario of conflict is more challenging. It relates to the conflict of constitutional law with international standards on the separation of powers and democratic governance. Cases falling into this category concern constitutional provisions on state organisation and state institutions. As an example, one may take the debate on the new Hungarian Basic Law.[15] As mentioned, the European Union and the Venice Commission have in the past voiced severe criticism of the new Basic Law. The criticism relates in essence to shortcomings regarding separation of powers and democratic governance. The Venice Commission points to the frequently used method of referring to 'cardinal laws', ie laws regulating in detail those matters that are only described in general terms by the Constitution and require a two-thirds majority of the Members of Parliament for their adoption and amendment.[16] The new Hungarian Basic Law envisages cardinal laws to regulate, among other matters, family policy, the defence forces and the police.[17] The Venice Commission recommended a more restricted use of cardinal laws because they would carve in stone a particular political choice, leaving practically no room for later changes.[18] Preventing political change puts the principle of democratic governance at risk.[19] Another critique concerns the curtailment of the

[13] For the case of the Interim National Constitution of Sudan with conflicts with provisions of the ICCPR, see O Köndgen, 'Shari'a and National Law in the Sudan' in JM Otto (ed), *Sharia Incorporated: A Comparative Overview of the Legal Systems of Twelve Muslim Countries in Past and Present* (Leiden, Leiden University Press, 2010) 218–19.

[14] *Öcalan v Turkey*, Application no 4622/99 (ECtHR, 12 May 2005).

[15] For a balanced view see A Jakab and P Sonnevend, 'Kontinuität mit Mängeln: Das neue ungarische Grundgesetz' (2012) 72 *ZaöRV* 79.

[16] Venice Commission Op 621/2011 (n 1) paras 22–27.

[17] On family law see art L(3), on the defence forces see art 45(2) and (5), and on the police see art 46(6) of the Hungarian Basic Law of 18 April 2011.

[18] Venice Commission Op 621/2011 (n 1) paras 22–27. See Hungarian Basic Law, art 24.

[19] Venice Commission Op 621/2011 (n 1) para 24.

powers of the Constitutional Court.[20] Here, the Venice Commission 'is concerned that a number of provisions of the new Constitution may undermine further the authority of the Constitutional Court as a guarantor of constitutionality of the Hungarian legal order'.[21] Lastly, the Commission criticised the vague formulation of the design of the ordinary judiciary, eg that it shall have a 'multi-level organisation'.[22] It is feared that vague institutional safeguards may threaten the independence of the judiciary.[23]

The second scenario is more challenging from a legal point of view than the first for two reasons. Other than in the first scenario, binding international standards on the separation of powers and democratic governance[24] are only just emerging.[25] At present, the lack of international binding standards on separation of powers and democratic governance limits the impact of international law on constitutional issues. Furthermore, even when such international standards would exist, states must be given a wide margin regarding the interpretation of the institutional consequences of the international standard. This is because there are multiple ways to organise governance in conformity with the principle of separation of powers and democratic governance, eg a presidential system or a parliamentary system.[26]

Nevertheless, with domestic constitutional law becoming an international concern of rising importance, international law has taken up the challenge of formulating standards for separation of powers and democratic governance.[27] There are a number of soft law instruments dealing with separation of powers and democratic governance, eg the UN Basic Principles on the Independence of the Judiciary:

> The independence of the judiciary shall be guaranteed by the State and enshrined in the Constitution or the law of the country. It is a duty of all governmental and other institutions to respect and observe the independence of the judiciary.[28]

[20] ibid paras 91–101.

[21] ibid para 97.

[22] ibid paras 102–10. See Hungarian Basic Law, art 25(4).

[23] Venice Commission Op 621/2011 (n 1) para 106.

[24] Depending on the legal tradition, the notion of separation of powers is regarded as a part of democracy, see, eg the (former) UN Commission on Human Rights, Commission on Human Rights Resolution 2003/36: Interdependence between democracy and human rights, 23 April 2003, E/CN.4-RES/2003/36: 'the essential elements of democracy include … the separation of powers'. In the context of the ECHR, which is of primary relevance here, the two notions should be distinguished for practical reasons.

[25] See section III below for a discussion of the Convention as a possible international standard for separation of powers and democratic governance.

[26] See D Kosař, 'Policing Separation of Powers: A New Role for the European Court of Human Rights?' (2012) 8 *EuConst* 33, 58, arguing that there is less consensus among CoE states in the field of separation of powers than in that of fundamental rights.

[27] For an overview see Democracy Reporting International, *International Consensus: Essential Elements of Democracy* (Report, October 2011), available at www.democracy-reporting.org/files/essential_elements_of_democracy_2.pdf.

[28] United Nations High Commissioner for Human Rights, *Basic Principles on the Independence of the Judiciary, Seventh United Nations Congress on the Prevention of Crime and the Treatment of Offenders, Milan, 26 August to 6 September 1985*, UN Doc A/CONF.121/22/Rev1 (1985) 59.

International soft law on judicial independence is also contained in a recommendation by the Council of Europe's Committee of Ministers[29] and Organization for Security and Cooperation in Europe (OSCE) commitments.[30] For example, as part of international standardisation, today the removal of a judge during his term of office is commonly regarded as a violation of the principle of the rule of law.[31] In this respect, the work of the Venice Commission is of crucial importance.[32]

Additionally, human rights bodies have long recognised, to a varying degree, the connection between a principled organisation of governance and a climate favourable to fundamental rights. For example, the Inter-American Court of Human Rights has held:

> The obligation to respect and guarantee such rights, which Article 1(1) [of the Inter-American Convention on Human Rights] imposes on the States Parties, implies … the duty of the States Parties to organize the governmental apparatus and, in general, all the structures through which public power is exercised, so that they are capable of juridically ensuring the free and full enjoyment of human rights.[33]

Similarly, the UN Human Rights Committee, in its concluding observations on a state report of Slovakia, noted 'with concern that the lack of clarity in the delimitation of the respective competences of the executive, legislative and judicial authorities may endanger the implementation of the rule of law and a consistent human rights policy'.[34] Since the principled organisation of government is relevant to the effective enjoyment of fundamental rights, it is no wonder that international human rights bodies have started to derive organisational duties from these rights.[35]

The connection between state organisation and fundamental rights is most obvious in relation to the domestic judiciary, which is supposed to adjudicate fundamental rights violations. Therefore, it is not surprising that pronouncements by international human rights courts often concern the organisation of the domestic judiciary.[36] Relations among the other branches of government have also been

[29] Committee of Ministers, *Recommendation on the Independence, Efficiency and Role of Judges*, Recommendation No R (94) 12.

[30] Document of the Moscow Meeting of the Conference on the Human Dimension of the CSCE, II (18), Moscow, 3 October 1991, para 19.2, available at www.osce.org/odihr/elections/14310.

[31] A Seibert-Fohr, 'European Standards for the Rule of Law and Independent Courts' (2012) 20 *Journal für Rechtspolitik* 161, 163.

[32] See Joakim Nergelius, Chapter 11.

[33] *Exceptions to the Exhaustion of Domestic Remedies (Art 46.1, 46.2.a and 46.2b American Convention on Human Rights)*, Advisory Opinion (IACtHR, 10 August 1990), OC-11/90, Series A No 11, para 23.

[34] UN Human Rights Committee, *Concluding Observations of the Human Rights Committee: Slovakia*, UN Doc CCPR/C79/Add. 79 (1997) para 3.

[35] For a detailed analysis in the context of the ECHR see III.A below.

[36] On the emergence of international standards with regard to the rule of law and the judiciary see A Seibert-Fohr, 'European Standards for the Rule of Law and Independent Courts' (2012) 20 *Journal für Rechtspolitik* 161.

the subject of international human rights proceedings. The over-concentration of power in the hands of the executive in a constitution has been recognised as a problem in the context of Article 25 ICCPR (right to vote) by the UN Human Rights Committee. In this respect, the Committee noted with regard to the new Constitution of Croatia that:

> significant amendments have been introduced in the Constitution and legislation so as to clarify the separation of powers between the three branches of the State, in particular moving from an over-concentration of power in the executive branch to a more balanced form of parliamentary oversight of the executive and strengthening of the independence of the judiciary.[37]

III. CONVENTION RIGHTS AS 'MINIMUM CONSTITUTIONAL GUARANTEES'

Section III situates and analyses the two scenarios of conflict between constitutional norms and international law in the context of the European Convention on Human Rights. It will be shown that the ECtHR has cautiously started to take up the challenge and in fact reviews domestic constitutional norms on their conformity with the Convention.

So far, there have only been instances of the first scenario of conflict, ie conflicts of constitutional norms with Convention rights as *limits to constitutional rule-making*. The ECtHR has not adjudicated on the second type of conflict, ie the conflict of domestic constitutional norms with Convention rights as *limits to institutional design*. I shall argue that Convention rights can be interpreted both as limits to constitutional rule-making and as limits to institutional design (on the level of constitutional norms). In other words, the Convention allows for a reinterpretation of its rights as 'minimum constitutional guarantees'. In this sense, Convention rights may, in addition to their traditional functions, be used as guarantees of a certain level of constitutionality *(Verfassungsstaatlichkeit)* within the CoE states.

A. Convention Rights as a Limit to Constitutional Rule-making

In the well-known case of *Sejdić and Finci* in 2009, the ECtHR has found domestic constitutional norms to be in violation of the Convention.[38] The Constitution of

[37] UN Human Rights Committee, *Concluding Observations of the Human Rights Committee: Croatia*, UN Doc CCPR/CO/71/HRV (2001) para 3.

[38] *Sejdić and Finci*, Application no 27996/06 *et al* (ECtHR, 22 December 2009). See S Bardutzky, 'The Strasbourg Court on the Dayton Constitution' (2010) 6 *EuConst* 309. For a similar case under the ICCPR see UN Human Rights Committee, Communication No 1744/2007 (15 January 2013) concerning the requirement under the constitutional law of Mauritius that prospective candidates of elections to the National Assembly had to identify themselves as members of one of the four categories of the Mauritian population.

Bosnia and Herzegovina, which was adopted as part of the Dayton Peace Agreement, stated that only members of the so-called 'constituent peoples' (Bosniacs, Croats and Serbs) could run for public office. In the case before the ECtHR the two complainants, a Jewish and a Roma citizen of Bosnia and Herzegovina, both held prominent public positions. They did not, however, declare their affiliation with the 'constituent peoples'. Therefore, they were ineligible to stand for election to the House of Peoples (the second Chamber of the State Parliament) and the Presidency. The Court found the relevant constitutional norm to be in violation of the non-discrimination provisions of the Convention (Article 14 ECHR and Article 1 of Protocol No 12 to the ECHR).

Another recent case is *Anchugov and Gladkov*, decided in 2013.[39] This case concerned two Russian applicants who were convicted for murder. By article 32(3) of the Russian Constitution they were barred from voting in elections to the State Duma and other elections. The ECtHR held that the disenfranchisement of the two applicants violated Article 3 of Protocol No 1 to the ECHR. The case is revealing because the government had in fact raised the objection that the ECtHR had no jurisdiction to hear the case due to the constitutional nature of the impugned provision.[40] The ECtHR correctly rejected that objection by pointing to Article 1 ECHR which did not exclude any part of domestic law from its jurisdiction.[41] Furthermore, the ECtHR pointed to Article 19 ECHR which establishes its own duty to 'ensure the observance of the engagements undertaken by the High Contracting Parties'.[42] The ECtHR repeated that it was not its task to review the constitutional provision in the abstract but only to review the effect the provision has on the applicants' rights in the *concrete case*. However, the distinction between an abstract review of the constitutional norm and a concrete review of the applicants' cases does not make much difference here. The impugned provision of article 323(3) of the Russian Constitution was phrased in plain terms, leaving no discretion to the authorities applying it. The disenfranchisement was automatic and indiscriminate by virtue of the constitutional provision. *Anchugov and Gladkov* is, therefore, an example of a case where the impugned Convention violation directly originates from a norm of the Constitution.

A third case, which has not yet been decided on the merits by the ECtHR, the Swiss minaret ban, falls into the same category. Article 72(3) of the Swiss Constitution provides in plain terms, '[t]he construction of minarets is prohibited'. This provision entered the Constitution by popular initiative. The initiative was adopted although the Swiss government, the Bundesrat, had prior to the initiative announced in public that it regarded the initiative as a violation of

[39] *Anchugov and Gladkov*, Application no 11157/04 (ECtHR, 4 July 2013).

[40] ibid para 48.

[41] ibid para 50.

[42] ibid para 51.

Convention law.[43] The case of the Swiss minaret ban has not yet been decided on the merits by the ECtHR. The literature almost unanimously considers the prohibition of the construction of minarets a violation of the Convention, in particular of the provisions on freedom of religion (Article 9 ECHR) and non-discrimination (Article 14 ECHR).[44] Here, too, the potential Convention violation stems from the constitutional norm itself. The constitutional provision arguably violates negative duties established by Convention rights.

Cases of this scenario fit into the prevailing view of the Convention as a 'constitutional instrument'.[45] The constitutional instrument approach to interpretation reflects the function of Convention rights as limits on public power in the contracting states. The limiting function of the Convention naturally applies to norms of domestic constitutional law, too. The function of Convention rights as a legal standard for constitutional provisions is, therefore, unproblematic in the first scenario of conflict. From the perspective of general international law it does not make a difference on which level of the domestic hierarchy of norms the violation of a Convention duty originates.[46] Thus, the ECtHR in *Sejdić and Finci* and in *Anchugov and Gladkov* was right to use the Convention as a standard to review the constitutionality of the provisions of the Constitution. The same approach would apply in the case of the Swiss minaret ban. The conflict of domestic constitutional norms with Convention rights *as limits to constitutional rule-making* can be treated according to the same logic as other fundamental rights cases.

B. Convention Rights as Limits to Institutional Design

The crucial question is whether Convention rights can be interpreted as limitations of institutional design (on the constitutional level). Here, it will be argued that such a reinterpretation is in fact possible.

[43] Bundesrat, *Botschaft zur Volksinitiative "Gegen den Bau von Minaretten"* (BBl. 2008, 7627), available at www.admin.ch/ch/d/ff/2008/7603.pdf.

[44] See A Peters, 'El Referéndum Suizo sobre La Prohibición de Minaretes' (2010) 25 *Teoría y Realidad Constitucional* 429. On the special problem of a Convention violation by constitutional norms adopted in a popular vote, see G Biaggini, 'Die schweizerische direkte Demokratie und das Völkerrecht' (2010) 65 *Zeitschrift für öffentliches Recht* 325, 337. Biaggini argues that the Federal Supreme Court has a duty to avert a conviction of Switzerland by the ECtHR. He refers to s 122 of the Act on the Federal Supreme Court allowing for the revision of a federal judgment adopted in violation of the ECHR if reparation is insufficient.

[45] The expression of the Convention as 'constitutional instrument' was first employed by Sir Gerald Fitzmaurice in his Concurring Opinion in *National Union of Belgian Police v Belgium*, Application no 4464/70 (ECtHR, 27 October 1975) Annex. For a recent authority see also *Al-Skeini and others v United Kingdom*, Application no 55721/07 (ECtHR, 7 July 2011) 53 EHRR 18, para 141. For a discussion of the elements of the Convention as constitutional instrument see A Peters and T Altwicker, *Europäische Menschenrechtskonvention* (Munich, CH Beck, 2012) 13–14.

[46] This is, of course, different from the perspective of the convicted state, From a state-based perspective the domestic constitution is the supreme normative order.

Fundamental rights can indeed have an institutional dimension, ie they can directly impact the design of institutions.[47] The Convention rights are no exception. Convention rights can be reinterpreted as internationally binding standards on issues such as the independence of the judiciary, prohibition of over-concentration of power in the executive branch, accountability of the executive, autonomy of the legislature and roles of political parties and the opposition. While in principle any Convention right could be reinterpreted institutionally, some are more likely to be used as limits to institutional design than others.[48]

It should be noted that the text of the ECHR does already (albeit in a very cautious manner) lay claims on the organisational design of the state and its institutions, which has implications for the structure and functioning of the judiciary,[49] law enforcement agencies[50] and the legislature.[51] In the jurisprudence of the ECtHR, the institutional dimension of fundamental rights is only gradually emerging. It has not yet been given the scholarly attention it deserves.[52] Historically, the institutional dimension of Convention rights was introduced when the ECtHR set up a 'duty to investigate' in cases involving severe violations of Convention rights.[53] Furthermore, procedural guarantees derived from substantive Convention rights, eg the right of access to documents in family law proceedings, fall under the institutional dimension.[54] The ECtHR has started to develop jurisprudence on issues of state organisation. Since 2002, when the ECtHR decided *Stafford v United Kingdom*, separation of powers issues have gradually gained more attention from the ECtHR.[55] The Court has repeatedly emphasised that it pays special attention

[47] On the institutional dimension of fundamental rights in the context of the German Basic Law see BVerfGE 35, 79, 115: 'The fundamental rights provisions of the Basic Law also incorporate an objective order of values ... Article 5(3) [freedom of scholarly activity] contains one such value decision. Its key function is to guarantee free scholarly activity both in the interest of the individual scholar's self-realization and for the benefit of the entire society ... The state is therefore obliged as a civilized nation to defend a system of free scholarly inquiry and to affirmatively provide for an institutional framework in which such inquiry can be carried out', quoted from DP Kommers, *The Constitutional Jurisprudence of the Federal Republic of Germany* (Durham, NC, Duke University Press, 1997) 437–38. See generally R Alexy, *A Theory of Constitutional Rights* (Oxford, Oxford University Press, 2010) 314, 323–33.

[48] Convention rights likely to contain an institutional dimension are Art 6 ECHR (judiciary), Art 3 of Protocol No 1 (legislature), Art 10 ECHR (media, university) and Art 11 ECHR (political parties). It must be left to a larger study to analyse the institutional dimension for each Convention right.

[49] See, eg Arts 5, 6, 10(2) ECHR.

[50] See, eg Art 11(2) ECHR.

[51] See Art 3 of Protocol No 1 to the ECHR.

[52] Similarly Kosař, 'Policing Separation of Powers' (n 26) 35, arguing that there is a lack of scholarly interest in the implications of the Strasbourg jurisprudence for the issue of separation of powers.

[53] In particular, but not limited to, cases concerning the right to life (Art 2 ECHR), *McCann and others v United Kingdom*, Application no 18984/91 (27 September 1995) 21 EHRR 97 para 157; *Silih v Slovenia*, Application no 71463/01 (ECtHR, 9 April 2009) para 192. See, in more detail, Peters and Altwicker, *Europäische Menschenrechtskonvention* (n 45) 23–24.

[54] The ECtHR based the right of access to documents on the right to family life (Art 8 ECHR), see *TP and KM v United Kingdom*, Application no 28945/95 (ECtHR, 10 May 2001) para 73.

[55] *Stafford v United Kingdom*, Application no 46295/99 (ECtHR, 28 May 2002) para 78. See on this development Kosař, 'Policing Separation of Powers' (n 26).

to the standard of separation of powers.[56] The ECtHR, however, has so far not looked into separation of powers' problems on the level of constitutional law. ECtHR cases on separation of powers issues have primarily concerned the design of the domestic judiciary. For example, the ECtHR indicated in Campbell and Fell that an ability of the executive to remove a judge during his term of office would give rise to a violation of the independence of the court (Article 6(1) ECHR).[57] Other separation of powers questions concerned the compatibility of judicial office with other tasks.[58] Additionally, the ECtHR has, for example, ruled upon the organisation of a police operation.[59]

Regarding democracy, the ECtHR has, for example, ruled on the compatibility of electoral thresholds with the right to free elections (Article 3 of Protocol No 1 to the ECHR). Electoral thresholds serve the public interest in institutional stability. The ECtHR held in *Yumak and Sadak* that electoral thresholds are, in principle, acceptable limitations of the right to free elections. However, an electoral threshold exceeding a 10 per cent level would violate the right to free elections (Article 3 of Protocol No 1 to the ECHR).[60] This, too, is an example of how the right to free elections serves as a benchmark for the international constitutionality of state institutions. That the state is, by virtue of the Convention, under a positive duty to hold regular elections (Article 3 of Protocol No 1 to the ECHR) offers another example in the context of democratic governance. The ECtHR has derived quite far-reaching consequences from this:

> It should also be noted that, in the context of Article 3 of Protocol No 1, the primary obligation is not one of abstention or non-interference, as with the majority of civil and political rights, but one of adoption by the State of positive measures to 'hold' democratic elections. In this regard the Court also takes into consideration the fact that the right to vote, the 'active' element of the rights under Article 3 of Protocol No 1, is not a privilege. In the twenty-first century, the presumption in a democratic State must be in favour of inclusion. Accordingly, the exclusion from the right to vote of any groups or categories of the general population must be reconcilable with the underlying purposes of Article 3 of Protocol No 1.[61]

The institutional dimension of Article 3 of Protocol No 1 to the ECHR can be used in the case of the Hungarian cardinal laws as well. It can be argued that the right to free elections is violated by removing some policy fields from a democratically elected (simple) majority. As another example for the institutional dimension of

[56] For a recent authority see *Volkov v Ukraine*, Application no. 21722/11 (ECtHR, 9 January 2013) para 103.

[57] The ECtHR held that, although a formal rule on non-revocability of judges during office is not required by the Convention, there must nevertheless be a de facto recognition of that principle, see *Campbell and Fell v United Kingdom*, Application no 7819/77 (28 June 1984) 7 EHRR 165, para 80.

[58] *Stafford* (n 55); see Kosař, 'Policing Separation of Powers' (n 26) 41–46.

[59] *McCann and others* (n 53) para 185.

[60] *Yumak and Sadak v Turkey*, Application no 10226/03 (ECtHR, 8 July 2008).

[61] *Sitaropoulos and others v Greece*, Application no 42202/07 (ECtHR, 15 March 2012) paras 67–68.

democratic governance, it can be mentioned that the ECtHR has set up a positive duty to safeguard media pluralism.[62]

In fleshing out the institutional and organisational content of the Convention rights, the ECtHR takes into account the opinions of the Venice Commission and the Commissioner for Human Rights of the Council of Europe.[63] Additionally, the Court engages in comparative analysis.[64] This is appropriate since, as was mentioned above, there is a multitude of reasonable organisational designs in conformity with separation of powers standards. As the few examples mentioned here make clear, the jurisprudence regarding the institutional dimension and, as a consequence, the conception of rights as minimum constitutional guarantees is still at an early stage.

C. Procedural Implications of Convention Rights as 'Minimum Constitutional Guarantees'

What are the procedural implications of reinterpreting the Convention rights as minimum constitutional guarantees? The first scenario of conflict does not pose any special procedural problems: if Convention rights are used as limits to constitutional rule-making (as in *Sejdić and Finci* and in *Anchugov and Gladkov*), the conflict between constitutional norms and Convention rights can be dealt with in the ordinary individual complaint procedure according to Article 34 ECHR (or, less likely, in an inter-state complaint on the basis of Article 33 ECHR). If the Convention violation by a constitutional norm has led or has the potential to lead to a large number of applications, the ECtHR may have resort to the 'pilot judgment procedure' introduced in *Broniowski v Poland*.[65] The purpose of this procedure is to reduce the Court's workload when there are, actually or potentially, a large number of applications sharing the same root cause. It allows the Court to select a complaint for priority treatment. The Court will then try to formulate a solution that can be extended to all pending or future cases raising essentially the same issue. According to Rule 61(3) of the Rules of Court, '[t]he Court shall … identify both the nature of the structural or systemic problem or other dysfunction as established as well as the type of remedial measures which the Contracting Party concerned is required to take at the domestic level by virtue of the operative provisions of the judgment'.[66] The use of the pilot judgment procedure seems appropriate only for cases where the constitutional

[62] See Art 10 ECHR and the accompanying jurisprudence of the ECtHR, in particular *Centro Europa 7 Srl and Di Stefano v Italy*, Application no 38433/09 (ECtHR, 7 June 2012) para 134.

[63] See recently, *Volkov* (n 56) paras 79–80.

[64] ibid paras 81–82.

[65] *Broniowski v Poland*, Application no 31443/96 (ECtHR, 22 April 2004) para 188. On this procedure see Rule 61 of the Rules of Court of 1 September 2012. The Rules of Court are available at www.echr.coe.int/Documents/Rules_Court_ENG.pdf.

[66] ibid.

norm itself is in violation of the Convention and a large number of applications is to be feared (note that this was not the case in *Sejdić and Finci* concerning the Bosnian electoral rules). Interestingly, the ECtHR did not have resort to the pilot judgment procedure in *Anchugov and Gladkov* on the disenfranchisement of convicts by a constitutional provision. As the Court itself remarked, some 734,300 prisoners are affected by it.[67] The decision not to apply the pilot judgment procedure here is difficult to understand as the judgment may give rise to a vast number of applications.

Things are more difficult with regard to the second scenario of conflict. The conflict between a constitutional norm and Convention rights as limits on constitutional design poses, in particular, problems of standing (or, in the terminology based on Article 34 ECHR, the 'victim requirement'). The ECtHR, in principle, does not exercise an 'abstract control of norms' but is concerned with the impact of Convention legal norms as applied to individual cases.[68] The number of people directly affected by, for example, the restructuration of the judiciary by constitutional amendment, is prima facie limited. The victim requirement is a central feature of the review mechanism under the ECHR to preclude *actio popularis* complaints.[69] This requirement must also be fulfilled in cases of individual complaints against constitutional norms.

The problem of standing limits the possibility for an international review of constitutional norms in the second scenario of conflict of constitutional norms. In principle, there are three ways to address the conflict of constitutional norms with Convention rights as limits on constitutional design. First, there is the inter-state complaint procedure under Article 33 ECHR. In that case the Convention is charged with safeguarding the European *ordre public* and there is no requirement of victim status.[70] The inter-state procedure remains a possible mechanism to enforce Convention rights as minimum constitutional guarantees, however, European states have in the past been unwilling to use this procedure against other states. It is therefore unlikely (though not impossible) that states will have resort to this instrument.

Secondly, the ECtHR may use an individual complaint against a domestic decision and merely point to the underlying constitutional origin or dimension of the problem. Thus, early on the ECtHR has used 'soft power' to address widespread or systemic malfunctions in domestic legal systems. The 2013 case of *Volkov v Ukraine* is an example.[71] The case concerned a Ukrainian national who was dismissed as judge at the Supreme Court. The Court concluded that the case not only revealed individual violations of Convention rights, but also disclosed systemic

[67] *Anchugov and Gladkov* (n 39) para 104.

[68] See R Harmsen, 'The European Convention on Human Rights After Enlargement' (2001) 5 *International Journal of Human Rights* 18, 33.

[69] See Peters and Altwicker, *Europäische Menschenrechtskonvention* (n 45) 268.

[70] ibid 282–84.

[71] *Volkov* (n 56).

problems as regards the organisation of the judiciary: In particular, the violations found in the case suggest that the system of judicial discipline in Ukraine had not been organised in a proper way, as it did not ensure sufficient separation from other branches of state power. Moreover, it did not provide appropriate guarantees against abuse and misuse of disciplinary measures to the detriment of judicial independence, the latter being one of the most important values underpinning the effective functioning of democracies.[72]

In a far-reaching move, the Court even recommended the 'restructuring of the institutional basis of the system'.[73] This path of using an individual complaint to deal with constitutional malfunction will only be available in rare circumstances.

A third, better way to tackle constitutional design problems may be the new advisory procedure envisaged by Protocol No 16 to the ECHR which was recently opened for signature.[74] This new Protocol, which is not yet in force, allows highest courts and tribunals of the contracting states to request an advisory opinion on 'questions of principle relating to the interpretation or application of the rights and freedoms defined in the Convention or the protocols thereto'.[75] The exact meaning of 'questions of principle' is unclear. It may be gathered from the 'Report of the Group of Wise Persons to the Committee of Ministers' and, based on the latter, from the Explanatory Report that advisory opinions should relate to important questions of general interest arising under Convention law.[76] Problems in the constitutional law of a contracting state arguably meet that threshold criterion of importance. It must be noted that advisory opinions are non-binding.[77] In sensitive areas such as constitutional law, the non-bindingness of a Court statement may, however, prove to be an advantage. The problem remains, though, that there must be some political will in the CoE state concerned to have its constitutional norms reviewed by the ECtHR since the advisory procedure can only be instituted by its highest courts and tribunals. One can imagine political circumstances where this option must appear as a mere theoretical possibility.

[72] ibid para 199. The case is exceptional, too, concerning the remedy ordered in the operative part: The Court ordered the applicant's reinstatement in the post of judge of the Supreme Court at the earliest possible date. On the problem of non-pecuniary individual remedies under the Convention see Peters and Altwicker, *Europäische Menschenrechtskonvention* (n 45) 288–89.

[73] *Volkov* (n 56) para 200.

[74] Protocol No 16 to the Convention for the Protection of Human Rights and Fundamental Freedoms, 2 October 2013. The text is available at www.conventions.coe.int/Treaty/EN/Treaties/Html/214.htm.

[75] ibid Art 1(1).

[76] See Explanatory Report to Protocol No 16 to the ECHR, para 9 (stating that the interpretation of 'questions of principle' is inspired by considerations similar to those for a referral of a case to the Grand Chamber, Art 43(2) ECHR). The text of the Explanatory Report is available at www.echr.coe.int/Documents/Protocol_16_explanatory_report_ENG.pdf.

[77] Protocol No 16, Art 5.

IV. LEGITIMACY

The reinterpretation of Convention rights as minimum constitutional guarantees would enable the ECtHR to review constitutional norms on their conformity with Convention rights both as limits to constitutional rule-making and as limits to institutional design (on the constitutional level). This raises legitimacy concerns that will be addressed here.

A. Guarding the Guardians?

A first objection runs like this: the ECtHR has no mandate to find a domestic constitutional provision in violation of the Convention.

It is clear that the Convention does not represent a super-constitution that could trump domestic constitutions. The ECHR is not a super-constitution for a number of reasons: first, it is incomplete (eg in the field of social and economic guarantees). Furthermore, the Convention neither 'constitutes' a distinct political community nor establishes public power.[78] In other words, it lacks the foundational element commonly attached to constitutions. However, as outlined in section I of this chapter, there is a trend towards convergence in relation to constitutional law in Europe, as well as a trend to make constitutional law an international concern. During the advancement of the constitutionalist project, legal questions with regard to domestic constitutional law will arise which, depending on their gravity, need to be settled by an independent institution guaranteeing uniform application.

The role of the ECtHR in relation to domestic constitutional law is limited, though. First, it must be borne in mind that the necessity of uniformity may be less urgent with regard to separation of powers and democratic governance, where often more than one design will be reasonable and in conformity with international standards. It is clear that many questions of constitutional design involve political choices that neither are nor will be fully determined by international law. In many cases there remains a 'corridor' of possible solutions that are compatible with Convention rights as minimum constitutional guarantees. The margin of appreciation is a suitable tool to delineate that 'corridor'. Secondly, even if reinterpreted as minimum constitutionality guarantees, the Convention rights do not require establishing a particular constitutional design. In other words, while the Convention continues to act as a limitation on constitutional law, it is unlikely that the ECtHR will ever positively mandate that some rule or institution be established *at the constitutional level*. This is because the Convention does not establish any duty to make a matter a constitutional issue in the first place.

[78] D Grimm, 'Types of Constitutions' in M Rosenfeld and A Sajó (eds), *The Oxford Handbook of Comparative Constitutional Law* (Oxford, Oxford University Press, 2012) 104, 108–9.

It does not even require including fundamental rights in the text of a constitution. Consequently, the ECtHR has held that no provision of the ECHR 'requires States to comply with any theoretical constitutional concepts'.[79] If it is up to the contracting states to decide what belongs in a constitution, it is all the more their choice as to what extent the constitution regulates specific state institutions. In addition, an assessment by an international court that the level of constitutional regulation is insufficient would require something akin to a 'common theory of constitutional law'. However, given the diversity of constitutional traditions in Europe, agreement on theoretical positions of constitutional law (especially regarding institutional issues) does not seem likely.[80] In sum, while the Court has the mandate to adjudicate upon Convention rights as minimum constitutional guarantees, it may not 'harmonise' domestic constitutions and their institutional design.

B. Institutional Legitimacy?

A second objection can be formulated as follows: adjudicating on minimum constitutional guarantees is an act of international constitutional law-making. The ECtHR does not possess the necessary institutional legitimacy to do this.[81]

Judicial review by an international court of domestic constitutional law is certainly a sensitive venture from the perspective of state sovereignty. Constitutional norms manifest a state's choice of its political, economic, social and cultural system. The adoption of constitutional law often requires super-majorities, endowing it with special democratic legitimacy.

As is the case of other international courts, the legitimacy of the ECtHR does not derive from a formal chain of legitimisation, ie through basing the acts of an institution ultimately on the consent and participation of national citizens.[82] In matters of legitimacy, one therefore needs to be careful not to require the impossible from an international institution. Armin von Bogdandy and Ingo Venzke have recently laid out several criteria for assessing the democratic legitimacy of law-making by international courts.[83] These criteria relate to the reasoning,

[79] *Kleyn and others v Netherlands*, Application no 39343/98 (ECtHR, 6 May 2003) para 193.

[80] See M Mahlmann, 'Grundrechtstheorien in Europa—kulturelle Bestimmtheit und universeller Gehalt' (2011) 46 *EuR* 469, discussing the fundamental rights part of a common European theory of constitutional law.

[81] On the concept of "institutional legitimacy", see A Buchanan and R Keohane, 'The Legitimacy of Global Governance Institutions' (2006) 20 *Ethics & Int'l Aff.* 405. For the Convention context see J-P Costa, 'On the Legitimacy of the European Court of Human Rights' Judgments' (2011) 7 *European Constitutional Law Review* 173.

[82] N Petersen, 'Determining the Domestic Effect of International Law through the Prism of Legitimacy' (2012) 72 *ZaöRV* 223, 232.

[83] A von Bogdandy and I Venzke, 'On the Democratic Legitimation of International Judicial Lawmaking' in A von Bogdandy and I Venzke (eds), *International Judicial Lawmaking* (Heidelberg, Springer, 2012) 477–509.

judges, procedure and role of domestic organs. The institutional legitimacy of international adjudication derives fundamentally from the quality of the court's reasoning. The legitimacy of adjudicating upon minimum constitutional guarantees, thus, hinges primarily upon fully reasoned decisions.[84] Reasoning in relation to Convention rights as minimum constitutional guarantees can be considered more demanding than that required for settling disputes. However, the focus on reasoning in cases involving Convention rights as minimum constitutional guarantees may not be sufficient for safeguarding institutional legitimacy. In cases where Convention rights are used as minimum constitutional guarantees, it seems appropriate to look for domestic 'allies' (eg the highest courts of the state concerned)[85] to relate to an existing or emerging consensus among the CoE states.

The record of the ECtHR on institutional legitimacy does not look too bad. Its adherence to the principle of subsidiarity is a decisive factor supporting the institutional legitimacy of the ECtHR.[86] As a consequence, especially in cases involving institutional issues of constitutional law, as argued above, the Court is well-advised to apply a wide margin of appreciation. The Court's cooperation with domestic organs is a second, crucial aspect of institutional legitimacy. In particular, cooperation with national organs is decisive for a successful change in the law in cases involving systemic problems.[87] Comparative legal analysis, which the ECtHR employs at least in more controversial cases, is an important element contributing to institutional legitimacy.[88] Especially in cases involving Convention rights as minimum constitutional guarantees, the Court should base its reasoning on comparative analysis of constitutional design. It is, however, of great importance that the ECtHR further refines its comparative methodology which, at present, sometimes lacks consistency or appears to be mere 'cherry picking'.[89]

[84] Committee of Ministers, *Report of the Evaluation Group to the Committee of Ministers on the European Court of Human Rights*, EG Court(2001)1, available at www.wcd.coe.int/ViewDoc.jsp?id=226195&Lang=fr: 'In the Group's opinion, a vital consideration must be to ensure that judges are left with sufficient time to devote to what have been called "constitutional judgments", ie fully reasoned and authoritative judgments in cases which raise substantial or new and complex issues of human rights law, are of particular significance for the State concerned or involve allegations of serious human rights violations and which warrant a full process of considered adjudication'.

[85] The importance of this type of 'collaboration' between the ECtHR and the domestic judiciary is rightly stressed by W Sadurski, 'Partnering with Strasbourg: Constitutionalisation of the European Court of Human Rights, the Accession of Central and East European States to the Council of Europe, and the Idea of Pilot Judgments' (2009) 9 *Human Rights Law Review* 397, 420–21.

[86] See High Level Conference on the Future of the European Court of Human Rights, Brighton Declaration (19 April 2012) paras 3, 11, 12, available at www.hub.coe.int/en/20120419-brighton-declaration.

[87] See Sadurski, 'Partnering with Strasbourg' (n 85) 420.

[88] See K Dzehtsiarou and V Lukashevich, 'Informed Decision-Making: The Comparative Endeavours of the Strasbourg Court' (2012) 30 *Netherlands Quarterly of Human Rights* 272, 277.

[89] See M Ambrus, 'Comparative Law Method in the Jurisprudence of the European Court of Human Rights in the Light of the Rule of Law' (2009) 2 *Erasmus Law Review* 353, 370.

C. Constitutional Pluralism?

There remains a last objection to be mentioned here. Interpreting Convention rights as minimum constitutional guarantees is counter-intuitive in times of constitutional pluralism.

Of course, the reaction to this objection depends on what is understood by 'constitutional pluralism', itself a highly ambiguous term. In its strictest formulation, pluralists believe that different legal orders are disjoint and incommensurate.[90] Thus, there can be no ultimate authority to decide in cases of conflicts of norms.[91] In its most general sense, constitutional pluralism implies constitutional orders are disjoint and sovereign regarding their ability to alter the normative situation of their subjects. Constitutional pluralism favours a horizontal view of constitutional orders and declines to accept a gravitational centre that could decide scenarios of conflict with supreme effect.

A majority of constitutional systems have, at least at first glance, adopted a pluralist approach towards the Convention. For example, the German Federal Constitutional Court has repeatedly held that the 'last word' belongs to the German Constitution.[92] The position of other Constitutional Courts is similar.[93] Other specificities of the ECHR also suggest a model of constitutional pluralism, for example, the margin of appreciation doctrine. From the perspective of most CoE states, constitutional pluralism, therefore, makes sense as an adequate description of the relationship between the domestic normative order and the Convention.

However, an argument based on constitutional pluralism is inherently problematic when it is made within the legal framework of the Convention. First, pluralism has a tendency towards epistemic particularism. This is contrary to the universalist ambition of Convention rights.[94] For example, it would be indefensible

[90] CF Sabel and O Gerstenberg, 'Constitutionalising an Overlapping Consensus: The ECJ and the Emergence of a Coordinate Constitutional Order' (2010) 16 *ELJ* 511, 546.

[91] N Krisch, 'The Open Architecture of European Human Rights Law' (2008) 71 *MLR* 183, 185.

[92] 'The Basic Law aims to integrate Germany into the legal community of peaceful and free states, but does not waive the sovereignty contained in the last instance in the German constitution. There is therefore no contradiction with the aim of commitment to international law if the legislature, exceptionally, does not comply with the law of international agreements, provided this is the only way in which a violation of fundamental principles of the constitution can be averted', German Federal Constitutional Court, 2 BvR 1481/04, 14 October 2004. The 'Berücksichtigungspflicht' (duty to take into account) is part of the pluralist conception towards the Convention by the German Federal Constitutional Court. The UK Human Rights Act 1998 follows a similarly pluralist approach: UK courts are required to 'take into account' ECtHR jurisprudence, but they may also (albeit in rare cases) decline to follow an ECtHR decision, see *R v Horncastle and others* [2009] UKSC 14, [2010] 2 AC 373.

[93] See, eg Austrian Constitutional Court, Judgment, 14 October 1987, VfSlg 11500/1987.

[94] On the role of universality in the Convention context see P Mahoney, 'Reconciling Universality of Human Rights and Local Democracy: The European Experience' in C Hohmann-Dennhardt, P Masuch and M Villiger (eds), *Grundrechte und Solidarität, Festschrift für Renate Jaeger* (Kehl, Engel, 2011) 156, arguing that the ECtHR constantly has to draw a line between matters which are to be decided at local level and matters so fundamental that they require universality.

for CoE states to reintroduce a criminal sanction for consenting homosexual conduct between consenting adults. According to the margin of appreciation doctrine held by the ECtHR, the invocation of pluralism is misplaced when a common European standard has emerged.[95]

Secondly, constitutional pluralism has the detrimental effect of 'othering'. 'Othering', here, refers to the process of differentiating between 'the own' and 'the other'. 'Othering' is frequently used as a strategy for domination. Whereas constitutional pluralism enhances the 'othering' of Convention law and stresses the differences among legal orders, the idea of a common 'minimum', contained in the view of the ECHR as 'minimum constitutional guarantees', seeks to bridge the gap between 'the own' and 'the other'. The view of Convention rights as minimum constitutional guarantees is more closely in-line with the Preamble to the Convention that speaks of the goal of developing a 'common understanding and observance of … human rights'.

V. ENSURING MINIMUM CONSTITUTIONALITY: A DESIRABLE FUNCTION FOR CONVENTION RIGHTS?

This chapter aimed to clarify how the ECtHR deals with conflicting domestic constitutional law. Conflicts of constitutional norms with ECHR law have become more likely, as evidenced by the Bosnian election rules case (*Sejdić and Finci*), the Russian prisoners' voting case (*Anchugov and Gladkov*) or the Swiss minaret ban (which has not yet been decided on the merits). However, there is an imbalance between the ambition to make constitutional law an international concern and the ability of international adjudicative bodies, such as the ECtHR, to solve conflicts with domestic constitutional law.

The main finding of this chapter is that the ability to review domestic constitutional norms depends on the functions ascribed to the Convention rights and their procedural operationalisation. In order to be able to review constitutional norms concerning the institutional design of CoE states, Convention rights must be reinterpreted as 'minimum constitutional guarantees' that intend to safeguard a certain level of constitutionality. Recent developments suggest that this function is indeed gradually gaining ground in the Court's jurisprudence. In the context of the ECHR, such a review of domestic constitutional law is least problematic if Convention rights are used as limits to constitutional rule-making. These cases follow the usual logic of international human rights review.

Far more challenging is the other scenario where the Convention rights are used as limits to institutional design (on the constitutional level). The recent case law of the ECtHR makes clear that the institutional setting has strong implications

[95] See A Legg, *The Margin of Appreciation in International Human Rights Law* (Oxford, Oxford University Press, 2012); JH Gerards, 'Pluralism, Deference and the Margin of Appreciation Doctrine' (2011) 17 *ELJ* 80.

for the efficiency of fundamental rights protection. To eradicate Convention rights violations at their roots, domestic institutions must meet minimum standards of constitutionality. The ECtHR, together with other international actors (such as the Venice Commission), can and should play a role in identifying and operationalising this international standard.

14

The Unconstitutional Constitution: A Timely Concept

CATHERINE DUPRÉ*

Az élet nem arra való, hogy mindig jól jarjunk.[1]

I. INTRODUCTION

MUCH PAPER AND ink has been dedicated to the study and discussion of European constitutionalism, which, scholars agree, is a new breed of constitutionalism, challenging the established theoretical and cognitive categories used to think about (and criticise) the nature of law, sovereignty and political power. These discussions have been triggered by the unprecedented development of European Union law, particularly since the 1992 Maastricht Treaty, with the creation of European citizenship, and the failed Constitutional Treaty of 2004, which propelled the concept of 'constitution' into the language of EU law. Scholars across Europe (as well as from abroad) have endeavoured to define this new creature; European constitutionalism has been understood as multilevel and integrated,[2] postnational[3] or coordinate.[4] Its novelty has been celebrated as a powerful

* I wish to thank to Stephen Skinner and Steve Peers for taking the time to comment on an earlier version of this chapter.

[1] Péter Popper (1933–2010).

[2] I Pernice, 'Multilevel Constitutionalism in the European Union' (2002) 27 *European Law Review* 511; I Pernice *et al* (eds), *Konstitutionalisierung jenseits des Staates: Zur Verfassung der Weltgemeinschaft und den Gründungsverträgen internationaler Organisationen* (Baden-Baden, Nomos Verlag, 2002). See also P Häberle, *Europäische Verfassungslehre* (Baden-Baden, Nomos Verlag, 2009).

[3] N Walker, 'The Idea of Constitutional Pluralism' (2002) 65 *Modern Law Review* 363; JHH Weiler and M Wind (eds), *European Constitutionalism beyond the State* (Cambridge, Cambridge University Press, 2003).

[4] CF Sabel and O Gerstenberg, 'Constitutionalising an Overlapping Consensus: The ECJ and the Emergence of a Coordinate Constitutional Order' (2010) 16 *European Law Journal* 511.

transformation,[5] but it has also been criticised for its lack of imagination and capacity to innovate.[6]

All the while, the democratic quality of European constitutionalism has remained largely in the background of these discussions, somewhere half way between a resigned acknowledgment of the EU democratic deficit and calls for greater democracy. Despite the recurring niggling reservations about the EU democratic character, the general feeling has been that, inside the European Union, democracy is by and large safe.[7] After all, since 1993 candidate countries have had to pass the stringent Copenhagen test and meet its wide-ranging conditionality criteria before being admitted to the EU. Moreover, the Lisbon Treaty drafters have created a novel type of alert and sanction mechanisms in Article 7 as a response to possible threats to democracy within the Member States, following the Austrian crisis.[8]

The coming into force of the Hungarian Basic Law in January 2012, the first new Constitution adopted by a Member State in the Lisbon European Union, has reactivated the discussions on EU democracy.[9] The Hungarian constitutional developments should arguably not be considered as an idiosyncratic feature of the small Central European country; on the contrary it is suggested that they are part of a number of warning shots about the fragility of European democracy.[10] While Hungarian constitutional developments since 2012 are not the primary subject of this chapter, they have to be integrated in the wider reflection on European constitutionalism and its connections to democracy. It is suggested that in addition to the ideas of constitution and constitutionalism, the concept of European constitutionality now deserves closer conceptual attention. In other words, European constitutionalism as a doctrine has to include a reflection and definition of its opposite, as it is not possible to fully define 'a' without defining 'non-a'. If a rule or behaviour may be described as constitutional (or perhaps designed as such), then other rules or behaviours, logically, can be assessed as being unconstitutional. This

[5] JHH Weiler, 'The Transformation of Europe' (1991) 100 *Yale Law Journal* 2433.

[6] I Ward, 'Beyond Constitutionalism: The Search for a European Political Imagination' (2001) 1 *European Law Journal* 24; U Haltern, 'Pathos and Patina: The Failure and Promise of European Constitutionalism in the European Imagination' (2003) 9 *European Law Journal* 14.

[7] In general, the connections between democracy and constitutionalism are not always self-evident, see J Elster and R Slagstad (eds), *Constitutionalism and Democracy* (Cambridge, Cambridge University Press, 1988); D Greenberg *et al* (eds), *Constitutionalism and Democracy: Transitions in the Contemporary World* (Oxford, Oxford University Press, 1993).

[8] W Sadurski, 'Adding Bark to a Bite: The Story of Article 7, EU Enlargement and Jörg Haider' (2010) 16 *Columbia Journal of European Law* 385.

[9] K Kovács and GA Tóth, 'Hungary's Constitutional Transformation' (2012) 7 *European Constitutional Law Review* 183; GA Tóth (ed), *Constitution for a Disunited Nation: Hungary's 2011 Basic Law* (Budapest, Central European University Press, 2012); A Vincze and M Varju, 'Hungary: The New Basic Law' (2012) 18 *European Public Law* 437. See also Norwegian Helsinki Committee, *Democracy at Stake in Hungary: The Orbán Government's Constitutional Revolution*, Report 1/2012; J Stolz, *Hongrie, l'Apprentie Sorcière du Nationalisme* (Paris, Editions du Cygne, 2012).

[10] I Pogany, 'The Crisis of Democracy in East Central Europe: The "New Constitutionalism" in Hungary' (2013) 19 *European Public Law* 341.

chapter, therefore, argues that it is time to accept the possibility, both in practice and at a theoretical level, that constitutions may be unconstitutional within the EU, and it discusses the key components and boundaries of this idea.

The first important distinction to make for the sake of conceptual clarity is between EU constitutionalism (specifically restricted to the EU institutions and rules as defined in the treaties) and Euro-constitutionalism, a much more inclusive and integrated approach to constitutionalism in Europe, embracing Member States' Constitutions and national constitutionalism and EU constitutionalism, together with the human rights requirements under the Council of Europe. The chapter argues that in this wider framework of Euro-constitutionalism, it is not only possible to devise a concept of an unconstitutional constitution, but that this apparently shocking oxymoron is arguably vital to thinking about constitutionalism in Europe, as it makes explicit the connections existing between democracy and constitutionalism. While this raises profound and complex theoretical questions, the chapter adopts a methodological approach that consists of identifying the existing ingredients of Euro-constitutionalism and bringing them together in order to discuss the usefulness and the limitations of this idea.[11]

Central to Euro-constitutionalism is what can be called a duty of democracy, according to which the only regime that constitutions can create within the European Union is a democracy. As demonstrated in section II, this duty has been gradually developed in Europe since 1789 in four key stages, with the latest stage being marked by the coming into force of the Lisbon Treaty in 2009. As part of this duty, a whole set of standards and criteria of constitutionality exists in various forms and at all normative levels; these are identified and briefly discussed in section III. Section IV considers the crucial issue of enforceability of the criteria and standards of Euro-constitutionality. The last section reflects on the effectiveness of protecting democracy through law and sanctions as devised under Euro-constitutionalism.

II. EURO-CONSTITUTIONALISM: DUTY OF DEMOCRACY

This section argues that, historically and politically, Euro-constitutionalism is born out of a commitment to (re)establish and enhance liberal democracy, and that it is, therefore, anchored in a compelling duty of democracy. This duty is historically rooted in the political project of the French Revolution of controlling the absolute monarch's powers through a set of key mechanisms and principles, namely, the requirement of a constitution separating the different branches of power

[11] It is important to note that while the primary object of study considered here are state constitutions, the EU 'constitution' may also be out of line with the wider Euro-constitutionalism. It would be a mistake to exclude this possibility on the basis of the supranational (and supra-sovereign) nature of the EU; constitutionalism as a doctrine implies that the sovereign is not always right, and this arguably applies to the supranational sovereign, as well as to the national sovereign.

and protecting human rights. The current version of Euro-constitutionalism is the product of a gradual evolution of these criteria and of constitutionalism in Europe that arguably took place in four stages, following key dates and events: 1789, 1949, 1989 and 2009.

A. 1789: 'We the Citizens' Constitutionalism

1789 is the founding moment of Euro-constitutionalism. The summer of that year was rich in revolutionary events that gave constitutionalism in Europe its initial features: the infamous Bastille was stormed on 14 July, the privileges of the aristocracy were abolished on 4 August and the Declaration of the Rights of Man and of the Citizen was adopted on 26 August,[12] which has become what is perhaps the foundational text of constitutionalism in Europe.[13] The 1789 Declaration arguably created the duty of democracy by inventing citizens and placing them at the source of sovereignty, giving them the power to control the monarch and to make law. The political regime arising out of these new arrangements was not explicitly called a democracy, but its aim was clearly established as 'the preservation of the natural and imprescriptible rights of man', and its ultimate guarantee rested in the right of 'resistance to oppression' (Article 2). The detailed organisation of the new regime had to be set out in a constitution, which under Article 16 had two compulsory components: it had to guarantee human rights and to ensure that powers were separate.[14] It took about two centuries to develop and refine the 'we the citizens' type of constitutionalism and to design the mechanisms through which constitutions could secure democracy, principally by increasing the franchise and establishing a clearer system of separation of powers with mutual checks as well as a broader range of rights.

B. 1949: 'Never Again' Constitutionalism

The next decisive transformation of constitutionalism was triggered by the realisation that 'we the citizens' constitutionalism had not been an effective barrier against the rise of dictatorship and war. 1949 can be used here as a dating device to capture the moment and spirit of this endeavour. As such, it encompasses several key dates, notably 1948 with the adoption of the United Nations Universal Declaration of Rights, 1949 with adoption of the West German Basic Law, and

[12] M Gauchet, *La Révolution des Droits de l'Homme* (Paris, Gallimard, 1989).

[13] P Häberle, '1789 als Teil der Geschichte, Gegenwart und Zukunft des Verfassungsstaates' in P Häberle (ed), *Rechtsvergleichung im Kraftfeld des Verfassungsstaates, Methoden und Inhalte, Kleinstaaten und Entwicklungsländer* (Berlin, Duncker und Humblot, 1988) 685; S Rials, *La Déclaration des Droits de l'Homme et du Citoyen* (Paris, Hachette, 1989).

[14] Article 16: 'A society where rights are not secured or the separation of powers established has no constitution at all'.

1950 with the adoption of the European Convention on Human Rights (ECHR). As a result of the commitment that 'never again' dictatorship and war could arise out of constitutions, political power became subject to a threefold increase in control. These included an emphasis on the symbolic and normative importance of the constitution as the supreme law, a detailed catalogue of fundamental rights binding on all branches of political power, and the creation of a mechanism of supranational control of states' action in relation to human rights with the ECHR and its Court.

This 'never again' type of constitutionalism was animated by a sense of the fragility of peace and democracy[15] and by the understanding that democracy and constitutionalism are closely related. It was the driving spirit which guided the adoption of the West German Basic Law and the development of its practice over the years.[16] The 'never again' approach to constitutionalism spread beyond the German borders and also guided the constitutional move away from dictatorships in the south of Europe (Spain, Greece and Portugal) and in post-communist states in Central Europe. Under this type of constitutionalism, constitutions have a dual overarching purpose: first to establish democracy (after dictatorship) and, secondly, to secure democracy in the long term. Since 1949, the resulting practice has been that the only type of regime established by a constitution in the European Union (or European Communities as it was then) was a (liberal) democracy. Crucially, the duty of democracy was binding on the law-maker but gradually, the constitution-makers (*pouvoir constituant*) behaved as if they were bound by this duty too, limiting their own freedom to adopt a constitution creating a non-democratic regime.

C. 1989: 'Conditionality' Constitutionalism

The de facto practice of establishing and preserving democracy through constitution-making set up during the previous stages arguably became a legal requirement under the conditionality type of constitutionalism. It is suggested that the turning point was 1989, understood here as embracing the collapse of the Berlin Wall and the end of communist dictatorships in Central and Eastern Europe,[17] the adoption of the first revised constitution in a post-communist state (Hungary), the creation of the Commission of Democracy through Law within the Council

[15] J Habermas, 'Learning by Disaster? A Diagnostic Look at the Short Twentieth Century' (1998) 5 *Constellations* 307.

[16] H Dreier, 'Artikel 1' in H Dreier (ed), *Grundgesetzkommentar* (Tübingen, Mohr Siebeck, 2004) vol I, 139; S Baer, 'Dignity, Liberty, Equality: A Fundamental Rights Triangle of Constitutionalism' (2009) 59 *University of Toronto Law Journal* 440.

[17] W Sadurski, *Constitutionalism and the Enlargement of Europe* (Oxford, Oxford University Press, 2012); H Grabbe, *The EU's Transformative Power: Europeanization through Conditionality in Central and Eastern Europe* (Basingstoke, Palgrave Macmillan, 2006).

of Europe in 1990 (also known as the Venice Commission)[18] and the adoption of a range of criteria to be met by candidate countries in order to join the European Union at the Copenhagen summit in 1993.[19] This new type of constitutionalism, which has been shaped by the EU accession requirements, can therefore be referred to as 'conditionality constitutionalism'.[20]

The Copenhagen criteria have determined those states eligible for accession and the pace of enlargement.[21] They have, therefore, shaped national constitutionalism in the candidate countries, which had to demonstrate to the EU that their constitutions (as well as their legislation) met the accession requirements. In other words, the *pouvoir constituant* in the candidate countries was more tightly restricted than ever before as it had to ensure that the constitution met these specific requirements.[22] Moreover, and this was perhaps not the intended result, the Copenhagen criteria (and their close monitoring by the EU) have arguably shaped EU constitutionalism by making explicit those criteria that the EU considered central to compliance with its normative expectations, ie the criteria of constitutionality. Compliance with the economic core of EU activity, the *acquis communautaire*, was to be expected as a requirement for admission into the EU. Interestingly and crucially, however, the Copenhagen criteria were also about democracy, with a requirement to have 'stable institutions guaranteeing democracy, the rule of law, human rights and respect for and protection of minorities'. Accession to the Council of Europe was often seen as a preliminary step to EU accession and ratification of the ECHR became an explicit requirement.[23] As a result, by imposing on its new Member States a duty of democracy, the European Union arguably also subjected itself, together with its existing Member States,

[18] J Jowell, 'The Venice Commission: Disseminating Democracy through Law' (2001) *Public Law* 675.

[19] Constitution-making in post-communist Europe was characterised by an unprecedented import–export process, which resulted in the new Constitutions being largely drafted following the model of those of existing Member States. See C Dupré, *Importing the Law in Post-Communist Transitions, The Hungarian Constitutional Court and the Right to Human Dignity* (Oxford, Hart Publishing, 2003); Y Mény (ed), *Les politiques du mimétisme* (Paris, L'Harmattan, 1993) and A Sajó, 'Universal Rights, Missionaries, Converts and "Local Savages"' (1997) 6 *East European Constitutional Law Review* 44.

[20] C Spinelli, 'Conditionality and Enlargement in the Light of EU Constitutional Developments' (2004) 3 *European Law Journal* 357; A Albi, 'Ironies in Human Rights Protection in the EU: Pre-accession Conditionality and Post-accession Conundrums' (2009) 15 *European Law Journal* 46.

[21] 'Stability of institutions guaranteeing democracy, the rule of law, human rights and respect for and protection of minorities, the existence of a functioning market economy as well as the capacity to cope with competitive pressure and market forces of the Union', Copenhaegen European Council 'Presidency's Conclusions' *EC Bulletin* 6-1993, 13.

[22] This first wave was followed by a series of constitutional amendments in candidate countries aimed at integrating their newly acquired national sovereignty within the EU supranational structure and logic, A Albi, '"Europe" Articles in the Constitutions of Central and Easter European Countries' (2005) 42 *Common Market Law Review* 399.

[23] There was some discussion at the time that the Venice Commission might be involved in monitoring the democratic quality of newly adopted Constitutions, see the Memorandum by the President, Part A, referred to in J Raue, 'Der Europarat als Verfassungsgestalter seiner neuen Mitgliedstaaten: Vom Beobachter zum Reformer in Osteuropa?' (2005) 126 *Schweizer Studien zum Internationalen Recht* 55.

to this duty and established an explicit set of EU constitutionality criteria to complement those contained in the Treaty of Maastricht, in force at the time (eg provisions on EU citizenship). As a result, the duty of democracy, by force of being binding on Member States, arguably became binding on the EU itself too.

D. 2009: 'Dignity Constitutionalism' under the Lisbon Treaty

2009 is the latest stage in the development of constitutionalism in Europe, the date being that of the coming into force of the Lisbon Treaty. Despite the fact that the 2009 Treaty is no longer labelled a constitutional treaty, the principle of EU constitutionalism has firmly taken root in the way its democratic quality is assessed. The combination of a commitment to a range of 'foundational values' (under Article 2 of the Treaty on European Union (TEU)) and human rights protection (under Article 6 TEU) with the possibility of a sanction in the event of a 'serious and persistent breach' (Article 7 TEU) lies at the heart of the 2009 type of Euro-constitutionalism. In this respect, despite its limited scope the EU Charter of Fundamental Rights plays the significant role of rendering visible all the fundamental rights to which the EU is committed. As both the Lisbon Treaty and the EU Charter prominently enshrine human dignity as their first value (Article 2 TEU) and most important right (Title I of the EU Charter), this type of constitutionalism can be called 'dignity constitutionalism' in order to reflect the new emphasis on respect for human dignity at the European level.[24]

As a result, constitutionalism is now not just about establishing and safeguarding democracy, it arguably involves protecting a special quality of democracy, ie one that places the individual at the centre of its activities as highlighted in the Charter Preamble, with human rights anchored in and interpreted in compliance with human dignity.[25] The principle of inviolability of dignity can be compared to a form of higher law, central to constitutional theory in order to distinguish between positive law and external benchmarks, that can be used as a point of reference to discuss the constitutionality of positive law both of Member States and of the European Union. EU constitutionalism is no longer self-referential; it is bound by the duty of democracy and the principle of inviolability of dignity. Thus, technically EU law must now comply with two types of external bodies of

[24] C Dupré, 'Article 1' in S Peers *et al* (eds), *A Commentary on the European Union Charter of Fundamental Rights* (Oxford, Hart Publishing, 2013). See also M Borowski, 'Artikel 1: Würde des Menschen' in J Meyer (ed), *Charta der Grundrechte der Europäischen Union* (Baden-Baden, Nomos, 2001) 85–94; S Rixen, 'Würde des Menschen als Fundament der Grundrechte' in FSM Heselhaus and C Nowak (eds), *Handbuch der Europäischen Grundrechte* (Munich, CHB Verlag, 2006) 335–60.

[25] C Dupré, 'Human Dignity in Europe: A Foundational Constitutional Principle' (2013) 19 *European Public Law* 319.

criteria, the ECHR[26] and the common constitutional traditions of the Member States.

The 2009 type of constitutionalism is therefore characterised by an unprecedentedly complex stage of development and integrated systems of constitutionalism, arguably brought together by an overarching duty of democracy. It is suggested that there are now three levels of constitutionalism: the EU level, with its distinct founding treaties, body of rights and separation of powers, both horizontal and vertical; the national level of constitutionalism; and the Euro-level of constitutionalism, embracing and integrating both other levels. Following from this, there are three often but not always overlapping sets of constitutionality criteria, the EU criteria, the national criteria and the Euro-criteria. The national criteria are relatively easy to identify in the sense that they are located in the national (mostly codified) Constitutions and their practice. The distinction between the EU and Euro-criteria is more difficult to establish, as the EU has set its own criteria to include those of the Member States by referring to the 'constitutional traditions common to the Member States and ECHR' (under Article 6 TEU). The key difference, however, arguably lies in these 'traditions', and in the ways in which they are, often selectively, reconstructed and reinterpreted.[27] Consequently, Member States' Constitutions must now comply with both EU and Euro-constitutionality criteria. Moreover and arguably, the European Union itself has to comply with its own constitutionality, as well as with Euro-constitutionality. Both requirements take their full significance in the case of adoption or revision of a founding constitutional norm (an EU Treaty or the Constitution of a Member State).

It is therefore suggested that post-2009 constitutionalism in Europe is no longer a descriptive doctrine with a cognitive value and role; it has become a system of beliefs in democracy, respect for human rights and dignity and a *pouvoir constituant*, both at the supranational and national levels, that has lost its freedom to create a regime that does not meet these criteria, or that deviates significantly from the increasingly complex criteria of constitutionality. The Venice Commission expresses this duty in its usual concise and eloquent style by noting that 'in Europe, democracy is the only accepted form of government. It is a condition for membership in the Council of Europe and the European Union and is presented as "the only system of government of our nations" in the 1990 OSCE Charter

[26] The ECHR is now fully and explicitly integrated in EU constitutionalism under Lisbon Treaty, Art 6. See W Weiss, 'Human Rights in the EU: Re-thinking the Role of the European Convention on Human Rights After Lisbon' (2011) 7 *European Constitutional Law Review* 64.

[27] Closer scrutiny of those common traditions is required. It has to be noted and remembered that in terms of both quantity (number of years and states) and quality, those traditions are much more about dictatorship than they are about democracy. Out of the current 27 Member States very few states can claim not to have been a dictatorship or at least leant towards dictatorial regimes at some point of their history since 1922. The EU phrase 'traditions common to the constitutions of Member States' is also to be read in the light of the normatively looser and vaguer phrase of 'common constitutional heritage' developed mainly by the Venice Commission; see *The Constitutional Heritage of Europe*, Science and Technique of Democracy No 18 (Strasbourg, Council of Europe Publishing, 1996). See also A Pizzorusso, *Il Patrimonio Costituzionale Europeo* (Bologna, Il Mulino, 2002).

of Paris for a new Europe'.[28] As discussed below, this is not a mere rhetorical incantation, as the duty is implemented through a set of constitutional criteria and standards of Euro-constitutionality.

III. STANDARDS AND CRITERIA OF EURO-CONSTITUTIONALITY

A number of standards and criteria of Euro-constitutionality have gradually emerged in parallel with the rise of the democracy duty discussed above. Respect for human rights is the clearest and easiest criterion of Euro-constitutionality to identify. It is to be found in most of the codified constitutions of Member States, in the EU Charter of Fundamental Rights and in the ECHR (and its Protocols). These foundational texts have been developed by supranational and national courts to form a uniquely rich and sophisticated body of rights. Overall, the logic driving the judicial elaboration of these criteria is the courts' common endeavour to develop a higher level of protection. This has been an explicit hermeneutic policy of the ECtHR, which has construed the ECHR as a 'living instrument'.[29] Similarly, Member States have historically kept the ECJ and the EU under close scrutiny to ensure that the EU human rights level of protection is not out of line with that of Member States.[30] Finally, the EU Charter makes it clear that its own rights have to be integrated in the existing practice of human rights and that the resulting implementation of EU Charter rights can go beyond the existing levels of protection.[31] As a result, any effort to identify the standard of protection in relation to a specific human right has to take into account the latest practice and case law development. Therefore, logically, in instances of conflicts between the levels of Euro-constitutionalism, what should prevail is the level providing the higher standard of protection. This logic also arguably applies to the *pouvoir constituant*, and constitution drafters, therefore, can either maintain the status quo or enhance the quality of protection; failing to do so may amount to a breach of Euro-constitutionality.[32]

Euro-constitutionality also involves a number of procedural and institutional standards. The overarching requirement is respect for the rule of law and separation of powers, with mutual checks. Unlike human rights, however, the standards' normative basis is perhaps less strong as they tend to be rooted in good practice

[28] European Commission for Democracy through Law (Venice Commission), *Opinion on the Amendments to the Constitution of Liechtenstein Proposed by the Princely House of Liechtenstein* (Opinion No 227/2002, 16 December 2002) para 6.

[29] *Tyrer v United Kingdom*, Application no 5856/72 (ECtHR, 25 April 1978) Series A no 26, 15.

[30] W Sadurski, '"Solange, Chapter 3": Constitutional Courts in Central Europe—Democracy—European Union' (2008) 14 *European Law Journal* 1.

[31] EU Charter, Art 52.3.

[32] This is due to the fact that Euro-constitutionalism, at the heart of which is respect for human rights, is driven by the living instrument logic originally constructed by the ECtHR and therefore aims for increasingly higher standards of democracy. More generally see C Dupré, *The Age of Dignity, Human Rights and Constitutionalism in Europe* (Oxford, Hart Publishing, 2015).

repeated across Member States in the EU (as opposed to being compulsory by virtue of a legal norm). They are, therefore, perhaps best referred to as 'standards' and can be identified in a range of ways. First, the Copenhagen requirements have been decisive in linking democracy to a particular institutional design, which was then adopted in all post-communist states, mirroring and confirming most of the established practice in the 'old' Member States. The ECtHR case law has also caused some very precise institutional arrangements to become compulsory through the interpretation of certain ECHR rights, such as the right to a fair trial under Article 7 ECHR. The ECtHR case law has further developed a set of procedural requirements through its doctrine of positive obligations, which can oblige states to take very specific procedural steps to ensure compliance with human rights, such as adequate training and equipment of police force, proper investigation of state killings or organisation of health systems (under Article 2 ECHR).[33] Finally, the Venice Commission has produced a substantial body of opinions, which have considerably fleshed out the foundational principles of the rule of law, protection of human rights and separation of powers.[34] While the Venice Commission's main role is to provide technical advice and assistance on institutional design and constitution-making,[35] its opinions make up a useful database of good or best practices, which has gradually acquired some persuasive authority.[36]

Paradoxically perhaps, while the *pouvoir constituant* has never been under such tight and explicit normative constraints in terms of substance, one of the grey areas of Euro-constitutionality concerns the rules through which a constitution may be amended or adopted in a constitutional way. Constitution-makers, while no longer completely free in terms of contents and bound by the duty of democracy, have remained largely free to adopt a constitution in the way they choose. The overarching principle and expectation is that the constitution is the law of the people, and not the law of a particular ruling party at a national level, or of a set of states at a supranational level.[37] In this sense, the EU's efforts to make the Lisbon Treaty the law of the people by opening up its drafting process to the public were remarkable (even if, as we know, ultimately unsuccessful and not generally followed through at the national level by systematic referendums).

The criteria and standards of Euro-constitutionality have been in a way victims of the success of Euro-constitutionalism, in that the difficulty in determining a benchmark of Euro-constitutionality primarily arises from their complexity and the fact that they may be intertwined in another set of rules, rather than in the

[33] More generally see A Mowbray, *The Development of Positive Obligations under the European Convention on Human Rights by the European Court of Human Rights* (Oxford, Hart Publishing, 2004).

[34] See www.venice.coe.int/WebForms/documents/by_opinion.aspx.

[35] On its website, the Venice Commission emphasises the 'non-directive approach' of its work: 'Although its opinions are generally reflected in the adopted legislation, the Venice Commission does not impose its solutions, but adopts a non-directive approach based on dialogue'.

[36] J Raue, 'Der Europarat als Verfassungsgestalter seiner neuen Mitgliedstaaten: Vom Beobachter zum Reformer in Osteuropa?' (2005) 126 *Schweizer Studien zum internationalen Recht* 55.

[37] Lisbon Treaty, Art 48.

lack of such criteria. This is particularly so, perhaps, in relation to the EU criteria, which are often embedded in the dense body of *acquis communautaire*. Similarly, the fact that a particular criterion may simultaneously be located at several normative levels will require a close examination of each level and effort to derive from them some sort of combined criterion.

The greatest difficulty, and risk, however, when seeking to determine the exact scope of a criterion of Euro-constitutionality is double standards. At the supranational level, there is a well- known discrepancy between the standards of constitutionality and democracy that the European Union expects of its (future) Member States and those which the EU is prepared to impose on itself.[38] Moreover, not all the current Member States were subjected to the same level of pre-accession scrutiny of the democratic quality of their Constitutions.[39] Once admitted to the EU, the double standards risk means that criteria of Euro-constitutionality may be used to single out a particular Member State, whose Constitution and constitutional practice may generate some political (and cultural) unease among some Member States or at the EU level, while perhaps not being so out of line with constitutional practice in another Member State. In this respect, the boundaries between a healthy level of constitutional pluralism and standards of Euro-constitutionality are sometimes quite porous and thin. The distinction between the two is, however, not subjective. While a good degree of constitutional pluralism is accepted and acknowledged as variations on a theme,[40] the theme itself can be identified as a combination of absolute human rights under the ECHR as endorsed by the EU Charter and minimum standards in terms of institutional design that are expected to be met.[41] Moreover, it is suggested that any assessment of possible breaches of Euro-constitutionality has to consider the alleged breach in its full context, both through a holistic (or systematic) reading of the constitutional text and by taking account of the wider political and cultural circumstances in which the disputed provision is to be implemented.

IV. ENFORCEABILITY

Euro-constitutionalism does not contain a fully worked out and centralised procedure for constitutional review comparable to that which exists in (most)

38 A Moravcsik, 'In Defence of the "Democratic Deficit": Reassessing Legitimacy in the EU' (2002) 40 *Journal of Common Market Studies* 603.

39 A Williams, 'Enlargement of the Union and Human Rights Conditionality: A Policy of Distinction?' (2000) 25 *European Law Review* 610; M Jorna, 'The Accession Negotiations with Austria, Sweden, Finland and Norway: A Guided Tour' (1995) 20 *European Law Review* 132.

40 Notably through the subsidiarity principle in the EU and the margin of appreciation doctrine in ECtHR case law.

41 This is very clear in relation to the Venice Commission: 'Fortunately, the Commission possessed the self-assurance to insist that democracy contains a set of absolute standards from which there is limited scope for deviation'. Jowell, 'The Venice Commission' (n 18) 682. The Venice Commission has therefore not hesitated to identify this deviation in specific cases and to criticise it expressly.

Member States. This is not to say, however, that the constitutionality standards and criteria discussed above are deprived of any normative strength. Since 1989, Euro-constitutionalism has developed a sense of distrust in Member States' ability always to do right and to behave in a democratic way.

A. Distrust

Historically, distrust has been a key trigger of constitutionalism, in that it has replaced the trust in governments in power to behave spontaneously in a democratic manner with a range of constitutional mechanisms and provisions designed to force states to behave in a democratic way precisely when they may be tempted not to do so. It is suggested that such distrust has occupied a central place in Euro-constitutionalism since 1989. This evolution has primarily been triggered by accession to the European Union of ten post-communist states.[42] The prospect of a large influx of Member States that had been dictatorships less than two decades before created a sense that the EU is no longer a (relatively) small club of democratic states, where states' good democratic behaviour could be taken for granted and trusted. This lack of confidence in the new Member States was arguably followed by the perception that the EU's nature and purpose in relation to democracy was not sufficiently clear and could also no longer be taken for granted, but needed to be explicitly stated in the founding treaty and normatively built in through the possibility of sanctions. This was done by the Lisbon Treaty through the combination of Article 2, spelling out the democratic values underpinning the EU, and Article 7, allowing for sanctions in case of serious breach. While states appear to be the primary targets of this constitutionalised distrust, it has to be noted that the EU's action in relation to human rights is no longer assessed according to endogenous and self-referential criteria, but (as discussed above) according to external benchmarks of constitutionality, as derived from the ECHR, and from the common constitutional traditions of Member States. To a large extent, existing enforcement mechanisms of Euro-constitutionality are designed to promote good communication and mutual checks.

B. Institutional Dialogue, Prevention and Monitoring

It falls beyond the scope of this chapter to offer a detailed account of all preventive mechanisms deployed on a routine basis to check compliance with Euro-constitutionality, so only two of them will be mentioned here. The first is a general monitoring process that goes on through both EU and Council of Europe

[42] W Sadurski, *Constitutionalism and the Enlargement of Europe* (Oxford, Oxford University Press, 2011), in particular ch 2.

channels and focuses primarily on human rights. Within the Council of Europe, discussion of the constitutional quality of constitutional reforms has primarily been carried out by the Venice Commission, as discussed above. At the EU level, formal and close monitoring takes place before accession and is part of regular checks on compatibility of candidate countries with the European Union. Within the EU, a lighter degree of monitoring is performed by the Fundamental Rights Agency,[43] which might be called upon as part of Article 7 proceedings.[44] The second mechanism has taken the form of a judicial dialogue among courts across Europe. The most formalised version of this dialogue is the preliminary reference proceedings under Article 267 of the Lisbon Treaty, which makes it possible (and in some instances compulsory) for Member States' courts to obtain a ruling on interpretation of a point of EU law by the Court of Justice of the European Union (CJEU).[45] Moreover, informal judicial dialogues have developed in two other ways. Historically, the first type of dialogue has arisen out of the so-called '*Solange*' ruling of the German Federal Constitutional Court and it has been used as a way for domestic courts to engage with the CJEU on the matter of standards of human rights protection within the EU. The second type of dialogue is more recent and has developed spontaneously between the two supranational courts in an attempt to minimise inconsistencies in interpretation on similar rights or issues.[46] Under the Lisbon Treaty, this originally informal dialogue is formalised in the sense that EU human rights now have to be constructed with regard to the ECHR, as explicitly required under Article 6 of the Lisbon Treaty and Article 52.3 of the EU Charter.[47] The multiplicity of participants in these dialogues revolving around issues of Euro-constitutionality can generate uncertainty as to who may have the last and authoritative word.[48] Their merit, however, is to anticipate and prevent

[43] P Alston and O de Schutter (eds), *Monitoring Fundamental Rights in the EU: Contribution of the Fundamental Rights Agency* (Oxford, Hart Publishing, 2005).

[44] W Sadurski, *Constitutionalism and the Enlargement of Europe* (Oxford, Oxford University Press, 2012) 87.

[45] M Bobek, 'Learning to Talk: Preliminary Rulings, the Courts of the Member States and the Court of Justice' (2008) 45 *Common Market Law Review* 1611. See also Additional Protocol 16 to the ECHR adopted on 2 October 2013, not yet in force. Its Art 1 reads: 'Highest courts and tribunals of a High Contracting Party, as specified in accordance with Article 10, may request the Court to give advisory opinions on questions of principle relating to the interpretation or application of the rights and freedoms defined in the Convention or the protocols thereto'.

[46] S Douglas-Scott, 'A Tale of Two Courts: Luxembourg, Strasbourg and the Growing European Human Rights Acquis' (2006) 43 *Common Market Law Review* 629; CF Sabel and O Gerstenberg, 'Constitutionalising an Overlapping Consensus: The ECJ and the Emergence of a Coordinate Constitutional Order' (2010) 16 *European Law Journal* 511.

[47] The next envisaged step is the EU accession to the ECHR: T Lock, 'The EU Accession to the ECHR: Implications for Judicial Review in Strasbourg' (2010) 35 *European Constitutional Law Review* 177.

[48] M Kumm, 'Who is the Final Arbiter of Constitutionality in Europe?: Three Conceptions of the Relationship between the German Federal Constitutional Court and the European Court of Justice' (1999) 36 *Common Market Law Review* 351; M Kumm, 'The Jurisprudence of Constitutional Conflict: Constitutional Supremacy in Europe Before and After the Constitutional Treaty' (2005) 11 *European Law Journal* 262. See also A Pliakos and G Agnanostaras, 'Who is the Ultimate Arbiter? The Battle over Judicial Supremacy in EU Law' (2011) 36 *European Law Review* 109.

possible breaches of Euro-constitutionality and to promote a fluid approach to constitutional review that is arguably suited to the complexity of these intertwined types and levels of constitutionality.[49] Finally, these various types and levels of dialogue can be understood as pedagogical tools to promote a practice and culture of constitutionality, as well as respect for human rights, through mutual checks and peer pressure. Compliance with Euro-constitutionality is, however, not entirely left to the above processes of dialogue and monitoring, and states can be sanctioned for breaches of constitutional criteria.

C. Sanctioning Breaches of Euro-constitutionality

In addition to constitutional review procedures existing in the Member States that may lead to annulment of an unconstitutional provision,[50] a number of proceedings can be triggered before both the CJEU and the European Court of Human Rights. A distinction can be made between what can be called routine procedures and exceptional procedures, which are meant to address breaches of human rights and constitutional values that are so serious that they might jeopardise democracy in Europe.

The routine sanction before the ECtHR is triggered by individuals who feel they have been victim of a breach of their ECHR rights by a state. The qualification of 'routine' used here is not meant to trivialise these breaches, but is used to highlight this form of sanction's relative ease of use and its ability to remedy a specific violation, generally by awarding damages to the victim. Importantly, individual petitions have triggered the vast majority of ECHR rulings. While these rulings are meant to affect only the parties to a particular case, states have usually been keen to respond to an adverse ruling by amending the contested legislation. The second routine procedure is the infringement procedure under Article 258 TEU, which can be triggered by the European Commission against a Member State and may lead to lump sum or penalty payments by the guilty Member State.[51] This procedure is not designed as a mechanism of constitutional review, but it may be initiated to address constitutional issues. This was illustrated by the recent case against Hungary, which was triggered by the Hungarian government decision to compulsorily retire senior judges, prosecutors and notaries at the age of 62

[49] The procedure under Protocol 2 Lisbon Treaty may be added to the overall picture, but it is too early to assess its use, see P Kiiver, 'The Early-Warning System for the Principle of Subsidiarity: The National Parliament as a Conseil d'Etat for Europe' (2011) 36 *European Law Review* 98.

[50] H Steinberger, *Models of Constitutional Jurisdiction*, Science and Technique of Democracy No 2 (Strasbourg, Council of Europe Publishing, 1993); H Schwartz, *The Struggle for Constitutional Justice in Post Communist Europe* (Chicago, University of Chicago Press, 2000); R Procházka, *Mission Accomplished: On Founding Constitutional Adjudication in Central Europe* (Budapest, Central European University Press, 2002).

[51] S Peers, 'Sanctions for Infringement of EU Law after the Treaty of Lisbon' (2012) 18 *European Public Law* 33.

instead of the normal age of 70.[52] The underlying concern in that case was that this decision breached the principle of judicial independence and the irrevocable status of judges, a key pillar of constitutional democracy in Europe. The CJEU addressed this issue purely in terms of EU law and held that this constituted a breach of Directive 2007/78.[53]

Euro-constitutionalism also allows for exceptional sanction procedures to address exceptional breaches, both at the EU level with Article 7 TEU and in the Council of Europe with the inter-state petition under Article 33 ECHR, according to which 'any High Contracting Party may refer to the Court any alleged breach of the provisions of the Convention and the protocols thereto by another High Contracting Party'. Significantly, both procedures are explicitly designed to remedy breaches of constitutionality, ie of human rights and the foundational values of the European Union under Article 2 TEU. Significantly, too, the sanction for a breach is not primarily of a pecuniary nature, but of a political nature, eventually culminating in possible exclusion from the Council of Europe (and presumably from the EU too), or in the 'suspension of voting rights of the representative of the government of [the guilty] Member State' (Article 7.2 TEU). Both types of procedure have so far been initiated very rarely, but this does not necessarily undermine their significance and may instead point to their deterrent effect, as well as perhaps to a generally satisfactory level of respect for human rights and democratic values.

In contrast with (most) Member States' constitutional order, where constitutional review is concentrated in one specialised court, there is no equivalent institution in the scheme of Euro-constitutionalism. A number of institutions, however, may be understood to perform a function of constitutional review, such as domestic constitutional courts, the ECtHR and the Venice Commission. In practice, as has been illustrated by the Hungarian situation since spring 2011, many of the above mechanisms can be spontaneously triggered in an apparently independent manner by the various actors described above. The Venice Commission has so far apparently played the largest role in this process. It was consulted no fewer than ten times about a whole range of constitutional reforms between March 2011 and October 2012 (time of writing), leading to very close constitutional 'assistance' and (hopefully) fostering of good communication between the Hungarian government and the Council of Europe, with each opinion discussing a key (problematic) issue of constitutionality.[54] At the EU level, three institutions

[52] Case C-286/12 *Commission v Hungary* [2012] EU ECJ. According to the CJEU, 270 senior Hungarian judges are targeted by this reform (10 per cent of the judiciary). According to the Hungarian NGO TASZ, 200 judges have already been replaced (*Le Monde*, 8 November 2012).

[53] Council Directive 2000/77/EC establishing a general framework for equal treatment in employment and occupation [2000] OJ L303/16.

[54] European Commission for Democracy through Law (Venice Commission), *Opinion on Three Legal Questions Arising in the Process of Drafting the New Constitution of Hungary* (Opinion No 614/2011, 28 March 2011); *Opinion on the New Constitution of Hungary* (Opinion No 618/2001, 18 March 2011); *Opinion on the Act on the Legal Status and Remuneration of Judges and on the Act on*

were actively involved in what can be (loosely) described as the review of the Euro-constitutionality of the Hungarian constitutional reforms. Chronologically, the first was the European Commission, which opened accelerated infringement proceedings (under Article 258) against Hungary on 17 January 2012 on three grounds (independence of the National Central Bank, independence of the judiciary and independence of the data protection supervisory authority). It was followed by the European Parliament, which adopted a resolution 'on the recent political developments in Hungary' on 14 February 2012, in which MEPs expressed 'serious concern at the situation in Hungary in relation to the exercise of democracy, the rule of law, the respect and protection of human and social rights, the system of checks and balances, equality and non-discrimination'.[55] The latest EU institution involved in this process was the CJEU, which delivered a ruling against Hungary on 6 November 2012 in relation to compulsory retirement of senior judges.[56] Last but not least, the Hungarian Constitutional Court delivered a ruling of unconstitutionality on this controversial statute in July 2012.[57] While these actions do not appear to have been concerted, it is perhaps not insignificant to observe that, in its February 2012 resolution, the European Parliament referred to Article 7 TEU and to the opinions of the Venice Commission delivered at the time. Similarly, the CJEU referred to the Hungarian Constitutional Court's ruling on the contested compulsory retirement of judges and decided (much against the Hungarian government's wishes) to proceed with its own procedure despite the fact that the domestic ruling invalidated much of the contested measure.[58] This set of procedures, therefore, illustrates that, in the event of serious and persistent concern about respect for Euro-constitutionality, they can be triggered in parallel, developing a kind of complementary and collaborative informal review process and ensuring close and sustained attention.

the Organisation and Administration of Courts (Opinion No 663/2012, 19 March 2012); *Opinion on Act CCVI of 2011 on the Right to Freedom of Conscience and Religion and the Legal Status of Churches, Denominations and Religious Communities* (Opinion No 664/2012, 17 March 2012); *Opinion on Act CLI of 2011 on the Constitutional Court of Hungary* (Opinion No 665/2012, 19 June 2012); *Opinion on the Act on the Prosecution Service and the Act on the Status of the Prosecutor General, Prosecutors and Other Prosecution Employees* (Opinion No 668/2012, 19 June 2012); *Opinion on the Act on the Rights of Nationalities* (Opinion No 671/2012, 19 June 2012); *Opinion on Act CXII of 2011 on Informational Self-determination and Freedom of Information* (Opinion No 672/2012, 18 October 2012); *Opinion on the Cardinal Acts on the Judiciary that were Amended following Adoption of Opinion CDL-AD(2012)001 on Hungary* (Opinion No 683/2012, 15 October 2012). Before 2011, the Venice Commission had only delivered one opinion on Hungarian constitutional matters, *Opinion on the Regulatory Concept of the Constitution of Hungary* (Opinion 6/1995, 10 November 1995).

55 European Parliament, Resolution 2012/2511 on the recent political developments in Hungary, point R1.

56 Case C-286/12 *Commission v Hungary* (n 52). Only one ground for infringement dealt with in this case has (so far) led to a ruling by the CJEU, with the second ground on the independence of the Hungarian Central Bank being suspended by the Commission, and the third ground on the independence of the data protection supervisor still apparently pending.

57 Decision 33/2012 (VII.17) AB határozat (Constitutional Court of Hungary).

58 ibid paras 43–47.

In conclusion, it is argued that, while neither complete nor perfect,[59] Euro-constitutionalism is equipped to address a whole range of possible breaches of constitutional standards and criteria, which can be monitored and sanctioned. Importantly, the existing range of mechanisms appears to include a gradation of responses depending on the seriousness of the breach. Whether they can effectively promote and safeguard democracy, however, is a separate question discussed below.

V. EFFECTIVENESS

The issue of the effectiveness of review and sanctioning of (un)constitutionality is discussed here from two perspectives. The first is the technical appropriateness of the existing mechanisms, most of which were not originally designed to ensure compliance with Euro-constitutionality as understood in this chapter. The other, perhaps even more important, is the faith in law underpinning the logic of Euro-constitutionalism.

A. Technical Appropriateness: An Incomplete System of Sanctions and Review

The question of effectiveness raises a whole range of technical issues, such as the lack of a centralised and purpose-built mechanism or institution to review Euro-constitutionality and sanction breaches as they occur; the adequacy of financial penalties to remedy breaches of democratic principles or human rights violations; and the oblique way in which the CJEU has to address breaches of constitutional criteria and principles by way of translation into the technical terms of EU law, as illustrated in the recent case against Hungary. Further weaknesses of this approach flow from the eminently political nature of the sanction proceedings under Article 7 TEU, with sanctions depending on unanimous voting, and under Article 33 ECHR, with experience showing that states have tended to be very reluctant to initiate such proceedings before the ECtHR. Moreover, the ultimate threat or possibility of exclusion from the EU and the Council of Europe in the event of serious human rights violations may well protect democracy for the remaining Member States, but will do little to redress those breaches in the concerned country, as was illustrated in the *Greece* case,[60] with Greece being deemed to have withdrawn from the Council of Europe as the military dictatorship took hold.[61] The more serious

[59] For instance, there is no procedure to stop medium or large scale violations of human rights (beyond remedies for individual victims) and the existing mechanisms described here are complex and take time to be deployed.

[60] Applications nos 3321/67, 3322/67 and 3323/67 by Denmark, Norway and Sweden of 20 September 1967, joined with Application no 3344/67 by the Netherlands of 27 September 1967.

[61] I Krateros, 'Greece' in R Blackburn and J Polakiewicz (eds), *Fundamental Rights in Europe: The ECHR and its Member States, 1950–2000* (Oxford, Oxford University Press, 2001) 355–81.

concern about effectiveness, however, has to do with the role of law itself, which raises what is called below the paradox of democracy through constitutionalism.

B. Faith in Law: Paradox of Democracy Through Constitutionalism

The paradox of democracy rests on two assumptions. The first is that democracy can be safely built and secured through law; the second is that constitutional democracy rests on a set of values that are deemed to be shared by all in the European Union.

It is suggested that faith in law has been the engine driving the reconstruction of democracy in Europe after the Second World War, as well as after the collapse of dictatorships in the south of Europe, and then in Central and Eastern Europe. This faith was in particular channelled into adoption of European Bills of Rights by way of the ECHR and, more recently, the EU Charter of Fundamental Rights. It was also channelled into the adoption of codified Constitutions in all new Member States joining the EU, Constitutions that were all drafted according to similar legal principles including separation of and mutual checks on powers, protection of human rights and 'Europe articles' organising the relationship between the state and the EU. Expectations of what could be achieved through constitutional law have been very high: it was believed that constitutions could create democracy after non-democratic times, with the expected quality of democracy almost totally relying on the quality of its law. In other words, the idea was that new (and often not self-evident) democratic values could be sown in post-war and post-dictatorial societies through legal reforms that would transform these societies and countries into 'stable democracies'. In short, with the right law properly monitored, it was believed that democracy would be safe. This kind of institutional optimism arguably became the hallmark of post-communist constitutional transitions,[62] and marked the turn to the conditionality type of constitutionalism after 1989. The Venice Commission, eloquently named 'the Commission of Democracy through Law', is exemplary of this faith in law's ability to (re)build and sustain democracy in the long term. This approach has not been without success and the smooth and controlled admission to the EU of ten post-communist states less than 15 years after the collapse of (for some countries) the longest and harshest dictatorships in Europe is an achievement that ought not to be underestimated. Moreover, Euro-constitutionalism has arguably delivered a very high quality of democracy and human rights protection, unprecedented and unrivalled in the world, considering its scope and the quantity of undemocratic 'traditions' in some of the EU Member States.

[62] P Kendé, 'L'Optimisme institutionnel des Élites postcommunistes' in Y Mény (ed), *Les Politiques du Mimétisme* (Paris, L'Harmattan, 1993) 237 and C Dupré, 'After Reforms: Human Rights Protection in Post-communist States' (2008) 5 *European Human Rights Law Review* 622.

However, this faith in law has an inherent weakness, which lies in the misconception that law alone is sufficient to build a stable democracy. This raises the well-rehearsed (and yet inconclusive) discussion about which comes first, law or culture. In the European context of post-war and post-dictatorship, the chosen approach was very much about law versus culture, ie the good law versus the bad culture (of dictatorship). While this has proven successful in formally establishing democracy and protecting human rights, the challenge is whether the law before (or versus) culture approach can be sufficient to sustain democracy in the long term, perhaps particularly when the very term 'democracy' no longer conjures up an ideal of and longing for freedom as it arguably did under dictatorial regimes. Moreover and crucially, this faith in law is arguably shaken when democracy can no longer deliver economic and material prosperity, at least to levels equivalent to those previously existing in non-democracy (as engraved in the sometimes distorted and selective memory of the many who see their standards of living decline under the democratic regimes) and/or to the levels promised by the EU or domestic governments.[63]

The second dimension of the Euro-constitutionalism paradox is that it rests on values that are assumed to be commonly shared within the European Union but, by definition, that are rejected (or at least loudly challenged) by non-democratic political parties. Since 2009, the EU rests on these values as indicated under Article 2 TEU. However, as the Europe-wide debate about the choice of these values (unleashed at the time of the drafting of the Constitutional Treaty) showed, their selection and the consensus about them are far from being self-evident. The core of the debate at the time concerned whether or not to include references to Christianity in the Constitutional Treaty.[64] It is suggested that other Article 2 TEU values, such as equality, protection of minorities and even democracy, may well be just as controversial if the rise of far-right parties across EU Member States can be used as an indicator. By definition, a 'serious and persistent breach' of some Article 2 values (to use Article 7 TEU terminology) would reflect and crystalise a worrying lack of consensus about the value of democracy or of, for instance, equality. In short, Euro-constitutionalism rests on a questionable faith in law to establish the right institutional framework within which democracy can flourish and on a belief in, and commitment to, a set of values that are not, by definition, necessarily shared by the critics of democracy.

[63] Topically, see P Krugman, 'Depression and Democracy', *New York Times*, 11 December 2011. Generally, see J Dine and A Fagan (eds), *Human Rights and Capitalism* (Cheltenham, Edward Elgar Publishing, 2006); D Nicol, *The Constitutional Protection of Capitalism* (Oxford, Hart Publishing, 2010).

[64] See, eg J Weiler, *Un'Europa Cristiana* (Milano, Rizzoli, 2003) discussed by AJ Menéndez, 'A Pious Europe? Why Europe Should Not Define Itself as Christian' (2005) 30 *European Law Review* 133.

VI. CONCLUSION

This chapter has constructed and discussed the concept of the unconstitutional constitution in the framework of a dignity-based type of Euro-constitutionalism following the coming into force of the Lisbon Treaty. Consideration of this concept has shed new light on the nature of constitutionalism in Europe, its connections to democracy and its 'toolkit' for dealing with breaches of democracy and human rights. This chapter has further highlighted the existence of procedures and mechanisms that considered together may form a useful apparatus for challenging and eventually sanctioning unconstitutional constitutional developments.

The concept of the unconstitutional constitution is still very much a work in progress that reflects the incomplete construction of Euro-constitutionalism as a prescriptive doctrine used to foster and protect democracy. In particular, as has been shown, existing sanctions are not always appropriate to redress breaches of constitutionality. Moreover, while the chapter has largely focused on states as the possible perpetrators of such breaches, a more fully developed understanding of Euro-constitutionalism should also consider the possibility of the European Union or the Council of Europe committing such breaches, as the logic of constitutionalism implies that their supranational status does not put them above the law.

Ultimately, this chapter has argued that the essential importance of the concept of the unconstitutional constitution is twofold. It makes it possible to address the possibility that not all constitutions are democratic, and it highlights an inherent weakness of such theoretical construction, the faith in law. As such it focuses timely attention on the crucial interaction of values and norms, as well as their foundations, in Europe today.

Index